Furthe
History

The Proceedings of the Third Annual
Construction History Society
Conference

Queens' College, University of Cambridge, 8-10th April 2016

Edited by

James W.P. Campbell

Nina Baker

Nicholas Bill

Michael Driver

Michael Heaton

Yiting Pan

Michael Tutton

Christine Wall

David Yeomans

Published by The Construction History Society
1 Scroope Terrace
Cambridge
CB2 1PX

www.construction.co.uk

ISBN 978-0-9928751-2-1

Formatting and layout by Yiting Pan
First printed by Lulu print on demand for the Construction History Society

Proceedings of the Third Construction History Society Conference
edited by James W P Campbell, Nina Baker, Nicholas Bill, Michael Driver, Michael Heaton, Yiting Pan, Michael Tutton, Christine Wall and David Yeomans

THE THIRD ANNUAL CONSTRUCTION HISTORY SOCIETY CONFERENCE

Organised by:

The Construction History Society

Hosted by:

Queens' College, University of Cambridge
&
The Department of Architecture, University of Cambridge

Organising Committee

Chair: James Campbell

Michael Heaton
Jonathan Lee
Yiting Pan
David Yeomans

Scientific Committee

Chair: David Yeomans

Antonio Becchi
James Campbell
Simon Pepper
Robert Thorne
Christine Wall

Editorial Committee

Chair: James W P Campbell

Nina Baker
Nicholas Bill
Michael Driver
Michael Heaton
Yiting Pan
Michael Tutton
Christine Wall
David Yeomans

Acknowledgements

The preparation of any conference takes an enormous amount of time and effort on behalf of a large number of people. I am hugely grateful to all those who have assisted in the planning of this, Third Annual Construction History Society Conference. In particular I would like to thank Yiting Pan who has worked so hard to put these proceedings together, having just completed her PhD. David Yeomans as chair of the Scientific Committee took on the unenviable task of collecting all the abstracts together and distributing them to the various members of the scientific committee for review. I am as always grateful for his sage advice and I would like to thank him and all the other members of that committee for their efforts in reviewing all these proposals. Once the papers were in the editorial committee took over and went painstakingly through every paper. Any errors remaining are my fault not theirs. I would like to thank all those members of the committee of the Construction History Society who give their time so generously to the society without any form of remuneration. They are Antonio Becchi, Michael Driver, Michael Heaton, Niall Bird, Alan Palmer, Michael Tutton, Nina Baker, Andrew Jackson, Jonathan Lee, Treve Rosoman, Christine Wall and the journal editors Hermann Schlimme and Bill Addis. Without their support the Society would not function. Lastly I would like to thank all those staff of the Architecture Department and Queens' College, in the University of Cambridge for hosting this conference, without whose aid none of this would be possible.

James W P Campbell
2016

Contents

Contents

The Middle Ages

The Sixteenth and Seventeenth Centuries

The Eighteenth Century

The Nineteenth Century

The Twentieth Century

Contents

Introduction

This is the third volume in the series that began in 2014 with the *Proceedings of the First Conference of the Construction History Society* (ISBN 978-0-9928751-1-4), followed by *Studies in the History of Construction: the Proceedings of the Second Conference of the Construction History Society* (ISBN 978-0-9928751-1-4) in 2015. The thirty-nine papers included in this volume are the result of a process that started nearly a year ago with a call for abstracts. Eighty-nine abstracts were received and reviewed by the scientific committee. Sixty-six were then accepted. In the end, only thirty-nine papers were received and accepted for inclusion and it is these that are published here. These papers thus represent a long process of selection and a considerable amount of work by a large number of people. They also represent a fair cross-section of the range of interests that fall within the general title of "Construction History", crossing disciplinary boundaries between engineering and architectural history, economic and social history, archaeology and the history of technology and all focused on the central problem of how we built the world around us in the past. The range is large, encompassing papers in subjects as diverse as Medieval nails and Geodesic Domes. Hopefully there will be something in here to entertain and inform every reader. The papers are arranged thematically rather than by author, to make it easier to browse and to bring together all the papers into a coherent whole. The volume starts with papers on general themes (those that are either theoretical or cover long periods) and then is arranged roughly chronologically.

The Building Industry

This volume begins with Andrew Rabeneck's survey of the development of the building industry. He identifies what he sees as a disturbing shift in the construction industry over the last few decades away from an industry led by professionals and tempered by Government regulation, to a process increasingly led by large manufacturing firms and international conglomerates. He calls upon construction historians to investigate how this has happened and to record what is happening. If Rabeneck's analysis is true, then architects and engineers will become increasingly marginalised by the interests of big industry. Nina Baker's paper, *Have the effects of its history resulted in a Scottish construction industry that differs from its counterparts in the rest of the UK?,* is similarly discursive and a call to arms. Here the topic is a single country, Scotland, and the question is whether there is anything in particular that sets it apart.

Sources

The next two papers examine the sources for construction history. In *Picturing Construction: photographical documentation of Belgian construction sites by late nineteenth and early twentieth-century contractors,* Inge Bertels looks at the possible sources for photographs of building construction in the period and why the photographs were taken or commissioned, showing how contractors themselves played an increasingly important role in taking photographs of their own work in action. Bill Addis's paper, *Are the traces left by structural engineers sufficient to assess their eminence?,* discusses the various factors a historian might use to determine the relative merit of an engineer in history and the sources that might aid in this pursuit. By no means exhaustive, it provides a useful and provocative introduction to the subject by an experienced engineer and historian, drawing heavily on personal experience.

Materials

Papers on materials are surprisingly rare in construction history and thus particularly welcome. I have gathered together three papers under this general theme in this section. The first two are remarkably similar and look at gypsum. The first paper by Vincenzina La Spina, Fernando Vegas, and Camilla Mileto concentrates on gypsum production in the Spanish Levant, that is the eastern coast of the Iberian Peninsula on the Mediterranean. As the paper shows, gypsum production covered a wide area of eastern Spain. They provide an excellent account of its extent, the ways it was extracted and processed and the uses in the local area, which included rendering, flooring and stabilisation of walls.

In Britain, gypsum is most commonly referred to as *plaster of Paris.* Tiffanie Le Dantec's paper provides an excellent account of why. While lime renders and plasters predominated in Britain, in Paris gypsum was the plaster of choice externally and internally. What is interesting is that, as Le Dantec shows, real *Plaster of Paris,* that is the external render used in Paris, was not pure gypsum at all, but a careful mix of gypsum and other ingredients that allowed the plaster to be worked and delayed its setting. In the twentieth century the lack of skilled labour led to the loss of the correct methods for making and applying this plaster which led in turn to its abandonment, gypsum only being retained for internal plastering as it is elsewhere today. As this paper shows, the loss was as much to do with technique as material.

The last paper in this section is also on technique. The techniques here are to do with the reinforcement of masonry to resist earthquakes. Modern concrete frame buildings have sometimes performed unexpectedly badly in earthquakes while traditional construction has sometimes exceeded expectations. This paper is part of a growing body of research looking at why this is the case. It takes two examples, one in Aquila, in Italy and one in Lefkada in Greece. Both are masonry buildings reinforced with timber to resist earthquakes. The paper shows how, by using these clever traditional methods, the buildings actually meet modern codes for earthquake design. The problem, as the paper highlights, and has been highlighted elsewhere, is that earthquakes are infrequent and thus it is quite possible for generations to forget why certain features were used in buildings and reject them as unnecessarily old-fashioned. This paper thus highlights the vital importance of a historical understanding for informing modern construction and preserving traditional techniques.

The Graeco-Roman World

Studies of the classical world have been notably absent from the previous volumes in this series. That is not to say that no research is going on in these areas, but rather that it has tended to be published elsewhere (usually in archaeological journals). It is thus a pleasure to be able to include three papers in this volume that hopefully represent a new trend and the start of more submissions in this area in the future. Shaher Rababeh and Rama Al Rabady's *Stone Architecture: Stone Dressing in Petra, Jordan,* provides an in depth analysis of the peculiar methods of cutting and finishing stone used by the Nabateans in Jordon. The second paper in this section by Rossana Mancini examines the masonry of Rome's Aurelian Wall, constructed in the fifth century AD. Here the material is brick rather than stone, and the paper looks at the sizes of bricks used and their coursing in detail. The last paper in this section by Carla Maria Amici, looks not at walls, but at roofs. It examines the fragmentary remains of huge concrete slabs in Hadrian's Villa at Tivoli and tries to reconstruct the floor/roof from which they have fallen. These are fascinating structures. Roman concrete was very strong, but of course unreinforced, so the floor must have relied on timber beams, or perhaps even trusses, to take the tension, but these have long since disappeared. As they were thick, the weight of the huge slabs must have been considerable and this paper will no doubt lead to others looking at the structural problems associated with supporting such a floor.

The Middle Ages

Medieval construction was largely ignored in the last volume, so it is good to have seven papers in this one. The first is by a truly international collaboration between Chris How from Australia, Caroline Bolle and Jean-Marc Léotard from Belgium and Artur Lapins from Latvia. The paper looks at the "bi-petal nail", a rare type of medieval nail that is distinguished by its strange head that looks like two petals from a flower, hence the name. Nails are just one of the aspects of the history of construction which are so common throughout history and yet have never been properly catalogued and analysed. Examples are shown here from Belgium and Latvia, providing an interesting case study of how the form was found in various times in various parts of Europe.

Ignacio-Javier Gil-Crespo's paper looks at timber reinforcement in Spanish castle walls. The incorporation of timber in masonry structures not only has a long history, but also continued as a practice until surprisingly recently in Europe. Indeed, it can still be found many parts of the world for protection against earthquakes, as we saw in Tonna and Chesi's paper in the section on Materials above. In the case of Spanish castle walls, the reason for inclusion was to strengthen the masonry against under-mining and bombardment. Buried deep in the walls, the timbers offered a short term gain as in time they rotted away, but fortification was about resisting imminent attack, rather than concerns about longevity.

The third paper in this section is also on Medieval walls, this time those build around towns. Alicia Sainz Esteban puts forward the idea that, in certain cases, these were not laid using conventional masonry techniques, but were instead constructed like pisé: that is, they were constructed using a timber formwork into which a mixture of rubble and lime mortar were poured, much in the same way as modern builders would pour concrete. This method explains the existence of putlog holes, which the author argues were used to hold the two sides of the formwork together. This is a controversial suggestion and certainly one that warrants further discussion. If true, it represents a considerable change in thinking about medieval rubble construction.

Like the previous papers, Michael Tutton's paper is also on masonry, but this time it is brick, not stone, and the problem is a particular one: the construction of brick helical staircases. Medieval stone staircases are comparatively common, even in brick buildings, but surviving brick staircases in Britain are very rare indeed, almost certainly because they were so much more complicated to build. Michael lists 24 examples of which 19 remain and details how many of them seem to have been built by Flemish or German bricklayers. The question is: are these the only examples? Hopefully if there are others, this paper will prompt people to publish them.

The next three papers deal with church architecture. The first, by David Wendland, looks at Late Gothic vaulting. These vaults show peculiarly complex and often playful arrangements of ribs and, as Wendland says, are sometimes "standing not because of, but in spite of their structural design". The question is how they were set out, and how their designers understood the limits of what was possible. Wendland proposes an intriguing and convincing solution, using surviving treatises from the sixteenth century by Rodrigo Gil de Hontañón and in the seventeenth century by François Derand, and interpreted by Rondelet in the early nineteenth century.

The next paper, by Agustí Costa Jover, Josep Lluis i Ginovart, Sergio Coll Pla, Albert Ferré Jover from the Department of Architecture, Universitat Rovira i Virgili looks at the extraordinary construction of the Cathedral of Tortosa, a process that involved the gradual replacement of an early twelfth-century Romanesque cathedral by a much larger gothic cathedral quite literally building around and above it from 1375 to 1757. Working from modern ground radar and laser scans of the existing structure, the paper shows in a series of enticing computer-generated drawings how the building progressed, engulfing the original as the older building was demolished from within. This was surely one of the most unusual phased demolitions in history.

The final paper in this section, by Antonio Luis Ampliato Briones and Juan Clemente Rodríguez Estévez, looks at the church of Santa María in Carmona, a town 30km from Seville and how the architecture of this late fifteenth century and early sixteenth century building relates to so-called "Seville Cathedral Gothic". The research is aided by laser scan models of the cathedral interior, a tool that is becoming increasingly popular in allowing detailed formal comparisons to be made between structures which had previously been too complex to easily survey.

Sixteenth and Seventeenth Centuries

The division between the Middle Ages and the sixteenth and seventeenth centuries is an artificial one. As the papers in the previous section showed, construction projects often flowed over centuries and the paucity of sources makes it difficult to trace changes of techniques from the twelfth to the thirteenth, thirteenth to the fourteenth, fourteenth to the fifteenth or fifteenth to the sixteenth centuries. While the birth of printing meant that treatises began to appear in the sixteenth and seventeenth centuries, as Wendland's paper suggests, it is difficult to see how much they represented the period that went before, or were promoting new possibilities. The most obvious differences were stylistic, with the increasing adoption of classical design and the problems and challenges that involved. English architecture in the sixteenth century was a curious mixture of traditional forms combined with half-understood classical references. One of the most striking features of the more lavish houses of this period in Britain are their huge windows, leading to the term "lantern houses". In an age when glass was expensive and the weather was colder than it is now, huge rooms with large expanses of glass in a northern climate must have been very cold in winter indeed. Dean Hawkes's paper addresses precisely this issue, using modern sun path diagrams to show that the rooms in Hardwick Hall were surprisingly carefully orientated to the sun to provide warm and pleasant conditions throughout most of the year.

Hardwick Hall was a new building, but even in new buildings it was common to re-use fragments of earlier buildings. The re-use of ships' timbers is an oft-cited example, although research has shown that timbers from ships were rarely re-used even in coastal areas and most so-called "ships' timbers" found in Medieval and seventeenth-century timber houses in Britain are usually just re-used building timbers. Michael Heaton's paper focuses on this re-use of parts of buildings, showing how window frames, doors, floor beams and even whole staircases were salvaged from demolished buildings and re-used elsewhere, providing puzzles for building archaeologists and traps for the unwary historian seeking to date properties from their stylistic details.

This period also saw the transition from craftsmen-led construction to the appearance of architects and engineers whose knowledge was based on books and who were responsible particularly for design. One feature of this new arrangement was delegation, with architects often having teams of draftsmen working on a number of projects simultaneously. The paper by Raúl Romero Medina and Manuel Romero Bejarano details how Hernan Ruiz the Younger (c. 1515-1569), one of the leading architects of the Spanish Renaissance, delegated the overseeing on site of his many projects to various individuals, allowing him to apparently oversee a bewildering number of projects simultaneously spread over a large geographical area. As the writers point out, this questions the role of "authorship" in building projects of this period. Indeed construction history continually challenges the architectural historian's wish to ascribe the details of building projects to single individuals. Today no single individual is responsible for the design of every aspect of a building and it is clear that to a certain extent this has always been the case: building is, and has always been, essentially a collaborative exercise.

Eighteenth century

Modern computer modelling is beginning to open exciting new methods of analysis of historic buildings and a number of papers in the current volume provide good examples. Often this analysis exploits relatively simple aspects of the computer's capabilities. Claudio Mazzanti's elegant paper, *A multidisciplinary study on the exposed brick walls of the baroque architecture of Penne in Italy,* uses simple computer graphics to clearly differentiate shaped bricks used in elaborate baroque decorative window and door surrounds, and places this brick manufacture in its context, providing an excellent study of building materials in use.

The period from the sixteenth to the nineteenth century sees the development of structural mechanics and the transformation of design from the use of trial and error and physical models to the mathematical modelling that underpins modern structural analysis. Capecchi and Tocci's paper looks at the three technical reports prepared by Roger Joseph Boscovich (1711-1785) in the mid eighteenth century. Boscovich was an extraordinary polymath, who was an astronomer, mathematican, physicist, philosopher, diplomat and politician. He was born in Dubrovnik in modern-day Croatia, but spent much of his life in Italy as a Jesuit priest. In 1742, as a then Professor of Mathematics, he was asked by the pope to investigate the cracking of the dome of St Peters. The three reports dealt with here are the result of that investigation and subsequent investigations of cracking of the domes of the Hofbibliothek in Vienna and Milan cathedral, each providing fascinating insights into the eighteenth century understanding of the structural mechanics of domes.

Nineteenth century

Much of the research currently being carried out in construction history appears to concentrate on nineteenth and twentieth century topics and this is reflected in the current volume by the fact that almost half the papers relate to this later period. This is no doubt partly driven by the greater survival of buildings and documents, making research both easier and more relevant. It is also partly driven by architects and engineers seeking to understand buildings that they are actively working on. The range of studies is as varied as the discipline. The section opens with two studies of iron roof structures. The first is the iron roof constructed over the Giulio Cesare Hall in the Palazzo Senatorio in Rome. The original timber roof by Giacomo Della Porta built in the 1570s had much decayed by the nineteenth century. The paper by C.F. Carocci and C. Tocci details not only the Polonceau trusses which were inserted to place it, but also the process of restoration illustrated by the surviving drawings from the period providing a fascinating insight into a nineteenth century restoration project. The second paper in this section is also on an iron roof, this time the astonishing glass and iron roof of the famous Gallery Vittorio Emanuele II (1865-77) in Milan. Iva Styanova's paper uses evocative 3D computer drawings to show us the construction of this seminal structure in detail.

The subject of Ronald Cox and Dermot O'Dwyer's paper *Education for Construction: Engineering Education in Trinity College Dublin in the 1840s* is apparent from the title. In a period when English engineers were still using comparatively little mathematical analysis, it is interested to see how much mathematics was being taught on this course. Just as the teaching and practice of engineering was changing in this period, so also was the building industry. Jelena Dobbels, Inge Bertels and Ine Wouters's paper, *The professionalization of Belgian general contractors (1877-1914): an analysis of the construction journal 'La Chronique des Travaux Publics, du*

Commerce et de l'Industrie' examines the changing nature of building firms in the nineteenth century and the various trade organisations and federations that rose up to serve them. *An English Company's Role in the 19th Century Water Supply to Cartagena* explores the surprising story of how an English company became involved in producing infrastructure in late-nineteenth-century Spain. The trade with Britain is also the subject of Virginia Flores-Sasso's *Timbers, palm boards and construction materials at eighteenth and nineteenth century's architecture in Dominican Republic*, that looks at the role European traders and companies played in supplying both timber and prefabricated houses to the Dominican Republic in the eighteenth and nineteenth centuries.

The last paper in this section, Louis Vandenabeele, Inge Bertels, Ine Wouters's *From de l'Orme's to Hetzer's arch roofs: engineering the elegance* traces the development of laminated arch roof structures from Philibert De L'Orme's treatise on carpentry in the 16th century to Friedrich Otto Hetzer's glue laminated arched roof structures developed in a series of patents from 1892 to 1907.

Twentieth Century

The last ten papers in this book are all on twentieth-century topics. The first paper, by Jonathan Clarke, looks at a key question in British construction: why steel frames remained more common in the UK than concrete ones in the early twentieth century and why concrete structures became more common in the 1940s. The second paper, by Fiona Smyth also concentrates on early-twentieth-century Britain, but from a completely different point of view, that of acoustics. The government's Building Research Station (BRS) operated for just three years, from 1923 to 1926. It was the first UK laboratory set up to test building materials and the testing included sound absorbency. The paper details the setting up of the lab, the facilities and how tests were carried out. Around the same time that this laboratory was testing materials, the French engineer Eugène Freyssinet was developing methods for pre-stressing reinforced concrete. Marc Sanabra-Loewe's paper provides an overview of this important subject and explores why it was more popular in the United States than in Europe after the Second World War.

1950s

The next four papers look at the 1950s. Before independence, 20-40% of architects worked for the Government in colonial India. S. Melsens, P. Mangaonkar-Vaiude, and Y. Joshi *Architect-entrepreneurs in post-independence Pune (India)* looks at the development of independent architectural practices in the post-colonial period. The paper by Francisco Javier Muñoz Fernández examines how British prefabricated house systems came to be licenced for use in Bilbao after World War II. Similar practices could obviously have been applied to other building types such as motels. The next paper by Laura Greco shows how prefabrication was considered for motel construction in Italy but rejected by Ente Nazionale Idrocarburi (National Hydrocarbons Agency) a.k.a. ENI. (formerly AGIP). The paper works extensively from the company archives to provide details of how their motels were constructed in situ reinforced concrete and the thinking involved. The next paper by Stefania Mornati draws on the same archive, this time to provide an overview of the office and administrative buildings in steel and concrete built by ENI in the 1950s. Both papers show clearly the importance of corporate archives in preserving records of building projects as a possible area for future research. The 1950s also saw the introduction of double-glazing in Belgium as detailed by the next paper, by Stephanie Van de Voorde. As the paper explains, double-glazing had been invented in the US in the 1930s, but it was not until the 1950s that it appeared in Belgium under the trade name "Thermopane".

1960s and 1970s

The last two papers deal with the 1960s and 1970s and both by chance both deal with domes. Will McLean's paper examines the extraordinary inflatable formwork systems of Dante Bini (1932-). The so-called Binishells involve temporary balloons and a net of reinforcement over which concrete is sprayed. The resulting structure is then allowed to set and domes can be built in a matter of hours. Spans of 36 metres have been achieved and Bini himself reported that between 1970 and 1990 over 1600 Binishells were constructed. Bini is still alive and his system is still in use today. David Yeomans's paper also looks at domes, but this time geodesic ones. The importance of the self-promoting maverick Buckminster Fuller is often debated, but no one can deny his success in publicizing what became known affectionately as "Bucky Domes". As Yeomans points out, although the idea was influential, geodesic domes were not in practice terribly practical structures. Nevertheless they did offer advantages in certain situations. Yeomans's paper shows how the British engineer Frank Newby, of the firm Felix Samuely and Partners built a series of these structures in the United Kingdom and the various technical problems and issues he solved.

Concluding Remarks

The thirty-nine papers summarized here thus provide an overview of the broad range of just some of the research being carried out in the growing field of construction history. When the First International Congress was held in Madrid in 2003 there were a large number of papers devoted to structural calculations proving that historic buildings stand up. There are none in the current volume and it is good to see that the subject has increasingly sought a wide variety of approaches to understanding how and why people built in particular ways in the past. Likewise this volume has managed to avoid any papers on methods of building conservation. An understanding of the History of Construction is vital to any conservation professional, but the discipline is devoted to providing that knowledge and not getting distracted into the discussion of repair methods and other aspects of conservation work. There are other outlets for research into those areas. What all these papers do have in common is that they demonstrate not only the progress that is being made in documenting and understanding the history of building construction, but also the enormous areas that remain to be explored in every period. As in every study, the more you begin to know about a subject, the more you realise how much there is left to discover and the enormity of the work that remains to be done.

James W.P. Campbell
Chairman
Construction History Society
April 2016

The Building Industry

The place of knowledge in construction

Andrew Rabeneck
Independent researcher

> "It is fruitful to view a society from the point of view of the structured distribution of knowledge related activities"[1]

In this paper I explore shifts that I perceive in the control of the intellectual capital of construction as it relates to materials, to products, to processes and to organization. I think this should be a fruitful area of research for construction history. I believe that the last hundred years have witnessed a wholesale move of intellectual capital away from the demand side of construction, those who control the decision to build, and towards the supply side, those who respond to that decision and do the building.

Construction knowledge

Knowledge is an important instrument of modern global capitalism; indeed economists and sociologists talk increasingly of living in a *knowledge economy*.[2] This economy challenges traditional concepts of identity and authority that explain the roles of actors in knowledge related activities, including construction. A significant social and cultural side effect of the shift I am examining is the marginalization of some actors in construction whose traditional authority derives from technical knowledge, particularly architects and engineers, who have hitherto been important instruments of the demand side and who have often been mainstays of construction history.

I will now outline the process by which this shift in knowledge has happened. Construction knowledge results historically from the evolution of strategies for building.[3] In order of appearance these strategies have been:

Trial and Error - the innate and the instinctual

Copying of whole structures - collective experience, ritual

Copying of parts using rule systems - abstract systems of order, aesthetics, memory, learning, collective success and failure; tacit knowledge of technique

Explicit prediction - rules based on science (materials, structures, calculation), aesthetics, theories; tacit knowledge remains but the organization of resources is in the hands of professionals serving decision makers

The knowledge gained at each stage is cumulative rather than successive; old strategies remain in use and co-exist within the multiple cultures of construction.[4] Knowledge is developed, transmitted, stored and exploited in various ways according to prevailing customs, social and cultural. Howard Davis's 2006 analysis of contemporary building cultures usefully illustrates the highly specialized social frameworks that support different approaches to construction.[5] In the long history of pre-industrial construction, knowledge was embodied in precedent, in conventions and in acquired skills that allowed sufficient understanding to complete buildings and infrastructure that met the expectations of those paying for them. Knowledge could be taught and transmitted; yet immediate control of the material resources remained with the artisans.

With urban development, though, as buildings departed from convention in scale, type or design artisanal knowledge became inadequate to address new risks of untried forms and techniques. Skilled intermediaries between demand and supply became important – architects and engineers socially aligned with the arts and sciences. The intermediaries gained power and influence over those who wanted to put up buildings, occupying a similar social position to other professionals in clergy, law or medicine. They survived the advent of industrialization, prospering by protecting building owners from unscrupulous artisans and builders. They eventually became institutionalized in the first half of the 19th Century, and their cultural influence continued to grow, peaking around 1970. But while the professions grew there were other effects of industrialization that took hold.

Population in England and Wales doubled in 50 years, from 10,164,000 in 1811 to 20,066,000 in 1861.[6] There was demand for housing in response to household formation, but also for welfare, commercial and industrial buildings. Construction in Britain grew in prominence, as it did in all industrializing economies, providing a source of employment and support for many families, and buildings of all types to sustain economic growth and provide for the comfort of a growing population, 77% of which was urban by 1901.[7]

Industrialization

Industrialization fuelled by population growth at first produced great amounts of surplus capital seeking opportunities for investment and growth. Much capital went directly into buildings, but at least as much went into infrastructure, roads, canals and later railways, as well as into the mechanization of the extractive industries and into the manufacture of building materials and products intended for wide distribution.[8] Some investment even went into the activity of construction itself with the growth of large contracting companies using machines and new management techniques.[9] Builders quickly adopted modern materials and products because they reduced uncertainty and represented value compared with artisanal outputs of uneven quality.

The greatest advances were made in products that are socially or culturally almost invisible: bricks, tiles, glazed ceramic wares, pipework, ironmongery, sheet metals, joinery, paint and glass. These are the products that allowed speculative builders to cope with massive demand. Fortunes were made also in mediating between the manufacture of these products and their markets: builders' merchants began to manage demand by responding to local preferences, and by providing credit to poorly capitalized builders.

These industrial developments involved a growth of proprietary knowledge including patented products and processes. So, when the first scientifically derived building materials appeared, their promoters relied on exclusivity via patents to maintain commercial advantage. A tipping point in the ownership of intellectual property came with the arrival of concrete building systems from 1890, a quite sudden phenomenon, widespread in both Europe and America, spearheaded by Hennebique, Coignet, Wayss and Freytag, Ransome and others. The entrepreneurs did the research, developed the processes, patented them and gained commercial advantage through their mastery of technique.[10] Most of what they built, factories, infrastructure and agricultural buildings remained culturally invisible at the time, but the pattern they established of industrial control over scientific knowledge and processes grew steadily. The massive risks of the new technologies had to be thoroughly controlled in all respects by their promoters, rather than by architects and engineers, who were often slow to understand the significance of scientific materials.

> 'The building industry up to 1914 showed little interest in any scientific understanding of the performance, compatibility and durability of materials. Apart from Portland cement and steel there were in 1920 no specifications for building materials.' [11]

Shifts in the social knowledge systems of construction continued through the first half of the 20C, well beyond expiry of the initial patents of the first concrete system builders in the early 1920s. The broad institutionalization of concrete technology was well under way from 1900 onwards.[11]

A habit of industrial control of technical knowledge was now well-established as the supply side of construction came to be dominated by large contractors often operating internationally and offering design-and-build contracts as well as by capital-intensive material and product manufacturing businesses dependent on increasingly global sources of raw materials.[12] This pattern of knowledge development, scientific and commercially valuable, threatened the long tradition of technical knowledge used by builders, contractors and artisans directed by architects or by developers on behalf of building owners.

Yet, despite a large shift of knowledge to industry with its R&D resources, the design professions remained powerful for two reasons: because of the cultural and social position of their practitioners, and because of the trust placed in them by a great and demanding patron, the state. First after World War 1 and again after World War 2 a growing share of the nation's budget was allocated to knowledge production in the form of education and scientific research to support reconstruction.[13] In Britain this took the form of government construction research, construction demand management through a large Ministry of Public Building and Works and direct large-scale investment in public housing and infrastructure.[14]

Professional resilience

During the 1950s the state's need to re-build and respond to rapid population growth elevated construction professionals to a plateau of power and influence that they enjoyed for 30 years. Urgent need for construction of all types, but above all housing, propelled architects and engineers into positions of power as public servants, until by the early 1970s more than 50% of the British architectural profession was directly employed by central and local government. The security afforded by their position, and the beliefs of modernists about the social power of architecture, affected the professional outlook– what architects were slowly losing in terms of technical mastery of construction due to industrialisation they were making up for through an eagerly professed social concern for the end users of schools, hospitals, universities and housing. They began to re-imagine themselves, not as master-builders controlling construction, but as social engineers with the power and the responsibility to improve people's lives and thereby build a better world.[15] The focus on this view of the task, the social and political potency it gave to architects, was mirrored by a relative neglect of traditional professional competences dealing with the more practical sides of construction.

The prediction and control of construction cost, and management of the construction process were early victims of this neglect, responsibilities enthusiastically picked up by quantity surveyors, emergent 'project managers' and contractors themselves, through design-build arrangements that challenged traditional professional roles in the name of cost certainty and technical know-how. The growing availability of proprietary building systems and materials, actively marketed, particularly to public sector clients, further eroded the professional authority of architects.[16] Meanwhil,e in the academy, architectural teaching grew increasingly remote from practice and beyond the control of the professional institutions that pretended to regulate it. Technical teaching diminished steadily from 1960 onwards and responsibility for practical education fell to the offices where graduates went for early experience.

Backlash against professionals

The growing power of design and build contracting, and a general expansion in property speculation caused anxiety and much debate within the architectural profession in Britain and in the USA.[17] But in the early 1970s construction professionals generally failed to anticipate the inevitable backlash against their power and influence, a backlash born of the disruption of global markets following dramatic oil price increases, with inflation and uncertainty about resources fuelling a revival of free-market economic ideology and fostering a deep hostility to professional monopolies. All professions, even the hallowed 'scientific community', came to be seen as creators of problems and generators of negative consequences. The very concept of professionalism was put under threat.[18] A decline in public trust and its replacement by an overriding notion of accountability led to a quite sudden hollowing out of the welfare state. The deadly combination of world recession and raging inflation in the mid-1970s forced Western governments to cut back drastically on key elements of the welfare state as their relative costs rose, notably public housing, now increasingly seen as unaffordable.

The rolling back of the state that gathered pace during the late 1970s and early 1980s included divestment of a huge body of publicly owned and delivered intellectual and professional capital related to design, construction and management of buildings. Responsibilities were transferred, diluted or lost as quickly as physical properties were sold to the private sector. The procurement skills of clients were dismantled as previously responsible government departments enthusiastically deskilled themselves. Private design and consultancy practices were invited to compete for public work on the basis of price rather than experience or qualifications. Such 'rationalisation' of procurement processes became politically popular in the freewheeling and relatively prosperous 1980s and 1990s. The promise was that free market procurement processes would be tested against robust, empirically based criteria. Unfortunately, the criteria actually used in this process became increasingly biased towards supply-side considerations, e.g. easy delivery at low cost, unaccompanied by any attempt to measure the longer-term value to taxpayers, clients and end users.[19]

Globalisation of capital markets

While the selling off of public knowledge has been going on apace, the industrialised building product and materials producers have been increasing their grip on global markets, massively helped by the deregulation of the capital markets around 1986, that freed up capital to move wherever it is needed. The new mobility of capital and its instruments of distribution represent a revolution in the political economy of construction: the extraction of raw materials, the manufacture and distribution of building materials, products and systems of construction, the organisation and execution of construction, the management of construction labour and not least the position of architects and engineers. Most significantly, new capital has fuelled a boom in global construction. By 2025, the global construction and engineering industry is forecast to have a value of $15 trillion, an increase of 70% since

2012, with just three countries accounting for 60% of the growth; China, the US and India.[20] Dynamic markets and mobile capital have been complemented by massive growth in shipping capacity, whether in bulk or in containers, making the effects of geographical distance completely insignificant for most materials and products.

The recent particular development and structure of the world's construction markets can be explained by the monopolies that First World manufacturing and construction firms have built up using the technologies that underlie the global built environment.[21] It took most of the twentieth century to embed First World products, materials and practices on a global scale.[22] Whether considering product standards of the ISO or codes of engineering practice, the First World is deeply embedded everywhere. So what gets built today in new and developing markets is whatever can unlock access to capital, regardless of point of origin or application. 'Investment grade' businesses, infrastructure and property are increasingly defined in terms of the criteria applied by the global underwriters of construction risks. Investment risk has been globalised to match global technology and track capital.

These recent developments represent the triumph of industrialization. The highly capitalized companies that dominate the markets may achieve their positions through mergers and acquisitions, but they also dominate research and development in their fields to preserve commercial advantage, thus controlling intrinsic knowledge. Since the abandonment of public leadership in construction knowledge in Britain, symbolised by the sale of the Building Research Establishment to its managers for £1.7m., there has been a diffusion of technical authority, and growing dependency on the knowledge of commercial firms.[23] Examples of such firms include the Austrian Wienerberger brick company, a global business with €3Bn annual revenues, exemplifying globalisation since the 1980s. With 15,000 employees, well capitalised and aggressively acquiring rivals in all world markets, Wienerberger dominates world brick and tile markets. It keeps tight control over technical knowledge, both for production and for use of its products, carefully managing its relations with specifiers in all markets. Another example, in architectural glass production, the Japanese NSG group which bought Pilkingtons in 2006, and which now dominates global production, operates in 28 countries and has a turnover of £3.7bn. But the biggest recent global move has been the 2015 merger of the French Lafarge and Swiss Holcim cement manufacturers, designed to create "the most advanced group in the building materials industry" (and to save the companies €1.4 bn annually). With a market capitalisation of €40bn and active demand management through its global control of sand and aggregate resources, the new company already dominates the cement and concrete knowledge that has positioned it so strongly.

Institutionalization of expertise

Such organizations challenge industrial society's traditional way of institutionalizing expertise, which is through professionalism. While society has generally positioned expertise in people rather than in things or rules, professionalism continues to survive, but its survival is precarious.[24] The commodification of expertise through computer software is an obvious threat, particularly among structural and mechanical engineers. Capital industry allows selective access to expertise through information systems, technical education, legal protocols and tools such as BIM, CAD and CAM. This access, presented as technical information and support, is in reality a subtle form of control. As these tools increasingly define the way things are, avoidance becomes futile; furthermore they are enthusiastically adopted by professional institutions and powerful clients, particularly governments; they enter the transactions between supply and demand. Nonprofessionals increasingly own and operate professional commodities.

The place of knowledge in construction

Insidious though commodification is, organization provides a much more formidable alternative to professionalism, though it mostly passes unnoticed. Just as machine-based division of labour destroyed skilled craft labour, so professional judgment is being replaced by the elaborate bureaucracies of multi-professional firms, in which professional knowledge is encoded in the structures of the organizations themselves. Actual expertise resides in the rules of these organizations, mediated by professional administrators, project managers, heads of discipline, and their ilk. Furthermore, organizational structures on the demand side now increasingly mirror those on the supply side – i.e. they resemble and seek out one another in mutual reinforcement, as witnessed in the contemporary procurement processes of both the public and private sectors.

So not only has direct control over knowledge of construction moved to the supply side, but the social and cultural context of its use, construction practice, is changing as well; the professional system is being replaced by a bureaucratic one, the rules of which are driven by the demands of large clients and the behaviors of major industrial firms. When a product manufacturer offers architects and engineers 'free' BIM templates and CAD details to download, the knowledge and assumptions embedded within them eclipse and replace the professional function. The World Wide Web, with its massive impact on data storage, transmission, diffusion and accessibility, is yet another significant instrument of the industrialization of knowledge.

Conclusion

For an individual professional to escape absorption by the organizational machine and to succeed in making original contributions that affect the nature of demand, is already hard and becoming harder by the day. For example, the authors collected in BRI's 'New Professionalism' issue offered an array of possible responses to the loss of professional authority, mostly centered on defense of the public good, championing sustainability of the national building stock and collaborative working.[25] But the purpose of this paper is to draw attention to the irreversible change in the social structure of construction knowledge, and the move to supply side dominance of it, mostly over the last century. The extent of the shift remains unresearched and underestimated and it is full of fascinating historiographical possibilities for construction historians.[26] Issues of identity and authority in the structure of construction knowledge remain vitally important to construction history; in any period they end up defining what may be built and how it may be built.

Note and references

[1] F. Machlup *The Production and Distribution of Knowledge in the United States* Princeton University press 1962

[2] The term was coined in 1962 by the economist Fritz Machlup. Sociologists of the social structure of knowledge systems, mainly funded by the U.S. Department of Education, include Burkhart Holzner, whose key book is *Identity and Authority: Explorations in the Theory of Society* (with Roland Robertson) London, Blackwell, 1980. More recently the economist Dominique Foray deals with the economics of the production and the management of knowledge in modern society, in his *The Economics of Knowledge*, Cambridge MA, MIT, 2006.

[3] A. Rabeneck, 'A model of social and technical change in building' pp75-87 in Lauri Koskela and Phil Roberts, (Eds) Proceedings of a Symposium: towards the Formation of Theory for the Built Environment, Salford 2007, University of Salford.

[4] The enduring quality of old technologies, and the important role of copying and replication in technical

development were elegantly discussed by George Kubler in *The Shape of Time: remarks on the history of things*, New Haven, Yale, 1962, and by George Basalla in *The Evolution of Technology*, Cambridge University Press, 1988. More recently David Edgerton has re-emphasised the principle in *The Shock of the Old; Technology and Global History since 1900*, London, Profile, 2006.

[5] Howard Davis *The Culture of Building*, Oxford, OUP, 2006.

[6] B.R. Mitchell, & P. Deane, *1962 Abstract of British Historical Statistics*, Cambridge, Cambridge University Press. p. 6.

[7] Andrew Rabeneck, 'The invention of the building industry in Britain' *ArtefaCToS*, vol. 4, nº 1, December, 94-121.

[8] One of few books describing the emergence of the modern building technology in Britain is Akira Satoh's *Building in Britain: Origins of a Modern Industry*, with Ralph Morton, Aldershot, Scolar Press 1995.

[9] What Akira Satoh does for construction technology, C.G. Powell does for construction's organisational development, *An Economic History of the British Building Industry 1815-1979*, London, Methuen 1980.

[10] A. Rabeneck 'The transformation of Construction by Concrete', *Nuts and Bolts of Construction History,* proceedings of the 4th International Congress on Construction History, Paris, 2012, vol.2, 627-635.

[11] Amy E Slaton, *Reinforced concrete and the modernization of American building, 1900-1930*, Baltimore, Johns Hopkins University Press 2001. Slaton describes the education in America, often by correspondence, of large numbers of concrete technicians who were snapped up on graduation, not by consulting engineers or architects, but by contractors and product manufacturers wanting to exploit the new technology.

[12] Two books deal with the international commercial expansion of construction; Marc Linder, *Projecting Capitalism: A History of the Internationalization of the Construction Industry,* Westport Conn. and London, Greenwood Press 1994 and Jeffrey Cody, *Exporting American Architecture 1870-2000*, London, Routledge, 2003.

[13] Fritz Machlup writing in 1962, gave as his reason for studying the production of knowledge the increasing share of the nation's budget allocated to the production of knowledge; the government's quest for social benefit through investment in knowledge production; and the shift in the labor force from physical to brain-work.

[14] Mark Swenarton, *Building the New Jerusalem*, Watford, BRE Press 2008. Introduction, pp. 1-11.

[15] Andrew Saint, *Towards a Social Architecture: the Role of School Building in Post-War England*, London, Yale University Press 1987.

[16] Stefan Muthesius and Miles Glendenning, *Tower Block: Modern Public Housing in England, Scotland, Wales and Northern Ireland* London, Paul Mellon Centre for Studies 1994.

[17] The debates on the professions crystalized into books only later, following vgorous polemics in various journals. Notable are Malcolm MacEwen's *Crisis in Architecture*, London RIBA Publications, 1974, and Brent Brolin's *The Failure of Modern Architecture*, London, Studio Vista, 1976.

[18] Attacks on professions and professionals were led by iconoclasts such as Rachel Carson, Jane Jacobs and later by Ivan Illich and E. F. Schumacher who initially inspired politicians to legislate against professional privilege. Later waves attacked government welfare and spending in general leading to the 'rolling back of the State'; see Harold Perkin *The Rise of Professional Society; England since 1880*, London, Routledge, 2002, particularly Chapter 10 'The Backlash Against Professional Society'.

[19] Frank Duffy and Andrew Rabeneck 'Professionalism and architects in the 21st century' *Building Research and Information* Vol. 41 No. 1, 2013 115-122.

[20] *Global Construction 2025; a global forecast for the construciotn industry to 2025.* London, Oxford Economics, 2013.

[21] Marc Linder, 1994, Chapter 9, The Emergence of a World Construction market and the Relative decline of

U.S. Firms.

[22] The processes of diffusion and institutionalisation are addressed in James Scott *Seeing Like a State*, New Haven, Yale, 1998, Chapter 3, Authoritarian High Modernism, and more recently in Keller Easterling *Extrastatecraft: the Power of infrastructure space*, London, Verso, 2014.

[23] David Parker *The Official History of Privatisation: Popular capitalism 1987-97* London, Routledge 2012, p. 386.

[24] Andrew Abbott *The System of Professions; An Essay on the Division of Expert Labor*, Chicago, University of Chicago Press, 1988. Abbott contrasts professionalism, commodification and organisation as social modes of institutionalising expertise.

[25] Bill Bordass and Adrian Leaman (Eds.) 'New Professionalism', special issue, *Building Research and Information* Vol. 41 No. 1, 2013

[26] A fascinating glimpse of the possibilities is given by Gilles Ragot's commentary on the Hennebique Archives, exposing the historiographical blunders of generations of architectural historians. 'The Hennebique Archives: Towards a New Corpus for Contemporary Architectural History', *American Archivist*, Vol. 59, Spring 1996. 214-220.

Have the effects of its history resulted in a Scottish construction industry that differs from its counterparts in the rest of the UK?

Nina Baker
Independent Researcher

Introduction

The construction of buildings and infrastructure constitutes one of the most important of economic activities of a country. Without this initial effort, little else beyond the most basic of subsistence agriculture can progress. Since the rebirth of the Scottish Parliament in 1999, many types of data, not previously available at all in a form that allowed extraction of information about Scotland, are now gathered by the Scottish Government. The legal, financial and educational systems in Scotland all differ structurally from those in the rest of Britain, so its construction industry might also be expected to show structural differences, both historically and currently.

The economic relationship between Scotland and the rest of the UK has varied from total isolation to total dependence. Economists consider Scotland a "region", as a geographically compact area with a population in millions and a labour force with more internal mobility than external (Krugman, 2003). Until the Act of Union (1707) Scotland was not only a separate nation, she was also physically isolated by poor transport links, as was true for at least another hundred years. This physical, economic and political isolation did not prevent movement of labour or ideas, but the nation remained very much itself. The industrial revolution brought Scotland to the forefront in Britain's manufacturing, particularly in the metal trades. The subsequent decline, from the early twentieth century, resulted in an outflow of manufacturing and its labour force. If manufacturing and its labour force was and is mobile, the same is not true for the output of the construction industry. Scotland's builders may follow the work abroad (although Krugman (2003) argues that the Scottish expatriate working population is peculiarly likely to return to Scotland at all stages of life), but the industry's products cannot. It is perhaps for this reason that technological change, economic control and planning regulations have remained different in Scotland.

To set the context for other research into the unique aspects of Scotland's construction industry, this review of literature and statistics aims to assemble data to consider the following:

- How did its constituent parts, structure and organisations change over time?
- What constitutes an industry in the eyes of its members and of outsiders?
- Is there evidence of a perception of a distinct entity for a construction industry in Scotland?

Due to the historically peripheral political status of Scotland, much of the available literature refers either mainly or exclusively to the development of the construction industry in England, even when the title of the work includes the word "Britain". This paper will draw together existing data to provide a new and coherent body of information for scholars.

Have the effects of its history resulted in a Scottish construction industry that differs from its counterparts in the rest of the UK?

Method

Data concerning industry structure and perceptions was sought by a literature search into:

- The general economic and industrial history of Scotland
- The Incorporations of trades
- The construction trades unions
- The construction industry employers' organisations
- The housebuilding industry

Statistical sources were searched for evidence of the extent of construction activity since earliest times, in the following categories:

- Numbers of participants
- Structural patterns: sizes of firms
- Access to materials and other inputs
- Output: housebuilding, industrial, commercial and infrastructural construction figures.

For evidence of levels of activity prior to the advent of systematic statistical collection, such as the first Statistical Account of Scotland, much has had to be inferred from remaining evidence.

Evidence of changing structure over time

Until modern times, many buildings were constructed informally, by the people who needed them, e.g. crofters constructing farm buildings. Major structures, from the earliest times, required at least some expert carpentry or masonry skills plus the aid of local unskilled labour.

There is implicit evidence for the extent to which surplus labour could be diverted from essential food production to undertake important building projects in the past. Prehistoric building effort in Scotland, such as Skara Brae stone village, in Orkney, with its interconnected family homes of worked masonry and wood, implies some masons who had acquired stone working skills over time. Probably such skilled workers were peripatetic, providing their services where required (Armit, 2003).

4750 years ago the economically pointless, but presumably culturally vital, structure of Maes Howe, Orkney, had taken 100,000 person hours to build and involved masons with advanced stone-working and structural skills, as well as huge amounts of unskilled labour, who would have had to be spared from food production, probably during the agriculturally crucial summer season. 3,000 years ago the climate cooled and the northern mainland population migrated to the warmer south, triggering the construction of many hill forts, as lowlanders attempted to defend their resources against incomers. Eildon Hill North, in the Scottish Borders, was the site of a huge hill fort, with 16 hectares of fortified enclosure and 500 associated stone houses, i.e. a "Town" of possibly 3-5,000 people. The total population of mainland Britain at that time was about 200,000, so this must have therefore been one of the largest single gatherings of people in the whole British isles. The labour and organization to build that must have been substantial.

Iron Age technical advances, such as iron ploughs (700BC) and rotary querns (200 BC), released some labour from food-production work. At this time, huge and structurally very sophisticated, stone Brochs and "Atlantic roundhouses" were providing settlements all over Scotland, again representing major amounts of construction work.

The Romans' departure from England, in 410AD, enabled the 'Scots' from Northern Ireland, to enter 'Scotland' for the first time. They built stone forts for prestige as much as for defence. The arrival of Columba in 563AD, to convert Scotland to Christianity, marks the beginning of church-building in Scotland. The building of churches and castles created a demand for unskilled labour, often compulsory for the local peasantry, overseen by skilled masons, who were also taking on some of the roles of engineers and architects.

The Norman King David 1 introduced the Feudal system of land tenure, which influenced patterns of urban growth in Scotland to the present day. The King is head of a feudal system and towns needed his permission to become a Royal Burgh to gain the privileges of raising taxes and holding markets. The layouts of older towns, with Mercat (market) crosses, Tollbooths and wide highstreets suitable for authorized markets, date from this system, and remain the underlying principle of the layout of most Scottish towns. Burgesses (freemen of a Burgh) were allocated plots of land along the highstreet and the right to build behind them, resulting in the narrow entrance lanes (closes, wynds or vennels) still to be seen and even replicated in modern tenements.

Scottish Incorporated Trades (guilds) enabled craftsmen to gain a say in the running of the Burgh, along with the Burgesses and guilds of merchants. The 13th Century provides the earliest records of master builders contracting for a building and employing other workers on a "measure and value" basis, assessed on completion. In 1222, Aberdeen had the first Dean of a merchant guild, with responsibilities for overseeing public works and for approving applications to build new buildings - the early planning application process (McWilliam, 1975). James 1 decreed (1424) that each trade should have a Dekyn (deacon) to oversee the quality of work of its members.

The trades' Incorporations oversaw the professional and social welfare of their members. The trades limited the number of new entrants by requiring a 7-year apprenticeship, followed by 2 years as a servant under a master, before the tradesman could offer his "Essay piece" for approval for entry to full membership or "freedom" to work. "Unfree" tradesmen could not carry on their trade within the Burgh. It was not unknown for Trades in the burghs to assist unfree men working beyond the burgh areas. A Glasgow mason was honoured by his Trade for his work to help the unfree masons in the area between Glasgow and Dumbarton.

The Wrights (woodworkers) building Glasgow cathedral were granted a Royal Charter in 1057 by King Malcolm III, enabling the governing structure of that craft to have state recognition. (Trades House) This is considerably in advance of the English craft guilds or livery companies which started in the 14th century. The Wrights' charter initially covered all the building trades, including the joiners, masons and coopers, but the latter two separated from the joiners in 1600. In some Scottish cities, slaters were incorporated into either the wrights (because of the woodwork required in a roof) or in the masons (because slate was stone). However, in Dundee the Slaters were a separate trade. Their earliest date is not now known because their "Lockit books" were destroyed in the 16th century.

Many of Scotland's castles and churches were built in the 13th-15th Centuries: Edinburgh (Great Hall 1510), Crathes (1596), Dunrobin (1236), Ravenscraig (1460), requiring enormous amounts of skilled and unskilled labour. There is evidence, from masons' personal marks, to show that skilled building workers were travelling from contract to contract, to supervise local unskilled labour. In 1503, a statute required all seaboard towns in Scotland to use their own money (the now controversial "Common Good" fund) to build seawalls of lime mortar and stone to protect against the English fleet. By the middle of the century, when many towns were enlarging, Elgin had to employ surveyors to mark out land for house building and Glasgow's population had tripled from that of a century previous.

The "Act Anent the uphalding of decayed landis within burghs" in 1594 pressurised owners of substandard property to maintain or rebuild, leading to a "great rebuild". By the end of the 16th Century, the religious reformation obliged parishes to build a kirk and a school in every parish. Most Burghs had Tolbooth towers, and markets, and harbours and bridges were being built to facilitate trade, reflecting Scotland's rising economy.

Throughout the 17th Century, Incorporated Trades formalized their constitutions and interactions with the Kirk, Burgh and merchants, by means of Seals of Cause. In 1659 the Dundee Master masons were allowed to "Combine" to protect jobs, at an agreed rate for agreed hours: 16s 8d per 12-hour day. This was highly unusual, as the burghs were generally terrified of "Combinations" like this, which were early forerunners of the closed shop trades union. Strenuous efforts to outlaw them continued right into the 19th Century.

The act protecting the textile industry from imports (1681) led to an early boom in industrial building, with many rural towns developing rapidly and building wool mills. This created a new type of work, which was to be very important to the building trades over the following two centuries: industrial and commercial structures.

Scotland's major cities expanded fast in the 18th Century, with concomitant infrastructure building. The Barony parish of Glasgow expanded from a population of 3,905 in 1755 (Gray, 1975) to 18,451 in 1791 (Sinclair, 1799), necessitating the building of 486 new dwellings in 1789-1799.

Following the 1715 Jacobite uprising, General Wade and Major Caulfield used soldiers to build hundreds of miles of road and tens of bridges to facilitate military access to the Scottish Highlands. Although they chose, for political reasons, not to use indigenous building workers for the construction of the roads, Major Caulfield set up a system of localized responsibility to ensure their future maintenance. The Turnpike Act of 1751 enabled the building of further hundreds of miles of toll roads in the Lowlands, with tollbooths (and "Turnpike" gates) at 5-mile intervals (McWilliam, 1975). In the 1780s the rapid expansion of industry needed factory villages for workers, such as New Lanark's model village, and mining towns in coal areas. Edinburgh and Glasgow expanded during the 18th century, each laying out "new town" areas. However, from 1739 to 1760s, there was a general economic depression, followed by a recovery in 1790, leading to another huge increase in infrastructure spending. This meant the system was under a sudden strain and, when war came in 1793, there was collapse of credit and the output of the brick making industry dropped 40% in 2 years. The draconian Highland Clearances of this period meant that cleared families went either to the cities (mainly Glasgow) or to the coasts, requiring a rapid development of coastal villages.

Scotland differed from England in how it dealt with poverty. In England, younger healthy or "outdoor" paupers were placed in obligatory apprenticeships to trades masters, administered under the Poor Laws by the parish, and known as parish apprenticeships (Walmsley, 1990). Surprisingly this also heralded a rare period when young women could get apprenticeships in the manual crafts, including metal working and building trades. However, the trades' Incorporations in Scotland still strongly controlled entry to the building crafts and this system of parish apprenticeships did not occur (Mitchison, 1988). There were instances of public and infrastructure work employing numbers of paupers as unskilled labourers, sometimes on a more or less "make-work" basis.

The end of the 18th Century saw the beginning of the general contractor type of firm with subcontractors, ending the earlier system of employing individual craft workers directly via an agent, master builder, architect or surveyor. In 1780, new rules required Government departments commissioning building work to use the new "Contract in gross" procurement system.

In 1803, a system of Commissioners for Highland Roads appointed Thomas Telford to extend Wade's road system. He reported that more than 1,000 bridges were needed on 780 miles of road, and that 200 new towns and planned villages should be developed at major junctions and river crossings. This major work extended into the first half of the 19th Century (McWilliam, 1975).

The first official census, in 1801 (Fig. 1), demonstrated that there had been a major increase in pre-industrial revolution urban populations. Burghs had to develop and expand, particularly requiring workers' housing and town houses for Lairds etc.

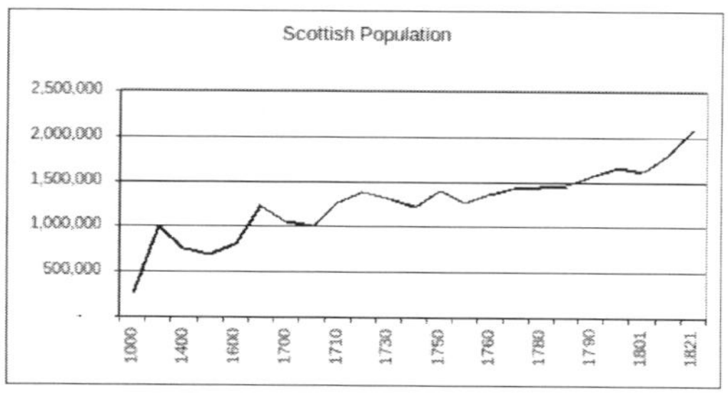

Figure 1. Scottish Population to 1821 (Sinclair, 1799 and censuses)

In 1846 the Act Abolishing Exclusive Trading Privileges ("Recissory Act") removed the political and monopolistic trading rights for the Incorporated Trades, which became welfare and social groups. This meant that all crafts could operate anywhere but also meant that there could be less oversight of standards for new entrants. However, apprenticeships, on similar lines to those used since the Middle Ages, continued to be the usual mode of entry for the next hundred years.

The 19th century saw the emergence of trades' unions and a measure of industrial organisation at all levels of the industry for both workers and employers. The employers acted vigorously to oppose "combinations" and unionisation for as long as possible and, with most construction work being small scale and short-term, levels of unionisation in the Scottish industry remained low. The industry was notoriously conservative both in technical practice and in conditions of work, with most workers favouring the specialised craft union over a whole-industry type of union common in the metal trades. The United Operative Masons of Scotland Society was started in1830 and, in 1844, bricklayers combined to prohibit piecework in Scotland (Marwick, 1936). The masons obtained the legal right to strike in 1836 and became the Scottish United Operative Masons Association, whose membership rose to 14,000 in 1877 with representation in 40 towns and cities (Jones, 1861). The masons were the only trade to be so widely represented at that time. Carpenters and joiners formed various unions from 1836 and became the Associated Carpenters and Joiners in 1861, in competition with another London-based union. Some plumbers joined unions based in England and some formed small local trade clubs but were not usually very highly unionised because of the small, itinerant nature of their jobs. There was a small Scottish Slaters' Society from the 1860s, operating mainly on the West Coast, a Scottish National Operative Plasterers union from 1888 and a Scottish National Federation of House and Ship Painters from 1887. The plasterers had about 1,000 members and their main activity was to employ quality control inspectors to ensure plasterers were not undercutting colleagues by 'scamping' on work. Bricklayers, joiners, glaziers, painters, plasterers, plumbers, slates and masons all had their own meeting places in Glasgow in 1861 but this was unusual and reflects the huge amount of work taking place there.

This level of organisation was not reflected in the firms themselves. Most firms were small, ephemeral and badly managed. Many kept no accounts and even the largest had no idea about market research or supply and demand. Anyone could call themselves a builder, or style themselves as undertaking any trade. Following the lead of Cubitts in England in 1815, some larger Scottish firms started to employ the full range of trades throughout the year, to provide all the work for a contract without subcontracting. Many became speculative builders in order to provide full employment (Bowley, 1966), but the practice was far less popular in Scotland and the industry remained dominated by small firms.

In 1834 the first forms of contract were agreed and the Institute of British Architects and the Builders' Society were founded. In 1850 the Architectural Institute of Scotland was founded. 1868 saw the founding of the Institution of Surveyors. Competitive tendering requirements, particularly for public works, led to dangerously low tenders and consequent bankruptcies, leading the Public Office of Works to draw up approved lists of potential tenderers. Previously, most subcontracting trades would provide their own materials but this became less common during this period, so that subcontractors were only paid for the labour they provided, but worked from more detailed plans under closer supervision (Bowyer, 1973).

The nineteenth century construction industry in Scotland had a huge cast of large and small companies (Morgan, 1990), which provide a lot of employment opportunities (Table 1) across the country, usually more than 10% of those in work. McAlpines employed 7,000 people in 1904, but there were many contractors with over 1,000 employees at that time.

Table 1. Numbers recorded in Decennial Census returns as working in construction related occupations

Year	Males in construction	Females in construction
1841	61904	158
1851	75440	187
1861	81457	184
1871	98184	324
1881	112572	560
1891	216244	819
1901	112528	681

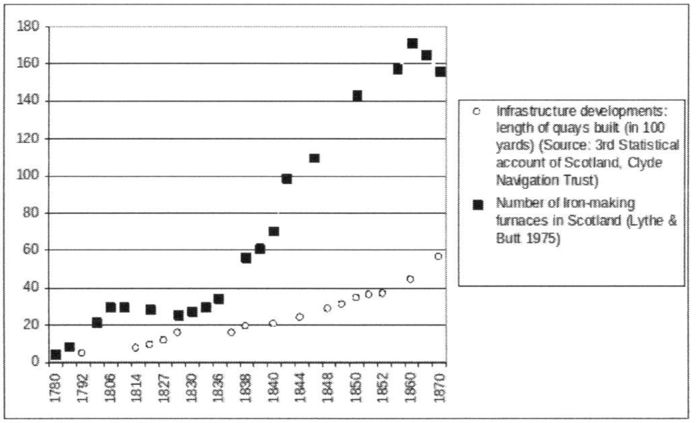

Figure 2. Industrial and infrastructural construction in the 19th Century in Scotland

Construction in the nineteenth century featured huge amounts of industrial and infrastructure works (Fig. 2). Nearly every major player of the time was involved in building or financing some part of the railways, but these were not always a sure way to success and the Talla water scheme bankrupted the previously large and successful company of Robert Young. The few firms founded over a hundred years ago which are still around today are those which were able to diversify successfully. Finance for builders came from many sources, large and small, formal and informal, and the ability of any builder to raise capital for a speculative venture depended upon the firm's own credit rating. Many small firms relied on informal credit and were chronically under-capitalised (Rodger, 1999). Such firms were therefore very susceptible to failure, and individuals commonly moved in and out of the contractor/journeyman roles.

For most of the 19th century the family firm was the normal model. However, very few survive to the present day, let alone in a form recognisable as a family firm. The advent of the limited liability company saved many small family firms in inheritance crises and bringing in a wider range of directors, often encompassing a wide network of interconnected families. Most of the firms were only capable of taking on small projects, but this period saw the start of widespread change with many large housebuilding and industrial contracts.

Few family firms lasted beyond the second generation and most of the Victorian firms were gone by 1918. One of the deciding factors was the Finance Act of 1910, which introduced an Increment Duty severely reducing income from the Scottish feu duties and ground rents on which many speculative builders relied for their reserve income (Slaven & Checkland, 1990). This prompted many firms to move into property management, and so survive the building slump at the start of the century but meant there was a very small industry remaining to deal with demand between the wars. Mergers and takeovers saw the disappearance of some previously important names and the spectacular collapses of formerly strong family firms. Smaller firms could not normally make that change and many folded, as they lacked the business skills. The interwar years featured huge growth, particularly in building by private contractors (e.g. Mactaggart & Mickel and Millers) for local authorities. The Scottish Housing Group brought together a number of firms to collaborate on erecting non-traditional housing.

The structure of the industry continued to include high numbers of small firms, with many individuals operating flexibly as employer or skilled employee to facilitate survival of such small firms. In 1930 there were 317 firms in Scotland with more than 200 employees each and 44,028 firms with less than 10 each. This pattern was uniform in all building trades (Milnes 1936) and areas of Scotland. Edinburgh (Fig. 3) in this period shows how medium sized firms predominated numerically. Interestingly Robertson (1936) commented that Edinburgh building practices at that time were likely to be less efficient than other parts of Scotland or the UK, due to the higher level of manual labour used in Edinburgh. Perhaps this explains why the shape of this graph is not as skewed to the smaller firms as would have been expected.

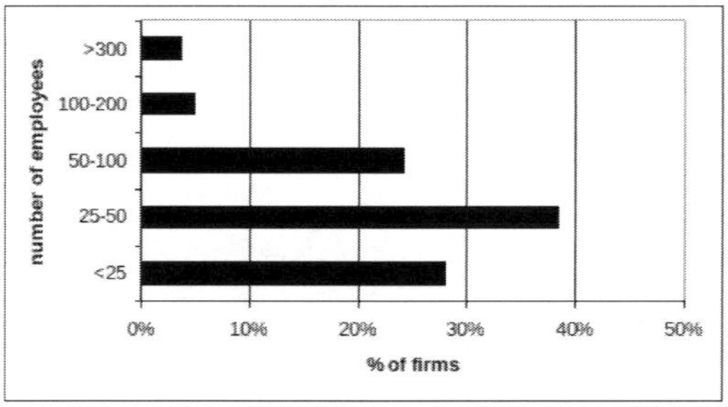

Figure 3. Structure of building industry in Edinburgh 1923-34 (Milnes, 1936)

There were fewer than 1,000 firms in Scotland (1935) who could build more than 100 houses/year and only 31 that could construct more than 1000/year. Many builders avoided public contracts because they were seen as either unfair or unprofitable. At this period the term "Contractor" applied strictly to public works contracting (roads, sewers etc.) and this group employed a larger percentage of unskilled labour than the "Building" firm. The pressure to take on novel methods and materials suited some companies, such as Melville Dundas and Whitson (concrete) and Robert Barclay Shaw (structural steel). However, the sector retained its reputation for conservatism, and small traditional builders could still find contracts, although they continued to be very vulnerable to economic cycles, against which they had insufficient resources to cushion themselves. In the interwar period, there was first a severe materials shortage and then a shortage of skilled labour, particularly bricklayers. Councils did not have their own building workers and the huge amount of public housing was mostly done under contract by private companies, such as Mactaggart & Mickel (Glasgow) and James Miller (Edinburgh).

The industry continued to be conservative in its practices, with unions resisting a national industry-wide union longer than some other industries. The Scottish Plasterers' Association refused the offer of a merger with the English National Association of Operative Plasterers in 1952 (Newman 1960). The Amalgamated Society of Woodworkers (ASW), believing that their special skills protected them against change, refused in 1959 to join with other unions to form an industry-wide union. This was not to come about until the Union of Construction, Allied Trades and Technicians (UCATT) formed in 1971, taking in the ASW, the Amalgamated Society of Painters and Decorators, the Association of Building Technicians and the Amalgamated Union of Building Trade Workers.

The Scottish Special Housing Association (SSHA), with its strong links to government subsidy and central organisation was superceded, at the end of the 1940s, by two umbrella groups: the Scottish Housing Group (SHG) operating mainly in the west and the Cruden Group in the east. SHG included Melville, Dundas and Whitson, John Lawrence, MacTagggart and Mickel, John Bisset and William Tawse, James Miller and W&JR Watson and was a cartel, aiming to exclude English contractors. The Cruden Group focused on novel methods and prefabrication and included Alexander Hall, Laidlaws, Alliance Construction and J. Wrights. These organisations helped bridge a gap until dominant companies could develop. In the 1950s the Miller Group (in Edinburgh) and

John Lawrence were major players, employing thousands of workers on site and in factories and taking ownership of building materials suppliers too.

The oil crisis of 1973 led to a 22% fall in construction output 1973-1981, particularly in the public sector. Construction had a slower upward trend than the rest of the Scottish economy (SPIC 2000). Thatcherite policies to encourage private ownership changed the direction of the housebuilding industry so that, from the 1980s, there was far more private, speculative housebuilding, although commercial and industrial construction stabilized and fell. In 2000 the Scottish Executive's Economic Report (2000) described the Scottish construction industry as less cyclic than it had been in the mid 1980s, and also less cyclic than its UK and European counterparts. By the end of 2015 the industry was considered to be in robust health, and indeed apparently the key driver in economic growth for the year, but with the perennial shortage of skilled labour. (Scottish Government, 2015)

The Scottish housebuilding market is also less overheated than that of the south east of England, where land shortage and house price inflation are problematic. When competitive tendering forced profit levels down to as low as 1.5%, many firms had to cease speculative building. Some moved into the Private Finance Initiatives field, where long-term stability was guaranteed by maintenance contracts for profit levels up to 15% (Corporate Watch UK, March 2004).

The modern construction industry now has huge numbers of very small firms and sole traders in Scotland, as in the UK generally (Fig. 4). However, Scotland has a lower percentage of sole traders and very small firms than the UK, but a higher percentage of larger firms.

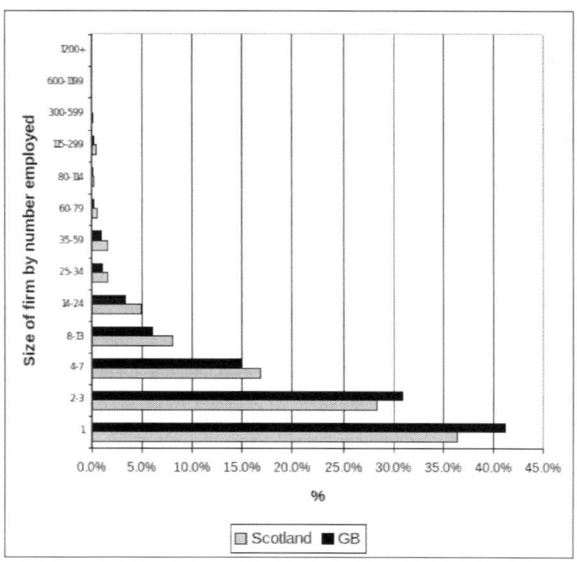

Figure 4. Structure of the Scottish and UK Construction Industries 2003 (DTI Construction Annual, 2003)

Conclusions

It can be seen that there was a distinct and distinctive Scottish construction industry from earliest times and that aspects have changed remarkably little over time. The pre-industrial revolution era was marked by very slow change in both technological and structural aspects of the construction industry. Materials, tools, contracting systems, the scale of work and control of manpower and means of production scarcely changed over hundreds of years. The new technology and massive movement of people during the nineteenth century affected these issues to some extent, but the Scottish construction industry profile remained one of a few large firms and a preponderance of very small local firms. The difficulty in getting finance to sustain smaller firms through slumps made the Scottish industry peculiarly resistant to technical and structural change. A single technological change which Scotland has, however, made its own from the late twentieth century, is the use of timber-frame housing, in which Scotland substantially outpaces the rest of the UK. It is still relatively conservative in outlook, with a less diverse workforce than in England. The Scottish construction industry retains a local character but is vital importance to national economic development.

Since the establishment of the Scottish Parliament, its interactions with the UK government remain variable, responding to conflicting demands for uniformity or difference in policy or implementation for Scotland. One area where a uniform policy impinges on a non-uniform situation is that of the effects of interest rate changes. Interest rates are among the fiscal measures used by the government to manipulate the market and control inflation. The well-known problem of house-price inflation in the South East of England is not uniform across the whole of the UK, but the mortgage interest rates are.

In Scotland, life and business may feel they operate in a separate "Nation", regardless of political formalities but, from the south of England, Scotland may seem like a tiny region of Britain and no different from, say, the English Midlands. Many of these differences have more or less relevance depending upon which end of the North/South telescope you look through, but Scotland retains much that is different.

References

[1] Bowley, M., *The British building industry*. Cambridge University Press, 1966.

[2] Bowyer, J., *A history of building*. Crosby Lockwood Staples,1973.

[3] Gibb, K., *Rebirth of the Market 1975 – present day and beyond,* in Homebuilders, RCAHMS, 1999.

[4] Gray, J.(editor), *Scottish population statistics including Webster's analysis of population 1755.* Scottish Academic Press, 1975.

[5] Jones, T., *UK First Annual Trades Union Directory*, 1861.

[6] Krugman, P., *Growth on the periphery: second winds for industrial regions?* Allander Series, Fraser of Allander Institute, 2003.

[7] Lewis, J. Parry, *Building Cycles and Britain's growth.* Macmillan, 1965.

[8] Marwick, W.H., *Economic developments in Victorian Scotland.* George Allen and Unwin, 1936.

[9] McWilliam, C., *Scottish townscape.* Collins, 1975.

[10] Milnes, N., *A study of industrial Edinburgh and the surrounding area 1923-34,* vol.1. P.S.King and Son Ltd, 1936.

[11] Mitchison, R., *The Poor Law. In: People and Society, vol 1, 1760-1830,* edited by Devine & Mitchison, John Donald Publishers Ltd. ISBN 0859762106, 1988.

[12] Morgan, N.J., *Construction Industry sector essay, in Dictionary of Scottish Business Biography Vol2*, edited by Slaven and Checkland, Aberdeen University Press, (1990).

[13] Newman, J.R., T*he NAOP Heritage, a short historical review of the growth and development of the National Association of Operative Plasterers 1860-1960.* NAOP, 1960.

[14] Owens, A., *Inheritance and the life-cycle of family firms in the early industrial revolution.* Business History, vol44, no.1, pp21-46. 2002.

[15] Robertson, M., *Building and contracting. Chapter VIII in A study of industrial Edinburgh 1923-34, vol 1,* edited by N. Milnes. P.S.King & Co Ltd, 1936.

[16] Rodger, R. (1999). Building Development, in *Home Builders* edited by Glendinning and Walters. RCAHMS.

[17] Scottish Executive, *Scottish Economic Report, January 2000, Scottish Economic Report January 2000.* Scottish Executive Papers, 2000. ISBN: 9780114972677

[18] Scottish Government, *State of the Economy - December 2015.* Scottish Government Office of the Chief Economic Adviser, 2015

[19] Sir J. Sinclair, *The statistical account of Scotland [1791-1799] drawn up from the communications of the ministers of the different parishes.* Creech, 1799.

[20] Slaven & Checkland (editors), *Dictionary of Scottish Business Biography v2*, Aberdeen University Press, 1990.

[21] SPIC, *The Construction Industry, Scottish Parliament Information Centre research note 00/37*, 22 May 2000.

[22] Trades House, *The Wrights.* Retrieved January 2016 from http://www.tradeshouse.org.uk/individual-crafts/wrights.aspx

[23] *UK construction industry overview,* Corporate Watch UK, quoting Bill Tallis of the Major Contractors Group. March 2004.

[24] Walmsley, J., *Provision for the non-ablebodied poor in the 18th and early 19th centuries: some evidence from 3 Bedfordshire parishes,* The Local Historian, vol 20, no.1, February 1990, issn 00245585, pp 9-19.

Have the effects of its history resulted in a Scottish construction industry that differs from its counterparts in the rest of the UK?

Sources for Construction History

Picturing construction. Photographical documentation of Belgian construction sites by late nineteenth and early twentieth-century contractors

---

Inge Bertels
Department of Architectural Engineering, Vrije Universiteit Brussel, Belgium

Introduction

In the past two decades various historians have addressed in different ways the use and abuse of photographs within architectural discourses and studied how the new nineteenth-century medium of photography not only documented, but also imagined and represented architectural and urban realisations and their histories.[1] Yet the analysis of this set of valuable images leaves many construction historians unsatisfied.[2]

Indeed, most of nineteenth-century architectural photography depicts buildings in their completed form at the time of inauguration or shortly after their occupation. Construction, demolition, maintenance or restoration works were only accidentally pictured as for many late-nineteenth-century photographers 'men at work' posed important technical problems for example, the need for long exposure times. Artistic arguments also played a role with the dominance of portrait photography, while most clients and architects were simply interested in the final masterpiece. However, recently scholars have shed light on valuable unknown and unstudied archival finds and photographic collections and revealed how photography can chart the architectural, conservation and engineering process.[3] Their research clearly demonstrates how nineteenth-century and early twentieth-century photographic reportages or close-ups of the construction process are highly valuable to understand ephemeral construction processes and techniques, and also enable us to understand how architects and engineers advertised and promoted their business via photographs.

Building upon earlier research into the history of the Belgian construction process and the principal actors involved,[4] this papers questions if, in a similar way to architects and engineers, contractors were also interested in this new nineteenth-century invention. Henceforth, the paper analyses a set of recently discovered late-nineteenth and early twentieth-century photographical reportages collected or ordered by construction contractors in the period 1875-1930 picturing their Belgian constructed oeuvre. The paper will not only analyse the content of the reportages, but also why, how and when these images were used. As such this contribution will also shed light on how contractors used contemporary photos to construct their representation and history.

The construction process photographed

Today, Robert Howlett's (1831-1858) iconic pictures of the construction of Isambard Kingdom Brunel's (1806-1859) Great Eastern steamship (built between 1854-1859) or Louis-Émile Durandelle's (1839-1917) various prestigious photographs of among others the construction site of the Opéra Garnier (built between

1861-1875) or the restoration works of Mont Saint-Michel (1872-1888) are world famous.[5] Yet, when Mike Chrimes published his *Civil Engineering 1839-1889. A Photographic History* in 1991 he tackled a topic of the construction process that many historians had overlooked. Indeed in Belgium today while the early history of photography is well known and studied from various perspectives,[6] the interaction between the development of photography and the construction and restoration process is hardly known. However, this research on architectural and engineering photography can provide an interesting framework to analyse contractors' photography.

Interestingly Mike Chrimes outlines the role engineers played in the emergence of photographic reportages and how engineers used this new visual medium in the long nineteenth century. Indeed, engineers most often characterised by their 'scientific curiosity and natural inventiveness' opted very quickly for photography as a tool for setting up detailed surveys or used it for accurate recording of tools, machinery and their engineering work. But they also used the medium to copy drawings, to record the results of experiments and to document their construction works in case of future contractual conflicts or structural problems. Last, but not least, photography became the tool *par excellence* to promote their business. Subsequently, alongside the development of architectural, engineering and construction journals, engineers sent photos of their work to commercial and technical journals as illustrations for articles and as advertisements of their work.[7]

The first engineering photographs usually pictured infrastructure soon after completion, as in Fox Tablot's photos of Brunel's Hungerford Suspension Bridge in London in 1845. But there are also early British examples of construction site photographs, as in the photo of the scaffolding at the base of Nelson's Column of 1843 and the 1847 daguerreotypes of the Kew Palm House under construction.[8] One of the first fully documented infrastructure projects is found in the photographic album of the Kiev Suspension bridge by Charles Blacker Vignoles (1793-1875) photographed by J.C. Bourne (1814-1896) and Roger Fenton (1819-1869), which was compiled between 1847 and 1852.[9] The album, including probably only a small number of the photographs of the entire photographic reportage, was also shown to Queen Victoria demonstrating its importance.[10] This is somewhat earlier than the photographs recording the reconstruction of the Crystal Palace in 1852-1853 which are often cited as the earliest complete photographic record of the construction of a building. The impact of the Great Exhibitio of, 1851, is difficult to conceive today, but it seized the popular imagination and was difficult for engineers and manufacturers to ignore. Many, after visiting its displays, must have been alerted to the possibilities that photography offered as a means of advertising products or recording construction".[11]

The development of photographic documentation of construction sites was very similar in France, the home country of Louis Jacques Mandé Daguerre (1787-1851), and where architects and engineers were involved in photography from the 1850s. The work of the French photographer Louis-Émile Durandelle (1839-1917) who became architectural photographer of large Parisian construction sites between 1860 and 1890 is notable[12] Besides portrait, art and architectural objects, he photographed various major construction sites thanks to "une voiture mobile" and captured the transformation of Paris during one of its major phases of metamorphosis working closely with the architects Charles Garnier (1825-1898), Gustave Eiffel (1832-1923) and Eduard Corroyer (1837-1904). Correyer became an advocate of photography as a practical tool for architects: "Corroyer encourage ses confrères à faire appel à des photographes sur leurs chantiers de construction et de restauratation puis à exposes ces photographes dans les salons professionels. La photographie est pour le le témoigne reel de l'édifice, elle ne peut mentir, à l'inverse du dessin d'architecture".[13] Durandelle photographed both new and restoration projects for Eduard Corroyer, which were used by Corroyer not only to document the contemporary state of buildings or sites and to develop his restoration projects, but also as a means to promote his own work.[14]

The use of photography to document architecture, engineering and construction works has also been examined by architectural and construction historians, for example Ruth Richardson & Robert Thorne,[15] Ellen Van Impe[16] and Dana Arnold,[17] in particular the relationship between the use of iconography (in it broadest sense) and text within architectural historiography and journals in the long nineteenth century. Dana Arnold reveals how in eighteenth-century publications this iconography influenced how histories have been formulated and constructed. Although these investigations have mostly looked at architectural publications over time, it is also valuable to interrogate how contractors used iconography and specifically contemporary photography. But it is also necessary to take into consideration that contractors used other textual and iconographical ways to communicate their construction works. Indeed, as is the case for architects and engineers, although photography was easily positioned within architectural and engineering milieus, recent historiographical research also warns against a simplistic analysis through clearly demonstrating that although photography increasingly takes over in practice and publications, engravings and drawings remained an important, and carefully considered medium..[18] Ellen Van Impe analysed, among many, Louis Cloquet's *Les Maison anciennes en Belgique* and demonstrated that photography [in this publication] is used to show either general views or details, as in masonry patterns or bricked up windows, either in the current state or the state prior to restoration. Orthogonal elevations, sections and plans are mostly drawn by the author, whereas more sketchy drawings reproduce depictions of the building under study, either from an older document to show specific details or, in some cases, they are a kind of 'evocative registration'.[19]

Photographical documentation of Belgian construction sites by late nineteenth and early twentieth-century contractors

The earliest photographs of Belgian construction sites are probably not commissioned by contactors themselves, nor by architects or engineers, but by photographers who were interested in the architectural and artistic production of the city. . One of the earliest photographs of a Belgian construction site is a by Jean-Frans Michiels (1823-1887) in which he captured the restoration works of the Brussels Town Hall undertaken between 1851 and 1852.[20] (Fig.1) In the print the wooden scaffolding used for restoration work on the tower is centrally placed, and rolling ladders and construction materials are also depicted. Michiels initially lived and worked in Bruges as a wood-carver, but then became a photographer and publisher. Later on he moved to Cologne and developed a reputation as an architectural photographer working in close collaboration with the publisher Franz Carl Eisen (1812-1861), where he documented the construction of the Cologne Cathedral and published albums of the new stained-glass windows.[21] These successful first attempts, together with falling prices and growing historical consciousness stimulated the development of photographic urban documentation projects. Among these are the well-known projects of the late 1850s and early 1860s by Edmond Fierlants (1819-1869), a Belgian apprentice of Hippolyte Bayard (1801-1887), who was officially commissioned by the urban authorities of Bruges, Antwerp and Brussels.[22] (Fig. 2) In Antwerp Fierlants was also commissioned by the city of Antwerp to document the monumental sixteenth-century city gates. This work was also required by the Royal Commission of Monuments who, at the time, were actively campaigning against the demolition of these historical gates to make way for a new boulevard.[23] Indeed in Belgium, major urban change became a subject of specific interest to both amateur and professional photographers, resulting in the iconic albumen prints of 1867 made by the French Louis Jospeh Ghémar (1819-1873) of the Brussels River Senne shortly before it was covered in brick and in Joseph Mascré's (1836-?) panoramic view of the construction site of the Brussels Palace of Justice in 1867. (Fig. 3)

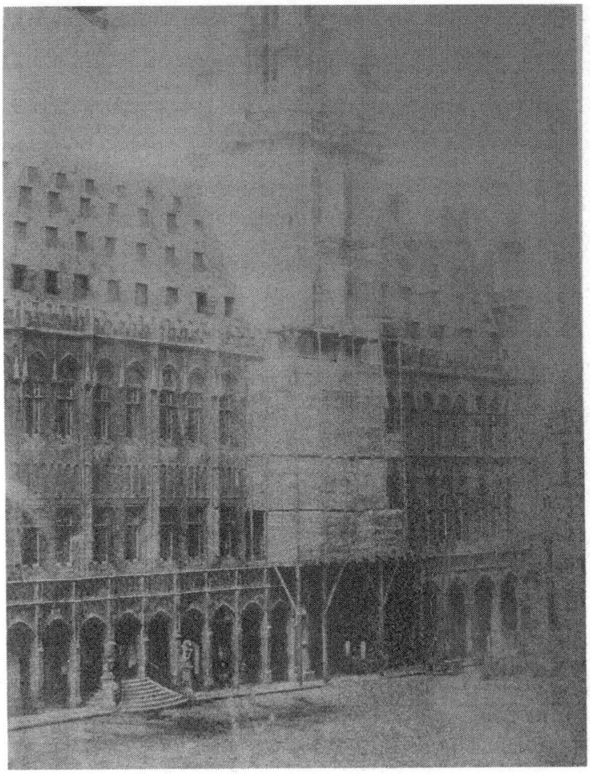

Fig. 1 Brussels Town hall under restoration, 1851-1852. Photographer Jan-Frans Michiels [FOMU].

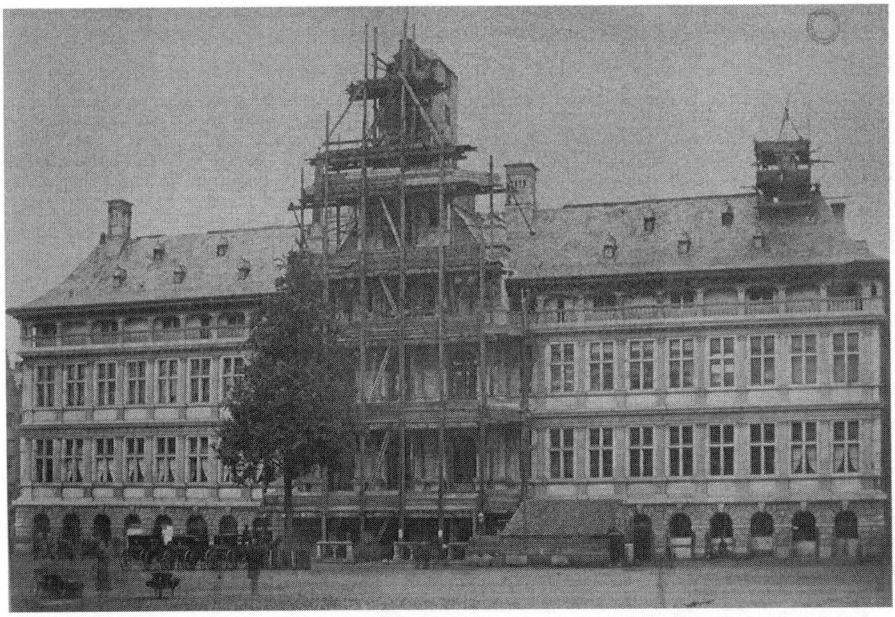

Fig. 2. Antwerp Town hall under restoration, 1865. Photographer Edmonf Fierlants [Private collection Berchem].

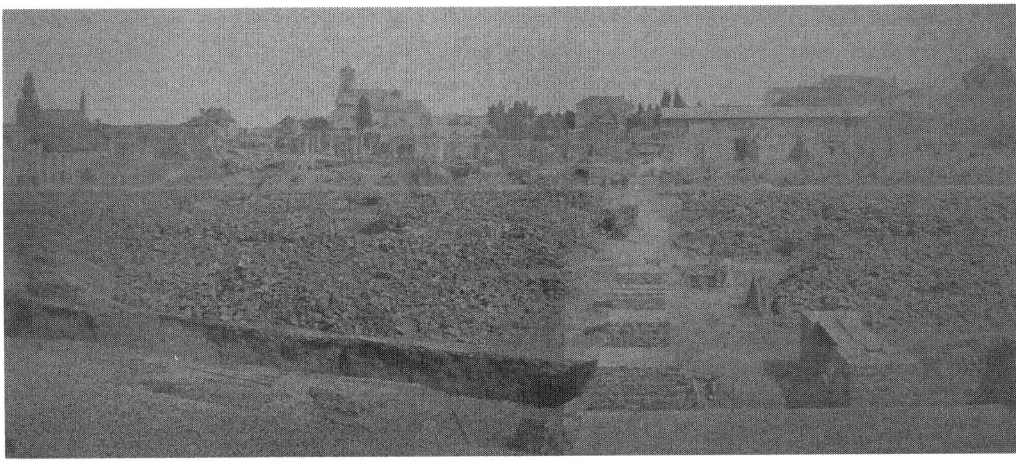

Fig. 3. Brussels Palace of Justice under construction, 1867. Photographer Joseph Mascré [FOMU].

This photographic evolution inspired contractors and the entrepreneurs Couvreux & Hersent commissioned, in 1877, a special photographic record of their infrastructure works carried out in Antwerp in the period 1877-1884. This album is up till now the first known complete photographic record of a construction site commissioned by the contractors themselves. Later on contractors also used photography to advertise their construction works. For example, contractors and construction firms were included in the photographic *Album de fabriques et de manufactures de la province d'Anvers offert à sa Majesté Léopold II à l'occasion du 50me anniversaire de l'Independence Belge* composed in 1880 by George Raynaud. (Fig. 4.1-2) But recently discovered archives of professional contractors organisations also bring to light three albums commissioned by the contractors themselves: two albums composed by the Antwerpse Confederatie Bouw (Antwerp Building Confederation) with projects and photos dating from the period 1899-1930 and one album composed by the *Association des Entrepreneurs Belges de Grands Travaux* (ADEB) in 1936.[24] (Fig. 11-12) The 1877 Couvreux & Hersent albums, and the 1899-1930 albums of the Antwerp Building Confederation are discussed in detail below.

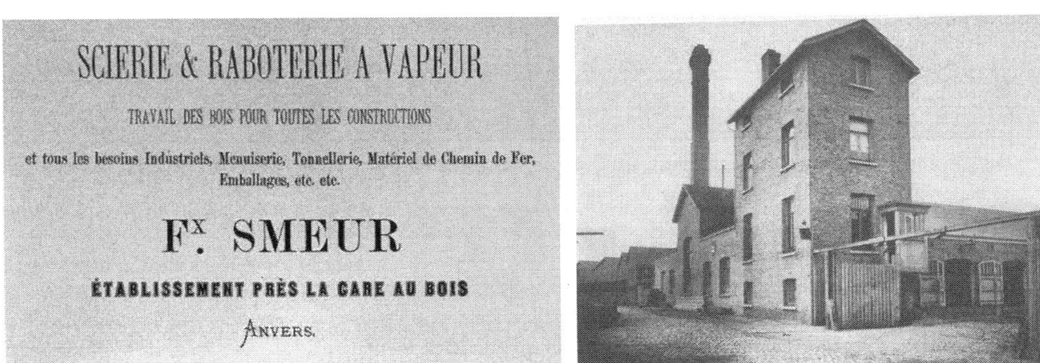

Fig. 4. 1-2. Scierie & Raboterie à vapeur de F. Smeur à Anvers, in: RAYNAUD, Georges (ed.), Album de fabriques et de manufactures de la province d'Anvers offert à sa Majesté Léopold II à l'occasion du 50me anniversaire de l'Independance Belge, Antwerp, 1880.

Picturing construction. Photographical documentation of Belgian construction sites by late nineteenth and early twentieth-century contractors

Couvreux & Hersent's Nouvelles Installations Maritimes d'Anvers (ca. 1877-1884)

The Antwerp Museum of Photography (FOMU) holds a highly valuable album entitled *Nouvelle Installations Maritimes d'Anvers* which was commissioned by the established French contractors Couvreux & Hersent. The album consists of 40 albumen prints (23.8 cm x 36.6 cm) bound together in a red leather album with gilded inscriptions[25] and documents one of Antwerp major nineteenth-century infrastructure works. From the 1860s onwards, major attention was directed towards the development of the Antwerp port infrastructure. In 1863 the toll on the river Scheldt was redeemed, which resulted in increasing port traffic. Subsequently, new infrastructure was needed to boost the strength of the Antwerp port in its competition with the ports of Rotterdam and Hamburg, and to offer commercial facilities, as did the English port cities.[26] The project included a connection between the existing *Bonapartedok* and *Willemdok* and the newly designed *Kattendijkdok* (realised in 1863), the *Houtdok* (1864), the *Verbindingsdok* (1869), and the *Kempisch dok* (1873). The master plan also included repairs and alterations to the quays which although appearing in earlier plans had been only partially realized. Now, after the reopening of the River Scheldt, these repairs became critical as there were major problems concerning silting of the quays, limited depth, and connection with the city canals.

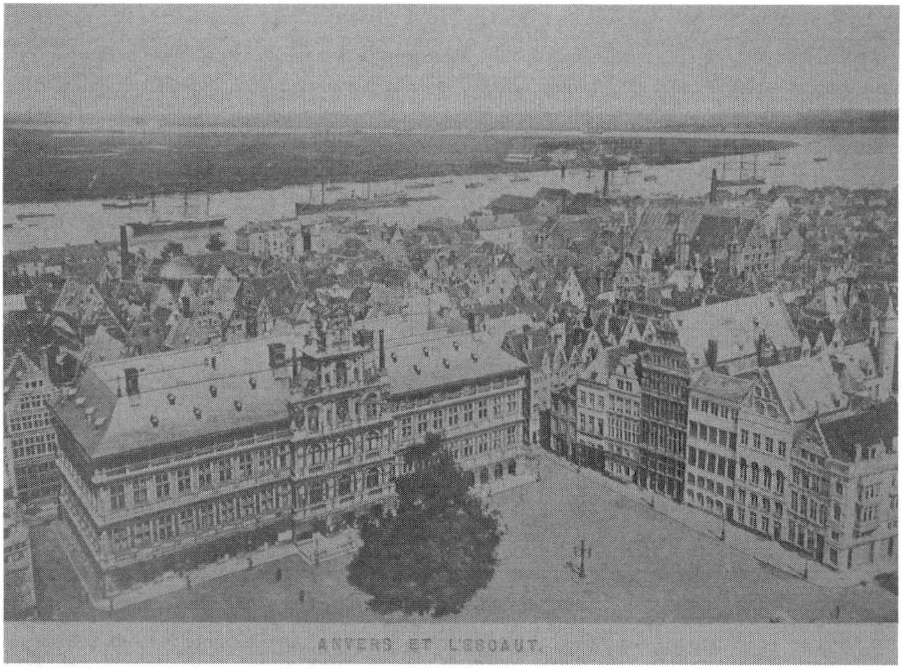

Fig. 5. View on the Antwerp Town hall and River Scheldt in Nouvelles Installations Maritimes d'Anvers. Photographer Gustave [FOMU].

Quay repairs and alterations of more than 3.5 kilometres were executed in the period 1877-1884 and the French contractors, Couvreux & Hersent, commissioned photography by Gustave Hergaux, a rather unknown photographer in Antwerp, but who had worked in Belgium and the Netherlands and probably also in Spain.[27] The album starts with several views of the historic River Scheldt (Fig. 5) and continues with the setting up of the construction sheds (Fig. 6). It further documents precisely the entire process, including the impressive movable cofferdams and scaffolding, (Fig. 7) the construction works and finally the newly constructed quays and locks.

(Fig. 8-9) The photographs in the album were carefully selected to reflect the contractor's expertise. On completion of the works a photo album was presented, in 1884, by the contractors to the Antwerp urban government and it is likely the album was also used to promote their work in France. Some views in the album document demolition works, but these are immediately linked to the ingenious new construction work and resulting prosperous port infrastructure. Historical research clearly demonstrates that via this photographic album the entrepreneurs Couvreux & Hersent not only documented their infrastructure works, but also constructed their own 'proper history'. What was not explicitly documented in this album, was the fact that in order to begin this extensive project major demolition work destroyed the oldest part of the historical city known as the *Werf* and the *Burchtplein. Het Steen* (the historic fortress) built circa 1200-1235, was one of the few buildings that survived but in all around 600 dwellings, were destroyed.[28] The result was that *het Steen* became an isolated building on the bank of the river Scheldt. Later, a promenade, including several metal storage sheds as well as a homogenous waterfront of houses and depots was realized.. This led to a number of civil protests and from 1882 a special urban commission (1882-1885) was established to supervise and encourage the preservation of what remained of the demolished, historical district. Photography was now used to document the historical architecture and artistic remains of the district alongside visual inspections, written inventories and drawings, and the preservation of a selection of art objects in the city's archaeological museum. . Antwerp city council also appointed the Antwerp based photographer Jos(eph) Maes (1838-1908)[29] to photograph the historic district under demolition.[30] (Fig. 10)

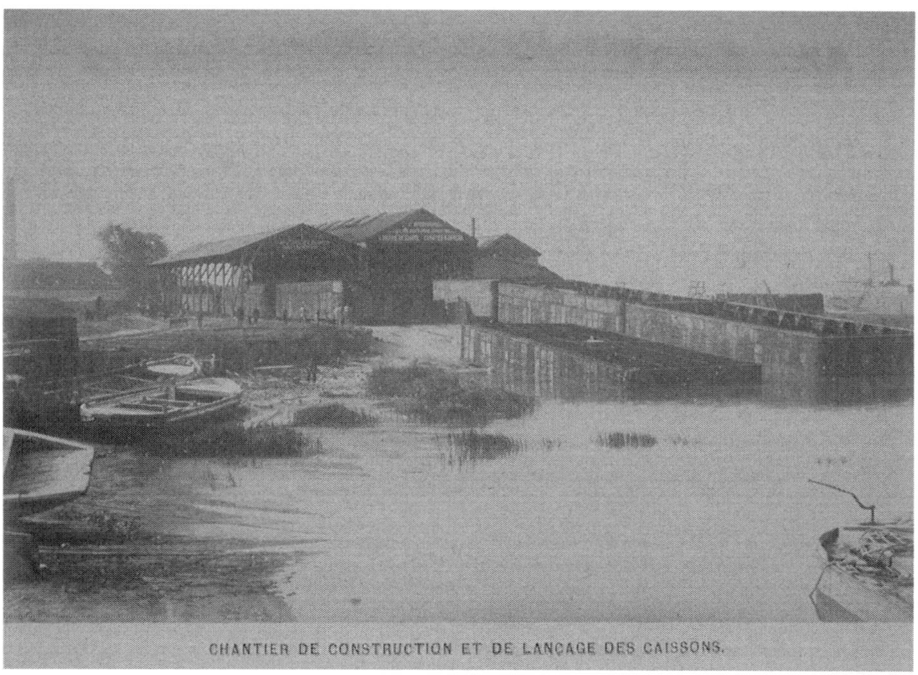

Fig. 6. Building sheds for the construction site of the rectification of the Antwerp quays in Nouvelles Installations Maritimes d'Anvers. Photographer Gustave [FOMU].

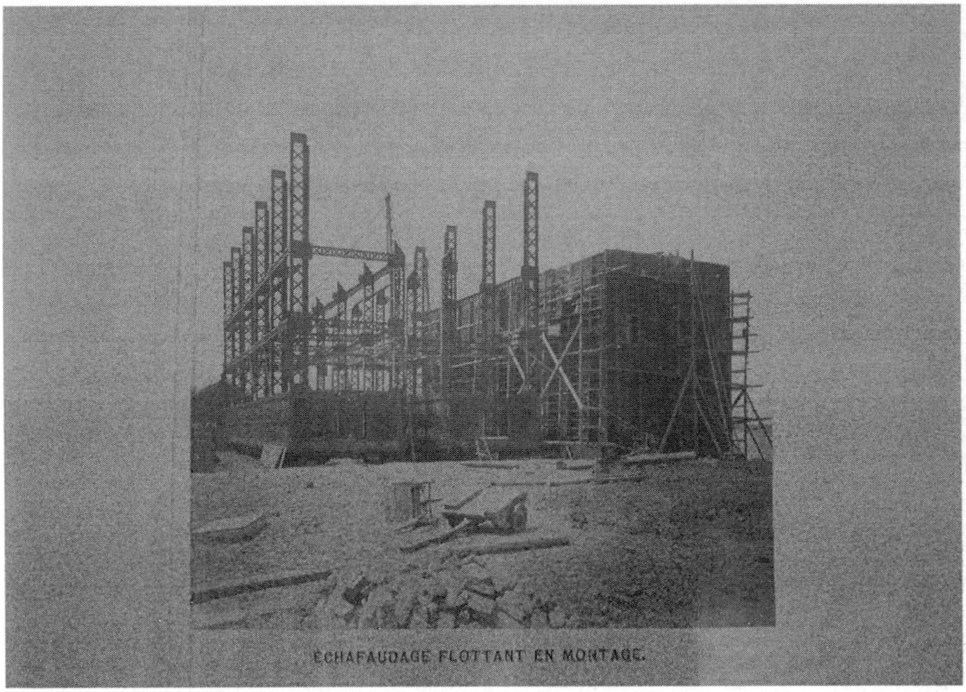

Fig. 7. Construction of the floating scaffoldings in Nouvelles Installations Maritimes d'Anvers. Photographer Gustave [FOMU].

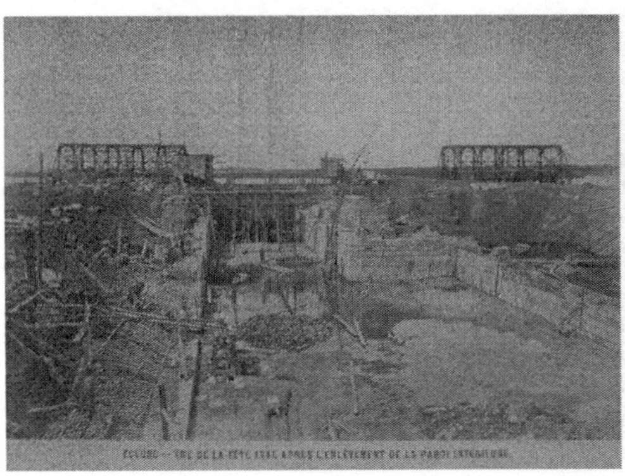

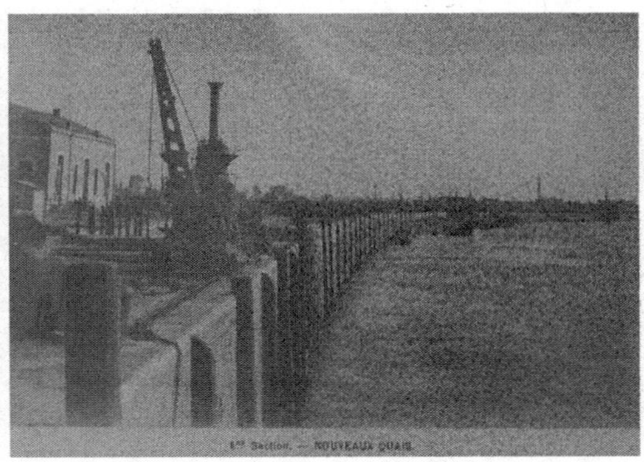

Fig. 8. Construction site of the new port infrastructure in Nouvelles Installations Maritimes d'Anvers. Photographer Gustave [FOMU]. (left) Fig. 9. New Antwerp quays constructed by entrepreneurs Couvreux & Hersent in Nouvelles Installations Maritimes d'Anvers. Photographer Gustave [FOMU]. (right)

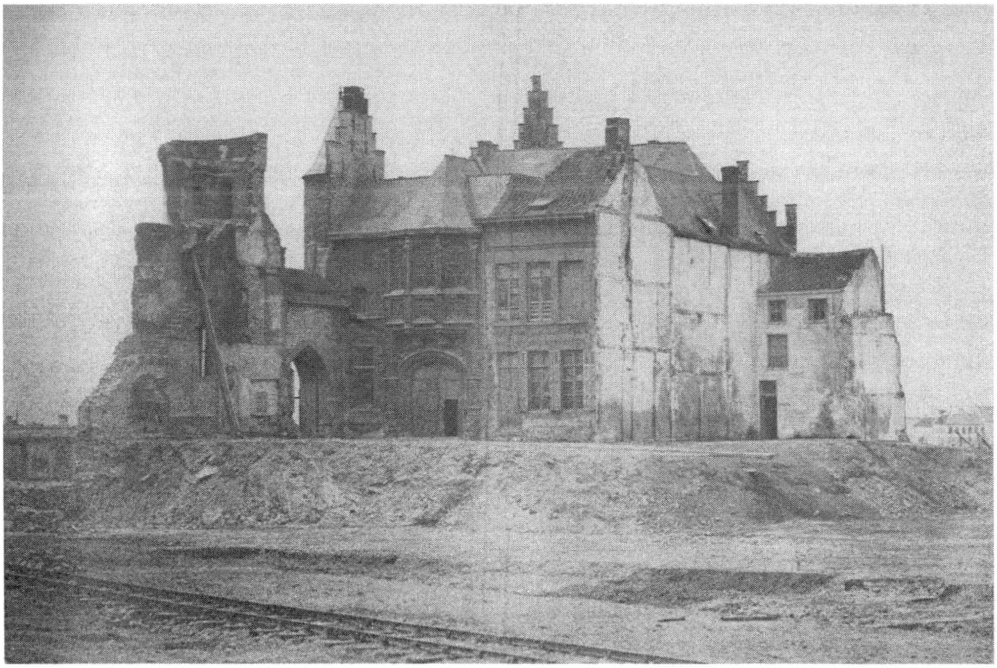

Fig. 10. View on the Steen and the demolished Antwerp historic district around 1882. Photographer Jos Maes [Private collection Berchem].

Tribute Album of the Antwerp Confederation of Construction in 1934

Of particular note are two photographic albums that were compiled in 1934 on the occasion of the sixtieth anniversary of the Antwerp Building Confederation (*Confederatie Bouw Antwerpen*).[31] The Antwerp confederation, named the *Cercle des Entrepreneurs de Travaux Publics*, was established in 1874 and was the first professional contractors organisation. The main goals of the professional organization were, to create and maintain professional standards, both internal and external, to establish clear customer-contractor obligations and to support the contractors' knowledge and education.[32] The Antwerp *Cercle* has undergone important changes and evolution since its inception , nonetheless it is still recognized as the historical core of the present-day Antwerp Confederation of Construction. To start with 75 Antwerp general contractors joined and its membership had increased to over 500 by the sixtieth anniversary in 1934. Over time the Antwerp Confederation celebrated its anniversaries and published various 'organisational homages', yet, as far as is known, no similar extensive photographic publications were made before or after the 1934 albums..

The two ringed albums (36 cm by 50 cm) comprise more than 300 black and white photos and document the growth of major construction sites in the early decades of the twentieth century (1899-1934) executed by members of the Antwerp *Cercle* . The photographer is not mentioned, but a visual analysis of the photos suggests that the organisations commissioned a professional photographer and that this series was probably supplemented with additional photos sent in by the various members themselves. Each photograph is accompanied by a caption providing information on the project and its constructors, while the architects or engineers, as conceptual creators, or the clients are mentioned to a lesser extent, . As such, the contractors are clearly identifying themselves with their 'built oeuvre' and claiming their part of the authorship.

Geographically the majority of the pictured projects are situated within the Antwerp region with a strong concentration in the Antwerp city and its surrounding areas. Projects in the south of Belgium, such as the re-building of the Liège quays, are also pictured. As well as construction photographs of member construction companies a broad variety of projects were included. The projects depicted ranged from major infrastructure works including roads, sewers, and water infrastructure, but also churches e.g. the Church of Our Lady of Lourdes in Edegem; schools e.g. the famous Seamen's school in the Antwerp harbour; theatres such as the Roma theatre in Borgerhout; factories e.g. Gevaert in Mortsel and major social housing and restoration projects e.g Sterckshof in Deurne and Hof van Liere in Antwerp as well as smaller housing projects. (Fig. 11-12) This visual documentation is a highly interesting source for building and construction historians but also clearly reveals the broad scope of general contractors' activities and undermines the frequent presumption that their portfolios were limited to major infrastructure projects.

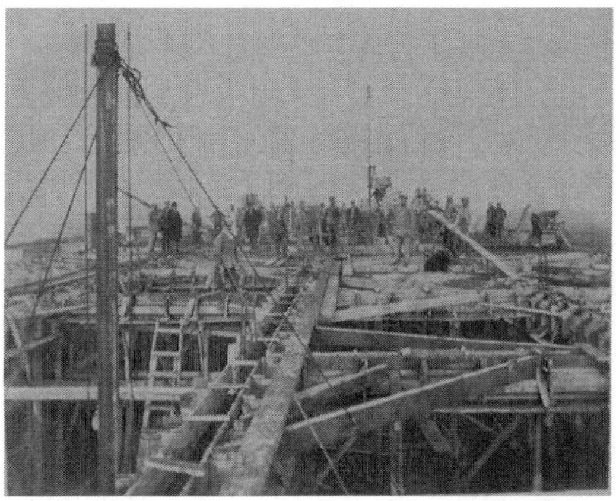

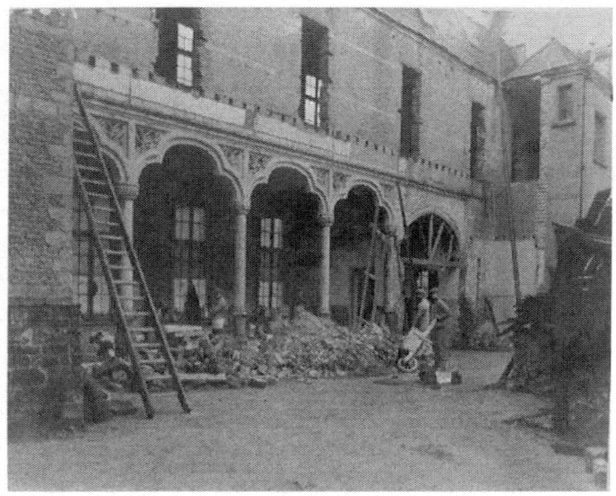

Fig. 11. Construction site of the Gevaert factory in Mortsel [Antwerp Confederation of Construction].(left) Fig. 12. Restoration project Hof van Liere in Antwerp [Antwerp Confederation of Construction](right)

Conclusions

This first attempts to understand how late nineteenth and early twentieth century contractors pictured the Belgian construction process demonstrates that, at varying rates of uptake, contractors used this new technology to document their projects and promote their core business to both clients and construction colleagues. As international architects and engineers, they clearly understood the strengths of photography and used it to create their own visual language, which in turn stimulated the creation of their entrepreneurial identites.

This paper is based on a limited range of sources, only photographic records and collections were consulted, in an attempt to initiate analysis of a subject of great complexity. Further research will benefit from comparisons with international examples, as well as research on the use of photography in relation to other visual and textual modes of communication. Specific attention should be given to specialised construction journals, which are still an underused source and hardly studied in Belgium.. A brief overview indicates that the introduction of photography here was rather late. *La Chronique des Travaux Publics, du Commerce et de l'Industrie* (°1877) for instance only published photographs at the very end of the nineteenth century with the first photograph appearing in the 48th issue of 1899 and overall photography was used infrequently.[33] However, the ongoing investigation of various contractors' archives in Belgium, may shed new lights on how photography was also used as a tool to regulate or control the contractor's business. I hope this paper will help to stimulate further research on the photographic documentation of nineteenth century construction sites in Belgium and beyond.

Acknowledgments

Special thanks to Mike Chrimes and Jelena Dobbels as well as to the archivists and curators of the consulted archives, museums and private collections.

References

[1] See among others: D. Arnold, 'Facts or Fragments? Visual histories in the age of mechanical reproduction', *Art History*, vol. 25, n° 4, 2002, pp. 450-468. Z. Böröcz and L. Verpoest (ed.), Imag(in)ing Architecture. Iconography in Nineteenth-century Architectural Publications. Leuven: Acco, 2008. H. Van Goethem, Photography and Realism in the 19th Century: Antwerp - the Oldest Photographs 1847-1880. Antwerp: Pandora, 1999.

[2] I. Bertels, Building the City, Antwerp 1815-1880. Unpublished doctoral thesis KULeuven, 2008.

[3] See among others: I. Bertels, Building the City, 2008. M. Chrimes, Civil Engineering 1839-1889. A Photographic History. London: Alan Sutton Publishing, 1991. J. Dobbels, "Aanzetten voor een erfgoedbeleid. De afbraak van het Antwerpse burchtgebied als casestudy vor de veranderende omgang met erfgoed (1863-1900)', Stadsgeschiedenis, 2011, Issue 2, pp. 130-146. B. Krikorian, 'Le fonds Durandelle à la bibliothèque des Arts décoratifs', Bibliothèques des Arts Décoratifs, 20 février-30 avril 2014, pp. 1-2. C. Leblanc, 'Louis-Emile Durandelle: La mémoire du Mont Saint-Michel', Bibliothèques des Arts Décoratifs, 20 février-30 avril 2014, pp. 3-8.

[4] I. Bertels, Building the City, 2008. I. Bertels, "Construction History in Belgium (2004-2014). From Attas to Zastasvni", A. Becchi, R. Carvais and J. Sakarovitch, L'Histoire de la construction. Un Méridien européen/ Construction History. A European Meridian. Paris: Association francophone d'histoire de la construction, pp. 25-48. I. Bertels and J. Dobbels, "ADEB 1936-2016. Quand une association du genie civil deviant la représentante des grandes entreprises de construction", in: Pestat, Y. and De Blieck, S., La Belgique construit 1936-2016, Brussels: AAM Editions, pp.10-31.

[5] M. Chrimes, A Photographic History. C. Leblanc, 'Louis-Emile Durandelle: La mémoire du Mont Saint-Michel', Bibliothèques des Arts Décoratifs, 20 février-30 avril 2014, pp. 3-8.

[6] F.J. Steven, T. Schwilden, and Claes, M.-C., Directory of Photography in Belgium 1839-1905, 2 vol., Antwerp-Rotterdam: de Vries-Brouwers, 1997. H. Van Goethem, H., Photography and Realism in the 19th Century, 1999.

[7] M. Chrimes, 1991,A Photographic History, pp. 1-13.

[8] Ibid., p. 3.

[9] Idem, p. 4. J. Vignoles, 'The construction of the Kiev Suspension Bridge 1846-1853', Engineering History and Heritage, Vol. 165, Issue EH1, 2012, pp. 21-45.

[10] Ibid., pp. 3-4.

[11] Ibid., pp. 4-5.

[12] C. Leblanc, 'Louis-Emile Durandelle: La mémoire du Mont Saint-Michel', Bibliothèques des Arts Décoratifs, 20 february-30 april 2014, pp. 3.

[13] Ibid.,, pp. 3-4.

[14] Ibid.,, pp.5-6.

[15] R Richardson & R. Thorne, The Builder. Illustrated Index 1843-1883. London: Hutton+Rostron, 1994.

[16] E. Van Impe, Architectural Historiography in Belgium 1830-1914. Leuven: Unpublished Doctoral Thesis, 2008.

[17] D. Arnold and L. Verpoest, "Introduction", in: B. Böröcz, Z. and L. Verpoest (eds.) Imag(in)ing Architecture. Iconography in Nineteenth-century Architectural Publications. Leuven: Acco, 2008.

[18] See for example Van Impe, p. 395 in Richardson and Thorne, 1994..

[19] E. Van Impe, Architectural Historiography in Belgium 1830-1914, pp. 397.

[20] F..J. Steven, T. Schwilden, and Claes, M.-C., Directory of Photography in Belgium 1839-1905, vol. 2, n° 24.

[21] Ibid., vol. 1, pp. 282-283.

[22] F. Steven and T. Schwilden, Edmond Fierlants 1819-1869. Photographies d'art et d'architecture. Brussels: Crédit Communal, 1988. H. Van Goethem, Photography and Realism in the 19th Century, pp. 44-51.

[23] I. Bertels and H. Van Goethem, "Veranderlijke stedelijke ruimte. De afbraak van de Spaanse omwalling in de negentiende eeuw", in: Antwerpen Versterkt. De Spaanse omwalling vanaf haar bouw in 1542 tot haar afbraak in 1870. Antwerp: UPA, 2009, p.136.

[24] The album is part of the collection of ADEB/VBA, but was at the time of consultation temporary archived in the Archives d'Architecture Moderne (AAM) in function of the preparation of the publication Pestat, Y. and De Blieck, S., La Belgique construit 1936-2016, Brussels: AAM Editions, 2015.

[25] Inscription on the frontispiece: "Nouvelles installations Maritimes d'Anvers. Couvreux & Hersent Entrepreneurs. 1877-1884".

[26] G. Vloerberghs, De Antwerpse stadsuitbreidingen, p. 109.

[27] F..J. Steven, T. Schwilden, and Claes, M.-C., Directory of Photography in Belgium 1839-1905, vol.1, p. 209.

[28] S. Van Aerschot (ed.) , Bouwen door de eeuwen heen in Vlaanderen. Stad Antwerpen, 3na. Turnhout: Brepols, 1990, pp. 352-358. D. Somers, Antwerpen, werf van de eeuw, Special issue of FotoMuseum magazine, 31 (2004) 31.

[29] F..J. Steven, T. Schwilden, and Claes, M.-C., Directory of Photography in Belgium 1839-1905, vol. 1, p. 267-268.

[30] J. Dobbels, "Aanzetten voor een erfgoedbeleid. De afbraak van het Antwerpse burchtgebied als casestudy vor de veranderende omgang met erfgoed (1863-1900)', Stadsgeschiedenis, 2011, Issue 2, pp. 141-142.

[31] The archives are part of the archive of the Antwerp Confederation of Construction, preserved in their Antwerp office.

[32] I. Bertels, "Building Contractors in late-Nineteenth-century Belgium: from Craftsmen to Contractors", *Construction History*, vol. 26, 2011, pp. 1-18.

[33] See the contribution of Jelena Dobbels on The professionalization of Belgian general contractors (1877-1914): an analysis of the construction journal La Chronique des Travaux Publics, du Commerce et de l'Industrie.

Are the traces left by structural engineers sufficient to assess their eminence?

Bill Addis
Co-editor of Construction History

Introduction

One reason for studying the history of structures is to understand how a building, especially an icon such as St Paul's Cathedral or the Crystal Palace works as a structure, and how it was constructed.

No less important an objective in studying the history of structural engineering is to evaluate the standing of a particular engineer or the significance of a particular structure. This may be with regard to the development or progress of the art of structural engineering; it may also concern the sheer originality of a structure and the creativity of the engineer.

This paper considers what evidence relating to a structure and the work of its engineers is likely to remain and be available to study in order to address the issues mentioned above.

There are several approaches to understanding the work and achievements of a structural engineer:

- Studying the structures produced by an engineer.
- Studying what was produced by the engineer (drawings, calculations, written work and oral evidence);
- Studying what was written or said about an engineer and their projects;

My concern is that conventional approaches to studying history, based on archival material and published literature, may not provide a complete or even a representative view of what engineers actually do, and make it difficult to discriminate between the good engineers and those who are less good.

What do structural engineers do?[1]

The precise activities of the structural engineer have changed over time and, even today, can vary greatly according to the nature of the project. Until recently, for example, bridges seldom involved a significant contribution from architects – engineers worked alone with the contractors. Now design teams for many bridges include architects.

For buildings, whose design teams are usually led by architects, engineers are rarely recognized for their contributions. It is often assumed that the design was made only by the architect. Indeed, even engineers often avoid affirming their contribution to the design of a building so that architects do not feel that authorship is disputed.

While an engineer's contribution to the design of a building can vary, the minimum input is to ensure the structure meets the requirements of the many design codes, regulations and standards relevant to building structures.[2] Today this is largely covered by design codes, such as the Eurocodes which cover the basis of design, actions on structures, design of structural elements in concrete, steel, composite steel and concrete, timber, masonry and aluminium, and also geotechnical and seismic design. Design codes such as these, specifically for large masonry buildings, have their origins in the sixteenth century.[3] Today's design codes are the accumulation and concentration of more than two hundred years of engineering design and construction experience. They provide a means of validating a design and ensuring that it will be safe. They do not, however, address the creative aspects of engineering design.

Before using the design codes to validate a design, the structural design engineer needs to conceive or invent and appropriate structural form (generally the most interesting part for many researchers) and the details of how it can be constructed. This process relies largely on experience, the engineer's intuitive understanding of the behaviour of structures and materials, usually augmented by a good understanding of the current theory of structures and materials.

Once the design is complete, there follows the process of preparing the drawings and the specification of materials and structural elements for delivery to the contractor who will building the structure. In addition, the design engineer usually has a role in monitoring the construction process until completion to ensure the structure is built as specified in the design documents. In terms of duration, this latter phase is often longer than the time taken to prepare the designs.

Researching the work of the engineer

Assessing the works produced by an engineer

When discussing the merits of structures, the criteria of structural excellence used, and their relative importance, are likely to vary from person to person. However, the ultimate purpose of such criteria need not be to establish some objective truth about this or that structure. Rather they are tools to enable people to argue with force and rhetoric about a structure and, by implication, the skills of its creator. The following are examples of criteria more directly concerned with engineering aspects of design:[4]

- Was the structure the first of its kind, with no direct precedent?
- Was the use of materials ahead of current practice?
- Did the engineer make innovative use of the structural theory available at the time?
- Did the engineer use an innovative design procedure, for example the use of scale models to test and predict the structural behaviour of the full-size structure?
- To what extent does the structure display evidence of the following skills and intentions of its designer(s):
- the skill and clarity with which structural actions, such as tension, compression, bending, truss and shell action, are used and expressed (or hidden);
- elegance or simplicity of connexions, structural elements or an entire structure;
- structural honesty, or dishonesty when that is appropriate;

- expression of an appropriate degree of solidity or delicacy;
- economy of material and appropriateness of a material to its structural function;
- awareness, exploitation and expression of each material's unique aesthetic;
- a design which succeeds in avoiding difficulties rather than surmounting them;
- juxtaposition and expression of materials and structural functions at connexions;
- expression in a structure's geometry or form, of the imposed loads, structural actions and internal stresses;
- expression of natural geometries such as the circle, catenary or parabola;
- selection of a structural form which sensibly anticipates the means by which it can be defined geometrically and justified by calculation or otherwise;
- allusion to structural precedents from history, other cultures or nature;
- degree of interaction and integration between loadbearing aspects of a structure and non-loadbearing aspects, such as cladding and building services;
- expression of the method of manufacture and assembly of the structure;
- devising of structural systems capable of repetitive manufacturing processes while retaining stimulating variation and irregularity;
- intelligent anticipation of production engineering problems at the design stage.[5]

Researching what was produced by an engineer during its conception

Drawings

These are the main means by which engineers communicate a design. Those produced during the development of a design may often be hand drawings which are rarely preserved; or rather they are kept only by engineers who can produce good hand drawings (many engineers do not, or cannot produce good hand drawings), and who want to keep a record of their emerging and changing design ideas.

The drawings produced for the contractors or manufacturers are formal, legal documents and do reflect the final design rather than stages in the design process.

This situation differs markedly from sketches and drawings produced by architects. Although they too produce final, contact drawings, they also keep large numbers of sketches and drawings which chart the progress of a project from the very beginning through its many intermediate stages before being finalised.[6]

Calculations

At each stage of a project, engineers make calculations to support their ideas. These calculations generally indicate the level of knowledge of the current theory of structures and materials, and can reveal how an engineer was thinking about the design or behaviour of a structure during its conception. Even today, initial calculations are likely to be approximate, often calculations made by hand.

The final calculations, like the drawings, can often form part of the legal documentation issued to the builder, especially for buildings with non-conventional structures. Their main function is to demonstrate that the structure was designed in accordance with appropriate standards, regulations and design codes of practice. They provide a full justification of the sizes and construction of all the structural components.

Written material

Are the traces left by structural engineers sufficient to assess their eminence?

Nowadays, during the development of structural designs, engineers produce many reports, often presenting different alternative options and their advantages or disadvantages. These reports can provide strong evidence of the skill of the engineer, but never are never published – indeed, they are usually treated as confidential documents, even after a project is completed.

After a project has been completed, many engineers publish articles in professional refereed journals[7] or less formal trade journals. However, this is generally done only when a project is particularly unusual, or large or innovative. And by no means do all engineers write papers even when a project might merit one. Engineers seldom write papers about 'ordinary' projects.

Again this situation is different from that of architects who nearly always publicise their works and generally use articles or books to advertise their skills and experience, particularly to help get further commissions.

Very few engineers write papers or books intended to communicate their approach to engineering design.[8]

Oral material

Engineers probably make their greatest contribution to the development of a structural scheme during discussions in design team meetings and among themselves. And such discussions usually involve a great many sketches, which are generally discarded. The traces of this important and highly creative part of the engineer's work seldom survive.

Project management

The success of most engineering structures, as viewed by the developer or building owner, is whether the building was delivered on time and within the agreed budget. Though other professionals are nowadays involved in these activities, the structural engineer has always played a major role on this aspect of a project. Although contractors and, nowadays, project managers, manage large projects once they are on site, a continuous dialogue with the structure design engineer is essential to ensure that the underlying concept of a structure is maintained.[9] As with most management activities, these can rarely be traced through published works; even the minutes of meetings may only record part of the story.[10]

Study what has been written or said about engineers and their projects

Before the mid-twentieth century, there were few examples of impartial assessments or critical comments made about engineering structures. However, for several decades now, there has been a growing number of awards for excellence in structural engineering given by organizations whose members are professional engineers. The following are some examples in the UK and internationally:

- Institution of Structural Engineers *
- Institution of Civil Engineers * **
- Royal Academy of Engineering **
- Structural Steel Design Awards *
- Concrete Society Awards *
- Structural Timber Awards *
- British Construction Industry Awards *

- International Association of Bridge & Structural Engineers (IABSE) **
- International Association of Shell and Spatial Structures (IASS) **

 * For individual projects ** For "Lifetime Achievement"

Generally the various award schemes have published the criteria used by the judges to assess the entries. The Structural Steel Design Awards, for example, give the following criteria:

The judging panel assesses all entries against the following key criteria:

Planning and Architecture

- Satisfaction of client's brief, particularly cost effectiveness
- Environmental impact
- Architectural excellence
- Durability
- Adaptability for changing requirements through its life
- Efficiency of the use and provision of services
- Conservation of energy

Structural Engineering

- Benefits achieved by using steel construction
- Efficiency of design, fabrication and erection
- Skill and workmanship
- Integration of structure and services to meet architectural requirements
- Efficiency and effectiveness of fire and corrosion protection
- Innovation of design, build and manufacturing technique

Such awards can give researchers a good insight into the quality of engineering designs, though, as mentioned above, they are usually awarded to a project rather than an individual engineer. Also, although the judging panels always include engineers, the judgements do not usually go into create detail about the nature of the engineering design quality (as listed in the previous section).

A further way in which individual engineers may be given recognition for their design abilities by their peers is that they are invited to deliver lectures or to write papers at conferences or for professional publications, or contribute chapters to books. However, such recognition gives little idea of what their achievements may have been. Furthermore, not all good design engineers are invited to make such contributions, and not all those invited were good designers.

Occasionally structures collapse and technical reports are written on the circumstances surrounding the event. These can provide valuable information, not only about the design and construction of the particular structure, but also about what the engineering community at that time generally did.[11]

Evaluating the work of an engineer or the historical significance of a structure

Evaluating the contribution of an engineer is rarely easy, particularly since individual engineers are never solely responsible for producing a design. Engineering design is a team activity and, especially today, the design of a structure is nearly always credited to a firm, not an individual. While architectural design is also usually a team activity, buildings are generally credited to an individual named architect. Nevertheless, there are good examples of books about the work and achievements of eminent structural engineers, though rather fewer in number than books about civil engineers.[12]

Evaluating the excellence and significance of an engineering structure is perhaps easier than the contributions of individual engineers. And there are many books and papers giving a critical assessment of individual engineering structures.[13]

Conclusion

This paper has summarised the range of evidence that is likely to be available to someone wanting to assess the eminence of a structural engineer or the excellence of a work of structural engineering.

For projects completed during the last few decades there is likely to be a good record of the designs of the structures themselves, especially where company archives have survived. For projects built before the twentieth century however, records of the engineering design are likely to be fewer or non-existent.[14] Evaluating such structures must rely on detailed surveys and assessments of the structure itself. Record design drawings are rarely 100% accurate and do not record changes to the design (especially details) that are devised and implemented on site to overcome problems discovered during construction. For this reason construction photographs can be invaluable since they provide a comparison between record drawings and what was actually built. Nevertheless, none of these give much indication of the engineer's intent and seldom divulge how the design progressed from initial ideas to what was actually built, which are the main skills of the structural engineer. The structure itself can reveal relatively little of the most important aspects and the full range of the structural engineer's skills.[15]

Notes and References

[1] The only book I know that directly addresses this question is Fritz Leonhardt, *Der Bauingenieur und seine Aufgaben*. Stuttgart, Deutsche Verlags-Anstalt, 1981.

[2] For discussion of the engineering design procedure and its use in studying engineering history, see Addis, Bill (2015), 'The epistemology of engineering design as a contribution to construction history.' *Proceedings of the Second Conference of the Construction History Society,* Cambridge, 2015. pp. 3-10.

[3] Huerta, S. (2010). 'The safety of masonry buttresses.' *Proceedings of the Institution of Civil Engineers, Engineering History and Heritage*, 163, pp.3–24

[4] For further discussion on these matters, see Addis, W., 'Structural Criticism and the Aesthetics of Structures.' *Congress Report, 15th Congress of International Association for Bridge and Structural Engineering*, Copenhagen (1996). pp. 121-126. Available online http://retro.seals.ch/digbib/view2?pid=bse-cr-002:1996:15::329 (Accessed 25/01/2016), and Addis, Bill, *Building: 3000 years of Design, Engineering and Construction*. London & New York: Phaidon, 2007.

[5] Arguably, one of the most important aspects is how the permanent structure is erected and whether or not the structural engineer fully considered this. This is what made many 19th-century engineers so special: they had to consider how to erect their structures and this has become largely forgotten by designers who become more and more detached from site practices. Most modern engineers design structures as 'wished-in-place' and they can end up being difficult to build. The designs for most major buildings are nowadays revised in discussions between design engineers and contractors; indeed, for many large projects contractors are employed to advise before the design has been completed to avoid the costly process of redesign.

[6] There are of course exceptions, I.K Brunel being one of them. He produced numerous sketchbooks that provide a wealth of information regarding the design development of his schemes.

[7] In the UK *The Structural Engineer* (published by the Institution of Structural Engineers) and the *Proceedings of the Institution of Civil Engineers* have published papers on many hundreds of individual building structures, but generally not giving independent assessment since they are written by their creators. Often the discussions of such papers (when published) provide a better insight as to the overall significance of a building or structure.

[8] Two exceptions are Ove Arup (*Ove Arup: a Philosophy of Design 1941-1981 Essays*, Edited by Nigel Tonks, Munich: Prestel 2012), and Peter Rice, (*An Engineer Imagines*. London: Artemis, 1994)

[9] Four of the worst structural accidents in the last 150 years were caused by contractors redesigning structures without consulting the structural design engineers: the collapse during construction in 1883 of the raised arm of the Statue of Liberty in New York (Eiffel's design was redesigned by the contractor to save money); the collapse of the first Quebec Bridge in 1907 (https://en.wikipedia.org/wiki/Quebec_Bridge consulted 28th February 2016); the collapse of the Tacoma Narrows bridge in 1947 (Addis, W. 'Design Revolutions in the History of Tension Structures', *Structural Engineering Review*, Vol.6, No.1, (1994) pp.1-10; the collapse of a suspended balcony in the Hyatt Regency Hotel in 1980, called 'the worst structural disaster in the United States' (Levy, Matthys & Salvadori, Mario, *Why buildings fall down*, New York and London: Norton, 1987, pp.221-230);

[10] A rare example in which the management of the design process as part of an overall project programme is discussed is 'Design towards convergence' by E. Happold, I. Liddell and M. Dickson (*Architectural Design,* Vol.46 No.7, 1976, pp.430-35).

[11] For example, *The Report on the Fall of the Cotton Mill at Oldham and Part of the Prison at Northleach.* London: HMSO 1845. More recently the partial collapse in 1968 of Ronan Point, a 22-storey tower block in East London, following a small gas explosion, was followed by many studies of the incident that will be of great value to future historians. (https://en.wikipedia.org/wiki/Ronan_Point Accessed 26th January 2016)

[12] Some examples are: David Cottam on *Owen Williams* (London: Architectural Association, 1986); in the early 2000s Thomas Telford published six books under the general title '*The Engineer's Contribution to Contemporary Architecture*': John Chilton, *Heinz Isler*. London: Thomas Telford. 2000; John Chilton, *Santiago Calatrava*. London: Thomas Telford. 2000; Angus MacDonald, *Anthony Hunt*. London: Thomas Telford. 2000; Remo Pedreschi, *Eladio Dieste*. London: Thomas Telford. 2000; Andy Brown, *Peter Rice*. London: Thomas Telford. 2001; David Yeomans, *Owen Williams*. London: Thomas Telford. 2001.

[13] Several German heritage structures have been described in publications by Germany's Federal Chamber of Engineers (Bundesingenieurkammer – similar to the UK's Institution of Civil Engineers) including Das neue Museum Berlin, Die Grossmarkthalle Leipzig, Der Flughafen Tempelhof, and Die Sayner Hütte. http://wahrzeichen.ingenieurbaukunst.de/publikationen/ . Other structures given critical appraisal include the Boat Store at Sheerness (Skempton, A.W., 'The Boat Store, Sheerness (1858-60) and its place in structural history', *Transactions of the Newcomen Society*, Vol.32, 1959-60, pp.57-78) and The Crystal Palace (Addis, Bill, 'The Crystal Palace and its place in Structural History.' pp.11-36 in Motro,_René (Ed.) (2009), *Structural Morphology and Configuration Processing of Space Structures*, Brentwood, Essex: Multi-Science Publishing

[14] Two rare exceptions are Milan Cathedral, for which records survive of a detailed inquiry in the late 14th century into its design and construction (see Frankl, Paul, *The Gothic*. Princeton University Press, 1960), and the Crystal Palace whose designs were published shortly after completion in 1851, and whose progress and construction were reported in detail every week in the *Illustrated London News*.

[15] Speaking personally, the engineer whose thinking, methods and skills I would most like to know more about is the Roman Emperor Trajan's engineer known as Apollodorus of Damascus who devised and constructed the huge concrete vaults in Trajan's market, baths (Thermae) which contained the prototype for the Pantheon, bridge over the Rhine and entire port at Ostia near Rome.

Materials

Gypsum in Spanish Levant: history of its production and use in local architecture

Vincenzina La Spina[1], Fernando Vegas[2], and Camilla Mileto[2]
1. Universidad Politécnica de Cartagena, Spain; 2. Universitat Politècnica de València, Spain

Introduction

Historically, gypsum is a construction material which has played a major role in both rural and urban architecture in the Spanish Levant, although its use is currently limited to rendering or plastering interiors and creating decorative details. In addition, the entire manufacturing process of raw gypsum for use in construction requires a great number of professionals, tools and techniques which have resulted, above all, in a highly characteristic local architecture where the material has many uses, both structural and decorative.

In the Middle Ages it was practically a homemade product, given that following extraction and heating in a furnace or kiln it was crushed using large wooden mallets before finally being sifted. Although the manufacturing process has become more efficient over the centuries, the basic traditional form of heating survived for a long time, and in rural areas the manufacturing process was practically the same as in medieval times up to the mid-twentieth century.

The aim of this article is to succinctly examine the process of transformation of raw gypsum from extraction to its use in various specific areas of the Spanish Levant. Special emphasis is laid on the geological features of the terrain which have encouraged the existence of deposits for extraction and on the traditional production process for powdered gypsum from medieval times until the mid-twentieth century, concluding with a detailed explanation of its multiple applications in local construction.

In geographical terms the areas of production are found in the Valencian Community and the Region of Murcia, specifically Rincón de Ademuz and surrounding areas of the cities of Valencia and Villena. The cities of Murcia and Campo de Cartagena, are places of particular interest in which several studies were carried out.

In addition, in chronological terms the modernisation of the production process due to the introduction of machinery, electric kilns, control systems, etc., and the Spanish Civil War (1936-40) with its generational change and the abandonment of rural areas, are milestones in the gradual oblivion of both traditional gypsum production and local construction techniques. Hence artisan produced gypsum was eclipsed by the development of new construction materials.

Historic deposits, quarries and extraction

Historic deposits and quarries

Gypsum ($CaSO_4$ $2H_2O$) is an evaporite rock formed through desiccation by evaporation of brackish waters and salt lakes or inner seas with no exit to the ocean, with thin water layers and under the effect of a dry climate. In general, this material resource is characterised by poor surface resistance, cleavage and solubility in warm water.

On the Spanish mainland there are numerous deposits of great geological and mineral importance, found mainly on the east side of the country. These formations mostly correspond to the Keuper (Triassic), Oligocene or Paleogene and Miocene (Tertiary) age. Gypsum from the Keuper and Miocene age are the most frequent, but gypsum from the Keuper age is more compact due to the longevity and the pressure it has been subjected to.

In the Valencian Community the deposits of Segorbe (Castellón), Tuejar, Chiva, Cofrentes, Llosa de Ranes (Valencia), Elda, Villena and Argot (Alicante), San Miguel de Salinas and Benejuzar (Alicante) should all be noted for their quality and reserves[1]. However, historically, the most important mine for the city of Valencia was “Niñerola”[2] in the town of Picassent, which already operated in Roman times.

In contrast, the distribution of the main deposits in the region of Murcia is varied but they are mainly found in the Carrascoy mountains, near Aljezares and Torreagüera; in the mountains of La Pila and La Garapacha in the north of the province; in the east in Totana and Lorca in the Espuña and La Tercia mountains, and in the northeast of the Algarrobo mountains in Campo de Cartagena. (Fig. 1)

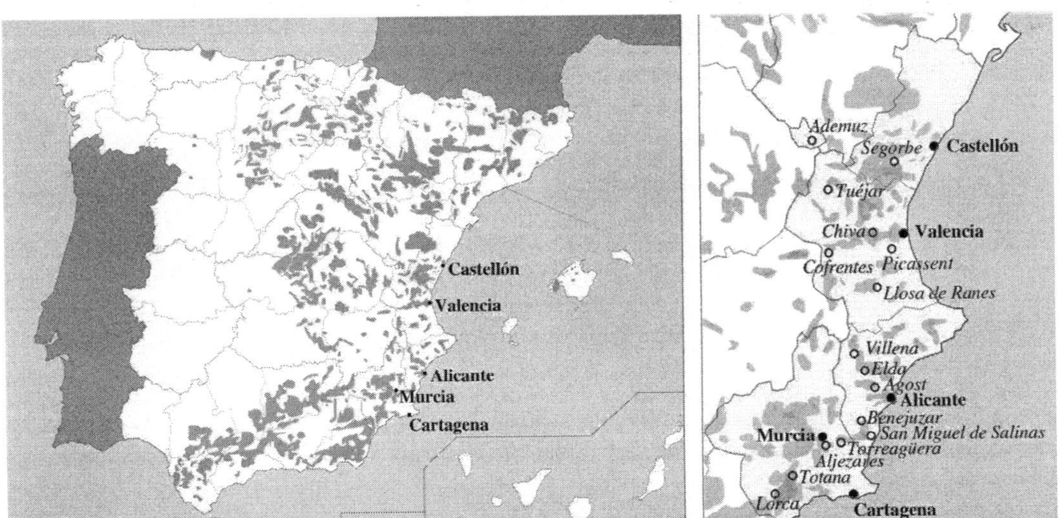

Figure 1. Location map of gypsum deposits in Spain (left) and in the Spanish Levant (right).Photo: La Spina. Instituto Geológico y Minero de España (IGME)

The operation of deposits

In the Middle Ages in Valencia there was full freedom to extract materials from quarries providing they were used for construction according to the privileges granted by King Jaime I in 1239 and included in the city legislation or *Fueros*[3].This was how raw gypsum was extracted, and production was generally intermittent, as quarries were only opened when there was a need to execute specific construction projects.

This type of operation was carried out mainly in rural contexts, co-existing for many centuries with industrial extraction. There are barely any written records for many of the sites quarried in the Spanish Levant in historical publications on mining or in the *Estadística Minera* censuses from the Instituto Geológico y Minero de España (IGME). This shows that the necessary licenses or permits were not requested since gypsum was extracted in a practically self-sufficient manner for domestic use by the inhabitants of a region as needed[4].

Traditionally, open quarries were the most common as they are less dangerous and more cost-efficient and accessible than underground ones. The 'quarriers' worked the more superficial and shallow sites extracting the gypsum manually with the aid of simple tools, digging and removing rubble until they reached a seam (or '*tetón*' as it is known to Spanish gypsum producers) with the aid of picks, pickaxes, iron and wooden wedges, bars, props, containers, shovels, etc. The material was removed downwards creating terraces that were accessed using survey methods, with the help of explosive charges (gunpowder) placed by '*barreneros*' in charge of drilling and blasting cylindrical perforations in the rock. These perforations were made with '*barrenas*' (rounded iron bars approximately 2.20 metres long and with straight edges at the ends), cleaned with a '*hisopo*' (1.50 metres long metal bar with one spoon-shaped end while the other was used to place a handful of esparto. After the detonation the larger fragments were broken up into smaller pieces using 4 or 5 kg iron mallets called '*almainas*' (or '*almádenas*'). Once the raw gypsum was extracted, either from underground or in the open air, it was transported in carts to installations where it was calcined and ground.

According to the historical literature consulted[5] in the province of Valencia most of the production was surface gypsum extraction, although there are exceptions, like Cerro de las Cuevas in Alfarp which was an underground mine in 1928[6]. Similarly, most of the sites in the Region of Murcia were also open air, for example in Las Yeseras (Campo de Cartagena, Murcia) or the quarry of Torreagüera (Murcia). However, it is worth noting the underground extraction of gypsum in Los Aljezares (Murcia) from large caves, like those in the region of Paris. According to W. Bierhenke[7], the first space in the cave was an enormous room with a 20 metres high vaulted ceiling and a circular opening through which the rock could be winched up from a winding tower with the ropes and baskets tied to the ends of the winch or '*malacate*'[8]. (Fig. 2) In addition, from this first cave other interdependent caves, separated by walls with partial openings forming columns to support the ceiling, were accessed.

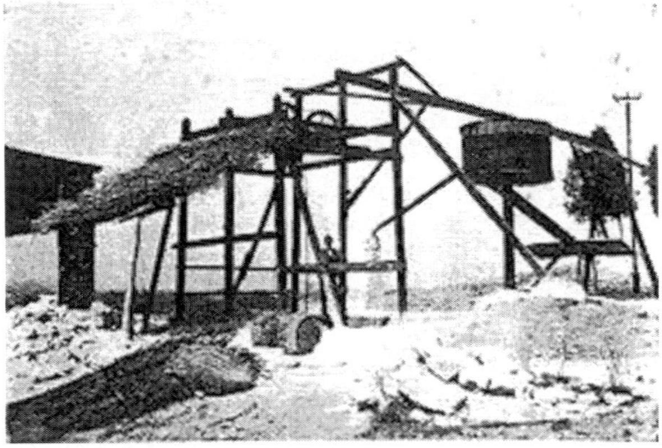

Figure 2. Gypsum mine in Aljezares (Murcia) in the early twentieth century. Photo: Bierhenke, Murcia, (Note 7) pp. 223-244.

Finally, the introduction into mining of large-scale machinery from the mid-twentieth century made it possible to work in deeper mines and where possible, even to transform underground mines into open air quarries and enable more earth to be transported.

Traditional production of powdered gypsum

Calcination or dehydration of the gypsum

The calcination or dehydration of gypsum consists in the removal of quarry water and the crystallisation within the raw gypsum. Traditionally this was carried out in rudimentary kilns, similar to those used to produce lime, known as Arab kilns, and found mostly near quarries, but also near large-scale or costly construction sites as it was possible to control the calcined material and prevent adulteration with earth or ash.

Kilns were generally simple cylindrical dry stone wall constructions of variable height, accessed via an opening at the front and built on sloping ground to facilitate loading and unloading from above, as in the case of those found in Rincón de Ademuz[9] (Valencia) (Fig. 3), in La Garapacha (Murcia) or in Rambla de Torreagüera (Murcia) Inside, large pieces of gypsum were used to create a false dome to form a hearth with an opening at the front to fuel the kiln, and on which pieces of raw gypsum were placed in descending order, simultaneously building a wall over the top opening of the kiln, finally filling all the gaps with remains and excess powder. The kiln was fuelled with logs, shrubs and branches, chosen to provide the best flame, although near La Unión and Cartagena '*carbonilla*' (coal residue) or coal was also used. The kiln had to be rendered inside and out with clay to prevent heat escaping from between the joins in the wall. In cases where there was a shortage of wood, kilns were built in a truncated conical shape[10] as in the case of those in Villena. (Fig. 4)

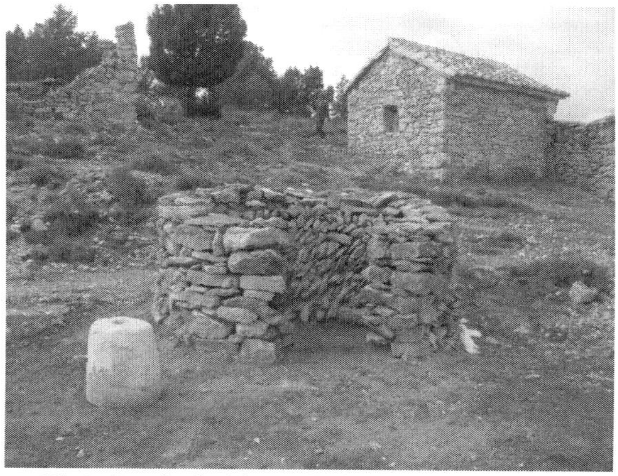

Figure 3. Traditional gypsum kiln in Rincón de Ademuz (Valencia), 2015. Photo:Vegas&Mileto

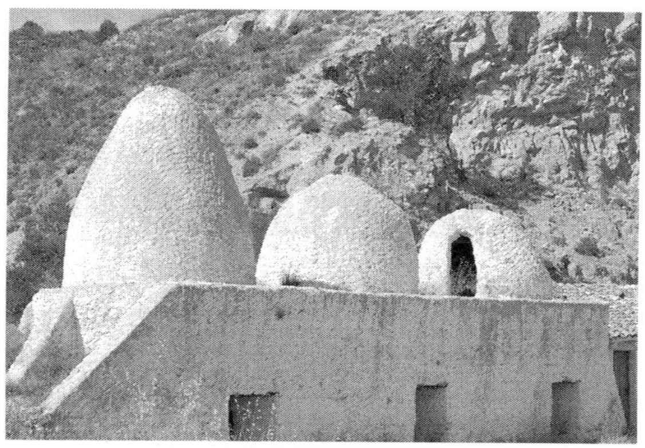

Figure 4. Photograph of a gypsum kiln in Villena (Alicante), 2010. Photo: http://www.villenacuentame.com/2010/07/los-hornos-de-yeso-del-cabezo-de-las.html

The calcination process consisted in first heating the rocks slightly to eliminate humidity and water not resulting from crystallisation, and subsequently increasing the temperature to complete dehydration. Calcination time, which oscillated between six and thirty-six hours, was a highly variable factor given that it depended on atmospheric conditions, the quality of the rock and the fuel used. Once the calcination was completed, whitish marks appeared on the upper part of the kiln, and these were covered in fragments of fine gypsum waste to prevent the escape of fumes and to redirect the draught. This operation was repeated several times and when everything went white the kiln was no longer fuelled[11]. Subsequently, the batch was once again covered with a layer of powder from the same gypsum in order to concentrate heat, ensuring slow and gradual cooling. Temperatures reached in this type of kiln were highly variable, with intervals ranging between 100°C and 1,000°C depending on location in the kiln. Consequently, heating with this method was always irregular since normally the raw gypsum above cooked poorly and the raw gypsum below heated too much, resulting in multiphase gypsum[12].

In short, the correct dehydration of gypsum depended above all on the experience of the gypsum producer who had to assess when the process had been completed, but also on the calcination time and atmospheric conditions, on the shape of the kiln, on the temperature reached and the type of raw gypsum[13], all of which are determining factors in the subsequent quality of the gypsum.

Equally, other types evolved from the simple kiln described, such as those built in Aljezares (Murcia)[14] until the mid-twentieth century. These were typically cylindrical double kilns, side by side, and as they were larger they had buttresses in the centre and on the corners as well as thicker walls made of masonry and '*láguena*' earth[15] which were rendered outside and tended to be protected with a roof.

In contrast, in Las Yeseras in Campo de Cartagena (Murcia) it would not be appropriate to only refer to them as kilns. These constructions consisted of a space for grinding and storage. Circular kilns partially embedded in the ground were placed at one end, in the centre a pillar to which the animal who pulled the roller was tied up, and on the opposite end two storage spots, one with a door halfway up the wall to sift the powdered gypsum and the other to store all sorts of gypsum[16].

Finally, similar installations mainly featuring several kilns or different constructions relating to the production of gypsum (mill, store, stacking and loading area) were also frequent in Villena (Alicante)[17].

Grinding, selection and transport

Once the kiln cooled completely, after approximately ten days, the most frequent action was to grind the calcined gypsum. The oldest method was simply breaking apart the raw gypsum using mallets and sticks, but when there were spaces beside mountain slopes near the kiln animal power was used. The soil was cleaned, prepared and hardened and the raw gypsum was spread once the larger rocks had been broken using mallets and sticks, finally grinding the gypsum in circles with a truncated-cone roller or a cylindrical bolus with a rough stone surface drawn by animals. In these spaces in La Garapacha and Torreagüera (Murcia), there was also a 1.10 metres high post in the centre to tie the animal and force it to go around in a circle[18]. (Fig. 5) However, from the mid-twentieth century these grinding spaces were gradually replaced with chain-driven crushers.

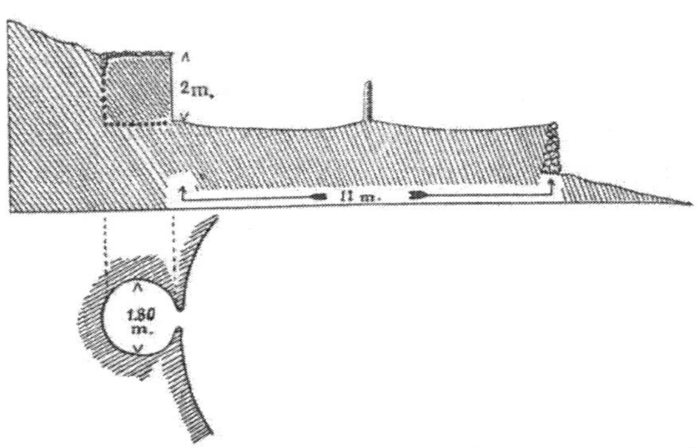

Figure 5. Diagram of a kiln and surrounding space in La Garapacha. Photo: Bierhenke, Murcia, (Note 7) pp. 223-244

Once the grinding concluded, the gypsum was removed from the grinding space and sifted, while any gypsum that remained was ground again in the grinding space[19]. Although sometimes it was not sifted, as was the case in Torreagüera (Murcia), but used immediately after grinding to make mortar and sifted only when the gypsum was going to be used to render walls. In a final phase the product that was ground and prepared for commercialisation was loaded in baskets onto animal-drawn carts and distributed.

When grinding was not carried out near kilns the dehydrated rock was transported to the construction site, as happened during the construction of the Temple in Valencia in 1763 where it was necessary to set up a temporary raw gypsum mill operated by a horse[20], or to more specific establishments known as 'gypsum factories'. The latter were the most frequent in the city of Valencia and there are records of the existence in 1510 of an industry for gypsum production in the "*algepsería*" in the square by the cathedral[21]. Equally, in later centuries, particularly in the eighteenth century, according to *Ramo de Providencias sobre el Abasto de yeso* in the city and its outskirts there were still gypsum mills, which were mostly simple wheels powered by animals. This was also the case in later times, as can be seen from the nineteenth century files of the *Policía Urbana*, and machines were even invented to obtain a more finely milled gypsum[22]. This continued until 1881 when gypsum factories were banned within a 150 metre distance from any dwelling, probably due to the constant inconveniences caused by this type of activity in the city.

Mediaeval supply of gypsum in the city of Valencia

In mediaeval Valencia, the gypsum market was smaller than the lime market, and more local, which meant that only in regions with an abundance of the material was there a gypsum market with a relatively wide scope of geographical influence[23]. However, the most striking information, without a doubt, is the presence of '*algepçeres*' (women gypsum producers). There were even times at which they had the monopoly over the supply of some public works as was the case of Isabel de Córdoba, '*castellana algepçera'*, who was almost exclusively in charge of supplying for building work on the cathedral in 1438-39. Other '*algepçeres'* from the city included Caterina, another woman called Isabel '*algepçera'* (probably *castellana*) and na Fariza, who was the wife of Isabel la Castellana's sole competitor for the work in the cathedral. In addition, just like na Fariza, Caterina was a widow and it was not unusual for widows to continue with their husbands' businesses after they passed away. However, these women were not the only suppliers for the numerous works being carried out in the city: documents in the archives show that there were also men, although little is known about them except their names and the amount of material they supplied.

Use of gypsum in local architecture

The widespread use of gypsum as a construction material with numerous uses in the Spanish Levant is undeniable, as attested to by the surviving historic and traditional buildings. This material has been used to render all sorts of interior surfaces, including floors, as well as façades. It has been used to construct interior partitions, built-in furniture and architectural elements such as doorways, windows, stairs, vault ribs[24] or fireplaces, and to execute structural construction elements such as floors, ceilings, vaults, pillars, rammed earth walls, etc.[25][26]

The professionals who took part in its execution varied considerably depending on the purpose of the gypsum: decorative, structural, for furniture, etc. and the location of the constructions, both urban and rural. This means the different construction techniques could be carried out by master builders, bricklayers and labourers, by simple local builders or even by the future owners of the buildings.

Renderings

Most of the constructions executed have been rendered on the interior with gypsum or a mix of gypsum and sand in order to maintain inhabited spaces clean. Although at present this is the only type of rendering which is still used in current architecture, historically it was also used to render the exterior of buildings. Evidence of this is found in the renderings of the façades of the historic centre of the city of Valencia from the eighteenth until the mid-twentieth century[27] (Fig. 6), as well as in many other Spanish cities and towns (Cuenca, Ademuz, etc.).

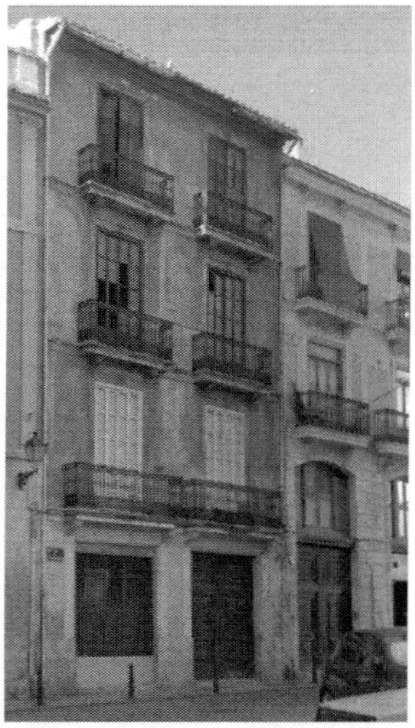

Figure 6. Image of a historic façade in Valencia rendered in traditional gypsum, 2015. Photo: La Spina

In these cases, the bricklayers were in charge of pouring the gypsum mix (gypsum and water or gypsum, water and some aggregate) with pointing, rectangular or square trowels. The mix was previously prepared by the '*peón de mano*' (hand labourer) in a trough (even without using any tools except his hands) and was immediately passed on to the bricklayer, who picked it up with a hawk or his hands. After the mixing the labourers had to clean the trough thoroughly with a scraper to eliminate all remains of dry gypsum if they wished to use it again. Equally, once the mix was spread a '*peón lavador*' (washing labourer) had to use wet rags to level out and smooth over any irregularities left by the rectangular trowel, running the rag up and down the entire wall to obtain a perfectly smooth and pore free surface.

In contrast, in rural areas the techniques were even simpler and at times more rudimentary so that gypsum mixes were applied and spread simply by hand in secondary buildings (stables, tool sheds, etc.). Other smoother and finer options were the renderings with trowels or with the help of guides in order to achieve a surface without marks.

Built-in furniture and indoor partitions

In the '*barracas*', typical traditional constructions in Valencian and Murcian orchards, as well as in the small rural houses of inland Spanish Levant, such as Rincón de Ademuz, it was not uncommon to find '*alacenas'*, built-in cupboards for the storage of different objects. These were usually built taking advantage of the corners of a room using reeds or flat stones placed against each other and finally polished with gypsum to form a smooth surface incorporated into the wall. Similar techniques were also used to make all sorts of interior partitions or furniture such as '*trojes'*, spaces defined by low walls used to store fruit and especially cereal (Fig. 7); balustrades, solid ledges; built-in shelves for plates, glasses and other utensils, built-in benches and fireplaces or chimneybreasts above the hearth.

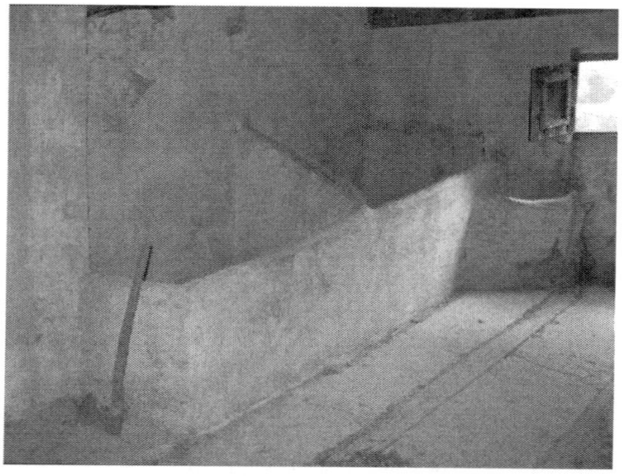

Figure 7. Photo of a 'troje' in a dwelling in Sesga (Rincón de Ademuz, Valencia), 2015. Photo: La Spina

Floors, ceilings and roofs

Equally, the traditional floors and ceilings of most of the Spanish Levant are built using wooden joists filled in with gypsum, well-poured on wooden formwork that can be restored, or on vaults made of ceramic brick and gypsum. This type of floor and ceilings, originally dating back to the sixteenth century, is characteristically used to save wood and make the best possible use of gypsum as a building material. In addition, when economic resources were scant, more often in rural areas, the gypsum on top became the floor of the house. For its use in construction the gypsum with a higher anhydrite content[28] was mixed with very little water in order to obtain high resistance gypsum, and oils such as linseed or olive oil were applied for greater waterproofing, an operation which was repeated periodically[29]. (Fig. 8)

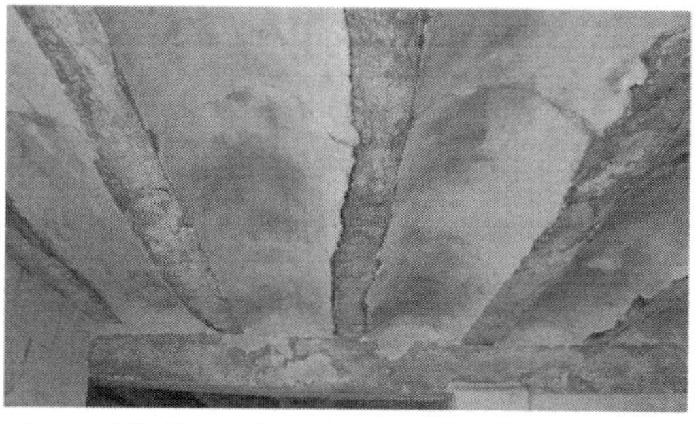

Figure 8. Ceiling with wooden beams filled in with gypsum in a dwelling in Sesga (Rincón de Ademuz, Valencia), 2015. Photo: La Spina

Pillars, walls and rammed earth walls

In the region of Rincón de Ademuz, traditional constructions characteristically have mass semi-formwork or formwork pillars which spring from bases or perimeter stonework loadbearing walls and which can withstand the load of up to four floors[30]. (Fig. 9)

Generally, pillars were built using vertical guidelines (4 or 6 cm strips of wood) which were placed between the corners of the future pillar to make these perfectly straight and vertical, stonework was subsequently added and secured with gypsum mortar, followed by gypsum rendering. Equally, in Murcia walls of houses were often stonework grouted with gypsum which was not even sifted, and was also rendered in the same material[31].

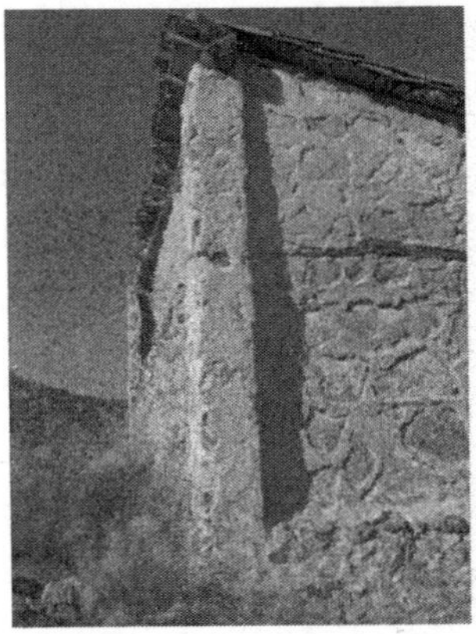

Figure 9. Gypsum pillars in a traditional construction from Rincón de Ademuz (Valencia), 2015. Photo: Vegas & Mileto

Finally, gypsum was also used in the construction of rammed earth walls. In most cases the gypsum was placed on the sides and corners of the moulds, adopting characteristic undulating shapes called '*brencas'* (Fig. 10) visible on the façades. With the use of gypsum the earth could be tamped, preventing shrinkage, improving the joints, reinforcing the weaker points and preventing cracks during drying[32].

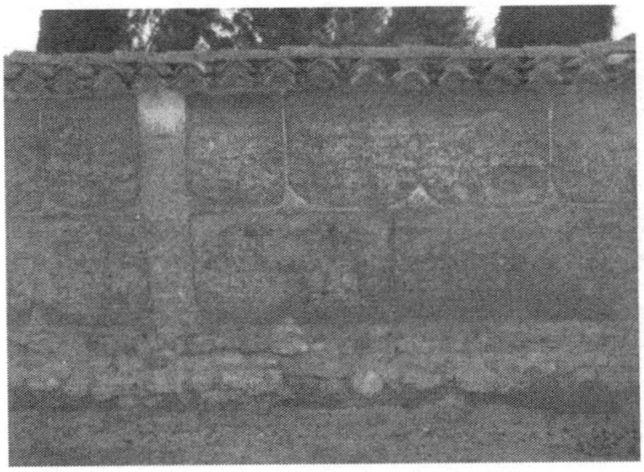

Figure 10. Rammed earth wall with gypsum 'brencas' in Rincón de Ademuz (Valencia), 2015. Photo: Vegas & Mileto

Conclusion

Without doubt, the great importance of gypsum in construction in the Spanish Levant is the result of two factors combined. It is partly due to the existence of deposits on the one hand, and on the other to the characteristics of the production process and its use in construction. The most notable characteristics are ease of extraction and grinding given the softness of raw gypsum; low fuel consumption as it only needs relatively short calcining time at moderate temperatures; immediate use following grinding as it requires no additional transformation; simple preparation of mixes as it is enough to add water, and the possibility of working with hands or rapid application as it hardens quickly, despite needing a greater number of building professionals working at the same time.

In terms of the calcination process there are slight geographical variations when heating the raw gypsum. The basic concept is the same, the only changes are in the size or shape of the kilns. In connection with this it is worth noting the tendency to unify all the phases of the building process in a single construction: calcination, grinding, sifting and storage, frequent in the area of Villena and Murcia, while in the city of Valencia the norm was to grind near the construction site or in the city, that is to say, near where the construction was to be executed. It is also interesting to note that women gypsum producers in mediaeval times continued the trade of their deceased husbands given that it was not necessary to have extensive knowledge in order to grind the gypsum.

Therefore, it can be concluded that there are many determining factors in the abundant and varied use of gypsum in local architecture. This unique characteristic becomes a trademark in itself, as well as a differentiating factor closely linked to the material resources available in the surroundings.

References

[1] D. Sanz Arauz, "Análisis del yeso empleado en revestimientos exteriores mediante técnicas geológicas" (Ph.D. Thesis, Universidad Politécnica de Madrid, 2009), p. 65.

[2] Also highlighted and supported by well-known Valencian botanist Antonio Cavanilles in A. J. Cavanilles, *Observaciones sobre la historia natural, geografía, agricultura, población y frutos del Reyno de Valencia* (2 vols), Madrid: Imprenta real, 1795. Vol 1, pp. 162-164.

[3] J. V. García Marsilla & T. Izquierdo Aranda, *Abastecer la obra gótica. El mercado de los materiales de construcción del territorio en la Valencia bajomedieval*, Valencia: Conselleria de Infraestructuras, Territorio y Medio Ambiente, 2013. p. 50.

[4] V. La Spina, L. García Soriano, C. Mileto & F. Vegas, "Gypsum quarries used in Valencian architecture: Past, present and future" pp. 411-418 in C, Mileto, F. Vegas, L. García & V. Cristini (eds), *Vernacular Architecture. Towards a Sustainable Future*, London: Taylor & Francis Group, 2014.

[5] Different historical publications and the *Estadística Minera* from 1861 to 1940 (IGME).

[6] VV.AA., *Estadística Minera*, Madrid: Imprenta Nacional, 1928. pp. 656-657.

[7] W. Bierhenke, "La obtención del yeso en Murcia", *Revista Murciana de Antropología*, no.16, 2009, pp. 223-244.

[8] According to the RAE dictionary this machine was often used in mines to extract minerals and water, with a drum above and the levers to which the horses are harnessed below.

[9] C. Mileto & F. Vegas, *Arquitectura preindustrial del Rincón de Ademuz, Homo Faber*, Casa Altas: Mancomunidad de Municipios Rincón de Ademuz, 2008. pp. 174-178.

[10] F. Ger y Lobez, *Tratado de construcción civil*, Badajoz: La Minerva Extremeña, 1898. p. 42.

[11] O. Puche Riart, L. F. Mazadiego Martínez, J.E. Ortiz Menéndez & J. F. Llamas Borrajo, "Yeserías históricas de Morata de Tajuña (Madrid)", *Materiales de Construcción*, vol.57, no.287, 2007. pp. 81-87.

[12] Sanz, thesis, (note 1) p. 32.

[13] Not all require the same firing according to seventeenth century Spanish treatise writer Fray Lorenzo de San Nicolás. Fr. L. de San Nicolás, *Arte y uso de arquitectura*, Madrid, 1639. p. 89b.

[14] Bierhenke, Murcia, (Note 7) pp. 223-244.

[15] '*Láguena'* is a fire-resistant reddish blue earth obtained from grinding soft slate.

[16] C. Martínez Hernández, "Las Yeseras", un paisaje geográfico cultural en abandono ligado al sistema constructivo tradicional", pp. 464-476 in *Proceedings of the IV Congreso Nacional de etnografía del Campo de Cartagena. La vivienda y la arquitectura tradicional del Campo de Cartagena,* Cartagena: Universidad Politécnica de Cartagena CRAI Biblioteca, 2015.

[17] C. E. Rizo Antón, J. García Guardiola & A. Luján Navas, *Arqueología Industrial en Villena: Contribución al estudio de las canteras de yeso del término municipal de Villena* (Alicante), Villena: Fundación Municipal José Mª Soler, 2001.

[18] Bierhenke, Murcia, (Note 7) p 236.

[19] Mileto & Vegas, Faber, (Note 9) p. 176.

[20] J. Villalmanzo Cameno, "El temple de Valencia: Historia de su construcción (1761-1785)" in VV. AA. (eds), *Iglesia y palacio del Temple: Síntesis de Arte e Historia*, Valencia: Del Sénia al Segura, 2008, p. 92.

[21] A. Nogales Espert, *La sanidad Municipal en la Valencia Foral Moderna 1479-1707,* Valencia: Ajuntament de Valencia, 1997, p. 242.

[22] One example is the machine designed by the gypsum producer Mariano Gonzalo de León in 1840, AHMV, *Policía Urbana*, file 21, box 57(64), 1840.

[23] García Marsilla & Izquierdo Aranda, Abastecer, (Note 3) p. 178.

[24] R. Marín Sánchez, *Uso estructural de prefabricados de yeso en la arquitectura levantina de los siglos XV y XVI* (Ph.D. Thesis, Universitat Politecnica de València, 2014).

[25] F. Vegas, C. Mileto, V. Cristini, J.R. Ruiz Checa & V. La Spina, "Gypsum as reinforcement for floors: conceptual approach", pp. 389-394, in Mariana Correia et al. (eds), *Vernacular Heritage and Earthen Architecture. Contributions for sustainable development*, London: Taylor & Francis Group, 2013.

[26] La Spina, García, Mileto & Vegas, Quarries, (Note 4).

[27] V. La Spina, *Vestigios de Yeso. Los revestimientos continuos históricos en las fachadas de la Valencia intramuros: estudio histórico, caracterización y propuestas de conservación,* (Ph.D. Thesis, Universitat Politecnica de València, 2015).

[28] Overcooked gypsum which has lost almost all the water from crystallisation and is almost insoluble.

[29] Vegas, Mileto, Cristini, Ruiz & La Spina, Floors, (Note 25).

[30] F. Vegas, C. Mileto, M. Diodato, J. García Soriano, C. Grau Giménez, "Traditional structures made with gypsum pillars: a reasoned hypothesis", in R. Carvais et. al. (eds) *Nuts & Bolts of Construction History* (3 vols), París: Picard, 2012.Vol. 2, pp. 509-516.

[31] Bierhenke, Murcia, (Note 7) p 238.

[32] C. Mileto, F. Vegas, L. García Soriano & M. Mestre Sabater, "Rammed earth construction in El Rincón de Ademuz (Spain)", pp. 181- 186, in C. Mileto, F, Vegas & V. Cristini (eds), *Rammed Earth Conservation,* London: Taylor & Francis Group, 2012.

Gypsum external renders of Paris: history and fabrication

Tiffanie Le Dantec
Laboratoire de l'école d'Architecture de Versailles /Laboratoire de Recherche des Monuments Historiques, Université Versailles-Saint-Quentin. Paris

Introduction

A research programme started in 2015 within the *Laboratoire de Recherche des Monuments Historiques* (LRMH) aimed at a better understanding of a very common material found on the facades of historical buildings in Paris and its surroundings: gypsum renders. The research programme aims on one hand to establish the true materiality of gypsum renders and find a way to replicate it or to repair it better; and on the other hand, it aims for a better understanding of the history of these renders and of the design of the Parisian facades.

The gypsum external renders of Paris are well known by the architects carrying out their restoration and by the city administration working on their conservation. However, nobody agrees on the composition of these ancient gypsum plasters, leading to numerous pathologies after ill-carried restorations. What everyone agrees on, however, is the general strength of this old material to resist weather erosion. Some renders are centuries old when restoration work begins.

Why were these traditional renders so resilient? Was it the way the gypsum was produced? Was it the way masons used gypsum on the facade? Was it the way the facade was designed? Or was it a combination of all those reasons? This article will shed some light on these questions.

To write this article, historic written literature was compared with a corpus of facades with gypsum renders and numerous visits of ruined buildings and restoration work. A geographical and historical review will set the context first. Then fabrication of 'Plaster of Paris', its application and architectonic details will be analysed to clear up the mystery of its strength.

Geography: the gypsum area

There are two main areas in France where gypsum is found easily, close to the surface and ready to be extracted: the regions of Paris and Provence. Those two regions have a built heritage of gypsum elements, mortars and internal or external renders from the Gallo-Roman period until the beginning of the twentieth century.

In the region of Paris, the use of gypsum in construction is linked to the accessibility of the raw material, easier to reach in the northern part thanks to outcrops, the most famous of them being Montmartre and Belleville, where gypsum has been extracted since the first centuries A.D[1]. Far from following the boundaries of the administrative region of Ile-de-France, the area of gypsum use can be obtained (Fig.1) by looking at built heritage and vernacular architecture past and present[2]. In culturally distinct areas with a strong local tradition of building with gypsum - such as Parisis, Goële, Multien, Orxois and Brie Française - gypsum outcrops widely.

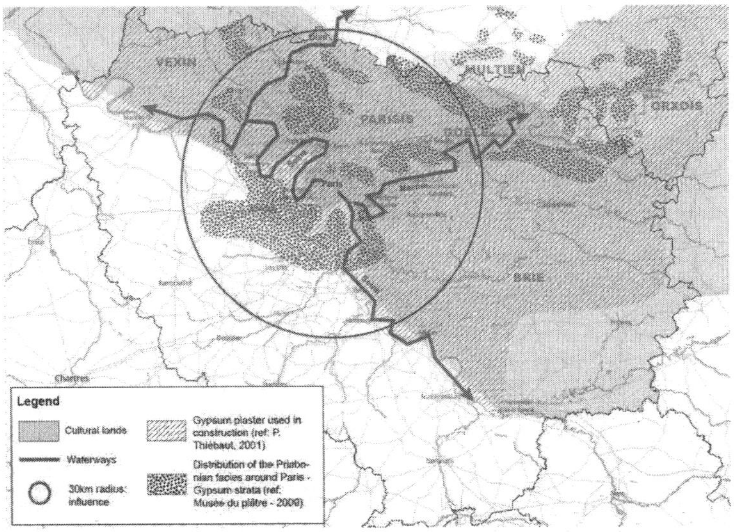

Figure 1: the gypsum area around Paris (Tiffanie Le Dantec, 2016)

The region's three major rivers, Seine, Oise and Marne, were also convenient for spreading the use of gypsum in construction. Historical urban centres with gypsum facades are a common sight all along their banks as far as Rouen, for the river Seine, where the historical city centre features gypsum-rendered facades. Furthermore, the sphere of influence of, for instance, Paris through the exporting of gypsum along carriageways from Montmartre is likely to have been the radius of around thirty kilometres around the city that could be covered by horse carriages within a day.

History of gypsum in architecture

Antiquity, from the first to the third century A.D: prefabrication.

Gypsum was used for construction as far back as the first century A.D: roof and wall tiles, bricks and ornamental elements have been found during archaeological excavations in the location of Gallo-Roman Lutece[3] (5th arrondissement of Paris). These were prefabricated elements, but according to the Greek author Theophrastus ('On Stones') and the Roman author Pliny the Elder ('Natural History, XXXVI Books'), gypsum renders were common in the Roman Empire, at least for internal finishes.

Middle Ages, from the fifth to the thirteenth century A.D.: new materials

The barbarian invasions were a period of intense migrations throughout Europe. The new Frankish population brought its own techniques for building: timber structure with cob on wooden lattices[4]. The Roman stone and gypsum masonry faded into history as the Roman Empire collapsed.

Middle Ages, from the thirteenth to the sixteenth century A.D.: gypsum renderings

The use of gypsum rendering instead of cob on wooden lattices started, in France, around the thirteenth century. Several reasons are proposed for the change. The urban densification of the left bank of the river Seine covered up the extraction sites for stones, mud and sand originally located there. At the same time, the growth of the city on the right bank and its extension to the North made the construction sites closer to gypsum quarries and production areas[5]. Gypsum was then chosen for its proximity to the new parts of the city.

A contemporaneous scholar, Bartholomew The Englishman, testified the wide use of gypsum in Paris in 1372: « *... où est le plâtre en grand foison, lequel est comme verre quand il est cru, et dur comme pierre. Et quand il est cuit et détrempé d'eau, il se convertit en cyment, dont on fait les parois des beaux édifices et les parrements des maisons* »[6]. ("...where gypsum is plentiful, behaving like glass when raw and as hard as a stone. And when it is baked and soaked into water, it converts to cement, from which we make the walls of the beautiful buildings and the facing of the houses." Translation, Le Dantec)

1667: King Louis XIV's order

In 1666, the Great Fire engulfed the wooden city of London, destroying most of it. Louis XIV feared the same would happen to Paris as most of the buildings were still composed of timber structures. In 1667, the 18th of august, the King ordered that all buildings must be covered with gypsum plaster, on the inside and on the outside, to prevent fire. The same law forbade corbelled constructions and gave a maximum height for facades. Owners not obeying would face fines and the destruction of their house. Thanks to this, Paris did not burn and the Golden Age of gypsum renderings began.

Sixteenth and seventeenth centuries: the golden age

Following 1667, the city covered itself up with gypsum. Paris was then the largest and most populated city of the western world, experiencing huge urban growth and much construction. Contemporaneous authors spoke of a city where 15 out of 16 houses had gypsum facades[7], and where three quarters of the *hôtels particuliers* were also made of gypsum, encompassing a wide band of the social strata. The use of gypsum was not only for external and internal renders, but also for mortar, filling of half-timbering structures, filling of timber partition walls, chimney ducts and stacks, floor slabs, stairs and ornaments.

The use of gypsum in every elements of construction in Paris was widely described by authors from the seventeenth century until the nineteenth century:

> *"Le plâtre est si utile et si employé dans la construction de nos maisons, que, par l'éclatante blancheur dont il les revêt, il fait de Paris une ville de plâtre. C'est à cette matière froide qui brave les atteintes de la flamme que notre cité doit sa tranquillité contre les accidents du feu."*

Raoul Boutrays, Lutetia, 1611

("Gypsum is so useful and so much used in the construction of our homes; its dazzling whiteness adorns them and makes Paris a city of gypsum. To this cold matter defying the wrath of the flames, our city owes its quietness against fire accidents." Translation, Le Dantec)

« À Paris et dans ses environs on en fait une immense consommation pour construire les maisons. (...) de manière qu'un bâtiment, depuis le sol du rez-de-chaussée jusqu'au grenier, peut être entièrement recouvert de plâtre, et paraître composé d'une seule pièce de cette matière. »

J. Claudel et L. Laroque, Pratique de l'Art de Construire, 1850. p77

("There is such a huge consumption [of gypsum] in Paris and its surroundings to build houses ... that a single building, from the ground floor to the attic, might be covered with gypsum, and seems to be made by a single piece of this material." Translation, Le Dantec)

Nineteenth century: industrialization

The first scientific investigations of gypsum were of Antoine Lavoisier during the eighteenth century, then Henri Le Châtelier during the nineteenth century. They helped develop understanding of processes such as the calcining of gypsum, the mixing, and the setting. Lavoisier wrote the formula of plaster hydration, a process known as mixing[8] :

$$CaSO_4, 1/2H_2O + 3/2\ H_2O \rightarrow CaSO_4, 2H2O$$

(Plaster powder) *(Water)* *(Gypsum)*

A better understanding of gypsum, led to a more efficient way to produce it. The first machines to grind it and calcine it were designed as soon as the end of the eighteenth century to produce a thinner powder, a whiter product. The first furnaces and grinder were used in the middle of the nineteenth century and largely spread in factories by the beginning of the twentieth century. Industrialization of the sector followed the galloping urbanization of Paris and its suburbs, with a higher demand for gypsum for everyday construction. An author compares production of plaster during the nineteenth century with the production of bread: '*le plâtre n'est pas, à Paris, sans analogie avec le pain. Paris a besoin chaque matin, de sa ration de plâtre frais.*'[9]

("In Paris, gypsum plaster is not without comparison with bread. Every morning, Paris needs its fresh bread supply." Translation, Le Dantec)

These new ways of production and use of machines slowly changed the materiality of the powder (Fig.2).

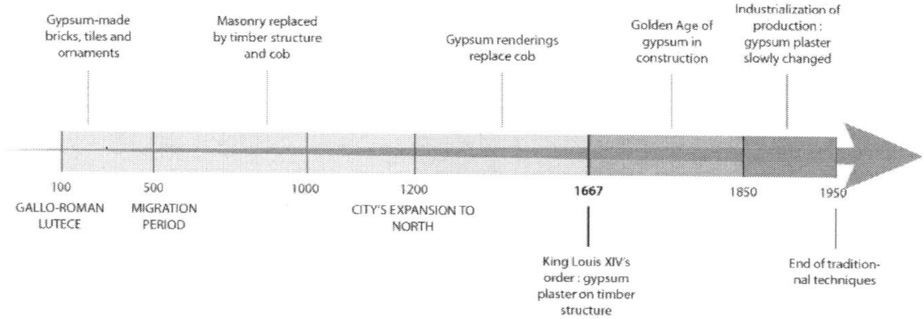

Figure 2: Timeline, history of gypsum around Paris (Tiffanie Le Dantec, 2016)

Twentieth century: crisis

Before the First World War, France was the principal exporter of gypsum and the principal producer. The quality of the "Plaster of Paris" was known worldwide[10]. After the war, gypsum in France did not adapt to the new market of building construction. The building construction required less competent workers, less ornaments, a better pace... The mason of Paris, a highly skilled worker, was suddenly not useful anymore and was replaced by migrant workers between the two wars. The masons tried[11] to change their material by using additives to slow the setting down and to increase its resilience but these chemicals were not monitored and very often led to the ruining of the facades. Architects and engineers no longer trusted gypsum plaster and stopped using it in construction.

The job evolved to become a single-tasked one, making the internal rendering of apartments became the daily life of plasterers. This job was exhausting and often subject to mockery as it was dirty and dusty, workers coughed and their body ended up crooked by the repeated contortions necessary for plastering ceilings. There is a song by Cavanna in the 1930's that goes: "*C'est le bon plâtre de paris, Qu'a fait crever mon mari*" ("The good plaster of Paris caused my husband's death." Translation, Le Dantec).

From then until now, gypsum plaster has had a bad reputation and being a plasterer no longer attracted young people. Gypsum evolved and became plasterboard in the 1960's, relegating wet gypsum plaster to restoration works.

Traditional making of Plaster of Paris

Plaster of Paris is a product obtained after calcination of gypsum stones in furnaces. The making of Plaster of Paris follows five steps: extraction, calcination, grinding, transportation and storage.

This article focuses on the timeline between 1667 and 1950 as traditional ways of producing plaster of Paris carried on quite late. The steps described below testify to skills existing centuries before 1667 which slowly evolved during industrialization from the 1850's until the 1950's.

Gypsum external renders of Paris: history and fabrication

Extraction

Gypsum is a common mineral, calcium sulphate dihydrate ($CaSO_4 \cdot 2H_2O$), found in four strata within sedimentary rocks in the Paris Basin. The three first strata are reachable thanks to outcrops shaped as hills: Montmartre, Belleville, Chaumont, Ménilmontant, and Charonne. Extraction of gypsum blocks was done in open-cast (Fig.3) or underground excavations. It is worth noting that any owner with gypsum outcrop located in his lot could extract it and sell it in his own name[12]. The owners of quarries were then found in any social group from peasants and craftsmen to merchants and noblemen and any institution. Gypsum was found easily and did not need any particular equipment to be extracted and sold. This explains why a map of past quarries has never been done, some quarries being just a hole in the ground.

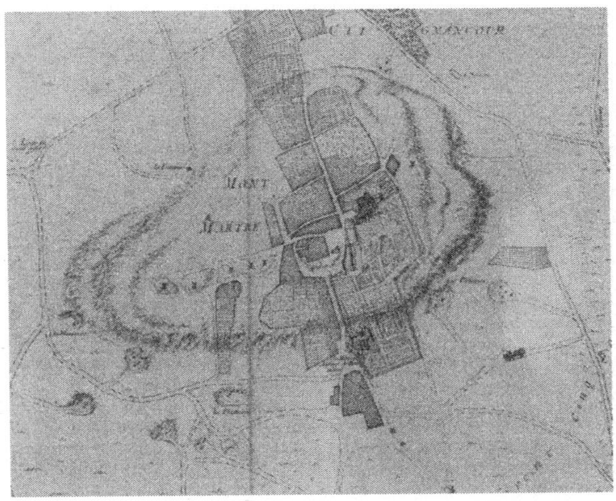

Figure 3: Quarries around Montmartre Hill (Paris en 1672 : fac-similé du premier plan de Jouvin de Rochefort, impr. Ch.Chardon aîné, 1870, Bibliothèque nationale de France, département Cartes et plans, GESH18PF37DIV3P60)

Roughly-cut blocks were extracted by the quarry workers and taken to the furnaces. Depending on historians and centuries, furnaces were located on the site of the quarry or on the construction site. Transportation of calcined gypsum from the quarry to the construction site could alter the material, so building workers preferred to heat it in the city. On the other hand the smoke was irritating and many complaints pushed the city to forbid furnaces[13] several times in its history.

Calcination

Gypsum stones must be heated to a temperature of 130°C so the calcination process occurs:

$$CaSO_4, 2H_2O - 3/2\ H_2O \rightarrow CaSO_4, 1/2H_2O$$

(Gypsum) (1, 5 water) (Plaster of Paris)

This low temperature, compared to calcination of lime (800°C), makes producing plaster easier.

From the eighteenth century[14] to the 1950's, a type of furnace called *four culée* was used to heat gypsum. The simplicity of these furnaces and their similarity with brick furnaces used by the fourteenth century[15] may let us think that they were used at the end of the Middle-Ages but we lack evidence. The stones were placed in a shed composed of three walls often made of gypsum stones and mortar with a high open gabled tiled roof. The stones were laid from the biggest to the smallest of top, in rows divided by vaulted holes where wood would be burned. (Fig.4). The heating process lasted around 12 hours: the stones became white as the water evaporated producing a thick smoke. Once cold, the furnace is destroyed and the stones put aside to be ground.

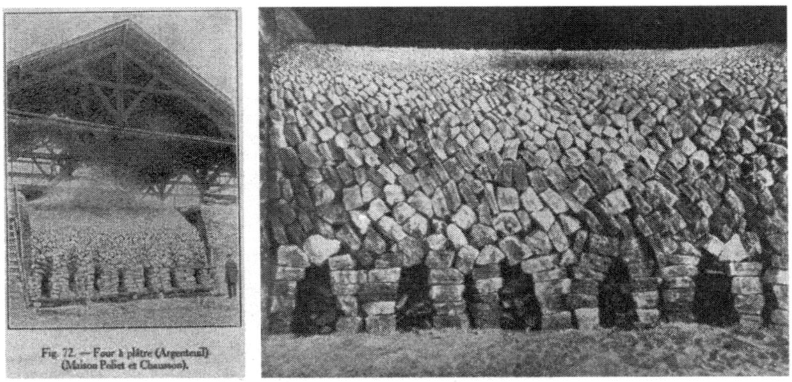

Figure 4: Traditional furnace and details of the layout of gypsum blocks. Left: Four à plâtre (Argenteuil), Paris, Hachette, 1932. Right: A gypsum furnace, Noisy-le-Sec, 1925, Photo Auguste Robin, Larousse, 1925.

Grinding

Traditionally, since Theophrastus to the beginning of the nineteenth century, grinding was done with a wooden staff, hitting the calcined gypsum blocks for hours, hence the still in use expression: *battre comme plâtre* (being beaten very hard). This exhausting job changed during the nineteenth century with the use of the animal-powered and then mechanical grinder, which made a much finer powder. Masons would complain as soon as the 1850s' saying that plaster came to the building site too fine and not suitable for construction[16].

Storage and transportation

Plaster produced on the quarry ended up as a rough white powder. Calcined gypsum spontaneously hydrates itself using the moisture in the air. Once calcined and ground it should be used within few days or it is called *éventé* (stale) and unsuitable for building. It can be stored in sealed barrels and moved with carriages but this way of transportation must not have been protective enough as gypsum plaster was not exported very far. Un-burnt stones were also exported to be heated where needed, but workers there lacked the skills to burn them well to make a good plaster and this solution did not lead to exportation either.

What is Plaster of Paris?

According to the different steps we have just followed, we have a clear definition of what Plaster of Paris powder comprises:.

- Gypsum : in at least four different forms according to the temperature the stones were at and their proximity to the flames :
  - Underburnt gypsum (< 130°C)
  - Hemihydrate **α** and **β** (130-150°)
  - Overburnt
    - Anhydrite III (200°C)
    - Anhydrite II (220-350°C)
- Calcium carbonate: resulting from of having sedimentary rocks (limestones) extracted at the same time as gypsum. Quarries had different amount of calcium carbonate in the gypsum strata, from 3 to 13% (Table.1).
- Coal and ashes: resulting from the burning of wood. Workers testified that replacing wood by coal or bituminous coal did not provide a plaster suitable for construction.
- Quartz and silica: resulting from dusty quarries, and beating on the ground... A wealthy owner[17] of quarries as soon as the eighteenth century complained that the dirtiness of his quarries and his workers would spoil the gypsum plaster.
- Lime perhaps, if the temperature in the furnace reached 800°C.

Different studies were done as early as the nineteenth century (Table.1) and more recently to clearly say what gypsum plaster comprises. The studies agree on saying that there is between 4 and 20% of calcium carbonate, a bit of quartz (not always), a bit of silica, some oxides, pieces of coals (Fig.5) and the rest is gypsum.

Table 1: Gypsum plaster exhibited at the 1878 Exposition universelle in Paris. In. Gustave Oslet, Cours de construction, Matériaux de construction et leur emploi, Paris, 1885, Archives du Musée du Plâtre

Name of the gypsum plaster	Calcium sulphate %	Calcium carbonate %	Magnesium carbonate %	Aluminium oxide and ferrous peroxide	Insoluble %	Water... %	Observations
Vitry	70.9	10.2	5.03	2.5	4.9	4.45	normal
Vitry	72.6	12	5.45	2.7	3.7	3.53	fine
Romainville	87.7	2.4	2.7	0.8	0.6	5.8	normal
Villejuif	77.95	8.5	1.9	0.6	4.8	6.25	normal
Bondy	79.05	9.9	2.3	1.5	4.4	5.83	normal
Bondy	83.4	6.9	2.3	1	2.4	4	fine
B-Le Comte	83.75	4.3	0	0.35	1.2	8.4	normal
Lamarche	88.45	3.75	0	0	1.6	6.2	normal
Bussières	84	7.15	0.4	0.45	1.05	6.95	normal
Moyenne	**80.87**	**7.23**	**2.23**	**1.1**	**2.74**	**5.71**	

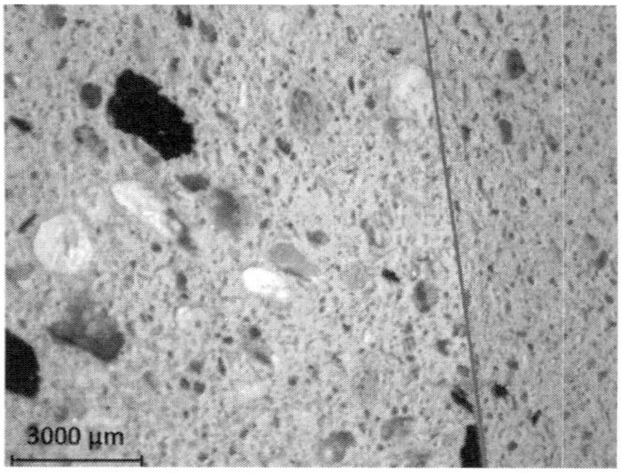

Figure 5: Two layers of rendering, charcoals and unburnt gypsum can be seen on left. Théâtre de la Renaissance, Paris. Binocular macroscope. (photography Jean Ducasse-Lapeyrusse, LRMH, 2015)

We also can conclude that plaster of Paris was a very rough powder, barely a powder at all judging by comments from nineteenth century masons who had to beat the plaster into pieces again on the construction site[18].

It is important to mention here that lime-based mortars were also used at the time in construction, but gypsum mortars were used even more in vernacular architecture. The prices for lime-based or gypsum-based plaster were roughly the same according to treatises from eighteenth century, but as gypsum mortar would have a quicker setting time, workers would choose it. Concerning renders, there are only gypsum-based renders in the region of Paris; there never were lime-based renders.

Traditional application of gypsum external renders

Masons and plasterers feature in the book by Etienne Boileau[19] describing all the statuses of professions in Paris from 1254 to 1271. Plasterers were the workers extracting and heating gypsum while the gypsum plaster was used by masons. A hierarchy of apprentice, companion and master masons used it to build an entire building from scratch.

Material preparation

Vocabulary of gypsum plasters : grinding and screening on site

The masons used gypsum plaster straight out of the barrel or jute bag. They screened it using two different sieves: a basket producing *plâtre au panier* (basket plaster) and a horsehair sieve called *sas* and producing *plâtre au sas* (horsehair sieve plaster). The basket had larger holes than the horsehair sieve and produced a rougher gypsum plaster.

Workers could also make a thinner plaster throwing gypsum plaster in the air with a spade: the layer of plaster stuck to the spade is called *fleur de plâtre* (flower of plaster). Another type of plaster was made putting plaster from the barrel through the basket then through the *sas*: instead of getting the thin plaster out of the last sieve, the worker will take the plaster on top of the horsehair sieve, which is called *crépis*.

Gypsum external renders of Paris: history and fabrication

Masons created the type of gypsum plaster they needed by beating the gypsum and screening it. These operations led to gypsum plasters with extremely different granularity.

Mixing plaster.

The mason gently sprinkled the gypsum powder on water until they merged and then mixed it with his trowel to obtain a paste. The amounts of water and plaster also depended on which type of paste the mason needed. Usually, a normal paste for a gypsum rendering would contain half plaster and half water. Masons put less water to have a more resilient plaster with less porosity and a quick setting: useful for joints. They put more water into the paste for pouring gypsum plaster into cracks and for some layers of renders.

Application of gypsum external renderings following treatises from the seventeenth, eighteenth and nineteenth centuries

Treatises[20] from 1691 until 1885 have been used to develop this model of traditional application of gypsum renders. This is how it was done before industrialization changed the material too much and before the knowledge of this manner of production and use disappeared. The application followed these steps:

- The wall, either made of rubble stones, bricks or timber-framed structure with stone, brick, or gypsum fillings should be brushed and soaked with water the day before the render is applied. Timber lintels and structures should be riddled with nails or grooved for a better bonding.
- Renders should never be applied in temperatures below 5°C or over 35°C, or when it rains.
- Ornamental features (mouldings) were always made before the renders were applied.
- The gypsum rendering was composed of four layers depending on the state of the wall (Fig.6):
    - *Renformi:* if in a bad state, the wall was put back in shape to insure its flatness. A compact gypsum paste was made to fill the holes and make the joints. Bumps were planed off.
    - *Gobetage*: A quite fluid gypsum paste is cast upon the wall with a wide brush, quickly the mason unified the layer with his hand. The layer is left to set.
    - *Crépi*: A quite compact paste is made with the *crépis*, the leftovers of gypsum on the top of the horsehair sieve. This gypsum plaster was cast on the wall with a brush, a trowel or the hand. The layer was then unified quickly with the back of the trowel. A *Berthelée* trowel was then used to groove the layer with its toothed side.
    - *Enduit*: A more fluid paste is made for the final layer with the plaster from the horsehair sieve. It was cast and spread with a trowel. Then, when the plaster set, the layer was cut with the sharp side of the *Berthelée* trowel in order for the whole wall to breathe.

Altogether, the layers can reach a thickness between 5 and 12 cm.

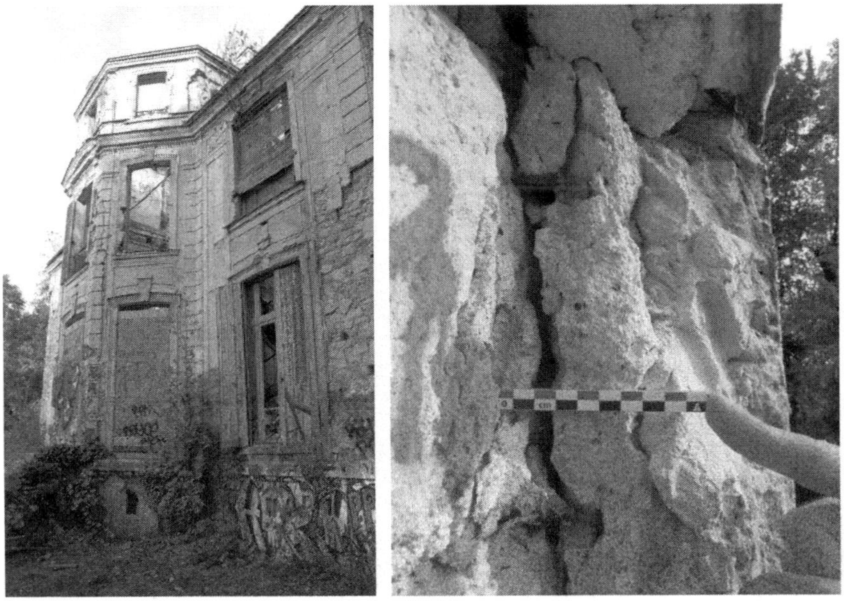

Figure 6: Goussainville, nineteenth century house. Left: general view. Right: detail on the layers of the rendering. (Tiffanie Le Dantec, 2015)

Each layer then had a different porosity and a different granularity. Research has still to be done to fully understand the way the layers work together to let the wall breathe: how is the moisture transfer insured from the wall to the outside but not the other way round.

Toward a gypsum architecture?

Gypsum plaster has many qualities. It is breathable; it helps moisture exchanges; it is fire-proof; and it is plastic. Its plasticity, in particular, allows it to accommodate seasonal movement of timber or stone structures. It has a good 'bounding', i.e. during setting, gypsum plaster expands and will fill all the voids and holes in the support. And it has good thermal insulation and soundproofing qualities, thanks to its porosity. But these qualities are nowadays overshadowed by a disadvantage: its solubility in water.

Features for avoiding water flow

Scientists working on the research programme will tell us in the coming years how the materiality or the application of those ancient gypsum plasters fought solubility. The design of the facade is also very important for avoiding rainwater flow over the facade. Moisture is not so much of a problem as long as it can dry. The real danger is a constant water flow slowly dissolving gypsum. Centuries of use of gypsum plaster architecture in the area of Paris have allowed masons and architects to solve the problem and led to facades being able to survive decades without damage.

In order to prevent the dissolving of the facade, some architectural features were necessary to resist water ingress:

- Rainwater flow: mouldings on the facade insured that flowing water did not wash the facade away, but encouraged formation of drops that would fall to the ground. Cornices on top, string-courses at every floor, and external window frames are part of these features.

- Water splash: when they meet a plane surface, raindrops throw other smaller raindrops around, causing dissolving of the render. This was prevented with a metal (lead or zinc) sheet over the string-courses and a different material for the base.

- Capillary rise: water from the ground rises through the foundations of the building and exits the wall, going through the mortar, joints and renderings to get out. This water is often in liquid form and cause damages to gypsum plaster.

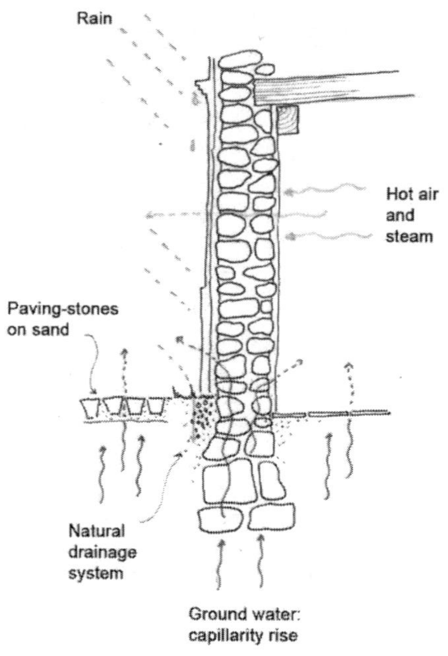

Figure 7: Cycle of water through seasons inside a stone wall with gypsum renderings (Tiffanie Le Dantec, 2015)

Conclusion

The long lost strength of gypsum external renders was certainly due to the heterogeneity of its composition, the highly skilled *savoir-faire* of the masons who knew, after five centuries practising gypsum plaster, how to make it last longer. The design of the facade, skilfully avoiding water flow on the surface of the renders also adds to what one can consider gypsum architecture.

The aim of this paper was to expose the first elements of research on the gypsum external renders of Paris. Its aim was also to ask questions, to be able to carry on research in this direction through the thesis and through the research programme led by the LRMH.

Among many questions, the main one is: how can people trust gypsum plaster again? After 100 years of despising plasterers and having a low quality material, how can young apprentices be made willing to practise this job once again and carry on the legacy of the skilled masons of Paris?

Acknowledgements

LRMH team: Jean Ducasse-Lapeyrusse PhD, LRMH civil engineer; Véronique Vergès-Belmin, LRMH research engineer and *Pôle Pierre* responsible; Stéphanie Celle, heritage architect, LRMH deputy director.

LéaV team: Nadia Hoyet, architect, PhD supervisor

Fondation des Sciences du Patrimoine : Emmanuel Poirault, director

Evan Chakroff, architect and author.

Notes and references

[1] Association des Géologues du Bassin parisien, «Les anciennes carrières de Paris et leur consolidation» in. *Les Roches au service de l'Homme. Géologie et préhistoire du Bassin parisien*, Bulletin d'information des Géologues du Bassin parisien, Mémoire hors-série n°7, publié avec le concours de Gaz de France, 1989, Condé-sur-Noireau
[2] Thiébaut, P., *La maison rurale en Ile-de-France*, Eyrolles, 2001
[3] Robin, S., Philippe Marquis, 'Aux origines du plâtre de Paris'», *Le Plâtre, l'Art et la Matière.* Créaphis, 2002, p.89
[4] Taté, T., *Historique du Plâtre*, **Congrès Technique International de la Maçonnerie et du Béton Armé**, 1928
[5] Robin, S., Philippe Marquis, *op cit*, p.89
[6] Barthélémy L'Anglais, *De proprietatitus rorum,* n.d.
[7] Ferroussat de Castelbon, E.H., *Réflexions sur la mauvaise qualité du plâtre et sur sa cause*, Paris, 1776
[8] Lavoisier, M., *Mémoires de Mathématiques et de Physique, présentés à l'Académie Royale des Sciences, par divers savants et lus dans les assemblées.* **Tome cinquième.** 1768 p.341
[9] Canet, M.M., 'Quatre générations de plâtriers dans le nord-ouest parisien, ruptures et continuités à la plâtrière Vieujot', *Le Plâtre, l'Art et la Matière*, Créaphis, 2002, p.47-57
[10] Gilardi,P., *Le plâtre, ses caractéristiques essentielles pour la construction*, 1933, Archives du Musée du Plâtre
[11] Encyclopédie des Métiers, *La plâtrerie, le Staff et le Stuc*, Vol.2, Les Compagnons du Devoir, 1994
[12] Guini-Skliar, A., *La pierre à bâtir dans l'architecture parisienne*, Tours, 1998
[13] Le Roux, T., 'Des fours à plâtre dans Paris, Histoire d'une parenthèse conflictuelle, 1765-1800', *Les Articles du Musée du Plâtre*, 2010
[14] Diderot et d'Alembert, *Recueil de Planches sur les Sciences, les Arts libéraux et les Arts mécaniques*, Paris, 1751-1772, Fig. 1
[15] Lafarge, I., *Le plâtre dans la construction en Île-de-France: techniques, morphologie et économie avant l'industrialisation*, Ph.D. Thesi, Université Paris I Panthéon-Sorbonne, 2013, p613.
[16] Claudel et Laroque, *Pratique de l'Art de Construire en Maçonnerie*, Paris, Carilian-Goeury et V. Dalmont,

1850

[17] Ferroussat de Castelbon, E.H., *Réflexions sur la mauvaise qualité du plâtre et sur sa cause*, Paris, Lottin Ainé, 1776

[18] Nadaud, M., *Mémoires de Léonard, ancien garçon maçon*, Paris, 1895

[19] de Lespinasse, R., et Bonnardot, F., 1879 - *Les Métiers et corporations de la ville de Paris - XIIIe siècle, le livre des métiers d'Etienne Boileau* ; Histoire générale de Paris, Imprimerie Nationale

[20] Treatises used to establish the traditional application of gypsum external renderings:

de'Aviler, A.G., *Cours d'Architecture*, (Paris: N. Langlois) 1691

Bullet, P., *Architecture Pratique*, (Paris: J.B Delespine, J-T Herissant) 1741

Diderot, D., et D'Alembert, J le R., *Encyclopédie ou Dictionnaire raisonné des Sciences, des Arts et des Métiers, par une société de Gens de lettres*, Original edition online: http://portail.atilf.fr/encyclopedie/, 1765

Patte, P., *Mémoires sur les objets les plus importans de l'architecture*, (Paris: Rozet), 1769

Lucotte,J, R., *L'Art de la maçonnerie*, (PariT: Imprimerie de Moutard), 1783

Rondelet, J,P., *Traité théorique et pratique de l'art de bâtir*, (Paris: Private), 1827

Biston, V., *Manuel théorique et pratique du Chaufournier.*, (Paris: Manuel Roret), 1836

Claudel, J., et Laroque, L., *Pratique de l'Art de Construire en Maçonnerie*, (Paris: Carilian-Goeury et V. Dalmont), 1850

Toussaint, M., et Magnier, M.D., *Nouveau Manuel Complet du Maçon, du couvreur, du paveur.* (Paris: Manuel Roret), 1864

Chabat, P., *Dictionnaire des termes employés dans la construction*, (Paris: Morel), 1876

Oslet, G., *Cours de Construction, Matériaux de Construction et leur emploi*, (Paris), 1885

Earthquake-resistant systems in traditional masonry construction: two examples from Mediterranean vernacular architecture

S. Tonna and C. Chesi
Polytechnic of Milan, A.B.C. Dept., Milan, Italy

Introduction

In the pre-modern age, before scientific computational procedures had been formulated, effective earthquake-proof structural solutions were developed following rules based purely on "common sense" and experience. This kind of knowledge, handed down from generation to generation, led to a definition of structural solutions that could cope with a variety of critical situations. Within this process, both the original morphology and the evolution over time of the most effective construction techniques were directly related to the level of criticality of local situations; in areas affected by severe and frequent natural disasters, therefore, it is only natural that special systems develop. In order for this to happen, however, it is necessary that memories of the natural event and knowledge of the damage are not lost. Risk awareness prompts local societies not to forget nor abandon traditional construction techniques, but rather to maintain and improve them. It follows that constantly recurring earthquakes fuel experience and play some kind of educational role by suggesting more effective construction solutions and restricting any misconceptions; at the same time, builders' insight is stimulated to understand the laws governing a building's response to ground motion.

The research presented here addresses some structural solutions developed within the context of vernacular architecture, which have proved effective in withstanding seismic actions. The issue is discussed with reference to a couple of examples that represent this ambivalence, Castelvecchio Calvisio (on the southern slope of the Gran Sasso Mountain, Italy) and Lefkada (one of the seven Ionian Islands, Greece). Both are characterized by high-level seismic hazard, yet associated with different return periods: 200 and 30 years, respectively. This situation led, in the former case, to alternately forgetting and rediscovering tradition and, in the latter, to the development of a structural system able to simultaneously withstand two kinds of criticality, namely, geotechnical and seismic.

As mentioned, the study focuses on the specific situation of vernacular architecture in critical areas, with the result that it is possible to highlight the profound connection with both the place where it was generated and with the no-alternative situation of learning to coexist with a native condition. The importance of studying these kinds of situation is clear, since it reflects local cultural heritage, a knowledge form which, normally, is not written but simply passed down orally; a tangible expression of a tradition refined over time in parallel with the peculiar calamities affecting a site.

Selection criteria and investigation methods

The two study cases are comparable in terms of local critical conditions: seismic hazard–which has importance for both with a geotechnical aggravating factor in the second case,[1] economy (shepherding in the Italian case, maritime activities in the other), and soil (rocky in Abruzzo and soft on the Greek island). After repeated on-site inspections and a study of previous works, it became possible to assume that both of these situations have contributed to developing distinctive building solutions which, despite the two situations being characterized by similar features, appear completely different. The Italian building tradition is based on a box-like behavior, with squat, low and compact buildings, whereas the Greek one consists in a lighter solution, with the presence of a sophisticated secondary structural system.

One of the most important issues influencing these traditional building types is earthquake frequency. With reference to an interesting concept expressed by P. Touliatos,[2] it can be stated that the quality level of the construction techniques is in proportion to the level of criticality typical of the area: where severe and frequent natural disasters take place, specific solutions need to be developed for the population to survive and continue to live in the same place. Such solutions require full continuity in memory of the seismic events, which implies that the return period of earthquakes corresponds, roughly, to the length of a generation. Fear of such events prompts local societies not to forget nor abandon traditional construction techniques, but rather to analyze, maintain and improve on them. Conversely, in those situations where earthquakes are a rare phenomenon and the period between two events far exceeds a generation's lifetime, both the population and craftsmen will lose any seismic awareness; consequently, structures, construction details and all the specific solutions will gradually lose importance, giving way to aesthetic issues and fashion trends. This process leads to a progressive reduction in the quality of construction details and to a forgetting of all the seismic protection solutions which had characterized earlier construction types, or even to a misrepresentation of them, with no understanding of their real meaning.

Several factors, not only loss of knowledge, contribute to such social phenomena, which can find evidence in analyses of the relationship between earthquake magnitude and damage level. In relation to the case studies discussed in the paper, for which relevant data are available for both such parameters, two meaningful plots have been obtained,[3] representative of a historical period that ends with the beginning of the Modern Age. (Fig. 1)

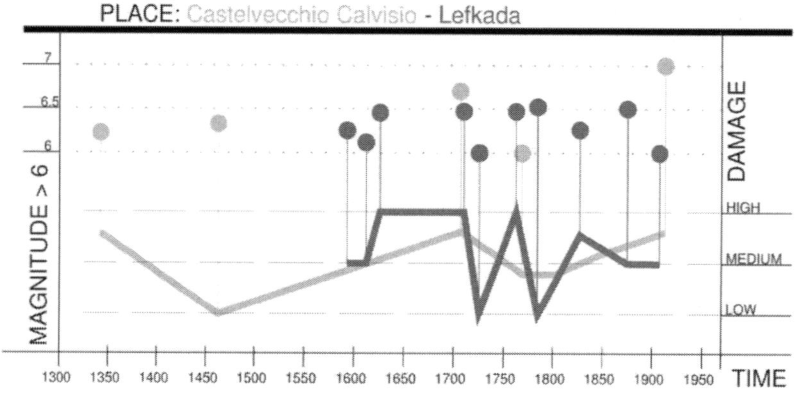

Figure 1. Simplified graphic representation of the relationship between earthquakes and damage at Castelveccio Calvisio and Lefkada from the 14th to the 20th century. (Source: S. Tonna, 2016)

Through the diagram, it is possible to highlight one first important aspect common to both cases: the damage level normally shows a positive trend just after a seismic event; subsequently, it keeps increasing over time. In this way, on the occurrence of the next earthquake, the construction system will not be appropriate to withstand it or, at the very least, will be somewhat weakened. Indeed, this behavior can be clearly recognized in the Italian example (Castelvecchio Calvisio), due to the time lapse between two subsequent seismic events, expecially between the second and the third (respectively in 1461 and in 1703) and between the fourth and the fifth (1762 and 1915). In both cases, the time interval roughly corresponded to 200 years, while, when the period was shorter, i.e., 1349-1461, it is possible to note a significant reduction, incongruous with respect to the greater severity of the earthquake.

In relation to the shape of the curve corresponding to the Greek case (Lefkada), different behavior is immediately apparent. The number of earthquakes was three times higher than in the previous case and, even if the magnitude values were roughly the same, the trend is markedly irregular, especially from the beginning of the eighteenth century to the first decades of the nineteenth.

Nowadays, the city of Lefkada is located in a lagoon, thanks to works carried out by the Venetians shortly after their settlement on the island (1684-1797). The new city was built following major reclamation work and the inhabitants were forced to move there from the old city location. The land on which they had to build their new houses was no longer rocky but soft soil. In 1704, an earthquake struck the island and caused severe damage: the nature of the ground had changed so the inhabitants had to rethink their building techniques. The following frequent earthquakes were a test for the new construction solutions and during the subsequent reconstruction work, people were able to improve the building's capacity of resistance. On January 19, 1825, during the British administration, a severe earthquake occurred and, due to a careful analysis of the buildings most affected and of the construction materials, well defined rules were imposed for new construction and repair works. With the subsequent earthquakes (in 1869 and 1914), the damage curve shows a homogeneous trend that can be estimated as average.

In conclusion, although earthquakes are unpredictable and many different aspects can affect a target area, knowledge of the damage mechanisms and the adoption of all necessary precautions, within a relatively stable political and economic context, make it possible to minimize their consequences on buildings. On Lefkada, the frequent recurrence of earthquakes has thus allowed the development of resilient buildings.

Features of the two case studies

At this point, an extensive description of the seismic protection elements will be given; this aims to provide the basis for a subsequent evaluation of their real effectiveness through the use of modern structural analysis tools. From a quantitative point of view, a simplified evaluation of seismic resistance level is developed. This was done by starting from a visual classification of masonry quality with reference to standard parameters and criteria.

The theme was initially examined with reference to the case of Apennine villages in the province of Aquila, Italy, which were affected by the 2009 earthquake. In order to go deeper into the debate on the effectiveness of building traditions developed on empirical bases, the analysis was extended to a second case, with different peculiarities yet analogous to the first example. Still belonging to the Mediterranean environment and in another critical area subject to frequently recurring major earthquakes and characterized by a specific traditional building system, is the Ionian island of Lefkada, where, as previously mentioned, critical environmental conditions also include soil-related problems, due to the former presence of marshland, subject over time to reclamation works.

Analysis of the building framework and seismic protection elements typical of these villages is based on the results of detailed survey work carried out in the field, supplemented by a study of local economic and historical conditions, an examination of historical earthquakes, and subsequent reconstruction and repairs.

Castelvecchio Calvisio, Aquila, Italy

Looking first at the urban scale, Castelvecchio Calvisio[4] was founded as a fortified village between the 12th and 13th centuries; it stands on a hill, is solidly rooted to the ground, and its urban profile is fully integrated into the natural environment: the ancient portion of the town was developed following the natural contour lines, commonly the buildings are no more than three storeys high and are anchored to the rocky soil as firmly as they are to one another.

The dominant building type is terraced housing arranged parallel to the contour lines; the old town is formed by jointed building units resulting in compact structural aggregates, further connected by covered walkways (*sporti*) and flying buttresses. (Fig. 2)

As to appearance, the chromatic aspect of the façades is the same as the limestone formation they rise from. (Figs 2-4)

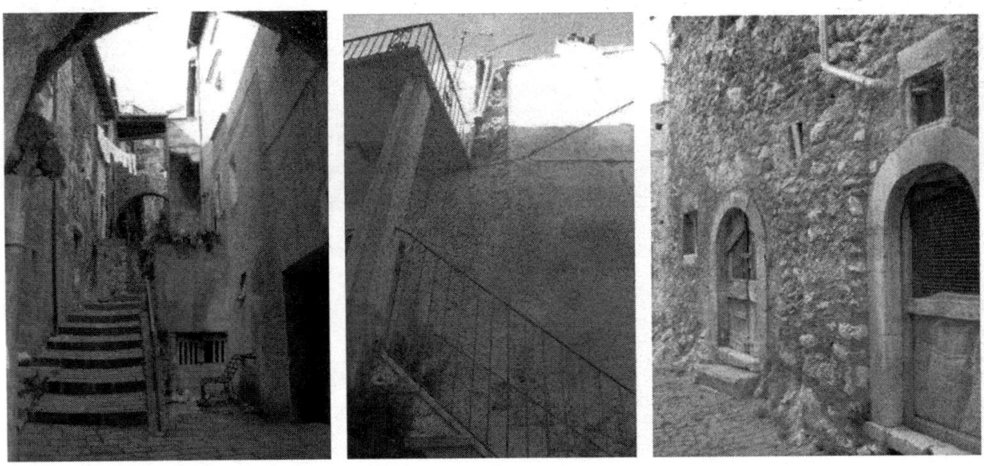

Figures 2. – 4. View from the street of the old town: compact structural aggregates, further connected by covered walkways and flying buttresses (left); Incorrect use of a "rue" (center); Foundations on rock (right) (Photos: S. Tonna, 2014).

Analysis of the construction details characterizing the village suggests that the builders were clearly aware of the need to conceive structures capable of withstanding seismic actions. Indeed, specific devices can be clearly recognized, suitable to contrast the tendency of the buildings to split apart under the effect of seismic forces. This is achieved mainly by providing each building with constraint actions transferred by outcropping rocks or adjacent units through the use of compressed elements, such as masonry arches, connecting walls, and buttresses. (Figs 2-4)

In the aggregates, the box behavior typical of single building units is accentuated, resulting in improved overall structural response. The same interpretation can be applied to the flying buttresses and covered walkways, since they aim to offer "*vaulted systems on an urban scale, with the thrusts reciprocally canceled within a sequence of opposing vaults and arches, both internal and external to the buildings*."[5]

The urban setting of the old town turns out to be itself a macroscopic seismic solution. The whole village behaves like a single building that can satisfactorily respond to an earthquake due to global box-like behavior and thanks to local reinforcing details: each structural unit often ends with a sloping wall or is clamped by sturdy buttresses whose purpose is to oppose horizontal thrust.

The urban layout is marked by interspaces, 50 - 60cm wide, between adjacent aggregates. It is assumed that this was done for hygiene purposes, i.e., water collection and disposal, or also to have seismic joints to protect buildings from hammering. These openings, called "*rue*", in most cases can no longer be recognized nowadays, as they have frequently been closed to extend internal rooms or have been used as waste deposits. (Fig. 3)

By analyzing wall cross-sections and sorting data in relation to the low level of damage recorded after the 2009 earthquake, the masonry quality can be evaluated in different ways. On the one hand, walls are not always assembled according to best practice; on the other, the masonry is unquestionably cohesive, with thicknesses varying from 50 to 60cm, consisting of one or two well-connected layers, with optimized values for the size of the segments. (Fig. 5) In several cases the presence of diatones, semi-diatones and wedge heels has also been highlighted (Fig.5); all of these elements help to increase the cohesion of the layers and to fill any gaps due to a lack of regularity. Such details, in addition to ensuring good cooperation between the wall layers, are a necessary condition for the inclusion of timber ties. Such elements play the role of tie rods and wall connectors, and are therefore of fundamental importance in relation to the box structure behavior. Timber ties are wooden elements inserted inside walls, following the wall perimeter, in order to produce a hoop effect for the building; instead, wooden or metal tendons (Fig.6) are linear structural elements that connect opposite walls, linking them to avoid relative displacements. Their presence can be recognized from outside the building, as they have external metal restraints of various shapes, according to the specific technology and artistic taste of the time.

On the first storey, the floors are mainly supported by barrel vaults made of light stone (a porous variety of limestone), while on the second, brick sheet vaults have been used, topped by lightweight infilling material. This system dates back to the 18th century; normally, simple wooden floors were in use, with the sole exception of some stone vaults. A few examples are still visible in some of the structural units.

The roof structure consists of "staked trusses", which support the joists and the roof cover (clay tiles). The truss elements are usually well connected to each other. Truss structures are particularly indicated in seismic zones because they do not produce horizontal thrusts onto the support walls. In this specific type of truss, a characteristic detail is present, clearly derived from the empirical knowledge of the damage mechanism: the specific term "stacked" comes from the fact that the entire system was anchored to the outer supporting walls, with the tie beam running through the wall and extending to the outside, where it was anchored by a wooden stake, "*which, in addition to preventing the tie beam from being pulled out, tends to make the wall vibrations synchronous*."[6]

Apart from the floors and the roof, most of the seismic protection elements and solutions adopted are based on a clever use of limestone blocks. Exceptions are the wooden elements inserted into the walls' external face to oppose the spread of earthquake-induced cracking, and by naturally curved wooden elements arranged in the stairwells to counter the splitting of interior walls.

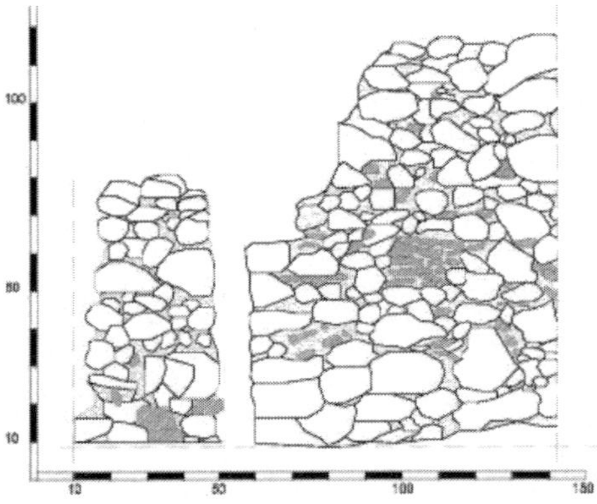

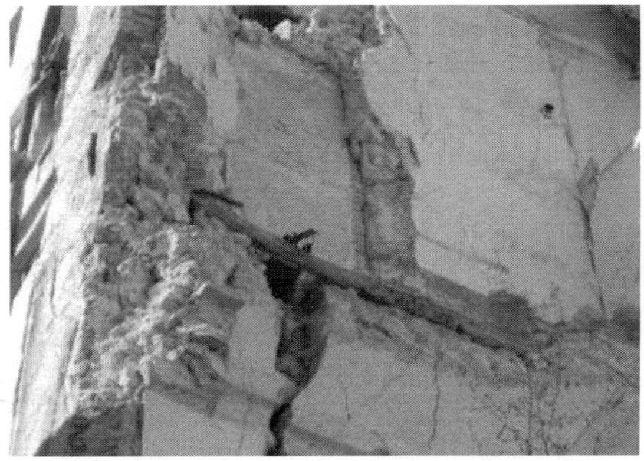

Figures 5. and 6. Section and external facing (left) (Source: S. Tonna, 2013); Wooden chain (right) (Photo: S. Tonna, 2013)

On the basis of the above classification, this masonry type can be compared to one of the standard types defined in the Italian building code, for which the reference value for the shear resistance is in the field 3.5 – 5.1N/cm^2. In the presence of diatones, semi-diatones and wedges, it is believed that the maximum value in the range (5N/cm^2) can be achieved. (Fig.5) Previous studies[7] have shown that, in the case of structures exhibiting a good box behavior, this resistance level is compatible with the actions generated by the kind of earthquakes that normally strike Mediterranean regions. Specifically, the analysis relating to traditional buildings in the Italian region between the cities of Aquila and Isernia, shows that the maximum value for ground acceleration (a_{SLV}) can be approximated as:

$$a_{SLV} = \frac{1}{2} \cdot \frac{\tau_d}{\gamma \cdot H}$$

on the basis of masonry shear resistance τ_d, density γ and total height H.

With reference to the problem under discussion, considering a typical three-storey building (ground floor and two upper storeys), the following values might be adopted:

$\tau_d = 5$ N/cm^2, $\gamma = 20$ kN/m^3, $H = 9$ m

thus obtaining a reference value of *0.29* (*g* units) for the maximum ground acceleration, which is in line with the expected values for the region (in the range 0.2-0.35*g*) as indicated in the 2013 European Seismic Hazard Model (ESHM13).

This explains why several buildings, despite being neglected and abandoned, have survived so far and still preserve their original appearance.

Lefkada city, Lefkada Island, Greece

As for Lefkada Island, one peculiar aspect is its capital city. The center of Lefkada city has preserved its original structure, which dates back to the 18th century and was specifically planned to allow for the drainage and natural flow of rainwater to the sea and to take advantage of a frequent wind condition that helps reduce humidity, with the air currents blowing from N-NW. With reference to studies developed at the National Technical University of Athens,[8] it is possible to briefly summarize the main characteristics of a typical traditional building.

This normally has from one to three storeys; at ground level a stone masonry structure is present, while the upper levels consist of a frame structure based on the mixed use of timber and clay bricks. All the floor slabs are timber structures and the roof is covered by tiles. Openings are arranged symmetrically in plan and, in order to protect timber structures on the upper levels from humidity, the outer façade is covered with wooden boards. (Figs 7 - 9)

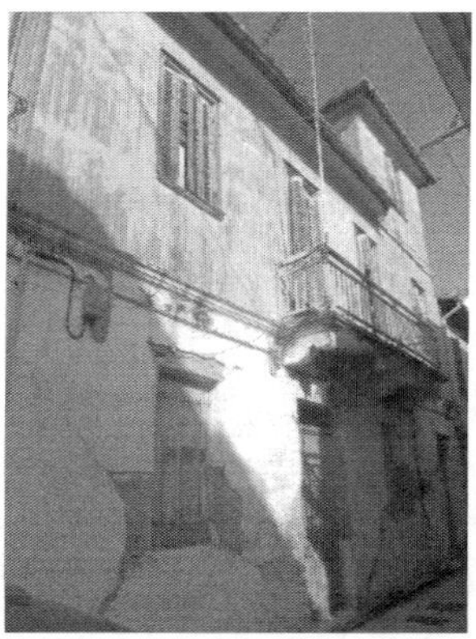
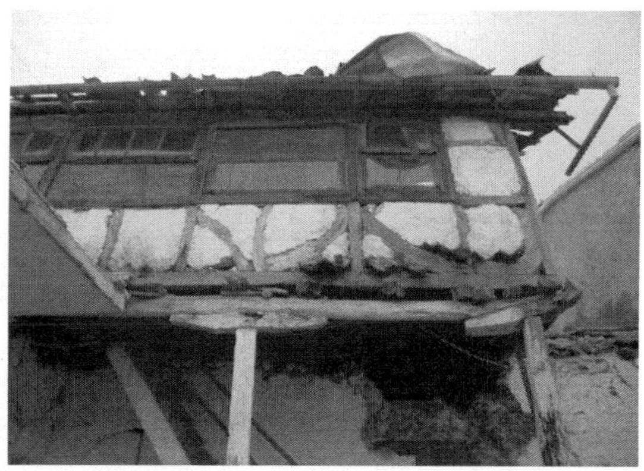

Figures 7. and 8. Lefkada traditional system: a three-storey house (left); an example with enclosed porch (right) (Photos: S. Tonna, 2016)

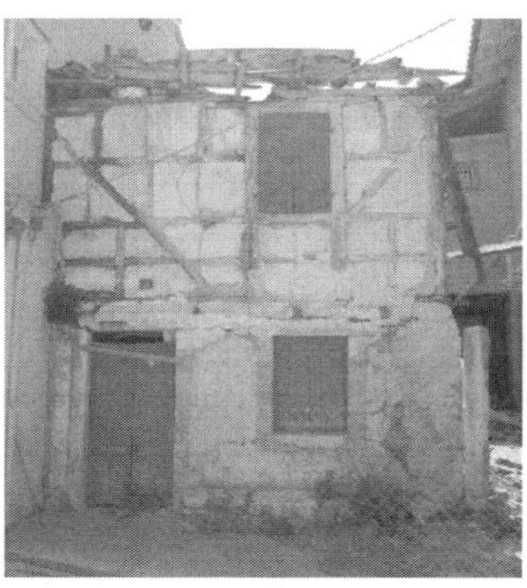
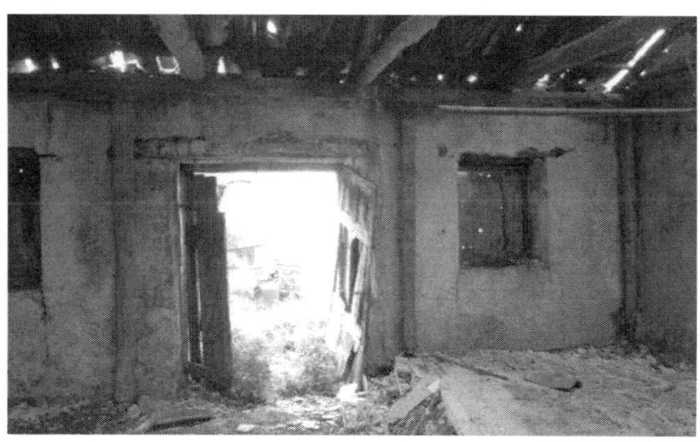

Figures 9. and 10. Lefkada traditional system: a two-storey house (left); internal view with detail of the timber columns in parallel to the ground floor (right) (Photos: S. Tonna, 2015)

The ground floor has a maximum height of 3m, and consists of stone masonry walls with a thickness in the range of 60 – 100cm, with the external leaf composed of roughly shaped elements, whereas those used in the corners are well-shaped; stones on the internal leaf are plastered. The space between the external leaves is filled with mortar and small pieces of stone and bricks.

In parallel to the masonry structure, a secondary structure is built, consisting of timber columns with a center to center distance of 2 – 3m. The slab timber beams provide connection of these columns to the masonry walls. Due to the low horizontal stiffness, this secondary system does not contribute to the seismic resistance; however, due to the strong connection to the slab, it does play a fundamental role in the case of a partial or total collapse of the masonry walls by providing support to vertical loads. It is therefore a passive protection system, which is activated in case of damage to the masonry, the primary resistance system; in addition, it allows masonry repair without interfering with the rest of the building. (Fig.10)

Timber floors play a double role, resisting both vertical loads arriving from upper levels, and those directly acting on them; such loads are transferred not only to the perimeter walls, but to the secondary timber structure as well. All the connections in the timber structure are extremely precise, with attention to detail.

Considering that economic resources have always been very limited in Lefkada, it can be assumed that the secondary system was also conceived with the purpose of increasing the structures' seismic performance in the sense of allowing easier and cheaper repairs to the damaged building.

For maximum effectiveness, this system requires the columns to rest on a stable supporting surface, not allowing for differential settlement; another requirement is that masonry on the ground level needs to be compact and well connected to the foundation walls.

The high level of soil deformability is a permanent condition for the urban area, and it may also affect the behavior of the sophisticated structural system conceived to resist earthquakes. Indeed, in the absence of a rigid base the passive secondary system might well lose effectiveness due to relative settlement and a consequent modification of stress distribution.

From analysis of the literature, it appears that the Lefkada foundation system has only been studied to a limited extent. However, thanks to a recent study,[9] it is now possible to formulate considerations on it, with the assumption that a couple of different solutions were systematically adopted depending on the availability of time and economic resources.

In order to explain the reasons and features of this foundation system, a clear understanding of the local soil condition is required. The foundation excavation depth was about 80 – 100cm, in order to reach the original lagoon bottom. In the past, neither efficient excavators nor drainage pumps were available; because of this, builders had to lay the foundation's lower surface relatively high in the ground, at a maximum depth of 150cm.

They were therefore forced to develop techniques that enabled the mortar to set in the presence of water or air, according to the situation; from this need, two different solutions were generated. Where the use of pozzolan cement or volcanic materials was permitted, a hydraulic mortar was used for the foundation walls, which could then be directly in contact with the ground. Where, instead, the use of such materials could not be afforded, a timber grid was used, providing a flat surface for the erection of walls; any contact with water was thus avoided. The grid extended homogeneously under the entire house perimeter; in the case of a higher water table level, additional timber layers were inserted, normally fixed to underlying ones.

From analysis of data recorded[10] during a recent earthquake that occurred in 2003, satisfactory results have been observed with both construction techniques. In the first case, indeed, the foundation system is a hard monolithic structure, almost a "concrete box" directly connected to the ground floor; in the second case, a hard wall is present, resting on a grid filled with sand, rocks and hydraulic mortar, which plays the role of a stiff surface for effective support of the upper structure.

From the above description, it can be clearly seen that the traditional Lefkada house provides an unconventional system with the building divided into two parts: a lower masonry structure and an upper timber part, directly connected to the foundation through the secondary timber system. This can be considered, in every way, a genuinely resilient solution; its relative potential is discussed below.

As already done for the first case study, the maximum value for the ground acceleration (a_{SLV}) can be approximated through some simplified numerical evaluations.

To this end, a typical house was selected, two storeys high, built according to tradition, with the ground floor in stone (wall thickness: 60cm) and the upper floors in timber-framed masonry (thickness of walls: 12cm); both the floors and roof are timber structures.

Therefore:

$$a_{SLV} = \frac{1}{2} \cdot \frac{\tau_d}{\gamma \cdot H} = \frac{1}{2} \cdot \frac{68.6}{10.4 \cdot 6.6} = 0.50g$$

The following values have been adopted for the parameters:

- shear resistance at the base of the masonry walls: $\tau_d =$ 68.6N/cm^2

- total building height: $H = 3.0+2.7+1.8/2 = 6.6$m

- average density for the walls over the entire building height: $\gamma = 10.4$kN/m^3.

The estimation of the average density comes from a weighted combination of the values relative to the ground floor masonry ($\gamma = 20$kN/m^3) and the upper floor timber walls ($\gamma = 12$kN/m^3 - 50 % clay bricks and 50% wood).

The value of 0.50 (g units) for the maximum ground acceleration is in line with the expected values for the region (in the range 0.4 - 0.5g), as indicated in the 2013 European Seismic Hazard Model (ESHM13).[11] In addition, it is worth noting that during the 2003 earthquake, the maximum acceleration recorded in the city of Lefkada was 0.43g.

The above calculations, although approximate, lead to a simple explanation for the system's seismic effectiveness: the high value of resistance is related to the strong mass reduction in the upper levels. This reduction has a twofold reason: from the first to the second storey, the thickness of the panels is reduced by 1/5 (from 60 to 12cm), while the material changes from masonry to timber (the density, correspondingly, varies from 20 to 12kN/m^3).

It should also be considered that the fundamental period[12] of these buildings does not exceed a value of 0.2s; the structure, therefore, as can be seen in the response spectra of the 2003 earthquake, is not affected by the high spectral amplification related to the deformability of the soil's surface layer.

The above simple yet significant quantitative evaluation confirms the intuition in the conceptual design of the Lefkada typical house, suggesting that large safety margins are offered, despite the high seismic hazard.

Conclusions

Analyses have shown that the traditional building techniques in the cases of both Castelvecchio Calvisio and Lefkada allow for resistance levels of the masonry structures that are basically on a par with the design requirements in force today. However, despite the common need to resist earthquakes, the "construction memory" has been handed down in different ways at the two sites: while the Greek tradition has perpetuated a well-established system to face the daily problems, in the Italian region around Aquila the seismic system has often been distorted to meet other needs; one in particular, adaptation to modernity with the consequent trend to abandon empirical, effective solutions. After the 2003 earthquake, the Lefkada historical center was ultimately preserved, despite major policies pushing for impactful interventions; in the Italian case, seven years after the major earthquake occurred in the area, general restoration plans have still not been implemented, especially in minor centers like Castelvecchio Calvisio. It seems important to underline that many construction details, which are effective, tested by time, and also economical, in most cases have not even been considered.

The analyzed case studies demonstrate the effectiveness of a multidisciplinary approach: the historical centers were analyzed within their own context considering all the major aspects that have influenced and characterized their structure. This is the basis for any conservation project and the starting point to enrich a data base of effective solutions which, with the necessary updates, could be applicable to new constructions.

Rather than being seen as a fragile system to be protected, the historical centers in seismic areas need to be considered as a knowledge source for defense against earthquake risk.

Acknowledgments

This work presents a synthesis of PhD thesis work by the first author, who wishes to express her gratitude to all those who have helped her become involved in their own research fields. Finally, special thanks also to A. Gillan for his contribution to the editing of this text.

Note and References

[1] S. Tonna, C. Chesi, E. Vintzileou, K. Katopodis, "Traditional building criteria in the Lefkada island: peculiarities of the foundation system" pp.1-10, in F. Peña & M. Chávez (Eds), Proceedings of the 9th International Conference on Structural Analysis of Historical Constructions SAHC2014, Mexico City, Mexico, 14–17 October 2014

[2] P. Touliatos, "Approach, identification and intervention in historic constructions. The technological point of view", Athens: NTUA, 2003. p.5

[3] S. Tonna, C. Chesi, "Implications of earthquake return periods on the building quality" pp. 784–793, in: C. Gambardella (Ed.), Proceedings of the XII International Forum "Le vie dei Mercanti", Best practice in Heritage conservation and management, Capri, Italy, 11-13 June 2015
[4] S. Tonna, C. Chesi, L. Marino, "The transumance architecture: handing down seismic knowledge while migrating" pp. 707-712, in Taylor & francis Group (Eds), Proceedings of International Conference on Vernacular Heritage, Sustainability and Earthen Architecture Versus 2014, Valencia , Spain, 11-13 September 2014
[5] M. D'Antonio, *Ita terraemotus damna impedire,* Gorgonzola (Mi): CARSA Edizioni, Global Print, 2013.p. 42
[6] Ibid., p.110
[7] S. Tonna, "Earthquake resistant systems: experience based construction techniques in vernacular architecture - Two study cases: the village of Castelvecchio Calvisio (L'Aquila, Italy) and the town of Lefkada (Lefkada Island, Greece)" (Ph.D. Thesis, Politecnico di Milano, 2014), pp.126-131
[8] E. Vintzileou et al, "Seismic behaviour of the historical structural system of the island of Lefkada, Greece", Elsevier Construction and Building Materials, **21**, 2007, pp. 225-236.
[9] S. Tonna, C. Chesi, E. Vintzileou, K. Katopodis, "Traditional building criteria in the Lefkada island: peculiarities of the foundation system" pp.1-10
[10] Learning from Earthquakes Preliminary Observations on the August 14, 2003, Lefkada Island (Western Greece) Earthquake, EERI Special Earthquake Report — November 2003
[11] J. Woessner et al, "The 2013 European Seismic Hazard Model: key components and results", Bulletin of Earthquake Engineering, Springer, 2015
[12] E. Vintzileou et al, (note 8), pp. 225-236

The Graeco-Roman World

Stone architecture: stone dressing in Petra, Jordan

Shaher Rababeh and Rama Al Rabady
Department of Architecture, Faculty of Engineering, Hashemite University, Jordan

Introduction

Petra is well known for its rock-cut architecture, a style of architecture that generated what could be termed 'flat' or 'shallow' architecture. Although the existing 800 rock-cut monuments[1] were influenced by other civilizations and incorporated elements and treatments from the Assyrian, Egyptian, Anatolian, and Classical architecture[2] it was the building engineering that distinguished Nabataean architecture. In his landmark book "*How Petra was Built: An Analysis of the Construction Techniques of the Nabataean Freestanding Buildings and Rock-Cut Monuments in Petra, Jordan*"[3], Rababeh informs us about the different building techniques that were used by the Nabataeans for constructing their cities, especially the capital of Petra. He suggests that the construction techniques used and developed by Nabataean builders were influenced by two important factors: their outside contacts, and the availability of certain building materials. As for the second factor, the most readily available building material was the sandstone. The Nabataeans carved in the Smooth, Honeycomb, Tear, and Disi sandstone layers[4]. These same layers were also quarried to provide blocks for freestanding buildings.

Using the sandstone had a prominent impact on the construction techniques used in Petra but also on the final appearance of its rock-cut facades. The stone dressing is generally characterised by the use of flat, textured, and linear finishing. Two theories have been developed to explain the flat dressed stone in Petra. The first is concerned with the carving technique and processes. It approaches stone carving as a progressive process that evolves through a typical sequence of carving, using different carving tools and techniques and to achieve specific goals of each phase. One of the strongest supporters of this theory is Rababeh[5] . According to him, Petra's stone carving underwent a process that was divided into a whole series of lesser processes; for each of which different tools were utilised to achieve specific dressing outcomes (Fig. 1). The hypothesis is valid for both self-standing buildings as well as the rock-cut monuments. For the former, while blocks of stone were being extracted from the quarry, they were roughly shaped. Later, block surfaces passed through a sequence of operations to give them accuracy and aesthetically desirable regularity[6]. Similar approach could be applied for carving monuments out of solid sandstone mountains to create various architectural structures because the stone has to go through several preparation phases to reach the desired stone dressing. In light of the absence of any written documents that describe the Nabataean dressing techniques, Rababeh reached this hypothesis through tracing existing evidences of the masons' tools and techniques that are still evident on the remaining facades. He analysed the facades through observing the traces left on the surfaces of the stone, making deductions from known parallels in antiquity, proposing hypotheses to describe the actual practice and then testing their accuracy. This involves examining the markings on the blocks, and noting the technical features which could be considered as evidence for the use of particular dressing tools.

Rababeh's theory supports the systematic and engineering qualities of Nabataean architecture. However, considering the various types of stones as well as the different carving tools that were used by the Nabataean, another theory advocates a connection between building materials and technical solutions. It suggests that the Nabataeans had a full comprehension of the stone types in their region and accordingly were able to employ the appropriate tools for each type; without going through a long carving process. For example, Paradise suggests that "*Nabataean dressing styles were more a function of rock type, substrate resistance, and hardness, more than any evolving iconography or progression of dressing technique.*" [7]. Thus, he provides a spectrum of all stone types that were used by the Nabataeans. He focuses on the mechanical and chemical properties of the carved stone and suggests that stone dressing was influenced by three correlated factors: integrity and hardness of the substrate (i.e., weathered and soft, indurated, ferruginous and hard); the substrate lithology (i.e., limestone, sandstone, basalt); and the carving tools (axes, hammers, chisels). Besides the pointed axe (pick) and the primary chisels (pointed and toothed chisels) that were usually used for soft sandstone, he highlighted the value of the bush hammer that was mainly used for dressing the resistant rock, especially the Precambrian basalts of Wadi Siyagh and Jebel Aswad (Schmidt hammer value R>90) to create a repeated fine-tooth impact depression.

Paradise's theory could be valuable for considering the ability of the Nabataeans to master the stone engineering based on its chemical and mechanical properties. The hardness of the stone suggests the use of specific tools and accordingly specific stone marks (mainly linear dressing for soft and medium stone because they used the axe, pointed and toothed chisels; and for rough hard stone (mainly basalt) they used the bush hammer). This study suggests that the 'hardness' factor could rightly affect the use of certain tools and accordingly the stone marking in Nabataean architecture. However, other factors could also affect the execution of stone dressing, one of which is the carving process and its techniques and tools. A process-based progression of stone carving is demonstrated by Nabataean rock-cut monuments. Based on existing, unfinished examples of monuments that have been carved out of sandstone monuments in Petra, several scholars claim that the carving process went through several phases. The Nabataeans adopted a top-down approach through which the carvers either start with cutting and smoothing the entire facade downwardly in order to prepare it for the next phase of shaping and detailing[8], or start with smoothing and carving from above using a series of horizontal platforms to conduct the two actions simultaneously[9]. In either case, it is clear that the Nabataean carving process evolved as a stylistic property that distinguishes Nabataean architecture from other Greco-Roman classical stonemarking. Accordingly, the current study revisits Rababeh's theory and focuses on the dressing of both stone blocks and rock-cut monuments in terms of: the dressing process and the sequence of operations to give them accuracy and aesthetically desirable regularity, carving tools and methods used for dressing, and the stone marks that distinguished Nabataean architecture.

Nabataean stone carving process and techniques

Nabataeans sought a flattened finish to their architecture. Flattening could be understood as "*the rough working of a surface to provide a flat finish rather than a smooth one*"[10]. Flattening mostly came in the form of linear marks (straight or curvilinear) or rugged texture. In cases of more complicated and detailed forms, fine dressing was sought to produce smooth surfaces using flat chisels as well as other carving tools. With reference to Rababeh[11], passing from the rough to the polished, smooth stone surfaces should have been developed through a complete linear process. Whether the piece progressed through the entire dressing process or stopped at specific stages depended on other factors that are not the subject of this study, but could be analysed in future research. Nonetheless, it is important to note that the dressing process went through four major phases: rough dressing, fine dressing, detailing and/or marking, and smoothing (Fig. 1). They could be illustrated as follows.

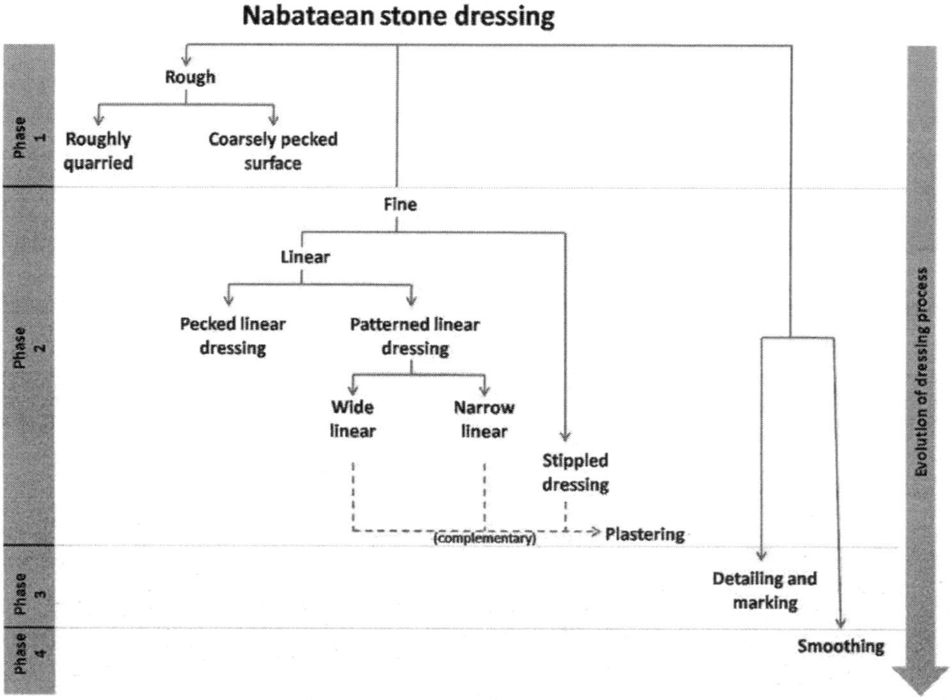

Figure 1 Evolution of the Nabataean stone dressing process as it evolves through consecutive phases

Rough Dressing

Once the block had been split and squared, the stonecutter started to give it its final shape and to test its flatness using different tools. Adam[12], following Leroi-Gourhan, divided these tools into two major categories: first, the tools involving direct percussion, which are used alone for squaring and for the rough shaping of faces. Examples of this category are the pick and hammer. The second category consists of tools involving indirect percussion, which are used in pairs, a punch or a chisel placed on the surface and struck by a precursor such as a mallet. Their use will be illustrated in the next section. In either case, a major factor that allows the use of these tools is the softness of the sandstone in Petra. At this initial phase of the dressing process, using the pick produced two types of rough dressing:

Dressing phase	Dressing marks			Dressing tool(s)	Examples
Rough	Roughly quarried			Pick	(a) 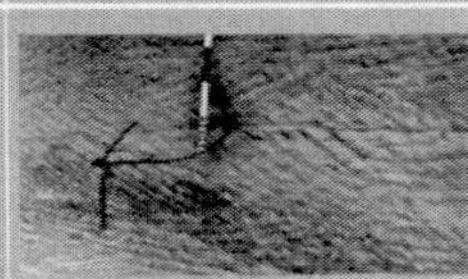
	Coarsely pecked surface			Pick	(b) 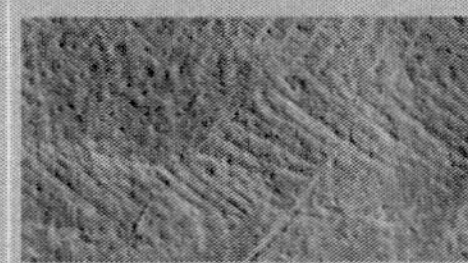
Fine	Linear	Pecked linear dressing		Point chisel, pick	(c) 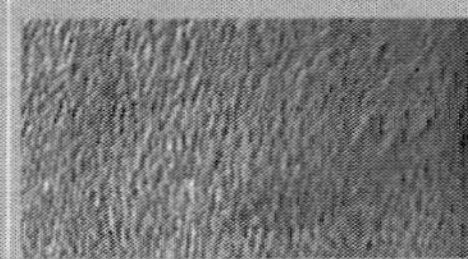
		Patterned linear dressing	Wide linear	Claw chisel (rectilinear) or roundel	(d) 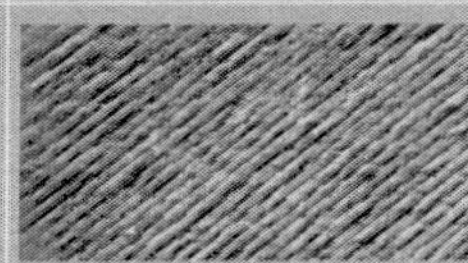
			Narrow linear	Claw chisel (sharp-toothed) or chemin-de-fer	(e) 
	Stippled dressing			bush hammer	(f) 
		Plastering		stucco or marble	(g) 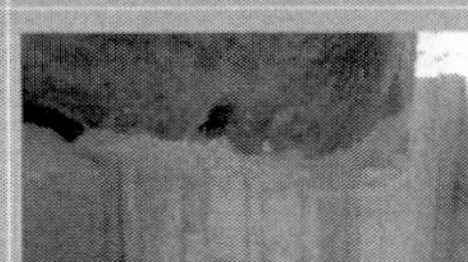
Detailing and marking				drill	(h) 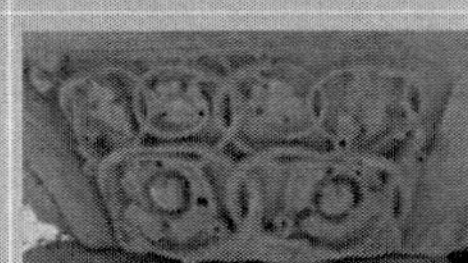
Smoothing				pounder	(i) 

Figure 2: Nabataean stone dressing process: tools and examples of each phase

- Roughly quarried stone represents the first stage of working a rock cut surface. It usually consists of long coarse straight or curved lines of peck marks, which might run in various directions (Fig.2a). These marks were left by the quarryman, and might have been done using a pick involving direct percussion. Harding was one of the first to report this technique. He stated that "*the Nabataeans' method of dressing stone is equally individual: they used a single ended pick and ran the cutting lines at an angle of 45 degrees across the face of the block, column rock face or whatever they were shaping*"[13]. Examples of this type can be seen in the ceiling of the Turkmaniyah Tomb.

- Coarsely pecked surface, in which the stonecutter started to roughly smooth the marks of the first stage that were left by the quarryman's pick (Fig.2b). Here the main concern was to remove the protruding parts and to make the surface as flat as possible to prepare for the next stage of fine dressing. Examples of this type can be seen in the interior of the Tomb of the Broken Pediment and the ceiling of Tomb 813.[14].

Fine Dressing

When the rough dressing of masonry walls, for drums, or for decorative elements was completed, they could have been refined using both direct and indirect percussion. In indirect percussion, the mallet and chisels were used for generating linear dressing. Amongst the most important chisels is the claw chisel. Hellmann, declares that a distinction should be made between two types of claw chisels[15]: the "*ciseau grain d'orge*" with pointed teeth and the "gradine" with straight-edged or rectilinear teeth. Therefore, it is obviously important to analyse the traces left on the stone blocks in Petra to distinguish the kind of tool used and to understand the stages of stone dressing. One piece of evidence is provided by the width of the grooves and the number of them per cm, as the distance between the grooves depends on the distance between the teeth of the claw chisel. Besides, while conducting his study in 2003, Rababeh met a stone carver, Dakhilalleh Qublan, who was working on restoring the arches of the east entrance of the "Great Temple". Qublan had a tool kit with a broad variety of chisels that were apparently used for the soft sandstone, specifically to knock the protrusions off the blocks[16]. It is suggested that the tools, involving indirect percussion such as a pick, point, tooth, and flat chisels, were probably used by the Nabataeans to rough out the block initially by knocking off protrusions.

In direct percussion, The Nabataeans sought a stippled dressing for their sandstones. They used the bush hammer which consisted of large toothed, flat headed hammers. Paradise claims that this tool was used at the very early stages in resistant rock and hard rocks, such as the granite and basalt[17]. It generated of new style of flat dressing with rugged texture. However, in cases of sandstone, the focus of this study, it is clear that the Nabataeans used the bush hammer in the early phases of stone dressing. According to Rababeh's theory that suggests a process-based dressing for the Nabataean sandstone, the Nabataeans would not be able to carry out a coarse texture using the bush hammer without going through a preparatory stage of fine linear dressing using the pick, tooth or point chisels. It is logical since the rough texture using the bush hammer appears to be condensely patterned on the sandstone, as opposed to the wide textured dressing of the basalt (Fig. 3)[18].

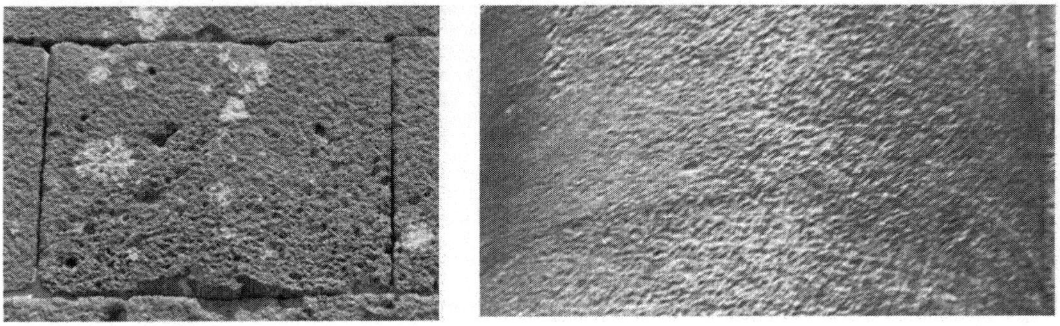

Figure 3 Use of bush hammer on basalt stone to produce rough texture as found in Umm el Jimal (left) and on sandstone to produce stippled dressing as found in Petra (right).

a. Linear dressing

Two types of lines can be observed: pecked linear dressing and patterned linear dressing: coarse and fine lines. It may be safely assumed that either a point or a claw chisel "gradine" with a mallet has been used for the coarse type. A similar example of coarse diagonal lines, carved by using a point, was found in Delphi[19]. However, one can distinguish a single point or pick from a toothed chisel by the regular spacing, as well as the fineness of the lines[20].

- Pecked linear dressing. The markings run in dotted straight lines (Fig.2c). The straight lines indicate the use of a mallet to strike on a point involving indirect percussion. If a pick had been used without a mallet, the markings would have been curved due to the movement of the workman's arm. Examples of fine pecked dressing can be seen in the façade of Tomb 343 on the right and left sides below the pediment.

- Patterned linear dressing. It appeared in two forms; depending on the width of the carved lines:

    - Wide linear dressing. It usually consists of horizontal, vertical, curved, or diagonal lines. The lines were carved in a regular pattern, and the composition of the grooves is homogeneous (Fig.2d). Their characteristics are similar to the lines carved on the freestanding blocks. For this type the stonemason used a claw chisel and mallet. It could be argued here that they could possibly used claw chisel with rectilinear teeth, with more widely spaced teeth. It appeares in four forms. The first is horizontal lines such as the ones that appear beneath the ceiling and the band of the Urn Tomb. The second is vertical lines that are found in the corners of the interiors of the tombs. Examples of this technique appear in the interior of most of the finished tombs, such as Tomb 813, the Obelisk Tomb, and the Urn Tomb. The third is curved lines that appear in the main chamber of the Corinthian. The fourth is tilted lines. Lines tilted at about 45 degrees are the most common type similar to those carved in the blocks used in the freestanding buildings. An example of lines at an angle can be seen in the interior walls of Turkmaniyah Tomb[21].

    - Narrow linear dressing. It is similar to the wide linear type, but the density of lines per cm is greater and the lines are finer (Fig.2e). Examples appear in the façades of Tomb 825 and Tomb 813. It seems probable that a sharp-toothed claw chisel was used for this type. Alternatively, the regularity of the carved lines in all of the rock-cut monuments led us to argue for the existence of another tool; a rasping tool, made of metal, like a hairbrush or a comb. This alternative tool could be used by hand or with a wooden mallet. The reason for suggesting this is the difficulty of obtaining regular fine lines in sandstone through an indirect percussion tool, especially as some narrow linear dressing also appears in a curvilinear form. In principle, it would be difficult to distinguish whether the marks are produced by a sharp-toothed chisel or the so-called *chemin-de-fer*[22]. The *chemin-de-fer* certainly exists now, and it is not certain it was used in antiquity[23], but traces of it at Petra can be distinguished from those of a sharp-toothed chisel, for example in the façade of Tomb 813, in which the fine lines are slightly curved, as if a tool like a hand plane or hairbrush was used. The curved lines show the use of a tool like a *chemin-de-fer* rather than a sharp-toothed chisel. The chief difference between them is that the sharp-toothed chisel involves more skilled labourers working over a longer time, while the *chemin-de-fer* involves unskilled labourers working and producing a higher output over a shorter time, particularly when the sandstone is sprinkled with water (i.e., being wet). As the sandstone in Petra is fairly soft, this would enable the stonemasons to achieve both regularity and fineness in their work[24].

Linear dressing (rough or fine, wide or narrow) remains the dominant stone dressing of the Nabataean sandstone in Petra and Heger. It evolved as a style that codifies the facade treatments of most rock-cut as well as self standing monuments[25]. In some cases, however, the Nabataeans utilised this rough surface as a base to hold plaster, stucco decorations, or marble (Fig.2g) as found on the facade of Tomb 825 according to Shaer & Aslan[26]. In other cases the lines received additional treatments using different tools to produce stippled dressing.

b. Stippled dressing

The next type of dressing occurs after the surface had been given a high degree of fineness, and the sculptor started to remove the fine lines from the elements which he intended to decorate. The surface then became stippled, with lines of tool marks visible (Fig. 2g). The surface of the interior of Tomb 813 is one example of this type of dressing. Similar examples can be seen in the facades of el-Khazneh, ed-Deir, and in the interior of Triclinium 21. In all these examples the stippled surfaces look as if they were produced with a bush hammer or similar tool with the teeth striking the stone directly[27].

Detailing and Marking

It seems certain that the Nabataean builders used a drill of some sort[28]. The use of the drill can be seen in both the rock-cut monuments and the freestanding decorative elements (Fig. 2h). McKenzie[29] noted some of these drill holes, which were still visible and left unfinished on the floral capitals of the Temple of the Winged Lions and the Khazneh. Treatment of the small details in Petra, therefore, often involved the drill. The tool may have been of one or more of three types[30]. The first one is based on a crank and flywheel similar to those used in Egypt in the Third Dynasty; the second type is the bow drill; and the third type is larger bow drill with a driving belt operated by a second workman[31].

After finishing this stage of dressing, the stonemasons started to mark the necessary symbols on the blocks to indicate their order in the building process. This technique was very common in Greek[32] and Roman architecture[33]. One important example of this technique can be seen in Petra showing the use of masons' marks, which consist chiefly of Nabataean letters and numbers: it appears in the west corridor of the Temple of the Winged Lions in the form of inscribed ashlars [34].

Smoothing

Smoothing is considered the last type of dressing. The finishing of most sculpted pieces either in the rock-cut monuments or the freestanding buildings indicates the use of rasps or grinding stones to smooth and then to decorate the final surface (Fig. 2i). The grinding tool must be harder than the stone surface to be ground. Since the stone surface in the rock-cut monuments consists of soft sandstone, a limestone grinder could have been used. In cases of limestone capitals and other elements, basalt grinders or other kinds of harder stones might have been used. Large grinders could be used to work on broad surfaces, but complex capitals needed small grinders or metal rasps.[35].

Conclusion

It appears from this study that Nabataean regions that are rich with sandstone, such as at Petra and Heger, witnessed the use of limited typologies of dressing that were fundamentally evolving from a linear configuration. The properties of the building materials, in this case the sandstone, played an instrumental role in defining a distinctive style of stone dressing that could not be found in any other regions. Nabataean areas that exhibit other types of stone, such as the limestone in Khirbet Al-Dhareeh or basalt in Umm el Jimal, did not utilise a linear stone dressing (Fig. 4). Most probably, the Nabataeans sought a unique style of stone dressing that differentiated the architecture in regions sharing a similar geological structure of sandstone, i.e., Petra and Heger. They could have also sought to distinguish their architecture from other imported architectural features, especially those that were borrowed from the Greco-Roman world. Although the Romans and Nabataeans share a sequential dressing process and similar dressing tools (see Table 1), it was the dressing outcomes of the rough and fine dressing phases that remain instrumental for generating a linear dressing style that characterises the Nabataean architecture and distinguishes their stonework.

It is clear that the Nabataeans were masters of stone engineering. The Nabataean masons were able to work with very sensitive type of stone to prepare blocks for free-standing buildings or make dressing of surfaces of the rock-cut monuments. They controlled the dressing of this stone through a typical sequential process that evolved from the rough quarried dressing to a more finely, detailed dressing. The gradual progression of stone dressing is a characteristic of stone working that is not necessarily limited to the Nabataeans. In studying the stone making techniques and processes of the Romans, scholars suggest that "*Successful carving is a methodical craft [in which each step] builds on its predecessor, progressing from initial quarrying, through roughing-out of the overall form, to more and more detailed work and eventually polishing*"[36]. Organising the stages and using the appropriate tool would significantly affect the final outcome of stone dressing. However, this does not suggest a standardised method for stone carving or a typical set of carving tools. Rather, Nabataean carvers used diverse methods to progress from the raw stone into the detailed dressing, depending mainly on their experience, the desired outcome, and more importantly, the properties of the material- in this case the sandstone. It is important to consider the Nabataean's values and technical achievements in this type of sandstone in future restoration works in Petra or similar historical sites around the world.

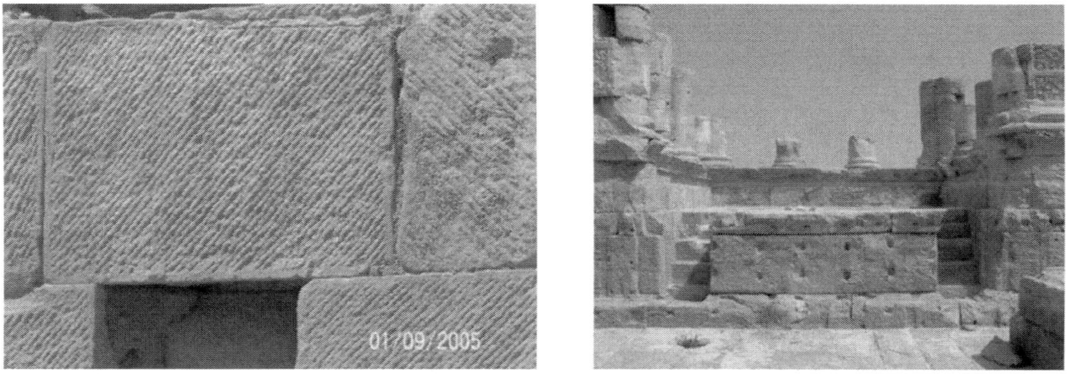

Figure 4 Comparison between the Nabataean stone dressing in Petra (left) and Khirbet Al-Dhareeh (right) with different styles of marking.

Table 1 Comparison between Roman stone dressing (according to (Wotton, Russell and Rockwell 2013) and Nabataean stone dressing.

Roman		Nabataean (Sandstone)				
Phase	**Tool(s)**	**Phase**	**Sub-phases**			**Tool(s)**
Squaring	• Quarry pick • Point chisel • saw					
Roughing-out	• Point					
Hollowing-out	• Point chisel • Quarry pick					
Rough shaping	• Point chisel • Flat chisel • Tooth chisel • Roundel	**Rough dressing**	Roughly quarried			• Point • Flat chisel • Mallet • Pick
			Coarsely pecked surface			
Fine shaping	• Flat chisel (smooth surface) • Tooth chisel (occasionally) • Roundel (undulating, rugged texture)	**Fine dressing**	Linear	Pecked linear		• Point • Pick • Mallet
				Patterned linear	Wide linear	• Claw chisel (rectilinear) • Roundel
					Narrow linear	• Claw chisel (sharp toothed) • Chemin-de-fer • Mallet
		Stippled				• Bush hammer
Detailing	• Drill • Flat chisel • Channeling tool • Flat chisel	**Detailing**				• Drill
Outlining	• Flat chisel • Roundel • Channeling tool • Drill					
Flattening	• Flat chisel • Tooth chisel					
Smoothing	• Flat chisel • Rasp • Scraper • Tooth chisel • Roundel	**Smoothing**				• Pounder

Notes and References

[1] Brünnow, R., & von Domaszewski, A., *Die Provincia Arabia, Vol. I*', (Strassburg, Von Karl J.Trübner), 1904; Brünnow, R., & von Domaszewski, A., *Die Provincia Arabia, Vol.II*', (Strassburg, Von Karl J.Trübner), 1909.

[2] Rababeh, S.,, 'Nabataean Architectural Identity and its Impact on Contemporary Architecture in Jordan', *Dirasat, Engineering Sciences,* 37, No. 1, pp. 27-53, 2010,

[3] Rababeh, S., *How Petra was Built*, (Oxford, Archaeopress), 2005

[4] Rababeh,S., 2010

[5] Rabebeh, S., 2010

[6] Rababeh, S., 2010, p 84

[7] Paradise, T., 'Nabataean Stone Dressing and Lithology in Petra, Jordan', *American Journal of Archaeology*, 114, No. 4, 2014.

[8] Hammond, P., *The Nabataeans: Their History, Culture & Archaeology* , Studies in Mediterranean Archaeology, 37, (Gothenburg: Coronet Books Inc.), 1973.

[9] for more information see Rababeh, 2005

[10] Wotton, W.B.R., and Rockwell, P.,'Stonemaking Techniques and Processes', 2013. http://www.artofmaking.ac.uk/content/essays/3-stoneworking-techniques-and-processes-w-wootton-b-russell-p-rockwell/ (accessed on November 29, 2015), p. 11

[11] Rabebeh, S., 2005

[12] Adam, J.P., *Roman Building: Materials and Techniques*. (London: Batsford), 1994, p. 33

[13] Harding,G., *The Antiquities of Jordan*, (New York: Thomas Crowell Company), 1967, p120.

[14] Rababeh, S., 2005, p. 93

[15] Hellmann,M., *L'Architecture Grecque I. Les Principles de la Construction*, (Paris: Picard), 2002, pp 82-83. See also Bessac, J. C., *L'outillage traditional du tailleur de Pierre: De L'Antique a nos jours,* (Paris: Center National de la Recherche Scientifique), 1986, 139-48, Figs.32, 33.

[16] Rababeh, 2005, p. 86, Fig 4.5

[17] Paradise, 2014

[18] The qualities of the basalt as an extremely hard stone and more difficult to cut and dress do not necessarily mandate the use of one unique carving tool (i.e., the bush hammer) to produce rough textures- as suggested by Paradise (2014). The cases of Umm Qais in Jordan, Bosra and cities of Jabal Druze for example, provide valuable examples of dressing the basalt stone to a fairly smooth finish and in some cases with fine decorative details. Saying that, it might be logical to consider other factors that could have influenced the rough dressing of the basalt stone in the Nabataean architecture. For example, in case of Umm el Jimal that witnessed the advent of the Nabataeans and was entirely built with basalt, Al Kurdi (Al Kurdi,N., 'Hard Building Material and Suitable Architecture: The case of Umm El Jimal- Jordan', *Architecture and Modern Information Technologies*, 1, No. 26, 2014, pp. 1-8.) suggests that the basalt stones were not finely smoothed and dressed because people in this area were not offered to pay for the time it took to attain fine and smooth stone dressing.

[19] Martin, R., Manuel D'architecture Grecque I: Materiaux et Techniques, (Paris, J. Picard), 1965, Pl. XVI. See also Pl. L112, which shows lines tilted at 45 degrees and lifting bosses at Delphi. For the use of the point see Bessac,,1988, p47, Fig.8

[20] Hammond, P., *The Temple of the Winged Lions Petra, Jordan 1973-1990*, (Fountain Hills, Arizona: Petra Publishing) 1996, p81 suggests that the typical Nabataean diagonal dressing would have involved toothed hammers, or special chisels (see (Rababeh, 2005, p. 88).

[21] See Rababeh, 2005, p. 93.
[22] Bessac, 1986, pp. 46-50; Rockwell,P., *The Art of Stoneworking: A Reference Guide*, (Cambridge, CUP) 1993, p. 22
[23] Ginouvés, R., & Martin, R., *Dictionnaire Méthodique de l'architecture grecque et romaine I. Matériaux, techniques de construction, techniques et formes du décor*, (Paris, Centre National de la Recherché Scientifique), 1985
[24] See (Rababeh, 2005, pp. 93-95).
[25] Rababeh 2010
[26] M. Shaer & A.Zaki, 'Nabataean Building Techniques with Special Reference to the Architecture of Tomb 825 (Tomb of the fourteen graves)', In M. Kuhlenthal, H. Fischer & B. L. *fur Denkmalpflege, Petra: die Restaurierung der Grabfassaden* , (Munchen: Karl M. Lipp), 2000, pp. 89-108
[27] Bessac, 1986, pp. 77-85, Rockwell, 1993. For more on these examples see Rababeh, 2005, p. 96.
[28] Lyttelton, M., *Baroque Architecture in Classical Antiquity,* (London, Thames and Hudson), 1974, p66 considered that there is no sign of the drill having been used. She based her suggestion on the capitals of the Qasr el-Bint.
[29] J. McKenzie, '*The Architecture of Petra',* (OUP), 1990, p. 51
[30] Bessac, 1986, pp. 231-252
[31] For images of these tools see (Rababeh, 2005, pp. 89, 91).
[32] cf.Martin, 1965, pp. 225-231; M. Hellmann, L'Architecture Grecque I. Les Principles de la Construction, (Paris: Picard), 2002., pp. 88-91
[33] Adam, 1994, p. 40
[34] Hammond P. 1996 p. 28. For more examples see Rababeh, 2005, pp. 91-92; Rababeh, 2005, pp. 96-98; Wotton, Russell, & Rockwell, 2013, p. 1
[35] Rababeh, 2005, pp. 96-98
[36] Wotton, Russell, & Rockwell, 2013, p. 1

Bibliography

B.de Vries, 'Umm al-Jimal Educational Project: A Curriculum Guide for Teaching Lessons on the Archaeology of Umm el-Jimal in Four Disciplines: Arts and Architecture, Civics, Geology and History', (The Umm el-Jimal Project and Open Hand Studios) 2012.

D. Arnold, *Building in Egypt: Pharaonic Stone Masonry*, (OUP) 1991.

G.Foerster, 'Masada V. The Yageal Yadin Excavations 1963-1965,' In J. Aviram, G. Foerster & E. Netzer, (Ed.) *Final Report: Art and Architecture,* (Jerusalem: The Hebrew University of Jerusalem), 1995.

G.Harding, *The Antiquities of Jordan*, (New York: Thomas Crowell Company), 1967.

J. P. Adam, *Roman Building: Materials and Techniques*. (London: Batsford), 1994.

J. Cl.Bessac, *L'outillage traditional du tailleur de Pierre: De L'Antique a nos jours,* (Paris: Center National de la Recherche Scientifique), 1986.

J. McKenzie, '*The Architecture of Petra',* (OUP), 1990.

M. Hellmann, *L'Architecture Grecque I. Les Principles de la Construction*, (Paris: Picard), 2002.

M. Joukowsky, 'History of the Brown University Excavations', In M. Joukowsky (Ed.),*Petra Great Temple Vol. 1*, (Providence, RI, Brown University, Petra Exploration Fund), 1998, pp 48-148.

M. Joukowsky, 'The Great Temple', Markoe, 2003, pp. 214-222.

M.Korres, *From Pentelicon to the Parthenon*, (Athens: Melissa), 1995.

M. Korres, 'The Ancient Quarries on Mount Pentelikon', In Y. Maniatis, N. Herz and Y. Basiakos (Eds.), The Study of Marble and Other Stones Used in Antiquity, London: Dorset Press, 1995b, pp. 1-7.

M.Lyttelton, *Baroque Architecture in Classical Antiquity,* (London, Thames and Hudson), 1974.

M. Shaer & A.Zaki, 'Nabataean Building Techniques with Special Reference to the Architecture of Tomb 825 (Tomb of the fourteen graves)', In M. Kuhlenthal, H. Fischer & B. L. fur Denkmalpflege, Petra: die Restaurierung der Grabfassaden , Munchen: Karl M. Lipp, 2000, pp. 89-108.

N. Al Kurdi, 'Hard Building Material and Suitable Architecture: The case of Umm El Jimal- Jordan', *Architecture and Modern Information Technologies*, 1, No. 26, 2014, pp. 1-8.

P.Bikai, 'North Ridge Project', ACORN, 14, No. 1, 2002, pp. 1-4.

P. Hammond, *The Nabataeans: Their History, Culture & Archaeology* , Studies in Mediterranean Archaeology, 37, (Gothenburg: Coronet Books Inc.), 1973.

Hammond, P., *The Temple of the Winged Lions Petra, Jordan 1973-1990*, (Fountain Hills, Arizona: Petra Publishing) 1996.

Rockwell,P., *The Art of Stoneworking: A Reference Guide*, (Cambridge, CUP) 1993.

Ginouvés, R., & Martin, R., *Dictionnaire Méthodique de l'architecture grecque et romaine I. Matériaux, techniques de construction, techniques et formes du décor*, (Paris, Centre National de la Recherché Scientifique), 1985.

R.Brünnow & A. von Domaszewski, 'Die Provincia Arabia', vol. I', Strassburg: Von Karl J.Trübner, 1904.

R.Brünnow & A. von Domaszewski, 'Die Provincia Arabia Vol. II', Strassburg: Von Karl J. Trübner, 1909.

R.Martin, *Manuel D'architecture Grecque I: Materiaux et Techniques*, (Paris, J. Picard), 1965.

S.Rababeh, *How Petra was Built*, (Oxford, Archaeopress), 2005.

S.Rababeh, 'Nabataean Architectural Identity and its Impact on Contemporary Architecture in Jordan', Dirasat, Engineering Sciences, vol. 37, no. 1,2010, pp. 27-53.

Woodford, S., *The Art of Greece and Rome*, (Cambridge: CUP), 1982.

T.Paradise, 'Nabataean Stone Dressing and Lithology in Petra, Jordan', American Journal of Archaeology,vol. 114, no. 4, 2014.

Wotton, W.B.R., and Rockwell, P.,'Stonemaking Techniques and Processes', 2013. http://www.artofmaking.ac.uk/content/essays/3-stoneworking-techniques-and-processes-w-wootton-b-russell-p-rockwell/ (accessed on November 29, 2015).

Al-Salameen, Z., 'The Nabataeans and Asia Minor', *Mediterranean Archaeology and Archaeometry* , 11, No. 2, 2011, pp. 55-78.

Some considerations on Roman building techniques in the early fifth century AD

R. Mancini
Sapienza University, Rome

Introduction

The aim of this study is to expand our knowledge of the building techniques practised in Rome in the first decades of the fifth century. Starting with an analysis of the largest construction project in the city at that time – the great Honorian heightening of the imperial wall of Rome – comparisons are made with other buildings of that era in order to reconstruct the building process. We are particularly interested in the materials used (mainly bricks and tufa blocks), their origins (whether new or *spolia*), how they were used, how scaffolding was constructed (through observing putlog holes) and recognising the various tasks of labourers put to work on this construction project. This study is part of a body of research on Roman construction techniques, a matter of interest to architects and archaeologists, particularly those that focus on Rome's Aurelian Wall[1].

Fifth-century buildings in Rome

In the early fifth century, from AD401 to AD403, the construction work to raise the height of the Aurelian Wall (AD271-AD275) commissioned by the Emperor Honorius began and was quickly completed[2]. Apart from this vast project of military architecture, the first half of the century also saw the construction of *tituli* influenced by the emperor's frequent presence, by the greater availability of the papacy's financial resources and, above all, the involvement of the aristocracy.

The churches of San Vitale (AD401-AD417), Santa Sabina (AD432-AD440), San Pietro in Vincoli (AD432-AD440) and Santi Giovanni e Paolo al Celio (AD401-AD417) all date from this period, built thanks to donations from private benefactors and, in some cases, with imperial grants as well. From AD380 to AD440, almost half the *domus ecclesiae* were expanded or replaced by large basilicas that aspired to fulfill a public role. Grand buildings were constructed during the papacies of Sixtus III (AD432-AD440) and Pope Leo the Great (AD440-AD461): San Sisto Vecchio (AD432-AD440) and San Pietro in Vincoli (AD432-AD440), as well as the abovementioned Santi Giovanni e Paolo and San Vitale. These new churches shared a number of features: they all had a standard layout, consisting of a nave ending in an apse, with a high upper wall with windows supported by arch-topped columns and two aisles.

The heightening of Rome's defensive wall, in contrast, proved a complex operation due to its extent and because these were improvements made to a structure that hadn't been built to bear further weight. The architects who had designed the previous circuit (commissioned by Aurelian in AD271) came across difficulties due to the choice of location, the acquisition of the land required and the presence of buildings, including monuments.

The difficulties involved in heightening the walls were no less imposing. The improvements did not merely stop at placing a new construction on top of the Aurelian defences; instead, a new structure encompassing what was already there was built. A rather complex construction was created that was structurally superimposed on the older wall and shared its purpose. The Honorian construction project almost doubled the height of the curtain walls between towers, creating an enclosed gallery[3]. This featured a series of arches that opened towards the city (Fig. 1), whilst the side facing out from the city was solid and featured a series of loopholes (Fig. 2). The towers' original command room was supplemented by another on an upper floor, with an indoor staircase connecting the two[4]. Each of these new rooms had eight archivolted windows, three on each of the two facades, facing towards the city and out from the city, and one on each side. Most of the old Aurelian windows of the lower room were walled up to become loopholes.

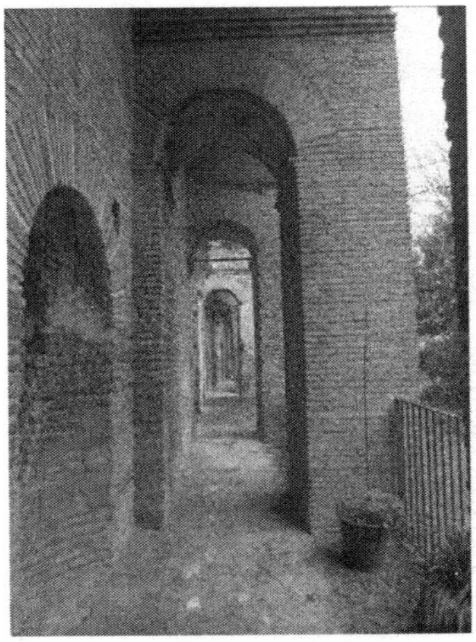

Fig. 1 Sector L, interior facing: Honorius' arcaded gallery, Rome city wall, 2015. Photo R. Mancini.

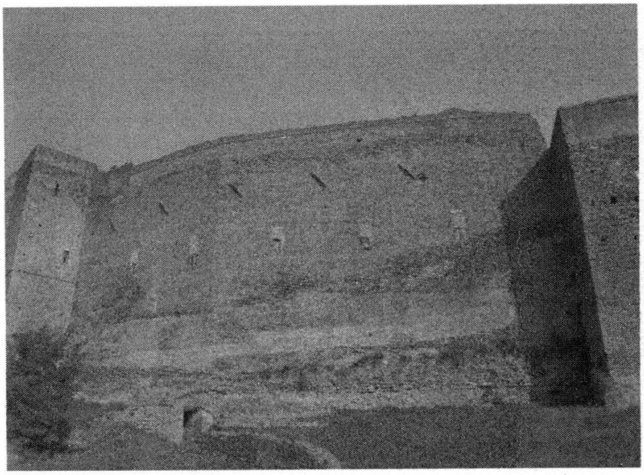

Fig. 2 Sector L, curtain L 10-11, external facing, Rome city wall, 2015. Photo R. Mancini.

The upper rooms led out to the open-air battlements through two archivolted doorways. The new command rooms were given cement vaulted roofs. The eight ribs of the cloister vault were arranged on an octagonal layout and four pendentives led from the square base to the polygon of the vault. The vault was covered with a four-pitch roof.

Construction techniques

All the masonry examined had an *opus caementicium* core clad in brick or *opus listatum* (tufa blocks and bricks). The bricks used for the curtain walls were generally sourced from whatever storage site happened to be used at the time and therefore vary in colour and size. This is why differences in height and size due to the use of *spolia* in the masonry are compensated for by the mortar which, with thicknesses that sometimes varied slightly and were not perfectly uniform, supported the wall layout, re-aligning the rows and ensuring they remained horizontal (Fig. 3). In the fifth century, brick was usually *spolia* and readily available, in that the city was undergoing a process of change. Large public buildings (such as amphitheatres and baths), as well as aqueducts, were gradually being abandoned for a variety of reasons, including a decline in the city's population. Residential districts were becoming depleted and large patrician homes were converted to other uses (often monastic). These buildings were stripped of their materials, which were used on new construction projects.

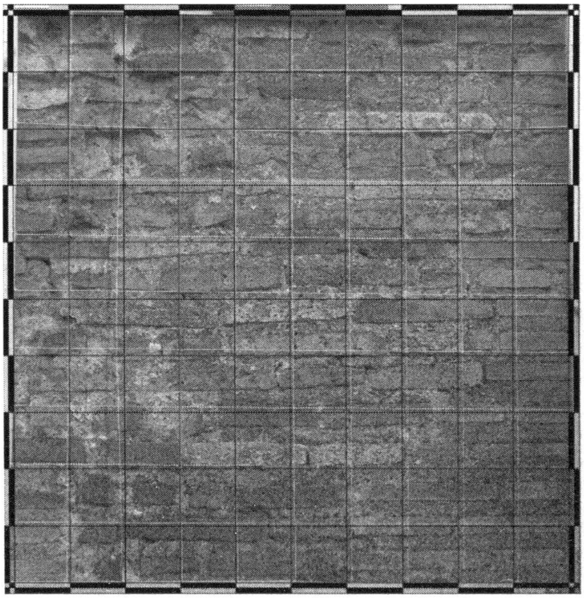

Fig. 3 Porta San Paolo, tower M1, Honorian masonry, Rome city wall, 2014. Photo A. Cannata.

As far as the Honorian alterations to the walls are concerned, the first phase of the project must have involved demolition work to remove the old crenellations that made it difficult to raise the height of the wall, incorporating them into the new structure. As we know, only rare traces of the third-century battlements survive and, while their disappearance may in part be attributed to the bad state of the fortifications at the time they were raised in height, we can also surmise their systematic demolition. We shouldn't rule out that some of the *spolia*, though just a small fraction, may have come from the existing Aurelian building. Indeed, it is possible that the bricks that were left over from the demolition of the third century crenellated parapet were re-used in the new structure as they were already found on site, as it is also plausible that the large amount of building materials removed in the fifth century to free up the area surrounding the wall, as described on the inscriptions above the city gates, were re-utilised for the alterations[5]. Indeed, in setting up the new construction site, it proved necessary to remove the 'extensive ruins' that now surrounded the wall and probably filled the moat that, either entirely or in part, surrounded the wall, a moat commissioned by Maxentius.

The construction method used for the masonry involved horizontal rows, presumably laid in this way by using strings that were stretched horizontally along each course of bricks and its corresponding cement core. The *modulo* used in this system of bricklaying can be recognised by the height of the series of three or five courses of brick (on the surface) and is a sign of a particular construction technique that uses perfectly bonded, horizontal courses to create the entire thickness of the cement wall in a stratigraphic succession of layers.

Among the fifth-century buildings entirely clad in brick we find – among others and apart from the Honorian alterations to the wall of Rome – the curtain walls of the church of Santi Giovanni e Paolo al Celio (AD401-AD417), of the Basilica of Santa Sabina on the Aventine Hill (AD432-AD440), the Basilica of San

Vitale (AD401-AD417) and the Basilica of San Lorenzo in Lucina (AD432-AD440). We also find *opus listatum* masonry (one or two courses of stone blocks, usually tuff, and a row of bricks). From the late fifth century to the early eighth century, brick cladding became quite rare, while *opus mixtum* was more common.

Moduli

Due to the variations in shape and size of the bricks used, the mortar bed helped to even out the pattern, tending to thicken until, in a number of buildings, it became higher than the height of the course of bricks. This is naturally reflected in the size of the *moduli,* which tended to increase in the fifth century. The mortar is pinkish-grey in colour and in some cases has pointing in the middle of the joint or, as in the previous century, is angled to such an extent that it leaves the upper edge of the lower row of bricks exposed. The *moduli* examined are 30-32 cm in San Vitale (AD401-AD417), 32-33 cm in the Honorian cladding along the Aurelian Walls (AD401-AD403), 35-36 cm in San Lorenzo in Lucina (AD432-AD440), 31-34 cm in San Pietro in Vincoli (AD432-AD440), 31-34 cm in Santa Maria Maggiore (AD432-AD440) and 31-34 cm in San Sisto Vecchio (AD432-AD440)[6].

The occasional use of large bricks (usually *bipedales*, square bricks two Roman feet long) continued to bind the external wall to the core and to distribute loads more uniformly within the wall's thickness. Linking brick courses are found from the second half of the first century BC and became common in the second and early third century AD.[7] Field literature concerning this matter states that they disappeared around the fourth/fifth centuries, but we do note some examples in the Honorian wall alterations, though sporadic. Their disappearance is traditionally attributed to the lack of large bricks. We come across the use of large bricks in the Honorian alterations even above and beyond the rare courses found, as we can see in the stretch between the Porta Appia and Porta Ostiensis gates, inside the gallery near the loophole niches (Fig. 4). In the first half of the fifth century, there was no lack of masonry with a cement core and *opus listatum* cladding. The materials were laid with a certain amount of care, despite the fact that the use of *spolia* involves, in any case, a certain degree of irregularity. Blocks of tufa are usually alternated with bricks (one or two courses of blocks and one of bricks). Alternating rows of brick and tufa blocks are found in the facades of San Vitale (one layer of brick for every layer of tufa), San Clemente and in San Giovanni a Porta Latina.

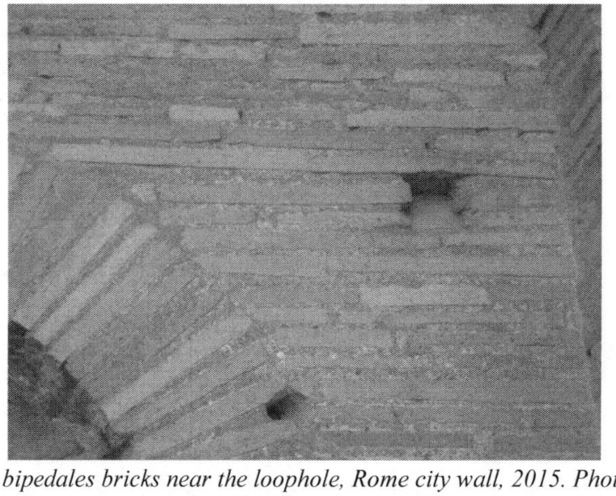

Fig. 4 Curtain L5-6 large bipedales bricks near the loophole, Rome city wall, 2015. Photo R. Mancini.

How the construction work was organised

How tasks were meted out

If we observe the curtain walls built in the fifth century along Rome's defensive circuit, we can see junctions between the different parts of wall that were built at the same time. Indeed, the new wall, like the Aurelian structure underneath it, was constructed using large groups of builders who worked simultaneously. This resulted in a number of vertical junctions, both within the core and on the facade. We know nothing about how the different core sections were connected, but by looking at the curtain wall facades we can understand what was done to the facing. Whilst a number of 'saw-tooth' junctions were made in the underlying Aurelian Wall in order to grip the curtain walls more firmly, these are found less often in the Honorian alterations, though they do exist and are well made (Fig. 5). 'Saw-tooth junctions' are the sign of a well organised construction programme, contradicting, at least in some sections of the circuit, what Richmond claims when he says that in the fifth century alterations "*...less care is taken to get the face of the Wall quite true from section to section, with the result that the junctions are ill-arranged, and invite those cleavages which strains have tended to create here and there*". However, Richmond also notes how the "*technique differs somewhat widely from Gate to Gate, or from section to section*".[8] Indeed, a direct analysis of the Honorian wall facing shows how certain construction methods and systems for choosing brick materials seem to characterise even only small sections of the alterations, such as portions of curtain wall.

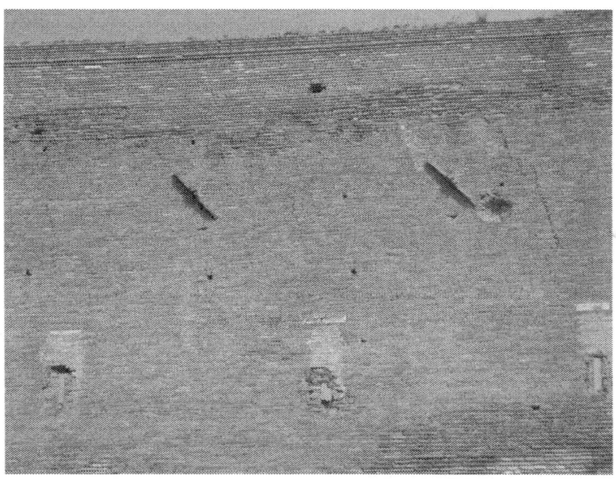

Fig. 5 Sector L, curtain L 10-11, external facing, showing the 'saw-tooth' junctions, Rome city wall, 2015. Photo R. Mancini.

As mentioned earlier, the gallery between the Porta Appia and Porta Ostiensis gates (sector L) boasts large bricks that are always placed at the same height compared to the niches where the loopholes are located. This is a particular feature that is repeated on the neighbouring four loopholes and that therefore cannot be considered random, but rather a specific *modus operandi* of a team of labourers, if not just one specific builder (Fig 4). By identifying the junctions, we can also work out how long the stretch of wall assigned to each group of labourers was: it was approximately 35 roman feet long, but also less when the wall has a curved surface (approximately 15 roman feet long – curtain L10-11).

The scaffolding

The Honorian construction project to raise the city's imperial defensive wall was organised in such a way as to be able to lean against the existing structure. In the case of the Honorian alterations to the wall, the scaffolding used must have been specially designed. If it leaned on the ground, it had to be detached from the wall for the first six metres in height, as there was no place to grip the Aurelian wall lower than the battlements (the scaffolding could lean against them but could not grip on to them in a more stable fashion). In this case, the construction of the scaffolding would have been rather complicated. However, we can't rule out that, rather than being anchored to the ground, except in a couple of places, the Honorian scaffolding may have been cantilevered. The distance between scaffolding levels varies from 140 to 160 centimetres. We still need to analyse a number of differences in the shapes of the putlog holes that are visible inside the fifth-century curtain walls.

Strengthening techniques

Honorius's builders strengthened the existing wall before raising it, as the old structure was carrying a load it had not been built to sustain. The only way we can glean information on how these improvements were carried out is by directly observing the building itself, particularly during restoration work and in areas where parts of the wall have previously collapsed, either recently or in the distant past. One of the reinforcement operations carried out was the thickening of the third-century defensive wall, carried out by building a structure that lay parallel to the older one and was simply placed adjacent to it, which ran along the side facing the city near the curtain walls and towers, designed to distribute the load of the new gallery partly along the new wall and partly along the old one.

On the top of curtain wall L4-5, south of Porta Appia gate, a deep furrow has been found running along the ramparts between the two towers, along the floor of the gallery (Fig. 6). This could be the junction between the old wall (facing out from the city) and the new one (facing inwards)[9]. It almost doubles the thickness of the previous wall that went from approximately 2 metres to around 3.70 metres in width at that point. In this way, the longitudinal arches running parallel to the battlements were placed on top of the new wall, while the diagonal arches that spread the weight of the barrel vaults that cover the gallery partly rested on the old wall and partly on the new one. The construction of a vaulted and arched structure that rests on two different structures that could only be partially solid built seems to have been quite a daring feat. The possibility that these two walls may have suffered a number of collapses is fairly probable and could be one of the reasons why some of the arches along the circuit have been lost.

The towers were also strengthened by doubling the thickness of the existing walls when they were raised, in order to adapt the old structure to the new load caused by the creation of a command room placed above the old one. We can see examples of this operation in towers L33, M12 and B8. In towers L33 and M12, one can clearly see the increased thickness of the wall, achieved by creating a new wall alongside it, facing inwards (Figs 7-8). The strengthened wall, featuring a facade of alternating rows of tuff blocks and bricks, could be attributable to reconstruction work carried out during Maxentius's reign (AD306-AD312). Tower B8 was restored in 1958 (Fig. 9), at which time it became possible to study the inner walls built to widen the whole[10]. In this case, too, the external wall that had been reinforced could date to the time of Maxentius. In both cases, pre-existing and supporting structures have similar thicknesses.

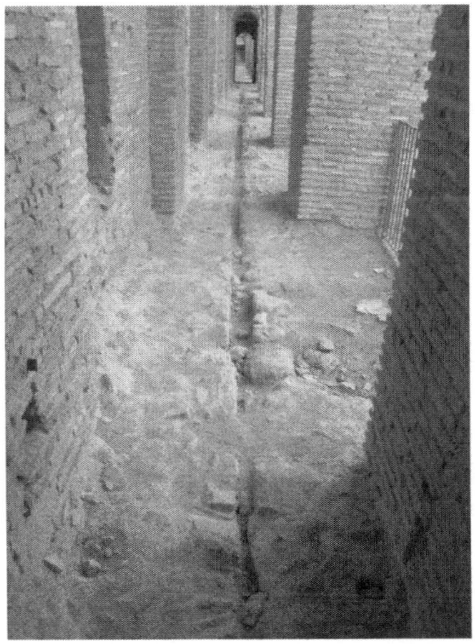

Fig. 6 Curtain L4-5, a deep furrow running along the ramparts, Rome city wall, 2015. Photo R. Mancini.

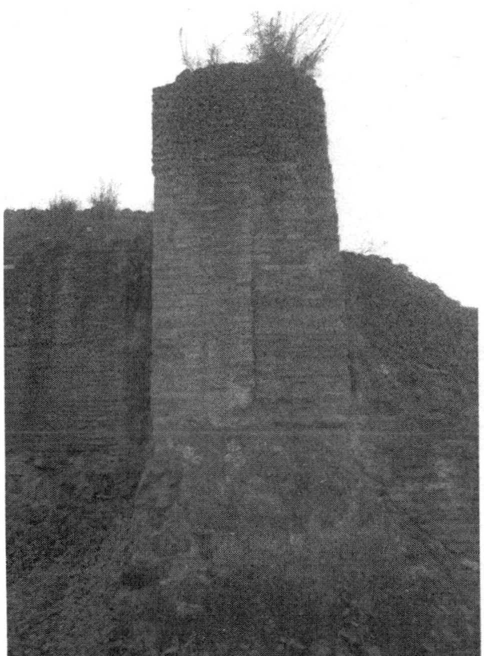

Fig. 7 Tower L33, the increased thickness of the wall, Rome city wall, 2010. Photo R. Mancini

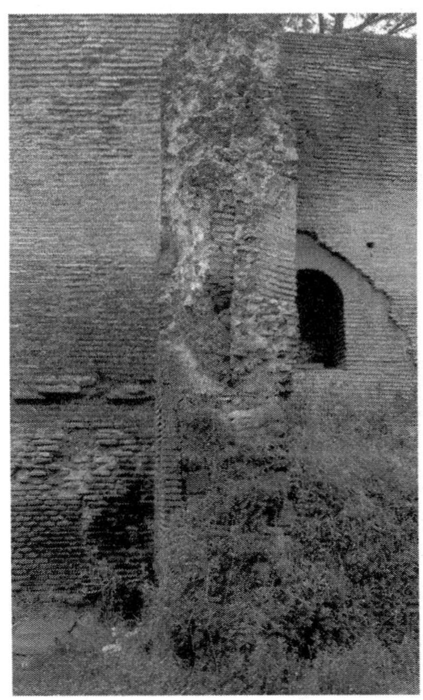

Fig. 8 Tower M12, the increased thickness of the wall, Rome city wall, 2014. Photo R. Mancini

We don't know if this type of reinforcement work was done to all the towers and near all the stretches of wall featuring covered galleries. Some doubts have been raised following the discovery of wall facing that would seem to be datable to the time of Aurelian, along stretches of curtain wall facing inwards towards the city, when a general doubling of the wall along the base of the gallery would have completely covered this facing. It is also worth remembering that the Aurelian structure did not always follow the same construction design and purpose and, as a consequence, the labourers working at the turn of the fifth century were forced to come up with a number of different methods to build over the older structure.

Richmond was the first to study the different types of fortification used in the third-century circuit, identifying three different types (A, B and C) that required different kinds of alterations in Honorius's time[11]. The first type (A) is a solid wall which was, according to Richmond, approximately 12 feet wide and 20 feet tall (the initial width of 12 feet would remove the need to double the width of the wall at the base when building the gallery), that in some sections of the circuit acts as a retaining wall for banks of earth that are almost as high as the wall itself. The second type (B) is entirely unusual, as it covers previously existing aqueducts. Richmond also observed the presence of occasional stretches of wall fitted with galleries that could be dated back to Aurelian's reign, between the Amphitheatrum Castrense and Porta Asinaria gate (of which only two arches remain) and in sector H (C-type wall), which it is presumed served as the main model for constructing the Honorian gallery.

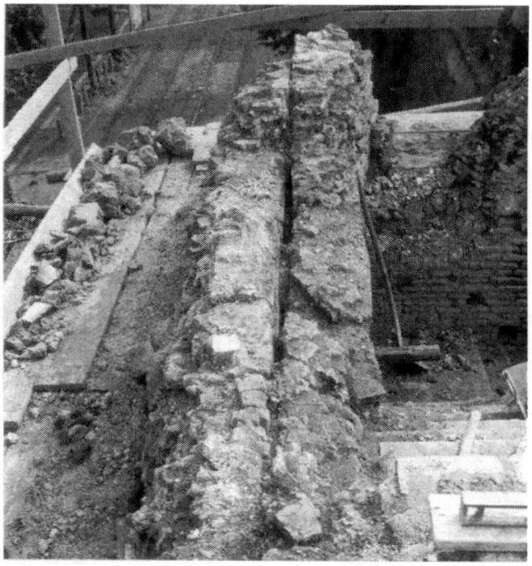

Fig. 9 Tower B8, the increased thickness of the wall, Rome city wall, 1958. Photo L. Cozza

As well as reinforcing the structure below, the new wall had to physically adapt to its different thicknesses and variations in direction, which are sometimes abrupt, sometimes almost imperceptible. Changes in direction were easily done by the Aurelian labourers given the simplicity of the structure they were building - a simple solid wall - but these same circumstances raised difficulties for the more complex Honorian project. Fifth-century work to thicken the walls may have also been carried out in order to make up for the inadequacy of the existing wall's thickness, which was not enough to allow the construction of covered battlements of a suitable width.

Where the wall acted as an embankment, Honorius's builders constructed a much simpler structure, without a gallery, mainly consisting of a continuous wall equipped with loopholes. Due to the irregular layout of the underlying circuit, the covered gallery bears traces of a number of bends that are more or less obvious (curtains A21-22, B3-4, B5-6, B9-10, F13-14, J3-4, K10-11) (Fig. 10). The heightening of the towers with the addition of a new command room involved the creation of a flight of stairs at the Aurelian floor height in order to reach the new rooms, with inevitable consequences for the vaults.

There are still a number of cases to be examined and it seems possible to assert that the fifth-century labourers dealt with the pre-existing structure on a case-by-case basis, without applying pre-arranged solutions, depending on the conditions of the old circuit.

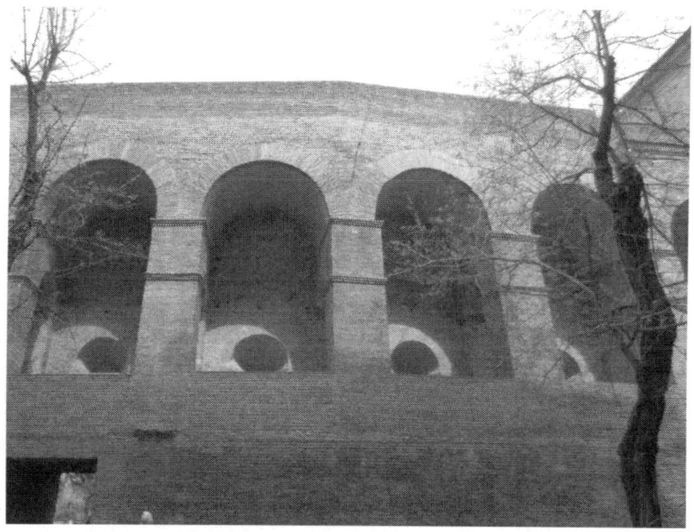

Fig. 10 Curtain B3-4, Rome city wall, 2014. Photo A. Cannata.

Conclusions

The fifth century faithfully continued Roman masonry construction techniques. Buildings created using masonry were solid, walls were made of faced concrete. While a number of different types of facing survived up until Constantine's day (*opus incertum, caementicium, spicatum, craticium, africanum, testaceum* and *vittatum*), only brick facing remained in the fifth century, becoming rare in the century that followed, as well as *opus listatum*[12]. Bonds between external curtain walls and their cores were less effective (courses of large brick binding the curtain wall facade to the core became rare). Large Roman *bipedales* bricks were still available in the fifth century, sourced from older buildings, and then became impossible to find in subsequent periods.

Most materials were taken from older buildings, in line with a tradition that, though very ancient, became commonplace from Constantine's day on, becoming a standard practice throughout the Roman world and becoming predominant during the early Middle Ages[13]. Curtain wall facades were irregular due to the use of brick and stone *spolia*, but the appearance of the surface seems well laid out, with a satisfactory horizontal uniformity of courses. The teams of labourers who worked on Rome's defensive wall (few compared to the total number) were still the heirs to the technical sophistication of the past, creating perfect junctions between curtain walls that are visible in certain parts of the Roman wall circuit.

Notes and References

[1] H. W. Dey, *The Aurelian Wall and the Refashioning of Imperial Rome. AD 271-855.* Cambridge: University Press, 2011; R. Mancini, *Le Mura Aureliane di Roma: Atlante di un Palinsesto Murario.* Rome: Quasar 2001, I. A. Richmond *The City Wall of Imperial Rome: An Account of its Architectural Development from Aurelian to Narses.* Oxford: Clarendon Press 1930, as well as the many contributions by Lucos Cozza which remains of enormous interest.

[2] "*Addebant pulchrum nova moenia vultum audito perfecta recens rumore Getarum, profecitque opifex decori timor, et vice mira, quam pax intulerat, bello discussa senectus erexit subitas turres cunctosque coegit septem continuo colles iuvenescere muro*". Claudian chose these words to praise the work of Honorius, and to inform us of the existence of his improvements to Rome's imperial walls. CLAUDIAN *De Sexto Consulatu Honorii Augusti,* vv. 529-536.

[3] There were already galleries running along the top of walls at the time Honorius commissioned these alterations. First and foremost there were, of course, a few stretches of the Aurelian fortifications, but there were also the walls of Carthage, those of Perga in Pamphylia, the praetorian fortress in Rome, that of Alba, the exterior walls of Constantinople and the wall of Terracina.

[4] For a detailed study of the Honorian towers, particularly as regards the vaulted roofs over the upper rooms, see L. Cozza, 'Osservazioni sulle Mura Aureliane a Roma', *Analecta Romana Instituti Danici*, 16. 1987, pp. 25-138 and P. Vitti, 'Tradizione romana e tradizione bizantina nelle tecniche costruttive delle volte fra V e VI secolo. Il caso delle Mura Aureliane', in *Archeologia dell'Architettura*, 18. 2013, pp. 88-113.

[5] The inscriptions on the gates of Porta Tiburtina, Porta Praenestina and Porta Portuensis, recording the Honorian alterations, state: "*Senatus popolusque Romanus imperatoribus caesaribus dominis nostris invictissimis principibus Arcadio et Honorio victoribus ac triomfatoribus semper augustis ob instauratos urbi aeternae muros portas ac turres egestis inmensis ruderibus ex suggestione viri clarissimi et inlustris comitis et magistri utriusque militiae Stilichonis ad perpetuitatem nominis eorum simulacra constituit* ...", C.I.L. VI, nn. 1188-90. The text attributes the restoration of the walls, gates and towers and the removal of an enormous amount of material, that had probably accumulated in the moat built by Maxentius, to the Senate and the People of Rome.

[6] R. Marta, *Tecnica Costruttiva a Roma nel Medioevo*. Rome: Kappa, 1989. p. 31.

[7] T.L. Heres, *Paries. A Proposal for Dating System of Late-atique Masonry Structures in Rome and Ostia.* Amsterdam: Rodopi, 1983. p. 48

[8] Richmond, *op cit*, p. 69, fn1.

[9] A. Ceccherelli, *Museo delle Mura*. Milano: Electa, 2007. p. 922.

[10] L. Cozza, 'Mura di Roma dalla Porta Pinciana alla Salaria', *Analecta Romana Instituti Danici*, 21. 1993, p. 101.

[11] Richmond, *op cit*, p. 69, fn3.

[12] Marta, *op cit*, p. 18, fn6.

[13] P. Galletti, 'Le tecniche costruttive fra VI e X secolo' p. 471 in R. Francovich, G. Noyé (Ed.), *La Storia dell'Alto Medioevo Italiano (VI-X secolo) alla Luce dell'Archeologia*, Florence: All'insegna del Giglio, 1994. On the probable closure of the brick-kilns in Rome and Lazio see P. Arthur, D. Whitehouse, 'Appunti sulla produzione laterizia nell'Italia centro-meridionale tra VI e XII secolo', *Archeologia Medievale*, 10, 1983, pp. 525-526.

The roofing system of the Tripartite Building at Hadrian's Villa, Tivoli (Italy)

Carla Maria Amici
Università del Salento, Lecce

The tendency to experiment with building design, which was typical of Roman architecture, is closely related to the experimentation that took place on-site, in the great building sites in the Late Roman Republic and Empire. There was an extremely close interaction between innovative spatial designs and the creation of the technical solutions needed to achieve them. From this point of view, a situation that was highly conducive to the development of new construction devices came about in Hadrian's Villa in Tivoli, Italy, the residence that Emperor Hadrian had built in the second quarter of the second century AD. Careful analysis shows that this was actually a gigantic building site that never stopped working. One particularly interesting case can be seen in the flat roofing system created for the three large rooms, between the Three Exedras and the so-called Stadium in Hadrian's Villa, known as the Tripartite Building[1] (Fig. 1).

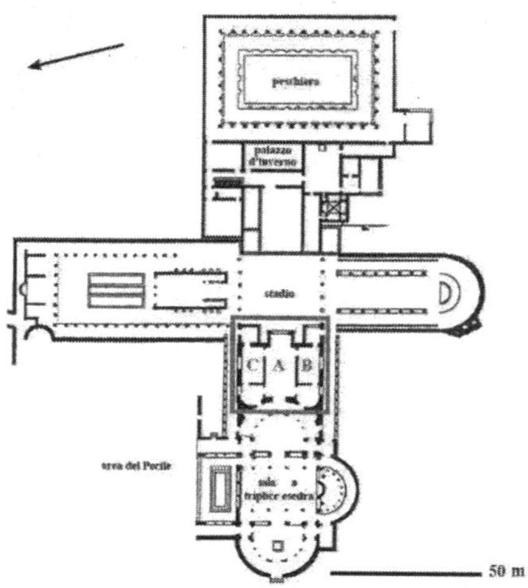

Figure 1 Tivoli, Hadrian's Villa. Layout of the complex called the Tripartite Building. A, B and C indicate the three rooms of the building with flat slab roofing. (from Salza Prini Ricotti 2001, with modifications).

The rooms measure about 16.20 x 6.88, 16.20 x 8.98, and 16.20 x 6.92 respectively, and their perimeter walls are 0.60 m thick, preserved to a height of about 8 m. On what is now the indoor floor level, which generally coincides with the original floor in *opus sectile*, there are many large fragments of *opus caementicium* paving slabs, with layers of *opus spicatum* and *cocciopesto*, and mosaic flooring between 55 and 77 cm thick, belonging to a flat floor (Fig. 2).

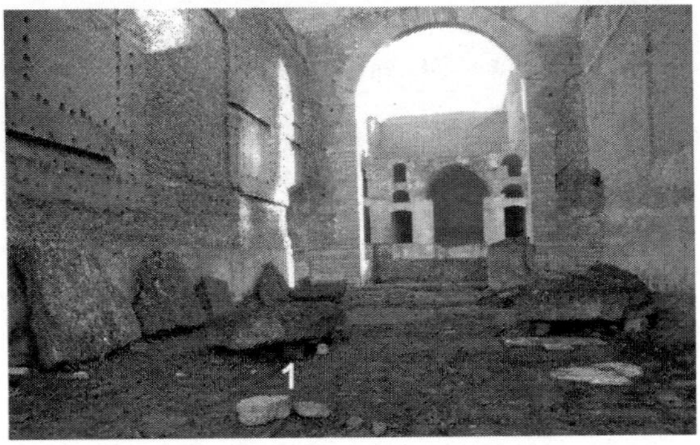

Figure 2 Tripartite Building, Room A; concrete slab fragments. The only fragment complete on three sides is marked with a ***1****.*

The limited breadth of the outer walls – about 60 cm – compared with the considerable thickness of the remaining floor slabs – about 70 cm – with their particular shape, has always been a problem for any convincing reconstruction of the roofing over these rooms. The fragments of concrete bear clear signs that they were cast in formworks, and were thus evidently modular slabs made on site. According to the currently accepted theory, proposed by E. Salza Prini Ricotti[2] and based on the only block with three sides that still remains, the 2.2-metre-wide blocks were placed up against each other until they covered the whole room. They were as long as the rooms they were in were wide, so about 7 metres in the two side rooms, and about 9 metres in the central one. They could be juxtaposed or superimposed in different ways on the vertical of the shared load-bearing walls, thus varying in size (Fig. 3). The construction system involved formwork measuring 2.2 m across and 7 to 9 m in length, depending on the size of the room. They were mounted on a "robust scaffolding" on which first the conglomerate was laid, and then a course of *opus spicatum* and one of *cocciopesto*, and finally the floor mosaic. Once the screed had taken hold, becoming almost monolithic, as the author describes it, the scaffolding was removed.

Without going into the precise calculations put forward to justify a solution of this type, even though expressing many doubts about the resistance to fracture in the central area of a concrete beam of this size, with a free span of about 9 m and weighing about 15 tons, it is noted that this reconstruction is based solely on an interpretation of the impression left by planks on the vertical sides of the only block of conglomerate that has preserved its original three sides (Fig. 2, n. 1) and, presumably, on the evident lack of holes for floor beams at the top of the walls as they are today.

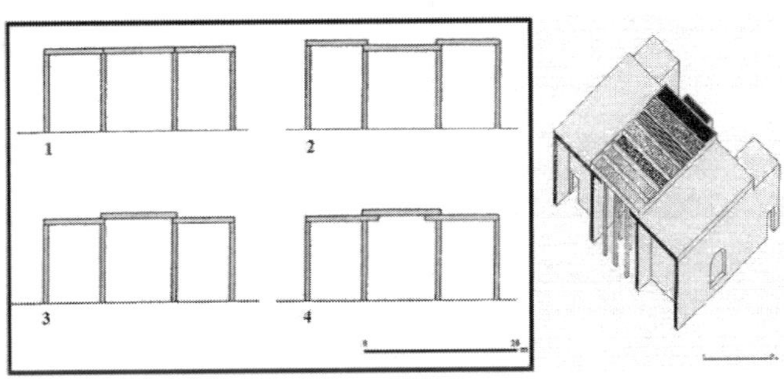

Figure 3 Alternative hypotheses for the positioning of the concrete slabs, with the construction scheme. (from Salza Prini Ricotti 1988, Figs. 12, 15).

Actually, on the surface of the smaller side of the slab it is possible to see the impressions left by the freestones of wall in reticulated work. These alternated with bands of brickwork, and constituted the facing of the outer walls (Fig. 4), against which at least this side was clearly cast. The horizontal trace was not caused by the joint between two formwork boards, but to the level where the opus spicatum was inserted, marking the overlapping of two layers.

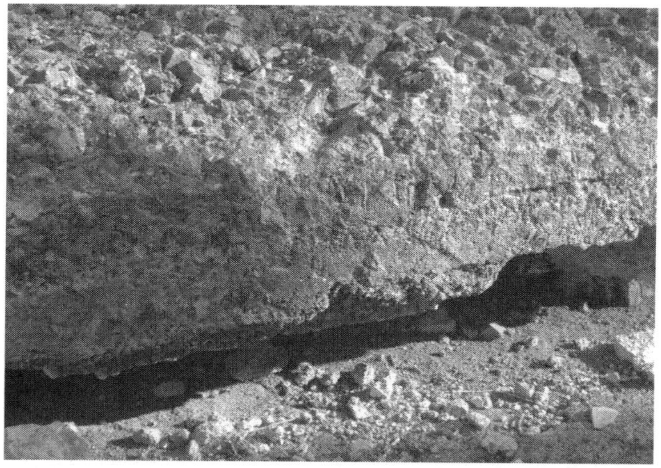

Figure 4 The wall of the shorter side of slab 1, Room A, which turned over when it collapsed; the impressions of the freestones of reticulated work against which the screed was cast can be seen in the negative.

This therefore rules out any self-supporting prefabricated elements resting on the top of the outer walls; it would be far more realistic to suggest an innovative system of constructing a traditional flat covering, built up in portions in formworks resting on a flat wooden support.

The outer walls of the long sides of the complex have been preserved up to a maximum height of about 8.50 m from the current floor level. The end walls of Rooms B and C, facing towards the Stadium, have been partially preserved, up to a maximum height of about 10 m. On the outer side of the end wall of the larger room, A, it is still possible to see the remains of the cornice, in *imbrices* and *tegulae,* that underscored the architectural design on the Stadium side, at a height of about 9.9 m. It is therefore possible to suggest robust flat ceilings, connected at right angles to the longitudinal walls of the three rooms. Their height in the side rooms was probably different from that of the wider central room, in order to create a balanced architectural design, the style of which can be hypothesised on the basis of many examples to be found in the vertical remains of the Villa.

Once these roofs were built, sectional formworks were placed on them, so that, even though they needed to ensure adequate contraction for the various layers of floor slabs, teams of workers could lay a number of casts at the same time. When these had contracted, the missing portions could be cast, after removing the timber formworks The width of the formwork, and thus of the individual elements of screed, is hypothetically calculated on the basis of the one remaining slab that still has three contiguous sides, which measures 2.2 m, but other solutions are equally possible. Bed mortar was poured evenly onto the continuous floor thus obtained, and the mosaic created on it, thus sealing the floor and making it completely even (Fig. 5).

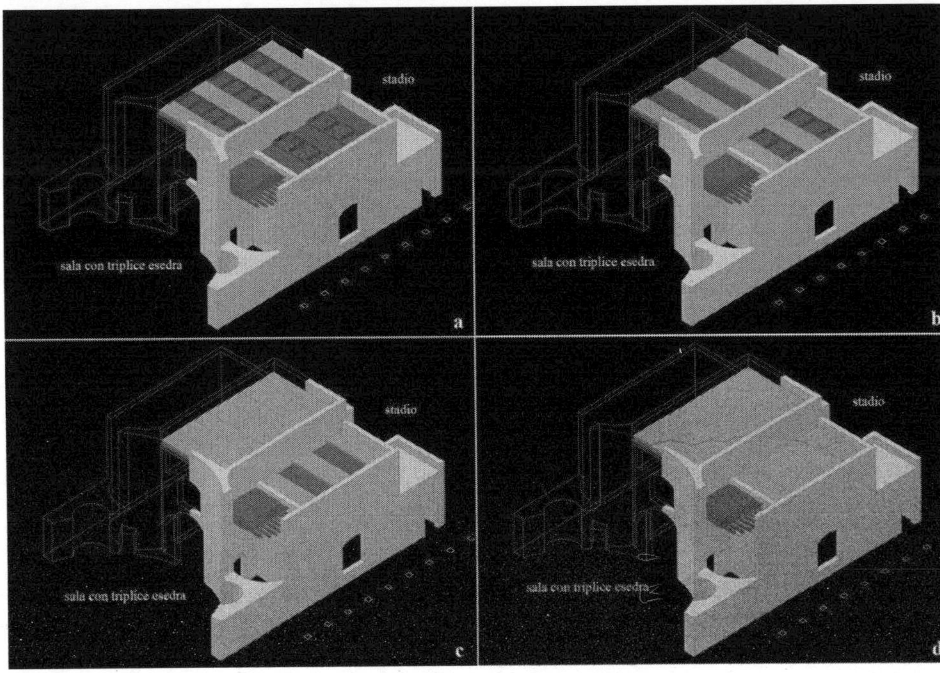

Figure 5 a-d, Reconstruction diagram showing the construction process using parallel formworks on the slab on the flat floor of the rooms in the Tripartite Building.

A detailed analysis of the fragments of the slabs in the three main rooms of the complex[3] gives us precise information about the structure and texture of the floor slabs, as well as data that can help in the reconstruction of the drainage system of the extradoses, of which there are now no traces in the outer walls.

The stratigraphy of the floor slabs is very similar in all the fragments examined. From the bottom up, there is a layer of conglomerate of pozzolanic mortar and aggregates of average size, mainly of fragments of clay, tufa and peperine stone (about 18-20 cm: *statuminatio*[4]); a layer of rough *cocciopesto* (about 15-18 cm: *rudus*)); a course of *opus spicatum* (about 5.4 cm); a further layer of *cocciopesto* (about 9-10 cm: *nucleus*); a layer of bed mortar for the mosaic (about 6 cm); fairly crude mosaic with white tesserae (about 4 cm); giving a total of about 56/63 cm. All the layers are extremely well-tamped and compact, clearly distinguishable one from the other, revealing a functional break between the casting of one layer and that of the next (Fig. 6). Overall, the estimated load per square meter is about 1 tonne, which would require a load-bearing floor with well-calibrated elements placed close together, perhaps resting on a longitudinal sleeper, even assuming that there is a certain coefficient of resistance to traction, once the mortar in the various layers had contracted.

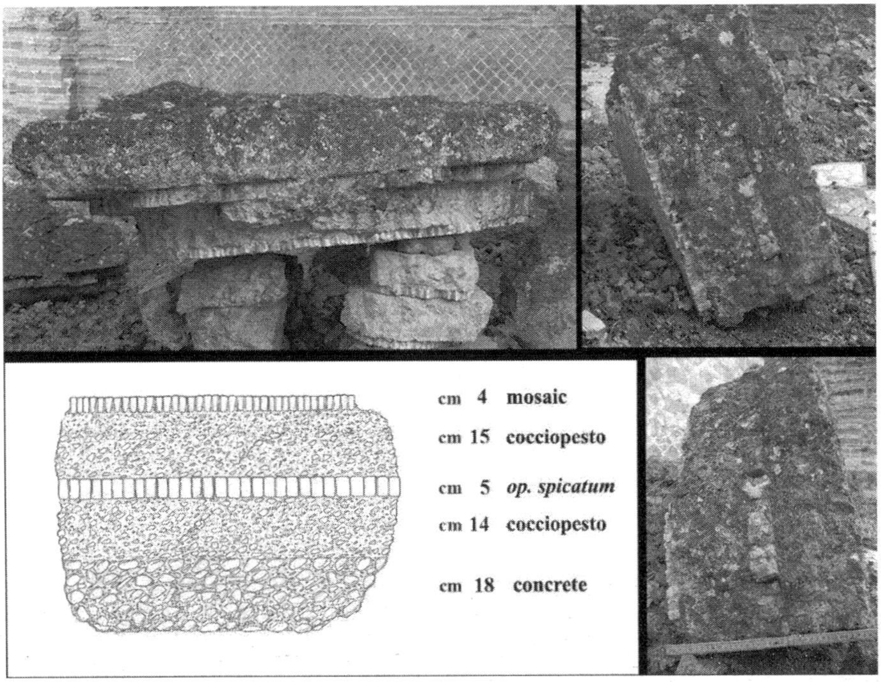

Figure 6 Fragments of floor slabs, broken into their horizontal layers upon collapse, and a schematic stratigraphy with the form and size of the individual layers.

The structure of this type of floor screed is the one typically found in the floors and terraces made for prominent buildings under Trajan and Hadrian, in which a layer of *opus spicatum* between two layers of *cocciopesto* ensures waterproofing, and prevents deformation due to settling and to the contraction of the mortar, while providing a resistant mesh that distributes the load of the upper layers uniformly. It became a standard construction technique, after solutions that were very similar, but applied and interpreted differently, had been tried out in the previous Augustan age[5]. The slabs did not necessarily have to be of the same size, but the length of the rooms, 16.2 m, was well suited for division into modules of about 2.20 m, considering that a formwork made of robust planks had to surround the castings of the initial portions of the floor screed (see fig. 5 a-d), and that the course of *opus spicatum* has differences of about 7 cm, which is the length of a brick in orthogonal projection. The repetitiveness of the measurements naturally made for faster work on the site, though changes could of course be made during construction.

In at least three of the slabs that have remained in place, the floor mosaic has been entirely or partially replaced by a layer of *cocciopesto*, of excellent quality, even though with bricks of considerable size. This is clearly a restoration of the terraced extrados, which was carried out on individual areas where the original waterproofing no longer proved sufficient or effective. Since in at least two of the cases examined the original location has been shown to be adjacent to one of the outer walls, it is likely that it was precisely the area where the vertical wall joined the horizontal floor that had created the greatest problems (Fig. 7).

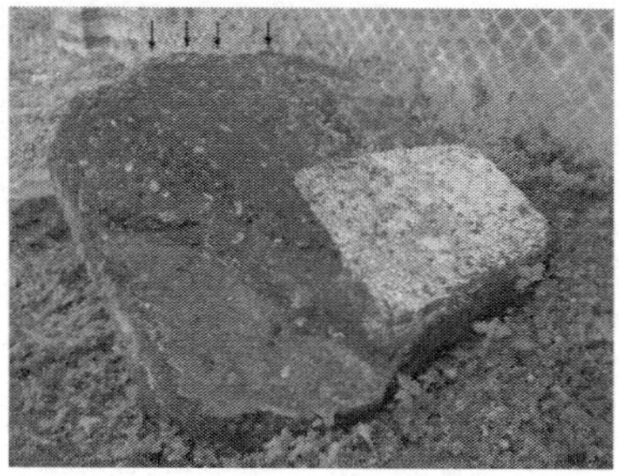

Figure 7 Slab with remains of the original white mosaic paving, restored with a layer of cocciopesto. The arrows indicate the strip that protected the band of contact between the horizontal plane and the outer wall.

The band of contact between the original mosaic and the new layer of *cocciopesto* is particularly precise, with excellent interpenetration, itself powerfully compacted in order to ensure perfect adherence to the layer below. Analysis of the mortar that forms the binder in the *cocciopesto* used for restoration (B) and of the *cocciopesto* that forms the layer below the mosaic, and thus of the original construction (A), has shown that both use a pozzolanic impasto of excellent quality. They are compact, well blended, with a high degree of hardness and excellent hydraulic properties due to the high concentration of $Al2O3$, $SiO2$ and $Fe2O3$, even though they are very different. In sample B, the hydraulic components are present in a significantly higher percentage, equal to that given by limestone, thus demonstrating excellent mastery of the processing techniques and dosing required for this particular purpose.

Restoration work was carried out here and there, only redoing the floor in places where it was damaged. It is possible that the mosaic floor of the terraced extradoses in the Tripartite Building, may have been preserved, even though with *cocciopesto* patches, so as not to spoil the view that one would have had from the complex above – the so-called Winter Palace – which was quite probably the emperor's apartment.

The analysis of a block that fragmented on collapse in the north-eastern corner of Room B provides precise information on the waste water system, which has apparently left no traces on the outer walls. The slab, which now measures about 120 x 130 cm, has two sides, at right angles that match the corner of the room. One of these contains remains of the perimeter strip, and a floor mosaic with *cocciopesto* infills. In place of a sharp corner, the various layers that make up the floor screed contain impressions and remains of 6-8-mm-thick lead sheathing, which formed the lining of a down-pipe made here in two segments, with one grafted into the other, about 26 cm in diameter (Fig. 8).[6]

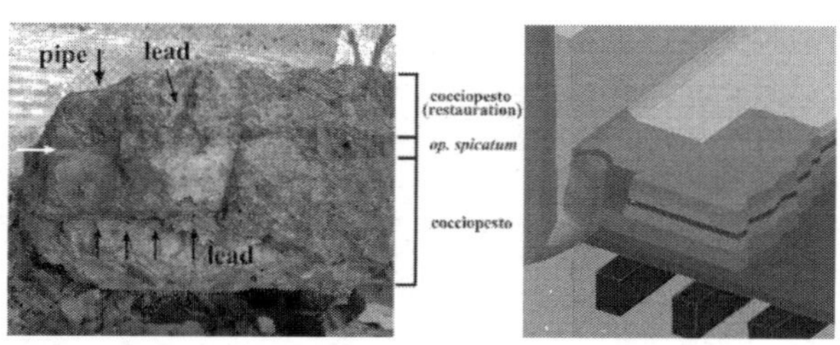

Figure 8 Edge of the slab and a restored view. The white arrow indicates the level where the top segment of the tube was inserted, corresponding to that of the opus spicatum.

The layer of *cocciopesto* that forms part of the floor of the extrados is restoration work, replacing the original floor mosaic (see Fig. 7). Despite the precautions that had been taken, there had evidently been leaks at the point of collection and drainage of the rainwater, and it is also possible that the end segment of the pipe was replaced, while the lead lining was restored.

Despite the presence of the connector, there is no trace of the down-pipe in the elevation that remains between Room A and Room B; this means that the water had to be discharged high up, on the outside. Dimensioned reliefs made by Hoffmann [7]– after the Stadium area next to the Tripartite Building was thoroughly cleaned – make it possible to reconstruct the original layout of the sewer system, which was later subjected to changes, additions and bypasses, which are often difficult to interpret.

On the basis of the data collected, it is possible to reconstruct the rainwater drainage system of the Tripartite Building, which brought together water from the extrados of Room A, with its double incline, into the ducts of the rooms B and C, and from there to the exterior. The drainage was either free, through a shaped drip channel, or through an external down-pipe set against the outer wall. In both cases, the water was collected and disposed of in the sewer pipe of the Stadium courtyard (Figs 9-10). It is no coincidence that, considering its position in the visual prospect and for people passing through, the large niche with large windows in the rectangular apse at the end of Room A was the architectural center of attraction of the whole complex. As a result, it was fitted all the way round on the outside with marble skirting, to insulate it from moisture.

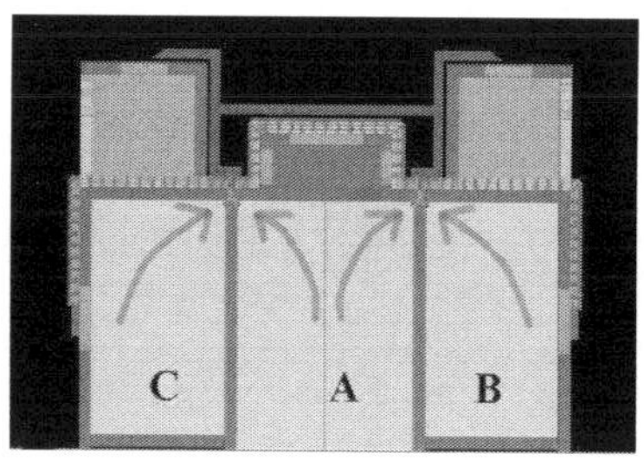

Figure 9. Planimetric reconstruction of the drainage system for rooms A, B and C of the Tripartite Building in relation to the layout of the sewer in the Stadium courtyard.

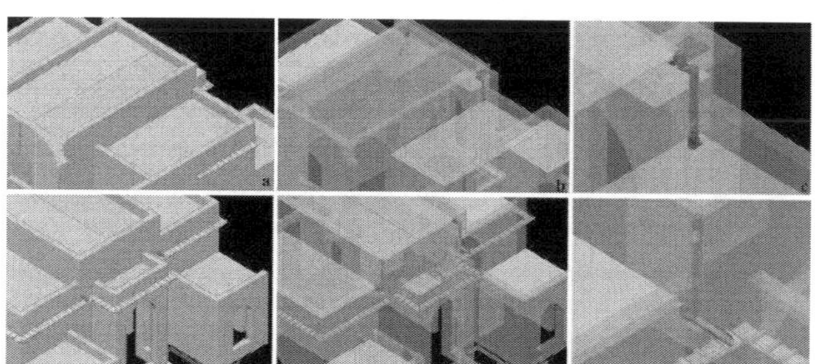

Figure 10 a-c. Axonometric reconstruction, from the southwest and southeast, of the inlets and drainage pipes on the terraced extradoses of rooms A, B and C, with details of the pipe layout.

The system adopted to create the terraced extrados of the Tripartite Building has not, so far as we know, been documented elsewhere, and it is unparalleled in terms of Roman construction techniques. It has all the characteristics of a building-site solution, put into practice in order to reduce the time required to build a floor that was challenging in terms of both shape and size, in a building that, considering its position and architectural features, was probably of key importance in a palace complex of unified design, of which it was an integral, if not essential part.

The division of the concrete floor into sections reduces the risk of cracks caused by the contraction of the mortar, but one critical aspect that is inherent in the waterproofing system should not be underestimated: the inevitable joints between the blocks meant that there was a clean vertical break, filled in only by the uniform layer of the mosaic flooring. The mortar and actual mosaic of the latter was about 10 cm thick and it was highly likely to crack along the lines between the blocks of conglomerate below if these were not placed in an absolutely uniform manner. It is no coincidence that the extrados of all three rooms were restored with *cocciopesto*, which was not superimposed, as is usually the case, but rather replaced the previous flooring. This was a much more expensive process but it made it possible to introduce suitable measures also for the extrados and for the joints between the modules below.

Ultimately, this device required strict management of timing and of the spaces, good coordination of all those involved, and careful, perfectly calibrated and uniform use of the materials. This clearly did not bring sufficient benefits for it to be adopted elsewhere, even though it is, to some extent, of disconcerting modernity.

Notes and References

[1] These rooms are part of a reception complex, next to the so-called Winter Palace, which is characterised by its unified but complex, innovative and sophisticated architectural design and its extremely elegant and sumptuous furnishings. The so-called Tripartite Building in particular has walls in *opus mixtum* of excellent quality, with unmistakable traces of wall cladding in marble, at least up to a considerable height, embellished with inserted bas-reliefs applied separately, and floors in opus sectile. See H. Kaehler, Hadrian und seine Villa bei Tivoli, Berlin 1950. pp. 55-68; M. De Franceschini, Villa Adriana. Mosaici, pavimenti, edifici, Rome 1991. pp. 211; E. Salza Prini Ricotti , Villa Adriana. Il sogno di un imperatore, Rome 2001. pp. 231-240.

[2] E. Salza Prini Ricotti, "Villa Adriana, un singolare solaio in piano in *opus caementicium*", Palladium, n.s. 1, 1988, pp. 11-16.

[3] The segments of slabs measuring at least 1.5 sq. m. were examined, giving a total of 33 elements, of which 11 in Room A, 9 in Room B and 13 in Room C. Other smaller fragments are however present.

[4] See Vitruvius, De Architectura, VII, 1, 5-6.

[5] Examples can be seen in the building that housed the College of the Augustales in Herculaneum, and, in the age of Domitian, in some floors of the Domus Augustana between the stadium and the Severan buildings.

[6] The lead remains had already been noticed and correctly attributed to the lining of a gargoyle by Salza Prini Ricotti, Eugenia (note2), p. 15, but without further details.

[7] A. Hoffmann, Das Gartenstadion in der Villa Hadriana, DAI, Mainz am Rhein 1980.

The Middle Ages

The Medieval bi-petal head nail

Chris How[1], Caroline Bolle[2], Jean-Marc Léotard[2], and Artur Lapins[3]

1. Warrnambool, Victoria, Australia; 2. Direction de Liege, Service de L'Archaeologie, Liege, Belgium; 3. Riga, Latvia

Introduction

Iron nails from the past two millennia are commonly found during European archaeological excavations. Most of the time, however, archaeologists pay little attention to these artefacts, which are often badly preserved and wrongly considered to be without significance, perhaps because of their supposed typological stability. In Belgium, for example, until quite recently interest in nails has been focussed mainly on the evolution of manufacturing techniques from the Industrial Revolution to the present day, together with their economic and social consequences[1],[2]. Consequently, as recently as 2014, a remarkable study was conducted on iron reinforcement used in the medieval roof frames of the Meuse basin, in which the nails received no attention [3].

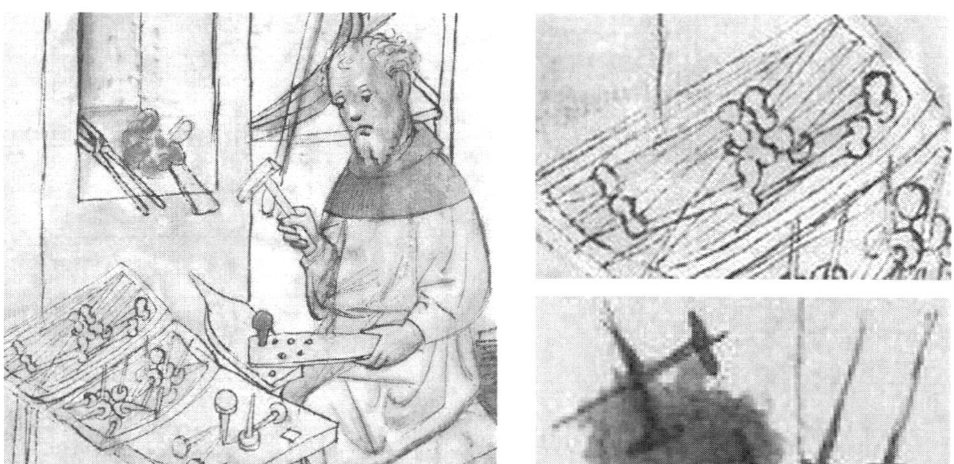

Figure 1. Top: Otto Nagler, 1425, making bi-petal heads from bar iron; tray of finished nails. Bottom right: Detail, Jorg Fluerrer, 1572, showing bi-petal heads and clasp nails. (Nuremberg Library)

However, a nail with an odd figure-of-eight - 'bi-petal' - head that features in a set of late medieval *Hausbuch* sketches in Nuremberg Library (Fig. 1) has shown-up in Liège in large numbers and in good condition during historic building examinations by the Walloon Region archaeologists. These fortuitous finds, together with examples from thirteenth century Riga and eighteenth century rural Latvia, can now help to put this sketch by an unknown artist into the context of the slow evolution of morphology of this type of nail. When a cut nail with similar characteristics appeared in England last year, what had first appeared to be an obsolete type began to emerge as one that had had a currency of at least seven centuries.

Generally, the paucity of medieval nail finds in identifiable condition sets up seemingly impassable obstacles to researching nails in Middle Ages building construction. In this case, however, the peculiar ground conditions in the Latvian capital and painstaking analysis by the Walloon Region archaeological team in Belgium have combined to allow this unusual find to relate part of the story of early nail development. This paper relates the story of the various finds and tentatively proposes a chronology of changes in use, reflecting the wide distribution of the bi-petal nail type. It also explores the probability of technological transfers or trading exchanges across Europe.

Methodology: Iron nails and building archaeology in the Walloon Region

One of the greatest challenges to this kind of study is the limited use of iron nails in medieval structures. In Wallonia, apart from churches and associated buildings, most structures were erected in oak using pegged joints. It is rare to discover well-preserved examples of historic nails, mainly because the structures in which they are found have been renewed or modified on various occasions. There is always a challenge in establishing a reliable chronological link between a mobile object, itself not datable, and its environment. Reliable discoveries require elements that belonged to one of the stages of a building process, or were clearly linked with it, and the absolute dating of at least one of these elements.

Thanks to the development of dendrochronology combined with accurate observations and an interdisciplinary approach, involving historians, art historians, architects, engineers, geologists, tradesmen and so forth, many wooden structures have been accurately dated during the past twenty years. This provides us with the opportunity to date the associated nails by indirect means and thus arrive at an understanding of the specifics, characteristics and roles of these iron items. To find that we had colleagues in Latvia , Britain and Australia who were carrying out similar research came as a pleasant surprise.

The bi-petal head nail

A set of sketches in Nuremberg Library provides some interesting insights into medieval wrought nail production, and a careful search of the sketches reveals two particular nail forms that are distinctive and offered some dating potential. These are the clasp nail and a curious nail with two protruding head lobes, which the authors have designated the 'bi-petal head'. This latter type, which shows in the 1425 sketch by Otto Nagler [4], is the subject of this paper. (Fig. 1) During recent archaeological investigations, many examples of similar medieval nails have been found in Liège, and some from similar and later periods had already been recovered from in and around Riga in Latvia.

Discoveries in Liège

In 2002, a medieval building was found to exist behind the nineteenth- and twentieth-century facades of two houses, Nos. 9 and 10 Emile-Dupont Square. Following detailed research, it was confirmed that the medieval structure had been part of the former infirmary of the Benedictine Abbey of Saint James. Its locality, characteristics, homogeneity and superior construction all supported this conclusion [5].

Despite a plethora of well-preserved wooden medieval structures (roof timbers, beams, timber frame walls, etc.), no metallic elements whatsoever were found in the eastern part of the original building. However, several nails were discovered in its western part, each being of bi-petal head type. These were situated in a vaulted panelled room which, from its context and by analogy with other Benedictine and Cistercian infirmaries, may have been a *dormitorium* for sick monks. (Fig. 2)

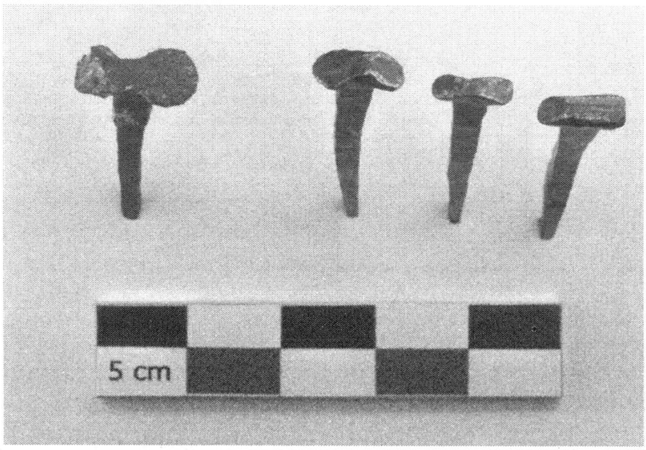

Figure 2. Liège, bi-petal head lining board nails. Left: A nail from infirmary of St James' Abbey. Right: 3 nails from Beaurepart Abbey. (Photo: Jean-Marc Léotard. SPW-DGO4)

This room, of about 8.5m in length, width and height, was delineated by two moulded and decorated peripheral trusses. (Fig. 3) Wooden panelling had been nailed to ten intermediate rafters whose visible portions were moulded and polychromatic; moreover, those bearing the linings (the main rafters, angle braces and lierne) were decorated with circular or square sculpted and painted wooden flowers (rosettes). Bi-petal head nails had been used to fix the lining boards to the rafters, and the rosettes to the trusses and to the lierne, and also for the floorboards. All the nails recovered have a similar form: the heads are comprised of two overflowing petals or lobes (in full bloom, larger than the shank in both directions) describing a figure-of-eight pattern. A section through the head shows that the base of the petals is almost flat; whilst at the top of the head, a very thin crest at the junction of the petals may sometimes be observed. The nails are of different lengths, related to the thickness of the elements secured. (Fig. 3, 1.1–1.3). Dendrochronological analyses of the roof frames yielded *a terminus post quem* of 1363–77. The timber framing walls sat on a wooden floor that was also fixed with bi-petal head nails and yielded a *terminus ante quem* of 1374–88. We concluded that these oak elements were contemporaneous with limestone façades characterised by windows with relieving mitre arches.

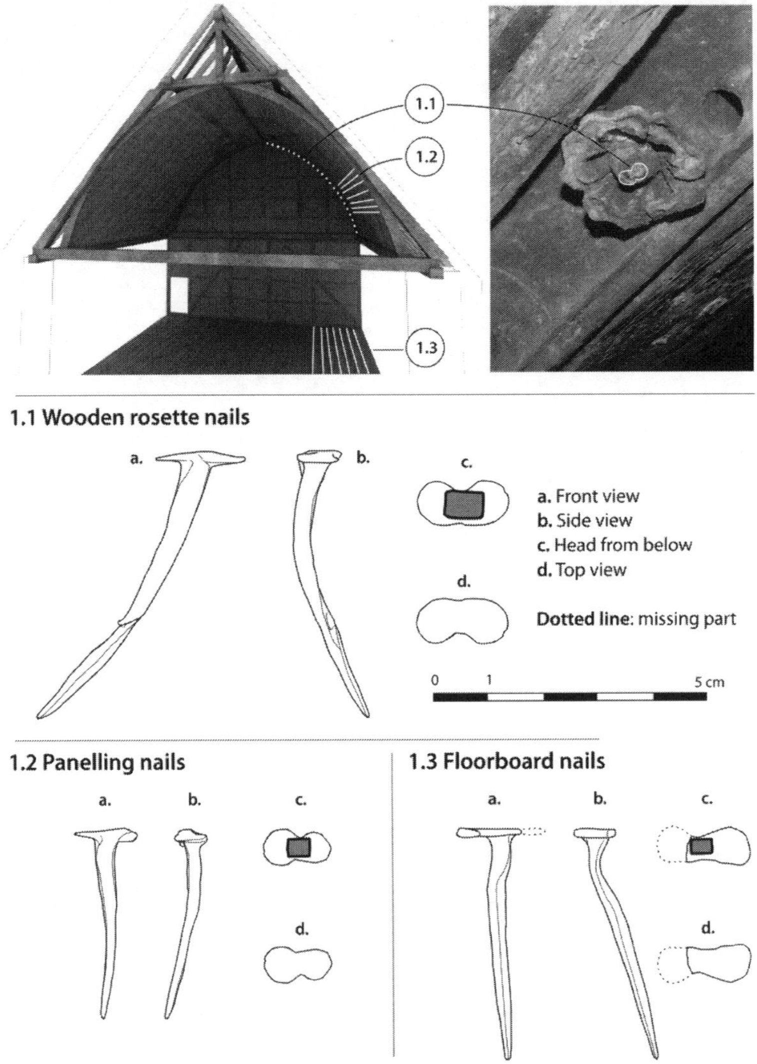

Figure 3. Model of 14th century dormitorium, St James Abbey; nail fixing rosette; 3 nails in room. (Modelling: Bolle & Silicium Lab; Photo: Geron; Surveys & infography: Lemaire. SPW-DGO4)

The discovery of this medieval building was deeply significant as it represents one of the few to have escaped the 1468 sack of Liège ordered by Charles the Bold, Duke of Burgundy. The find encouraged further research on buildings with similar features, especially mitred windows. As a result, the medieval origins of former canonical and convent houses have been revealed, going back to the fourteenth and fifteenth centuries. In one of these buildings, the south wing of Beaurepart Abbey (currently the Bishop's residence), many bi-petal head nails have been found in the eastern part of the roof frame. Again, these had been used in a panelled room that probably had a specific function, on the basis of its east-facing orientation, elegant windows and current use as a chapel. In this instance, many of the lining boards were still in place. (Fig. 4). These boards were profiled from beech, a lightweight wood, and featured intersecting V-jointing; the oak rafters that they covered were dendro-dated to the first half of the fifteenth century. The lining boards were nailed at each end. Although less overflowing than those found in St James' infirmary, the heads of the nails are of the figure-of-eight shape, suggesting that a similar manufacturing process had been used. (Fig 4, 1) This type of nail seems to have been laterally constrained, parallel with the widest dimension of the shank section, giving to the head an irregular rectangular shape. (Fig. 4, 1.1–1.3) Additionally, the underside of the head petals is generally not flat, but shows a slope at the connection with the shank.

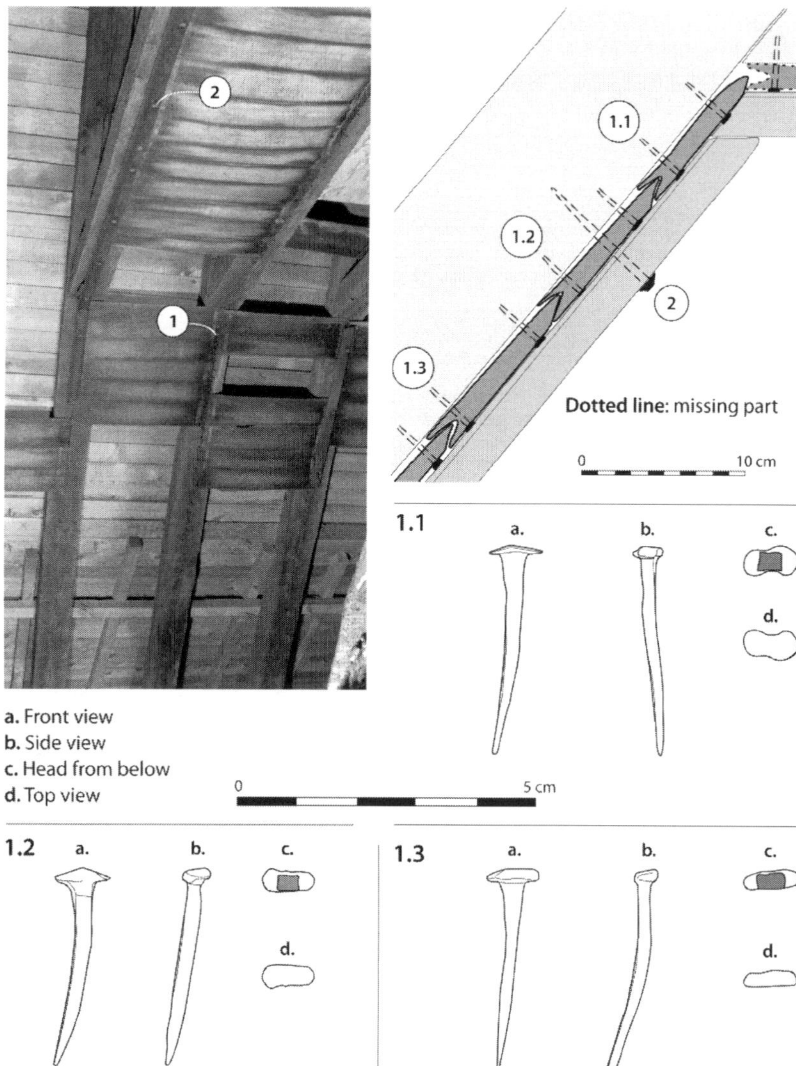

Figure 4. Panelled room, south wing, Beaurepart Abbey. (1) Bi-petal head nail cross-section. (2) Joint cover nail. (3) Bi-petal head nails. (Photo: Jean-Marc Léotard; Surveys: Caroline Bolle; Graphics: Jean-François Lemaire. SPW-DGO4)

Taken together, this information indicates the use of a specific technical process to standardise the head shapes. From this we conclude that the obore would have required a special hole shape, but this might be best determined by experiment. The lengths of all the nails found are rigorously the same, both in accuracy and standardisation.

A further type of nail was found on the same panelling at Beaurepart Abbey. These nails are larger and were used to fix the oak joint covers. (Fig. 4, 2) In this type the section of the shank is square, the shape of the head is approximately circular (or polygonal), its bottom is flat and the top forms a regular pyramid of four slopes with a flat summit. It is interesting to note that the two types of nails found in Beaurepart Abbey were contemporaneous and served different roles. It is clear that the bi-petal nails were not intended to be visible, so had to be as flat as possible; their shape is the result of technical necessity rather than aesthetics, while the pyramid form was visible and protruded.

The elongation of the head in both types of bi-petal head nail, at Saint James' and at Beaurepart Abbey, was created from the longest side of the shank, which necessarily has a rectangular section. In each case, the goal was probably to create a large area of contact with the fixed item, either at its surface or, more likely, inside, and simultaneously to achieve a nail head flush with the fixed item or slightly above its surface. For this reason, we conclude that our rare well-preserved examples were specifically used in decorative and boarding work.

Two further examples of bi-petal head nails were recently found on a rafter of the south wing of Saint Paul's cloister in Liège, dendro-dated to 1532–33. In this instance, the nails were on the upper surface of a piece of wood used to fix roof laths. As in the bishop's residence at Beaurepart Abbey, the petals are less overflowing, yet clearly present. The choice of nail and shape was obviously strictly practical.

A study of the dimensions of bi-petal head nails serves as another perspective. Thanks to the Walloon Region's building studies, we know a little about medieval metrology and it should be interesting to know whether nail makers used the same reference measurements. The main difficulty is to collect a sufficiently large sample of well-documented nails in a fairly good state of preservation. The discovery of a set of fifteen nails in Beaurepart Abbey has revealed significant standardisation of length (35 mm) with a narrow standard deviation (circa 0.5 mm), offering promising insights.

Discoveries in the Baltic

At the other end of central Europe, the buildings of present-day Latvia have been damaged in many wars, so nails of medieval origin are found only during archaeological excavations, rather than in standing buildings. Nails with intentionally flattened heads that date to the thirteenth to sixteenth centuries have been found in medieval castles in Riga, the capital, as well as in castles of various orders such as at Bauska, Salaspils, Selpils, Koknese and Aluksne. (Fig. 5)

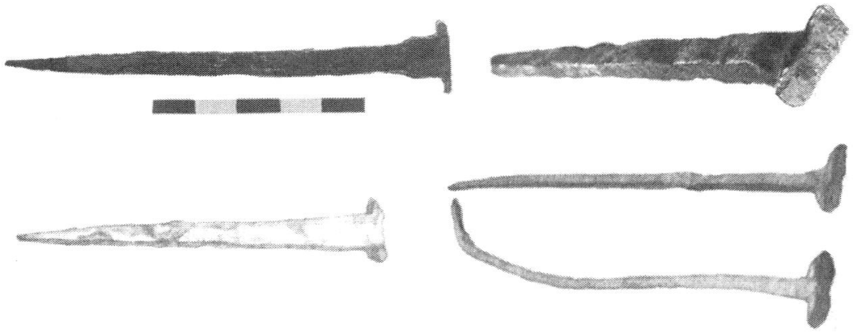

Figure 5. Two finds from Riga, circa 1200. Top: Nail from Liepaja Castle dig, circa 1600. Bottom: Two nails from Trakai Island Castle, circa 1600. (Photos: Arturs Lapins)

The development of Riga as a town from about 1160 is primarily associated with the Hanseatic League. During the early medieval period, settlers from Baltic Sea ports formed several enclaves of various Latvian groups. This left a legacy of north German framing (*Fachwerk*) and other artefacts. Being a port, Riga is a place where western European traditions have always been found, however it is a reasonable assumption that nail finds from the old city represent nailing techniques from areas mainly around north German ports, reflecting Saxon traditions and technology. Two significant finds have been archaeologically dated to 1180–1240 and 1250–1300, both in Marstalu Street, Riga. From these it is possible to see an early development of the bi-petal head nail. (Fig. 6) The same type of nail has been found during the excavations of Riga Castle. (Fig. 7)

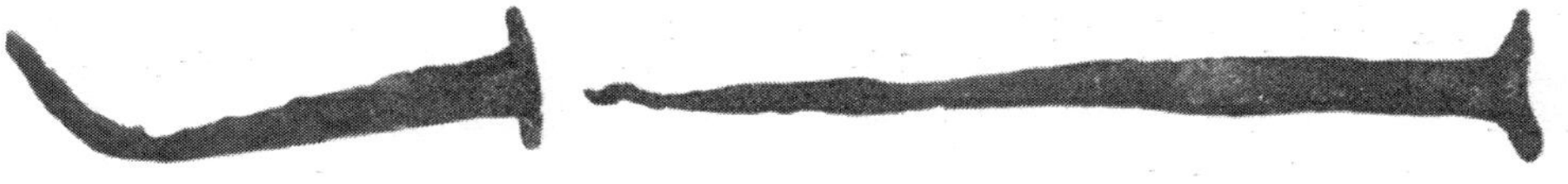

Figure 6. Turaida Church nail, circa 1600, and door nail from Adazu Basilica, circa 1700. (Photos: Arturs Lapins)

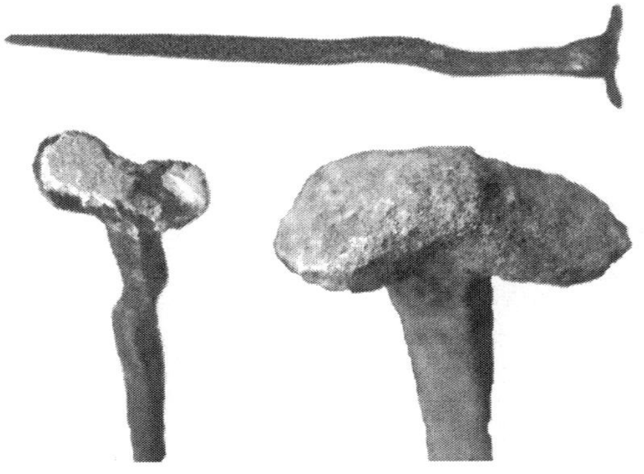

Figure 7. Top: Side view, bi-petal head. Riga Castle, circa 1780. Bottom left: Well-developed bi-petal lugs. Bottom right: Earlier, crested version, St Jacob's Tower, latter half 1700s. (Photos: How & Dirveiks)

The Medieval bi-petal head nail

A characteristic of Riga's medieval iron finds is their colour. Due to the specific properties of the local sandy soil, a rust-inhibiting phosphoric mineral known as vivianite is formed. When first excavated it is bright blue, but within a few hours it becomes grey and after several more hours it turns to powder. Accordingly, the term 'blue nails' has emerged to refer to the excavated artefacts, often still in recognisable condition.

Most of the finds near Riga indicate that bi-petal head nails were used alongside the more usual round-headed nails. It is not clear whether some heads were formed by the nailer during production or flattened just before driving into the wood. As can be seen in surviving later seventeenth- and eighteenth-century wooden items, local carpenters and joiners were not averse to leaving nail heads exposed; they are visible not only on the surface of basic construction components, such as rafters and joists, but also on floorboards, wall linings and door mouldings. Nevertheless bi-petal heads could be hidden more easily by sinking their heads into the wood grain.

Of the bi-petal head nails dating from the medieval period and a little later, a few have been found with ends shaped as rounded lozenges, similar to the Belgian samples, while others have squarer ends to the projecting lugs, as if deliberately squared off. Later samples tend to have marked side dimples and rounded lugs, essentially the same as those found in Belgium. It is not apparent how these lugs were forged but, for the main part, the shoulders beneath the heads are markedly square. A recent find from St Jacobs Tower, from the seventeenth century, provides a clue as to how the forging may have been done. (Fig. 7)

Purpose and prototypes

What was the purpose of this unusual bi-petal head? Our best guess is that it was akin to that of the clasp nail, but whereas clasp nails were provided with downward pointing 'wings' to grip the timber fibres, the bi-petal head reduced the risk of splitting the wood, and the lugs on either side were intended to close over any incipient cracks in the timber immediately under the head. This made it eminently suitable for use as a lath nail, and for linings and door panels. A fortuitous find of a late medieval nail from Esslingen, near Stuttgart, indicates that the bi-petal head was produced by first splitting the top of the shank and then the two 'wings' were peeled back. The hack iron incision mark is clearly visible in this specimen. (Fig. 8)

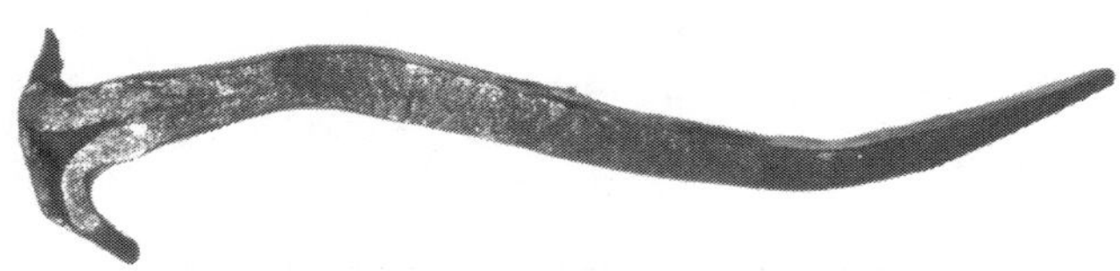

Figure 8. Clasp nail, circa 1420 to 1510, from Esslingen. (Photo: Chris How)

Nails similar to this include the 'strong' form of the clasp nail found in Britain, as described by Richard Neve in 1703 and studied in a previous paper [6]. Although the bi-petal head is a wrought nail type that was apparently never used in Britain, a cut form closely resembling it recently appeared in an assemblage dated to circa 1890. Research by Tools and Trades History Society member Mr Richard Jones has shown this to have been used in clog manufacture.

The linkages

Besides the bi-petal head nail type, a link between Latvia and Liège is evident in the preparation of the lining boards used in their buildings. Boards of similar size and with the same system of V-jointing to those at Beaurepart Abbey have been discovered in a 1740's manor house in central Latvia, yet made from rowan wood and not beech. (Fig. 9)

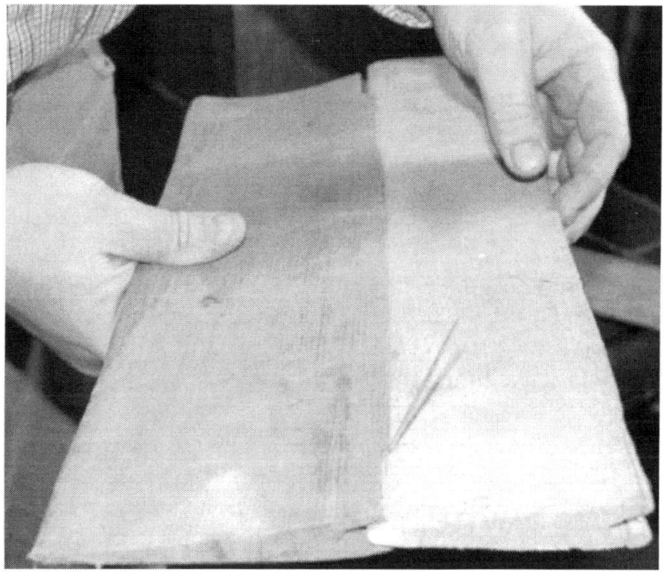

Figure 9. V-jointed lining boards from Tazu Muiza, central Latvia. (Photo: Chris How)

One reason why bi-petal head nails and V-jointed boards appear in both areas may be that Riga was linked with the north German ports of the Hanseatic League from 1241 until the end of the fifteenth century. Most of its rulers up to the Reformation were Catholic Archbishops from those areas, but one came from Vechten (Utrecht), in what is now north Holland, and another was from Auge, Normandy. There is even a direct link with Liège through Johannes von Walenrode, Archbishop of Riga 1393–1418, who went on to become Archbishop of Liège in May 1418 and died there the following year [7]. The expected German settlement linkage must therefore be seen in the context of a wider tradition of major constructions throughout Christendom, since the ecclesiastical rulers of both cities were prince-bishops.

Conclusions

This unusual type, the bi-petal head nail, has been shown to have been widely distributed in Europe, both in place and time. There is a tantalising possibility arising from the St Jacob's Tower find of 1560 that an earlier development of this type may have led to the design of a clasp form of head, since so far the earliest clasp nail finds have been from around 1500. The lucky finds of early medieval nails preserved in Riga's sandy ground suggest the start of this typology, and links between the German States and the Lowlands, add credibility to the idea that these nails followed a Low German pattern long before the modern states came into being.

The curious similarity between V-jointed lining boards could be pure coincidence or the long retention of a simple, medieval predecessor to the tongue and groove technique. We would ask that members of the Construction History Society involved with medieval buildings keep us informed of any chance finds reflecting either the use of the bi-petal head nail or similarly grooved lining boards.

Notes and references

[1] Hansotte, G., 'La clouterie liégeoise et la question ouvrière au XVIIIe siècle'. Brussels: *Editions de la librairie encyclopédique*, 1972.

[2] Hansotte, G., 'La métallurgie wallonne au XVIe et dans la première moitié du XVIIe siècle, essai de synthèse', *Bulletin de l'Institut Archéologique Liégeois*, LXXXIV, 1972, pp. 21–42.

[3] Maggi, C., 'Fers et bois dans les combles médiévaux et modernes du sud de la Belgique. Contribution à l'histoire de la construction en Europe occidentale' (Ph.D. thesis, Université de Liège, 2014).

[4] *Die Hausbücher der Nürnberger Zwolfbrüderstiftungen*, manuscript in Staatbibliotek Nürnberg, Ott Nagler, 1425.

[5] Bolle, C., Léotard, J-M., Coura, G., Charlier, J.L., & Henrard, D., 'Belgique/Liège/Liège. L'infirmerie de l'abbaye de Saint-Jacques' in C. Bolle, G. Coura & J.-M. Léotard (Eds) *The Archaeology of Buildings in Perspective: How to better understand, preserve and restore buildings,* **Études et Documents, Archéologie, 35**, 2014, pp. 366–69. (Namur)_

[6] How, C., 'The British cut clasp nail' in J. Campbell (Ed.), *Proceedings of the First Conference of the Construction History Society,* 2014, pp. 231–38. (Construction History Society)

[7] Archbishop Johann Walenrode, see http:// catholic-hierarchy.org/bishop/bwalenr (Consulted on 10 January 2016).

Wooden reinforcing chains in Spanish Medieval fortifications

Ignacio-Javier Gil-Crespo
Research Center "José Joaquín de Mora"-Cárdenas Foundation

Introduction

The walls of castles and fortresses have always played a key role: they had to resist not only mechanical actions, but also attacks with projectiles and battering rams. And so, to make them able to withstand attacks from enemies' walls had to be reinforced with internal wooden chains. This reinforcement also served to stabilise the walls in the event of a breach occurring, preventing them from collapsing and facilitating their fast reconstruction. The wooden reinforcing methods followed would be differ, depending on the technique used by builders to construct the walls. In rammed earth, formwork or masonry walls, branches and beams are laid inside the earth or the lime and rubble. In stone masonry walls and ashlar or brick walls, the wooden beams reinforce the internal filling. Authors such as Vitruvius or Philon of Byzantium had already referred to this *poliorcetic* building technique in ancient times. They recommended the use of wooden beams inside the walls to reinforce them; and it was during the Middle Ages that their recommendations were followed and fully applied.

Nowadays, we can still visit some Spanish Medieval fortifications in which the wooden reinforcement is clearly visible. The ruination of castles often reveals the building 'section' of the walls, and so, we can see the reinforcing system, study it and trace it. Usually, wood has rotted and fallen away through with time, and the only thing that remains is the imprint it has left on the wall mass. Despite this loss, there are some cases in which wood itself has been preserved, or the reinforcement design can be recorded.

Reinforced Walls Building Tradition: from Babylon to Medieval Europe

Commonly, walls are not just built with masonry or "hard" materials, but they are frequently reinforced with vegetable fibres: straw, branches or wooden square beams. The first aim of this reinforcement system was to help support the bricks and avoid shifts and movements while the mortar dried, and to make the wall one single unit but with a certain amount of elasticity, allowing the wall enough flexibility to settle without cracking.

However, it is one thing to improve the structural behaviour of masonry walls and control the movements and shifting due to the drying of mortar, the reinforcement of the walls using wooden chains embedded in the rubble or the masonry is different. In this case, the aim is then (also) to make the wall able to withstand external actions, i.e. the attack of a battering ram during a siege, for example.

Wall reinforcement using wooden ties is an ancient construction practice. In Mycenaean fortifications some wooden beams were embedded in the wall mass, giving the curtain wall "une sorte d'ossature" made by builders embedding transversal and longitudinal timber in the walls at different heights.[1] Wooden reinforcements were used in ancient Greek architecture, although not systematically, to increase the resistance of the walls against the battering of a ram and to reinforce the brick or ashlar masonries. [2]

Gaulish cities were surrounded by walls built with stone and earth masonry bonded by timber ties. In fact, a passage in Caesar's *De Bello Gallico* (Book 7, paragraph 23), describes the wall construction technique of the Gauls and adds: "it possesses great advantages as regards utility and the defence of cities; for the stone protects it from fire, and the wood from the battering ram, since it [the wood] being mortised in the inside with rows of beams, generally forty feet each in length, can neither be broken through nor torn asunder".

Ancient Greeks and Romans learnt from their conquests, they studied other people's constructions and developed the science of the poliorcetics and fortification. Philon of Byzantium wrote his treatise on fortifications and in it he offered some recommendations on the planning of fortresses, the nature of the ground onto which to build these fortresses and the size, form, elements and materials to be used in the construction of the walls so as to make them strong enough to stand a siege and to repel an attack of the enemy. He also recommended the face of the walls be built with stones or stones with salient bosses in the most exposed areas in view of an attack with siege engines: "timber ties of oak should be buried in the walls of both curtains and towers, the timber being placed end to end and forming horizontal chains at vertical intervals of 6 ft. The presence of these ties greatly facilitates the repair of any part of the wall which may be damaged".[3]

In Vitruvius's *De Architectura Libri Decem* (Book 1, chapter 5) we find some recommendations about the choice of the best place to build a city and the form, size and reinforcements needed in order to guarantee the solidness and strength of the defensive walls. Amongst other building items, Vitruvius suggests putting some charred olive wood "binding the two faces of the wall together like pins, to give it lasting endurance". For Vitruvius, olive wood is an almost ever-lasting material, which even when buried in the earth or immersed in water neither decays nor weathers and remains sound and useful. Notwithstanding the authority of Vitruvius, in the Spanish translation of his work made by Joseph Ortiz in 1787 an additional recommendation is given: "it will be a very dangerous mistake to put such long beams, with their extremes in the outer sides of the walls, as someone has drawn because they will be exposed to fire and surely collapse".

Byzantine builders learnt about the various aims of reinforced masonry (stone and brick) from Ancient Babylon and classical poliorcetics. First, the insertion of wooden chains allows for the stabilisation of the building during the first stages of construction, especially during the drying of the mortar. Second, this reinforcement balanced forces and trusses improving the seismic behaviour of the walls, arches and vaults. And third, the wooden chains reinforced the walls where external actions (such as warfare, the beating of the sea ...) were worse. This is the case, for example, of the monastery of Prinkipo (6-8th centuries), where there is an oak structure of 20x20 cm square beams that have been embedded in the mortar of the wall, at five regular intervals. Also the turrets of the walls of Constantinople were reinforced with wooden beams laid inside a brick structure.[4]

Commonly, Byzantine fortresses were built with a facing of stone and brick and a core of mortared rubble. To join the two materials and to keep them together, a system of wooden beams was usually set, a system which is still visible in Metabloe, Selifer, Susurkuk, the tower of Isaak Angelos in Constantinople and the castles of Achyraous and Lopadion built by the Kommeni.[5]

The works on construction and poliorcetics written by ancient authors such as Vitruvius, Vegetius and Philon of Byzantium became well known and highly respected by Medieval builders, especially since the 13th century. For instance, Amaury de Montfort built the castle of Houdan (Seine-et-Oise) between the years 1105 and 1137 following Vitruvius's recommendations on the layout of the keep, or Vegetius's ideas on the flanking towers built in the walls.[6] The descendants of Guillaume le Conquérant, the Plantagenet, dukes of Normandy, built most of the French castles in the 12th century. Guillaume le Roux, son of Guillaume le Conquérant, ordered the construction of the castle of Gisors (Eure). The builder was Robert de Bellême. The castle is located on an artificial mound 20 m high and it has a keep (20 m high and 25 m in diameter) and a surrounding chemise (70 m in diameter).[7] "A number of wooden beams are bedded in the rubble of the chemise to reinforce the cementing of the masonry; this also follows the principles recommended by Vitruvius (1, 5) and Philon of Byzantium (3, 3)".[8]

During the restoration works, Viollet-le-Duc observed that the walls of the castle of Coucy were built with a wooden chain in their internal part: "toute la maçonnerie était chaînée au moyen de longrines de bois de 0,20 à 0,30 m d'équarrissage, noyées dans l'épaisseur des murs, suivant la méthode encore en usage pendant le XIIe siècle. Au-dessus de la voûte du premier étage, ce chaînage se reliait à une enrayure également en bois".[9] Following Viollet, Choisy pointed out that "its use goes back to the most distant Ancient times, and it was for the same reasons: to distribute the effect of impacts during attacks".[10] The castle of Verclause was built around the year 1220 (experts have been able to date it using dendrochronology). A wooden chain with pieces 20-30 cm of section and joined together was laid inside the masonry. The chain was set at at least three different heights in the tower with bow-plan.[11]

Wooden Reinforcement in Spanish Medieval Castles

In the Middle Ages, from the 8th to the 15th centuries, the Crowns of Castile and Aragon were continuously enlarging their territories while re-conquering areas that belonged to the Muslim realms. And between the 12th and 15th centuries they were also fighting amongst themselves. Therefore, we can define this period as a latent state of war. Throughout these 800 years, numerous defensive constructions were built: watchtowers, city walls, castles, fortresses, fortified churches... Building techniques were various and some of them were in use for a long time while others were only specific to particular periods. For instance, stone masonry walls were built in every single period and always following, more or less, the same building principles, while formwork masonry is apparently specific to the 12th and 13th centuries, and rammed earth was mainly used in the palace-castles of the 14th and 15th centuries. This is the general rule; and of course there are exceptions to that rule. Rammed earth had been in use since the 10th-11th centuries and, very soon, builders learnt to use it to reinforce weak points in the walls, such as corners, that were usually built with stone masonry but without any ties. Many walls lost verticality and so builders began to put some wooden ties in the corners, as it can be seen in the castles of Autol, Arnedillo and Clavijo (La Rioja).[12]

Nevertheless, there is a construction invariant in all of these building techniques: walls were usually reinforced with wooden branches or beams embedded in the masonry, the rubble or the rammed earth. In some cases, these branches were only laid along the wall and in other cases a wooden chain was designed and built. The use of wooden chains was not only to horizontally reinforce and strengthen the wall, but they were also bracing systems to support turrets or echaugettes or to join corners and construction joints (i.e. between different materials).

The castle of Soliedra (Soria) was built on an ancient Muslim fortress —whose foundations still remain— and was still in use during the war between the Infante Alfonso de la Cerda and the Crown of Castile at the end of the 12th century: the Infante asserted his title to the Crown of Castile. Later on, the castle was intentionally destroyed. The building technique used in this castle was stone facing masonry filled with rubble. The corners were reinforced by laying various layers of wooden beams which are still visible today. There are four or five horizontal beams in each layer and, finally, two intervals of chains in the remaining sections of the tower (Fig. 1).

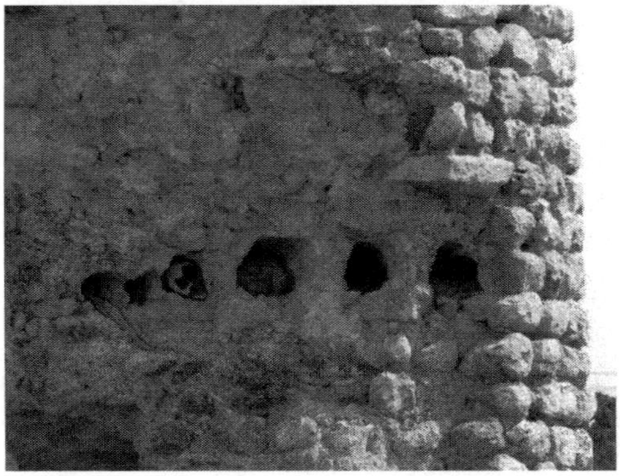

Figure 1. Wooden beams bedded in the rubble of the walls of the castle of Soliedra

Castles built with formwork masonry. 11th-13th centuries

With the conquest of Toledo in 1085 by King Alfonso VI, the Crown of Castile enlarged significantly its territory. Therefore, at this time many new towns and cities were built in the newly acquired territory so as to control —demographically, militarily and economically— the *extremaduras* (the southern bordering territories of the Christian kingdoms); new city walls, Romanesque churches and fortresses were also built. One of the most used building techniques was formwork masonry. This kind of technique allows express construction, durability and resistance against siege warfare, employing vernacular materials without needing to use previous and specialized works (as is the case with ashlar masonry).

Moreover, during the 12th and 13th centuries, the Crown of Castile was at war in different borders of the Iberian Peninsula. First, between the years 1118 and 1124 the Crown of Aragon conquered the Ebro valley and bumped into Castilian borders in the area that is today the province of Soria. Dynastic quarrels and a lack of definition of the borders ultimately resulted in a long-lasting war between the Crowns of Castile and Aragon until they finally reached peace and were united under one crown by the Catholic Monarchs by the end of the 15th century. Second, in 1157 Alfonso VII died and his kingdom was divided into the Crowns of Leon and Castile. In the year 1230 Ferdinand III, also called Saint Ferdinand, inherited the thrones of Castile and Leon and secured the permanent union of both crowns, but until then several wars were fought and borders had to be fortified and strengthened to withstand the enemies' attacks. Third, the Almoravid and Almohad Islamic Empires became strong in the Mediterranean and the Southern Iberian Peninsula after a period of weakness of the *taifa* kingdoms. The Battle of Las Navas de Tolosa (1212) allowed Castile to win over the Guadalquivir valley and conquer the cities of Cordoba and Seville. To round up this period in Spanish history, several civil wars occurred in Castile during this time. And throughout all this battling and fighting, building activity was strong, many new castles were constructed and the ancient ones rebuilt, restored or reinforced.

The complete process to build a wall with formwork masonry is as follows. The wall is founded on the bedrock. If not, then a stone foundation is built to avoid mines and underground attacks. Next various materials —rubble, pebbles, boulders... and lime—are poured into a wooden formwork. Once the operation is completed, the box is successively moved to the next stage. Walls are commonly 1.80-2.40 m wide. Finally, the last part of the wall is built, a thicker and intermittent area, which is where the wall-walk and the battlements were built. In the lower parts of the wall, when the slope of the ground would not allow builders to put the formwork in both faces, only the boards of the external face were set and the material was poured against the rock; that was the case, for example, of the walls built in the city of Segovia.[13] It was not always that the lateral formwork was erected, and so the joints into the "pouring-boxes" were sloped. The rammed earth construction technique is similar, but it differs in that the material is usually compacted and the face is a lime-crusted layer.

In both techniques the only connection between the successive boxes is by friction. Therefore, in order to brace the successive masonry boxes, it was very common to put wooden ties embedded in the rubble, in the low parts of the walls.

The border castles between Castile and Aragon of Peroniel del Campo and Soria still have these chains, or their imprint can still be seen. In both cases there are wooden beams 15x9 cm that were laid horizontally at each construction level (Fig. 2). The construction process was as follows: first, the fronts of the formwork were set and they were braced using needles made with a couple of thin branches. Builders then tied the vertical timber joining the boards of the formwork. Over the needles, the wooden chain was then laid to place and support them and, afterwards, the masonry was poured in the box.

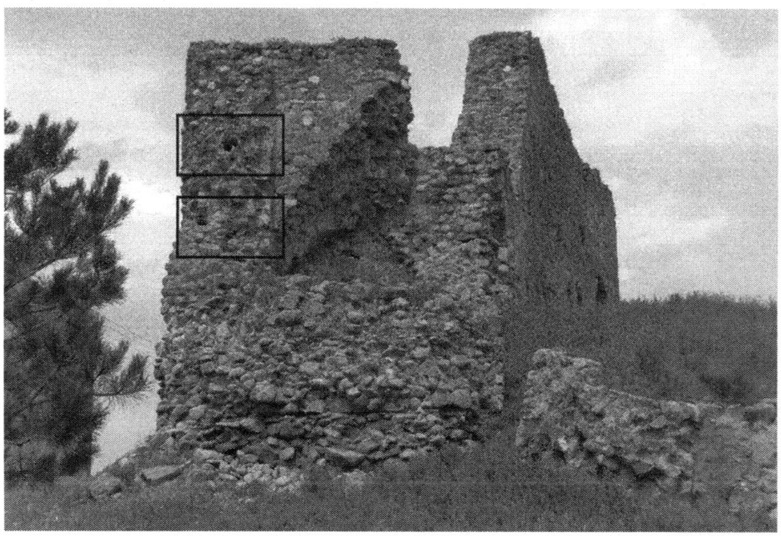

Figure 2. Tower of the gate of the castle of Peroniel del Campo, in where the wooden chains has been signed

Structurally speaking, in defensive architecture the main forces are perpendicular to the wall (projectiles, missiles, rams...) and they have to be resisted by the width of the wall and the internal ties and chains. The friction between two formwork masonry boxes is not always enough to resist the attack of a siege machine or the stones thrown by a trebuchet. This is why there is a wooden chain in the external border of the rubble. The medieval castle of Soria was demolished in the year 1813 —after the Peninsular War against the French— using powder and dynamite. The remains of the walls reveal that the force of the explosions displaced the Medieval formwork masonry boxes horizontally but the wooden chain provided resistance (Fig. 3).

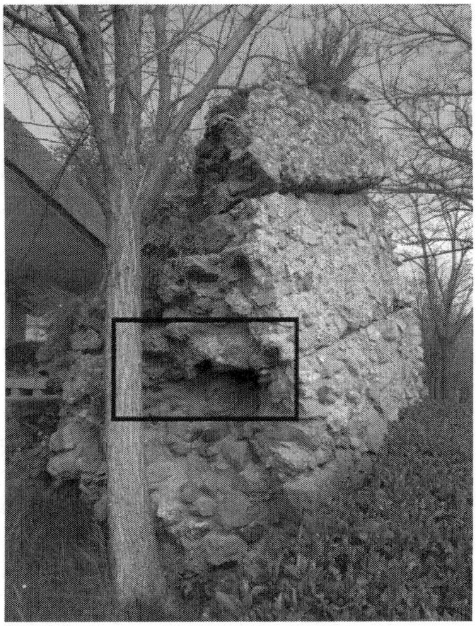

Figure 3. Negative of the wooden tie in the rests of the walls of Soria, after the explosions and demolition of 1813

The castle of Saldaña (Palencia) was built in the 11th century and was named after Juan Alfonso de Alburquerque who lived there in the 14th century. The building technique used in this castle was the same, with the difference that in this case the faces were built with ashlar. Each interval of formwork masonry was reinforced with two rows of wooden chains and, in the lower parts, the beams were connected with ties to the interior of the wall (Fig. 4).

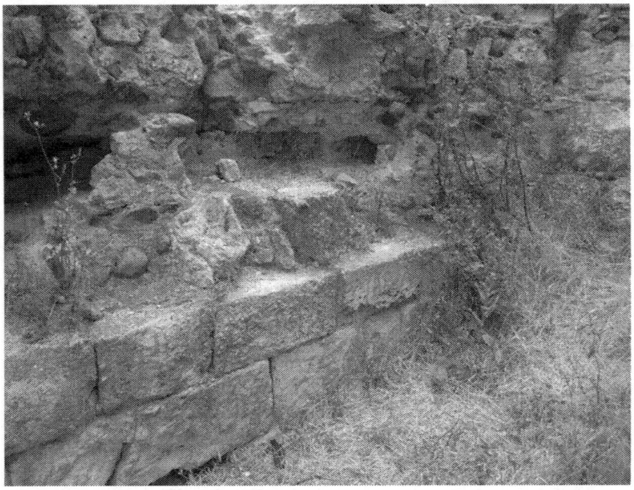

Figure 4. Hollow of the wooden chain placed in the rubble of the formworked masonry of the castle of Saldaña, visible when external ashlars have disappeared (generally, they have been stolen and reused in other constructions)

This system was also employed in other defensive buildings such as the tower of La Pica (Soria) or the castle of Turégano (Segovia). The most complex reinforced system is that of the external encincture of the castle of Turégano. The flanking towers are built with walls of formwork masonry of rubble, small stones and lime. The towers are filled with rammed earth all the way up to the wall-walk and parapet. The low part of some of the walls were reinforced with wooden chains of 20x20 cm square beams over which builders added other rectangular beams (about 5x15 cm) that join them with the internal fill of rammed earth. This system is completed with other vertical timbers (Fig. 5).

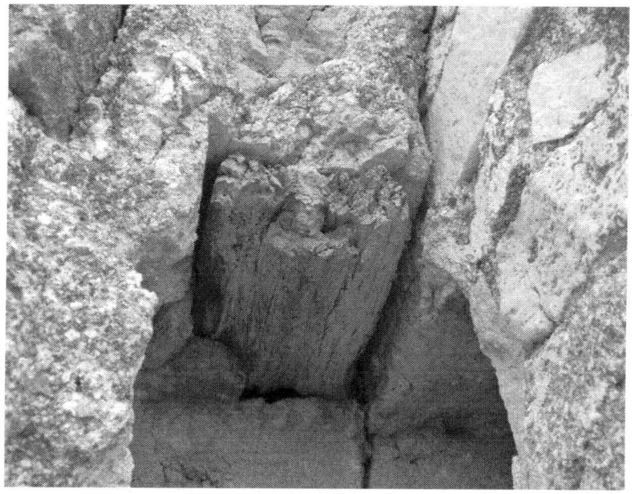

Figure 5. Negative laid by the wooden chains of the turrets of the outer walls of the castle of Turégano

Castles built with rammed earth. 14th and 15th centuries

After the Civil War of 1356-1369, also known as the War of the Two Pedros, the crown of Castile passed to the Trastámara Dynasty. They progressively transformed the lands of the Crown (public) into large private estates, on the one hand to free the Crown of the responsibilities of governing and to have a more effective control over the territories; but also to show their gratitude to the various noblemen that had stood by their side and had helped them during the wars. These new estates would see the building of several *alcázares* or castle-palaces.

Many of these castles were built using the lime-crusted rammed earth technique. The upper battlement and the parapet walk were built with stone and mortar for masonry that protects the top of the rammed earth walls from erosion. Late Medieval Christian Castilian fortifications have used rammed earth with only dry earth and a mix of earth and lime. The formwork used in these fortresses tends to be continuous, but there are many cases of closed boxes of formwork in which to ram the earth. Earth is the sole material in most cases, but there are masonries in which it is combined with brick in rows and buttresses.

As for the putlog holes, they tend to be placed in the immediately inferior constructive level and formed by the imprint of the putlog and placing stones over the beam. This system facilitates the extraction and later reuse of the beams. They usually have a rectangular section. This putlog system simplifies the bracing system used in Islamic construction which was based on half-beams, nails, wedges, Saint-Andrew crosses and rows which are abandoned inside the earth. In addition to simplifying the manufacture, the advantage of passant and rectangular putlogs is that they serve as scaffolding and can be reused as the building work progresses. Separation between the axis of the putlog holes tends to be constant in each castle because putlogs were reused constantly along the building construction.[14]

Another important constructive characteristic of Castilian rammed earth is that there is an internal reinforcement system. This system usually consists in a wooden chain that is placed inside the earth at the same time as the earth is rammed. This wooden reinforcement is also used in the corners, where logs are set at 45-degree angles between the two walls that meet at the corner. The ties are also set in the joint of elements with different materials or constructive elements, such as turrets.

The castles of Serón de Nágima (Soria) and Palenzuela (Palencia), although separated by more than 200 km, are similar in both size and typology. They were presumably built at the end of the 14th century or the beginning of the 15th century. Their walls are 2.70 m wide, equivalent to nine Castilian feet. Both castles have a square plan with towers in the corners: two in Serón and three —perhaps four— in Palenzuela. In the case of Serón, part of the north, part of the west and the south walls are preserved, as well as the low part of the southeast tower and part of the southwest tower. Walls have deteriorated immensely and parts of them have even collapsed. In the case of the castle of Palenzuela, the building preserves three of the possibly four corner towers it had and some parts of the curtains in between them.

Some beams of the perimeter wooden chain set along the walls are preserved in Palenzuela. With the collapse of the external layer of lime-crusted rammed earth, it is possible to see the wooden chain at every constructive level or, at least, the imprint it left. Branches are placed just underneath the putlogs, behind the lime-crusted external layer and parallel to the front of the wall. The chains seem —the ruins are in bad shape— to be continuous along the walls of the towers and especially in the corners (Fig. 6).

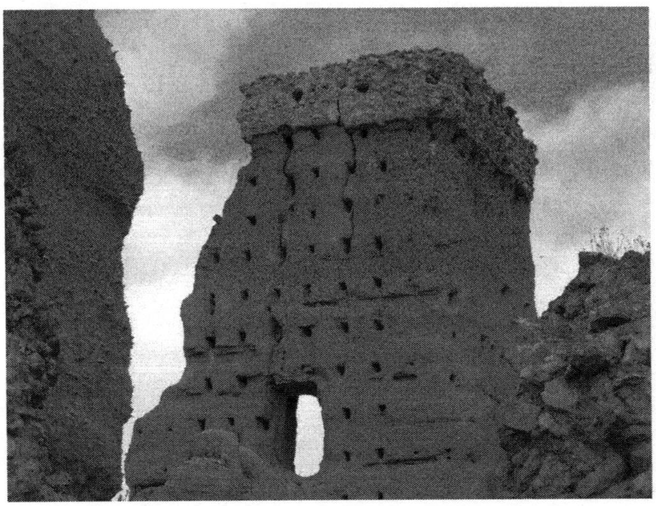

Figure 6. Tower of the castle of Palenzuela, where the wooden reinforcements of each rammed earth level are visible when the external lime crusted layer has disappeared

In the collapsed remains of Serón it is possible to see the "section" of the wall, and it reveals the use of a couple of wooden chains on each constructive level: the first is placed on the low part of the rammed earth layer and the second is set underneath the putlogs of the following level (Fig. 7). In addition to these wood elements, of which only the trace or the imprint inside the earth remains, other items have been found embedded inside the wall. They are wooden rough logs, about 8 to 10 cm in diameter. They appear mainly in the corners or in encounters between the castle walls. Perhaps their role was to lock the joint between perpendicular walls. After the March 2011 collapse, some rough logs have been found inside the ruins of the rammed earth and have been collected for laboratory analysis. The same system was used in the castle of Monreal de Ariza (Zaragoza), Aragon's border castle near Castile and very close to Serón (Fig. 8).

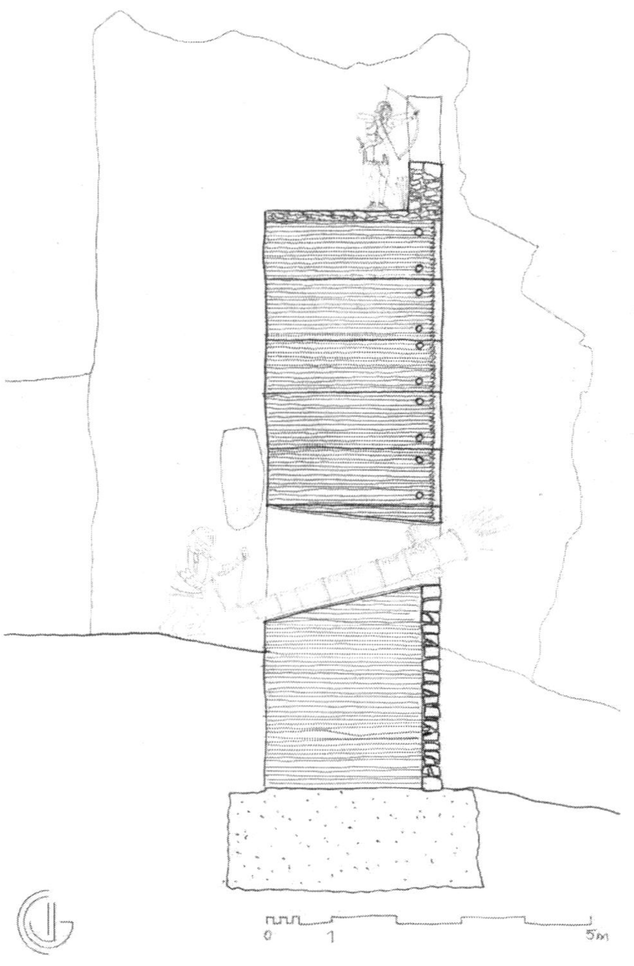

Figure 7. Section of the west wall of the castle of Serón de Nágima. First levels have an external layer of ashlars (they were stolen at the beginning of 20th century) and the upper levels have two wooden chains each one, placed behind the lime crusted external layer

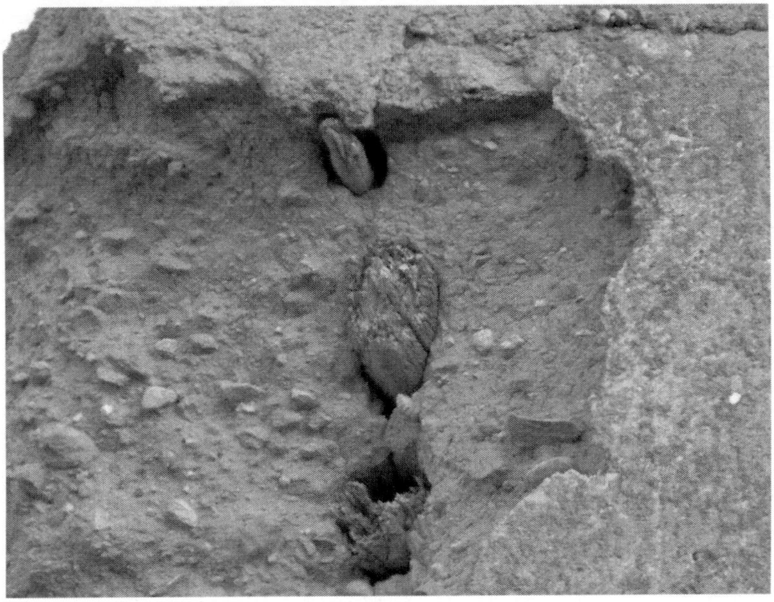

Figure 8. Some wooden beams placed inside the rammed earth walls of the castle of Monreal de Ariza

Finally, the castle of Fuentidueña de Tajo, near Madrid, shows the use of wooden ties to brace cantilevered turrets or echaugettes. Despite the information present in the first documents dating from the 12th century, the castle was restored and reused in the 14th and 15th centuries, when it was property of Don Álvaro de Luna, Constable of Castile. The current remains include a curtain and part of the 14-meter-high keep. The walls were built with rammed earth while the echaugettes were built with brick and stone masonry. In the inner part of the hedges of the keep there are some wooden pieces that are inside the masonry. The function of these wooden beams is to support and to reinforce the brick masonry of the cantilevered turrets in the keep's corners. There are two systems of wooden ties in the echaugettes. First, there are some wooden beams placed radially in the turrets. They seem to connect the external face of brick or masonry to the internal rubble. The second system ties the echaugettes to the rammed-earth walls by laying two or three parallel beams at every constructive level (Fig. 9).

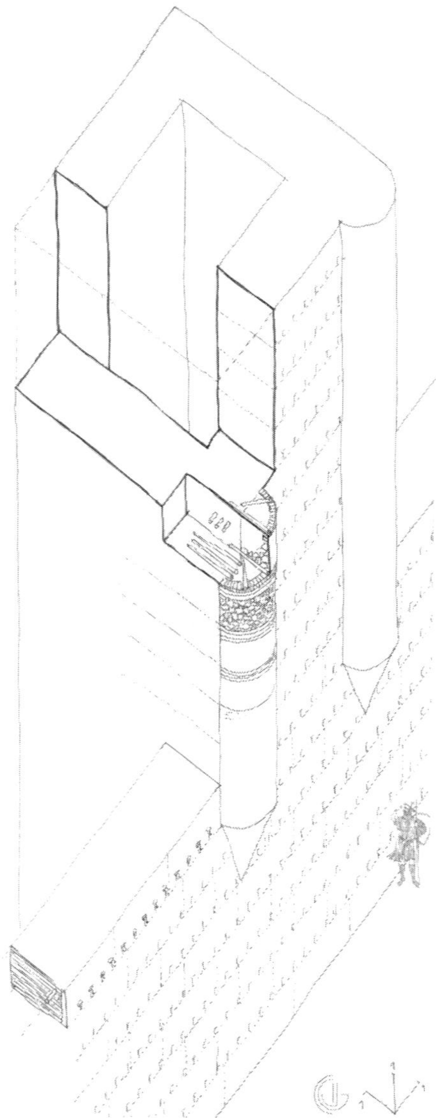

Figure 9. Axonometric analysis of the wooden ties for the echaugettes of the castle of Fuentidueña de Tajo

Conclusions

Historical architecture has been reinforced with vegetable fibres to achieve three main goals. The first one is to improve the flexibility of the masonry walls against movements, either seismic or, more commonly, due to mortar drying. The reinforcement of the beds of mortar between courses of bricks was born in Ancient Mesopotamia and Egypt and it is still been used today in traditional architecture. Byzantines reinforced their walls also to avoid cracks derived from the lack of volume when the mortar dries. The second function is to connect several parts of the building so as to distribute stress evenly, i.e. vaults and walls, or to connect different materials or volumes of the buildings as well the external layer with the rubble core of the wall or the cantilevered turrets with the walls. The latter is to give more resistance to the wall against external attacks. Military walls protect a secure enclosure against the external enemies who want to enter to occupy the city or the fortress by breaching the walls. When the wall is hit by a battering ram or a projectile, the internal reinforcement will distribute the bump and, in the case of the wall collapsing, will avoid the complete ruining of the whole building, holding the remains and facilitating quick reconstruction.

This poliorcetic technique was born in Mycenae and was used by the Greeks and the Romans (who learnt it also from the Gauls) and it became generalized during the Middle Ages —by influence of ancient books on architecture written by authors such as Philon of Byzantium, Vitruvius or Vegetius— to the point of constituting an accurate "wooden skeleton" for the masonry. Governors and builders followed their recommendations on the defence of fortresses and cities and used them systematically in every building technique and in every historical period.

References

[1] A. Choisy, *Histoire de l'Architecture*, Paris: Gauthier-Villars, 1899, vol. 1, pp. 227-228.

[2] R. Martin, *Manuel d'architecture grecque*, Paris: Picard, 1965, vol. 1: p. 32.

[3] Cited by: S. Toy, *Castles. Their construction and history,* New York: Dover, [1939] 1985, pp. 21-22.

[4] E. Mamboury, 'Le couvent byzantin de femmes à Prinkipo', *Échos d'Orient,* no. 19 (118), 1920, pp. 200-208.

[5] C. Foss, 'The defenses of Asia minor against the Turks', *Greek Orthodox Thological Review*, no. 27, 1982, pp. 145-205. C. Foss, 'Byzantine Malagina and the Lower Sangarius', *Anatolian Studies*, no. 40, 1990, pp. 161-183.

[6] F. Gébelin, *The châteaux of France,* New York: Putnam, 1964, p. 39

[7] J.P. Panouillé, *Les châteaux forts dans la France au Moyen Âge*, Lille-Rennes: Editions Ouest-France, 2015, pp. 9-10.

[8] Gébelin, *Châteaux,* (Note 6) p. 44.

[9] E.E. Viollet-le-Duc, *Essai sur l'architecture militaire au Moyen-âge*, Paris: Librairie d'Architecture de Bance, 1854, p. 98. E.E. Viollet-le-Duc, *Description du château de Coucy*, Paris: B. Bance, 1857.

[10] Choisy, *Histoire* (Note 1) p. 717.

[11] P. Bernardi, *Bâtir au Moyen Âge*, Paris: CNRS Editons, 2011, pp. 191-192. M.P. Estienne, 'Les chaînages de bois du donjon de Verclause (Drôme)' pp. 257-262 in J.M. Poisson, J.J. Schwien (Eds), Le Bois dans le Château de pierre au Moyen Âge. Actes du Colloque de Lons-le-Saunier, 23-25 octobre 1997, Besançon: Presses Universitaires Franc-Comtoises, Picard, 2003.

[12] B. Cabañero Subiza, 'Los castillos de La Rioja construidos frente al dominio del Islam. Notas sobre su origen', *Cuaderno de invesigación histórica Brocar*, no. 19, 1990, pp. 19-40.

[13] E. Herrero García, M.Á. Martín Blanco, 'Hipótesis del sistema constructivo de la muralla de la repoblación cristiana de la ciudad de Segovia', pp. 801-810, in S. Huerta and P. Fuentes (Eds), Actas del Noveno Congreso Nacional y Primer Congreso Internacional Hispanoamericano de Historia de la Construcción, Segovia, 13 – 17 de octubre de 2015, Madrid: Instituto Juan de Herrera, 2015.

[14] I.J. Gil-Crespo, 'Late medieval rammed earth technique in the fortifications of Castile, Spain', pp. 185-192, in B. Browen, D. Friedman, T. Leslie, J. Ochsendorf (Eds), Proceedings of the Fifth International Congress on Construction History, Chicago 3-7 June 2015, Chicago: Construction History Society of America, 2015.

Constructive similarities and differences in the walls in "*Comunidades de Villa y Tierra*" in the Diocese of Segovia, Spain

Alicia Sainz Esteban
University of Valladolid, Spain

Introduction

Historical context

From the eleventh to the thirteenth centuries, the Iberian Peninsula was immersed in the Reconquest. The Christian monarchs were trying to regain territory from the Islamic kingdoms using different strategies. In the eleventh century, the border between the Christian and Muslim kingdoms was situated on the line of the River Douro. To the south of this geographical limit was no-man's-land which was unpopulated for a long period of time (Fig. 1). The new, or repopulated, towns in this area were repeatedly attacked during the tenth century by the Moors, which forced the population to flee[1]. It was an unstable area, where the towns had little protection and were not safe, and where the control over the territory was not assured. The model used to advance to the north of the River Douro, repopulated through ecclesiastical interventions, or interventions by the nobility, was not working in this new territory, so a new and different focus was needed. The geography was also important in the conquest of this area: divided from east to west by the mountains of the '*Sistema Central*', a mountain range of approximately 600kms in length which formed an important obstacle.

Repopulaion started in 1072[2], further encouraged by the retaking of Toledo in 1085 by king Alfonso VI. The repopulation evolved into a network of new or repopulated towns that all had a similar structure and which extended from the River Douro to the River Tagus (Fig. 2). This network, called the *"Comunidades de Villa y Tierra"*, was made up of councils, geographically extense communities that had a principal town, the *"Villa"* and a subordinate territory, the *"Tierra"*, dotted with small villages. Some of these towns had very extensive territories, as in the cases of Salamanca, Segovia or Ávila, where the surface area was over 8,000 km^2. The principal towns of these councils had a centralising, administrative and military function. At the same time an important change was happening in the forms of territorial control, the system used to the north of the River Douro. Fortresses governed by Lords subject to the King, were replaced by fortress towns governed by councils, with a *tenente*, a mayor and a defensive wall in case of danger that even included the inhabitants of the surrounding villages. The model from the north of the Douro, with castles and towers spread around what had now become the territory of councils, although it had been functional in the frontier fighting, had now lost all sense with the appearance of councils. The delegation of power by the monarchs of Castile and of León to the councils led to the apparition of new social relationships, that is: "a set of rights that allow the councils to be defined as collective lordships".[3]

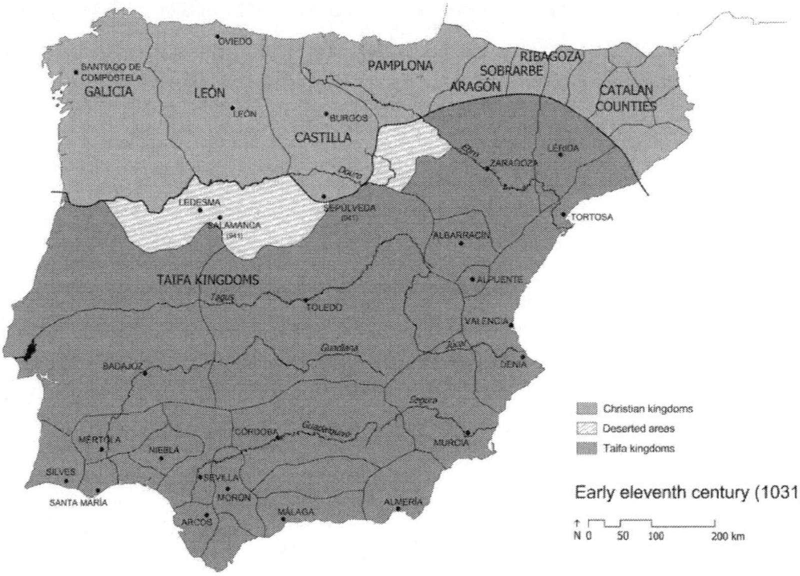

Fig. 1. Situation of the Iberian Peninsula in the eleventh century. (Own creation, according to J.L. Martín[4])

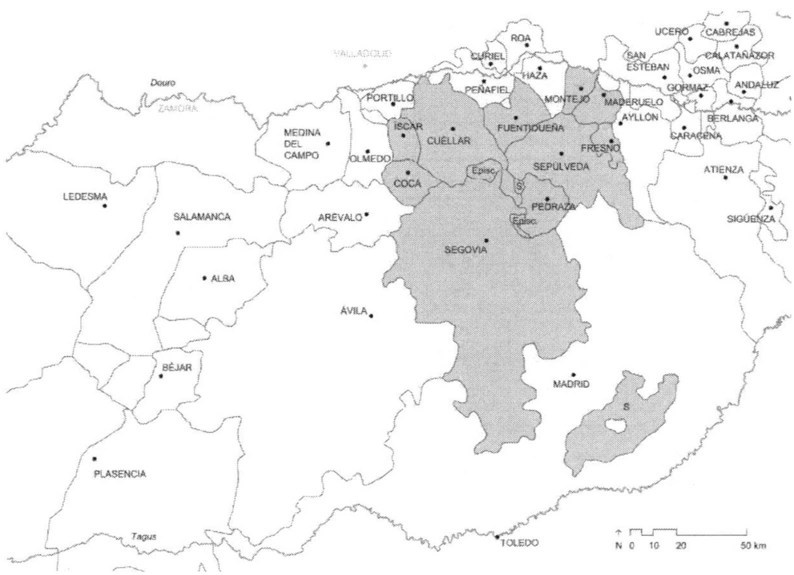

Fig. 2. Distribution of the 'Comunidades de Villa y Tierra', between the rivers Douro and Tagus. The shaded area corresponds to the territory under the influence of the Diocese of Segovia. (Own creation, according to G. Martínez[5])

The towns which were the seats of these councils were favoured from the legal point of view, as they possessed highly advantageous charters that had been written with the aim of attracting population to a deserted and unsafe territory.[6] The charter of Sepúlveda, dated 1076, set out highly beneficial rules for the inhabitants, who did not pay market taxes and where robbery or murder may not turn out to be too costly. These advantages attracted a population of very diverse origins who spontaneously came together, according to their origins, in districts that were organised into parishes. These factors gave rise to a very singular society that enjoyed a great deal of freedom and autonomywhich was unusual for the time[7]. There were also advantages from a political point of view because, although each town depended directly on the king, the government was greatly autonomous as well as having a participative nature, allowing the inhabitants of the town, and the surrounding villages, to participate in the decisions made by the council, at least in the early stages of the formation of this system[8].

The towns that formed the nucleus of each council were strongly protected by perimeter walls[9]. The villages, on the other hand, had no walls, but the people could go to the town at times of danger, even with their livestock. The town walls were usually extensive, covering a large surface area that enclosed not only the urban buildings, but also areas dedicated to pasture and cultivation. The walls currently conserved can act as witness to this; such is the case of Sepúlveda, with 50Ha of walled land. The aim of this study, which was part of my PhD, is to compare the walls of some of the towns in this network of councils, in particular those under the influence of the Diocese of Segovia. They are Fuentidueña, Cuéllar, Coca, Sepúlveda, Íscar, Pedraza, Montejo de la Vega de la Serrezuela, Fresno, Maderuelo and Segovia, all currently in the Province of Segovia, except for Íscar, which is in the Province of Valladolid.

State of conservation of the walls under study

The state of conservation of the walls is varied. Over the last few centuries, the town walls in Spain have mostly been demolished. Torres Balbás[10] explains how the walls were demolished because they were old, useless and in the way, and indicated that countless walls and gates were demolished in the first thirty years of the nineteenth century alone. Nowadays, the situation has changed, though cases of abandonment and destruction still occur due to a scarcity of economic resources or a lack of interest. Of the towns under study here, there are a few cases of ruined walls, such as Fuentidueña, where the walls still survive over a great part of their circumference, but in a state of progressive deterioration. In other cases, only some parts of the wall are abandoned or deteriorated. Some of these constructions have recently been restored, or partly reconstructed. Such is the case of Cuéllar, where, in 2007, the wall underwent a restoration that included the reconstruction of parts of the wall. It was done in two phases, the first including most of the wall and the second, focusing on the part of the wall between the *Torre de Santiago* and the *Plaza del Estudio*. This restoration included the building of new stretches of wall to complete it. The analysis of the original stretches of wall becomes more difficult after such a restoration has been done, as many interesting elements of construction are hidden. All the walls have had new buildings added on to stretches, hiding the wall as part of the construction, even making the doors and windows necessary for a house, modifying the wall's form with interventions and repairs. In some cases, as in that of Íscar, the town wall has not been conserved there is only the walled fifteenth century castle, but noextensive town walls similar to those of other towns. Some towns, such as Pedraza, have well conserved walls, although they are not complete. Coca conserves several stretches of wall that have been restored in several interventions.

Methodology

The methodology used in this study was mainly the direct analysis of existing structures. Fieldwork allowed the remaining defensive architecture to be analysed. The material to be worked on and analysed later was obtained through data acquisition *in situ*, taking measurements and photographs. The technique of orthophotography provided elevations to scale that allowed measurements and analysis at a later date (Fig. 3).

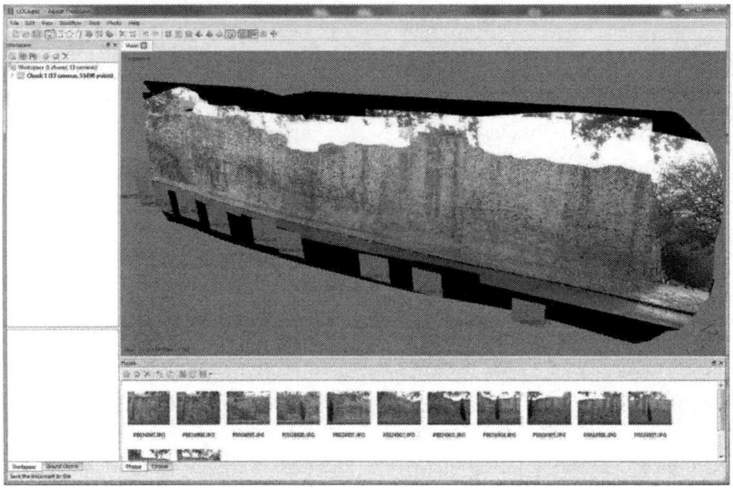

Fig. 3. Image of the Agisoft PhotoScan software, made up of several photographs, in which a rectified elevation of the interior face of the wall at Coca can be seen. (Own creation)

The downloading of georeferenced, numerical and raster data, through the internet, from such institutional sites as the Land Registry or the National Geographic Institute, was very useful in complementing fieldwork and allowing general analyses to be carried out of the positioning of the walls, their course and morphology. Such data are very useful for analysing the walled structure as a whole, providing information on the formation of the urban layout, closely linked to the course of the wall. The study of the current plots provided valuable information concerning the course of the wall. Satellite orthophotography was of great use both before and after the fieldwork in the analysis of the course of the wall.

The analysis of historical sources to discover more data surrounding the repair or maintenance of the walls throughout history is important, although we are dealing here with sources from later epochs than the construction itself, and such data usually include measurements and rules from previous centuries. The charter of Sepúlveda provides information concerning the freedom the inhabitants of that time possessed and what the social structure of the time was like, aspects which can help to determine who was responsible for the maintenance or repair of the walls. The Land Registry of the *Marqués de la Ensenada* reflects the characteristics of the villages of the Crown of Castile in the eighteenth century. It sets out information organised into such sections as jurisdiction, geographical situation, qualities and types of soil, properties, expenses, artists, labourers, etc., and also provided data concerning the importance of the defensive constructions.

Similarities

In this historical context of construction and reconstruction of towns as the *"Comunidades de Villa y Tierra"*, in which the towns share the same territorial structure and the same political and social organisation, the following question could be asked: Are there also similarities in the way these defences were built? The different aspects that these walls have in common from the construction point of view will now be dealt with. The aspects in which different construction solutions were used will be set out later.

Formwork technique

The formwork technique of gravel or stone cemented with lime is present in all the cases studied. In some it is the main system used while in others, there are other, equally important techniques being used. The use of formwork using gravel cemented with lime is very common in the Iberian Peninsula, with variations in both materials and form at the time of execution. It consists of large rectangular blocks, locked together as if they were bricks, of about 250-300cm long and 120-130cm high, and a depth corresponding to the thickness of the wall. These great blocks are made with a mould, the formwork board (Fig. 4), constructed with several rows of vertically placed boards separated by the desired thickness of the wall. When the formwork is made at ground level, supports are used in the first rows to hold up the formwork of boards. One of the short sides of the formwork is closed off by the previously constructed part of the wall, while the opposite end must be closed off using boards or a stone wall. When the formwork is being constructed at height and it is not possible to support it from the ground, it is supported by timbers placed transversally across the horizontal timbers which project from the formwork below and support the vertical timbers which in turn support the shuttering boards. The vertical timbers are tied at the top with rope. This mould is then filled with a mixture of stones, earth and lime which is inserted as if it were concrete. When it is set, the mould is removed and the next block is then constructed.

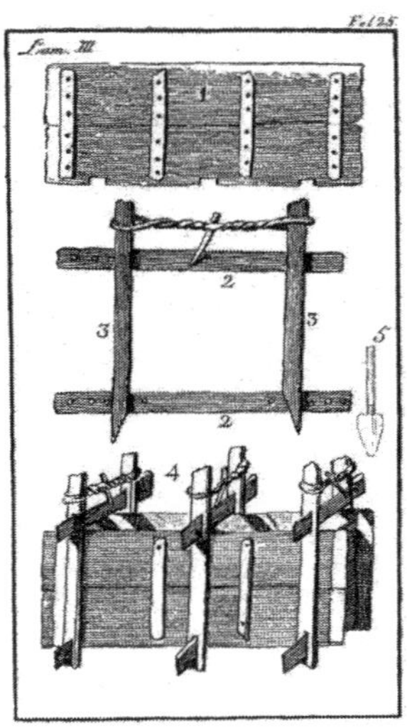

Fig. 4. Drawing by Juan de Villanueva showing a formwork board[11].

The marks left by the formwork are visible in the walls studied. The horizontal limit marks of the blocks are generally more visible than the vertical ones. A great irregularity can be observed in many cases in the execution of the wall, so the rows are not completely horizontal, and nor are the sizes of the formwork identical. In the case of Coca, irregular rows can be seen, without strict, calculated alignments, while in Fuentidueña there are stretches of wall with a great disorder in their formwork[12].

The horizontal timbers used for each formwork are always three in number and are always put at the base of the block. In the sections that have survived, the mark of the horizontal timbers is visible, and the timber itself is even conserved in many cases inside the wall. However, in many cases, only the putlog hole survives. When a channel is made to set the horizontal timber, variations can be seen in the supporting structure made from groups of stones, flat stones or tiles.

In some cases, before filling in the mould, stones are set down against the boarding to provide an ordered elevation of stones once the mould has been removed. This technique was used in the wall of Fuentidueña.

In the cases studied, the marks of the timbers used in the formwork can be seen in the wall, and it is possible to measure the height of the board. The heights obtained vary, but the most frequent are between 25 and 30 cm. In some cases they can be higher, but this is less common. It is surprising that the marks of the formwork have been conserved, when these walls normally have very deteriorated surfaces, with parts falling off or totally ruined.

Figure 5 shows a stretch of wall from Coca. The visible constructive elements have been drawn directly on the photograph: the horizontal and vertical lines forming the great rectangular blocks are visible. Also visible are the putlog holes at the base of each section. In this case, not all the putlog holes are visible as many are hidden beneath recent repairs and cannot be easily located, but they do have concrete positions along the wall, separated by a regular distance of 80-90cm when in the same formwork, and 60-75cm between putlog holes of one formwork and another.

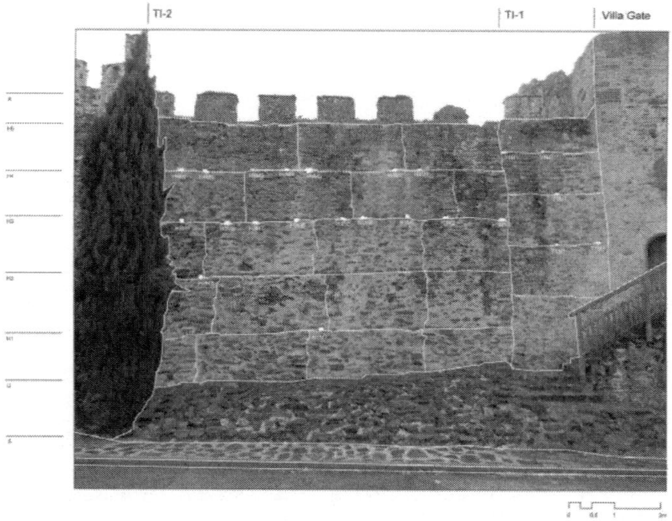

Fig. 5. Image of the northwest section of the wall of Coca, subject of the analysis of the constructive elements. (Own creation)

Absence of a base in the walls

One of the most striking aspects of sections of some of the walls under study is the absence of any base. In the cases of Fuentidueña, Coca, Cuéllar and Sepúlveda, stretches of wall can be seen that were built using formwork blocks, but without any effort being made to create a base. In some of these cases, it may be because the base is hidden by the accumulation of sediments on both sides of the wall. As for Fuentidueña (Fig. 6), it is clearly visible how the stretch of wall is built directly on the rock below. In the case of Cuéllar, no differentiated base or foundation can be seen.

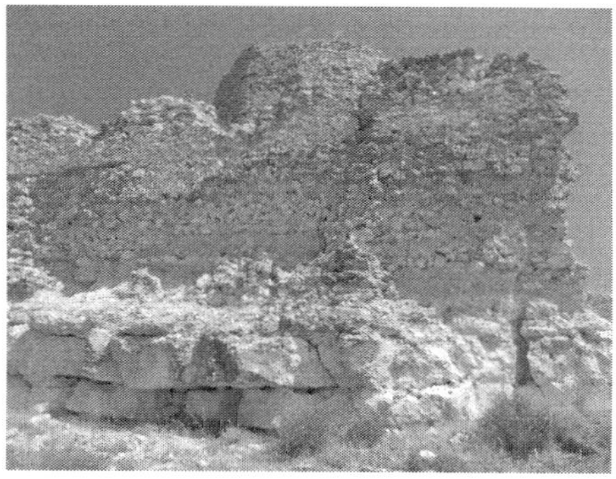

Fig. 6. The wall of Fuentidueña is built directly upon the ground. No differentiated foundation can be observed. (A. Sainz 17/06/2014)

In Segovia, the wall has, mainly in its towers, a base using different forms and material. Miguel A. Martín Blanco[13] describes the bases of the wall's towers, stating that they are discontinuous with respect to the tower. He also stresses the existence of cantilevers, ledges at the base of the towers which make the presence of the base itself more evident and which lead one to believe that they are older parts of the wall that have been taken advantage of at a later stage. In Coca, there is a stretch of wall in which a base built with reused materials is also visible.

Battlements

Several of the walls studied conserve examples of battlements. In Fuentidueña (Fig. 7), crenellations of a similar size with regular separations can be seen at the top of the wall. The size of each crenellation is between 55 and 60cm in height and width, with a relatively square proportion. The separation between each is 60 cm, identical to the width of each crenellation. In Coca, they are bigger, 100cm wide and 75cm high. Those in Cuéllar have been restored and partly rebuilt to allow the passage of people along the walkway. The restoration shows wide crenellations with narrow separations between them. Old photographs show the battlements in very bad repair and it is difficult to determine what the original proportions may have been.

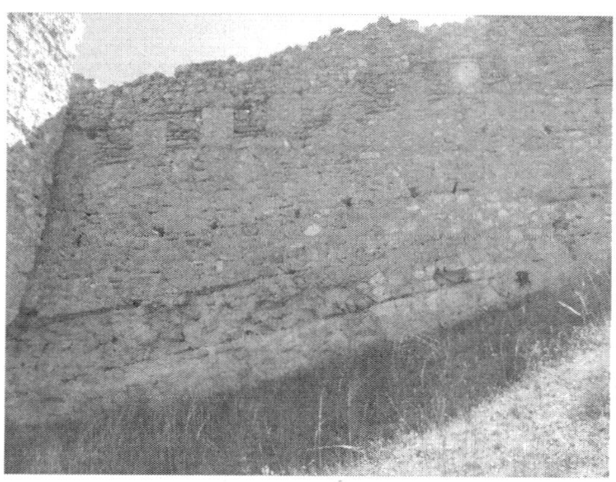

Fig. 7. Battlements visible in one of the stretches of wall in Fuentidueña. At the base, it can be seen how part of the material has fallen away. (A. Sainz 17/06/2014)

Absence of decoration

The absence of decoration in the studied walls is evident. There is no sign of any attempt to incorporate symbols, marks or other decorations to represent or transmit messages. In both Fuentidueña and Cuéllar, there are homogeneous stretches of wall built with the same continuous material, without decoration. In Sepúlveda, changes can be seen in the materials used, but no decorative interest is appreciable; the use of different materials does not have an aesthetic end; on the contrary, they seem to have reused materials from older constructions.

Some decoration, or at least changes in material and construction system, can be seen in the gates. In Cuéllar, the presence of bricks is only seen in the gates and the towers close to the gates. Brick reinforcements can be seen at the corners of the *San Basilio* gate, as well as brick courses in the tower with a similar rhythm to the height of the blocks. In Coca, brick decoration can be seen in the *Villa* gate, the only remaining gate. Coca also has bricks in the battlements of some towers. No decorative elements can be appreciated in the stretches of remaining wall.

Limited defensive resources

There is an important limitation in the defensive elements of the walls studied. Only towers and battlements can be seen as systems for improving the walls' defences. In general, massive towers were constructed along the walls, with better views for vigilance, and to hamper any enemies assaulting the town walls. The battlements are another defensive element used to improve the defensive capacity. However, there is scarce evidence of loopholes or other defensive measures in the walls studied. The walls of Cuéllar do have some loopholes in the upper section, built of stone. A loophole is also visible in one of the towers in Maderuelo. On the other hand, geometry is not used to design the wall, it simply adapts to the terrain. There is no sign of moats or machicolations or other defensive solutions. The only visible elements are some improvements of this kind in the gates, possibly added at a later stage. In some cases, such as Fuentidueña, the semicircular towers are currently separated from the wall, and seem to have been added later, which would suggest that, at first, the towers did not even exist.

Differences

Different techniques and materials used to make the formwork

When making the formwork board, its base is sometimes prepared to hold the horizontal timbers. The base of the block is prepared with two separate lines of stones to form a channel in which to put the horizontal timbers. In Coca, lines of stones can be seen that prepare the base of the block. In other cases, such as Cuéllar or Fuentidueña, the preparation of the base is not visible and no channel is expressly built to hold the horizontal timbers. The form of the putlog hole is exactly right for the horizontal timber used, with all its irregularities. Figure 8 shows one of the types of putlog hole that can be seen in these towns.

It is usual to find different techniques used for each formwork board in the same wall. In Cuéllar, flat horizontal timbers can be seen. In Fuentidueña, the use of paired rods can be seen[14]. In Coca, the use of horizontal timbers with a rounded section can be seen. In all the cases, different solutions for the same wall can be observed, even in the same sections. The technique used in the wall of Coca is different from the rest. In one side of each formwork board, a column of flat stones closing off the formwork is visible, built to form part of the formwork. This technique is not found in other cases studied.

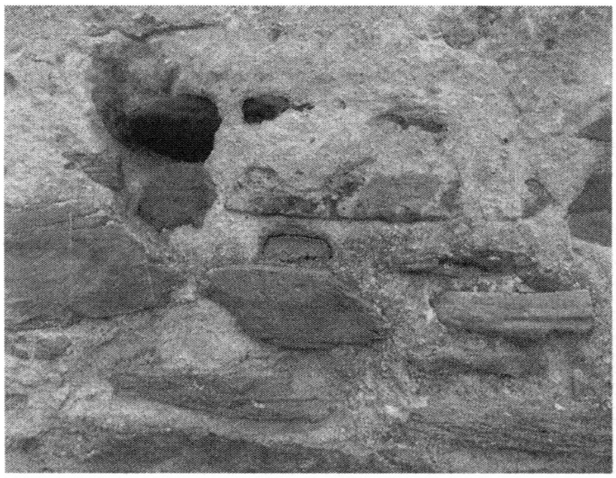

Fig. 8. Putlog hole in the wall of Coca. The horizontal timber is visible. (A. Sainz 02/02/2014)

The putlog holes are a witness to the way the formwork was done and various examples can be identified. The simplest is that made with no prior intervention, the horizontal timber is simply put in place and the material is poured in. In other cases, a channel is built using stones, or a flat stone is used as support above the horizontal timber. Tiles have also seen to be used. The use of bricks is also common in the putlog holes, but not in the cases studied here.

Various materials were used in the construction of the walls studied. In general, irregular unsculpted stones were used. Dressed stones are only found in gates and some towers. The stones used are normally limestone. In Coca, the use of red quartzite can be seen and is only present in this wall. Rounded river stones are also found in some parts of the wall in Coca. Reused stones can also occasionally be seen. The presence of reused granite stones, or other rock, can frequently be seen in Segovia in the base of towers, as well as some stretches of wall. Dressed granite can also be seen in Coca at the base of some stretches of wall and one of the towers was built almost exclusively in this way.

Constructive sections

The construction of the walls by sections is perceptible in Coca, the vertical lines in the formwork showing the vertical constructive interruption being evident[15]. (Fig. 5) In other cases, this division is not so evident; in Fuentidueña, an interruption that is not completely vertical is visible in one of the formwork boards, the interruption being more irregular and disordered, perhaps less planned[16].

Towers and gates

The towers are a fairly heterogeneous aspect in the walls studied. Although in most cases the materials and technique are similar to those used in the formwork, it is usual to find towers with different horizontal sections and very varied dimensions. Fuentidueña has five semicircular towers, built with formwork, and of a large diameter, reaching eight meters in some cases (Fig. 9). In the same set there are also rectangular towers with modest dimensions. The distance between towers is not constant either and it is difficult to identify a concrete pattern. The situation in Coca is similar. The existing towers are also semicircular and rectangular (Fig. 10), and even polygonal. The distance between towers is more regular in this case, around 20 to 25m. Worth noting in Cuéllar is the absence of towers along large stretches of wall that are over 100m in the southern part of the walled town.

As for Segovia, Miguel A. Martín Blanco[17] describes the variety of types of tower, whose floor cross-sections are rectangular, polygonal and semicircular. In this author's opinion, the coexistence of different tower types could suggest the existence of a prior wall that had been modified over the centuries.

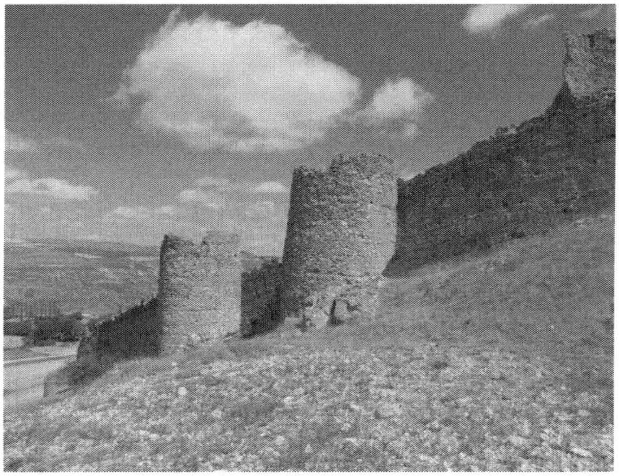

Fig. 9. Semicircular towers added to the wall of Fuentidueña (A. Sainz 13/08/2014)

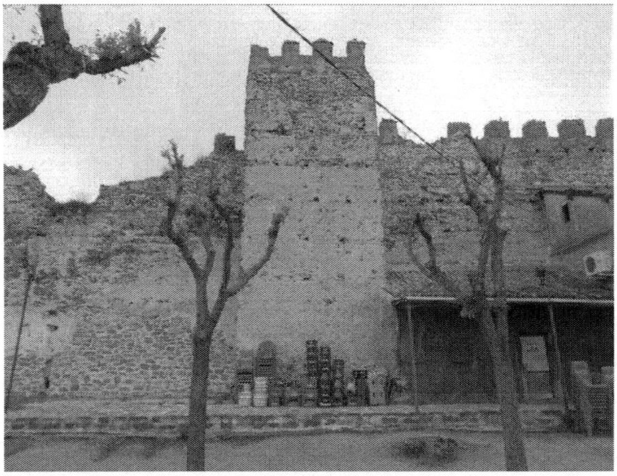

Fig. 10. Rectangular tower in Coca (A. Sainz 27/04/2015)

One of the most heterogeneous and varied elements of the studied walls are the gates. Whilst similarities can be found in the stretches of wall, the gates seem to have undergone a more important evolution and have reinforcements, additions, modifications, coats of arms and decorations, although this last is very modest. All these modifications spring from different origins and also from different epochs, so the variety in the solutions is more evident.

General dimensions

The thickness of the studied walls varies between approximately 90cm and 200cm. The thicknesses analysed are more generally small, if we think about the usually massive nature of defensive architecture. Parts of the wall of Fuentidueña are 90cm thick. In Coca, they reach 200cm, while this thickness is surpassed in Cuéllar. The height of the formwork is not so easy to compare, as it is hard to determine where the base of the wall is, taking into account the fact that, in some cases, part of the wall is now buried. The height of the walls from today's visible ground level is between 5.5 and 6.5m in Fuentidueña, reaching 10m in Coca.

Conclusions

The most important similarity found in these walls is the use of formwork. This system is used in all of them and, although it is found in defensive architecture in other parts of the Iberian Peninsula, it is interesting that it is also found in the walls of these towns, together with other common elements. Although there are differences in the dimensions of the formwork, they are still very similar, with relatively constant dimensions, 250-300cm in width and 120cm in height. One noteworthy similarity is that, in all the cases, formwork with three horizontal timbers was used. On the other hand, although the construction system is the same, there are differences in both the execution of the formwork and in the way it was filled, ordering the contents in different ways and making the putlog holes using different construction methods. The execution of the formwork shows notable differences, both among the walls of different towns and sections of wall in the same town. This begs the question of why, in one section of wall, in formwork of close proximity, are there different methods of formwork being used. The answer may lie in the presence of several teams of builders working at the same time, with different techniques and methods of formwork, going from one job to another. The use of formwork itself could indicate the construction of the wall without the need for specialised professionals, as happens in the case of dressed stone, where master masons were needed. The lack of order may indicate the absence of calculations at the time of building, the absence of a figure that could plan the work and coordinate the builders. In this sense, the construction by sections detected in Coca may indicate planning, where the sections were divided up beforehand or where the construction was previously limited to a particular length.

The towers present the most important differences within each walled town, as mentioned previously, and it is easy to see different floor cross-sections. Each type of tower is present in each town and in different parts of the wall, which allows comparisons to be made between the types. The case of Cuéllar is worth noting, where towers are scarce and far apart, there being long stretches of wall without any towers. This heterogeneity in the towers may be due to their typological evolution in adapting to defensive improvements over time, even in the same wall.

Acknowledgements

This study forms part of my PhD and I would like to take this opportunity to thank the *Fundación Juanelo Turriano* for the grant conceded to me enabling me to carry it to a conclusion.

Constructive similarities and differences in the walls in "Comunidades de Villa y Tierra" in the Diocese of Segovia, Spain

Translation from Spanish: Alan Hynds.

Notes

[1] J.M. Ruiz Asencio, 'La provincia de Valladolid en la Alta Edad Media' pp.9-64 in *Historia de Valladolid, Valladolid Medieval,* vol. 2, 1980, p.20. and G. Martínez, *Las Comunidades de Villa y Tierra en la Extremadura Castellana,* Madrid: Editora Nacional, 1983, p. 446.

[2] J.M. Monsalvo, 'Frontera pionera, monarquía en expansión y formación de los concejos de villa y tierra. Relaciones de poder en el realengo concejil entre el Duero y el Tajo (c.1072-c.1222) ', A*rqueología y territorio medieval*, vol.10, no.2, 2003, pp. 45-126, p.62.

[3] E. Portela, 'Del Duero al Tajo' pp. 85-106, in J.A. Cortázar (coord.), *Organización social del espacio en la España medieval. La Corona de Castilla en los siglos VIII a XV*, Barcelona: Ediciones Ariel S. L., 1985, p.113.

[4] J.L. Martín, *Manual de Historia de España, La España Medieval,* vol. 2, Madrid: Historia 16, 1993, p. 192-193.

[5] Martínez, Comunidades (Note 1) pp. 10-15.

[6] F. Benito, *La formación de la ciudad medieval,* Valladolid: Secretariado de publicaciones e intercambio editorial, Universidad de Valladolid, 2000, p.68.

[7] Monsalvo, Frontera, (Note 3) p.83.

[8] Monsalvo, Frontera, (Note 3) p.71.

[9] Benito, Formación, (Note 5) p.78.

[10] L. Torres Balbás, 'Las murallas que caen', *Arquitectura,* vol. IV, pp.77-84, p. 77-79.

[11] J. Villanueva, *Arte de albañilería,* Madrid: Oficina Don Francisco Martínez Dávila, 1827, p.24.

[12] A. Sainz Esteban and F. Jové, 'Aproximación al sistema constructivo de las murallas de Fuentidueña, Segovia' pp.55-64 in F. Jové, J.L. Sainz, (Eds), *Construcción con tierra. Investigación y documentación. XI CIATTI 2014. Congresos de arquitectura de tierra en Cuenca de Campos,* Valladolid: Cátedra Juan de Villanueva, 2015, p.63.

[13] M.A. Martín Blanco, 'Discontinuidades y pervivencias en la muralla de Segovia' pp- 145-180 in I.J. Gil Crespo, (Ed.), *Historia, arquitectura y construcción fortificada. Ensayos sobre investigaciones recientes,* Madrid: Instituto Juan de Herrera, 2014, p. 149.

[14] A. Sainz Esteban, Jové, 'Aproximación al sistema constructivo de las murallas de Fuentidueña, Segovia' in Jové, Construcción (Note 12) p. 62.

[15] A. Sainz Esteban, 'Sistema constructivo de las murallas en las comunidades de Villa y Tierra. Los casos de Coca, Cuéllar y Montejo (Segovia)' pp. 1541-1550, in S. Huerta, (Ed.), *Actas del Noveno Congreso Nacional y Primer Congreso Internacional Hispanoamericano de Historia de la Construcción,* vol. III, Madrid: Instituto Juan de Herrera, 2015, p. 1544.

[16] A. Sainz Esteban, Jové, 'Aproximación al sistema constructivo de las murallas de Fuentidueña, Segovia' in Jové, Construcción (Note 12) p. 63.

[17] M.A. Martín Blanco, 'Discontinuidades y pervivencias en la muralla de Segovia' in Gil Crespo, Historia (Note 13), p.146.

Brick staircases: the Rye House Group and beyond

Michael Tutton
Independent scholar

Introduction

There are probably no more than two dozen spiral, or winding, staircases made entirely of brick surviving in England. Most are concentrated in the eastern counties where the 14th Century renaissance in brick took hold, having leapfrogged over the channel from the Low Countries where it had a longer pedigree.[1] If we compare this figure of 24 with the many thousands of similar staircases in stone or timber to be found in churches, castles, fortified and unfortified houses of the late 14th and 15th Centuries, it becomes clear that the brick spiral staircase is rare indeed. Even in substantial early brick buildings such as Queens' and St John's Colleges in Cambridge, Eton College, Herstmonceux and Tattershall Castles and many more, the stairs are of stone.[2] Why are these brick stairs so rare? And what is the rationale behind their procurement and commissioning? The answers to these questions are: Exacting and high levels of bricklaying skills and status respectively. This paper brings together the strings of previous research and investigations and thus draws on secondary sources, although not exclusively so.[3]

The Staircases

Listed geographically from north to south. I have designated three types: (a) a continuous barrel-vaulted spiral; (b) a stair carried on a series of arches, and (d) indeterminate at the time of writing. RH indicates the Rye House Group. All were built in substantial high status brick buildings.

Tower-on-the-Moor, Woodhall Spa, Lincolnshire, (b). A surviving stair turret only with some fragments of wall, a hunting-lodge for Tattershall Castle. Before 1450, a stair carried on a series of arches rather than a winding vault. Mentioned by Smith and seen by him pre 1975,[4] but now collapsed as seen from a photograph taken in March 2014.[5] Bricks were already being taken from the site as early at 1472 for Tattershall Castle.[6]

Tattershall Castle, Lincolnshire, (d). Slim evidence of a stair similar to that at Tower-on-the-Moor c1450.[7] Attached to the outer face of the north-east octagonal turret is the scar of a former attached building hinting at a brick spiral stair. Other stairs in Tattershall Castle are of stone as mentioned in the introduction.

Hussey Tower, Boston, Linclonshire, (b). Wight dates it c1510 but Smith suggests slightly later than Tower-on-the-Moor, i.e. second half of 15th Century.[8] The tower once derelict but recently restored for a local museum. The stairs are carried on a series of brick arches, there is an integral moulded and sunk handhold, a feature common to brick staircases. (Fig.9)

Caister Castle, Norfolk, (d). The remains of a defensive fortress on the Norfolk coast.[9] Built by Sir John Falstoft from c1432. The great tower is 90 feet high (27.5m) with the stair turret rising a further 8 feet (2.5m). The staircase is problematic, the listing description states "The staircase of bricks and the moulded handrail cut into the wall have been removed above the first floor which is now accessed via a C20, timber, winder stair." There is certainly a brick staircase lower down, although this is not a spiral staircase. The form of the main staircase in the turret may have been brick or stone. Wight mentions that 122 stone steps were removed in 1782 for use as a parapet (?) elsewhere, and that stone was used for the newel of the stair turret,[10] although there are no specific sources given.

Drayton Old Lodge, nr. Norwich, (d). Also built by Sir John Falstoft. A much ruined hunting lodge just north of Norwich. Complete by 1437.[11] Smith includes it on his map of brick-built newel stairs but does not otherwise mention it,[12] until 2014 when he conjectures that it may have been brick to the first floor or wholly of timber.[13] The County H.E.R. states: "Southwest tower formerly had staircase, now all gone, ..."[14] The Lodge is currently undergoing repair and would repay further close investigation of the inside of the tower.[15]

Cow Tower, Norwich, (d) (Fig.1). An artillery tower, part of the City defences c1398.[16] The earliest example, a hybrid with a stone newel, so not entirely of brick construction. Nevertheless, with all other elements in brick it is sufficiently important to be included. These stone newels are coeval and not added later, the Building Accounts for 1398-99 give detailed costs: "To the same [Robert Snape] for 30 nowels price 3d a piece, 7s 6d."[17] The staircase is in poor condition, although it was complete in 1809[18], there are only 7 newels in-situ and the vault above appears to have collapsed although there is the hint of an arch higher up. This may have been a type (b) staircase similar to Tower-on-the-Moor and Hussey Tower. There is no handhold. There is no access beyond the entrance gates, but the interior of the tower and the start of the staircase can be clearly seen through the gates. The Cow Tower in Norwich is an exception here, quite why such a complicated and high status stair should be included in a military building of precise purpose is something of a mystery. But there are other elements equally mysterious in the Tower that await satisfactory answers.[19]

Kirby Muxloe Castle, Leicestershire, (a) (Fig.2). 1480-83, built by William Hastings a favourite of William IV. Bricks were being manufactured in October 1480 under the supervision of a Fleming, Anthony Yzebrond.[20] There are two staircases in the gatehouse and two in the surviving west tower, one of which is ruinous. There are no handholds.

Oxburgh Hall, Norfolk, (a) (Fig.3). 1482, when Edmund Bedingfield obtained licence to crenellate from Edward IV.[21] Staircase in north-west turret of gate tower, some 80 ft (24.6m) high serving the ground, first floor and the roof. A fine well preserved staircase with integral sunk handhold, there is a moulded base to the newel atop a larger diameter pedestal and tall lamp niche on the ground floor. The vault brickwork, particularly lower down, has been filled flush, painted to match the colour of the base brick then intricately lined in white paint to reproduce finely pointed work. This may be a 19th Century restoration although Wight says the gate tower survived the 18th and 19th Century rebuilding and restorations.[22]

Welle Manor Hall, Upwell, Norfolk, (d). A 14th Century Hall House, much altered c1480 and later[23]. The house has a rear stair turret with brick spiral stairs to the attic. To the north are two free-standing towers which flanked the former courtyard entrance in the perimeter wall, although all of this is now gone. These towers also contain brick spiral staircases and date to c1480.[24] When Wight (note 1) saw this house she described it as "remains, partly ruinous, ...". The house was substantially restored and extended in the later 20th Century and is now a private residence.

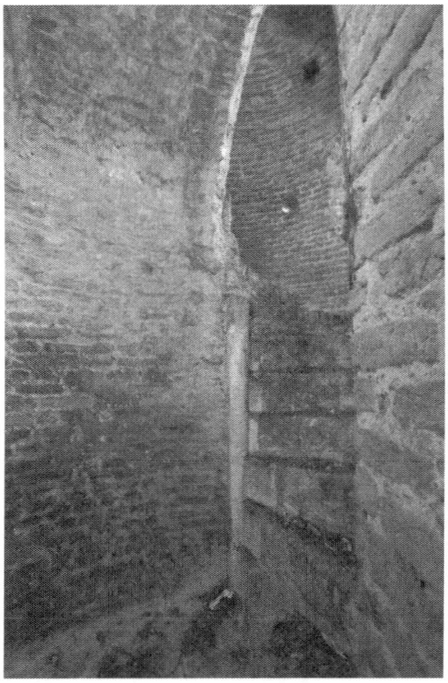

Figure 1. Cow Tower, Norwich, 1398. Brick stair with stone newel. Note the arch radiating from just above the dark hole or putlog in the upper right-hand. (M.Tutton)

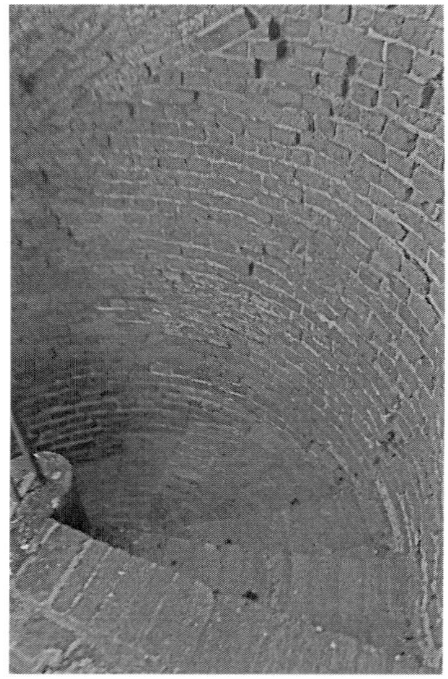

Figure 2. Kirby Muxloe Castle, 1480-83. One of the four brick staircases in the castle. The vault is seen at the top left-hand. (Jeremy Polanski, Flickr, Creative Commons Licence)

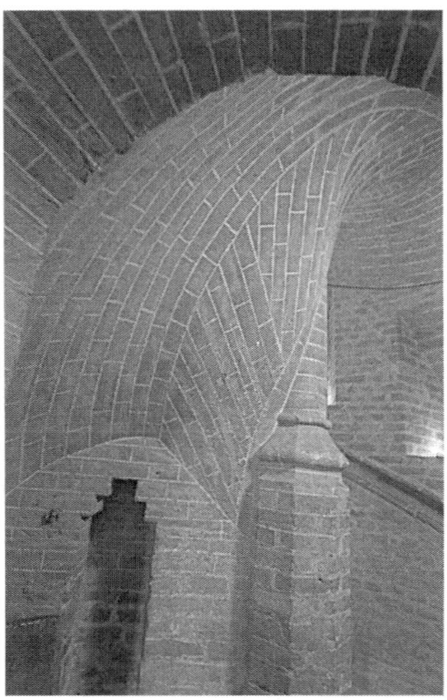

Figure 3. Oxburgh Hall, Norfolk, c1482. Bottom of the staircase with the base of the newel, lamp niche and handhold. Note the lining out of the pointing to the underside of the vault. (M.Tutton)

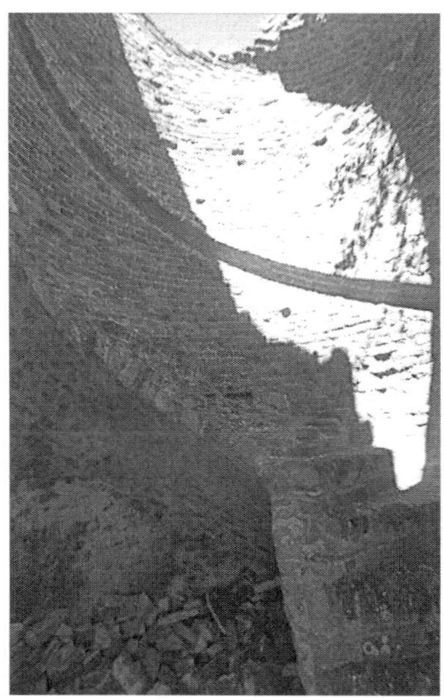

Figure 4. The ruined staircase at Someries Castle, Bedfordshire, 1464-71. (M.Tutton)

Leiston Abbey, Suffolk, (d). An early 15th Century gatehouse to an earlier monastic complex dating to the 1360s. The north turret of the brick gatehouse survives to second floor level and probably had a further storey. It certainly has a staircase, or the remains of one.[25] Further investigation is necessary to establish the form of the staircase.

Buckden Palace, Cambridgeshire (formally in Huntingdonshire), (d). Former palace of the Bishops of Lincoln, extensively rebuilt by Bishop Thomas Rotherham in 1472-80, of which the great tower and gatehouse only are now extant. I am reliably informed, that a brick staircase existed here some 40 years ago.[26] Also Smith is fairly adamant that a brick stair, or the remains of one, exists at Buckden.[27] However the plan of the gatehouse and great tower show only one spiral staircase in the north-east turret of the great tower,[28] and this is stone according to the listing description: "North-east turret has a stone staircase, partly restored, with moulded stone hand-rail and stone newel."[29] In the opposite turret there now exists a recent metal fire escape stair. The people who run the site state that there is no brick staircase there now, we can assume then that the staircase is now lost.

Someries Castle, Bedfordshire, (a) (Fig.4) RH. 1464-71, the ruined gatehouse and chapel of a larger complex, probably a fortified manor house, started by Sir John Wenlock, who completed the gatehouse. On his death in 1471 the estate passed to, Archbishop, Thomas Rotherham who continued, after a break from 1471-75, work on the chapel attached to the gatehouse.[30] The staircase is in the gatehouse at the southern corner. In 1966 it was climbable to the first floor, although Smith says "with difficulty".[31] It is now unfortunately partially collapsed with the entire newel and part of the inner vault missing, although it would still be possible to climb some way up, albeit keeping tight to the outer side against the shaft, it is however not accessible for safety reasons. The staircase has a sunk handhold, although this is damaged with most of the semi circular rail broken off.

Faulkbourne Hall, Essex, (a) RH. Sir John Montgomery added to an earlier timber-framed house when he obtained licence to crenellate in 1439. This was continued by his son Sir Thomas from 1449 and this includes the north-east tower with its attached stair turret and brick stair complete with sunk handhold. An illustration was included by Lloyd, although in general he gives these staircases only passing reference.[32] Faulkbourne Hall is a private residence and is generally not accessible.

Hertford Castle, Hertford, Hertfordshire, (d). Vague evidence of a fragment of concave brick handhold in a bastion tower in the walls,[33] probably 15th Century.

Rye House, Hertfordshire, (a) (Fig.5) RH. A fortified manor house, 1443,[34] built by Sir Andrew Ogard a naturalised Dane. Similar to Someries Castle, this is a gatehouse of a much larger complex, now all gone above ground, although in this case the gatehouse is intact. The stair is in the southern corner and has a sunk handhold. The steps are unfortunately heavily and uncharacteristically restored with Staffordshire blue bricks which creates an unpleasant contrast with the red bricks.

Hatfield Old Palace, Hertfordshire, (d). Former palace of the Bishops of Ely, built by John Morton, 1480-90. The surviving east wing of a quadrangular block, now an entertainment venue for Hatfield House. The west front projecting porch has a stair turret. Smith states "The Hatfield Palace examples are plastered over, but the form of the spiralling barrel-vault is almost certainly evidence for a brick stair."[35]

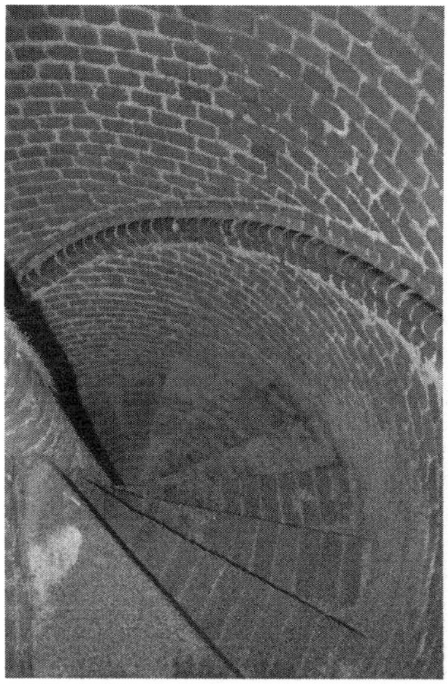

Figure 5. The Rye House, Hertfordshire, 1443. The handhold is particularly fine. The newer darker bricks to the treads are replacement Staffordshire blues and the tread in left foreground is faced up with sand and cement. (M.Tutton)

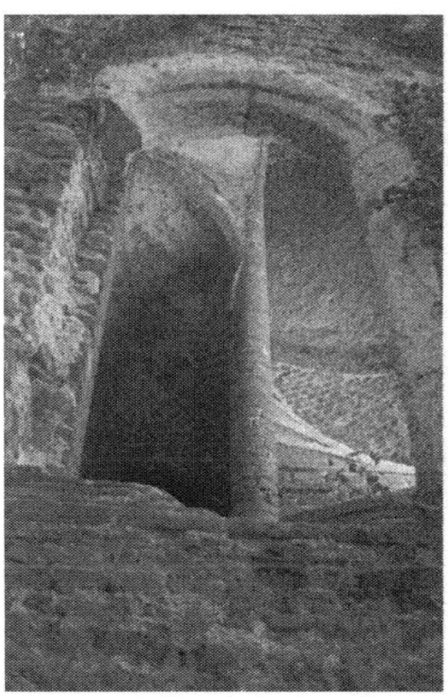

Figure 6. Nether Hall, Royden, Essex, c1460. Note the timber leading edges of the steps and clear evidence of plastering. (M.Tutton)

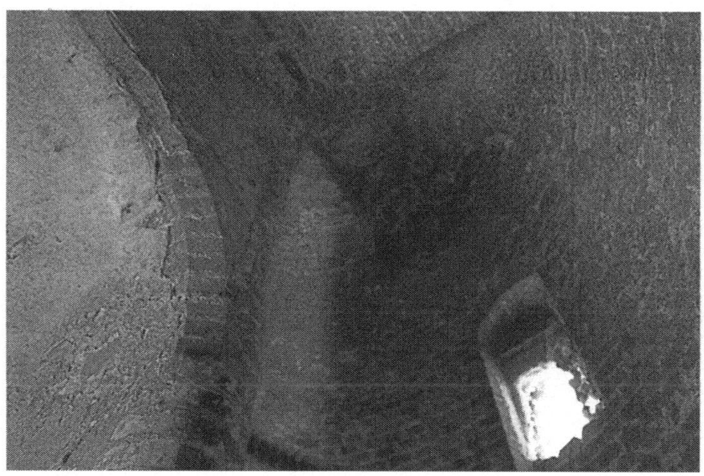

Figure 7. Nether Hall, Royden, Essex, c1460. The arched arrangement to the lower part of the stair. (M.Tutton)

Nether Hall, Royden, Essex, (b) (Figs 6 & 7), RH. Built by Thomas Colte, begun late 1460s.[36] Again the ruined gatehouse of a fortified manor house now all destroyed except for a section of curtain wall and the moat. The stair is located in the right-hand 3 storey tower which is virtually intact, the other is partially collapsed. The stair has a sunk and moulded handhold and is supported on arches rather than a barrel-vault, unusually the steps have timber leading edges, probably Oak or Elm, it is not known if these go all the way to the top but it is possible to climb the staircase to the parapets.[37] Ryan states "... the lower part of the stair has a spiralling barrel vault, but the upper part is constructed on arches which radiate from the central newel, so has reversed what is there."[38] Also of note is clear evidence of plastering.

Moot Hall, Maldon, Essex, (a) (Fig.8) RH. Built by Robert Darcy, it is sometimes known as Darcy's Tower. Possibly 1424-25[39] although Wight dates it a decade later.[40] Almost certainly part of a larger complex, virtually all physical trace of which is now lost. Excepting the Cow Tower in Norwich, this is the earliest brick staircase in England, of the type and period we are concerned with and along with Oxburgh Hall, the best preserved of those seen to date. The staircase from ground to first floor was sealed off in 1810 by the insertion of a floor at first floor and a partition on the ground floor. It was not opened up until the late 1960s. In 1810 a new timber staircase was inserted at the front of the building to the first floor to enable easier access to the court on that floor.[41]

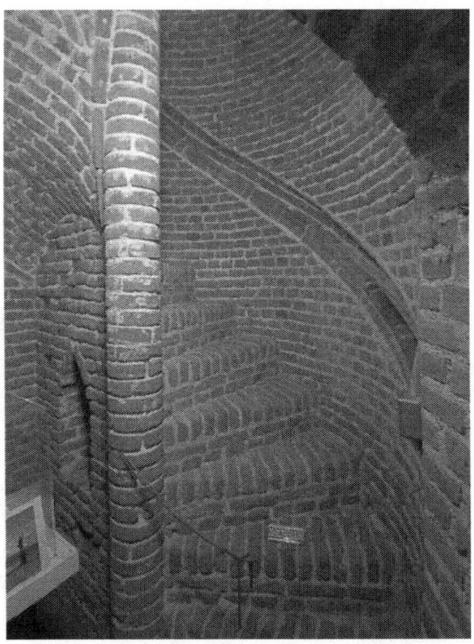

Figure 8. The Moot Hall or Darcy's Tower, Maldon, Essex, 1424. (M.Tutton)

Eastbury Manor House, on the outskirts of east London, although there is no brick stair here and slightly late at c1556-73. It has a pair of brick staircase shafts, both had timber stairs, but only the service stair survives. The principle shaft, which now contains a modern steel stair, has a moulded countersunk brick handhold of the type common with brick spiral stairs. (Fig.9) This feature is absent in the service stair where a rope would probably have been utilised.

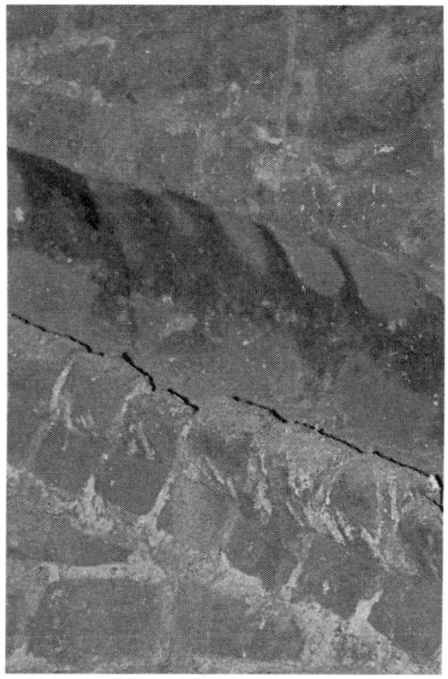

Figure 9. Eastbury Manor House, Barking, East London, c1556. The handhold to the higher status timber stair. (M.Tutton)

Wayneflete's Tower, Esher Place, Surrey, (a). 1475-80, A bishops' palace of which only the gatehouse remains. Built by William Wayneflete Bishop of Winchester.[42] The gatehouse has had later windows inserted, including in the stair turret, which break through the shaft in an ungainly manner, possibly by William Kent.[43] Wayneflete employed the master mason John Cowper, to build his house, who also worked at Kirby Muxloe Castle and Buckden Palace.[44] The staircase has all the attributes of the standard brick winder, although the sunk handhold is less refined than others.

Wayneflete's or Fox's Tower, Farnham Castle, Surrey, (d). 1470-75,[45] another residence of the bishops of Winchester. Although resembling one at first sight, this is not strictly speaking, a gatehouse, rather it was built to provide extra and more comfortable accommodation. There is slim documentary evidence only for a brick staircase. Thompson working from the manorial accounts and rent books states: "In 1477 the tower's staircase (*novus gradus novi Turris*) was tiled,"[46] at the date of recording, this could well mean 'bricked' or constructed in brick. Wight tantalisingly quotes: "In 1450s William Burgess was paid for making brick stair in a new tower, £1. 11s 8d."[47] Odd because of the date, unfortunately there is no specific source given.

Laughton Place, East Sussex, (b) (Fig.10). A surviving tower only of a larger house, built by Sir William Pelham in 1534, on an earlier moated site.[48] He employed Fuller White who had earlier worked at Esher Place under John Cowper. White built a different type of brick staircase, which is carried on closely joined radiating brick arches. This differs from the other arched staircases at Hussey Tower and Nether Hall, which have more widely spaced arches with a section of vault between. There is no sunk handhold.

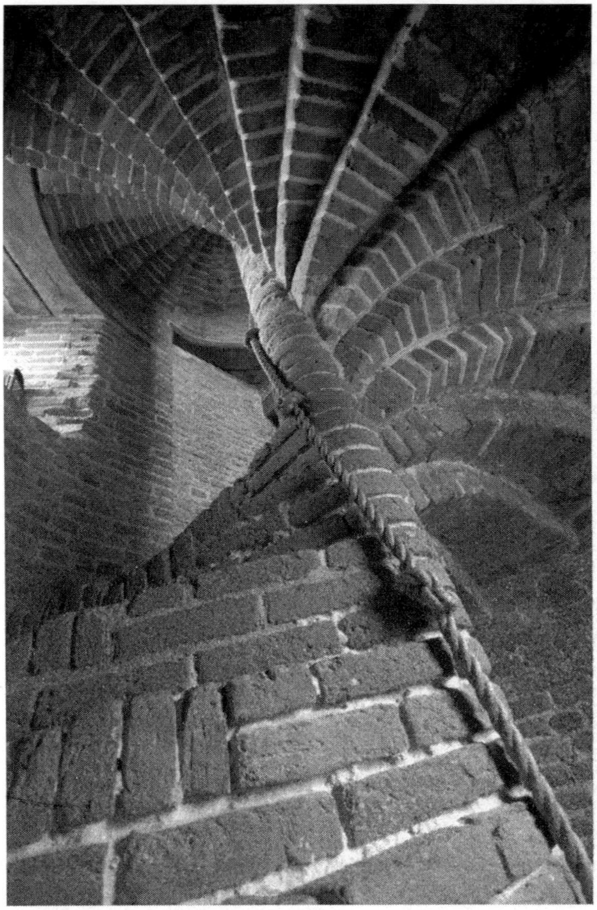

Figure 10. Laughton Place, East Sussex, 1534. (Victor Bayon, Flickr, Creative Commons Licence)

Discussion

Adding together the above examples we arrive at 19 definite brick spiral staircases and 7 possibilities, some of which require further investigation. Other strong possibilities are, or were: Denston Hall, Suffolk, although the gatehouse tower now demolished; Hadleigh Deanery Tower, Suffolk, which survives; Hunsdon House, Hertfordshire, built 1447, later a Royal residence of Henry VIII, now much altered and reduced but parts surviving. These may repay further close scrutiny and research. There may be others of course, as yet undiscovered and unrecorded, but they cannot amount to many. The reason for this scarcity must be the high degree of skill required to build them. It is one thing to lay bricks, rub and cut bricks for details and even corbel tables and the like. But to set out complicated formwork, cut bricks and lay them for a spiral stair with a continuing rising barrel-vault, finished in facing brickwork, is no mean task. Not to mention, in most cases, a highly crafted sunk handhold rising in a parallel line with the going of the steps. There must have been a very limited number of craftsmen with the skills and expertise to produce such work. It would also have been expensive.

A stone vaulted spiral staircase was easier to build and less expensive, contrary to popular opinion, bricks in this period were not cheap. The early stone stair required rough formwork to construct the vault in a rubble mix concrete upon which to place the steps. The newels were usually procured separately from a mason or direct from the quarry. On removing the formwork the underside of the vault would be plastered smooth, a task well within the capabilities of the average plasterer. The newel staircase, where the newel and step are one piece of stone, was easier still. These staircases were by far the norm for the period, and for some two centuries earlier. Here each step with integral newel was usually obtained direct from the quarry according to specification. It was then simply winched into place as the shaft was built around it, with the outer bearing within the shaft, requiring just simple timber props for temporary support whilst the surrounding masonry cured.[49] Stone spiral stairs were as common in East Anglia as elsewhere, evidenced by their existence in many parish churches, fortresses and houses. Indeed it has been forcefully argued that no part of East Anglia is so far from sources of stone that its procurement and transport was in any way prohibitive.[50]

The Rye House Group

The Rye House Group, as noted above, are: Someries Castle, Faulkbourne Hall, Rye House, Nether Hall and Maldon Moot Hall. The group was so named by Terence Paul Smith for similarities in decoration such as corbel-tables and diaper and other brick patterns externally.[51] Although the Moot Hall has none of these,[52] they are all, nevertheless linked by their staircases, which are, with the exception of Nether Hall, near identical. This can be seen from the illustrations, although the Rye House stair rises clockwise and the others are all anti-clockwise. This perhaps a whim of Andrew Ogard, for there is no real significance as to whether a spiral stair rises clockwise, or anti-clockwise.[53] The other link that Smith postulates is that this group was all the work of a single group or *atelier* of craftsmen.[54] Even taking into account the anomalies above, there appears to be no strong argument against this assertion.

Soldiers, Bishops and a Lawyer: The Links Between the Buildings and the Staircases Within

The desire for something exceptional in building was not uncommon and a brick staircase was seen as something highly fashionable, unusual and expensive. With the exception of the Cow Tower in Norwich, and other rare early examples, such as the 12th Century stair in St. Botolph's Priory, Colchester built of Roman bricks. We can assume that Sir Robert Darcy, was the leader in this fashion. He was a highly influential lawyer associated with the eastern ports from Berwick-upon-Tweed southwards, would have been familiar with the early brick industry in Hull and most probably had travelled overseas to the Low Countries, the Netherlands, Denmark and northern Germany.[55] He was elected Parliamentary Burgess for Maldon in 1422. He was not the first to build in brick in the 15th Century, but was surely the first to commission a brick staircase in the house he built in Maldon, possibly as early as 1424. The remains of the house are now called the Moot Hall, also known as Darcy's Tower. He was closely associated with other brick builders in Essex, Sir Lewis John, Sir John Tyrell and Sir John Montgomery, all three soldiers who had served in France. The latter of Faulkbourne Hall, also with a slightly later brick stair. All were immensely wealthy. John, Tyrell and Darcy were knights of the shire of Essex as well as serving together in other formal government and legal capacities.[56] There were also associations through marriage of Darcy's children with Tyrell's and possibly Montgomery's.

That these men were well travelled and thus influenced by the traditions of northern Europe's extensive use of brick is clear. Indeed Sir Andrew Ogard of the Rye House was himself a Dane. Ogard in turn was associated with Sir John Falstoft of Caister Castle, and cross-county associations surely existed, particularly within the Rye House group. It is fairly certain that Robert Darcy arranged to bring over Flemish or German bricklayers to construct his staircase, if not the whole house. There is plenty of evidence that alien brick craftsmen were working in East Anglia in the period and Smith cites extensive instances of this.[57]

And so the links continue and spread their web. Richard Bennington who built Hussey Tower and Ralph Lord Cromwell who built Tattershall Castle and Tower-on-the-Moor were both justices of the peace in south Lincolnshire and surely exchanged ideas, the stairs at the former and the latter are both similar in type.[58] William Wayneflete Bishop of Winchester was born in Wainfleet, Lincolnshire, hence his adoptive name. He was responsible for much brick building at Eton College where he was Fellow and Provost from 1440-47. He is also credited with the towers at both Farnham Castle and Esher Place, now both know as Wayneflete's Tower. The latter certainly with a brick stair and the former with documentary evidence of one. He is closely associated with Tattershall, close to Wainfleet, where his arms are displayed on the church and he knew Ralph Lord Cromwell the builder of Tattershall Castle personally.[59] He was an extremely powerful and influential person becoming Lord Chancellor of England in 1456. Wayneflete took into his service, sometime in the late 1470s, John Cowper a master mason who had been apprenticed at Eton College. He is inextricably linked to Wayneflete at Esher (and probably Farnham) and Tattershall on the church. He doubtless also found work at Tattershall Castle. Whilst there he was employed by Lord Hastings at Kirby Muxloe Castle with its four brick staircases, he is also linked to Buckden Palace.[60] Another powerful prelate and brick builder was Thomas Rotherham Archbishop of York and on two occasions also Chancellor of England. Before being appointed to the See of York he was Bishop of Lincoln and is responsible for much building and rebuilding at Buckden Palace the site of a brick staircase. He inherited the estates of Sir John Wenlock, a soldier who fell at Tewkesbury, in 1471. Wenlock was the builder of Someries Castle and Rotherham continued his work there, although not responsible for the staircase, which must be attributed to Wenlock, he would undoubtedly have much admired it.

Conclusion

Not all the staircases in the list have established links, but cross-fertilisation must be assumed, fashions travel. These staircases were commissioned by wealthy men to impress and celebrate their equally impressive brick residencies, hunting lodges and gatehouses and they surely influenced one another. Their rarity, there are very few now and there never were many, is due to the high degree of craftsmanship required to construct them. There were very few workshops capable of this work with the high degree of finish required. The number of craftsmen appears to have been static for a period and then dwindles with the required skills ever more scarce. This in turn was due to the expense of such staircases, the limitations of the material and the time taken to construct them. The fashion lasted little more than a century and by the time Clement Sysley came to build his mansion, Eastbury Manor House in Barking, in c1556 the appetite had gone. Although he incorporated a brick handhold in the higher status stair, he opted for the much less expensive and more quickly erected option of a timber stair. Brick never really represented a threat to stone and timber in staircase design and construction. In construction history terms these examples must be seen as rare and often beautiful phenomena that never took hold. The surviving examples are exceptional, even in ruin. They deserve further research and closer inspection particularly in comparison with their continental counterparts.

Notes and References

[1] For general works on the history of brick in England see: Nathaniel Lloyd, *A History of English Brickwork,* London, H Greville Montgomery, 1925, (1983 edition, The Antique Collectors Club Ltd.); Jane A Wight,

Brick Building in England: from the Middle Ages to 1550, London, John Baker, 1972; Terence Paul Smith, *The Brickmaking Industry in England 1400-1450,* Oxford, B.A.R., 1985; R W Brunskill, *Brick Building in Britain,* London, Victor Gollancz, 1990.

[2] Terence Paul Smith, 'Rye House, Hertfordshire, and Aspects of Early Brickwork in England', *Archaeological Journal,* Vol. 132, No.1, 1975, p.138.

[3] Between the deadline for submission for this paper and actual presentation some of the sites will be visited for further investigation. Further details and illustrations will therefore be offered in the presentation of the paper.

[4] Smith (Note 2) p. 137 and 138 note 114, recorded as a personal observation by him, see also Wight (Note 1) p.86. Smith also notes this staircase in 'The Early Brickwork of Someries Castle, Bedfordshire, and its place in the history of English brick building', *Journal of the British Archaeological Association,* 1976, Vol. 129, p.46.

[5]https://flickr.com/photos/infraredd/13225335873/in/photolist-qT72CF-atpJSP-m9FiAi-m9EsUT-m9G9ij-m9ErRk-m9Fga6/ (Accessed 22nd December 2015).

[6] Wight (Note 1) p.306.

[7] Smith, 1976 (Note 4), pp.46-7.

[8] Wight (Note 1) pp.299-300. Smith, 1976 (Note 4), p.47.

[9] Wight (Note 1) pp116-122

[10] Wight, (Note 1) pp120-21.

[11] Terence Paul Smith, 'Drayton Lodge: A fifteenth-century hunting lodge near Norwich', *Information,* Vol. 127, 2014, pp.7-17

[12] Smith, 1976, (Note 4) p.47.

[13] Smith (Note 11) p.10.

[14] Norfolk Heritage Explorer: http://www.heritage.norfolk.gov.uk/record-details?MNF7854 (Accessed 22nd December 2015).

[15] Historic England, *Heritage at Risk,* East of England Register, 2015, p38.

[16] A D Saunders, 'The Cow Tower, Norwich: An East Anglian Bastille?', *Medieval Archaeology,* Vol. 29, 1985, p.109; and Smith, 1976 (Note 3) p.45.

[17] ibid., p.109.

[18] Wight (Note 1) p.340.

[19] Brian S Ayers, Robert Smith and Margot Tillyard, 'The Cow Tower, Norwich: a detailed survey and partial reinterpretation', *Medieval Archaeology,* Vol. 32, 1988, pp.184-207, with a contribution by T P Smith. Note: There is no interpretation let alone a reinterpretation of the staircase in this paper.

[20] John Goodall, *Ashby de la Zouch Castle and Kirby Muxloe Castle,* London, English Heritage Guidebook, 2011 (2nd revised), p.24.

[21] Wight (Note 1) p.342.

[22] ibid., p.343.

[23] http://www.britishlistedbuildings.co.uk/en-221825-welle-manor-hall-upwell-norfolk#.VoAn5FLOVTU (Accessed 27th December 2015)

[24]http://www.heritage.norfolk.gov.uk/record-details?MNF22171-Welle-Manor-Hall-Upwell&Index=2&RecordCount=1&SessionID=0ea48536-46e7-467c-8e71-6e5eacd91499 (Accessed 27th December 2015)

[25] List entry: http://www.historicengland.org.uk/listing/the-list/list-entry/1014520 (Accessed 10th January 2016).

[26] David Kennett tells me that he walked up it some 40 years ago, personal communication.

[27] Smith (Note 2) p.138 and (Note 4) p.48.

[28] http://www.buckden.cambs.info/local_info/buckden_palace.asp (Accessed 28th December 2015).

[29] http://historicengland.org.uk/listing/the-list/list-entry/1130324 (Accessed 28th December 2015).

[30] Terence Paul Smith, Someries Castle, *Bedfordshire Archaeological Journal,* Vol. 3, 1966, pp.35-51; Smith (Note 4) pp.42-58 and 'Someries Castle: Some reconsiderations', *Bedfordshire Archaeological Journal,* Vol. 5, 1970, pp109-112.

[31] Smith, 1966, (Note 30) p.41.

[32] Lloyd (Note 1) pp. 86 and 371.

[33] Clapham and Godfrey, n.d., *Some Famous Buildings and their Story* (Westminster) p.141-5, referred to in Wight (Note 1) p275 also Smith (Note 4) p.48, note 27.

[34] Smith (Note 2) p.129.

[35] Smith, 1976 (Note 4), p48, note 26. Smith's plural may indicate more than one staircase.

[36] Wight (Note 1) p.265.

[37] Personal communication.

[38] Pat Ryan, *Brick in Essex from the Norman Conquest to the Reformation,* Chelmsford, Pat Ryan, 1996, p.61

[39] ibid., pp.52-53.

[40] Wight (Note 1) p.262.

[41] Michael Tutton, 'The Moot Hall or Darcy Tower, Maldon, Essex', *Information,* 132, forthcoming 2016.

[42] http://historicengland.org.uk/listing/the-list/list-entry/1286940 (Accessed 1st January 2016).

[43] http://waynefletetower.co.uk/architectural-development-of-esher-place/ and for photographs: http://castlefacts.info/castledetails/photos.aspx?uin=13467 (Both accessed 15th December 2015).

[44] Wight (Note 1) p.382.

[45] M W Thompson, 'The Date of "Fox's Tower," Farnham Castle, Surrey', *Surrey Archaeological Collections,* Vol. 57, 1960, p.87.

[46] ibid., p.88.

[47] Wight (Note 1) p.383.

[48] http://www.historicengland.org.uk/listing/the-list/list-entry/1043133 (Accessed 1st January 2016).

[49] Michael Tutton, 'An Outline of the History and Development of the Staircase' and James W P Campbell, 'The British Staircase' in Campbell and Tutton, eds., *Staircases: History, Repair and Conservation,* London, Routledge Taylor & Francis Group, 2014, pp.33-37 and 76-83 respectively.

[50] Smith, (Note 1) *passim.,* and Ryan, (Note 38) pp.65-7.

[51] Smith, (Note 1) pp.16, 18, 37 and 38.

[52] Tutton (Note 41).

[53] Guy Neil, 'The Rise of the Anti-clockwise Newel Stair', *Castle Studies Group Journal,* Vol. 25, 2012, pp.113-174.

[54] Smith, (Note 1) pp.16, 18 and 37.

[55] Ryan, (Note 38) p.68.

[56] ibid.

[57] Smith (Note 1) *passim.*

[58] Terence Paul Smith, 'Hussey Tower, Boston: a Late Medieval Tower House of Brick', *Lincolnshire History and Archaeology,* Vol. 14, 1979, p.35, cited in Ryan, (Note 38) p.67.

[59] Thompson (Note 45) pp.89-90.

[60] John Harvey, *English Mediaeval Architects: A Biographical Dictionary down to 1550,* Gloucester, Alan Sutton Publishing, revised 1984, (first 1954) pp.73-4.

Load bearing matters: considerations on geometrical and structural design in Late Gothic vaults

David Wendland
TU Dresden

In late Gothic architecture, the design of ornate vaulted ceilings is a guiding theme. Vaults were built which were extremely complex and apparently, from the structural point of view, often very audacious. They were realized over large spans, sometimes with remarkably low fleche, creating extremely intricate spatial figurations. Although these masterpieces of architecture have fascinated generations of scholars, there are still open questions on how they were designed and built, and, in particular, how their builders conceived their mechanical behaviour in order to achieve structural safety.

Some particularly clamorous examples are vaults that have no ribs at all – "Diamond Vaults" consisting only of a folded shell with sharp arrises – or vaults with ribs that have spatial curvature. In the latter, the looping ribs obviously deny their original structural function (due to their curvature they cannot take relevant normal forces) – let alone such examples where their intersections occur in different levels and some ribs even end suddenly in plain cuts (Fig.1).

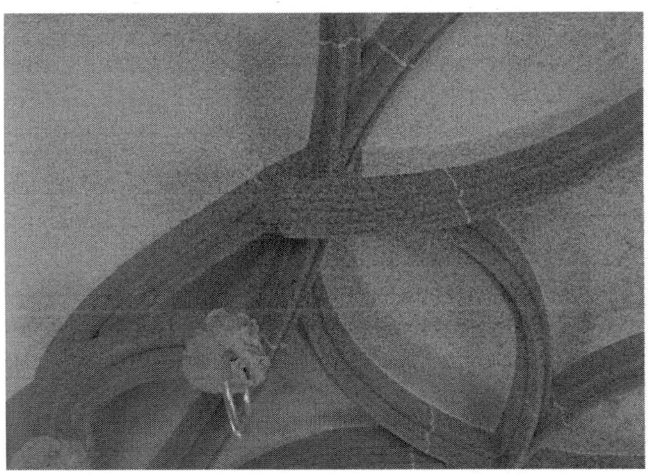

Figure 1. Detail of the vault with looping ribs in the Sacristy of St. Anna at Annaberg. The formation of the ribs plainly contradicts their traditional structural function (M. J. Ventas Sierra, D. Wendland).

Looking at these daring vault constructions, one often wonders how these structures can withstand even their own weight. In this paper, we want to ask how *their builders* might have thought that these structures could stand safely. Our aim is to propose some hypotheses for discussion.

Load bearing matters: considerations on geometrical and structural design in Late Gothic vaults

Unfortunately, only very few sources available on the "structural theory"[1] in the context of late Medieval and Early Modern architecture are available, hence we know little about how builders imagined the mechanical behaviour of their structures. The only source associated with late Gothic design and building practice containing explicit statements on structural design and mechanical behaviour of vaults is the treatise on church design attributed to the Spanish architect Rodrigo Gil de Hontañón.[2] The interpretation of this text can be supported by some elements of other treatises by Late Gothic architects, and in particular by later treatises that are associated with modern architecture, but turned out to be helpful to understand the design principles for buttresses in Gothic architecture.[3] In any case, it appears hard to believe that the complex vaulted structures in late Gothic were built without a precise notion about their mechanical behaviour – besides that the good actual performance of most of them show that these notions were at the least not entirely wrong.

As we know, the stability of vaults is intrinsically connected to their shape. Of course, the abutments must be sufficiently sustained to resist the lateral thrust; but the strains within the vault itself are usually very low, while the main concern of load bearing and structural safety is the stability.[4] Consequently, we usually find the geometric concept of vaulted structures closely linked to the structural concept. For instance, in Frei Otto's grid shell at Mannheim (1975) the shape is entirely designed according to the membrane surface that represents the figure of stability of the spatial roof structure under its own weight. A similar example is the funicular design developed by Antoni Gaudí for the Colonia Güell church (1898-1914).[5]

But this occurs also before the modern mechanical science was available for the structural design. As prominent example, we can refer to the design of Christopher Wren's great dome of St. Paul's cathedral, where during the design process the cross-section of the dome was correlated to the curve of the catenary, introducing the recent discovery of the stability figure of the arch under its own weight.[6]

Another prominent vaulted structure where the geometrical design can be shown to be intrinsically linked to the structural concept, is the dome of Ste-Geneviève in Paris, by Jean-Baptiste Rondelet.[7] This design was largely disseminated also through Rondelet's treatise 'L'Art de Bâtir',[8] which became one of the most influential books on Construction and Structural Design in Architecture during the 19th Century. As a matter of fact, Rondelets treatise clearly states how the shape and the structural performance of vaults are supposed to be linked. His theory on vaults provided the base for some of the most prominent wide-spanned vaults in the nineteenth century, such as the Mole Antonelliana in Turin (completed in 1888), the new vaults for the central nave in Cologne Cathedral and the neo-Gothic vaults built by Johann Claudius von Lassaulx – it was further disseminated for instance by Georg Moller and by the authors of Breymann's treatise on construction, thus circulated and apparently remaining generally accepted by architects until the beginning of the twentieth century.[9]

For the last group of examples, it is interesting to point out that we are dealing with a structural theory that is obsolete in respect to the contemporary development of mechanics, and even extremely problematic to the point of being grossly wrong: These buildings are standing not because, but in spite of their structural design. Therefore, the structures based on the application of the theory developed by Rondelet and his followers are symptomatic for the methodological challenges that we have to face when trying to understand the choices made by the designer in his historical context:[10] We find that the project is not determined by our knowledge on structural behaviour in this day and age, but by the notion the builders had in their time within their particular knowledge society – hence, it is necessary to comprehend the latter if we seek for understanding the choices that determine the built object we analyze.

Design principles in Late Gothic vaults

If we state that the connection between geometric design and structural concept in vaults has been very common even before the development of the modern theory of mechanics (while the good reasons for doing so can be precisely described only in modern times), we may find at the least surprising that, according to the current interpretation of its design principles, this is not supposed to be the case in Late Gothic vaults.

Based on the interpretation of drawings showing the geometric concept of late Gothic vaults, and on texts that are associated with the tradition of the Gothic design practice, but are of much later date, Werner Müller has reconstructed a design process which he himself characterized as an "algorithm".[11] It is a closed geometric procedure that starts from a given figure of ribs or arches in the plan, where they are traced as straight lines. Upon this figure, the curve system is defined by a uniform radius for all arches, which is determined according to fixed rules. Hence, the only variables are the figure in plan, and the choice whether some arches are "rising" (starting with vertical tangent from the springing) or "falling" (drawn with a horizontal tangent at the vertex). From this autonomous development of the curves, the intersections of the ribs would result in different levels and spring in different height from the walls, according to their relative path lengths from the springing or from the vertex – phenomena which can in fact be regularly observed in complex late Gothic vaults (Figs 5, 7, 9).

It is beyond doubt and for a long time generally recognized that the geometric concept of Gothic vaults is by principle based on autonomous curves, which describe plane curves usually defined as circle segments or, in some cases, oval arches composed by more than one circle segment.[12] Hence, the curves of the arches are given a priori and never derive from projection to, or intersections of, geometrically defined surfaces, as it occurs in vaults of other periods and styles. However, the quasi "automatic" procedure of developing the spatial system of the curves, as supposed by Müller, is questionable. First of all, there are too many examples of vaults which have been surveyed and analyzed where this scheme doesn't apply, so it definitely doesn't reflect any general practice. Further, it cannot be supported by the contemporary written sources; those texts where it is explicitly described date from the eighteenth century when late Gothic vaulting was since a long time out of practice (this regards in particular the so-called *Prinzipalbogen*). In fact, the exaggeration of the tendency of uniform radii is typical for the perspective taken in the Gothic Revival,[13] and the further step proposed by Müller fits very well in the architectural discussion of the late twentieth century, when the theoretical bases of parametric design were formulated. Another major concern is that this supposed design procedure is essentially a closed process – it is a somewhat strange procedure for creating buildings, as it doesn't allow reacting upon complex boundary conditions, it excludes any criteria related to the proportion system of the entire building (although it turns out that proportion systems were of very high interest in that time), and – which is our concern here – , it also excludes a priori any design criteria linked to the structural performance of the vault.

For the so-called Principal Arch design, Jos Tomlow proposes an interpretation in terms of a more "open" procedure, highlighting the use of the graphic design procedure which can be seen in the contemporary drawings, and which could solve many of the mentioned problems.[14] But from our analyses based on surveys, we would rather think that the design method was based on the determination of many of the intersection points in first place, and the successive arrangement of the spatial curve system upon these nodes. In particular, the analysis of Diamond Vaults, where on one hand the effects of the building process on the shape could be clarified, and on the other hand the design of the curves are not influenced by the constraints from the design of any stone elements, gives way to hypotheses on the criteria for these design choices that turn out to correlate well not only to the features observed on the built objects, but also to some sources. These are, in particular, the passages dedicated to Gothic vaulting in the treatise of Philibert de L'Orme and most notably the treatise attributed to Rodrigo Gil.[15]

In fact, in many cases we observe that the positions given to the intersection points of the system of arches cannot be explained as consequence of the development of a spatial system of autonomous curves. Sometimes we can identify the impact of decisions that clearly created constrains on the construction which are even clearly visible and must have caused considerable difficulties in the execution. Hence, we may suppose that they are due to design choices which were imposed to the workmen and considered to be important.

Diamond Vaults in the Albrechtsburg at Meissen – an attempt of creating the perfect vault?

The building of the Albrechtsburg, the new palace of the rulers of Saxony, started in 1470; it is one of the most innovative residential buildings of its time. One of its most outstanding features is that originally all ceilings of the building, on four stories, were conceived as masonry vaults. In the final execution, all ceilings of the ground floor and the first two upper floors were vaulted, as well as the stairway towers which are entirely built in masonry. Such a superposition of vaulted ceilings, instead of the usual wooden beams, is challenging regarding the thrust acting on the outside walls. It is therefore remarkable that no buttresses appear on the outside walls: in reality, the wall, while plane on the outside, is buttressed towards the inside by a system of niches and wall projections.

All original vaults in the Albrechtsburg, including the ramps of the two spiral stairway, are "Diamond vaults", which are characterized by their folded surface with ridges between the groins, creating ceilings with subtle patterns of light and shadow (Fig. 2). This peculiar type of brick vaults has been developed specially for this building; in the following it was used in many buildings throughout central-eastern Europe.

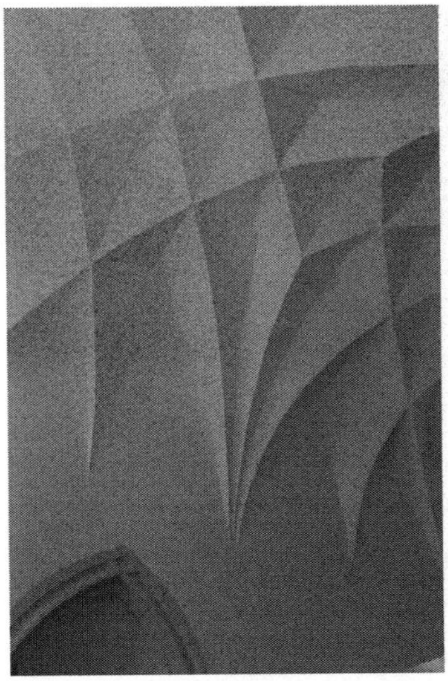

Figure 2. Albrechtsburg in Meissen; Diamond vault in the second floor (M. J. Ventas Sierra, D. Wendland)

The masonry shells of the Diamond vaults were built free-handed on centring arches supporting only the groins. The centring system consisted of vertical poles, between which the centrings of the single arches were hung. It was possible to clarify this in first place through the geometric analysis, showing on one hand the discontinuous course of the arches between the intersection points, and on the other hand the relatively precise position of these intersection points. This picture correlates very well with the unique description given by Rodrigo Gil in his text and drawing, of the assembly process of a complex rib vault. Finally, we could also show in practical experiments carried out in full scale that such a device is very practical and leads to the same geometrical features as they can be observed in the original.[16]

If we envision the information flow from design to realization, in particular regarding the crucial stage of building the temporal support which serves also as guide for the construction of the vault, it seems likely that the positions of the intersection points (in particular their height, and therefore the length of the poles) was transmitted explicitly, using the tracing floor provided *in situ* mainly for adapting the project to the real dimensions of the perimeter where the vault was to be built. In consequence, we may suppose that these specifications were formulated even in a rather early stage of the design process, and not generated solely by the intersection of circles which would have been a rather imprecise and error-prone geometric procedure.

In a vault in the second floor of the palace which we discussed elsewhere in detail (Fig. 2),[17] we find that the ridges of the formeret arches are positioned according to the curve system of the vault itself, by projecting the nearest intersection point or the corresponding height of the nearest groin orthogonally to the wall. While there is no obvious reason for forcing these points exactly to that position – for instance, there are no windows or similar boundary conditions at the impost of the vault – we could observe that this decision must have caused considerable difficulties in the execution of the vault masonry. We could ascertain this, once again, in the full-scale experimental reconstruction of this vault, and also from the analysis of the surface flow in the respective portions of the vault.

In this vault, there is no apparent reason for the choice of the radii of the arches, but it is possible to show a very straight-forward procedure which could define at first the heights of the intersecting points (using a semicircle on the diagonal of the bay), and successively determine the radii. A main feature of this geometric concept, according to this hypothetic reconstruction, is the division of a semicircle in three parts in order to determine the heights of the lateral nodes of the curve system. This leads to a division of the vault in a central portion and two lateral portions, where the nodes separating these different portions are defined by a secant with an inclination of 60°.

A similar arrangement appears more explicitly in the Great Hall of the Albrechtsburg, around the central umbrella of the vault (Fig. 3). Here, the nodes of the radial arches departing from the central pillar turn out to be located according to secants with the inclination of 60° (Fig. 3, left).

This positioning of the intersection points that belong to the first row of bifurcations in the ribs of the umbrella in respect to their springings, and then again in the summit of the radial groins in respect to the base of the pillar, is clearly not derived from the plan with an autonomous development of the curve system, but must have been specified by purpose in the elevation of the arches – which is also possible in the known graphical procedure used in Late Gothic vault design, where in superposition with the plan the arches are represented in undeformed elevations. There is no obvious reason to define the nodes of the vault as primary feature by means of a secant with the inclination of 60°, nor can we find any explicit statement on this matter in the contemporary sources. However, the general picture strongly reminds some peculiarities in vaulted structures of the nineteenth century which are based on Rondelet's theory of vault mechanics, already mentioned. Could this perhaps offer us an approach to the interpretation?

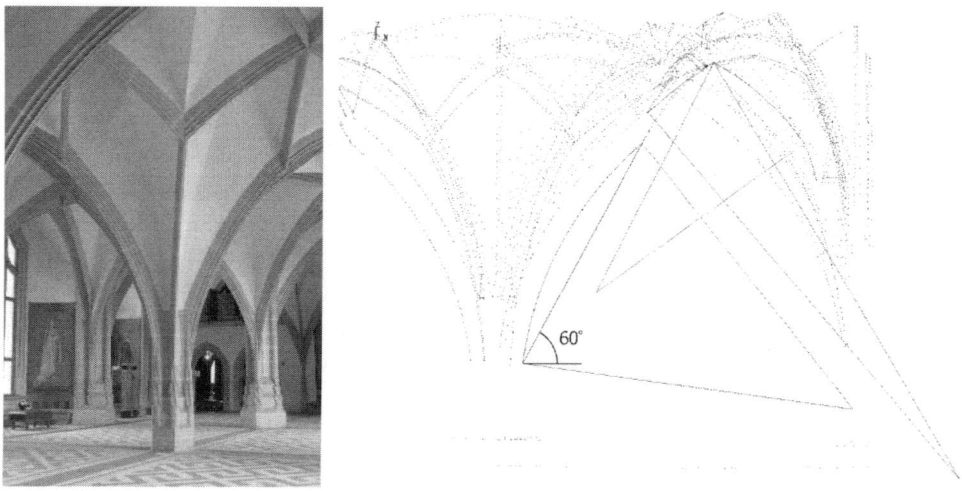

Figure 3. Vault in the Great Hall of the Albrechtsburg at Meissen: The geometric analyses show that the intersection points around the central umbrella are defined by secants inclined to 60° (M. J. Ventas Sierra, D. Wendland).

This theory is based on the idea that the equilibrium of the vault can be described by the interaction of some parts that exert thrust, and other parts having the ability to stabilize the vault and counteract the thrust. Through the arrangement of the "pushing" and the "resisting" parts of the vault, it is supposed to be possible to build vaults which are stable or even which don't exert any lateral thrust – a topos which we can find already in treatises of the eighteenth century: The idea is utopian, as we know, but beyond doubt extremely appealing.

The property of the "pushing" and the "resisting" portions of the vault depend partly on their construction detailing (e.g. the masonry texture), to a greater extent on the distribution of the loads, and most important, on the geometry of the vault. In fact, according to Rondelet and his followers, the limit between the counteracting parts of the vault is supposed to be located at the point where the joint between the arch voussoirs is inclined by 45°, which means that the position of this "fracture joint" is situated at the fourth part of the curve of the semicircular arch. Hence, in order to assess the mechanical behaviour of the vault it is sufficient to compare the extension of the portions below and above this joint, which can be carried out simply according to their projection in the plan: If the proportion between "resisting" and "pushing" parts is equal, the vault is stable and, according to this peculiar theory, would not even exert any lateral thrust. Beyond that, a still more direct way to exclude any lateral thrust to the abutment would be to build vaults that consisted only of the "resisting" parts without the "pushing" parts.

Although Rondelet cites all important authors from the emerging modern mechanical theory, his methodology in demonstrating his ideas is definitely not according to the contemporary mathematical efforts, let alone the results (in particular the supposed absence of horizontal reaction forces in consequence of the counteracting rotation moments). Hence, from the references given by Rondelet himself we must state that the origin of his ideas is not clear. Some items are not new: For instance, the idea of strategically applying extra loads to certain parts of the vault, which he proposes in order to enhance the resisting properties of the lower portions, virtually has been since ever in the repertory of vault design – it is, for instance, the original purpose of the "Tas-de-Charge" (and the origin of the term denominating this construction). The "fracture joint" already constitutes a principal element of the kinematic model of the arch formulated by de la Hire, who, however, refers to common knowledge as base of this assumption. Apparently, both ideas have been present before and resumed by Rondelet. But perhaps the most interesting trace is a reference to the older structural rules formulated by François Derand (1643),[18] which Rondelet pretends to improve in his theory.

Derand's rule is known as a geometric procedure to determine the size of the abutments according to the shape of the arch. As Santiago Huerta shows, it appears in treatises already around 1600 and was apparently used for the design of the buttresses of Gothic vaults.[19] It consists in dividing the arch in three parts, extending the secants of the lower parts downwards to the double length, and taking the end point of these segments as outer edge of the abutment. In a semicircular arch, the resulting buttress is one fourth of the span, having the secant an inclination of 60°. The idea beneath this procedure supposedly is that of equilibrium: the lower portion of the vault may corbel to the inside as far as it is bedded towards the outside.

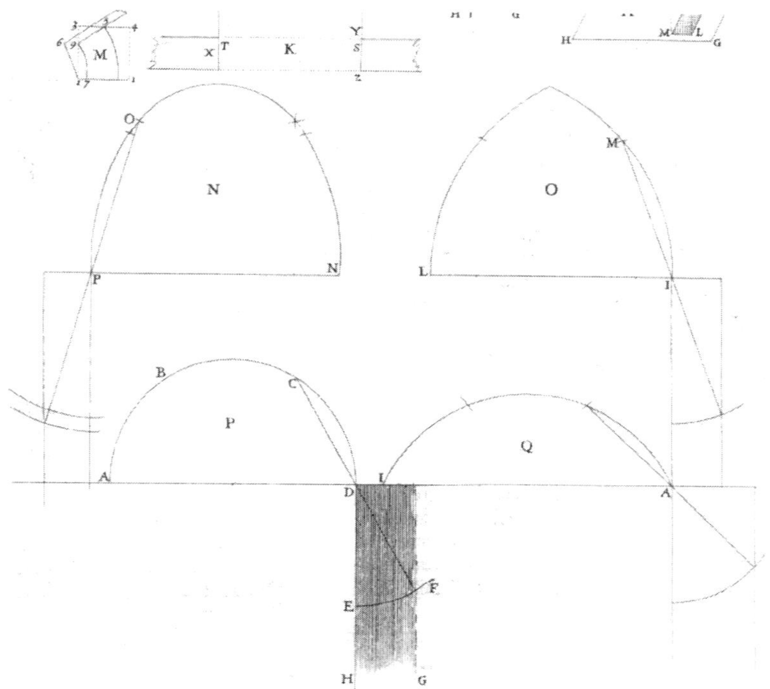

Figure 4. Geometric procedure given by Derand for determining the strength of the abutment according to the shape of the arch (Derand 1643, 11).

It so happens that also the idea of counteracting parts in vaults apparently was known already to the builders of late Gothic vaults: In fact, in the treatise attributed to Rodrigo Gil we read that the vault consists of parts which "carry" and parts which "are being carried", and that the stability of the vault is obtained through the equilibrium of these parts.[20]

Load bearing matters: considerations on geometrical and structural design in Late Gothic vaults

It seems appealing to simply put these two concepts together: Could it be that late Medieval and Early Modern architects believed that the stability and the thrust of vaults could be controlled by the ponderation of "resisting" and "weighting" parts, like Rondelet still conveys, which are, however, divided by a pivot situated at the third part of the semicircular arch and marked by the 60° secant, integrating Derand's rule? There is absolutely no written source proving that, for instance, Arnold von Westfalen, architect of the Albrechtsburg, made such considerations in the design of his vaults. But if we could assume so, it would explain many choices in the design which otherwise remained obscure. In first place, the central umbrella in the vault of the Great Hall would consist solely of "resisting" parts, as the nodes are arranged by secants with the inclination of 60°. If we then observe how the vaults are divided in lower and upper portions by the geometry of the arches, we can state that the entire vault of the Great Hall, with the umbrella as dominant part, seems to consist predominantly of "resisting" parts, and, if ever, only few "pushing" parts, which, if we reason in the same way as Rondelet does, would result in a vault without thrust. This, again, would justify the audacious superposition of four vaults in one building and the apparent understatement in the abutment of the structure.

For supporting this idea, we may point out that many instructions in Rodrigo Gil's treatise correlate well to the vaults in the Albrechtsburg. But more important would be to confirm these observations in a larger number of cases – while at present, we are able to discuss only very few examples.

Tiercerons in the vaults of Freiberg and Annaberg

The nave of the parish church of Freiberg, one of the most emblematic late Gothic architecture in Saxony, was completed around 1500, according to the scheme of the "hall church" with very slender pillars and walls. The buttresses are barely visible on the outside, but project also to the inside of the lateral nave. This system reminds the Albrechtsburg; in fact, the church in Freiberg was built under the same patrons only few years later. In the three isles of the naves, the vaults are equal in height (19.2 m) and also in span (ca. 8 m), and, except for small variations, have the same rib figuration. The plan of the bay is approximately square; the rib system consists of diagonal and transversal ribs, to which a secondary figure is added that is supported by long tiercerons springing at a much lower level. It is conspicuous that some ribs spring with an obtuse angle (as if the span of the arch were much larger than the actual span between the supports), while others, namely the tiercerons, start with a vertical tangent – and not directly attached to the pillar, but displaced in such a way that the intrados of the rib starts in the void (Fig.5)

According to the geometric analyses, the arches have a uniform radius.[21] While the transversal and cross ribs run more or less continuously, the other ribs show significant discontinuities at the intersection stones – once again, in many cases the positions of the intersections are guiding the curve system. In particular the striking discontinuity at the vertex of the tiercerons must have been imposed by a deliberate choice in the design: The tiercerons are located considerately below the rest of the vault, and in the elevation their curves completely independent of those of the upper ribs. Again, the curves of these tiercerons, while "detached" from the rest of the vault, describe one third of a semicircle: their springing and their summit are connected by a secant with an inclination of 60° (Fig. 6). So, here again we may dare to suppose that the geometric design of the vault could possibly reflect the distinction between lower "supporting" parts (mainly the tiercerons and longitudinal arches) and upper parts "being supported": this would be a possible approach to understand the structural design of the vault, and would definitely explain the discontinuities in the rib system we described.

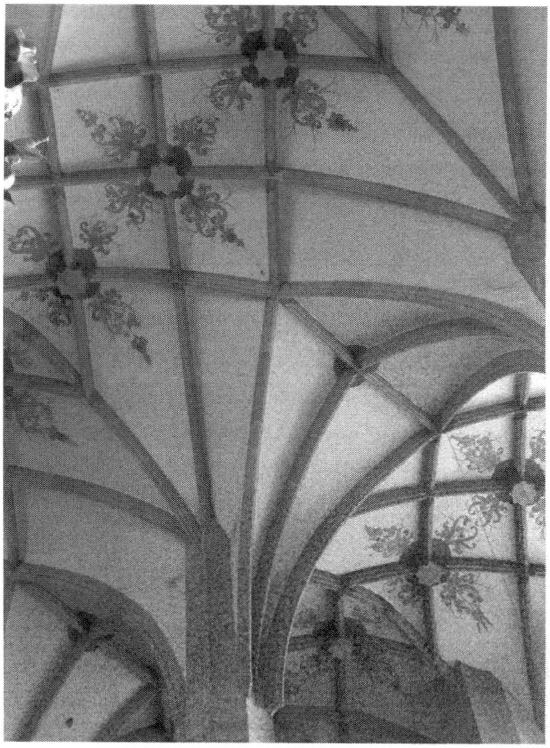

Figure 5. The vault in the Parish Church at Freiberg, Saxony. Note the discontinuities in the intersections of the ribs and the "detached" position of the tiercerons (M. J. Ventas Sierra, D. Wendland).

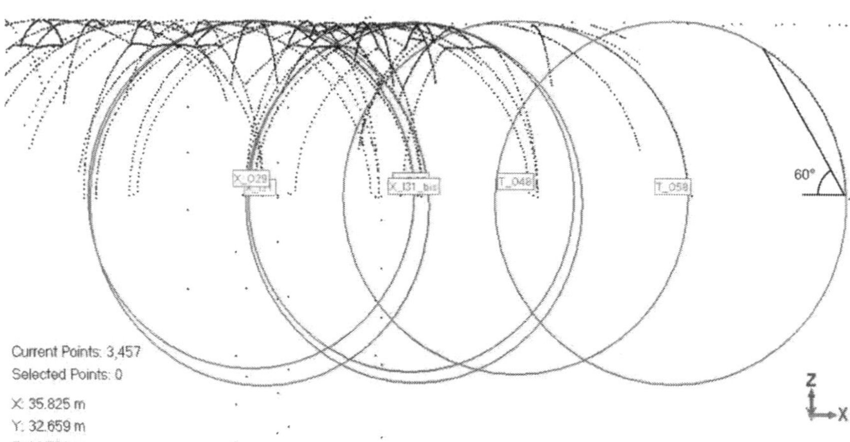

Figure 6. Geometric analysis of the survey data, showing that the tiercerons are defined by a secant inclined to 60° (M. J. Ventas Sierra, D. Wendland)

Load bearing matters: considerations on geometrical and structural design in Late Gothic vaults

For the sacristy of St. Anne's church at Annaberg in Saxony, in 1519 Jakob Heilmann designed a vault which had to cope with rather difficult conditions: While the transversal span of the rectangular space measures 6.90 m, the total height is of only 5.20 m, constraining to a rather low fleche.[22] Moreover, the vault is heavily loaded: it carries the floor of a large gallery and even part of a superposing structure of a transversal nave. Heilmann, who is notable for his particularly artistic vault constructions,[23] responds to this with a design that blatantly challenges our notion of structure. At the main supports, the ribs virtually spring from the void; most ribs have double curvature and are connected at the intersection stones in a way that denies any notion of force transmission (see above, Fig. 1). The diagonal arches are divided in two parts with loose ends hanging downwards, carrying heads of lions holding iron rings in their teeth, as if wanting to carry something.

The main structural element of this vault is the masonry shell spanning over the curving ribs. But still, it is clear through the detailing of the stone elements and its very systematic relation to the masonry shell that the rib work still is supposed to play an essential part in the structure.[24] In the whole complexity of the rib system, there is only one group of ribs that according to its shape and design could be considered to be seriously involved in load bearing: These are the tiercerons, located in pairs in the outer portions of both bays of the vault. They describe plane arches, starting nearly vertically from very low springings and running continuously to their common vertexes, where the connections to the successive ribs is, here again, discontinuous. Also the geometry of the tiercerons is, surprisingly enough, the same as in Freiberg: they are generated as the third part of a semicircle, hence, by means of a secant inclined by 60°.

Possibly the term "tierceron" refers to this geometric condition of "one-third arch" and perhaps once more we can interpret these arches as part of the "resisting" portions of the vault. Referring to ongoing studies on this building, we may add that also the detailing, especially the design of the stone elements of the massive tas-de-charge, can be interpreted in terms of ponderating parts that "supports" and parts that "are supported", just as Rodrigo Gil explains.

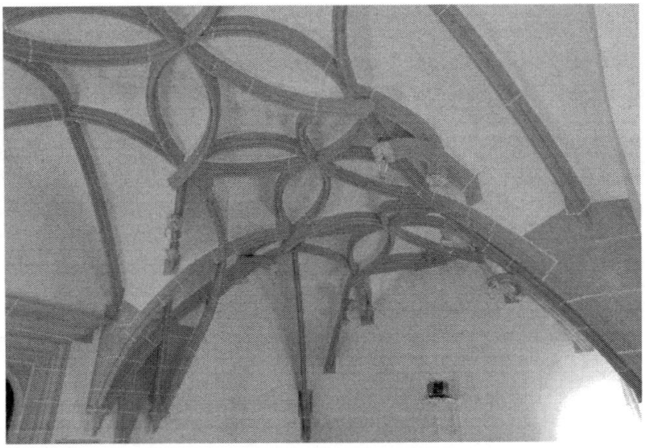

Figure 7. The vault in the Sacristy of St. Anne's church in Annaberg. Only the tiercerons rise as plane arches whithout interruption (M. J. Ventas Sierra, D. Wendland)

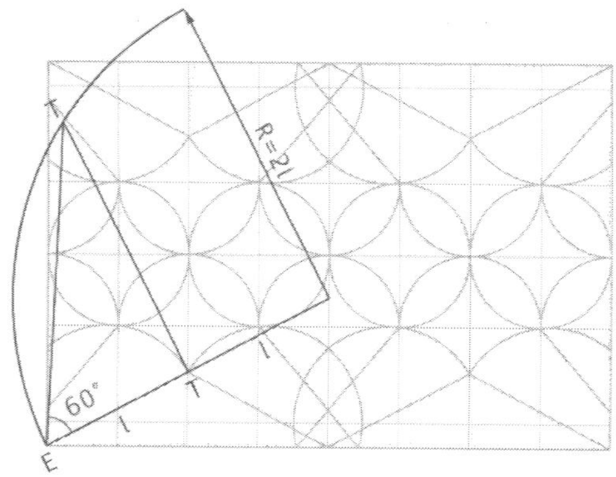

Figure 8. Geometric definition of the tierceron: By the "third-part" of the semicircle, the radius as well as the position of its summit can be determined (M. J. Ventas Sierra, D. Wendland).

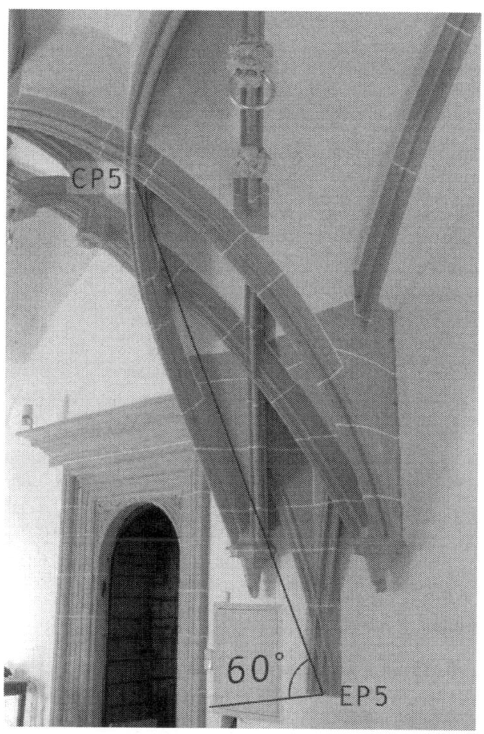

Figure 9. In the complex springer as a whole, the relation between the springing and the intersection of the long curvilinear ribs (CP5) is also related by an angle of 60° (M. J. Ventas Sierra, D. Wendland).

Some concluding remarks

As stated before, the existing database on the geometry of late Gothic vaults is far from being sufficient for any kind of statistic evidence for this idea. At present, we can only propose it as possible interpretation in some case studies.

In the ongoing research, this interpretation can be confirmed by a closer view to the construction detailing. Moreover, there is some evidence that the very isolated assertions on vault mechanic contained, for instance, in the treatise attributed to Rodrigo Gil, correlate to the actual design practice in late Gothic vaults. Beyond that, the approach to structure we sketched would solve the problem of possible connection between geometric and structural design. Therefore we want to put the idea of "supporting" parts of vaults, defined by a third-part of the semicircle or a tangent inclined to 60°, to discussion.

As a final example, we propose this perspective to one of the most prominent vaulted structures in architectural history, Brunelleschi's Cupola in Florence – which we could also consider a late Gothic vault, finished some 35 years before the building of the Albrechtsburg started. We want to point out just one isolated aspect, namely the curve of the inner shell, which during the planning was subject to a heavy dispute between Filippo Brunelleschi and Lorenzo Ghiberti. The diagonal section of the intrados describes one-third of a semicircle, with an tangent inclined to 60°, as shown in the graphic by Giovanni and Michele Fanelli (Fig.10).[25] [FN] Could it be that the geometric design of the Cupola aimed to create a vault without thrust, by composing it only of "resisting" parts?

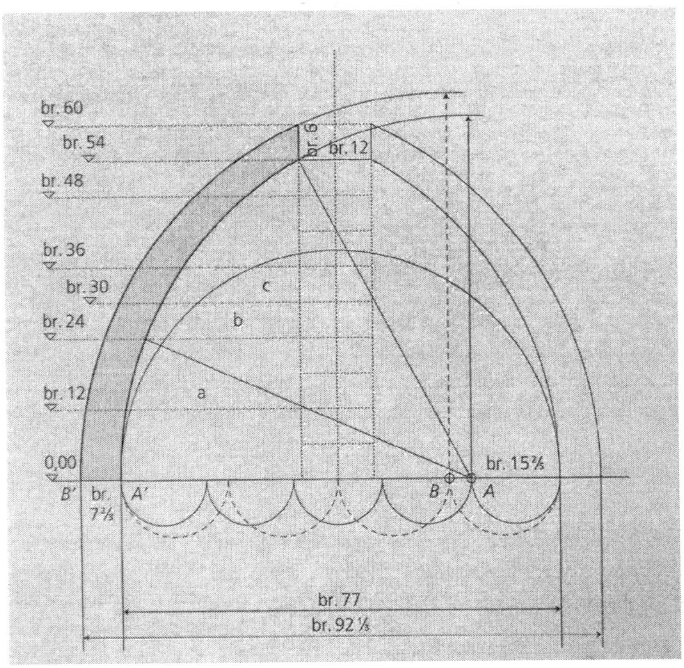

Figure 10. Scheme of the geometric design of Brunelleschi's Cupola in Santa Maria del Fiore (Fanelli 1984). According to the radius of 61.6 braccia *and the height of 54* braccia, *the inclination angle of the secant in the corner of the intrados is 60.3°.*

Acknowledgements

This research is carried out within the ERC Starting Grant "Design Principles in Late-Gothic Vault Construction – A New Approach Based on Surveys, Reverse Geometric Engineering and Reinterpretation of the Sources", which is receiving funding from the European Research Council under the European Union's Seventh Framework Programme, ERC grant agreement n° 284373.

Notes and References

[1] Here we refer to a common idea for describing and predicting the structural performance shared within the group of people involved in the design of buildings.

[2] Parts of this treatise are handed down to us in a manuscript of the 17th Century: Madrid, Biblioteca Nacional Ms. 8884: S. García, 'Compendio de Arquitectura y Simetría de los Templos, conforme a la medida del cuerpo Humano. con algunas demonstraziones de Geometría Año de 1681'. On the passages dedicated to the mechanics of arches: S. L. Sanabria, 'The Mechanization of Design in the 16th Century: The Structural Formulae of Rodrigo Gil de Hontañón', JSAH vo. 61, no.4, 1982, pp. 281-293; S. Huerta, *Arcos, bóvedas y cúpulas: Geometría y equilibrio en el cálculo tradicional de estructuras de fábrica*, Madrid: Inst. Juan de Herrera, 2004.

[3] Huerta, *Arcos* (Note 2); S. Huerta, 'Technical Challenges in the Construction of Gothic Vaults: The Gothic Theory of Structural Design', pp.163-195 in U. Hassler, C. Rauhut, and S. Huerta (Eds): *Construction Techniques in the Age of Historicism: From Theories on Gothic Structures to Building Sites in the 19th Century*, München: Hirmer, 2012.

[4] S. Holzer. *Statische Beurteilung historischer Tragwerke*. vol. 1: *Mauerwerkskonstruktionen*. Berlin: Ernst & Sohn, 2013.

[5] J. Tomlow, *Das Modell / The Model / El Modelo - Antoni Gaudís Hängemodell und seine Rekonstruktion*, Stuttgart: Krämer, 1989.

[6] J. Heyman, 'Wren, Hooke and partners' pp.3-9 in S. Huerta, (Ed.), *Proceedings of the First International Congress on Construction History*, Madrid 2003, Madrid: Instituto Juan de Herrera, 2003; J. Heyman, 'Wren's Domes' pp.209-218 in J. Campbell et al., (Eds), *Proceedings of the First Conference of the Construction History Society*, Cambridge 2014; R. Graefe, 'Zur Formgebung von Bögen und Gewölben', *Architectura*, 1986, pp. 50-67.

[7] M. Trautz, *Zur Entwicklung von Form und Struktur historischer Gewölbe aus der Sicht der Statik*. Stuttgart: Universität Stuttgart, Institut für Baustatik, 1998; D. Wendland, *Lassaulx und der Gewölbebau mit selbsttragenden Mauerschichten. Neumittelalterliche Architektur um 1825-1848*, Petersberg: Imhof, 2008.

[8] J. B. Rondelet, *Traité théorique et pratique de l'art de bâtir*, fifth edition, Paris 1812-14. The first edition appeared from 1802 onwards.

[9] Wendland, *Lassaulx* (Note 7); D. Wendland, 'Systematic underestimation of the thrust of vaults among some builders of the 19th century', 2008, http://elib.uni-stuttgart.de/opus/volltexte/2008/3454/.

[10] This matter was first pointed out by J. Heyman: 'On the Rubber Vaults of the Middle Ages and Other Matters', *Gazette des Beaux-Arts* 71. 1968, pp.177–88.

[11] W. Müller and N. Quien, *Erdachte Formen, errechnete Bilder: Deutschlands Raumkunst der Spätgotik in neuer Sicht*, Weimar: VDG 2000, pp. 7, 9.

[12] One of the first scholars who described this in great clarity was Robert Willis. Cf. Wendland, *Lassaulx* (Note 7).

[13] D. Wendland, 'Johann Claudius von Lassaulx' Gewölbe "aus freier Hand" – Die Wiedererfindung der

gotischen Architektur und die Entwicklung der technischen Literatur', pp. 92-117 in U. Hassler, C. Rauhut, and S. Huerta (Eds): *Construction Techniques in the Age of Historicism: From Theories on Gothic Structures to Building Sites in the 19th Century*, München: Hirmer, 2012.

[14] J. Tomlow, 'On Late-Gothic Vault Geometry', pp. 193-217 in H. Nowacki and W. Lefèvre (Eds), *Creating Shapes in Civil and Naval Architecture: A Cross-Disciplinary Comparison*, Leiden / Boston: Brill, 2009, as well as in earlier publications.

[15] D. Wendland, 'Reverse Engineering und Experimentelle Archäologie – Forschungen zu Bau, Planungsprinzipien und Entwurfskriterien spätgotischer Zellengewölbe', pp. 10-37 in K. Schröck, D. Wendland (Eds), *Traces of Making – Entwurfsprinzipien von spätgotischen Gewölben – Shape, Design and Construction of Late Gothic Vaults*, Petersberg: Imhof, 2014.

[16] ibid.; for a detailed study of Rodrigo Gil's description, D. Wendland, ‚Zum Bau figurierter Gewölbe - eine Anleitung im Werkmeisterbuch des Rodrigo Gil de Hontañón', pp. 244-272 in S. Bürger, B. Klein, and K. Schröck (Eds), *Werkmeister der Spätgotik: Personen, Amt und Image*, Darmstadt: WB, 2010.

[17] D. Wendland, Reverse Engineering (Note 15).

[18] F. Derand, *L'Architecture des voûtes, ou l'Art des traits et coupe des voûtes*. Paris: S. Cramoisy, 1643.

[19] Huerta, Arcos (Note 2); Huerta, Technical Challenges (Note 3).

[20] D. Wendland, Reverse Engineering (Note 15).

[21] The surveys are carried out by M. Aranda Alonso, M.J. Ventas Sierra, and the author.

[22] The surveys are carried out by M. Aranda Alonso, C. Mai, M. J. Ventas Sierra, and the author.

[23] D. Wendland, M. Aranda Alonso, and A. Kobe, 'The Vault with Curvilinear Ribs in the "Hall of Arms" in the Albrechtsburg Meissen: Studies on the Concept, Design and Construction of a Complex Late Gothic Rib Vault', pp. 459-468 in J. Campbell et al., (Eds), *Proceedings of the First Conference of the Construction History Society*, Cambridge 2014.

[24] D. Wendland, 'Tragende Teile: Gedanken zur Konzeption von Rippenwerk und Schalenkonstruktion in einigen spätgotischen Gewölben', pp. 132-143 in G. Zumpe (Ed.), *George-Bähr-Forum Jahrbuch 2014/2015*, Radebeul, 2015.

[25] G. and M. Fanelli, *La Cupola del Brunelleschi*, Firenze: Mandragora, 1984, p. 177.

The construction-deconstruction process of the Cathedral of Tortosa

Agustí Costa Jover, Josep Lluis i Ginovart, Sergio Coll Pla, Albert Ferré Jover
Department of Architecture, Universitat Rovira i Virgili, Spain

Introduction

The Cathedral of *Santa Maria* of Tortosa (1345-1757) is one of the most important Gothic buildings of Catalonia (Fig. 01). Its construction involved the progressive replacement of the existing Romanesque Cathedral (1178), in a process of construction-deconstruction. Both buildings co-existed until the early eighteenth century, as did the near examples of Girona (1312)[1] and Barcelona (1317)[2], among others.

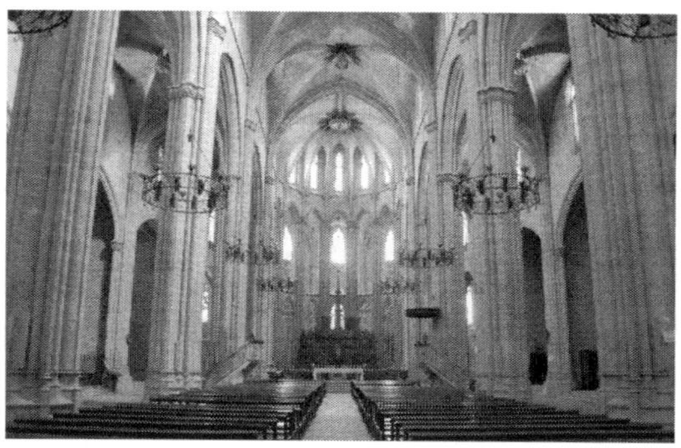

Fig. 01. The Gothic apse of the Cathedral of Tortosa.

The building chronology of the apse of Tortosa cathedral is partially recorded in the *Llibres d'Obra* (construction accounting books) which are kept in the chapter house archive of Tortosa cathedral (ACTo.). This valuable primary source compiles several years of accounting records about the construction. The building chronology of the Gothic apse has been precisely determined by Josep Lluis i Ginovart[3] and Victoria Almuni[4] on the basis of the primary sources and the analysis of the built masonry: this article presents the latest advances in the study of this process by means of topographical, geophysical and analytical techniques, enhancing present knowledge beyond traditional historiography.

The exact locality of the Romanesque building was unknown, so a geophysical survey of the subsoil was performed using Ground Penetrating Radar (GPR). This technique is commonly used in heritage constructions, and in Spain it has been applied with good results in the temples of Girona[5], Valencia[6] or Tarragona[7]. The first results[8] identified the old foundation of the so-called *pilar major* (main column) (Fig. 02a), a big, multifunctional temporary element, the existence of which had already been discovered in 2011 by Lluis i Ginovart & Almuni[9]. The GPR also identified the remains of the rest of the ancient Romanesque cathedral (1178) (Fig. 02b), the construction model of which is proposed in our article of 2014[10].

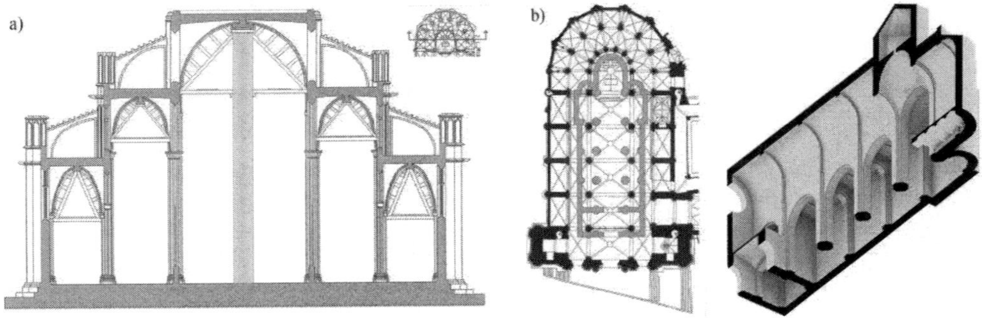

Fig. 02. Hypothesis from the GPR. a) Pilar major, b) Romanesque cathedral.

This assessment is completed with a limit analysis of the structure of the apse, according to the theoretical framework established by Heyman[11], through which the equilibrium conditions during the construction process are analysed, identifying the phases when it could have been necessary to use some temporary system of buttressing to compensate the thrusts of the vaults and to guarantee the stability. In respect of composition, the apse is defined by a heptagonal floor plan having a three-level double ambulatory covered with ribbed groin vaults. The unit of measure for the apse is the Tortosa span (23.23 cm)[12].

Methodology

The investigation involved two main stages. Firstly, the geometry of the Cathedral of Tortosa was defined by means of a Terrestrial Laser Scanner (TLS), and underground remains were identified by means of Ground Penetrating Radar (GPR). The location of the *pilar major* and the rest of the ancient Romanesque building enables a virtual simulation of the process of construction-deconstruction.

Secondly, the study is completed with an assessment of the equilibrium conditions using graphic statics techniques at the different construction stages. This verifies the need for temporary elements to guarantee equilibrium until the structure was completed. The assessment is focused on the apse, since it is where the work began and where the main decisions about the design of the new Cathedral were taken. In addition, it is the most complex part of the building.

Surveys

Two topographic surveys were carried out using TLS. The first survey (2013)[13] focused on the indoor spaces, while the second survey (2014-15)[14] analysed the outside of the apse. Both surveys used very similar devices and offer the same data acquisition accuracy. A tolerance of 3mm has been allowed for the joining of the different point clouds. Firstly, the station readings were processed with the software Cyclone (Fig. 04.a) in order to obtain the complete point cloud of the apse. Secondly, based on this point cloud, the software 3DReshaper was used to define a mesh (Triangulated Irregular Network). The mesh density was set to an average triangle size of 2.5 cm (Fig. 04.b). Lastly, the 2D-geometry of arches and vaults was defined on the basis of the 3D mesh[15].

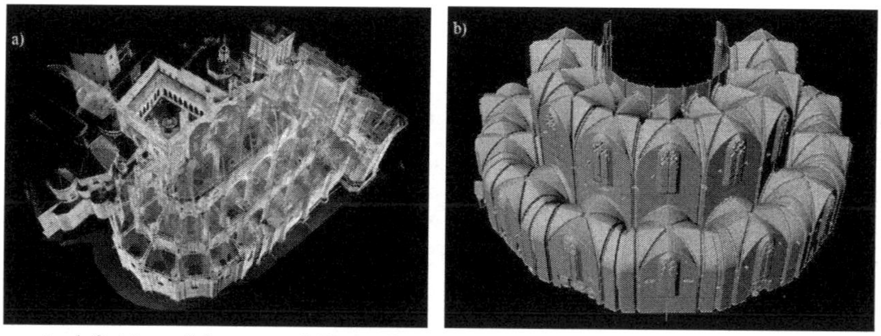

Fig. 03. Geometric definition of the apse. a) Point cloud, b) 3D mesh

The geophysical survey was performed between 2012 and 2013[16]. A GPR IDS Hi-Mod 200-600MHz, with a resolution of 0.018 x 0.2m, was used. It enabled alternative visualizations, with greater detail (600MHz, 60 ns.) or greater depth (200MHz, 90 ns.). The effective depth obtained ranges between 8m (600MHz) and 2.3m (200MHz), with a a velocity of 0.095m/ns.

Calculation strategies

There are currently many analysis and prospecting techniques which can provide this information, but their implementation can be complex and costly in some cases. In the context of masonry structures, the widely known limit analysis by Heyman allow analysis of the equilibrium conditions of a structure by knowing its materials and geometry, as pointed out by authors such as Block[17], Ochsendorf[18], Boothby[19], O'Dwyer[20] and Huerta[21]. The historical background and the theoretical framework are provided by Huerta[22], Roca[23] and Theodossopoulos[24], who analyse the state of play regarding the different analysis techniques. The lower bound theorem enables the equilibrium approach, so the aim of the study is to analyse possible solutions, instead of searching for the 'real' state of the structure.

On the basis of their structural function, we can make a distinction between thrust-generating elements (arches, vaults and flying buttresses) and thrust-countering elements (enclosing walls, pillars and pinnacles). The only supported element is the top roofing, which rests on the vaults. Two strategies to calculate the pressure lines have been used: (a) characteristic cross section analysis by means of a spreadsheet, and (b) detailed analysis by means of manual graphic statics.

In order to analyse the characteristic cross section – Strategy (a) –, we have examined the basic structural cross section of the apse at the different construction stages by means of a spreadsheet, allowing identification of a wide range of possible solutions. This approach involves a higher degree of simplification and does not allow checking of the effects of asymmetric situations, because it is limited to cases where the vaults on both sides of the cross section concerned have already been built.

As for the detailed analysis – Strategy (b)–, we have examined the building stages of each level's first vaults. The pressure lines were manually calculated using CAD software, providing a thorough analysis of each arch. In this case we did not calculate results ranges, since the structure can be regarded as stable if there is one valid solution.

Simulation of the process of construction-deconstruction

Building stages and historical chronology

The building of the apse can be divided into three main stages, with some sub-stages (Fig. 04). First of all, the ring of radiating chapels was built around the original Romanesque cathedral, which was still in use by then. The chapels were built in sequence from the gospel side to the epistle side. They were covered with square-based ribbed vaults between 1383 and 1424. The keystones of these vaults are at a theoretical height of 45 spans (1045.35 cm).

The second stage involved the building of the nine vaults of the ambulatory between 1424 and 1434. The two first vaults have a square base, while the seven remaining vaults have a trapezoidal base, and their keystones are all at a theoretical height of 72 spans (1672.56 cm). Unlike the radiating chapels, the ambulatory vaults were built symmetrically from the foot of the apse towards the choir.

Lastly, the chancel was built between 1435 and 1441. The *Clau Major* (main keystone) was placed in the apse centre at a height of 100 spans (2323 cm) and then the vaults were closed, starting with those located at the foot of the apse, which are bigger than the rest. The *pilar major* presumably helped to balance the thrusts of the ambulatory chapels and chancel chapels, and also supported the scaffolding system.

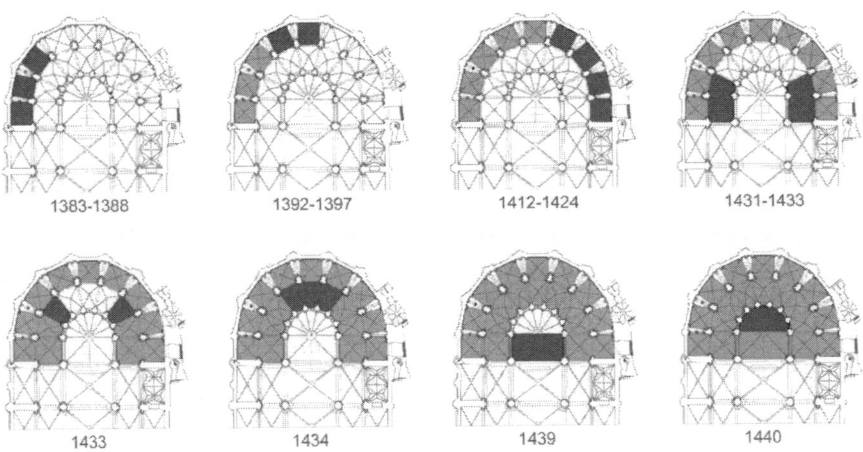

Fig. 04. Building stages of the apse in Tortosa cathedral (1345-1441).

The central body was built between 1441 and 1757, following the height parameters established by the apse. There is a central nave and two side aisles surrounded by chapels.

Apse construction (1347-1441)

The construction of the cathedral started with St. Peter's chapel, at the gospel side (Fig. 05). The initial work (1347-83) resulted in the first stretches of the enclosing wall. The chapels were completed one by one from the gospel side towards the epistle side (1383-1424).

The ring of radiating chapels did not coincide in space with the pre-existing Romanesque structure, which remained unaffected. The closeness between both masonries raises the possibility that shores or other temporary elements were placed on the Romanesque structure, particularly during the vaults construction.

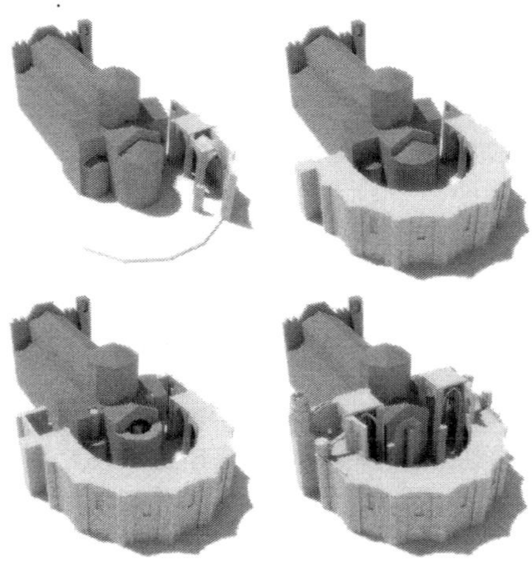

Fig. 05. Construction sequence of the apse (1345-1441)

Once the ring of radiating chapels was completed, the construction of the ambulatory began (1424-34). It is at this point that the modular proportion changed from (9/5) to (9/6), and remained so until the end of the construction work. The ring of pillars between the ambulatory and the chancel encircled the Romanesque apse without affecting it in any way. Construction work on the pillars presumably began when the chapels were still being built, and we know that the first stretches of the first-level enclosing wall were already finished in 1426. The building of the first-level pinnacles and flying buttresses began that same year, parallel to the vaults.

The construction of the arches separating the ambulatory from the chancel started in 1427. These arches, as well as the first vaults of the ambulatory, rest on the pillars that are located on the foot of the apse. According to our previous model, these pillars coincided in space with the enclosing wall of the Romanesque apsidioles. As a consequence, part of the Romanesque masonry had to be demolished. Thus, the new pillars were placed at the centre of the apsidioles, encircled by enclosing walls which were demolished at a later point in time. Once the pillars at the foot of the apse were placed, the ambulatory vaults were built on a higher level, so there was no more interference between the two buildings.

The vault of the Romanesque apse was demolished in May 1428. The construction of the *Pilar Major* began in August of the same year. The placing of the main pillar also signalled the start of construction of the ambulatory vaults, since this pillar must have been the main element that countered the vault thrusts while the apse structure was being built. The ambulatory vaults were built very quickly (1431-34), closing the space symmetrically from the foot of the apse. A provisional enclosure was placed in the altar area to maintain worship in the original Romanesque cathedral.

The Gothic apse was completed without any further impact on the original church, since the latter had a lower height and was contained in the new volume. Thus, the construction of the chancel (1434-41) began after completing the ambulatory. The placement of the *clau major* (main keystone) on the *pilar major* (main column) on Sunday 27 September 1439 triggered the closing of the chancel vaults. The *pilar major* served a double function as a supporting element and also as a staking out aid to accurately define the location of the great keystone. Besides, it supported the centrings and scaffolding necessary to build the vaults while ensuring overall stability. The vaulted space was closed from west to east, thus completing the structure of the Gothic apse, which was consecrated in April 1441.

The model proposed includes a dome in the Romanesque transept which must have been very close to the side arch separating the nave from the apse. However, this side arch was at a higher level than the dome, so both elements could coexist.

It was also in this period that the construction of the nave's first pillar began at the epistle side. According to our model, this pillar did not coincide in space with any supporting element of the Romanesque structure; therefore, it had only a minimum impact at ground level. The foundation excavation must have exposed the foundation of the Romanesque structure, as is apparent from the direct sources available.

Central body construction (1441-1757)

After completion of the Gothic apse, work began on the first structural line (1441-95). There are no written records confirming the overlap of construction and deconstruction work, but the construction sequence indicates that the Romanesque cathedral was enclosed in the Gothic building and continued to be used (Fig. 06). The Romanesque structure was not affected by the perimeter walls or by the partition walls between chapels. The sections of the central body were closed one by one from the chapels towards the central nave, following the same construction sequence as Mallorca Cathedral[25].

Therefore, the Romanesque building remained almost unaffected until the pillars of the central nave were built. These pillars were erected with minimum demolition, by drilling through the roofing of the Romanesque side aisles. Once through this roofing, the Gothic vaults of the side aisles could be built without demolishing the Romanesque structure. The side chapels of the central body's first section were finished in 1454.

According to the construction accounting books, the Romanesque dome was dismantled after roofing the side aisles. This allowed the central vault to be closed (1494-96), thus completing the first Gothic section. Next, the lower level of the Romanesque structure was removed. Some kind of rain protection must have been put into place, since some time passed between the removal of the Romanesque dome and the reclosing of that space with the new Gothic vault. This need for protection against the rain only concerned the area of the central vault, since the remaining indoor spaces were already covered.

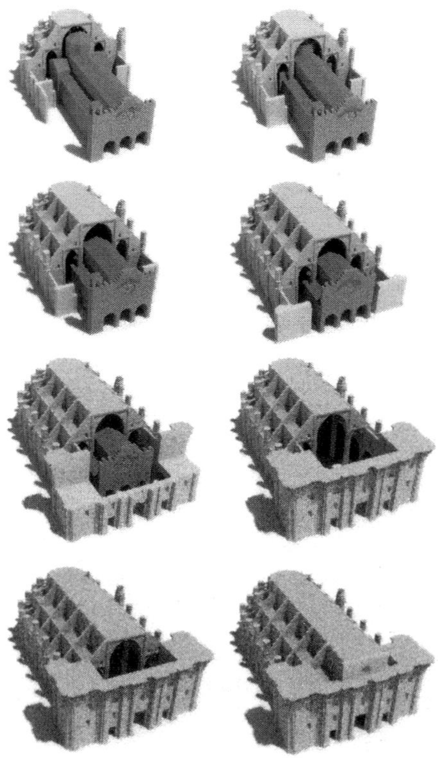

Fig. 06. Building stages of the main body (1441-1757)

The construction-deconstruction process of the next two sections (1495-1575) was carried out in a similar way, except that, in the absence of a dome, the roofing of the Romanesque cathedral was removed after finishing the Gothic vaults. On the one hand, this ensured protection against the rain and the elements: on the other hand, the Romanesque structure could be used as a supporting element, considerably optimizing construction resources.

The cathedral was reconsecrated in 1597. At that point, the Gothic construction – the heptagonal apse and the three first sections of the central body – probably coexisted with the last section of the Romanesque cathedral and its main façade.

Construction work on the Baroque façade (together with the dismantling of the Romanesque façade) did not start until the beginning of the 17th century. Both façades coexisted until the beginning of the 18th century, since the new façade was built outside the Romanesque building. The dismantling of the Romanesque façade started in January 1703[26]. Finally, the top of the Baroque façade and the last two sections of the central body were completed. This change in the order of construction-deconstruction must have also had an impact on the temporary elements and on the progress of the construction work. Whereas in the former, sections the scaffolding system could rest on the Romanesque structure, in the last two sections conventional systems had to be used. Lastly, following the complete disappearance of the Romanesque building, the Tortosa Gothic cathedral was consecrated again to Saint Mary in 1757.

Limit analysis of the apse (1345-1441)

Structure characterization

The structural model is complex, since there are four different impost line heights which define the arches' springing at the chapel vaults (Fig. 07). At the first roofing level, each pillar in the ambulatory receives the thrusts from: 1) the arch located on the same axis, 2) the diagonal ribs, 3) the side arches, and 4) the bonders. At the second roofing level, these pillars also support the diagonal arches and the transverse arch of the ambulatory vault, which are at a greater height. Thus, the pillars must adapt to changing stresses during the construction process, with thrust forces alternating on both sides. The design of the ambulatory was changed during construction, so that the side arches, bonders and diagonal arches were all built on the same impost line. The modular ratio in height also changed from (9/5) at the chapels to (9/6) at the ambulatory[27].

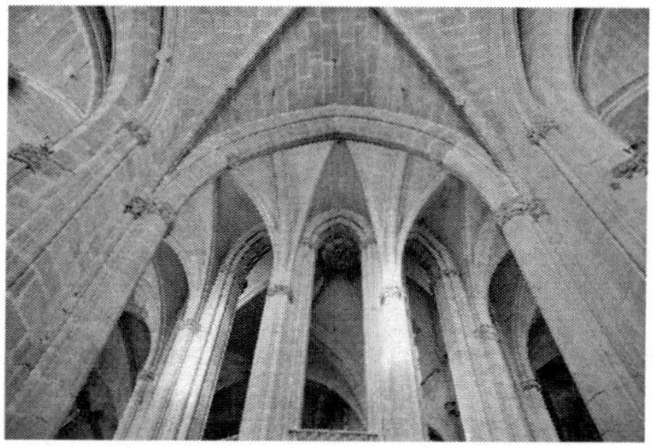

Fig. 07. Arch springing at the vaults.

In order to define the materials used – particularly for the roofing –, we refer to authors such as Bassegoda[28], who describe the usual practice in southern Gothic architecture, and also the test bore made during the writing of the *Pla Director* (Master Plan)[29]. The vaults' springing is solid up to a height between one third and two-thirds of the rise, depending on the geometry. The filling layer covering the extrados is filled with *gerres* (ceramic jars). On top of that there is a 20-40 cm thick lime mortar layer known as *trespol*, forming a horizontal plane which supports the top roofing (originally built with ceramic tiles). This layer arrangement is also detailed in the construction process of one the ambulatory vaults[30]. The vertical structure, as well as the pinnacles and flying buttresses, are all built with sandstone masonry. Due to the lack of experimental data, the specific gravities of the main materials are taken from bibliographic references[31]. These gravities are as follows: sandstone: 24 kN/m^3; *trespol*: 22 kN/m^3; lightweight filling: 2 kN/m^3.

Results

The calculation models have been defined on the basis of the building stages as established for each level of the Gothic apse. Thus, six models are defined for the intermediate building stages, and a seventh model for the cross section of the complete apse:

-Level 1: chapel vault (1).

-Level 2: enclosing wall (2), pinnacle and flying buttress (3), ambulatory vault (4).

-Level 3: enclosing wall (5), pinnacle and flying buttress (6), chancel vault (7).

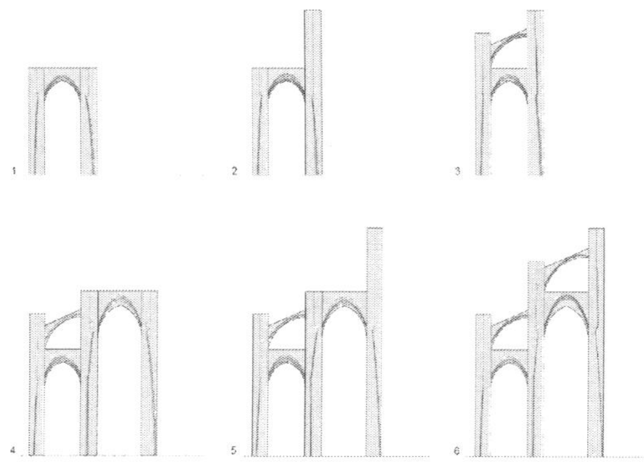

Fig. 08. Results from the characteristic cross section analysis (a).

The number of considered hypotheses depends on the number of elements involved in the calculation and on the equilibrium conditions, with a range of 10-14 combinations for each building stage. The magnitude of the thrusts is so small in relation to the weight of the countering system that the different hypotheses entail very minor variations in the location of the pressure lines in the countering system (Fig. 08). Several stable solutions can be found, though in some cases the pressure line is barely contained within the base of the pillar, meaning the structure would be at its limit. This is the case of the chancel pillar in the building stages (4) and, specially, (5) and (6).

A detailed analysis enables comparison of the results with the spreadsheet, and also assessment of the effect of any asymmetry situations resulting from the vaults not being built simultaneously (Fig. 09). After calculating the thrusts of each arch and rib, the stability of the pillars on their two main axes is assessed. The differences between different cross sections are irrelevant, which is why the results for the first cross section are shown. The analysis reveals minor differences relative to previous results.

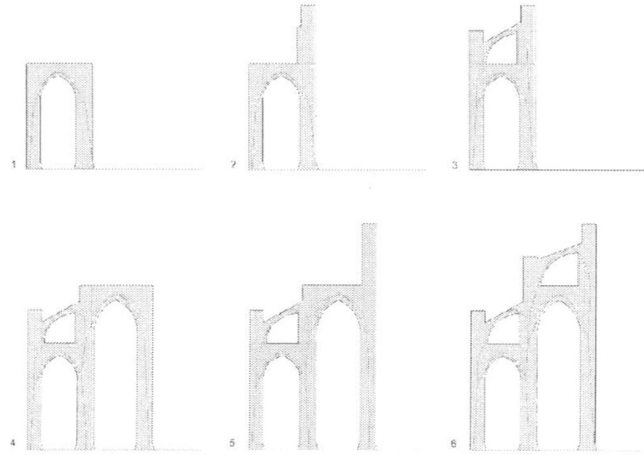

Fig. 09. Detailed analysis results (cross sections).

Additionally, the results for the pillars' transversal axis enable checking of the negative effect of the asymmetry situation resulting from the vaults not being built simultaneously (Fig. 10a). In the chapels' pillar, the pressure line is outside the middle third but far from the cross section limit. As for the pillar located between the ambulatory and the chancel, the result is more unfavourable, since the pressure line is very close to the cross section limit. Otherwise, both strategies enable a stable solution considering the completed apse (Fig. 10b).

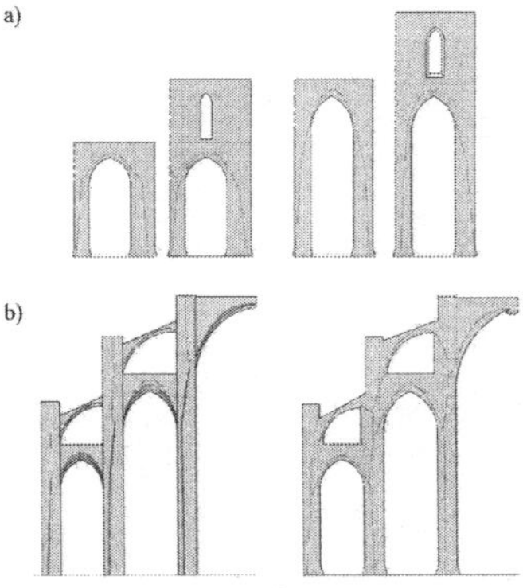

Fig. 10. a) Transversal sections, b) Results for the finished structure.

Evaluation of the stability

From a structural point of view, the equilibrium is mainly assessed through an analysis of the tipping conditions at the base of the supporting system. The TLS survey showed that the vertical elements are perfectly plumbed, indicating that they have not been subject to displacement and the structure is perfectly balanced. This is consistent with the results of the analysis of the complete structure.

Conversely, the intermediate building stages resulted in some situations where the pressure lines were barely contained within the pillars cross section at the base. The vaults thrust against the apse perimeter – both the thrust from the chapel vaults and from the ambulatory vaults – was countered without any problem, even though the flying buttresses and the pinnacles had not been built yet. In this respect, the external reinforcement of the perimeter wall is an entirely optimized solution.

The thrusts towards the chancel's centre, however, were more difficult to counter, particularly in the case of the chancel's pillars, which are taller. The pressure lines are very close to the limit at the pillars' base in all cases, even considering extreme scenarios with a minimum thrust from the vaults. The results are the same for the transverse axis of the pillars, when only the vault on one side has been built. This asymmetry situation makes it very difficult to find a stable solution.

Conclusions

Tortosa Cathedral has been analysed using a combination of methods. Historical, geophysical (GPR) and geometric (TLS) data, together with limit state analysis data, have enabled determination of the process of construction-deconstruction. The volumetric assessment has revealed the difficulties and advantages of the co-existence of the two buildings, which made possible the continued use of the Romanesque cathedral as a place of worship and as a temporary support for the Gothic structure that replaced it..

The assessment of the equilibrium at the stages of construction has completed our understanding of the building process of the Gothic apse. The finished structure does not have any equilibrium issues, but during the intermediate building stages the set of forces was not yet complete and may have caused stability problems. Therefore, the pressure lines calculated, reveal that it was necessary to use temporary thrust-countering systems in order to ensure the stability of the whole structure. Thus, the *pilar major* (main column) must have played a key role in construction, balancing the horizontal forces from the vaults by means of props which might also serve as supporting elements for the scaffolding system. Besides, the co-existence with the Romanesque cathedral leads us to believe that the latter was also used as a support for props and scaffolds during construction, thus reducing the cost of temporary systems.

References

[1] G.E. Street, *Some account of gothic architecture in Spain*, London, Albemarle Street: John Murray, 1865. p. 318

[2] J. Bassegoda i Nonell, *La catedral de Barcelona: su restauración 1968-1972*, Barcelona: Editores Tecnicos Asociados S.A., 1973. p. 55.

[3] J. Lluis i Ginovart, A. Llorca, *Pla Director Sancta Maria Dertosae. Tortosa*. Bisbat de Tortosa. Departament de Cultura Generalitat de Catalunya, 2000; J. Lluis i Ginovart, *Geometría y diseño medieval en la catedral de Tortosa: la catedral no construida* (Ph.D. thesis, Universitat Internacional de Catalunya), 2002.

[4] V. Almuni, *L'Obra de la Seu de Tortosa : 1345-1441*. Tortosa: Cooperativa Gràfica Dertosense, 1991; V. Almuni, *La Catedral de Tortosa als segles del gòtic* (2 vols). Barcelona: Fundació Noguera, 2007.

[5] M. Dabas, C. Camerlynck, P. Freixas i Camps, 'Case History: Simultaneous use of electrostatic quadrupole and GPR in urban context: Investigation of the basement of the Cathedral de Girona (Catalunya, Spain', *Geophysics*, 65 (2), 2000, pp. 526-532; P. Freixas, *La catedral de Girona, redescobrir la Seu Romànica. Els resultats de la recerca del Projecte Progres*. Ajuntament de Girona. Girona, 2000.

[6] V. Pérez Gracia, et al., 'GPR survey to confirm the location of ancient structures under the Valencian Cathedral (Spain)'. *Journal of Applied Geophysics*, 43, 2000, pp.167-174.

[7] J.M. Macias, A. Muñoz, I. Teixell, 'A la Recerca del Temple d'August, les intervencions arqueològiques a la catedral de Tarragona', *Plecs d'Historia Local*, nº 146, 2012 juliol/agost, pp. 2-4.

[8] J. Lluis i Ginovart, A. Costa Jover, G. Fortuny Anguera, 'Elementos auxiliares de construcción en la arquitectura gótica. El 'pilar major' de la catedral de Tortosa', *Informes de la Construcción*, *67*(537), 2015, e057.

[9] J. Lluis i Ginovart, V. Almuni i Balada, 'La clave de la clau. El cierre constructivo del presbiterio gótico' pp. 733-742, in S. Huerta (Ed.), *Proceedings of the Séptimo Congreso Nacional Historia de la Construcción, Santiago de Compostela* 2011, Madrid: Instituto Juan de Herrera, 2011.

[10] J. Lluis i Ginovart, A. Costa-Jover, S. Coll-Pla, 'La reconstrucción de un palimpsesto románico mediante técnicas no destructivas', *Informes de La Construcción*, 66 (536), 2014, e045.

[11] J. Heyman, The Stone Skeleton. International. *Journal of Solids and Structures*, 2, 1966, pp. 249-279; J. Heyman, *The Stone Skeleton*. Cambridge: Cambridge University Press, 1995.

[12] J. Lluis i Ginovart, G. Fortuny Anguera, A. Costa Jover, P. Sola-Morales Serra, 'Gothic construction and the Traça of a heptagonal apse: The problem of the Heptagon', *Nexus Network Journal: Architecture and Mathematics*, 15(2), 2013, pp. 325–348.

[13] Campaign 2013, Josep Lluis i Ginovart, Agustí Costa, Josep M. Puche. Equipment: Leica Scan Station C10. Time-of-flight with a maximum instantaneous speed of 50,000 points/sec and wavelength of 532 nm. Laser class 3R (IEC 60825-1). Field-of-View: 360° Horizontal, 270° Vertical. The range accuracy of single

measurements is: position (6 mm), distance (4 mm), horizontal/vertical angle (60 µrad/60 µrad; 12"/12"). Target acquisition: 2 mm standard deviation up to 50 m.Imaging: built-in camera, 4-megapixels per each 17° x 17° colour image.

[14] Campaign 2014-15, Josep Lluis i Ginovart, Agustí Costa, Sergio Coll. Equipment: Leica Scan Station P20, Ultra-high speed time-of-flight enhanced by Waveform Digitising (WFD) technology. Wavelength 808 nm (invisible) / 658 nm (visible). Laser class 1 (in accordance with IEC60825:2014). Field-of-View: 360° Horizontal, 270° Vertical. 3D position accuracy: 3 mm at 50 m, 6 mm at 100 m; linearity error: smaller than or equal to 1 mm. Angular accuracy: 8" horizontal; 8" vertical. Target acquisition: 2 mm standard deviation up to 50 m. Imaging: built-in camera, 5-megapixels per each 17° x 17° colour image.

[15] J. Lluis i Ginovart, A Costa, J.M. Puche, S. Coll, 'Assessment of the construction process of the Cathedral of Tortosa', *Journal of Architectural Conservation, 20*(3), 2014, pp. 156–169.

[16] R. Sala, *Memòria d'Intervenció. Prospecció geofísica a la catedral de Tortosa*. SOT Prospecció Arqueològica (Roger Sala, Ekhine Garcia, Robert Tamba), 2013.

[17] P. Block, M. DeJong, J. Ochsendorf, 'As Hangs the Flexible Line: Equilibrium of Masonry Arches', *Nexus Network Journal*, *8*(2), 2006, pp. 38–47.

[18] J. Ochsendorf, *Collapse of masonry structures* (Ph.D. thesis, Department of Engineering, Cambridge University, Cambridge, 2002).

[19] T.E. Boothby, 'Analysis of masonry arches and vaults', *Progress in Structural Engineering and Materials*, *3*(3), 2001, pp. 246–256.

[20] D. O'Dwyer, 'Funicular analysis of masonry vaults', *Computers & Structures*, *73*(1-5), 1999, pp. 187–197.

[21] S. Huerta, 'Mecánica de las bóvedas de fábrica; El enfoque del equilibrio', *Informes de la Construcción*, Vol. 56, nº 496, marzo-abril 2005, pp. 73-89.

[22] S. Huerta, *Arcos, bóvedas y cúpulas. Geometría y equilibrio en el cálculo tradicional de estructuras de fábrica*. Madrid: Instituto Juan de Herrera, 2004; S. Huerta, 'The Analysis of Masonry Architectures: A Historical Approach', *Architectural Science Review*, vol. 51, 4, 2008, pp. 297-328.

[23] P. Roca, M. Cervera, G. Gariup, L. Pelà, 'Structural Analysis of Masonry Historical Constructions. Classical and Advanced Approaches', *Archives of Computational Methods in Engineering*, 17(3), 2010, pp. 299-325.

[24] D. Theodossopoulos, & B. Sinha, 'A review of analytical methods in the current design processes and assessment of performance of masonry structures', *Construction and Building Materials*, 41, 2013, pp. 990–1001.

[25] J. Domenge i Mesquida, *L'obra de la seu. El procés de construcción de la catedral de Mallorca en el tres-cents*. Palma: Institut d'Estudis Baleàrics, 1999.

[26] Acta from 19 January 1703. R. O'Callaghan, *Anales de Tortosa III*, Tortosa: Imprenta Católica de Gabriel Llasat, 1888, p. 184.

[27] J. Lluis i Ginovart, & A. Costa Jover, 'Design and medieval construction: The case of Tortosa catedral (1345–1441)', *Construction History*, *29*(1), 2014, pp. 1–24.

[28] J. Bassegoda i Nonell, 'La construcción de las bóvedas góticas catalanas', *Boletín Académico. Escola Técnica Superior de Arquitectura Da Coruña*, 11, 1989, pp. 30–38.

[29] J. Lluis i Ginovart, A. Costa Jover, 'La bóveda y el trespol. Cobertura y estructura del gótico meridional', pp. 529–536, in S. Huerta (Ed.), *Proceedings of the Octavo Congreso Nacional de Historia de la Construcción. Madrid, 9-12 de octubre de 2013*. Madrid: Instituto Juan de Herrera, 2013.

[30] Almuni, La Catedral (Note 4) Vol2, pp. 584-587.

[31] CTE, DB SE-AE; J. Murcia, *Seismic analysis of Santa Maria del Mar church in Barcelona* (Master's thesis, Universitat Politècnica de Catalunya, 2008).

The first design project for the church of Santa María in Carmona (Seville, Spain): hypothesis on the creation of a new architectural typology in the Spanish Late Gothic

Antonio Luis Ampliato Briones and Juan Clemente Rodríguez Estévez
University of Seville, Spain

Introduction

In the last third of the fifthteenth century, embracing the initiative of other major towns in the archbishopric, Carmona embarked on the construction of a large Gothic building to house its main church, inspired by the monumental cathedral in Seville. Following the Christian conquest of Carmona in 1247, the parish of Santa María had taken up residence in the town's old mosque. Like the cathedral in the city of Seville, the new Gothic project was conceived as a modernising initiative and triumphant expression of the church. The close ties between the local and ecclesiastical elites of Seville and Carmona, coupled with the involvement of the cathedral master builders, meant that the new work was a particularly mature interpretation of the cathedral model.

As part of an interdisciplinary investigation into the church of Santa María in Carmona undertaken by a research group that has spent the last decade analysing the Gothic cathedral in Seville and its influence in south-west Spain, this paper presents the key results relating to the first design project for Santa María.[1] First of all, we delimit the various sections of the work built according to the successive design projects and offer a hypothesis about the typology that was originally conceived and then radically altered. We then interpret the work in light of its model, the cathedral in Seville, through a dialogue that enables us to clarify important aspects about both buildings.

The Seville Cathedral model and its impact on the archbishopric

Begun around 1433, Seville's cathedral was conceived as a vast stone mass to replace the old and dilapidated Almohad mosque that had been used as the seat of the archbishopric since 1248. Presiding over a city which since the discovery of America had consolidated its status as a metropolis, the cathedral was completed in 1506 when the last stone of the dome was placed. However, following the collapse of this dome in 1511, the works continued for another decade.[2] The extraordinary technical and economic effort required—something only within the reach of one of the richest archdioceses in the Iberian Peninsula—gave rise to an original building, with no direct typological antecedents, (Fig. 1) that obeyed the particular conditions in which the project was forged. The Almohad building destined to be replaced had been a Christianised space, a repository for the customs and traditions that had marked the life of the seat of the archbishopric for two centuries. The new Late Gothic building was obliged not only to incorporate the enormous Islamic oratory—making it the world's largest church at the time—but also to maintain the close and unique relationship that existed between the building and the urban fabric that surrounded it and formed part of the actual cathedral grounds, all of which constituted an anomaly in the Gothic tradition. Moreover, the new design also had to resolve the complex institutional organisation that had existed since the thirteenth century whereby the king and the archbishop each occupied their own specific place within the sacred space, which was divided into two equally powerful areas—the Royal Chapel and the cathedral's liturgical space—a pre-eminence now disputed by the Cathedral Council, the major sponsor of the new Gothic building.[3]

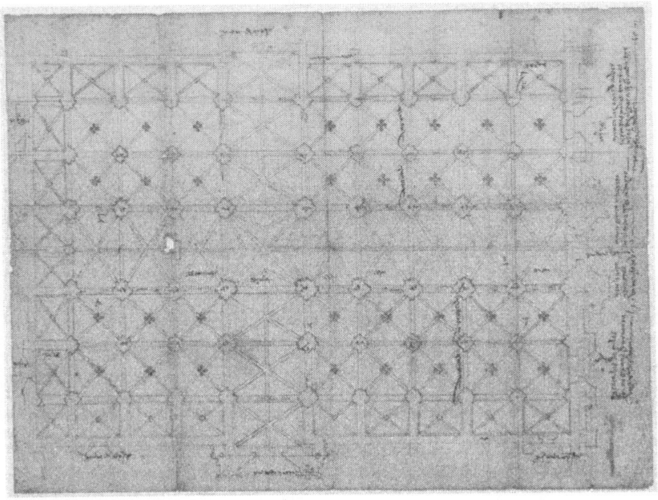

Figure 1. Floor plan of Seville Cathedral known as the 'Bidaurreta Plan', mid-fifthteenth century. Archives of the convent of Santa Clara de Bidaurreta, Oñate, Guipúzcoa, Spain.

The result of all this is the building which, in essence, has reached us today. It is a building with a nave and four aisles, side chapels, a flat-ended chevet, and a large crossing crowned by a dome. The interior space is imposing and serene, with none of the tension of the traditional Gothic, (Fig. 2) while the exterior volumes are robust and orthogonal, the characteristic echeloned nave and aisles, flat-roofed vaults and horizontal buttresses lending the complex a distinct, recognisable profile in the works that followed its example.

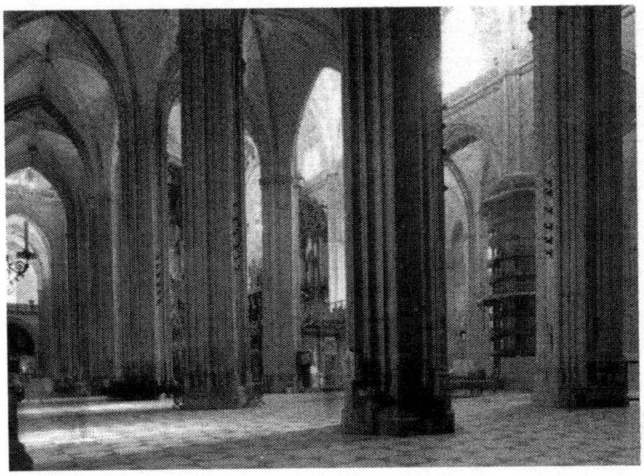

Figure 2. Interior of Seville Cathedral. Photo: A. L. Ampliato.

Although parts of the design were redefined at specific points during the building works, the cathedral is essentially the product of a single project.[4] On the rectangular floor plan of the church a great cross was drawn, composed of the nave and transept, both of them higher than the aisles and characterised by a ridge rib running down the apex of their vaults. This great cross with its evident symbolic value introduced a certain centrality around the two elements that constituted its main core, the choir and chancel, linked by the Way of the Cross. Meanwhile, the side chapels would continue around the entire chevet, their presence reinforced by a raised platform with ornately carved parapets, lending emphasis to a 'rectangular ambulatory' destined to accommodate the Royal Chapel. In the event, this chapel, surrounded by endless controversy, was not completed until the mid-sixteenth century and adopts a distinctly Renaissance design.

The essence of this design project was included in the so-called Bidaurreta Plan, (Fig. 1) which is thought to reproduce the original design attributed to Maestro Ysambarte, recorded as active at the cathedral in 1433.[5] Of French descent, this architect played a central role in disseminating the Spanish Late Gothic, both in the Crown of Aragón and Castile. His renovation of Palencia Cathedral introduced a spatial conception whose duality we believe offers a crucial insight into the design of the building in Seville.[6] In any case, the execution of the works fell to his successors, first Carlín de Rouen (1435-1449) and then Juan Norman (1449-1478), who built the section from the entrance to the crossing as well as the beginning of the pillars and the chapels around the chevet. During a second phase, Juan de Hoces (1478-1496), Simón de Colonia (1496-1498) and Alonso Rodríguez (1496-1512) completed the east side of the church.[7]

In the last third of the fifthteenth century, the cathedral model was disseminated through the construction of several large parish churches in the archbishopric of Seville, giving rise to what has come to be known as Seville Cathedral Gothic.[8] Oscillating between the strong identity of the model and the diversity of the local circumstances, a heterogeneous landscape gradually emerged in which the church of Santa María in Carmona occupies a unique place.

The town of Carmona, 30 km from Seville, had strong historical connections to the capital.[9] Its local elites and church maintained close ties with Seville, whose cathedral boasted illustrious canons like Maese Rodrigo de Santaella and Juan de Vílchez, who played a crucial role in the new project. Supported by both the local clergy, through the so-called Universidad de Beneficiados, and the municipal council, the work was begun with direct input from the cathedral master builders. According to the chronological data available, the plans for the Cathedral Gothic phase must have been drawn up by Juan de Hoces in the 1480s, with the actual works commencing in 1496 under Alonso Rodríguez.[10]

Construction phases of the Priory of Carmona and identification of the first section

The priory of Santa María in Carmona (Fig. 3) is the product of a long construction process that was overseen by several generations of master builders. Only approximately 40 per cent of the Cathedral Gothic design was completed, specifically in the first three sections of the nave and aisles commencing at the entrance facade since, as was the case with the cathedral itself, the works in Carmona were executed in reverse order. The fourth line of pillars therefore constitutes the boundary of this first area as well as being the line that marks the beginning of the transept. The vaults over this transept (including the dome), and indeed the rest of the chevet, correspond to a second construction phase during which significant changes were made to the original design project.[11] In contrast to the fidelity with the cathedral model of the master builders Juan de Hoces and Alonso Rodríguez, who executed the works in the first area, Diego de Riaño's design for the chevet, begun in the 1530s, represented a radical change. During his career, Diego de Riaño, another master builder who worked on Seville Cathedral, in his case following the completion of the main building, evolved from the use of a Late Gothic idiom nearing the end of its course to early incursions in the new Renaissance language.[12]

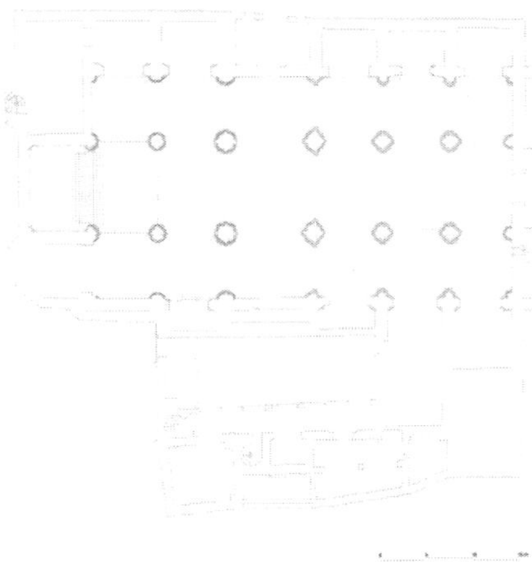

Figura 3. Floor plan of Santa María in Carmona. Drawing by A. L. Ampliato, P. Gimena & E. Acosta.

The two areas of the building that correspond to these two construction phases present radically different formal characteristics. In the first three sections, the Gothic language maintains some of its more traditional principles, (Fig. 4) but this formal regularity nevertheless conceals an interesting and highly refined systematisation of the language through the introduction of numerous spatial markers (subtle modifications in the moulding) which evidence an enormous spatial sensitivity.[13] In contrast to this classical serenity, the language used by Riaño in the chevet clearly reflects the sophisticated experiments that were taking place in the Iberian Peninsula during the early decades of the sixteenth century. (Fig. 5) Particularly notable in this other area are the constant formal variations in all of the elements based on a series of common guidelines. Thus, the space becomes a place dominated by an apparent desire to avoid two identical elements. This is literally the case of all of the vaults over the nave and in particular of the pedestals, since in the entire chevet no two are the same, not even the ones in symmetrical positions.

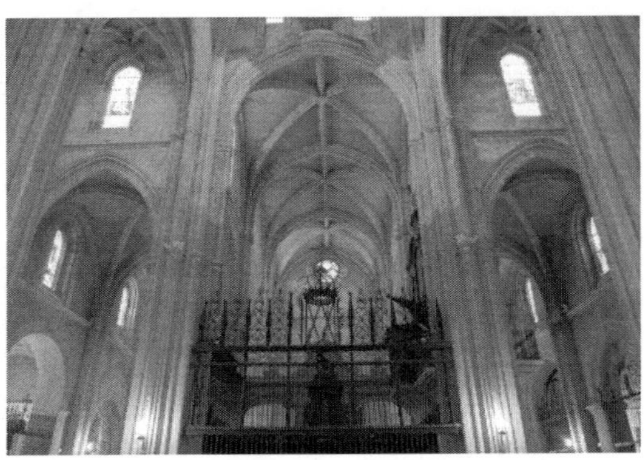

Figure 4. Details of the first sections in Santa María in Carmona. Photo: A. L. Ampliato.

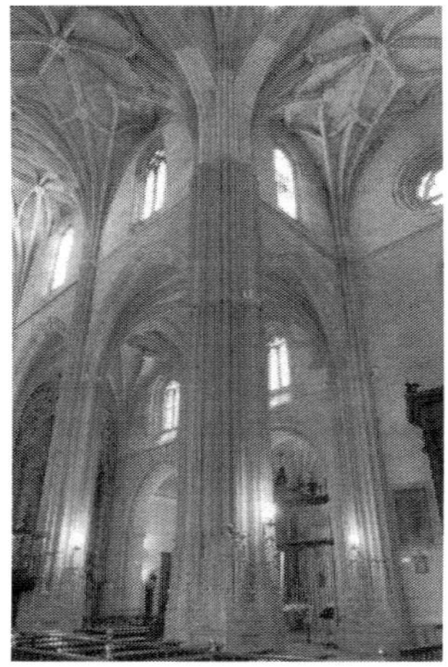

Figure 5. Details of the chevet of Santa María in Carmona. Photo: A. L. Ampliato.

The changes introduced in the 1520s in the design for the Carmona priory also affected its typological layout. (Fig. 6) Maintaining the nave-and-two-aisle basilica structure, the nave was extended by one module to place the new chancel beyond the perimeter initially planned, creating a projecting prism-shaped volume. Additionally, the chancel floor was raised considerably, with access via a grand flight of steps.[14] This new layout for the chancel provided a direct view of the altar for a large part of the congregation, grouped in the aforementioned sections since the choir, in keeping with the Spanish tradition, was relegated to the module in front of the transept. However, these changes make it more difficult to perceive the intentions of the Cathedral Gothic design, especially the position defined for the original chancel. In order to formulate a hypothesis on this, we must seek out the signs that may exist in the built work, and in this process of investigation architectural drawings provide a crucial aid.

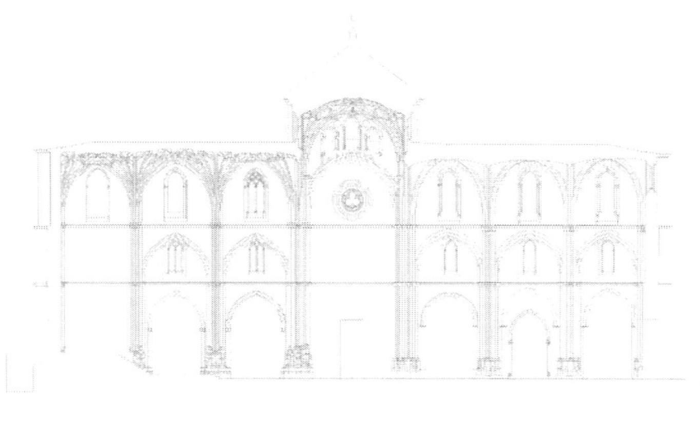

Figure 6. Longitudinal section of Santa María in Carmona. Drawing by A. L. Ampliato, P. Gimena & E. Acosta.

Hypothesis on the Cathedral Gothic design for Santa María in Carmona

In the context of the research project concerning the church in Carmona, a new architectural survey has been undertaken based on the exhaustive collection of data using a Leica total station. Drawings are an essential tool for understanding architecture. In the design project, the architectural drawing generates knowledge because it establishes the logic for the complex building processes. A drawing of what has already been built provides an insight to the building because it partly reproduces the original processes.

The point cloud obtained from the data collected reflects the actual building that exists with extraordinary precision. However, the building that exists lacks geometric precision because of the vicissitudes of the construction process and subsequent deformations of a pathological nature, etc. In creating drawings, we are constantly faced with the need to strike that difficult balance between respecting the demand for precision with regard to what exists and reflecting the regularity (or regularities) that prevailed during its genesis. In processing the information gathered, we created a series of interim drawings (walls, pillars, arches, vaults, etc.) in which, in the manner of a journal, we annotated the graphical representation of the architecture with details of its original geometric characteristics, particular morphology and the most notable alterations observed.

We began our search for the original church plans by focusing our attention on the first three sections of the building, where there are several interesting variations in the design of the pillars on line four with respect to those on lines one to three, presumably related to the succession of the first two master builders, Juan de Hoces and Alonso Rodríguez. The pillars on line four seem to introduce a great emphasis on the transept, probably motivated by the incorporation of a dome which may not have been planned initially.

The building process followed at the church in Carmona may therefore have parallels with that of the cathedral itself in Seville. In our opinion—although this is open to debate—the transept represented in the Bidaurreta Plan (Fig. 1) lacks a dome, the only spatial accent being the variation in the design of the central vault through the incorporation of tiercerons.[15] Apart from other considerations which fall outside the purpose of this paper, this hypothesis is supported by the fact that the pillars represented in the plan, including the four central ones, all have the same dimensions, Some time after 1496, Alonso Rodríguez and Simón de Colonia altered this original layout by including a high dome supported by four considerably larger pillars, in line with the spatial innovations that were being tentatively introduced in the centre of the Iberian Peninsula, some of them by Simón de Colonia himself.[16]

In Carmona, the two central pillars on line four display a clear formal continuity with the pillars on line three, while their morphology is considerably more complex on the side facing the transept. The central issue stems from the fact that the form of the side pillars on this line is based on a literal translation of the drawing of the central ones, as the data painstakingly collected reveals. (Fig. 7) This translation in turn interrupts the formal continuity between all the wall pillars in the aisle, since the ones in the previous lines already displayed significant variations with regard to the corresponding central ones. The position of the side pillar on line four is strangely forced, since the vertical rib supporting the vault's diagonal rib is embedded in the wall, thus distorting that corner of the vault. Interestingly, all of these issues emerge in a strictly symmetrical manner, in both aisles, which confirms their deliberate, systematic nature. The reason for this layout is not clear, although the mostly likely explanation is that it obeys a desire to obtain a certain visual uniformity in the pedestals visible from the transept. All of this allows us to formulate a hypothesis on the configuration planned for the transept in the first construction phase, according to which it would project slightly from the total width of the nave and aisles, as indeed is the case in Seville Cathedral and is shown on the Bidaurreta Plan. (Fig. 1)

A second group of observations enables us to identify a clear continuity in the design of the aisle windows in the chevet with respect to the side windows in front of the transept, with the exception of a few small variations in the dimensions. Both the geometric configuration of the carved opening in the wall and the position of the colonnettes are identical in both cases. By contrast, the form and dimensions of the clerestory windows in the chevet are completely different from those of the corresponding windows in the sections in front of the crossing. Furthermore, without exception all of the colonnettes in the chevet windows, both the clerestory ones and those lower down, have cylindrical shafts and pedestals, while the ones in the lower windows of the north aisle have prism-shaped pedestals, as do all the windows in front of the crossing. All of this indicates a certain building continuity in the areas around the chevet with respect to the first sections of the church.

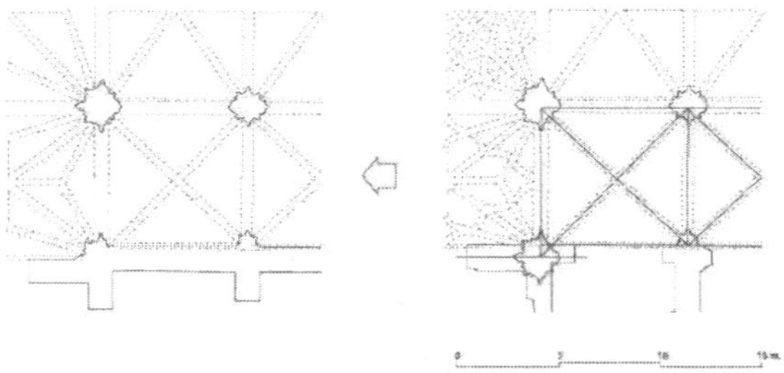

Figure 7. Geometric analysis of the pillars and walls enclosing the crossing in Santa María in Carmona. Drawing by A. L. Ampliato.

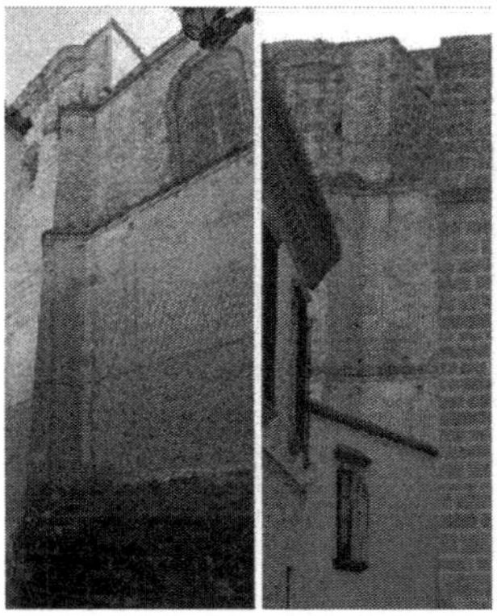

Figure 8. External buttress corresponding to the seventh line of pillars in Santa María in Carmona. Photos: A. L. Ampliato.

To conclude this series of observations, we finally come to the exterior north buttress corresponding to the seventh line of pillars. As can be seen in the general floor plan, (Fig. 3) this element adopts a diagonal position, which is clearly contradictory in the context of what was actually built. From a structural point of view, and since this is a nave-and-aisle organism, a corner buttress may only be placed diagonally if all the affected vaults, including both the immediate one and those of the adjacent sections, are of the same height. If any of the adjacent vaults are higher, flying buttresses are required at the top to carry their thrust, in which case the buttress would have to be placed at right angles to the wall to support them. In fact, the position of this buttress on line seven, initially diagonal, is rectified after the second cornice, where it becomes orthogonal and is slightly recessed in order to rest on the wall between chapels. (Fig. 8) The lower diagonal part therefore obeys an earlier design in which the nave vault, between the pillars on lines six and seven, would have been similar in height to the aisle vaults, and all three would therefore have formed a last transverse aisle, lower in height, just in front of the flat wall in which the chevet culminates. Together with the elongated aisles, this last transverse aisle would have created a rectangular ambulatory around the original chancel, whose only position would have corresponded with the first module of the chevet nave, just behind the crossing; in other words, exactly the same position as the chancel drawn in the Bidaurreta Plan for Seville Cathedral, which with notable transformations has been preserved to this day.

The hypothesis about the first Cathedral Gothic design for Santa María in Carmona is graphically represented in a floor plan and section. (Fig. 9) The drawing incorporates complementary elements, such as the roof finials, borrowed from other examples of this architectural phase and Seville Cathedral itself, our only aim being to offer a visualisation of the typological structure of the overall complex, which is the true focus of our interest.

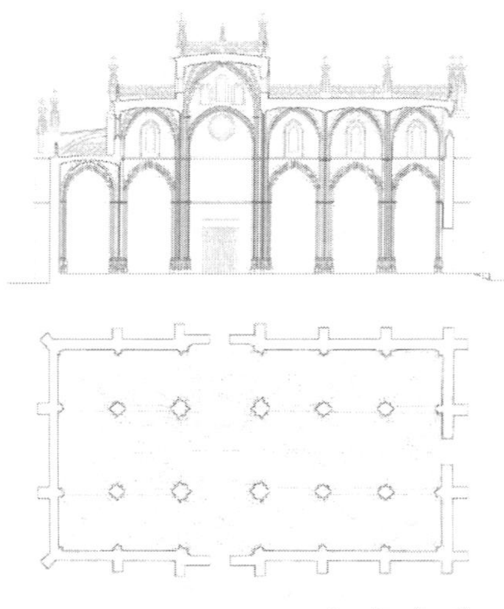

Figure 9. Graphical hypothesis on the first design project for Santa María in Carmona. Drawing by A. L. Ampliato.

Conclusions

The signs detected in the priory of Santa María that we see today in Carmona enable us to formulate a reasoned graphical hypothesis regarding the configuration planned in the first Cathedral Gothic design project, an incomplete project in which the chevet was radically altered. What we present is an ideal graphical reconstruction that emphasises the typological structure and only considers other formal aspects in a secondary manner.

Except for the logical reference supplied by Seville Cathedral, the design for Carmona had no clear antecedents at the time and its clarification is an important discovery since it sheds light on the typological structure of the aforementioned cathedral itself. In light of Santa María in Carmona, this vast and rather unusual organism emerges as the product of a deliberate design project which was shared by the successive generations of master builders who ran the workshop and which served as the basis for defining a model that could be replicated in smaller buildings. The space in Carmona may therefore have been conceived as a reduction of the essence of its model, Seville Cathedral, with a rectangular perimeter, flat-ended chevet, and an ambulatory composed of an orthogonal nave and aisles around a chancel situated in a module of the nave, between four pillars, preceded by the choir on the other side of the transept.

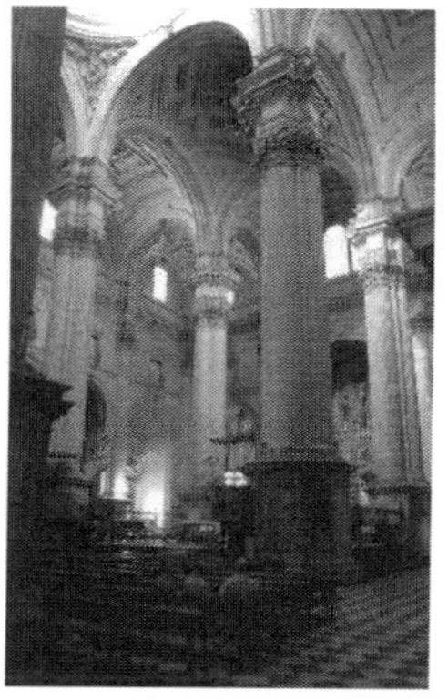

Figure 10. Interior of the chevet of Jaén Cathedral. Architect, Andrés de Vandelvira, second half of the sixteenth century. Photo: A. L. Ampliato.

Furthermore, the experience of Santa María in Carmona also anticipated a certain evolution in ecclesiastical space in southern Spain that would achieve a notable impact at the height of the Renaissance. Built in one of the most important cities in the kingdom, Seville Cathedral itself would, to a greater or lesser extent, influence other major cathedrals of the sixteenth century, such as those in Las Palmas de Gran Canaria, Salamanca and, on the other side of the Atlantic, Mexico City.[17] The trail blazed by the Seville model is even discernible in some of the most important examples of Renaissance architecture in Spain, such as Jaén Cathedral designed by Andrés de Vandelvira in the second half of the sixteenth century. (Fig. 10) Reduced to a nave and two aisles compared with a nave and four aisles in the Seville building (and in this case adopting the general configuration of a hall church), the typological structure of Jaén Cathedral is identical to the priory in Carmona, with a flat-ended chevet, a chancel that occupies a single module between four pillars adjacent to the crossing, and a rectangular ambulatory of nave and aisles around it.[18]

Notes and references:

[1] This work was conducted within the framework of the national R&D&I project 'Seville Cathedral Gothic: Architecture and City in the Spheres of Influence of the Cathedral of Seville' (Ref. HAR2012-35152), whose lead researcher is Antonio Luis Ampliato Briones.

[2] For the most recent data obtained about Seville Cathedral, see A. Jiménez, *Anatomía de la catedral de Sevilla*, Seville: Diputación Provincial de Sevilla,2013.

[3] J.C. Rodríguez, *Los canteros de la catedral de Sevilla. Del Gótico al Renacimiento*, Seville: Diputación Provincial de Sevilla, 1998, pp. 34-48.

[4] J.C. Rodríguez, 'Cambio y continuidad en el proyecto gótico de la Catedral de Sevilla', *Laboratorio de Arte*, no. 23, 2011, pp. 33-64. A. Jiménez et al., *La catedral gótica de Sevilla. Fundación y fábrica de la obra nueva*, Seville: Universidad de Sevilla, 2006, pp. 394-408.

[5] B. Alonso & A. Jiménez, *La traça de la Iglesia de Sevilla*, Seville: Cabildo Metropolitano, 2009.

[6] J. C. Ruiz, 'Ysambart y la renovación del gótico final en Castilla: Palencia, la capilla del Contador Saldaña en Tordesillas y Sevilla', in A. Jiménez (Ed.), *Magna Hispalensis: los primeros años*, Seville: Avla Hernán Ruiz, Catedral de Sevilla, 2008, pp. 37-58. J. Ibáñez, *La capilla del palacio arzobispal de Zaragoza en el contexto de la renovación del Gótico final en la Península Ibérica*, Zaragoza: Museo Diocesano, 2012, pp. 15-65.

[7] On the cathedral master builders, see T. Falcón, *La catedral de Sevilla. Estudio arquitectónico*, Seville: Diputación Provincial, 1980, pp. 121-137. Alonso & Jiménez (Note 5), pp. 123-170.

[8] J. C. Rodríguez, 'El gótico catedralicio. La influencia de la catedral en el arzobispado de Sevilla', in A. Jiménez (Ed.), *La piedra postrera. Simposium Internacional sobre la catedral de Sevilla en el contexto del gótico final,* Seville: Tvrris Fortissima, 2007, Vol. I, pp.175-255.

[9] M. González, *Carmona medieval*, Seville: Fundación Lara, 2006.

[10] M. Fernández y López, *Historia de la ciudad de Carmona*, Seville: Gironés y Orduña, 1886, pp. 28-30. All the available records summarised in A. L. Ampliato & J. C. Rodríguez, 'Un nuevo levantamiento arquitectónico y algunas hipótesis de base para el estudio de la Iglesia Prioral de Carmona', *Laboratorio de Arte*, no. 27, 2015, pp. 43-57.

[11] The specific delimitation of these two major phases was examined in A. L. Ampliato & J.C. Rodríguez, 'La iglesia de Santa María de Carmona. Hipótesis sobre su evolución tipológica y constructiva des una perspectiva interdisciplinar', in S. Huerta & P. Fuentes (Ed.), *Actas del Noveno Congreso Nacional y Primer Congreso Internacional Hispanoamericano de Historia de la construcción, Segovia 2015*, Madrid: Instituto Juan de Herrera, 2015. Vol. I, pp. 103-113.

[12] On Diego de Riaño, the most complete record to date is that of A. Morales, 'Diego de Riaño', in *El ciclo humanista. Arquitectos I. Proyecto Andalucía. Artistas andaluces y artífices del arte andaluz*, Seville: Publicaciones Comunitarias, 2011, Vol.25, pp. 191-225. On his work in Carmona, Ampliato & Rodríguez (Note 10).

[13] A. L. Ampliato, 'Tramas, nudos, desenlaces: apuntes sobre posibles huellas de control espacial en la arquitectura del gótico catedralicio sevillano' in B. Alonso & J. C. Rodríguez (Ed.), *1514. Arquitectos tardogóticos en la encrucijada*. Sevilla: Universidad de Sevilla, 2016, pp. 495-502.

[14] There are documents recording the various legal conflicts that emerged at the time as a result of this occupation of external urban spaces, Fernández (Note 10), pp. 331-335.

[15] On the issue surrounding the possible existence of a dome in the original cathedral plan: Alonso & Jiménez (Note 5), pp. 22, and Rodríguez (Note 4), p. 51.

[16] Alonso & Jiménez (Note 5), pp. 141-146.

[17] On the relationship between Seville Cathedral and those of Las Palmas and Salamanca, see: J. C. Rodríguez, 'El maestro Alonso Rodríguez', in B. Alonso (Ed.), *Los últimos arquitectos del Gótico*, Madrid: Grupo de Investigación de Arquitectura Tardogótica, 2010, pp. 302-306/311-317 and Castro, 'La catedral de Sevilla como modelo: la catedral de Salamanca', in A. Jiménez (Ed.) *La catedral sin la catedral. XVIII Avla Hernán Ruiz*, Seville: Diputación Provincial, 2011, pp. 59-115. In relation to the Mexican cathedral: L. J. Cuesta, *Arquitectura del Renacimiento en Nueva España. Claudio de Arciniega, Maestro Maior de la obra de la Yglesia Catedral de esta Ciudad de México,* Mexico: Universidad Iberoamericana, 2009, pp. 175-228.

[18] A detailed spatial analysis of Jaén Cathedral in A. L. Ampliato, *Muro, orden y espacio en la arquitectura del Renacimiento andaluz. Teoría y práctica en la obra de D. Siloe, A. Vandelvira y H. Ruiz II*, Seville: Universidad de Sevilla y Consejería de Obras Públicas y Transportes, 1996, pp. 163-170.

The Sixteenth and Seventeenth Centuries

The environment of the Elizabethan House: Hardwick Hall

Dean Hawkes
Darwin College, University of Cambridge

Introduction

Hardwick 'New' Hall was built between 1591 and 1599 and is one of the most important houses of Elizabethan England. It was the home of Elizabeth, Countess of Shrewsbury, familiarly referred to as "Bess of Hardwick", and the work of the architect Robert Smythson (1536-1614). It stands on a hilltop and is immediately adjacent to the "Old' Hall that was itself under construction between 1587 and 1598 [1]. The appearance of the house is remarkable, with walls of local stone pierced by enormous mullioned windows and six turrets that rise high above the roofline (Fig. 1). The exterior observes and dramatically demonstrates the principles of strict symmetry that were an important aspect of the architecture of the English renaissance, but this conceals a surprising asymmetry and complexity of interior organisation. An examination of the plans of the house shows how this organisation is founded on the observation of what we may now recognise to be principles of environmental design. This paper presents an environmental analysis of the house with particular emphasis on the conditions of Bess' personal first floor apartments, as they might have been experienced when they were occupied by Bess between 4th October 1597, when she moved into the house, until her death there on 13th January 1608.

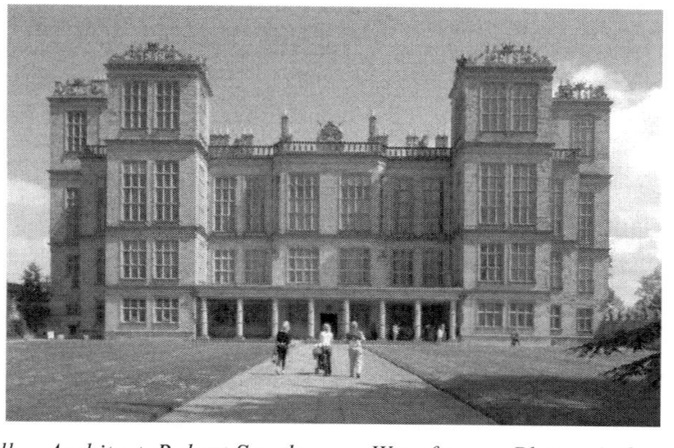

Figure 1. Hardwick Hall. Architect, Robert Smythson. West front. Photo: Author.

In providing shelter for their occupants, buildings mediate between the variable and unpredictable external climate and the desire for more constant and moderate conditions within. To understand a house constructed four centuries ago we must, therefore, construct a description of the climate of that time. It is then necessary to develop an understanding of the internal environment that would have been sought by the inhabitants of a great Elizabethan house. This leads to an analysis of the organisation, construction and equipment of the house as these relate to its environmental qualities.

Climate and Comfort in Elizabethan England

At the end of the sixteenth century, meteorology in its modern sense was unknown. Instruments for the measurement of temperature and atmospheric pressure were yet to be developed [2]. But climate was keenly observed by other means and from these we may construct a description of the conditions in which Hardwick was conceived and inhabited. The most notable fact to register is that at this date England was in the depths of the so-called Little Ice Age that extended from the fourteenth to the nineteenth centuries [3]. In the period 1580-1620 proxy records have been used to reconstruct descriptions of the conditions that were most probably experienced [4]. These indicate that England suffered from extremely cold winters with deep frosts and frequent snowfall, but also from warm summers and drought. The average annual temperature has been estimated to have been 1 degree Celsius below that of the late twentieth century and the winters considerably colder. It was under these conditions that Hardwick was built and first inhabited by its elderly owner.

This was exactly the time of Shakespeare (1554-1616) and vivid descriptions of contemporary climate may be found throughout his works. To contrast winter and summer we have:

> When all aloud the wind doth blow,
> And coughing drowns the parson's saw;
> And birds sit brooding in the snow,
> And Marion's nose looks red and raw,
> *Love's Labour's Lost*
> Act V, Scene ii

> Shall I compare thee to a summer's day?
> Thou art more lovely and more temperate:
> Rough winds do shake the darling buds of May,
> And summer's lease hath all too short a date:
> Some times too hot the eye of heaven shines,
> And often is his gold complexion dimm'd;
> *The Sonnets*, 18

These capture the sense of the coldness of those Little Ice Age winters and periods of great summer heat tempered, then as now, in England by the unpredictability and brevity of our summers.

At a time when the environment within a building was more closely connected with the external climate that in our time, its occupants would have had a much keener perception of the annual cycle of the seasons and of the daily passing of the hours than our twenty-first century experience, cushioned by elaborate environmental control systems. Comfort was perceived quite differently from our modern expectations. The Shakespeare scholar Jonathan Bate has emphasised how,

> "In an age of candle and rush-light, nights were seriously dark. The night was accordingly imagined to be seriously different from the day. The very fact of long hours of light itself conferred a kind of magic upon midsummer night." [5].

In developing an understanding of the environmental expectations and perceptions of the Elizabethans, we may infer a similar awareness of the thermal environment in which interiors were more responsive to external conditions. Indeed, we might assume that the experience of 'comfort' was complex and diverse, with activities expanding and contracting in time and space. This is the basis upon which we may examine the environment of Hardwick.

Hardwick Described

The primary source for describing Hardwick is the house itself. Although four centuries old, its form and construction remain relatively unchanged [6]. Significant documentary sources are the Building Accounts [7] and the comprehensive Inventories of 1601 [8], compiled just four years after Bess first moved in.

The overall configuration of the plan is strikingly simple (Fig. 2). It consists of a rectangle that is elaborated by the addition of six projecting turrets. A massive masonry spine wall runs the entire length, slightly offset from the long axis. This is most clearly seen at second floor level. The plan is oriented with its long axis close to the north-south cardinal. At ground and first floors the double-height Hall subdivides the plan, defined by thick masonry walls. The complex detailed planning of the house is then superimposed upon this essentially simple diagram.

The accommodation is broadly arranged with servants' quarters at ground level, the principal family rooms on the first floor and the great rooms of state on the second floor. At ground floor the north of the plan is principally occupied by the kitchens, large and small, and the associated buttery, scullery and larders. The only exception to these domestic places is the Chapel, whose lower level occupies the north-east turret. To the south of the Hall lie the Pantry and a smaller, associated chamber. The remainder of this wing contains domestic apartments, including, significantly, the Nursery.

Before outlining the principal apartments of the upper floors it is appropriate to discuss the building's two staircases. These are both on the east side of the house. The north stair winds a complex route to the first floor from where it enters the north turret to proceed to the second floor, giving access to the staterooms and then on to roof level. The south stair is a much grander, ceremonial event. It rises from ground to first floor in a generous dog-leg arrangement to arrive at a spacious landing at the entrance to the Countess of Shrewsbury's personal apartments. From there it proceeds southwards and terminates in a dramatic sweeping turn in the brightly lit south turret at the entrance to the High Great Chamber, the most significant room in the house.

Returning to the internal planning of the house, the first floor is divided into north and south parts by the double-height volume of the hall. The whole of the south end is occupied by Bess' personal apartments and those of the closest members of the household. These rooms will be the subjects of detailed discussion later. To the north of the hall is the Low Great Chamber, a magnificent formal room, and the little dining chamber, both conveniently placed above the kitchens. The second floor houses the most important ceremonial rooms of the house. Arriving from the long, elaborate progress of the main stair, the point of arrival is the magnificently decorated High Great Chamber. This measures 19.75 metres in length and between 9.75 and 15.00 metres in width. It occupies the entire the south-west corner. Immediately by the entrance a door leads into the Long Gallery, which, at 61 metres, extends the full length of the east side of the plan. The remainder of this floor, the Withdrawing Chamber, Best Bedchamber and other associated chambers, constituted in effect a state suite, which it has been surmised, was created in anticipation of a visit by the Queen [9]. Above these rooms is an attic storey, accessed by the north stair that reduces their ceiling height. This originally did not cover the Withdrawing Chamber, but was extended over that at some date before 1764 [10], reducing its ceiling height. Finally the north stair arrives at roof level in the north turret from where access is made to the roof, the 'leads' in contemporary usage. In the sixteenth and seventeenth centuries these were commonly used for outdoor exercise and other recreations.

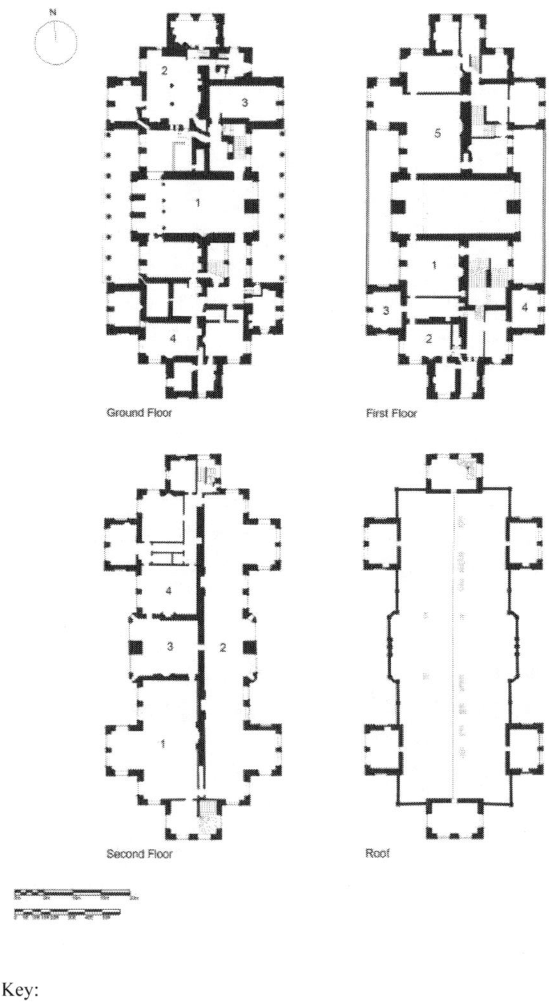

Room Key:

Ground Floor: 1. Hall. 2. Kitchen. 3. Chapel. 4. Nursery

First Floor: 1,Bess' Withdrawing Room. 2. Bess' Bedroom. 3. William Cavendish's Room. 4. Arbella's Bedroom. 5. Low Great Chamber.

Second Floor: 1. High Great Chamber. 2. Long Gallery. 3. Withdrawing Chamber. 4. Best Bedchamber.

Figure 2. Hardwick Hall. Floor plans. Author

Fireplaces and Windows

The twentieth century British architect Peter Smithson wrote of Hardwick, "What's nice about [the plan] is that it indicates the thick spine wall, where the fireplaces are ... and the perimeter bay windows that let in the light." [11]. This is an elegant characterisation of the environmental essence of the house in which numerous fireplaces in the thermal mass of the masonry core compensate for the heat loss through the windows. If we exclude the four hearths in the roof turrets, the house as built had 31 fireplaces. The great windows are, perhaps, the most striking aspect of the appearance of the house and it is said that early in its existence it acquired the soubriquet, "Hardwick Hall, more glass than wall". The High Great Chamber is the glassiest room of all with eight great windows, each consisting of 12 individual lights. But elsewhere appearances can be deceptive and careful examination shows that no less than 30 of the windows, in a total of 156, approximately 19 per cent, were constructed 'blind' over inner masonry walls [12]. In the detailed analysis that follows it is proposed that these arrangements were not arbitrary, but were integral to the environmental logic that informed the entire design.

Orientation and insolation

A key factor in environmental analysis is the relationship between a building and the sun's passage across the sky. As a universal constant, this has not changed between the sixteenth century and the present. Hardwick stands at the latitude of 53 degrees and 10 minutes north and longitude of 1 degree and 19 minutes west. Its elevation is 151 metres above sea level. At the date of Hardwick's construction life was regulated by sun time as it was observed at each location. At Hardwick the key factors may be summarized as follows (Table 1).

Table 1. Solar Data for Hardwick, Latitude 53° 10' N

	Winter Solstice	Autumnal & Vernal Equinox	Summer Solstice
Sunrise			
Time	08.20	06.00	03.40
Azimuth	132°	180°	48°
Sunset			
Time	15.40	18.00	20.20
Azimuth	228°	270°	312°
Altitude			
at Noon	13°	37°	60°

Data compiled by author.

People living at the end of the sixteenth century would have been deeply aware of the facts represented by the sunpath diagram and the table above. In a largely agrarian society, much of their life was spent out of doors and buildings, by their nature, admitted a sense of daily and seasonal cycles to their interiors.

The orientation of the long axis of Hardwick is tilted just 6 degrees to the east of due north. If the plan is superimposed on the polar sunpath diagram (Fig. 3) we may observe how orientation informs the planning the building. The benefit to the southerly rooms is immediately apparent. At the ground floor the nursery is in a particularly advantageous place at the south-west corner with windows in adjacent south and west facing walls. Alternatively the location of the kitchens and larders at the north end of the house is clearly practical in providing cool storage and preventing solar warmth from exaggerating the heat of the cooking fires. At first floor the entire southern end of the house is devoted to Bess' own apartments and those of her closest family and servants.

The second floor contains the great ceremonial and staterooms and is the most luminous part of the house. The High Great Chamber (Fig. 4) was the site of feasts and entertainments and its location and organisation are finely calibrated to provide the best setting for these events. This magnificently decorated room is where the principal meals of dinner and supper were served, in direct response to the constraints of available natural light, at late morning and afternoon respectively [13]. This is the most highly glazed room in the house and, in the summer months, would be flooded with light from midday until sunset as the sun moved towards the west. The Inventory of 1601 [14] does not mention the presence of any curtains at the windows of the room, so its brightness would have undiminished. Nor is there mention of any fixed or permanent source of nighttime illumination. The Inventories tell that the Great Hall had fixed candlesticks and that others were kept nearby in the Pantry and Buttery. This suggests that the High Great Chamber would have been lit by some of the 25 portable candlesticks that were identified as kept in the Porter's Lodge. The contrast between summer and winter would have been extreme. The sole heat source is the magnificent fireplace set in the spine wall, equipped with, as the Inventories list, "a payre of brass Andyrons, a fier shovel, a payre of tonges." The presence of "Andyrons" indicates that the fuel burned was wood and we may conclude that the fireplace brought relatively little comfort to the room on a cold winter's evening. This probably encouraged the household to retreat early to smaller, more congenial places. There is some evidence that great rooms at this period were differently decorated according to the season and Thornton (15) has pointed out that the Hardwick Inventories refer to two pairs of "hanginges" for the High Great Chamber, one of tapestry the other of woolen cloth. The former still hang in the room, the latter have disappeared. If they were ever in use the room would have had a very different atmosphere according to the season.

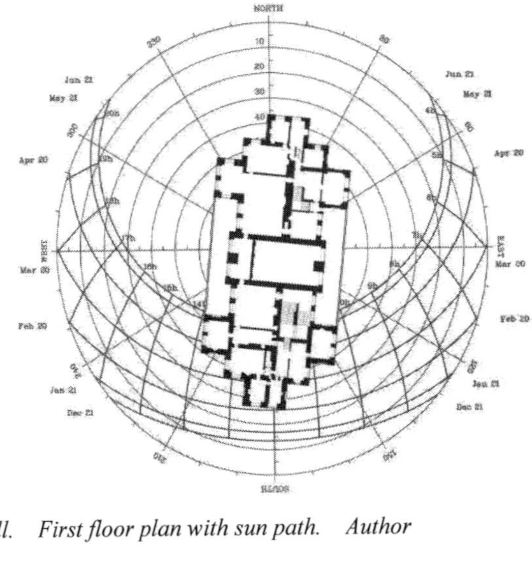

Figure 3. Hardwick Hall. First floor plan with sun path. Author

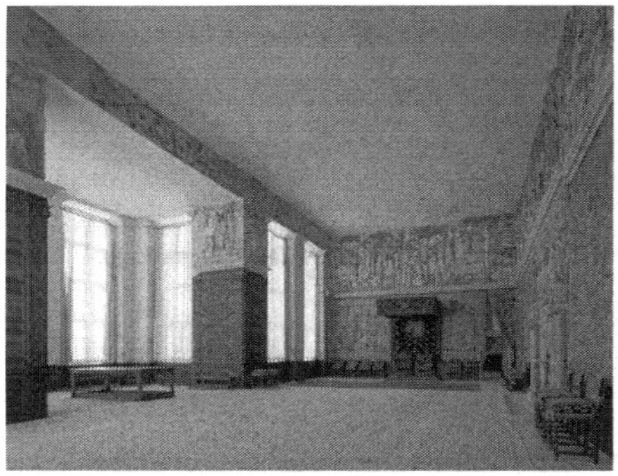

Figure 4. Hardwick Hall. High Great Chamber. Photo: © National Trust Images/Nick Guttridge.

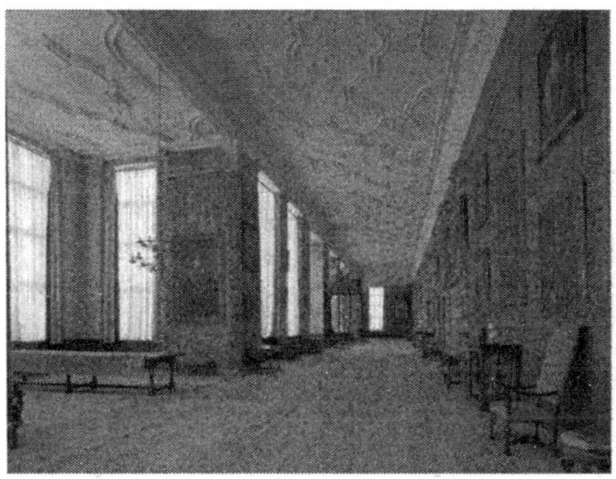

Figure 5. Hardwick Hall. Long Gallery. Photo: © National Trust Images/Nick Guttridge.

The Long Gallery (Fig. 5) occupies the length of the east side of the second floor. This was where Bess and other senior members of the household took daily exercise, most particularly in inclement weather. The easterly orientation makes this an ideal place to be in the morning. In comparison with the High Great Chamber not all of the windows are glazed. The two north-facing lights in the turrets are blind [16] providing these spaces with just east and south light and excluding the disadvantageous north aspect. The walls of the gallery are faced with a set of tapestries, illustrating the biblical story of Gideon and the Midianities, bought by Bess in 1592. They remain insitu to the present day. The room was quite sparsely furnished, but was notable for the number of cushions, some specifically placed in the window bays. This suggests that these were attractive places to sit on sunny mornings. Again no curtains are mentioned in the Inventories. There are two fireplaces in the spine wall, comparable with that of the High Great Chamber. These were also equipped with andirons, a fire shovel and tongs. They are located in the narrow part of the gallery, not opposite the window bays. This would help them to provide a small field of warmth within the vast space, to allow a walker to pause for some comfort as she traversed the gallery on a cold day. There is an account of an event that took place on 7th January 1603 that suggests that the Gallery had an at least tolerable environment in the depths of winter. Sir Henry Bronker, a commissioner sent by the Queen, came, apparently unannounced, and recorded,

> "I arrived at Hardwick and found the house without strange company. My Lady of Shrewsbury after she had my name, sent for me in her gallery where she was walking with La: Arbella (Bess' granddaughter) and her son William Cavendish." [17]

The accommodation of the second floor is completed by a suite of sumptuous bedrooms that were intended for the most important visitors.

Finally, the rooftop 'leads' were, in effect, a great outdoor room (Fig. 6). When weather permitted they would be used for exercise and other recreations and entertainments would take place there n the summer months. The roof turrets could play a part in these. The four turrets oriented east and west have fireplaces and could thus offer additional comfort. The south turret is given special significance by Bess' arms above the entrance. This does not have a fireplace, but is glazed to east, west and south and becomes almost a solarium on sunny days (Fig. 7).

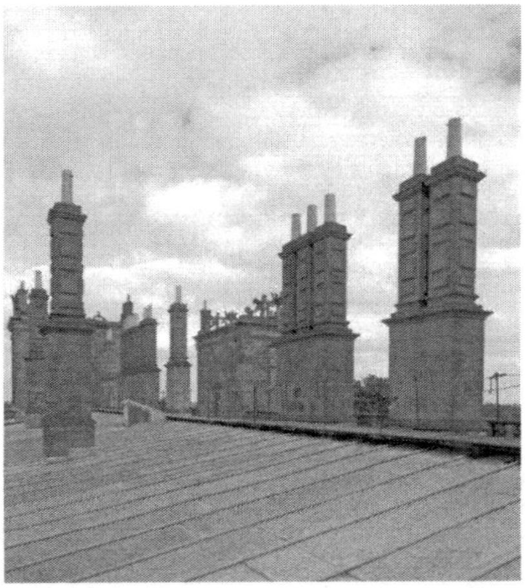

Figure 6. Hardwick Hall. Roof, the 'Leads'. Photo: Author.

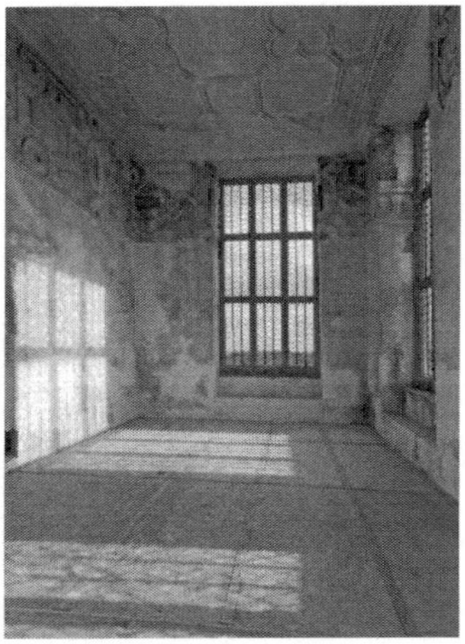

Figure 7. Hardwick Hall. South Turret Interior. Photo: Author.

Bess' Apartments – a house within a house

The first floor of the house (Fig. 8) is protected from the elements by the floors below and above and is the location of the most intensively occupied rooms. To the north of the double-height volume of the Hall is the Low Great Chamber, the largest of the apartments, 13.00 metres long and between 9.75 and 14.75 metres wide, with the fully glazed turret almost a room in itself measuring 6.00 by 5.00 metres. This was lavishly furnished and decorated as a setting for dining and recreation by the household. To the south and connected by a gallery above the Hall are Bess' most intimate apartments, which also housed her closest family members and companions. These are especially significant in a study of the historic environment. Their significance is declared by the entrance to Bess' Withdrawing Chamber that opens from the wide landing of the great stair. This is brightly lit from the east by two large windows. The door is surmounted by a plaster cartouche that presents the head of a soldier set in a deep frame (Fig. 9).

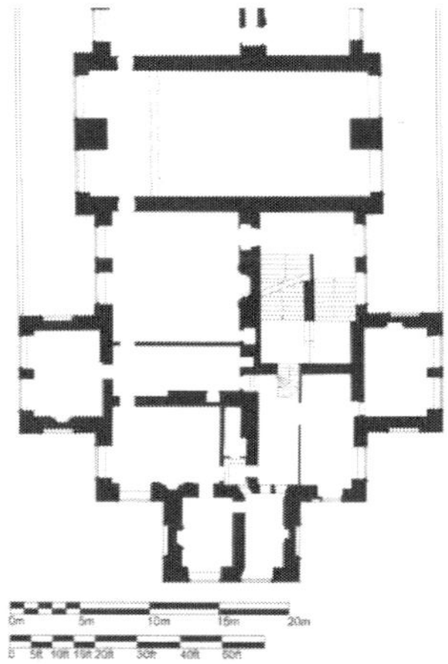

Figure 8. Hardwick Hall. First floor plan, Countess of Shrewsbury's Apartments. Author.

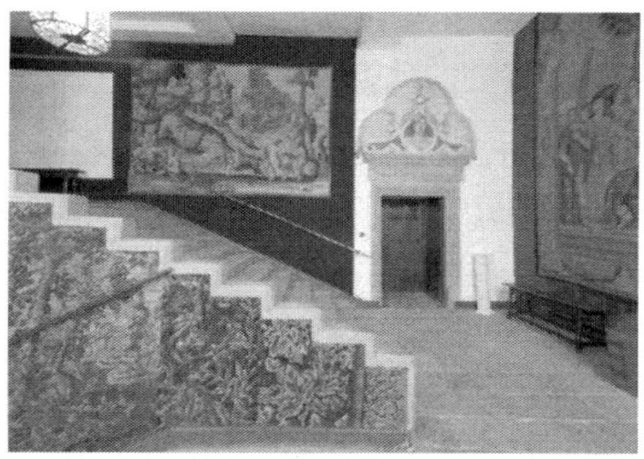

Figure 9. Hardwick Hall. Entrance to Countess of Shrewsbury's apartments. Photo: Author.

The Withdrawing Chamber itself is 9.75 meters deep and 9.25 metres wide. The floor to ceiling height, as throughout this floor, is 4.50 metres. The fireplace is on the inner, wall and there are two, west-facing windows, each of nine lights (Fig. 10). Although a relatively private place, accessible to only to the closest family members and servants, this was a key room in the house and the comfort of its principal occupant would have been a priority. The 1601 Inventory lists a number of seats with, " ... a chayre of black lether guilded, a footstoole of wood, a foot turkie Carpet ..." ". This is clearly Bess' own chair, with the added comfort of the carpet-covered footstool. Two other chairs are listed, plus, " ... too Chares for Children ..." ", eleven "Stooles" of various material and a number of "forms" and numerous cushions of fine material. Other items including a cupboard and various chests providing storage for small items. There was also an "inlayed borde", a table that was, as was the practice, covered by carpets. The principal decoration was six hanging tapestries that survive to the present day. The fireplace is described as, " ... an Iron Chymney, with a back of Iron..." its surround displays the Hardwick arms. There were the usual andirons, fire tongs and shovel. The Inventory also lists three "skreynes". At this date this could refer to either a large folding screen that would be used to define a small area within a room or it could be a smaller free-standing item that was used to provide protection from the heat of a fire [18]. It is likely that the three referred to here were of the latter kind and were used to protect the faces of the occupants of the three chairs as they sat by the fire.

As the sun path diagram shows, the west-facing windows do not admit sunlight in the winter months, as they are obstructed by the projecting turret, but are bright from mid afternoon until sunset throughout the summer months. Unlike the great public rooms on the second floor, these windows were curtained, "...too Curtins of darnix..." [19]. This was, most probably, to provide some thermal protection on winter's evenings. In a room of this size there are distinct 'environmental zones' with different lighting and thermal conditions, dependent on the season and time of day. The relatively high ceiling and the clear view of the sky allows daylight to reach deep into the room. On a bright summer's afternoon the area close to the windows would be particularly pleasant, warm and bright. In winter, on the other hand, the reach of heat from the fire would extend only a short distance and the useable space would contract to the inner part of the room. Thermal comfort would also be associated with dim light. On lighting at this time, Thornton observes, "...It is difficult for us to conceive how little light there normally was...after dark. ...In fact, the strongest light in a room after dark would mostly come from the fire." [20].

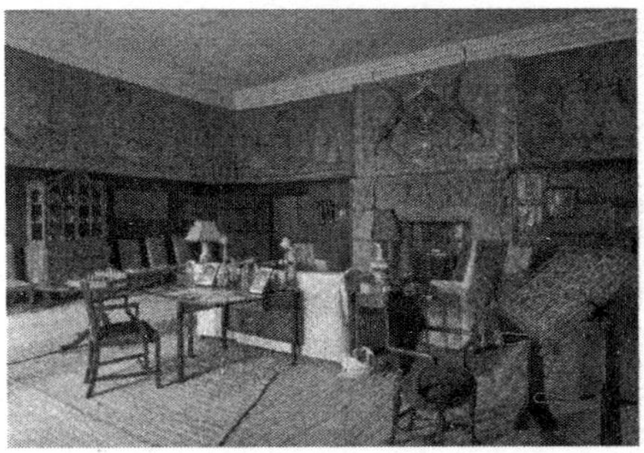

Figure 10. Hardwick Hall. Bess' Withdrawing Chamber. Interior in present state. Photo: © National Trust Images/Andreas von Einsledel.

Bess' Bed Chamber was the most intimate and complex environment in the house. Thornton describes the efforts that were made to provide protection against the cold of the Little Ice Age by the layers of curtains to the windows and enclosing her bed, along with the depths of covers upon it and carpets on the floor [21]. The room, which measures 7.75 metres by 5.50 metres, is deeply embedded into the body of the house. Its only external surfaces are the two walls containing the west and south facing windows. These provide ample daylight. The fireplace is in the south wall adjacent to the window. This arrangement ensures that the room is highly protected against the elements. In addition to listing numbers of chairs, stools, writing desks and chests, the Inventory records that "My Ladie Arbells bedsted" was also in the room, although she also had a personal chamber nearby. The arrangement of all of these items is not clear, not least the position of the beds. It is probable that these were in the inner part of the room and that the daytime activities took place at the south west corner. Thus receives the best of afternoon sunlight at all seasons and in winter is also within reach of the warmth of the fire.

There is uncertainty regarding the exact use of the other rooms in Bess' group. The arrangement at Fig. 9 is based on that suggested by Durant and Riden [22]. This proposes that Arbella's chamber was in the south east turret and describes the chamber in the south west turret, that is entered from Bess' Withdrawing Chamber, as "Chamber where my Lord's arms are", that may have been the apartment of Bess' son, William Cavendish. It is assumed that the rooms in the south turret were occupied by Bess' personal attendants and maids. All of these chambers have windows in just one wall, the others being blind, which is more appropriate to their dimensions and uses. Arbella's chamber in the south-east turret was furnished with damask and silk wall hangings and a canopied bed with curtains of silk and taffeta with ample mattresses, quilts and covers. There is no explicit reference to curtains, but the Inventory includes, "ten pieces of Darnix", that might have served this purpose. In other respects the room appears to have been quite sparsely furnished with only a cupboard, a square table and a stool, plus a number of cushions, suggesting Arbella spent more time elsewhere. The fireplace had the usual fire shovel and tonges. The Inventory suggests that William Cavendish's chamber in the south-west turret was also primarily used as a bedroom.

Conclusion

The aim of this paper has been to reach behind the striking appearance of Hardwick Hall to discover the environmental principles that, in some measure, inform its complex internal planning. One of the surprises and delights of the house is that the strict biaxial symmetry of the exterior conceals an internal arrangement that is, on first encounter, of perplexing complexity. This is quite unlike the Italian works of his near contemporary, Andrea Palladio (1508-80), where exterior symmetry derived from exact internal symmetry, and differs even from Smythson's own earlier great house at Wollaton (1580-88). The reasons for this are most certainly many, but the analysis presented here suggests that what we now refer to as 'environmental' considerations were hugely influential.

The orientation of the building, with its long axis almost exactly on the north-south cardinal, establishes a fundamental differentiation between the environments of the spaces to north and south of the central Hall. Throughout the house the orientation of the principal rooms may be interpreted by reference to their specific uses. The bright morning light of the Long Gallery and the flood of afternoon light into the High Great Chamber precisely accord with the times when they were most used. Most convincing of all is the location and arrangement of Bess' personal apartments at the south of the first floor. Here they provide protection and comfort at all seasons for their elderly inhabitant and the closest members of her household. In addition, the analysis shows how the dramatic 'glassiness' of the exterior was quite precisely calibrated by the construction of blind windows to fine-tune the environment of individual rooms.

In the late sixteenth century the notion of 'comfort' was certainly a much different from our present expectations. But this study of Hardwick Hall helps to show that, in the depths of the Little Ice Age, it was possible for an architect and his remarkable client to reconcile the elaborate expression of status and rank and the highest ambitions of formal composition with subtle accommodation of human needs.

Acknowledgements

I should like to thank the following for their assistance with this project. Dr. Nigel Wright, Building and Collections Manager, The National Trust, Hardwick Hall, for allowing access to the house. Nigel Coote, Plowman Craven & Associates, Surveyors, Harpenden, for supplying the digital survey of Hardwick. Stan Finney, Department of Architecture, University of Cambridge, for help with CAD. Luke Kon, Darwin College, Cambridge, for drawing the digital plans.

References

[1] These building dates are from the Hardwick Building Accounts as published in David N. Durant and Philip Riden, *The Building of Hardwick Hall, Part 1: The Old Hall, 1587-91, Part 2: The New Hall, 1591-98*, Chesterfield: Derbyshire Record Society, Vol. IV, 1980, Vol. IX, 1984.

[2] See W.E. Knowles Middleton, *Invention of the Meteorological Instruments*, Baltimore: Johns Hopkins University Press, 1969.

[3] Brian Fagan, *The Little Ice Age: How climate made history, 1300-1850*, New York: Basic Books, 2000.

[4] See Mike Hulme, 'Climate', in Bruce R. Smith (ed.), *The Cambridge Guide to the Worlds of Shakespeare*, Cambridge: Cambridge University Press, forthcoming 2016.

[5] Jonathan Bate, 'Introduction to A Midsummer Night's Dream', in Jonathan Bate and Eric Rasmussen (Eds.), *William Shakespeare: Complete Works*, London: The Royal Shakespeare Company/Macmillan, 2007.

[6] See Mark Girouard, *Robert Smythson and the Elizabethan Country House*, New Haven: Yale University Press, 1983.

[7] Durant, Riden, Note 1.

[8] Lindsay Boynton (Ed.), *The Hardwick Inventories of 1601*, London: The Furniture History Society, 1971.

[9] See Mark Girouard, *Hardwick Hall*, London: The National Trust, 1989, revised edition 2002.

[10] Girouard, Note 10.

[11] Peter Smithson, *Conversations with Students: A space for our generation*, Catherine Spellman and Carl Unglaub (Eds.), New York, Princeton Architectural Press, 2005.

[12] The numbers of fireplaces and blind windows are calculated from the detailed survey of the house carried out in 1998 by Messrs. Plowman Craven, Surveyors, Harpenden.

[13] Girouard, Note 10.

[14] Boynton, Note 8.

[15] Peter Thornton, *Seventeenth-Century Interior Decoration in England, France & Holland*, New Haven and London: Yale University Press, p.106.

[16] The opening in the south-east turret would appear to have been constructed 'blind', but the different construction of the closure of the opening in the north-east turret suggest this might have been a later alteration.

[17] Cited in David N. Durant, *Bess of Hardwick: Portrait of an Elizabethan Dynast*, London: Peter Owen Publishers, revised edition, 1999. The original is in the Cecil Papers at Hatfield House.

[18] See Thornton, Note 16, pp. 255-256, for a discussion of fire screens.

[19] 'Darnix' was a woolen fabric used for curtains and wall hangings. From 'Doornick', the Flemish name for Tournai.

[20] Thornton, Note 16, p.268.

[21] Peter Thornton, 'A short Commentary on the Hardwick Hall Inventory of 1601', in Boynton (Ed.), Note 8, p. 15.

[22] Slightly different plans are offered by Boynton to accompany the 1601 Inventories (1971), Girouard in the National Trust Guidebook (1989) and Durant and Riden to accompany the Building Accounts (1984). The plan here is based the last of these. This is also presented in David N. Durant, *The Smythson Circle: The story of six great English houses*, London: Peter Owen Publishers, 2011.

Spolia Britannica: The historical use of salvaged building materials in Britain

Michael Heaton

University of Bath, UK

Abstract

Using case studies from the author's professional work as an archaeological surveyor of historic buildings in southwest England, the thesis examines evidence for the historical use of salvaged materials in British buildings; compares it with accounts of the same in architectural, economic and cultural histories; and argues that the material is more common and of greater archaeological potential and historical significance than the limited anglo-centric literature would suggest.

The thesis demonstrates that salvage was culturally endemic throughout England and probably the whole of Britain throughout the later Middle Ages and the early Modern periods and was facilitated by sophisticated markets, distribution networks and possibly customary 'linear' exchange; that, in addition to its iconographic and economic value, salvage was an important vector of technological and stylistic diffusion and development; and that salvaged architectural details – or spolia – were employed creatively by Catholic and other minority owners as expressions of cultural affinity and political legitimacy. That creative use reaches its ultimate expression in the 'ruins' of Bradenstoke Priory in Wiltshire , which were re-sculpted using salvaged materials by a succession of Catholic and latterly antiquarian owners during the late 17th , 18th and 19th centuries, before partial demolition – for salvage – by William Randolph Hearst in 1929.

Introduction

Architectural salvage is an established subject of academic study, in which Britain hardly features. The re-use of materials and architectural details from older buildings was widespread in late imperial Rome, medieval Islam and Europe and was instrumental in the development of Renaissance architecture in Italy[1], but the extent and manner in which that operated in Britain has not been addressed, despite salvaged materials being a common component of historic buildings in this country. Whilst several authors[2] have referred in passing to the re-use of monastic building materials in the late 16th century, few[3] identify anything other than economic utility in the practice. Admittedly, Britain is at the edge of the Classical and Renaissance worlds and a late recipient of their influences, but the purposeful use of salvaged materials and *spolia* has been demonstrated in 17th century Ireland[4],which is geographically more distant than Britain from the Classical world and lacked direct contact both with it and Francethroughout the Medieval and *Ancien Regime*[5]. There is therefore no obvious geographical reason for its absence from Britain.

Culturally, however, Britain became increasingly distinct from its two nearest neighbours and the rest of the Catholic world after the Reformation, and by the middle of the 18th century was the only industrialised economy in the world and well on the way to becoming the first urbanised one. But not every Briton embraced iconoclastic Protestantism or the rationalism of the economic revolutions that followed it[6]. Many clung to – or adopted - the old ways, others ignored or were by-passed by the march of Reason. Their eccentricity, unrecorded historically, remains manifest in their material artefacts and buildings: specifically their use of salvaged materials, structural assemblies and architectural details.

This paper, derived from the author's MPhil thesis, draws on a broad cultural history and case studies to demonstrate that the purposeful re-use of salvaged building materials and architectural details has been as common in Britain as the rest of Europe. Furthermore, in addition to the iconic, aesthetic and economic use manifest elsewhere, the exchange of such material in Britain appears to have had important social agency and its use influenced the development and dissemination of architectural forms and construction technology.

Current understanding

The architectural literature on salvage, and on *spolia* in the Mediterranean in particular, is substantial and supported by a large number of extant Roman, medieval, Islamic and Renaissance buildings. It is a broad and well-established subject that does not bear repetition here. Suffice to say that salvaged materials and *spolia* were employed to confer cultural legitimacy on the host buildings, often during periods of cultural change. Britain hardly features in that literature. Colvin, Salzmann or Airs, for example – make passing reference to the re-use of materials from monasteries and Crown buildings throughout the Middle Ages into the 17th century, but attribute it to economic utility or vandalism. More recent studies detect other motives, but without developing them: Howard suggests that the motives for demolition were more complex than simple economic expediency and nihilism and that "*..the destruction of the monasteries ... formed part of a much wider interchange and re-use.*"[7] Stevenson observes that 17th century Londoners were familiar with "*the symbolic charge that it* (i.e. salvaged building stone) *could carry*" citing John Stow's reference of 1603 to the practice of using "*stones taken from the Jew's house in 1215*" [8] - i.e. 400 years prior to the material's incorporation in 17th C London tenements. Moss demonstrates the use of salvaged Romanesque masonry, the latter as *spolia* in the Classical sense, was practiced by the Protestant Ascendancy of 17th century Ireland[9] under circumstances their English cousins would have recognised. Most recently, and intriguingly, Fancelli reports that *spolia* was an essential component of the 'fictitious ruins' – i.e follies – of *giardini inglesi* – English Gardens – as fact that has escaped most English writers ![10].

Broader cultural history reveals the apotropaism of 17th century Londoners to be evident in the behaviour of the wider populace. Fragments of the Boscobel Oak in Cumbria, in which Charles II is reputed to have hidden, were retained after felling by superstitious Royalists for apotropaic use in their houses[11]. Similarly, Duffy relates the hoarding of religious relics – structural and liturgical – by unreformed parishioners in the later 16th century[12]; whilst Airs deduces an early reticence to build on formerly religious sites, for exactly the same reason – the material fabric of the buildings was clearly deemed to be imbued with metaphysical properties[13]. In the Mediterranean it might have been the detail of the re-used epigraphy or sculpture: in Britain, as Stevenson notes above[14], it appears to have been the material itself. A comparable function for portable material possessions was identified by Malinowski in his anthropological study of Polynesia[15]. This, and subsequent archaeological studies of European societies[16], observed that the ritualised non-economic 'linear' exchange of objects and artefacts was a social activity that tied communities together: the objects themselves were of no economic or functional value, but their exchange was a matter of public communal obligation. In Polynesia it was large conch shells or 'kula' necklaces; in prehistoric Europe it was *Spondylus* shells; in the Hebrides, pieces of white Iona marble at Early Christian *cenobia* indicate an association with the parent monastery and disciples of Columba[17]. Might this also have applied to other building materials? Dennison[18] has identified possibly totemic re-use of fragments of Sheriff Hutton Castle throughout the Post-medieval houses of the adjacent village, and the present author is undertaking a similar survey of Abbotsbury. To modern Western eyes, buildings and their components are functional and/or decorative; but to historical or non-Western communities they can also be totemic of activities with a wider societal function, as Ochsendorf has demonstrated for mountain footbridges in the Andes[19].

Similarly, archaeology reveals a more nuanced and fulsome picture of the use of salvaged building materials, which are encountered in most archaeological excavations of Roman and later sites in Britain; whilst archaeological surveys of extant buildings record its use into the early 19th century. For example: Stocker and Everson's study of Lincolnshire churches[20] identified three forms of re-use – 'Casual', 'Functional' and 'Iconic' and concluded that the phenomenon is nationwide and likely to extend beyond their early 16th century cut-off date and ecclesiastical sphere. Thorpe and Cox's unpublished surveys of buildings in Devon[21] support that assertion, identifying chronologically and typologically specific patterns of salvage re-use: It does not occur in the primary fabric of major medieval or non-domestic buildings of any age; it occurs only in the secondary fabric of major medieval buildings, i.e. in modifications, and in the primary fabric of Post-Dissolution houses, becoming increasingly common in late 17th and 18th century houses and particularly in urban houses. The use of salvaged material, therefore, appears to have been selective and structured.

Nonetheless, given that churches and monasteries underwent centuries of recurrent architectural remodelling, it is remarkable how *little* architectural detail there is within their surviving foundations and wall cores exposed by excavation: where has it all gone ?. Those monasteries were components of complex socio-geographic systems, of which their religious function was merely a part, albeit a fundamental one[22]. Perhaps, just as those secular communities contributed to the establishment and maintenance of the monasteries, they also took part in their cyclic re-building and eventual dismemberment. The few contemporaneous accounts of dismemberment that survive, such as Hailes Abbey or Reading Abbey [23], imply no criminality on the part of the 'wreckers', they are simply financial analyses of the economic diminution and wide social re-distribution of a Crown asset. Is it possible that the monasteries were dismembered, not solely because of vehement anti-Catholic or anti-monastic sentiment, but because it was customary to do so?

The extent to which the British were also routinely engaged in the despoilation of others' secular buildings is made clear in Rakoczy's studies of the Civil War[24]. She demonstrates that dismemberment and dispersal of buildings was conducted on an immense scale that required experienced organisations and a well-established legal framework, exactly as was the case in continental Europe[25]. It is highly improbable that the capabilities necessary sprang up 'overnight' in the midst of Britain's bloodiest ever civil conflict. They must have been long established. Furthermore, she avers that salvage and re-use also had extra-economic significance in the quasi-religious context of the Civil War, where appropriation of an enemy's building fabric and other property was an acceptable totemic alternative to complete destruction of otherwise desirable residences. Is this not an architectural and post-medieval manifestation of the 'linear' exchange systems identified by Malinowski and others, albeit under confrontational circumstances?

Archaeology and a broader reading of cultural history, therefore, reveal glimpses of customs complementary to those of continental Europe and a material resource of some historical significance. The following case studies demonstrate some of the ways in which that significance is manifest in extant British buildings.

Case Studies

No.28 High Street, Shalbourne, Wiltshire

This small 18th century brickwork house is notable only for the asymmetry of its principal elevation and internal layout, enforced by the position and scale of its staircase, which takes up nearly 30% of the house's floor space. (Fig.1). Unlike comparable houses in the village, the stair of No. 28 is a grand open-well structure positioned at the centre of the house. It is formed entirely of modified salvaged members of an oak cross-frame of later medieval type. This represents, surely, more than simply the opportunistic use of salvaged timber, because it required - or facilitated - the design and construction of an atypical staircase and building layout. It would undoubtedly have been easier, cheaper and more space-effective to have adhered to vernacular practice by constructing a narrow winder stair in one of the internal corners. The salvaged frame might have been free, but its use necessitated construction of a larger than normal staircase that consumed a larger amount of high grade joinery timber and floor space. Nonetheless, the staircase lent the interior of the house an air of grandeur not evident in its external appearance, implying architectural and/or social aspirations.

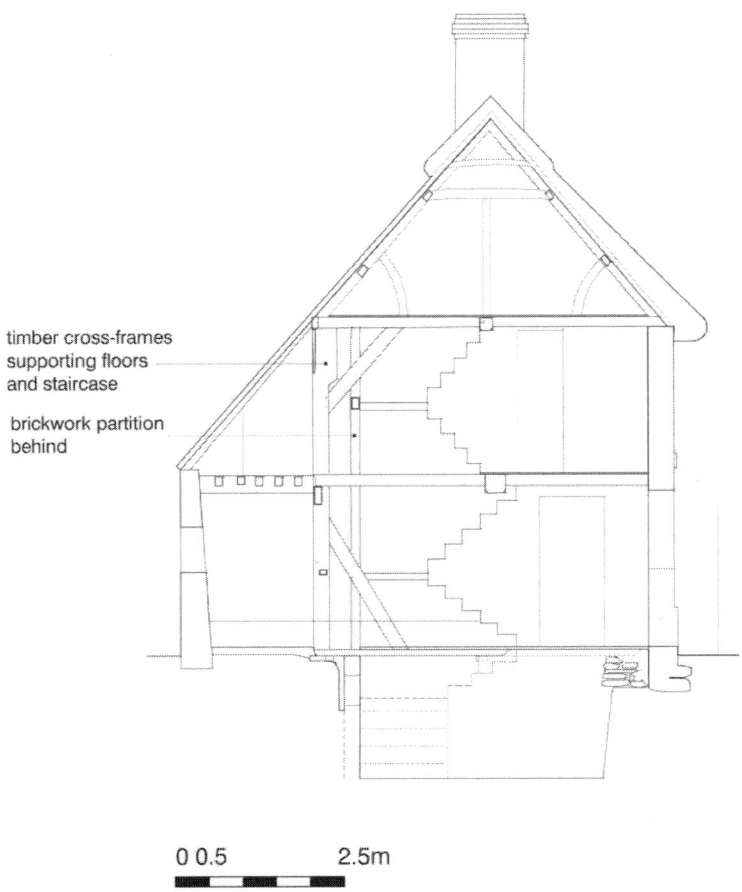

Figure 1. No. 28, Shalbourne, Wiltshire. Composite sectional elevation showing re-used wall frame members forming stair enclosure

Netherhams Farm, Low Ham, Somerset

Netherhams Farm[26] encompasses, *inter alia*, an extensive landscaped garden, a miniature church and the remains of two unfinished baroque mansions. The first, commenced in the late 16th century for Edward Hext MP, accompanied the ¾ scale Perpendicular parish church, but was unfinished at Hext's death in 1624. The second, commenced in 1689 by Hext's Catholic son-in-law John Stawell, is depicted on a survey of 1779 that also records the presence of a dovecote on the summit of the hill that overlooks Netherhams Farm c. 1 mile from the south, and annotates the nearby stream '*Paradise*' – i.e. a landscaped stream[27]. Colvin deduces French influence in the design of the house[28], possibly the hand of one Jacques Rousseau (1630-93,) but the elevation shown on the 1779 survey is clearly a baroque English house. Stawell died in 1692[29] with the mansion unfinished and his estates forfeited. The house and stables were quarried by the Mildmay family for their new house at nearby Hazlegrove, surviving as picturesque ruins until c.1925[30].

Colvin notes *in situ* architectural details of the Stawell mansion within the fabric of the extant farm yard walls, but close examination reveals that many of those details cannot be *in situ* because they are arranged randomly. Nonetheless, the main barn and adjoining walled yard, present in 1779, incorporate much salvaged architectural masonry positioned for maximum visual effect. In the example shown, the door opening was possibly functional, but the window frame surmounting it does not pass through the wall and is therefore purely decorative. (Fig.2). Whilst that degree of decoration might seem anomalousfor farm buildings, at the time of its construction Netherhams Farm was the centrepiece of an extensive designed landscape and stood outside the door of the parish church. It was a highly visual and public architectural statement.

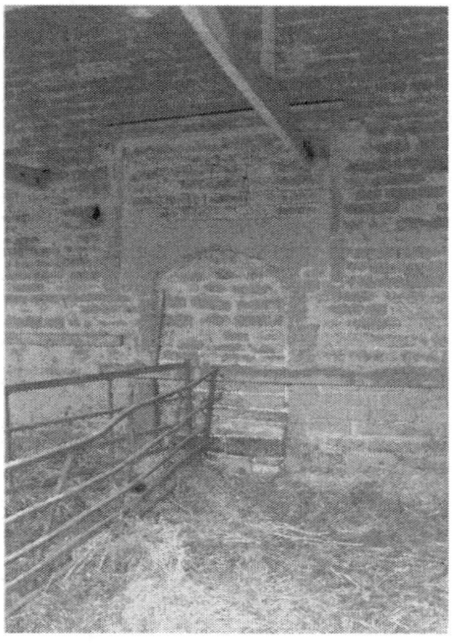

Figure 2.Netherhams Farm. Re-used door and window frames in barn wall. The door, though now blocked, could have functioned; the window could not

It is reasonable to assume that the barn and the rest of the farm complex was built c. 1689-1692 for Stawell, incorporating *spolia* from the ruins of his predecessor's house, possibly under the supervision of a French architect. The Stawells were Catholics who had supported the Stuart cause during the Civil War and the Glorious Revolution, with John Stawell possibly dying for his allegiances. He had good reason to proclaim his family's legitimacy, and in that regard his use of *spolia* is analogous to that of his religious and political counterparts in Ireland[31] and, indeed, Roman and Renaissance practice. As a Catholic, Stawell would have been sensitive to the iconographic value of salvaged architectural details, even those of his Protestant in-laws[32]. His mansion was designed by a Frenchman who would have been familiar with the architectural practices of the Italian Renaissance with regards the use of *spolia*. Rousseau might have had difficulty persuading his English patron to adopt a foreign architectural template for the mansion during difficult times, but the farm buildings facing it might have been an acceptable canvas on which display their shared appreciation of fashion and symbolism. To the owner, the country house of the late 16th and 17th century was "*...symbolic of his knowledge and intelligence, as well as his wealth and power....The cultural contemporary mind delighted in anything that was strange or curious, particularly if it were later revealed to have hidden meaning..*" [33]

Cockington Court

Cockington Court has been owned by only three families between the Norman Conquest and 1932: Fitzmartin (c. AD1066), Cary (c. AD1394) and Mallock (c.AD1654). The Carys became major landowners, but forfeited Cockington Court during the Civil War and their Catholic members continued to support the Stuart cause after the Glorious Revolution[34]. They had acquired nearby Torre Abbey at the Dissolution, to which they moved in 1662, ceding Cockington Court to the Mallocks[35], wealthy *parvenu* merchants who became prominent and politically astute landowners and parliamentarians throughout the 17th and 18th centuries.

The building's interest lies in the structure of its first floor. It has been dated to AD1673 on historical grounds[36], so was installed by the Mallocks. All the beams and joists were salvaged from a building – or buildings of slightly different dimensions, many with varying and highly complex joint forms. Dendrochronology suggests a date of AD1599 for the earliest of them[37]. (Fig.3) The whole structure, covering an area of c. 227 square metres, had been used for less than a century elsewhere before its installation at Cockington Court. The most likely candidate is nearby Torre Abbey, but most of the floor structure was first assembled c. 50 years after the closure of the abbey and remained in its primary setting for less than a century. If Torre Abbey was the source, therefore, it was being remodelled at great expense two generations after the Dissolution[38] by the Carys.

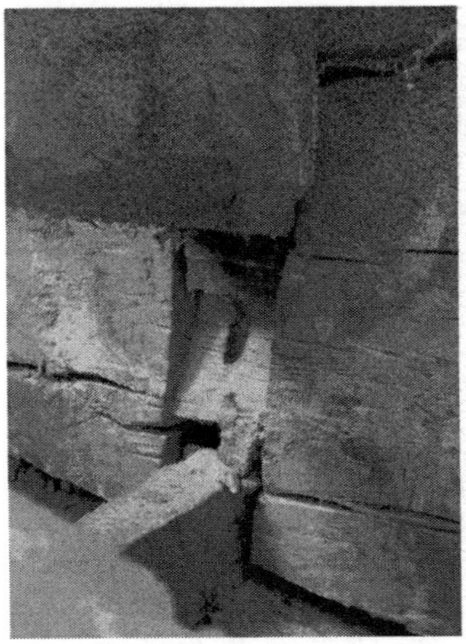

Figure 3. Cockington Court. Example of re-used floor beam with full-depth socket only partially occupied by secondary floor and ceiling joists.

The dispossessed Carys might have benefited financially from sale of the floor, but this might also have been an example of *'conspicuous waste'*[39] enacted publicly by the recently deposed family as a last act of *noblesse oblige* that confirmed their customary status despite their reduced circumstances. It would have been understood by the 17th century society accustomed to religious and royal processions[40]. What did the Mallocks gain? It is unlikely that their motives were financial or that they were interested in the associational value of fabric from a former monastery, but it is possible that the use of salvaged materials was a studied public exercise in prudence, intended to contrast them with their dissolute Catholic Royalist predecessors. They were now the new lords of several manors in England's principal maritime county just as widespread deforestation caused by ship building for the Civil and Dutch wars was becoming apparent. Evelyn's *Sylvarum* was commissioned by the Admiralty in response to that deforestation, and the Mallocks were the sort that would have read it.

A major church

Of the many unexplained conundra[41] in the layout and fabric of Christchurch Priory church, the Pulpitum is the most visually arresting. (Fig.4). This enormous structure does not fit the church: it is wedged asymmetrically between the two east piers of the Crossing, which have been brutally chopped to accommodate it, so it was made for a different monastic or cathedral church[42]. It was in place in 1787[43], but neither its source nor exact date of arrival are recorded[44]. Whilst most of the geographically proximate monasteries have been lost or display no evidence of a pulpitum[45], Winchester Cathedral was in an almost constant state of refurbishment throughout the 17th – 19th centuries and had its Perpendicular stone pulpitum removed during Inigo Jones' minor re-ordering in 1638[46]. The Christchurch pulpitum is stylistically and metrically compatible with it.

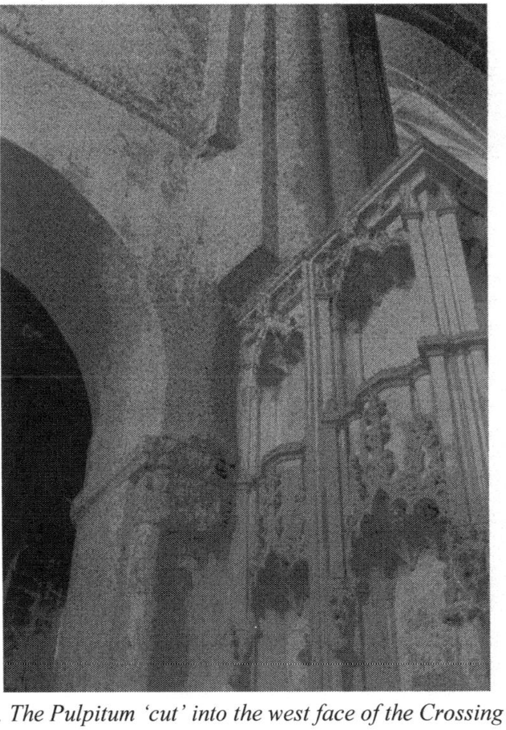

Figure 4. Christchurch Priory. The Pulpitum 'cut' into the west face of the Crossing piers

Assuming Winchester was the source, the act of salvage and re-location was also a public manifestation of the relationship of the two churches. Prior to the Dissolution, Christchurch Priory was the wealthiest monastery on the south coast and, though situated within Winchester Diocese, was not hierarchically or financially related to it. That changed in the 16th century, with the former priory church becoming subservient to the Cathedral and, eventually, supporting the Diocese financially through its precept payments. Materials were therefore moving down the hierarchy, whilst money flowed up. It is redolent of the culture of exchange inferred above from the archaeological evidence of excavated monasteries. That the exchange was not recorded by either church suggests it was customary.

It also suggests, perhaps, that the iconoclastic Puritanism of the early 17th century was held less fervently – at least at Christchurch. Embellishment of a former monastic church in the early-mid 17th century with decorative fabric ran counter to the Puritanism of the time and the indigenous anti-Catholic sentiment assumed by Masinton and others[47] . Indeed, it suggests that the parishioners embraced or resumed the old-fashioned tendencies of Charles I confidently, on the eve of the Civil War. Had their intent been simply to reduce the floor area of the church or separate *Word* from *Sacrament*, a timber or plaster screen would have been quicker and cheaper[48]; demolition of the east end of the church – as at Bath and Malmesbury - would have served the same purpose and turned a profit in an area lacking freestone. The parishioners of Christchurch took a more conservative path. This is *spolia* on a monumental scale undertaken at a time of cultural change comparable to late Imperial Rome or Renaissance Europe. The logistical effort involved in moving and installing this monumental structure demonstrates it was acquired for its associational value, if not its iconic significance, and that the salvage industry identified by Rakoczy for the later 17th century was active before the Civil War.

A monastic ruin

Bradenstoke Priory is the *casus belli* of building conservation in Britain. Leland described it as already ruinous in 1542 and by the 17th century only the 'cellars' and 'Priors' Hall' survived*[49]*. The hill-top ruins became a part of Wiltshire's historic landscape, the subject of antiquarian attention, romantic painting and archaeological investigation.(Fig.5) It achieved national attention in 1929, when William Randolph Hearst purchased it with the express intention of quarrying it for architectural details to augment St Donats in Glamorgan[50]. But was the building Hearst demolished part of a medieval priory? William Haywood, describing the structure in 1897, identified "*modern barrel vaults*" and several other perplexing features, but crossed-out that term before reading his account to the RIBA[51].

During the preceding four centuries it had passed through the hands of some notable builders[52]. It was owned and garrisoned during the Civil War [53] by the regicide Sir John Danvers (1588-1655), who constructed the artillery defences that later formed the kernel of a formally-designed landscape garden with the priory ruins at its dramatic northern edge[54]. Danvers was a cultured man and "*professed papist*"[55], who had travelled throughout Europe and accumulated crippling debts through his extravagant tastes in architecture and gardening[56]. His father was one of Inigo Jones' clients for his trip to Rome c. 1613 acquiring architectural prints[57]. Aubrey tells us "..*Twas Sir John Danvers....who first taught us the way of Italian gardens* and that Danvers' son-in-law, Viscount Purbeck, had offered to give him a "*view*" – i.e. a drawing - of the priory ruins for his proposed history of North Wiltshire, but it was not forthcoming[58]. Nonetheless, the offer suggests Danvers had had something to show-off.

By 1732 the remains were occupied by a Germanicus Sheppard, " *a colourful character...a devout Catholic....who died after a fall from his horse in 1758*"[59], to whom the Buck Brothers dedicated their 'view' (cf. Figure 6, below). At an unknown date, possibly 1758 but certainly by 1772, the estate was owned by the Methuen family of Corsham Court who retained it till 1863. In addition to their economic power, the 17th and 18th century generations of the Methuens were diplomats to Spain, Italy and Portugal, amateur architects, acquisitive patrons of the arts and, probably, Catholics: Sir Paul Methuen (c. 1672 – 1757), the second to bear the title and the first to embrace architecture as an activity, attended a Jesuit school in Paris[60]. Between 1863 and 1917 it was owned by the enthusiastic amateur architect Sir Gabriel Goldney, before coming to the attention of William Randolph Hearst through the promotional efforts of *SPAB* in 1929. The rest is received conservation history.

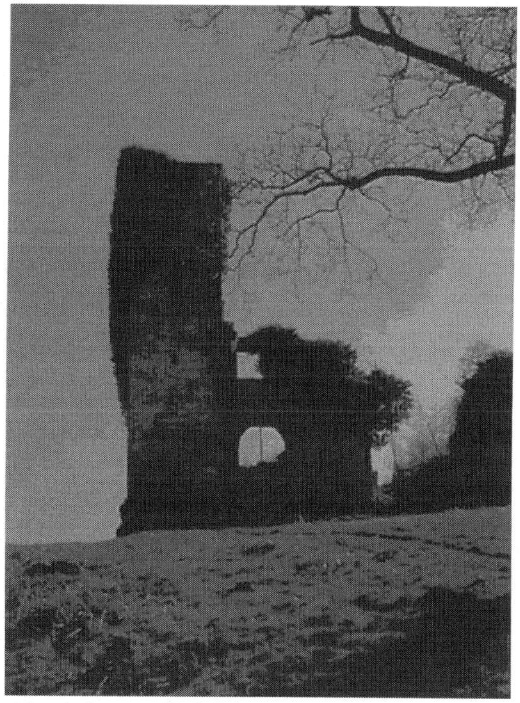

Figure 5. Bradenstoke Priory. The skyline profile left by Hearst in 1929.

Archaeological and historical analysis of the surviving fabric, however, suggests Heywood was correct and that some, if not all of those owners, left their mark. Simple comparison of the many antiquarian views of the west elevation reveal it to be of multiple phases of construction and embellishment. (Fig.6) Most of that was demolished by Hearst, but the surviving fabric incorporates many details inconsistent – if not incompatible – with medieval construction. The most obvious anomaly is the tower and adjoining ground floor elevation. Present in 1732 but architecturally distinct from the rest of the building in being decidedly Italianate, the tower is unparalleled in a medieval British monastery and positioned for maximum skyline profile, but was not referred to by Leland [61]. The adjoining 'broken' wall stubs (cf. Figure 7: A) are in fact fully closed primary masonry (i.e. built like that) and its winder stair has no access openings at floor levels. (Fig.7). There are many similar anomalies, including an incomplete vaulted ground floor supported by an internal brickwork flying buttress, and most of it is constructed using salvaged material.

Top: The engraved version of the Buck Brothers' depiction of 1732, commissioned by Germanicus Shepherd. The Buck Brothers and their engravers rationalised or omitted anomalies, just as portrait artists did, but they faithfully recorded the presence of the tower – if not its roof form – and the two door openings at the bottom left hand corner, with one blocked-up more or less as it is today. In that respect, their depiction is a faithful one. The tower and the 'blocked' door had been added before 1732.

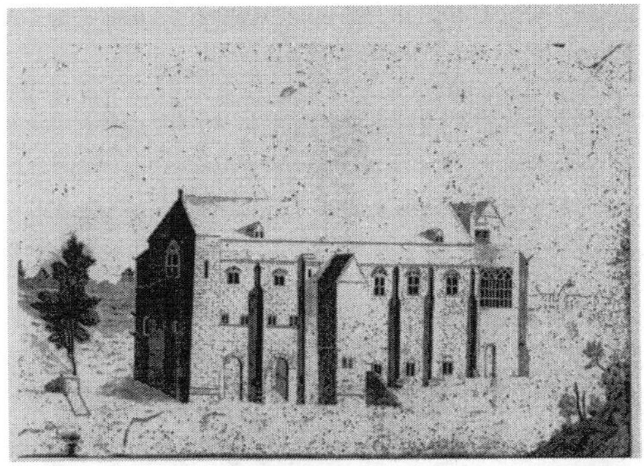

Middle: Buckler (Snr) watercolour of 1808, commissioned by Richard Colt-Hoare for his Antiquities of Wiltshire. The Bucklers' depictions are 'archaeologically' accurate in recording without interpretation. They indicate the presence of the 'blocked' door opening at the far left hand end of the elevation and, more importantly, the presence of three arcade arches that were not there in 1732 or 1917 (below). Examination of the existing fabric reveals the notches for those arcades, demonstrating Buckler's accuracy. The building had, therefore, been embellished between 1732 and 1808.

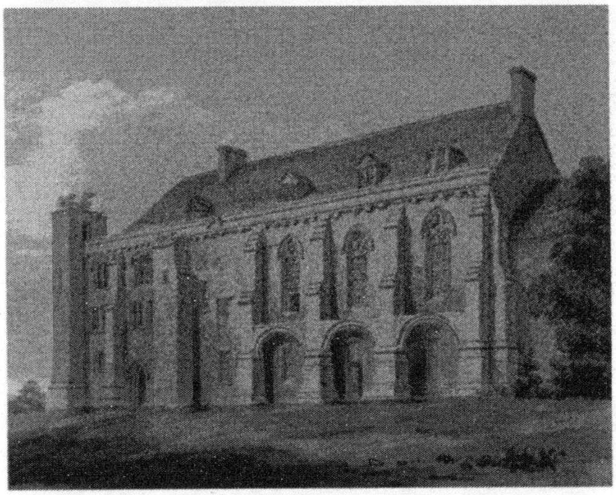

Bottom: RCHME photograph of 1917 taken during Brakspeare's investigations. The elevation corroborates Buckler's record, except for the arcade arches, which had presumably been removed by Goldney. The most important detail of this and Buckler's depiction is the relationship between the parapet and the tower door, which demonstrates that the tower could not have been functional. The medieval ruins had, indeed, been embellished.

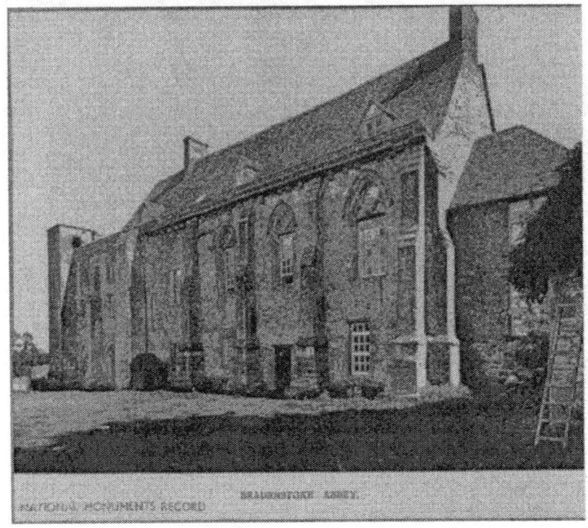

Figure 6. Bradenstoke Priory. The Priors' Hall as recorded by Buck in 1732 (top), Buckler in 1808 (middle) and Brakspear in 1917 (bottom)

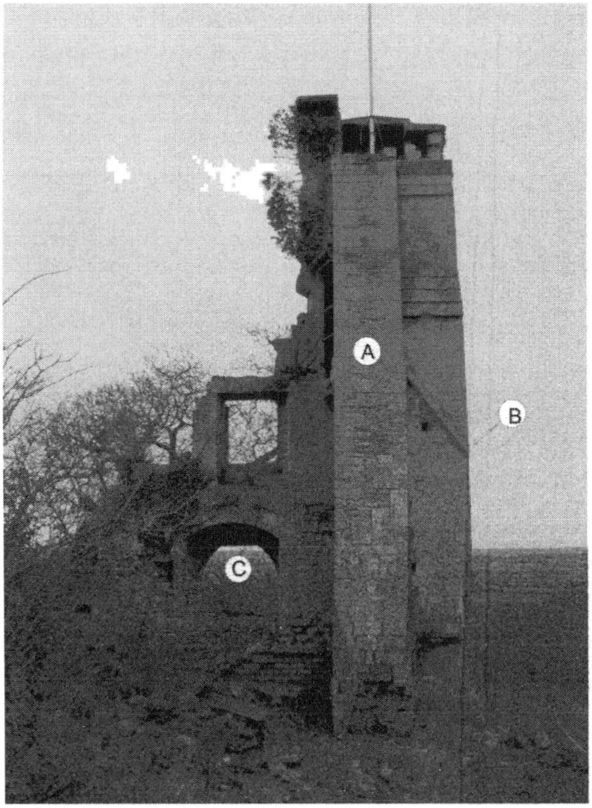

Figure 7. Bradenstoke Priory. Rear elevation of the tower showing the many non-functional 'architectural' details: A, wall 'stub' of fully closed masonry; B, verge fillet for non-existent pentice; C, door opening with internal reveals that do not reach the ground

The fabric Hearst left behind, therefore, had been added to the medieval remains as a folly prior to 1732 and the ensemble then heavily modified between 1732 and 1808, with both phases using salvaged material positioned to evoke a Gothic(k) interpretation of Classical antiquity and the early Renaissance architecture of Italy. By who is not known, but of its many 16th and 17th century owners Sir John Danvers is the most likely candidate, whilst the 18th century embellishments correspond with the Methuen's dabblings in architecture. This is salvage developed to fulfil a creative function, a grotto-like folly essential to *I giardini inglesi.* If Danvers was indeed the first to introduce Italian garden design to Britain, this is probably the *giardino inglese,* whilst his internal flying buttresses anticipate Piranesi by a century and are possibly one of the earliest essays in Gothic(k).

Whilst Danvers couldn't erase his name from Charles I's death warrant, he could broadcast his affinity with the cultural and religious affinities of the monarchy to those who understood the allusion, whilst indulging his passion for garden design and Mediterranean architecture. Unlike his Irish contemporaries, Danvers' intended audience was his peers and betters, not his tenants. The Methuens were relatively new members of the land-owning class, like the Mallocks at Cockington Court, but by the mid 18th century they were well-established diplomats and privy councillors. They had little to prove but perhaps they had aesthetic impulses that could not be expressed publicly at Corsham Court. Was Bradenstoke the canvas on which they indulged their Catholic tastes with *spolia*?

Discussion

The polemical and aesthetic motives of Stawell, Danvers and the Methuens match European and Irish patterns of *spolia* and need little explanation here. These buildings and a host of others demonstrate that the use of salvaged materials and *spolia* in particular was as widespread in 16th – 18th century Britain as it was in continental Europe and the Mediterranean and possibly indicates a wider familiarity with European architectural writing than has hitherto been assumed. Nonetheless, it is significant, in the British context, that its secular use appears to have appealed principally to Catholics[62]. In addition to illustrating the iconophilia we might expect of recusants in 17th and 18th century Britain, this also suggests that European architectural mores were being communicated to Britain through Catholic channels.

At the vernacular level, most re-use was undoubtedly economical[63]. However, it is possible that such materials are not solely tokens of wealth, but that they were the wealth itself. This is suggested by critical examination of Hoskins' hypothesis of the 'Great Rebuilding'[64] , in which he attributes the appearance of the Yeoman House directly to the redistribution of land wealth at the Dissolution, despite there being little historical evidence of commoners benefiting directly[65]. As with the forced sales of Royalist lands a century later, the 'lots' were too big for the peasantry and soldiery to afford or use. The building materials, however, were of immediate use to them. It is more likely, therefore, that salvage was the medium or currency through which some of the value of monastic and royal estates was transferred to the commonality. Rather than simply being 'evidence' of wealth redistribution, the material fabric of the Yeoman House was the wealth itself. The 16th century yeomanry or 17th century soldiery didn't need to own land in order to build on it, but they did need materials.

The emergence of Hoskins' Yeoman House undoubtedly owed much to the availability of salvaged materials: might not its form and higher standard of fit-out also have been a direct result of the abundance of such materials and emulation of the buildings from which they were sourced? The castles, palaces and monasteries were the architectural tip of a social, economic and technological pyramid through which aesthetic mores and construction technology trickled. But how ? The mechanisms of stylistic and technological transfer, socially and geographically in Britain, have not been explained[66]: How did the gentry or yeomanry copy architectural details fixed to 40' or even 20' high buildings ? how was the stereotomy of the ribbed vault transferred from monastic nave to rural porch without the use of foreign language treatises on Descriptive Geometry ? how was the 'secret notched lap joint' made commonplace ? Howard has demonstrated the influence monastic layouts had on the architecture of larger 16th and 17th century houses of the gentry and aristocracy[67] and Lazanski[68] has demonstrated the widespread distribution of architectural details such as window frames and floor structures. Is it not possible that vernacular construction technology benefited directly? The better-surviving examples of late medieval monastic architecture, such as Cleeve Abbey in Somerset, demonstrate that late 16th century secular developments, such as well-appointed and ceiled ground floor rooms, glazed windows or open-well staircases were a monastic innovation. As Lazanski has demonstrated[69], the despoilers of those buildings would have witnessed at first hand, probably for the first time, enviable levels of comfort and, more importantly, the structural and technical details necessary for its realisation, which they carried away in accordance with time-honoured custom.

This assertion is supported by dendrochronology. Wild and Moir's holistic analysis of 177 accurately dated houses in Surrey[70] remarks on the speed with which structural and technological innovations were adopted in the mid to late 16th century. The insertion of upper floors over formerly open halls, the more economic use of timber as narrow modulus beams and joists, and developments in joint form occurred "*within a generation*".

This they attribute, *pace* Hoskins, to the rapid vertical distribution of monastic real estate wealth. Within a generation ? In our own times we have witnessed a similar privatisation of public wealth[71] with little popular manifestation of it, despite infinitely higher levels of financial liquidity and accessible credit compared to the 16th century. Back in the 16th and 17th centuries, the financial institutions and mechanisms necessary for the transfer and realisation of land wealth to the 'Yeomanry' *within a generation* did not exist[72]. The material fabric of the donor buildings was the only way that wealth could have been transferred.

Those three trends – the iconic, the aesthetic and the customary uses of salvaged building materials and architectural details - represent the British use of salvaged materials and *spolia:* a *Spolia Britannica.* They demonstrate that in at least this one respect, Britain - or at least some of it - was not substantively different from its continental and Catholic neighbours.

Notes and references

[1] The literature on Classical, Islamic and Renaissance salvage and *spolia* in particular is substantial, but some of the principal authorities are: Alchermes, J., 1994, 'Spolia in Roman cities of the late Empire: Legislative rationales and architectural re-use', *Dumbarton Oak,* 48 pp167-178; Bernard, J-F., Bernardi, P., and Esposito, D., (Eds) 2008, *Il Reimpiego in Architettura: Recupero,Trasformazione,Uso.* Collection de L'ecole Francaise de Rome 418 (Ecole Francaise de Rome, Universita 'La Sapienza' Roma); Brenck, B., 1987, 'Spolia from Constantine to Charlemagne: Aesthetics versus Ideology', *Dumbarton Oaks,* 41 pp103-109; Greenhalgh, M., 2009, *Marble Past, Monumental Present: Building with Antiquities in the Medieval Mediterranean.* (Leiden, Brill); Ousterhout, R., 1995, 'Ethnic Identity and Cultural Appropriation in Early Ottoman Architecture, *Muqarnas,* 12, pp48-62; Ousterhout, R., 2003, 'Architecture as Relic and the Construction of Sanctity: The Stones of the Holy Sepulchre', *Journal of the Society of Architectural Historians,* 62, pp4-23; Payne, A., 1998, 'Creativity and bricolage in architectural literature of the Renaissance', *Res* 34 pp 20-38; Waters, M.J., 2015, 'Reviving Antiquity in Granite: Spoliated columns and the development of the Roman Renaissance, ' in Lex Bosman (Ed), *Architecture in Pieces: the representation of architecture by means of spolia. (*Tournhout: Brepolis)

[2] Cf. Airs, M., 1995, The Tudor and Jacobean Great House: A building history (Stroud, Sutton); Briggs, M.S., 1952, Goths and Vandals: A study of the destruction, neglect and preservation of historical buildings in England. (London, Constable); Colvin, H.W., *et al*, 1963-1982, *History of the Kings Works.* (London, HMSO); Salzmann, L.F., 1952, *Building in England down to 1540.* (Leicester, University Press).

[3] Specifically: Harris, J., 2007, *Moving Rooms: The trade in architectural salvage.* (Yale, Paul Mellon Centre for Studies in British Art); Howard, M., 1987, p26, *The Early Tudor Country House: Architecture and Politics 1490-1550.* (London, George Philip); Stevenson, C., 2006, 'Occasional Architecture in Seventeenth Century London', *Architectural History,* 49, pp 35-74.

[4] Moss, R., 2008, 'Appropriating the Past: Romanesque spolia in 17th century Ireland', *Architectural History,* 51, pp 63-86.

[5] Cf. Bernard, J-F., Bernardi, P., and Esposito, D., (Eds) 2008, *Il Reimpiego in Architettura: Recupero,Trasformazione,Uso.* Collection de L'ecole Francaise de Rome 418 (Ecole Francaise de Rome, Universita 'La Sapienza' Roma)

[6] Duffy, E., 1992, *The Stripping of the Altars;* 2001, *The Voices of Morebath* (Yale); Haigh, C., 1981, 'The Continuity of Catholicism in the English Reformation,' *Past and Present,* No. 93, pp37-69.

[7] Howard, 1987, *The Early Tudor Country House: Architecture and Politics 1490-1550,* p. 26. (George Philip).

[8] Stevenson, C., 2006, 'Occasional Architecture in Seventeenth Century London', *Architectural History,* 49, pp35-74.

[9] Moss, R., 2008, 'Appropriating the Past: Romanesque spolia in 17th century Ireland', *Architectural History,* 51, pp 63-86.

[10] Fancelli, P., 'De Spoliis in Fictas Ruinas', in Bernard *et al,* 2008, pp 661-674

[11] Harris, E., Harris, J., and James, N.D.G., 2003, *Oak: a British history,* p 141. (Exeter, Windgather Press)

[12] Duffy, 1992, *The Stripping of the Altars*, p 562 (Yale); 2001, *The Voices of Morebath,* pp 143,162,177 (Yale)

[13] Airs, 1995, p27. Admittedly, some new owners were wary of repossession during the fluid politics of late 16th century England.

[14] Stevenson, *op cit.*

[15] Malinowski, B., 1922, Argonauts of the Western Pacific: An Account of Native Enterprises and Adventure in the Archipelagoes of Melanesian New Guinea, p 81. (London, Routledge and Kegan).

[16] for instance: Renfrew, C., 1969, 'Trade and Cultural Process in European Prehistory', *Current Anthropology,* Vol 10 No 2/3, pp151-169; Shackleton, J., and Elderfield, H., 1990, 'Strontium Isotope dating of the source of Neolithic European Spondylus shell artefacts,' *Antiquity,* 64, No 243, pp312-15; Gregory, C.A., *Gifts and Commodities.* (New York: Academic Press); Weiner, A.B., 1992, *Inalienable Possessions: the Paradox of Keeping-While-Giving.* (Berkeley: University of California Press)

[17] Aston,, M., pers comm.

[18] Dennison, E., pers comm.

[19] Ochsendorf, J.A., 2006, 'Engineering Analysis for Construction History: Opportunities and Perils', *Proceedings of the 3rd International Congress on Construction History, Cambridge* Vol 1, pp89-107.

[20] Stocker, D., and Everson, P., 1990, 'Rubbish Recycled: A study of the re-use of building stone in Lincolnshire', in D.Parsons (Ed), *Stone Quarrying and Building in England AD43-1525.* (London, Phillimore/Royal Archaeological Institute)

[21] All 'grey literature' reports accessed at Devon County HER, and will eventually be available through the OASIS on-line library.

[22] Howard, 1987, *The Early Tudor Country House: Architecture and Politics 1490-1550,* p 142 (London, George Philip); Luxford, J., 2014, 'Architecture and Environment: St Benet's Holm and the fashioning of the English Monastic Gatehouse,' *Architectural History,* 57, pp 31-72.

[23] Preston, A.E., 1935, 'The Demolition of Reading Abbey', *The Berkshire Archaeological Journal,* 39 No. 2, pp 107-144; Lazanski, D, 2013, 'The Destruction of Hailes Abbey: a case study in pillaging at the dissolution.' MPhil Dissertation, University of Bath.

[24] Rakoczy, 2007.is her PhD thesis. She also edited a book of the same title in 2008.

[25] Bernard *et al, op cit,* 2008.

[26] Wilson-North, 1997, 'Low Ham, Somerset: Relic gardens of the 17th century and development of the landscape' (Exeter, RCHME); Bond, J., and Iles, R., 1991, 'Early Gardens in Avon and Somerset', in A.E. Brown (Ed), *Garden Archaeology ,* (CBA Res Rep 78); Aston, M., 1978, 'Gardens and Earthworks at Hardington and Low Ham', *Proceedings of the Somerset Archaeological and Natural History Society,* 122, p 78.; Colvin, H.W., 2001, 'Lord Stawell's Great House in Somerset', *Architectural History,* 44, pp 332-340.

[27] Brown, J., 1999, *The Pursuit of Paradise: A Social History of Gardening and Gardeners.* (London, Harper Collns).

[28] Colvin, o*p cit*

[29] Collins, A., and Brydges, Sir E., 1812, *Collins's Peerage of England,* 9, p 425. (London, Collins)

[30] Wilson-North, *op cit*

[31] cf Moss, *op cit*

[32] But as Gardiner, J.E., (2014, *Music in the Castle of Heaven: A Portrait of Johann Sebastian Bach,* p374 (London, Penguin)) observes, with respect to the Lutheran J.S.Bach, symbolism affected everyone in pre-Enlightenment Europe, Protestant and Catholic.

[33] Airs, M., 1979, 'The English Country House in the Sixteenth Century,' *Oxford Art Journal,* 2, pp 15-18

[34] Watkin, H. R., 1920, *The House of Stuart and the Cary Family: James II and Torre Abbey.* (Exeter, James G. Commin).

[35] Jenkins, J.C., 2010, 'Torre Abbey: locality, community and society in medieval Devon', DPhil Thesis, University of Oxford.

[36] The floor fits the floor plan created in 1673, as indicated by a date stone in the northernmost gable of the front elevation.

[37] Bridge, M., 2011, 'Cockington Court, Cockington Lane, Cockington, near Torquay, Devon: Tree-ring analysis of timbers. Scientific dating report.' (English Heritage Research Report Series 120-2011).

[38] Cf Howard, M., 2003, in D.Gaimster and R. Gilchrist (Eds), 'Recycling Monastic Fabric: Beyond the Act of Dissolution,'*The Archaeology of Reformation 1480-1580.* Archaeology of Reformation Conference February 2001. (Leeds, Maney); and Howard, M., 2007, *The building of Elizabethan and Jacobean England.* (Yale).

[39] Belk, R.W., 1984, 'Cultural and historical differences in concepts of self and their effects on attitudes towards having and giving', in T.C.Kinnear (Ed) *Advances in Consumer Research,* 11, pp 754-763

[40] cf. Stevenson, C., 2006, 'Occasional Architecture in Seventeenth Century London', *Architectural History,* 49, on the temporary architecture of Stuart processions.

[41] Cf Polk, B., 1994, *Christchurch Priory.* (London, Academy Editions). The Nave roof is also wholly salvaged

[42] Pulpitums are specific to monastic or cathedral churches

[43] Drawing held by the Society of Antiquaries, dated 1787.

[44] Druitt, H., 1919-1932, *Christchurch Miscellany,* (Christchurch, Private), does not mention it in his anthology of the churchwardens' accounts.

[45] Hearn, M.F., 1975, 'Romsey Abbey: A Progenitor of the English National Traditional in Architecture', *Gesta,* 14, No.1, pp 27-40.

[46] Lindley, P., Brodrick, A., and Darrah, J., 1989, 'The Great Screen of Winchester Cathedral I', *The Burlington Magazine,* 131, No. 1038 (Sep. 1989), pp 604-617.

[47] Masinton, A., 2008, 'The Destruction of the Monasteries: Dissolution and Continuity of Space in Tudor Yorkshire,', in L. Rakoczy (Ed), *The Archaeology of Destruction.* (Cambridge Scholar Publishing), pp 239-260.

[48] Lath and plaster partitions and blockings were installed elsewhere in the church in the 17th and 18th centuries.

[49] Jackson, J.E. (Ed), 1862, *Wiltshire: The Topographical Collections of John Aubrey,*
AD1659-70 (Devizes, Private).

[50] Harris, J., 2007, *Moving Rooms: The trade in architectural salvage.* (Yale), presents a potted history of Allom and White.

[51] Haywood, W., 1897, 'Account of Pugin travelling scholarship to Somerset and Wiltshire'. RIBA Archive Ref. X(079) P 72.033.4/5.

[52] Succinct accounts of a complex history of ownership and tenure are given in Pugh, R.B., (Ed), 1956,

Victoria County History of Wiltshire, Vol 3, p 275; and RCHME, 1998, 'Bradenstoke Priory and Clack Mount', (non publication survey report, Royal Commission on the Historical Monuments of England).

[53] Hobbs, S., 2003, 'Clack Mount.', *Wiltshire Archaeological and Natural History Magazine,* 96, pp 101.

[54] Creighton, O., 2000, 'Early castles in the medieval landscape of Wiltshire', *Wiltshire Archaeological and Natural History Magazine* 93, pp 55-60.

[55] Lee, S., 1900, *Dictionary of National Bibliography, 1885-1900,* Volume 14. (accessed through http:wikisource.org on 28.10.14)

[56] Kelsey, S., 2004, 'Sir John Danvers (1588-1655)', *Dictionary of National Biography* (Oxford).

[57] Mowl, T., and Earnshaw, B., 1995, *The Rise of Puritan Classicism under Cromwell.* (Manchester).

[58] Britton, J., 1847, Aubrey's Natural History of Wiltshire. (London)

[59] Devizes Museum, Bradenstoke Heritage Collection.

[60] Schweizer, K, W., 2004, 'Methuen, Sir Paul (c.1672-1757)', *Oxford Dictionary of National Biography. N* (Oxford Univerity Press, On-line Edition*)*

[61] Britton, *op cit*

[62] The religious affinity of the owners was discovered after the case study buildings had been chosen.

[63] Bernardi, P., in Bernard *et al,* 2008, pp503-516, demonstrates this was not always the case, especially during war.

[64] Hoskins, W.G, 1952, 'The Rebuilding of Rural England, 1570-1640', *Past and Present,* 4 pp 44-59. His theory is recurrently challenged, but Wild and Moir's recent dendrochronology (2013) supports its basic chronological premise.

[65] Gentles, I., 1973, 'The sale of Crown lands during the English Revolution,' *Economic History Review,* New Series Vol 26, No. 4, pp 614-635; Howard, M., 1987, *The Early Tudor Country House: Architecture and Politics 1490-1550,* P 138 (London, George Philip).

[66] The huge subject of construction technology transfer is not addressed by any English language authorities and we do not know of an English equivalent of Villard de Honnencourt.

[67] Howard, op cit and 2007, The building of Elizabethan and Jacobean England. (Yale, Paul Mellon)..

[68] Lazanski, *op cit*

[69] *Ibid,* p 64

[70] Wild, R., and Moir, A., 2013, 'Key dating features for timber-framed dwellings in Surrey', *Vernacular Architecture,* 44, pp 46-61.

[71] i.e. the British utilities companies in the late 1980s

[72] Gentles, *op cit*

Traces and architects in the 16th century architecture of Spain: the case of Hernan Ruiz in Jerez De La Frontera

Raúl Romero Medina[1] and Manuel Romero Bejarano[2]

1. UNIR- International University of La Rioja, Spain; 2. University of Seville, Spain

Introduction

Hernan Ruiz the Younger (c. 1515-1569) was one of the leading architects of the Spanish Renaissance. As a master builder of the Archiepiscopacy of Seville he was in charge of a large number of works, so high that it seemed impossible that anyone could take on so much work.

This paper examines one of the aspects of the labour organization of the period that has received little attention to date, namely that of the auxiliary architects. Thanks to a document located in the archive of Protocols of Jerez de la Frontera, we now know how an architect who lived more than 100 kilometres away from some of the works he was responsible for was able to control them. In 1567, the architect Francisco Rodriguez signed a contract in which he agreed to work as the assistant of architect Hernan Ruiz in all the works that the latter was in charge of in Jerez; five churches altogether. In it, he agreed to take the responsibilities of the senior master, which included drawing plans, building according to the plans that Hernan Ruiz sent and outsourcing to other stonemasons.

Meanwhile, Hernan Ruiz would make an annual one-day visit to make sure that the five works were progressing as planned. As we can see, the chief architect left all the work in the hands of the assistant architect, therefore the concept of authorship of the works is seriously undermined by the discovery of the document mentioned above. In fact, one can speak of a co-authorship of the building plans and full responsibility of the assistant architect. Thanks to our knowledge of the work of Francisco Rodriguez as a senior architect of the Episcopacy of Cadiz, we can establish the characteristics of his style and determine to what extent the works so far attributed to Hernan Ruiz are really his.

A brief summary of the lives of Francisco Rodríguez and Hernan Ruiz II

There is a document from 1567 in which Francisco Rodríguez agrees to get involved in being the assistant stonemason of Hernan Ruiz II in the construction of several parish churches in Jerez de la Frontera (Cádiz): San Salvador, San Miguel, San Juan de los Caballeros, San Mateo, San Marcos, Santiago y San Lucas.

Son of a master builder from Jerez called Antón Rodríguez, grandson of a master builder called Francisco Rodríguez the Elder, and nephew of Alonso Rodríguez, who was a senior stonemason of the Seville Cathedral, Francisco Rodríguez spent his childhood and youth in Málaga, where his father was working and where he studied architecture. He was the senior stonemason of Cádiz from about 1536 to 1569. He was the builder of several parish churches in this area Medina Sidonia, Vejer, Tarifa y Gibraltar, as well as the Santo Domingo

Monastery in Sanlúcar de Barrameda (Sancho de Sopranis 1964, 55*et seq*). He became so important that he was nominated senior stonemason of the Hospital de las Cinco Llagas in Seville. However, Martín de Gainza had been nominated too, and he finally got the job(Morales Martínez 1997, 77-98). He worked in the construction of San Miguel parish church in Jerez as an assistant architect of Hernán Ruiz II. He died in Medina in 1569. He had no sons, only a daughter, called Francisca Rodríguez.[1]

Hernan Ruiz was one of the most important architects in Spain in the second half of the 16th century. A member of a dynasty of construction masons, he was born in Córdoba in 1514. In this town he completed his first projects as the front of San Pedro parish, the tower of San Lorenzo parish church, the baptismal chapel of San Nicolás de la Villa parish church and he also finished the construction of the main chapel of the Cathedral. From 1557 to his dead in 1569, he was the senior mason of the Seville Cathedral, where he designed the chapter rooms, the Giralda´s weathercock (Seville Cathedral tower) and the vault covering the Royal Chapel. As a result of his work as a senior mason, he could take part in many constructions, the most important being the repair of Santa María de Gracia´s church in Espera. He did a lot of civil works and managed the construction of the Hospital de la Sangre in Seville, where he designed the magnificent edifice which is currently the Parliament building of Andalucía. All his work was influenced by Serlio and by his own ability to be creative and to experiment with classic architecture, as shown in his *Architecture Manuscript*, unpublished up to the 20th century (Morales Martinez 1996).

The constructions

A letter from Hernan Ruiz to Archbishopric administrator is attached to the document mentioned above. In this letter, the cordobés stonemason explains that Francisco Rodríguez was a skillful builder capable of designing and managing work.[2] Judging by these words, Francisco Rodríguez was engaged as an assistant architect because he had to manage the building, but it also makes clear that he could design too.

Having mentioned the reasons, Francisco Rodríguez got an agreement with the stewards to manage and deal with the work.[3] That meant that not only the Hernan Ruiz´s stonemason could plan but another person could be employed to do the same. That is why it is thought that his presence was not required on a daily basis, which is logical when it comes to Francisco Rodríguez, who did this but also worked as a senior stonemason of the Bishop of Cádiz at the same time.

As the document is complex, we can only talk about the importance of each stonemason when we try to analyse the work and we are going to focus on San Miguel sacristy. The work had to start around 1547 and the first floor was not completed until 1551, according to an inscription which was found in the entablature. This was built by Pedro Fernández de la Zarza based to a design of Martin de Gainza and it is the lower area, with a square floor plan, which is extended to the east through a narrow rectangular room which was the presbytery. On the elevation, the rectangular area is surrounded by four columns of a giant order, with fluted shafts and composite capitals, whereas the small rectangular room is "ástilo" (undecorated). The northern and southern walls follow the same plan: between the columns, we can see a shining arch which leans on boxed pilasters.

There is an inscription placed in the stone altarpiece of the San Miguel sacristy which states that the sacristy was finished on the 30th of September in 1564.[4] That seems conclusive proof of the date of the end of this room and that was what most historians have concluded from Grandallana onwards (Grandallana, 1885). However, the documents we have consulted seem to contradict what appears on the inscription, since after the year written on the inscription we can prove the purchase of 1900 cartloads of stone. This would be far too much stone to account for the remaining works, if we take into account that after the sacristy they only built the ante-sacristy over the stairs to agree with the semanero´s room as well as the vault of this room, the current archives and the courtyard which was covered with wood and bricks. Besides, the fact that quarry material (which adds up a total of 469 cartloads of stone) was bought in 1506 is quite significant, both in the contract of sale of stones and in its bill. About this, it is three times that for the new sacristy, which was already built.[5] Moreover, there is no clear indication in both documents about the amount of material or any stonecutting the main master/builder and, at the same time, a foreman of the work,[6] is responsible for this matter and he is Francisco Rodríguez. As we see, technical problems stopped the construction. It would be possible, therefore, to think that a particularly difficult element had arisen, because of this absolute obedience to Rodriguez´s decisions that the stonemason showed since the mason had to buy the amount of necessary stone (they knew the amount the required as they worked) and he also had to supervise every single stone that arrived at on site.[7] We see, as well, that the workshop is mentioned in the contract, that is, a place where the stone is worked carefully because every piece was critical to the whole.

From all the architectural elements that have been conserved in San Miguel parish, only the dome of the sacristy and the vault of the stairs up to the semanero´s room needed a special care in stonecutting. That is why we think that the work was not finished in 1564. Thus, there is a contradiction between the inscription in the room and the documents and we are going to try to give an explanation for this confusion. The date painted on the altarpiece in the sacristy, as the earlier historians believed, is right but it is not completely right. This date refers to the date at which the dome was completed, but only its inner part because the outside is covered by a thick structure, which is adapted to fit the internal hemisphere. This fact accounts for the payments for stonecutting. Both this structure and the vault of the stairs up to the semanero´s room were designed by Hernan Ruiz with the support of Francisco Rodríguez. They are very complex and until then there wasn't anything similar in this area and for this reason there are no references to the stonecutting which was usually used at work.

There is a document from 1567 that proves the use of these two elements continued after 1564. In this document, Francisco Rodríguez asks for his salary to the archbishopric administrator of Seville, which he had not done before because he was waiting for Hernan Ruiz to visit all the works in Jerez which were being managed by him, one of which was San Miguel. Rodríguez was, actually, an architect under the supervision of Ruiz, because he had done some work which had been approved by the cordobés stonemason, who was satisfied with what he had done.[8] If we take into account that, apart from San Miguel, Hernan Ruiz was in charge of (only in Jerez) repairing and enlargement of another six churches, we can draw the conclusion that his job only involved supervising in a superficial way because in one day a year it is very complicated to go to the churches mentioned above and stay there enough time to check them in any detail. There is a document in the Archivo de Protocolos de Medina Sidonia that could prove this. On 1st of February 1570 Ana de Esquivel, Francisco Rodriguez's widow, conceded something to Martin Delgado, who was the foreman of San Miguel's church[9] to receive in her name what she was owed from the work stewards.[10] In that document, it is said that Rodríguez had died at the beginning of November 1569 and that there were several objects, which had been left in Jerez. These were property of the master builder including a bed and a work-table.[11]From this information, we can say that Francisco Rodríguez had a studio in Jerez where he could sleep. In this studio, he had the right material to do his working drawings/templates.

When Hernan Ruiz and Francisco Rodriguez died in 1569, there was a change in the management of the sacristy work. From then on Martin Delgado is identified as the work master/builder,[12] a master builder who had studied "architectural techniques". Although he was not creative, he was working in Jerez from the last years in the 16th century to the first years in the 17th century and he had already been working as quantity surveyor under the supervision of Ruiz and Rodríguez. He did the stone vaulting outside the sacristy. The supply of stones stopped in 1575 suggesting that the work finished that year.

The structure built by Fernández de la Zarza and Gainza extends the original, which results in more light permeating into the building. In an attempt to elevate the aforementioned structure, a smooth pedestal is added on top of the cornice, finished in 1559. A downward break is made to accommodate the window pilasters. In addition, a serrated structure, which coincides with the pendentives, is added to the corners. This makes the second cornice—which is projected out over the original one—look more dynamic. The bases of the arches on the eastern and western walls are paneled. The window pilasters are paneled as well, and have a narrow rectangular band on the inner side, which ends in two semicircles. The band has a circle in the middle, tangent to the rectangle into which it is inserted. This motif, which Francisco Rodríguez would use in other works[13], appears in Hernan Ruiz's *Manuscript of Architecture* and, consequently, a clear relationship may be established with this source (Hernan Ruiz 1997). The four arches that support the dome rise from this base and have a corbel at the keystone. A series of pendentives enable the transition from the square into the triangle. The arch in the western wall has considerable depth and is paneled in the reveal. (Fig.1) The arch over the apse of the sacristy has a double coffered vault. Each panel contains a flower decoration (a rose) except for two of them that have a coiled snake, located on both sides of the lower part, near the window. This is how the extension of the central space is concluded in this direction. It should be noted that the analysis of the lower body revealed that the same procedure was utilized on both sides of the lower part. Above the centre of every single arch, there is a window made up of a rounded arch. The ones at the eastern and western walls are blind windows due to the presence of other constructions behind them. In the external part, these arches have two paneled pilasters of Composite order which support a cornice. There are two smaller ones near them of the Tuscan order with paneled shafts which carry the same semicircles and circles found at the entablature. The window arch itself is very richly decorated in its straight part with embossed semicircles and circles. On its curved part, however, the arch has five panels, each of which contain a cherub.

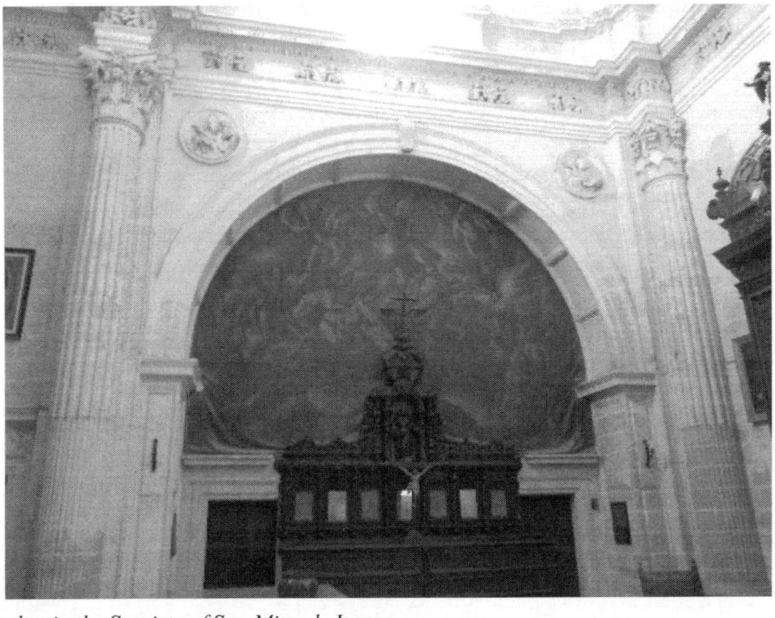

Fig. 1 Lower arches in the Sacristy of San Miguel, Jerez.

The window corresponding to the eastern wall is surrounded by two big elliptical windows. These two windows have the same geometric decoration seen in other areas.

The pendentives have been analysed by Francisco Pinto who notes that they have such a highly geometric quality that they are like solid vaults (Pinto Puerto 2001).[14] These pendentives are richly decorated. (Fig.2) Each carries a medallion representing an evangelist and a flower decoration (rose). Pinto in his thesis notes that this decoration in the pendentives appears in an number of place the Hernandez Ruiz's architectural manuscript. In fact, the decoration appears eight tines in the manuscript.[15] On page 105 of this manuscript, we can see exactly the same details of decoration that are found in San Miguel´s church in Jerez de la Frontera.

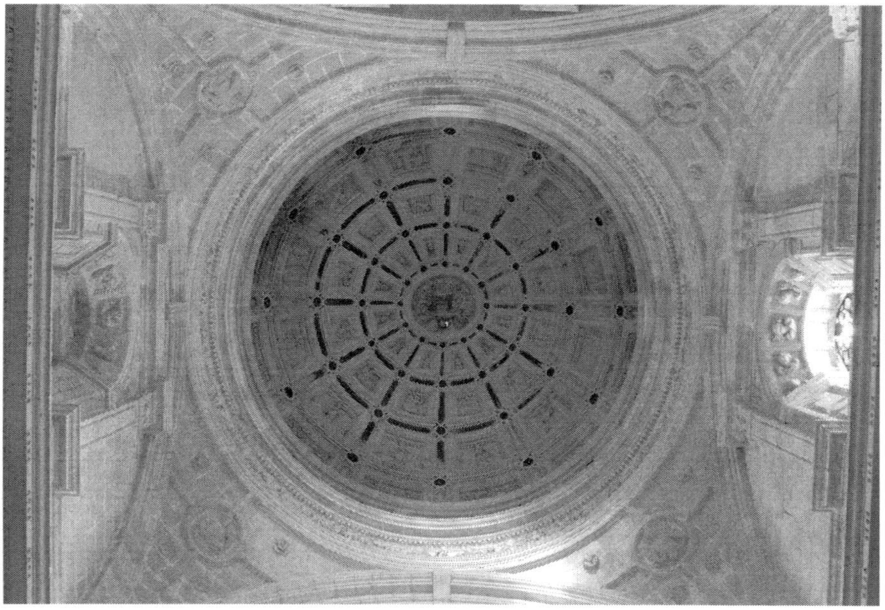

Fig. 2 The Dome of the Sacristy if San Miguel, Jerez

The pendentives carry an entablature consisting of an architrave with many moldings. The frieze is decorated with *rinceaux* and *putti* and the cornice decorated with water drops. As Pinto highlights, the entablature is so powerful that the inclusion of a tambour is needed in order to fully appreciate the hemisphere from the floor and he compares the vault with the aforementioned Manuscript of Architecture by Hernán Ruiz (Pinto Puerto 2001).[16]

In addition to the observations in Pinto´s text, it is worth noting that in the drum there are fours arches, one placed in the centre of each wall of the sacristy. In the panels of the dome, separated by bands of colours, there are rows of different representative figures whose iconography is analysed here from the lowest to the uppermost. The first row is not visible from the floor of the sacristy. It is the only area where the panels are framed by an ovolo molding. The panels represent the twelve apostles. The second row conists of angels playing various instruments. The third row consist of angels holding the instruments of the Passion of Christ instruments. In the fourth row consists entirely of angel's heads and in the keystone Christ is blessing between clouds and angels. The whole seems to be designed to cerate a feeling of dematerialization of the dome, the reducing size of the elements as we go up making it appear higher that it really is. It is important to note that Hernan Ruiz built other similar domes in Jerez, for instance, the Royal Chapel of the Seville Cathedral, in the main sacristy of Santa María de la Oliva de Lebrija and the Casa Profesa church of the Jesuits (today Annunciation church) in Seville. In fact, Ruiz´s manuscript contains no fewer than eight versions of the inside of the dome which are similar to the one in the San Miguel church in Jerez.[17] These models of decoration all seem to be based on the print of the Agrippa's Tomb (and other buildings from Roman Age) that Serlio (1552) reproduced in his prints.[18]

Interpretation of the outside of the dome is more difficult and we are unclear whether Ruiz or Rodríguez designed this. In the book of architecture of the cordobés architect and in two domes built according to his directions, the church of Santo Domingo Monastery in Sanlúcar de Barrameda and the Anunciación church in Seville, we can see carefully made external decorative elements including vases or torches. In this way, the dome is endowed with a grand exterior, something that does not happen in the Jerez example.

In fact, the exterior of the dome of the San Miguel sacristy is largely undecorated. If we look at it from the street, we can see that this dome is curved but it is almost completely hidden by the octagonal structure below. The windows are surrounded by articulated and the corners by piers supporting vases with tall pyramidal tops topped by spheres. The visible surface of the dome is plain, except at the top where it is completed with a coarse lantern. The reasons of this "vandalism" on the outside of the dome is not clear. It could be noted that Martin Delgado, the one who was responsible belongs to a generation of architects (from the last decade of the 16th century to the beginning of the 17th century), which was influenced by Juan de Herrera style which not rich in decoration. The completion of this feature was delayed waiting for the completion of other rooms that were considered more important but which were never completed.

Notes and References

[1] APNMS. 1569. Blas Montesinos. Fol. 456 y ss. August 18, 1568.Francisco Rodriguez, main builder, and his wife Ana de Esquivel, give their son-in-law, Alonso de Alfaro, half the house where they lived, as a part of her daughter´s dowry, Francisca Rodríguez. The house was situated in Medina Sidonia, in the Puerta de Jerez.

[2] *"para la prosecuçion de las obras que están comensadas y de las que se an de comensar di razón y traça a francisco Rodrigues maestro mayor de la dicha çibdad* (de Jerez) *al qual señale y señalo con facultad de vuestra merçed por maestro de las dichas obras y aparejador de ellas en my ausensya el qual digo que es abil y sufisiente y de su abilidad y sufisençia estoy satisfecho para la governasyon de las dichas obras según my administrasyon y por que las dichas obras son de calidad y travajosas y çientificas en su governasion e traça conviene la persona del dicho francisco Rodrigues por la espirençiaque del se tiene y estando en las dichas obras bastara una sola visita mya una vez cada año".*APNJF. 1567. Oficio XIII. Miguel Jiménez. Fol. 465 vto. y ss. July 30.

[3] *"a las obras de las dichas yglezias durante los días de my vida todo el tienpo que fuere menester para dar la horden y las trasas que convengan a las obras que a la sason labraren para que vayan bien asentadas e que yo sea obligado e nos obligamos a poner aparejador que en las dichas obras de las dichas yglezias e cada una de ellas labraren e sean abiles y sufisientes para que trasen o trasas que se les dieren las entiendan*APNJF. 1567. Oficio XIII. Miguel Jiménez. Fol. 465 vto. y ss. July 30. *It is a complex document which is used by Francisco Rodríguez to apply for being nominated as the foreman in the building of some churches in Jerez. The first one is the transfer of a letter written by Hernán Ruiz to the vicar of the archdiocese on the 13rd of November in 1566. Thesecondoneisthecontractlength.*

[4]"ACABOSE ESTA SACHRISTIA AÑO DE MILL QVINIENTOS Y SESENTA Y QUATRO A TREINTA DE SEPTIEMBRE".

[5] *"para la sacristia nueva que se haze en la dicha yglesia".*

[6]A.P.N.J.F. 1566. Oficio XII. Martín de la Cruz. Fol. 90 y ss. January 20. The stonecutter Juan Pérez de Villanueva sells more than four hundred cartloads to the butler of San Miguel´s parish who was the priest Andrés López Farfán. The kind of the stone cut is not indicated. The price was five reales for each cartload of the first 100 and six reales for the rest. The price included the transfer of everything to the studio, which was near the work. In this document it is said nothing about a dead line in the delivery.

[7] *"a la puerta del taller de la dicha sacristia"*A.P.N.J.F. 1566. Oficio IX. Rodrigo López de Arellano. Fol. 780 y ss. Nov. 17. We have underlined that. It is about the payment letter of the stonework bill of sale mentioned in the note before. For that reason we know that finally 469 cartloads and half a stone cartload were delivered.

[8] *"por que las dichas obras son de calidad y travajosas y çientificas en su governasion e traça* (por lo que) *conviene la persona del dicho francisco Rodrigues por la espiriençia que del se tiene y estando el en las dichas obras bastara sola la visita mya una vez cada año"*A.P.N.J.F. 1567. Oficio XIII. Miguel Jiménez. Fol. 465 vto. y ss. July 30. It is about a fragment of the letter that Hernán Ruiz wrote to the vicar of the archdiocese. There is a extensive document included in the letter in which Francisco Rodríguez asks the curia for his salary)

[9] *"aparejador de la obra de la yglesia de señor san myguel de la çibdad de xeres de la frontera".*

[10] *"de los mayordomos que son o fueren de las fabricas de de las yglesias de la dicha çibdad de xeres el trigo e maravedis que le deban de salario en cada un año por que tenya cargo de las obras de las dichas yglesias".*

[11] *"una cama de lienço e un escriptorio"*A.H.P.C. Protocolo Notarial de Medina Sidonia. 1570. Blas de Montesinos. Lost numbering. Besides Martin Delgado, Alonso Martin stayed as the attorney because of the document. The document only tell us about him that he was from Jerez. We know the date of the master death because of the public scribed statement who claimed that he knows the widow and the master had died. Regarding the furniture that the master owed, Ana de Esquivel says in the document that the attorneys were so powerful that they could act if it was required.

[12]A.P.N.J.F. 1575. Oficio IX. Leonís Álvarez. Fol. 87 vto. January 17. It is about a stonework bill of sale (we will talk about it later) in which it is said that the stonework had to be as Martin Delgado, the work builder, wanted to.

[13] We find the same reason in Santa Maria Coronada´s Church in Medina Sidonia at least in two elements designed by Francisco Rodríguez: the choir and the monumental doorway of the temple through which we can access the cloister.

[14] *"la solución estereotómica adoptada para estos elementos se basa en una bóveda baída resuelta por hiladas redondas: las pechinas serían el resultado de construir esa bóveda hasta los puntos de tangencia con los paramentos verticales, a la altura de los cuales ya disponemos de una planta circular".*

[15] Particularly on pages. 78, 90, 92, 95, 97, 103, 105 y 109, tome I.

[16] *"este tambor se configura como un elemento neutro, sin apenas decoración, donde llaman la atención los casquetes esféricos de cerámica vidriada de color azul cobalto, muy característicos del arquitecto cordobés* (with reference to Hernan Ruiz) *[...] La superficie esférica de la cúpula se soluciona mediante una retícula de meridianos y paralelos, definidos por unas líneas oscuras rehundidas, que se cruzan formando el artesonado. De esta forma se invierte la composición tradicional, donde los nervios son elementos corpóreos y los casetones son los vacíos resultantes de la red de paralelos y meridianos, tal y como está ejecutada la cúpula de la Capilla Real de la catedral hispalense* (designed by Hernan Ruiz). *El nuevo efecto lo encontramos recogido en las cúpulas de las iglesias del manuscrito* (by Hernan Ruiz) *donde se observa la cada vez más definida presencia del casetón sobre un fondo neutro, que aparecen como gruesos nervios de meridianos y paralelos. En nuestro caso, cada una de las superficies limitadas por ellos se constituyen como casetones aislados sobre un fondo oscuro, creando una fuerte sensación de desmaterialización. Los*

cruceros van disminuidos, remarcando las intersecciones mediante estrellas cuyo centro está ocupado por los mismos casquetes esféricos, azul cobalto que se habían dispuesto en el tambor. Este recurso cromático aligera enormemente la solidez de la cúpula, haciendo aún más patente la distribución del artesonado [...] El aspecto exterior de esta cúpula es de una gran severidad. Se trata de un prisma octogonal, que oculta la forma esférica de la cúpula, en cuyas caras aparecen alternativamente el vacío de los vanos del tambor y la geometría de los contrarrestos"

[17] *Specifically on pages* .78, 90, 92, 95, 102, 105, 107 y 109, tome I.

[18] Fol. VII, XVIII y XIX. In the first case it is done in the Pantheon engraving whereas the other two ones are temples from Roman Age which have been identified)

Bibliography

A.J. Morales Martínez, "La construcción del Hospital de las Cinco Llagas. Crónica de un monumento inacabado", en El Parlamento de Andalucía. Sevilla. Parlamento de Andalucía. 1997, pp. 77-98.

A. J. Morales Martínez, *Hernán Ruiz "El Joven"*. Madrid.: Akal, 1996

F. Pinto Puerto, *Las esfereas de piedra. Sevilla como lugar de encuentro entre arte y ciencia en el Renacimiento.* Sevilla: Universidad de Sevilla, 2001.

H. Ruiz, *Libro de Arquitectura.* Sevilla: Fundación Sevillana Endesa. 1997.

H. Sancho de Sopranis, "La arquitectura jerezana en el siglo XVI", *Archivo Hispalense*. Sevilla. 1964. Nº 123. pp. 55*et seq*.

L. Grandallana y Zapata, *Noticia Histórico-artística de algunos de los principales monumentos de Jerez.* Jerez de la Frontera: Gautier Editor, 1885.

S. Serlio, *Tercero y quarto libro de arquitectura. Edición de Francisco de Villalpando.* Toledo: Iván de Ayala. 1552.

The Eighteenth Century

A multidisciplinary study on the exposed brick walls of the baroque architecture of Penne in Italy

Claudio Mazzanti

Department of Architecture, University "Gabriele D'Annunzio" of Chieti-Pescara, Italy

Introduction

Penne, an historic town in the Abruzzi Region (Italy), has several baroque churches and palaces built or transformed between the seventeenth and eighteenth centuries: the main examples of this architecture are the Cathedral, the churches of Santa Maria del Carmine, Santa Maria di Colleromano, San Panfilo, Sant'Agostino, San Giovanni Battista, the Santissima Annunziata, San Domenico, San Giovanni Evangelista, San Ciro and Santa Chiara; among the noble residences: the palaces de Dura-del Bono, Titone-Abbati, Aliprandi, Ferdinando Castiglione and Teseo Castiglione. All these buildings, which stand out for their original Baroque expressive language, can be interpreted as an 'scenic apparatus' carefully designed in the urban system of this city (Fig. 1), almost exclusively characterized by the use of brick as building material.

In the façades of some of these churches and palaces there are eye-catching effects that was possible to realize through details in exposed brick.

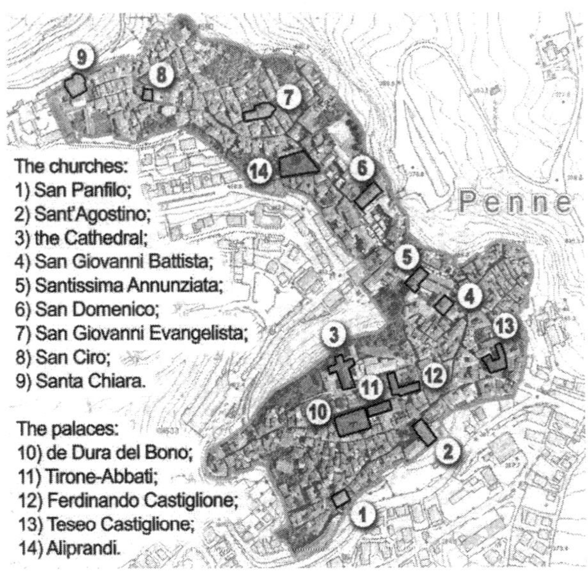

Figure 1. The urban centre of Penne and its main examples of the Baroque architecture: the churches and the palaces.

The History of the city from Pinna Vestinorum to the Farnese State

The urban centre of Penne, originally called Pinna Vestinorum[1] and corresponding to the current Abruzzo region has always been very important in Central Italy. : It was one of the strongholds of the Vestini people, that in the fourth century BC was opposed to the will of expansion of Romeandin and before being defeated in 302BC the city preferred to ally itself with Rome's enemies but later, even under Roman rule, it continued to play a prominent role[2].

After an interim phase of decline, during the Middle Ages, Penne became one of the main settlements in the area; initially the city was under the control of the Lomgobards as part of the Duchy of Spoleto; in 773, it was proclaimed the capital of the Province of Penne, as a bishopric, at the behest of Charlemagne.

This village, called *Civitas*, was mentioned in 968 in the parchment of Otto I, the emperor of the Holy Roman Empire; starting around 1130, Penne became part of the Kingdom of Sicily. Initially small, already in this period it begins to expand and to be fortified. In the later centuries, the city always prevailed over surrounding towns: this domination began through the acquisition of some neighbouring fiefs; then it involved a wider area, called Judicial Province of the Abruzzo Ultra. Its influence was not only due to its size and the number of inhabitants, but also due to the presence in the zone of many religious settlements[3].

In the fifteenth century Penne was looted and destroyed during the conflict between Alfonso of Aragon and Rene d'Anjou because of the possession of the Kingdom of Naples; it was soon rebuilt and in the sixteenth century it became the capital of a vast estate in Abruzzo, initially controlled by the Medici for a short time and then, for three centuries, known as the 'Farnese State' of Abruzzo: when the Kingdom of Naples was annexed to the domains of Charles V, the emperor gave the Duchy of Penne, Campli, Leonessa, Cittaducale and Montereale, as a gift to his daughter Margaret, who married Alessandro de' Medici; after the latter's death, Margaret married Ottavio Farnese: the spouses, accompanied by the Butler Giovanni Aliprandi, took possession of Penne, the chief town of the Farnese State.

During the Margaret period, Penne became an important centre of political power in the Abruzzo region, and many fine palaces and civic structures were built during this time. The feudal rule of the Farnese covered a large territory over which Penne administered the justice by its captains, to carry out the *mero et mixto empire*, paying to the Kingdom of Naples the taxes for the military defence.

Penne continued to be the chief town of this area even after 1734 when Charles, son of Elizabeth Farnese, was proclaimed King of Naples and the possession of the State handed entirely to the Bourbons; this is attested also by the title of the Urban Cadastre, drafted in 1757 by Saverio de Mattheis, member of a noble family of the place: *Pubblico e General Catasto di questa fedelissima Città di Penne capo de' serenissimi Reali Stati farnesiani*. The feudal possession, with Charles III returned to be submitted to the Royal Property; consequently, Penne slowly began to lose its original pre-eminent role.

The urban development

Since its origin, the urban centre of Penne included the areas of Colle Sacro, with the ancient cathedral, and the hill of Santa Croce with the Castle; also the areas of Colle Cappuccio and Colle Romano developed significantly through the first half of the seventeenth century.

This increase in building was interrupted by a violent epidemic of plague that lasted seventeen months, from October 1656 to March 1658, killing nearly three thousand people and deeply affecting the significant process of urban development which until then had characterized the city[4]. Its urban structure, previous to the fatal event, is known to us through a 'descriptive cadastre' of the early seventeenth century[5], preserved in the Municipal Archives of Penne.

The residences of the great landowners and the noble families were traditionally located in the most important areas of the town, also for their strategic value. These buildings stood out from other buildings because of their size, the formal characteristics of their façades and for their relationship with the urban system, in which there were manyopen spaces, mostly for vegetable or roof gardens.

The eighteenth century saw important changes to the type of building and the original medieval urban layout. Large open spaces were occupied and existing buildings both noble and religious were modified. This radical transformation was implemented along the main streets of the city, through the modification or replacement of the old urban fabric through the creation of more complex architectural compositions. Referring to the current names: via Muzio Pansa, with the palaces Del Bono, Tirone and Castiglione; Corso Martiri Pennesi, in which stands the palace Aliprandi, with its Baroque façade of great dramatic effect; Corso Alessandrini, with the impressive late Baroque front of the Church of the Annunziata.

The whole urbanization of Penne is mainly characterized by the use of bricks which were used to build both the religious and the civil buildings to pave all the roads[6]. In the nearby Apennine mountains, the buildings are characterized by the use of stone extracted from the local quarries[7]; otherwise, in the foothills where Penne is located, there are many clay deposits. In these hilly areas still remain today some of the ancient brick-kilns, with their traditional chimneys: they may be similar to archaic architecture, simple and rudimentary, which resembles the shape of bevel pinions, typical in the zone[8]. The Italian word *pignone* derives from the Latin vulgar *pinnione*, from which comes *pinna*: 'pinnacle'; some historians connect this term with the ancient name of the city: Pinna, cited above. The word *penn*, with the meaning of pinnacle or tip, also exists in other ancient European languages and also could be link to the shape of the chimney.

Penne has kept its homogeneous architectural image, in which prevail the surface characteristics and colour of the terracotta: in the buildings, in the urban environments and, more generally, for the texture and the look of the whole town. The material is used for façades, roofs and decorative elements and its extensive use bricks was noted in the mid-nineteenth century by the English painter Edward Lear during his voyage in the Abruzzo region[9]; in his memoirs, he depicted Penne for its fine buildings[10] and for the narrow streets of the old centre, which he described as very steep, but well paved with bricks[11].

Penne the 'Town of bricks'

The widespread use of bricks in every historical building and paving gave Penne the appellation of the 'Town of bricks'[12]. Therefore, the knowledge of the construction technique of these buildings is very interesting and allows us to add new information concerning the development of the architecture of Penne over the centuries.

Our historical study was multidisciplinary and concerned the art, the architecture and the construction, as well the drawing and the different forms of representation: in addition to the archival research and the direct analysis of the buildings, we used the computer graphics 3D, involving other researchers coordinated by Professor Catherina Palestini, in the Department of Architecture of the Gabriele d'Annunzio University of Chieti-Pescara.

The systematic study of the historical feature also by means of the three-dimensional representation allowed us a deeper understanding of the design of these façades, with the related technical problems, the geometric rules of proportion and composition, as well as the effects of light and colour variations. This study focuses on the great variety of types of bricks and other pieces to be used in building: our analysis is based on the morphological knowledge of the material, relative to the size and the type of bricks used throughout the ages, examining several construction elements, with different states of preservation: the wall surfaces, the openings, the mouldings and the decorative elements. The design details and the colours of the different solutions studied allow us to identify and date the construction process.

Through careful measurements carried out on the walls of the old buildings, we get some results: the bricks used in Penne can be chronologically catalogued according to their size[13]. In particular, in the area surrounding the Cathedral and along the route that connects the via Muzio Pansa with the Duomo Square, we observed numerous traces of materials taken from the Roman buildings, reused in the medieval buildings[14]: the length of the bricks is just over 1.5 Roman foot (average: 47.7 cm / 18.78 inches); the width is about one Roman foot (on average 30.5 cm / 12 in); the thickness, regardless of the mortar, is reported to be 6 to 6.5 cm / 2.36 to 2.56 in: the latter measure also characterizes the bricks used in the medieval buildings, but these bricks have dimensional variability and their manufacture is not very accurate.

In Penne, brick was used both with archaic techniques[15] and more elaborate methods .The mixture of styles is due to the presence in this area of foreigner workers, especially from Lombardy; therefore also the dimensions of the elements used in the medieval buildings (length about 30 to 31 cm / 11.81 to 12.20 in; width 15 cm / 5.90 in) may refer to the module appeared in northern Italy since the ninth century[16].

The Municipal Statute of the sixteenth century, called *Codice Catena*, in the *Chapter LIII* of the *Book IV*, entitled *De modulis fornaciarum*, established the standard size for the bricks, referring to a standard sample kept in the Government Palace[17]. According to this rulebook, the bricks were to be stamped with the symbol 'C'; unfortunately, we do not have the standard sample or a trace of bricks made by the above mark; so either they may still be embedded in the walls and therefore unidentifiable, or the standard was ignored. It is likely also that the rule of to stamp the bricks, in order to certify their compliance with the defined standard dimensions, has been added to the *Codice Catena* later, maybe in 1457, or in 1468 as the text was updated again.

In the Abruzzo region, as in the rest of the Italian peninsula, there was a progressive decrease in the size of the bricks[18]; from the Middle Ages to the eighteenth century. in the Baroque period Neapolitan and Roman architects worked in this area along with those of Lombardy and Ticino[19]. At this time, in the Kingdom of

Naples the official unit of length was the Neapolitan span, equal to about 26,33 cm / 10.37 in; the bricks most common in the buildings of Penne constructed in this period have an average length of one Neapolitan span: width 11,5 to 12,5cm / 4.53 to 4.92; height 4.5 to 6 cm / 1.57 to 2.36 in.

The Baroque period

In the eighteenth century Penne was deeply transformed: brick was used for cornices and gable-ends looking drawn and sinuous, demonstrating the versatility and the technical capacity of the workers. For this reason the bricks are in various thickness and shape, especially for the construction of columns, doorways and windows. In the same way, the capitals were made by bricks, appropriately sculpted. Most of the interventions were reconstructions, transformations or formal adjustments.

The phenomenon is particularly evident in the religious Architecture, from the renovation of decoration, the addition of altars and chapels, the transformation of the interior space, to the total reconstruction in new forms. The reason of this general renewal could be the change of aesthetic and cultural conditions, supported by a period of relative political stability[20]. The insides of the churches were rebuilt; the walls were plastered with abundant decorations and the classical architectural order was always added; the liturgy apparatus was enriched with the inclusion of monumental altars, confessionals, canopies and tabernacles; instead, the vaults were built in place of the wooden ceiling. However in most cases the original medieval forms of the exterior of the churches were preserved, for example the facades of the church of Santa Maria in Colleromano and the Cathedral. The Baroque façades constructed in this period was those of San Ciro, San Panfilo and the Santissima Annunziata, each of them with exposed brick wall[21].

In Penne there was an intense building activity that deeply changed the appearance of the town, mainly with the modernization of existing buildings and rarely through a real transformation of the urban plan. Such interventions often disregard practical reasons and are due exclusively to purposes of social representation.

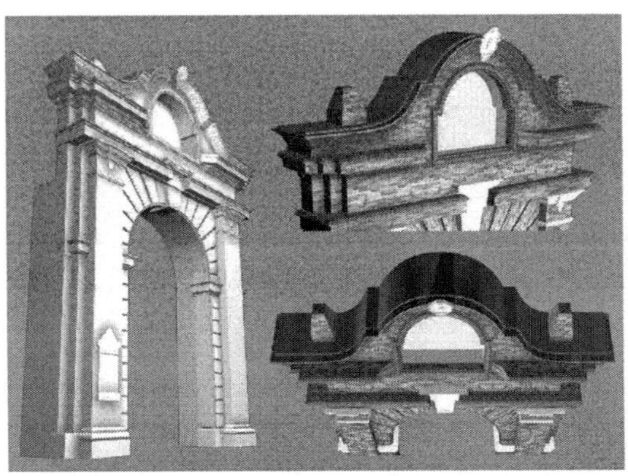

Figure 2. The urban gate of Porta San Francesco.

Among the public works, one of the most important is Porta San Francesco (Fig. 2), the entrance from the southeast to the town: it already existed in the medieval city wall and before of its modernization, done by the Neapolitan architect Francesco di Sio[22], it was called Porta San Nicola. In 1780 the old building was replaced by a ashlars arch, framed by pilasters and topped by a mixtilinear pediment over a niche that contains a sacred effigy. This urban gate has a surface wall which appears extremely accurate: in it there is the use of bricks smoothed and layers of mortar very regular, with a thickness greater than that of the same bricks.

However, already a few decades before, all the façades of the stately mansions built or transformed in the eighteenth century, all in Baroque style, begin to take on a new and important urban value, which is independent of the peculiar significance of each of these buildings. Many of them show plastered surfaces, according to the aesthetic of the time, but some interesting fronts are with the exposed brick wall.

The façades without plaster

The de Dura del Bono palace stands in the area of the Cathedral, along the via Muzio Pansa: this building dates from around the mid-century[23]. The surface treatment of its urban front continues the medieval tradition of building the exterior in exposed brick, the only stone details are the capitals and friezes of the jambs. This building can be considered as the 'baroque monument' to the brick, because this technology has been applied here with a remarkable three-dimensional expression; the warm colour and uniform of the façade is due to a type of brick that had a very accurate manufacturing and firing. This building designed by architect Francesco Di Sio shows full mastery of the compositional rules and the expressive possibilities of the material[24]. It is one of the most interesting examples of the Baroque civil architecture of Penne. A string course, which connects the main balcony at the smaller ones, separates the different levels of the façade; the windows are adorned by alternating triangular pediments and curved, while the large central window is surmounted by a broken pediment where the frame sags articulating the architectural shape, typically baroque. A series of rusticated pilasters give rhythm to the whole, highlighting the front through light and shade effects. The portal, in the middle of the façade, is the element of great interest, formed by two pairs of columns, constructed with curved bricks; instead, the Ionic capitals are carved in stone. Above the portal there is a long and sinuous balcony, supported by corbels stone (Fig. 3); the whole construction is made by standard bricks and others properly shaped. (Figs 4-5)

The cornice, to the top of the façade, consists of a flat strip, above which there is a sequence of brackets, also in brick, which support a large projection of the eaves with a series of mouldings (Fig. 6).

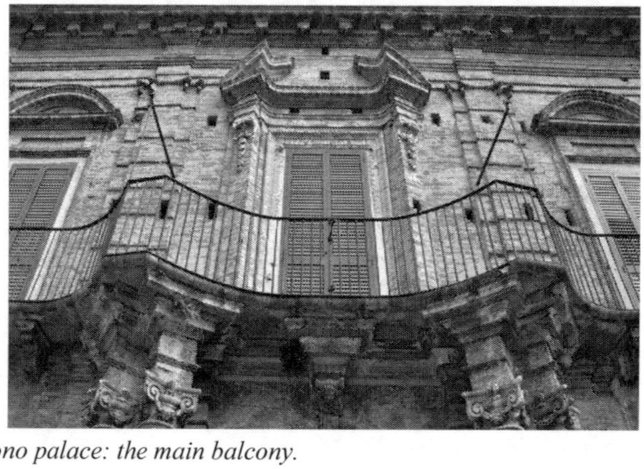

Figure 3. De Dura del Bono palace: the main balcony.

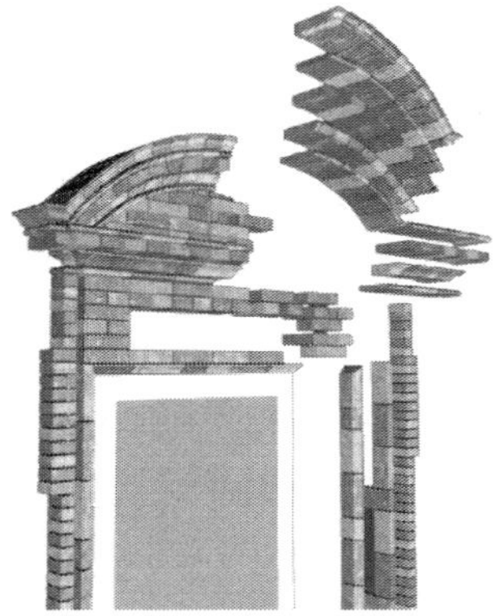

Figure 4. De Dura del Bono palace: exploded view of the window with a curved pediment.

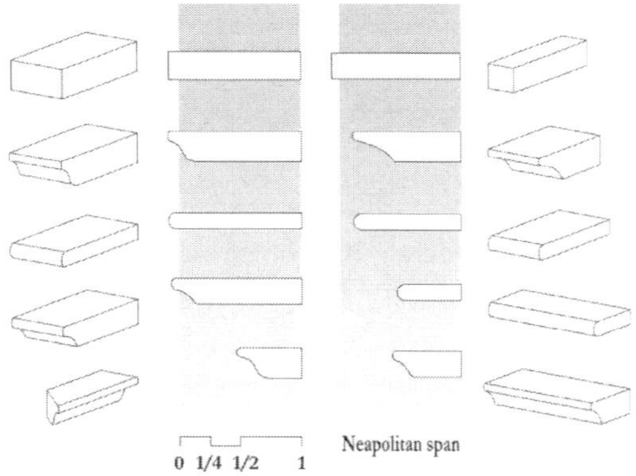

Figure 5. De Dura del Bono palace: different kinds of bricks.

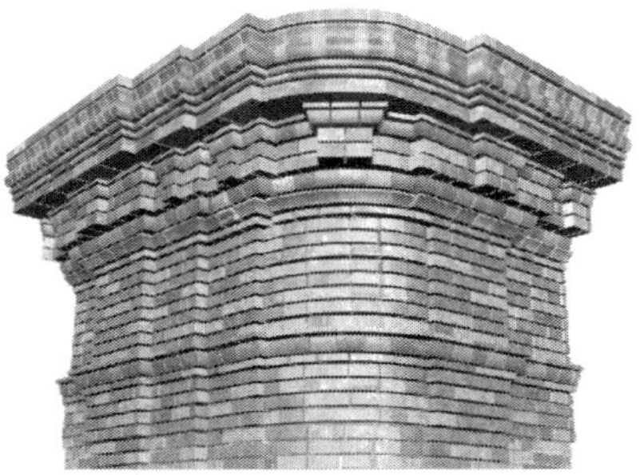

Figure 6. De Dura del Bono palace: the corner part of the cornice.

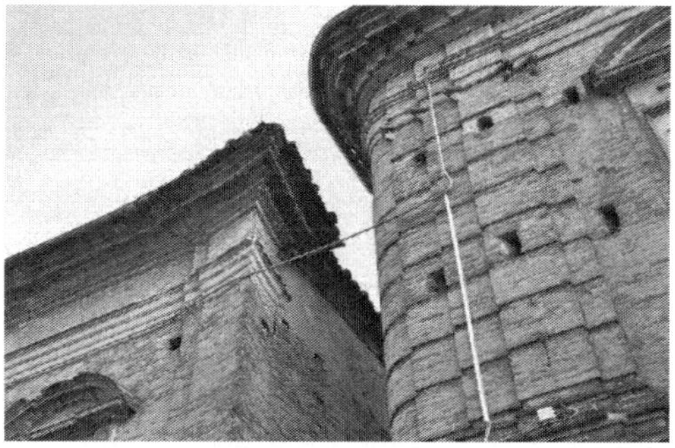

Figure 7. The corners of the palaces de Dura del Bono and Tirone, in via Muzio Pansa.

The design of the corner of the building is very interesting as it is in direct visual relationship with that of the adjacent Tirone palace (Fig. 7); these buildings were not designed as isolated cases, but as elements of an urban system[25].

We don't know the date of construction of the Tirone palace; however, we could assume that it was the result of the unification of some small buildings in the first few decades of the eighteenth century. This is evidenced by a document concerning the acquisition of a house in 1770 to be incorporated into the new building complex under construction; in the document there is also the specific request to create a partition by cob[26]. The walls of the building denotes a minor technical accuracy; in fact, we have found bricks reused from other older buildings and blocks of unfinished stone in the footing (Fig. 8).

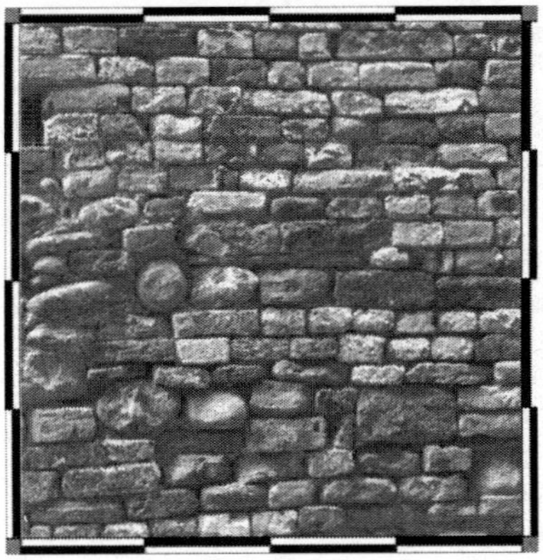

Figure 8. Tirone palace: analysis of the footing of the wall, by a square sample of 4 Neapolitan spans side.

The size of the bricks that we have seen, are highly variable; in particular, we have also verified the use of a brick of large dimensions: length 45 cm / 17.72 in; width 23 cm / 9.05 in; thickness 5 cm / 1.97 in. Generally, the building looks unfinished in its architectural elements. Some researchers suggest that this building, after completion, should have been finished with a thin layer of plaster[27], which might would mitigated all the imperfections of the construction.

Other buildings of this period, in fact, were plastered, like the palace Leopardi, in the Luca di Penne Square, who has an impressive baroque façade. A secondary front, in via Leopardi, has a secondary door in baroque style, entirely in exposed brick (Fig. 9).

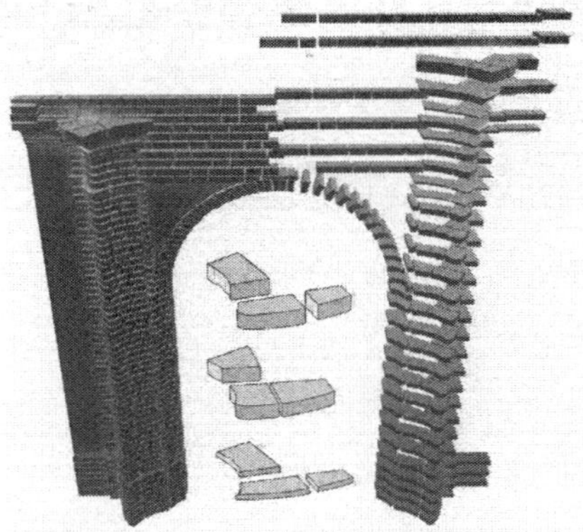

Figure 9. Palace Leopardi: exploded view of the secondary door, in via Leopardi.

The church of the Santissima Annunziata has the most meaningful façade of Baroque-stile[28] in Penne's religious building The construction of the front of this church was one of the last eighteenth century work in the town centre: it was modernized in the baroque style from 1733, on the initiative of the Compagnia della Pietà; the façade, with exposed brick wall, was built later, in 1801, in a phase already neoclassical; nevertheless, it is considered one of the highest expressions of the Baroque of Penne. Some researchers suggest that the author was Pietro Castiglione; however, he was probably only the Prior responsible for the build; others suggests the architect Francesco di Sio[29]. The urban front of the church, which reminds some projects of Francesco Borromini or Carlo Rainaldi in Rome, shows columns detached from the wall, with Tuscan capitals; this columns, completely built with brick, support a massive cornice, with cantilever elements; in the upper part of the façade there are other smaller columns, also by brick except for the Ionic capitals, of carved stone. The texture of the wall is quite precise; the skilful use of the brick in the front gives interesting effects of light and shade, even without elaborate ornaments (Fig. 10).

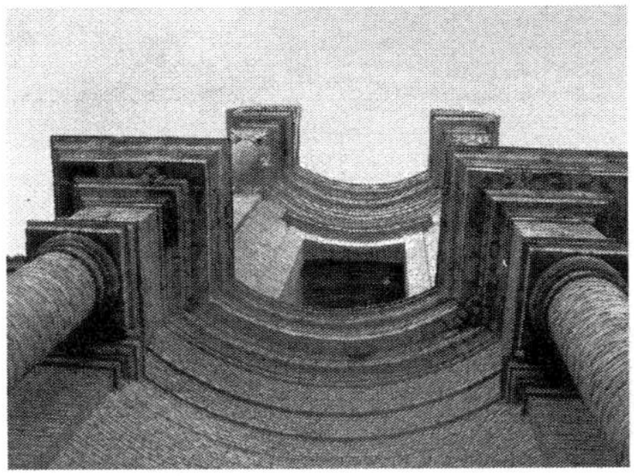

Figure 10. The church of the Santissima Annunziata: the upper part of the front.

Conclusions

The ancient edifices are an important heritage for their symbolic value, their artistic qualities and because they are the result of a heterogeneous construction process through a series of changes and rebuilding, which are the effect of the different historical events. Without sufficient archive data and reliable documents, the scientific method of analysis must consider the apparently secondary and less important aspects that nevertheless are the key to its understanding, because they are the expression of the events and of the ancientness of the building.

Our study includes both archival investigation and the direct analysis: besides the traditional survey, we have used also the 3D computer graphics to better understand the design of these façades especially with regard to the related technical issues, the rules of geometry and proportion as well as the lighting effects and the colour variations.

Generally, the baroque churches and palaces of Penne doesn't show complex geometric shapes: the basic module for the architectural design was the square[30]. However, the geometry was very important in order to draw the curved elements and by the digital drawing, we have also verified the existence of geometric patterns at the base of the brick masonry.

This methodological approach could be an important contribution for the scientific investigation in the field of the history of the construction. We have combined topics of the history of architecture and the theory and practice of drawing, in order to propose experimental methods of analysis through the knowledge of the historical monuments.

References

[1] M. Buonocore, A. Staffa, *Pinna Vestinorum*, Chieti: L'Erma, 2010.

[2] C. Rivera, et al, *Penne e l'area vestina nel bollettino di storia Patria*, Penne: Brioni, 1991, p. 23.

[3] U. Russo, E. Tiboni, (Eds), *L'Abruzzo dall'Umanesimo all'età Barocca*, Pescara: Ediars, 2000.

[4] V. Gentili, *Quadro di Città di Penna, o saggio storico statistico su Città di Penna*, Napoli: Minerva,1832, p. 27.

[5] G. De Caesaris, *Gli ordini di Margarita d'Austria per li suoi stati d'Abruzzo*, Casalbordino: De Arcangelis, 1934, p. 11.

[6] R. Mancini, *Viaggiare negli Abruzzi*, v. III, L'Aquila: Textus, 2006, p. 269.

[7] F. Rodolico, *Le pietre della città d'Italia*, Firenze: Le Monnier, 1965, p. 230.

[8] M. C. Forlani, *La prima industrializzazione in Abruzzo e le fornaci per laterizi*, in *Archeologia industriale in Abruzzo*, L'Aquila: Stabilimento litografico Gran Sasso, 1985, pp. 33-38.

[9] M. Costantini, *Penne un profilo iconografico*, Penne: Brioni, 1992, p. 164.

[10] E. Lear, *Illustrated Excursions in Italy*, v. I, London: Thomas McLean, 1846.

[11] M. Latini, *L'uso del laterizio nelle pavimentazioni di alcuni centri antichi abruzzesi*, in G. Biscontin, D. Mietto, (Eds), *Proceedings of VIII Convegno Scienza e Beni Culturali: Le superfici dell'architettura: il cotto. Caratterizzazione e trattamenti*, Padova: Libreria Progetto, 1992, p. 161-166.

[12] S. Bonamico, G. Tamburini, (Eds), *Centri antichi minori d'Abruzzo: recupero e valorizzazione*, Gangemi, Roma 1996, p. 69.

[13] C. Varagnoli, *Architettura di mattoni in Abruzzo*, in Biscontin, Mietto (Note 11) *Le superfici*, p.151.

[14] C. Varagnoli, *La costruzione tradizionale in Abruzzo*, Roma: Gangemi, 2008, p. 147.

[15] C. Forlani, *Territorio e costruzione: le abitazioni di terra*, Rimini: Maggioli 1982, pp. 54-55.

[16] Varagnoli (Note 13) *Architettura di mattoni*, p.152.

[17] De Caesaris (Note 5) *Gli ordini*, p. 33.

[18] Varagnoli (Note 13) *Architettura di mattoni*, p.153.

[19] S. Benedetti, *L'architettura dell'epoca barocca in Abruzzo*, XIX Congresso di Storia dell'Architettura, L'Aquila: Ferri, 1980, p. 275-312.

[20] L. Bartolini Salimbeni, 'L'architettura barocca e il Sei-Settecento in Abruzzo', in *Profilo socio-culturale del Seicento e del Settecento in Abruzzo, Rivista Abruzzese*, LV, 2002, pp. 233-254.

[21] A. Rubini, *Penne e le sue chiese*, Penne: Giancarlo Ambrosini, 1981.

[22] F. Battistella, 'Note su alcune fabbriche attribuite a Francesco di Sio architetto napoletano attivo in Abruzzo fra il settimo e il nono decennio del XVIII secolo', in *Rivista abruzzese*, XLII, 1989, pp. 97-184.

[23] L. Bartolini Salimbeni, *Sviluppi dell'architettura barocca a Penne*, XIX Congresso di Storia dell'Architettura, L'Aquila: Ferri, 1980, p. 319.

[24] Mancini (Note 6) *Viaggiare*, p. 290.

[25] A. Ghisetti Giavarina, et al, *Terra Vestina: L'Area Vestina della Provincia di Pescara*, Pescara, Carsa: 1992, p. 90.

[26] Battistella (Note 22) 'Francesco di Sio', p. 163.

[27] Varagnoli (Note 14) *La costruzione*, p. 157

[28] Bartolini Salimbeni (Note 23) *Sviluppi*, p. 322.

[29] Battistella (Note 22) 'Francesco di Sio', p. 112.

[30] Benedetti (Note 19) *L'architettura*, p. 276.

Three technical reports of R.G. Boscovich on the statics of domes

D. Capecchi[1] **and C. Tocci**[2]
1. Dipartimento di Ingegneria Strutturale e Geotecnica, Sapienza Università di Roma; 2. Dipartimento di Architettura e Design, Politecnico di Torino

Introduction

Boscovich devoted to the statics of domes three reports written on the occasion of his intervention in the debates developed in the eighteenth century on famous structural disputes: *Parere* [1] (Opinion) which was followed by *Riflessioni* [2] (Thoughts) for St. Peter's dome, *Scrittura* [3] (Writing) for the Imperial Library of Vienna and *Sentimento*[4] (Impression) for the Cathedral of Milan.

The most important of the three reports is *Parere*, not only for the intrinsic value of its mechanical content but also because of the difficulty of the topic. Boscovich was in fact asked to express his judgment on the stability of the immense Vatican dome – which showed signs of distress – and to propose interventions that could control the progression of cracking phenomena. In the case of the Cathedral of Milan, the problem consisted of evaluating the response of an existing structure to a new load. For the Library of Vienna, the problem was, in some ways, similar to that addressed for St. Peter's dome, but it occurred on a significantly different scale.

The three reports, while showing significant differences – due also to Boscovich's personal scientific growth (more than twenty years separate the first report from the last) – are all characterized by the explicit assumption of mechanics as a tool for analysing structural problems of architecture. Therefore, in addition to their scientific value, which can be summed up in the methodological cogency and the thorough discussion of mechanical issues, the three reports allow for reflection on the complex relationship between science and architecture which, in the eighteenth century, shows a growing involvement of expertise in statics in building design.

Parere on St. Peter's dome

Parere and *Riflessioni* were printed in late 1742 and early 1743.[5] *Parere* had been commissioned by Pope Benedetto XIV increasingly worried because of the alarming rumours about the spreading of cracks which had been circulating since the completion of the dome in 1590, rumours that became persistent in the first half of the eighteenth century. *Riflessioni* was published as a reply to the objections addressed to *Parere* following a meeting ('Congregazione') of experts that had been called by the Pope on January 22. The objections, and above all the harsh criticism received by the physicist Giovanni Poleni – who would finally be charged with the design of the restoration project – and by three Neapolitan mathematicians – Bartolomeo Intieri, Pietro Di Martino and Giuseppe Orlandi –, were the cause not only of the rejection of *Parere* but also, most likely, of its subsequent critical disapproval by historians.

Parere can be divided into three parts: the first considers the present state of the dome and its damage, in the second the causes of the surveyed damage is sought, in the third remedies are proposed.

In the first part of the report, cracks are listed with the aim of identifying the movement that could have produced them. The list is very detailed, as is the explanation of the correspondence between cracks and suggested mechanism. The main cracks, i.e. those sufficient to explain the establishment of the mechanism, are shown in Fig. 1, while the kinematic mechanism (that Boscovich calls a "system"), consistent with the surveyed crack pattern, is illustrated in Fig. 2. The base of the drum, cracked vertically, moves with the buttresses of the drum as a rigid body. Another rigid body models the inner part of the base, the drum and the attic. Finally, the great ribs act like a single rigid body too, carrying a piece of the dome. (It is worth noting that such a rigid body assemblage must be repeated for the sixteen ribs that form the dome). Fig. 2b shows the plan drawn by three mathematicians in their original figure 2.[6]

In the second part of the report, Boscovich identifies the causes that could produce the identified mechanism, essentially in the excessive thrust exerted by the dome and not effectively counteracted by the metal hoops and by the weight of the drum and buttresses. This can be proved by a balance of virtual work, i.e. using Galilean terminology, a balance of 'moments'. The application of the principle of virtual work is not trivial because of the presence of the hoops.[7]

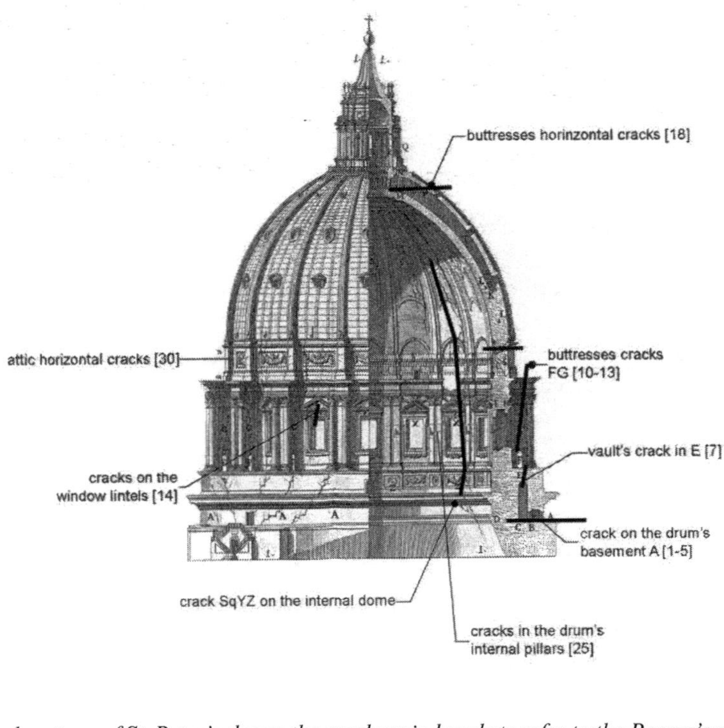

Figure 1. The crack pattern of St. Peter's dome; the numbers in brackets refer to the Parere's paragraphs (authors' elaboration from 'Parere').

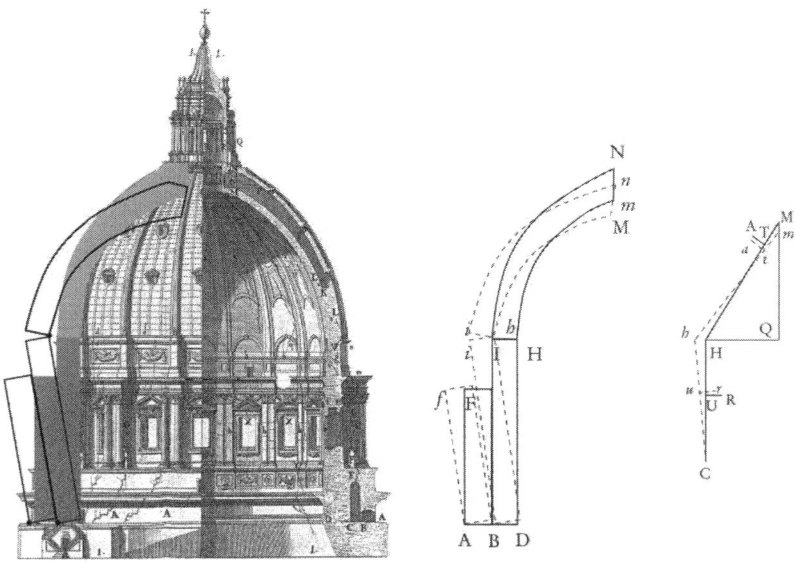

Figure 2. (a) Failure mechanism of St. Peter's dome. (b) & (c) Plans of the three mathematicians (authors' elaboration from 'Parere').

The results of the calculations performed in *Parere* (reported in Table 1) reveal a substantial imbalance of the thrusts against the resistance which Boscovich comments upon as reported below:

> "This imbalance, incessantly pressing on the drum and hoops, has forced the former to bend, and the latter to dilate and stretch, and would have overthrown that and broken these, if the contrast of the tip N, which can neither move inwards without further disruption of the lantern, nor outwards without breaking out much and separate in OP the ribs' walls, would not have held back the movement and the breaking. However, since the weight's imbalance never ceases to press and separate the parts, even making use of every small earthquake's shock, or thunder's rumble, or lightning's strike each of which by itself will be insufficient to disrupt a building of such magnitude, a ruin beyond repair can be feared if effective remedies are not adopted in time".[8]

Table 1. Thrusting and resisting normalized 'moments' (in roman pounds and kN)

	lb	*kN*
Lantern	2961060	10041
Dome with ribs	6412590	21745
Thrusts		*31786*
Drum	1266690	4295
Attic	867444	2942
Buttresses	574555	1948
Base	752686	2552
Hoops	2674918	9071
Resistances		*20808*
Imbalance		***10978***

As far as remedies are concerned, Boscovich concludes that the best and cheapest one is the introduction of new metal hoops, to be placed not only on the dome (at the abutment, in an intermediate position at the top) but also on the drum. Additionally, he also proposes the restoration of the damaged wall portions, and the addition of spurs and statues above the buttresses – as previously suggested by Vanvitelli in 1742.

Critical remarks about Parere

We mentioned above the criticism by the Neapolitan mathematicians and Giovanni Poleni. The former asserted that if there was such a great imbalance of resistance against thrusts, as found by Boscovich, then the dome would have already collapsed.[9] The latter argued, more diplomatically, that the kinematic mechanism proposed by Boscovich was unrealistic since it did not take into account the three-dimensional nature of the problem, in which the drum is a cylinder and not a linear segment.

Giovanni Poleni's criticism can be easily rejected by considering the movement of each of the sixteen great ribs, i.e. of portions corresponding to 1/16 of the entire dome instead of 1/6, as Poleni does.[10]

As far as the Neapolitans' criticism is concerned, the question is more subtle. To our knowledge, Boscovich, Le Seur and Jacquier were the first scholars to analyse a masonry structure other than arches using rigid body kinematics and the virtual work principle. The main difficulty with respect to the classical analysis of de la Hire [11] and Couplet [12] on the stability of arches, is that in the complex three-dimensional geometry of the dome, an opening mechanism 'by way of pomegranate' cannot be observed but only guessed, taking into account the surveyed crack pattern. The onset of the mechanism suggested for the dome implies that the tensile strength of masonry be overcome along both the meridional planes of the dome and drum (which identify the sixteen vertical slices of the mechanism) and the circumferential planes (which instead identify, within each slice, the parts in relative motion). Surely the tensile strength has been exceeded where the cracks have already opened, but it is still effective in the undamaged portions of the dome; and other resisting contributions derive from the interaction between the different meridional slices at the crown of the dome, where compressive forces prevail. The circumferential interaction recognised by Boscovich therefore introduces resisting contributions that oppose the onset of the collapse mechanism. These contributions, difficult, if not impossible, to quantify are, above all, of uncertain mobilization. This induces Boscovich, for safety reasons, to neglect them entirely.

> "It is not possible to carefully assess the resistance opposed by parts to separation. It depends largely on the quality of cement, and the diligence of the work. Only two things can be stated in general: the first is that architects have to rely as little as possible on the resistance created by the tenacity of parts in great buildings, and the less they have to rely the larger the building is".[13]

But disregarding the circumferential interaction, the 'imbalance' between thrusts and strengths obtained by Boscovich must not be intended as a demonstration of the impossibility of equilibrium for the dome, an obviously unacceptable result, but as a measure of the reliability of the dome's geometrical configuration and its reinforcing devices (metal hoops), in the cautionary hypothesis that resisting contributions, which are essential to ensure stability in the current situation, could suddenly fail – for example, because of exceptional actions such as those due to earthquakes [14]: "The imbalance would have certainly knocked down the great dome, had there not been more and more new parts to detach and crush with the spreading of cracks".[15]

It would therefore appear that Boscovich pursues with his analysis the dual aim of explaining, on one hand, the complex crack pattern surveyed on the dome and identifying, on the other hand, the strictly sufficient conditions of stability, i.e. the conditions under which the equilibrium of the dome is guaranteed, neglecting even the factors of problematic evaluation. The first objective is achieved through the use of a mechanism that derives from the survey of the actual crack pattern. The second objective assumes as its starting point the remark that it is not safe to rely on what cannot be clearly recognized and, consequently, that the safety assessment of the dome must be quite separate from anything that is not susceptible to a quantitative evaluation.[16]

Scrittura on the Imperial library

Boscovich's report on the Hofbibliothek (Imperial Library), now the National Austrian Library, dates back to March 1763. Although classified as a printed work, it is a manuscript text, surely hand-written, preserved as a single copy at the Austrian library itself and its first printed publication is that of the National Edition of the Works and Correspondence of Ruggiero Giuseppe Boscovich.[17]

The report contains the advice provided by Boscovich for the court architect Nikolaus Pacassi in occasion of the restoration of the Library (Fig. 3) carried out from 1763 to 1769, in order to address the structural problems, which occurred less than thirty years after the completion of the construction.

Scrittura is substantially similar to *Parere* and is divided into the same methodological steps – from surveying the damage, to building a consistent mechanical model, to proposing repair interventions. However, it does not include an explicit safety analysis such as that performed for St. Peter's dome. Moreover, the scale of the problem and its complexity are different, or better still, incomparable.

The main damage, as described by Boscovich, is essentially localized (i) at the intersection between the walls of the longitudinal gallery and the transverse wing (where the two orders of walls are disconnected because of different out-of-plumbs) and (ii) in the elliptic dome (cracked along its meridional lines) and its abutments.

Boscovich has no hesitation in identifying the main cause for such damage:

> "I think the most important cause of the troubles were the same that produced all the damage of St. Peter's dome in Rome, i.e. the horizontal thrust of the dome itself. The thrust has been aided here by the weight of the roof, which in part rests on the dome, in part pushes over the lateral walls".[18]

The thrust of the dome can in fact explain both the cracks of the dome itself and the monolithic outward rotation of the walls of the transverse wing. Boscovich does not exclude that the rotation could be in part due to local plastic strains of compressed masonry, somewhat comparable to settlements of the longitudinal walls of the gallery.

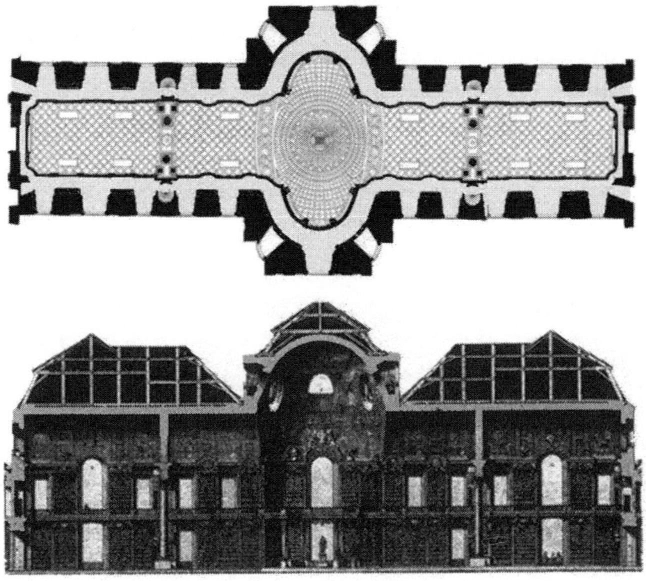

Figure 3. Plan and section of the Hofbibliothek (authors' elaboration from 'Edizione Nazionale delle Opere e della Corrispondenza di Ruggiero Giuseppe Boscovich').

Several other causes, which are undoubtedly significant, although difficult to quantify, can be associated with the thrust of the dome.[19]

Consistent with his damage analysis, the remedies Boscovich suggests aim primarily [20] at containing the thrust and proposing once again the solution suggested for St. Peter's dome, i.e., the introduction of metal hoops on two different levels, just above and below the windows. The reference to St. Peter's is not only an opportunity to polemically recall his disputes with the Marquis Poleni. It also offers a persuasive demonstration of both the devastating effects of the thrust of domes and the effectiveness of metal hoops (which, in the Vatican dome, were capable of controlling the outward movements).

> "Metal hoops restrained the thrust of the great dome of St. Peter's in Rome, ... Marquis Poleni who denied the thrust, for political purposes, and said that hoops were not necessary, required nonetheless that the already designed hoops be placed on the dome, ... He was then very intrigued when he saw, after the other books of his work had already been printed, that one of the ancient metal hoops, placed during the construction of the great dome, was broken because of a vigorous tension, and detached in a site for 5 fingers, in another for three, ..."[21]

Critical remarks about Scrittura

We do not know if the lack of an explicit evaluation of structural safety in the *Scrittura* is due to the greater difficulty of the theme of the elliptical dome with respect to the hemispherical St. Peter's dome. However, whatever the reason for such an absence, the interesting part of *Scrittura* is found in the interpretation of the structural troubles and in the discussion of the constructional aspects.

The former confirms Boscovich's ability in finding a strict correlation between the surveyed damage and the possible causes, the latter showing a remarkable maturity with respect to the previous report about the statics of St. Peter's dome.

The peculiarities of the static behaviour of the elliptical dome when compared with the hemispherical one – essentially resting in the lack of axial symmetry for the stress distribution – are clearly identified, but, above all, are interpreted by taking into account the overall plan of the building and the structural constraints it can introduce. This allows Boscovich to deduce, by simple logical reasoning, what in St. Peter's he had recognized through an explicit structural analysis and to retain such a deduction as being as reliable as a direct calculation.

The mastery of constructional aspects undeniably marks a maturation with respect to the Roman report and, perhaps, obtains a solid contribution from that experience. This is evident from the explicit references Boscovich makes to both constructional solutions for the restoration due to Luigi Vanvitelli and temporary machineries invented for their execution (on the basis of the renowned scaffoldings of Nicola Zabaglia).

Sentimento on the dome of Milan's Cathedral

Sentimento was delivered on February 24 1765. It contains Boscovich's opinion about the project drawn by Francesco Croce in 1764 for the construction of the Great Spire [22] above the dome of Milan's Cathedral. The report – together with those given by the other experts asked for by the *Veneranda Fabbrica del Duomo* [23] (G.B. Beccaria, F.M. de Regi, F. Martinez) to supervise the Croce's project with regard primarily, but not only, to structural aspects – is contained in the report that Ambrogio Nava prepared for the restoration of 1844.[24]

Boscovich's report is very concise and gives the impression of a mastery of structural problems, as regards both conceptual and constructive issues. The structure of the text itself shows Boscovich's self-confidence. After briefly describing his methodology, the measurements he performed and some assumptions that his personal experience allowed, he states sharply, with reference to the demands of the *Veneranda Fabbrica*, his 'impression' that:

> "the designed spire can well subsist both in itself and with reference to the rest of the temple and, if executed, it will find a resistance much greater than the forces tending to make it suffer in itself and causing troubles for the other parts of the temple as well".[25]

and aims to expose its fundamental principles without excessive details.

Boscovich's calculation methodology is based, as for the Vatican dome, on the principle of virtual work, which requires the identification of potential failure mechanisms that the construction of the Great Spire could cause. For the calculation of the virtual work ('moment') of the metal hoops, Boscovich refers to the theorem already established for St. Peter's dome, crediting himself with the authorship of such a theorem, which had been considered collective in *Parere* [26].

The description of the structures of the lantern (paragraphs 12-20) seems aimed, as well as the description of the damage detected in St. Peter's dome, at searching for the collapse mechanism (Fig. 4).

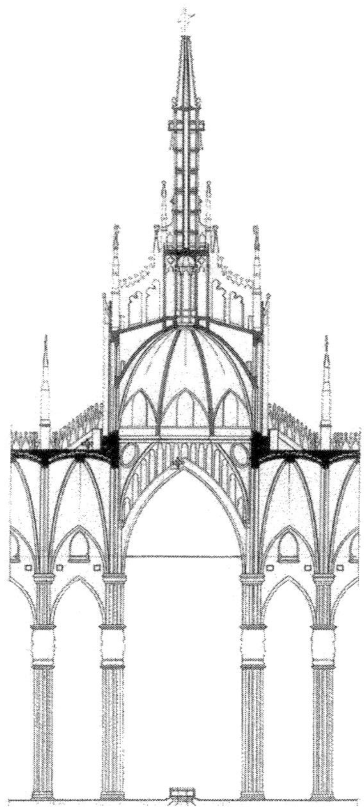

Figure 4. Cross section on the transept of the Milan's Cathedral. Just below the dome, the continuous plane formed by vaults can be seen (author's elaboration from '... e il Duomo toccò il cielo').

After evaluating the stability of the spire and lantern, Boscovich begins the structural analysis of the dome (paragraph 40). The dome has no drum and, moreover, the thrust of the ribs is absorbed without any trouble by the rigid plane formed by the cross-bar vaults which cover the church just below the abutment of the dome.

According to Boscovich, in this case, two failure mechanisms are possible. The former is shown in Fig. 5a: the ridge splits into two parts that can rotate relatively, the upper part, with the lantern, thrusting outwards, the bottom one, with chains, resisting. The latter is shown in Fig. 5b: the lantern drops pushing the ridge outwards and making it rotate around the outer edges, which causes a rise of its centre of gravity. In this way, the rib and the entire dome act as resistance.

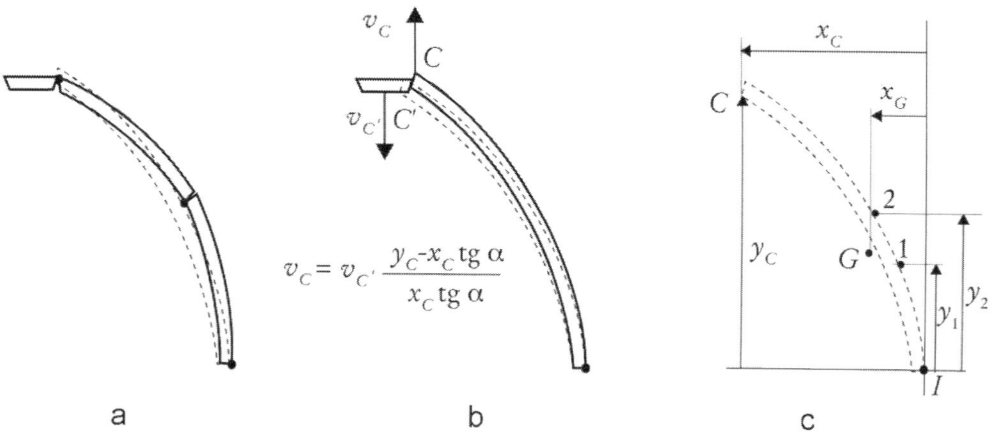

Figure 5. Collapse mechanisms of the dome (authors' drawing).

Boscovich affirms that the first mechanism is impossible, without further detailed explanation: but the reason is clear and depends on the presence of the walls above the marble ridges preventing outward opening. On the contrary, he thinks the second mechanism possible because the joints between marble voussoirs are inclined enough, in the upper part, so as to allow the sliding of the lantern, even though this requires overcoming very high frictions.

Once the failure mechanism has been identified, Boscovich can calculate the associated virtual displacements and, successively, the 'moments'. In the report for St. Peter's dome he had been very precise in describing the calculations that also led to the normalization of the values with respect to a reference point.

For Milan's cathedral, unfortunately, the documents that Boscovich says he attached to his report no longer exist, including those pertaining to the calculation of the 'moments'. Without these documents the exact interpretation of the failure mechanism adopted by Boscovich is somewhat uncertain. It is worth noting that the sliding of the lantern can occur only by overcoming high frictions, but these are not taken into account. As far as this aspect is concerned, Boscovich stresses a very interesting point that can emphasize the same kind of reasoning developed in the analysis of St. Peter's dome (i.e.: significant resistant contributions are neglected for safety reasons, in order to test, so to say, the geometric reliability of the configuration of the structure) and, after recalling how the resistance is four times the amount of the thrusts, he states:

> "Yet the *toughness of the parties is not taken into account* here, although it is considerable …; the *other frame of iron tie-rod is not taken into account*, although it will be infallibly present at the top of the apparent lantern … and being higher than 30 braccia from the support, it gives by itself a 30 million resistance; *another great contribution is not taken into account*, i.e. the fact that in this movement, instead of an hinge opening correlative to what was mentioned in N. 10, the top of the dome's arch, loaded by the weight of the lantern and of the spire, should slide on the wedge plane, while rotating around the abutment corner, …."[27]

Critical remarks about Sentimento

The methodology followed by Boscovich for the Cathedral of Milan is only partially similar to that used for St. Peter's dome. It differs from a theoretical point of view, because the problem is not analysing a damaged state but rather assessing the structural response to a new load condition. It differs from a methodological point of view, because, since the structure does not seem to have suffered damage, the role of analysis is rather modest, while in the case of St. Peter's dome it was, perhaps, the most challenging part.

Moreover, the two structures, although both vaults with stiffening ribs, differ in both geometrical and constructional features. In the Cathedral of Milan the drum is completely absent and the dome is directly supported at the height of the covering vaults of the aisles; furthermore, the ribs are made of marble in the Cathedral of Milan and of brick in St. Peter's dome.

Although apparently simpler, and perhaps much easier to address because of the possibility of avoiding an accurate analysis of the disrupted state, the problem that Boscovich has to face in formulating his "Impression" on the Great Spire of the Milan's cathedral is characterised, in truth, by a deep theoretical difficulty as far as the aspects of structural modelling are concerned, by virtue of the particular approach he uses. In fact, while in the case of the Vatican dome the crack pattern itself – carefully surveyed and interpreted by Boscovich – suggested the most likely failure mechanisms, in the case of the Cathedral of Milan the possible mechanisms must be foreseen and this constitutes a complex modelling problem.

Nevertheless, Boscovich demonstrates that he can deal with this problem with ability even greater than that already exhibited in the Roman querelle. As for the Vatican dome, he not only assumes several failure mechanisms, but also parametrically analyses the more likely mechanism by considering different positions of the fracture close to the abutment and assesses the stability of the dome for each position. Boscovich's analysis therefore predates the famous rule of *maximis et minimis* that Coulomb would explicitly formulate with reference to circular arches.[28] This proves Boscovich's extraordinary maturity as a structural analyst.

Conclusions

Boscovich's three static reports are extraordinarily important scientific texts. The flawless methodological articulation of the three reports is associated with a deep discussion of the mechanical aspects and, above all, a strict correlation between the different phases of the investigation. Thus, the analysis of the crack pattern of the Vatican dome – and, albeit with slight differences, of the Hofbibliothek – becomes central to the definition of the mechanical model and this, in turn, is the starting point for the definition of the repair interventions.

Similarly, the survey of geometrical and constructional aspects of the dome of Milan's cathedral leads to foreseeing the possible failure modes and allows for the formulation of a judgement on the structural safety of the building in the presence of the new spire.

It is precisely in the constant reference to architecture, and its constructional features, that Boscovich's maturity as a structural analyst is found, more so than in his remarkable knowledge of statics. The adoption or exclusion of a failure mechanism, as well as the introduction of specific assumptions for the mechanical behaviour of different structural portions, and even the simplifications adopted in the calculations, all descend from a careful constructive analysis of the building which characterizes the mathematical treatment by a significant adherence to the physical nature of the problem.

This is even more surprising if we think of how new the application of mechanics to architecture was at the time; while statics had in fact acquired, in the second half of the eighteenth century, a form quite similar to the present discipline, its applications to structural analysis were nevertheless still quite sporadic. From this point of view, Boscovich's three reports are documents of great interest, not only for the history of mechanics but also, and perhaps above all, for the history, which remains to be written, of the structural design of architecture, arising as crucial steps of a process that, not by chance beginning with the Enlightenment century, would reveal an increasingly stronger involvement of statics skills in architectural design.

Notes and references

[1] R.G. Boscovich, F. Jacquier and T. Leseur, *Parere di tre mattematici sopra i danni, che si trovano nella cupola di S. Pietro*, Roma: Pallearini, 1742. p. 36.

[2] R.G. Boscovich, F. Jacquier and T. Leseur, *Riflessioni de padri Tommaso Le Seur, Francesco Jacquier dell'Ordine de' Minimi, e Ruggiero Giuseppe Boscovich della Compagnia di Gesù, sopra alcune difficoltà spettanti i danni, e risarcimenti della Cupola di S. Pietro*, Roma, 1743. p. 64.

[3] R.G. Boscovich, *Scrittura sulli danni osservati nell'edificio della Biblioteca Cesarea e loro riparazione*, manuscript, 1763. 18 ff.

[4] R.G. Boscovich, 'Sentimento sulla solidità della nuova guglia proposta per la cima della cupola del duomo di Milano ....', 1765, in A. Nava, (Ed.) *Relazione dei restauri intrapresi alla gran guglia del duomo di Milano nell'anno 1844 ed ultimati nella primavera del corrente 1845*, Milano: Valentini, 1844. pp. 53-64.

[5] D. Capecchi, (Ed.) 'Perizie di Statica', (CD-ROM) in *Edizione Nazionale delle Opere e della Corrispondenza di Ruggiero Giuseppe Boscovich*, 2010, vol. IX/II; D. Capecchi, C. Tocci, 'Le perizie sulla Cupola Vaticana di Le Seur, Jacquier e Boscovich', *Palladio*, January-June 2011, Rome, 2011. pp. 43-58.

[6] Boscovich, *Parere*, (Note 1) p. 36.

[7] ibid., pp. 23-24. The virtual work of the weights, whether acting in favour of or against stability, is simple to calculate. The calculation of the virtual work done by the hoop in tension is more complex. Since there are no suggestions in the literature, Boscovich proposes a rule that, in modern language, states that the virtual work L of a hoop, acted upon by a constant tension force N and subjected to a change Δr of its radius, is given by the relation $L = 2\ \pi\ N\ \Delta r$. The reasoning developed by Boscovich to justify such a rule is simple and convincing although not completely rigorous, so that the logical status of the rule is that of a principle rather than that of a theorem.

[8] ibid., p. 30.

[9] G. Poleni, *Memorie istoriche della gran cupola del Tempio Vaticano e de'danni di essa, e de' ristoramenti loro, divise in libri cinque*, Padova: Stamperia del Seminario, 1748.

[10] Capecchi, *Cupola Vaticana*, (Note 5) p. 49.

[11] P. De La Hire, *Traité de Mécanique, ou l'on explique tout ce qui est nécessaire dans la pratique des arts, & les proprietés des corps pesants lesquelles ont un plus grand usage dans la physique*, Paris: Imprimerie Royale, 1695; P. De La Hire, 'Sur la construction des voutes dans les edifices', in *Mémoires de l'Académie Royale des Sciences*, Paris, 1712. pp. 69-77.

[12] C.A. Couplet, 'De la poussée des voûtes', in *Mémoires de l'Académie Royale des Sciences*, Paris, 1731. pp. 79-117; C.A. Couplet, 'Seconde partie de l'examen de la poussée des voûtes', in *Mémoires de l'Académie Royale des Sciences*, Paris, 1732. pp. 117-141.

[13] Boscovich, *Parere*, (Note 1) p. 30.

[14] The strong earthquakes that occurred in Central Italy in 1703 and 1706, severely striking L'Aquila and Sulmona, were felt in Rome as well.

[15] Boscovich, *Riflessioni*, (Note 2) p. 58.

[16] All of these considerations, moreover, allow for the clarification of an interpretative question that emerges from *Parere* about the actual configuration of the collapse mechanism suggested by Boscovich. Such a mechanism would indeed be different from that shown in Fig. 2 of *Parere* as we have observed by repeating the calculations of Boscovich. See: Capecchi, *Cupola Vaticana*, (Note 5).

[17] Capecchi, *Perizie*, (Note 5).

[18] Boscovich, *Scrittura*, (Note 3) § 52.

[19] ibid., § 57.

[20] Boscovich also suggests the introduction of tie-rods at the bottom and top of the transverse wing walls, and the repair of all minor cracks.

[21] Boscovich, *Scrittura*, (Note 3) § 67.

[22] D. Capecchi, C. Tocci, 'Il Sentimento di Ruggiero Boscovich sulla Gran Guglia del Duomo di Milano', *Palladio*, January-June 2012, Rome, 2012. pp. 115-128; E. Brivio, F. Repishti, (Eds), ... *e il Duomo toccò il cielo*, Milano, 2003.

[23] The *Veneranda Fabbrica del Duomo di Milano* was established in 1387 by Gian Galeazzo Visconti to supervise the construction of the cathedral, replacing the *Superstantia S. Maria Maggiore*, created the year before by the archbishop Antonio da Saluzzo.

[24] A. Nava, *Relazione dei restauri intrapresi alla gran guglia del duomo di Milano nell'anno 1844 ed ultimati nella primavera del corrente 1845*, Milano: Valentini, 1844.

[25] Boscovich, *Sentimento*, (Note 4), § 11.

[26] ibid., § 6.

[27] ibid., § 49.

[28] C.A. Coulomb, 'Essai sur une application des règles de maximis & minimis à qulques problème de statique relatif à l'architecture', in *Mémoires de mathématique et de physique*, Académie Royale des Sciences, Paris, 1776.

The Nineteenth Century

The Giulio Cesare Hall in Palazzo Senatorio in Campidoglio. Notes on the late XIX century construction-site.

C. F. Carocci[1] and C. Tocci[2]

1. Dipartimento di Ingegneria Civile e Architettura, Università di Catania; 2. Dipartimento di Architettura e Design, Politecnico di Torino

Introduction

The opportunity to analyse the late nineteenth century construction-site in the Palazzo Senatorio in the Campidoglio was provided by the involvement of both authors in the latest repair and restoration project of the gable roof standing directly over the Giulio Cesare Hall, today seat of the city council.

The roof is different from the two symmetrically adjacent roofs (that cover the building's side rooms slightly projecting from the main body toward the square) due to its greater span (13.00 m) and lower slope (21°). (Fig. 1) Eleven composite Polonceau trusses form the main structure of the roof. (Fig. 2a) One meter below their supports, a walkable metal grid rests on the upper chords of riveted iron trusses with curved intrados that form the centring supporting the barrel vault, with end coves, which covers the city council hall (Fig. 2b).

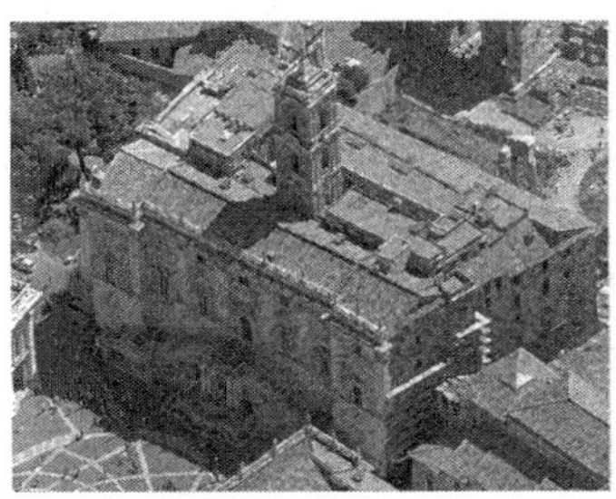

Figure 1. Top view of the Palazzo Senatorio. Google Maps.

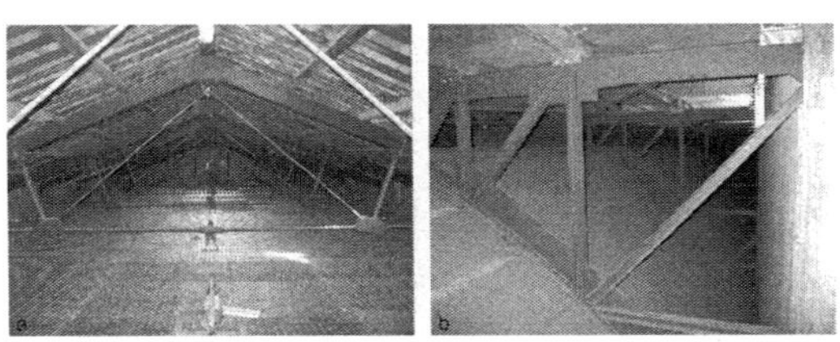

Figure 2. The composite Polonceau trusses of the roof (a) and the iron trusses supporting the vault of the Giulio Cesare Hall (b).

Both the roof structure and the vault were built at the end of the nineteenth century to replace the old wooden queen trusses (still visible in the two side rooms) and masonry barrel underpitch vault springing from the longitudinal walls of the Palazzo.

In 2009, following the failure of one of the Polonceau trusses and fearing severe and pervasive structural deficiency, the Municipality began a study aimed at developing a project to restore suitable safety conditions.[1] Design criteria and intervention techniques – which made it possible to preserve the nineteenth century structural conception, with minor changes aimed at correcting design defects and repairing (or replacing) damaged elements – were defined in accordance with the results of an accurate cognitive phase.

The comparison between the archival data – in particular the graphic documents pertaining to the late nineteenth century project – and the current situation, directly surveyed, made it possible to recognize not only the substitution interventions performed on the main structures – the vault and the roof – but also the associated actions undertaken on the masonry walls to create the supports for the new structures.

These transformations date back to June 1893, when the collapse of localized portions of plaster from the intrados of the hall's barrel vault started the process that would lead to the decision to replace the great masonry vault with a metal one having the same shape, and dismantle even the sixteenth century timber trusses substituting them with composite Polonceau trusses.

After a brief historical outline of the main building phases regarding the Palazzo Senatorio, the paper describes first the late nineteenth century construction-site and then offers some basic details of the recent survey with the aim of integrating the knowledge framework emerging from the archive documents.

The Palazzo Senatorio in Campidoglio: historical data

The Palazzo Senatorio, seat of the Senate of the Free City of Rome, was built in the mid-twelfth century on the ruins of two Roman buildings: the Veiove Temple (196 BC) and the Tabularium, the city's public archive (78 BC).

In its most ancient configuration, the building's façade overlooking the square appeared with two rows of windows, with a battlement on the top and was flanked by a high tower. In the early XIII century, the arcaded hall on the ground floor was probably connected to the square by a stepped ramp.[2] Towards the square, there was another loggia upstairs,[3] facing the audience hall for the Senator and the General Council – covered by a wooden trussed roof and decorated with frescoes depicting coats of arms, garlands and stripes.

During the fourteenth century, Palazzo Senatorio took on the appearance of a fortress: loggia arcades were filled and two buttressing towers built. In the fifteenth century the towers of Martin V (in the square) and Nicholas V (towards the Forum) were added and three Guelph cross windows were opened on the first floor; the second floor loggia was cut by a balcony on corbels (the *corridore*), still visible in the early sixteenth century views.[4]

The great transformations of the square, started in 1537 when Paul III asked Michelangelo for a project for the Campidoglio, led to the elimination of the two-level grand loggia with superimposed arcades built in 1520, at the behest of Senator Squarcialupi as a monumental entrance on the right side of the façade. (Fig. 3a)

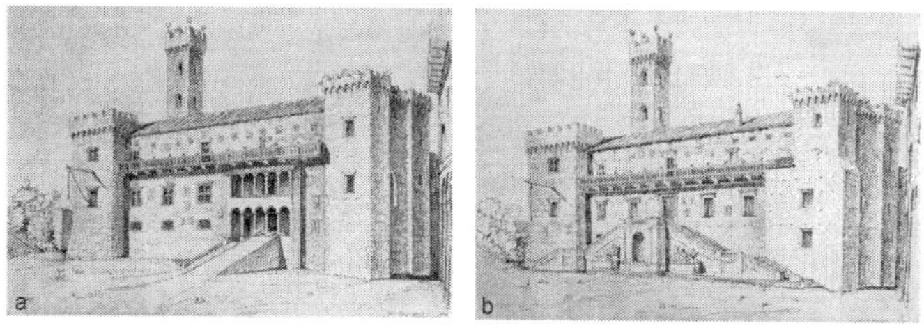

Figure 3. The Palazzo Senatorio in 1520 with the so-called Loggia Squarcialupi (a) and in the middle of XVI century with the first double staircase by Michelangelo (b). C. Pietrangeli 1959.

In Michelangelo's project, Palazzo Senatorio was connected to the square by the sculptural double stairway (Fig. 3b), built before the death of the architect between 1542-54; while Palazzo Nuovo was erected directly opposite Palazzo dei Conservatori (completely renewed) to enclose the new urban space, in the middle of which the architect had already placed the equestrian statue of Marcus Aurelius. (Fig. 4)

After 1564 and until 1593-98, Palazzo Senatorio underwent major interventions with significant changes with respect to the original plan by Giacomo Della Porta, successor of Michelangelo as the Architect of the Roman People. In particular, the late sixteenth century configuration of the Senator courtroom (today the Giulio Cesare Hall) was built between 1573 and 1578 by unifying the two superimposed levels of the medieval palace, defining the space with a great barrel vault and designing the two rows of windows of different sizes that characterize the main façade.[5] (Fig. 5)

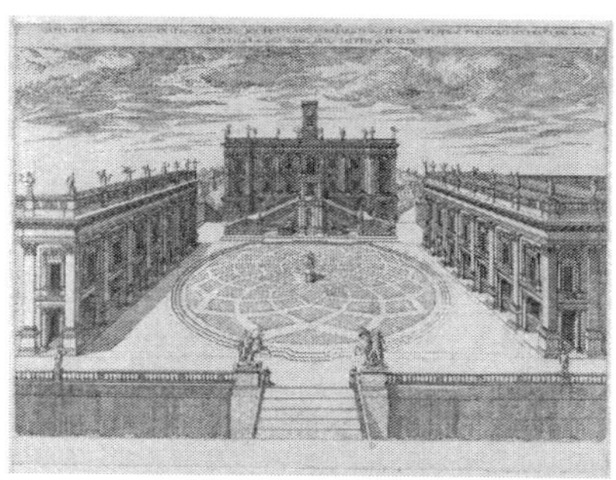

Figure 4. View of Campidoglio square in the Michelangelo's project (E. Du Perac, 1569); Palazzo Senatorio presents two superimposed levels.

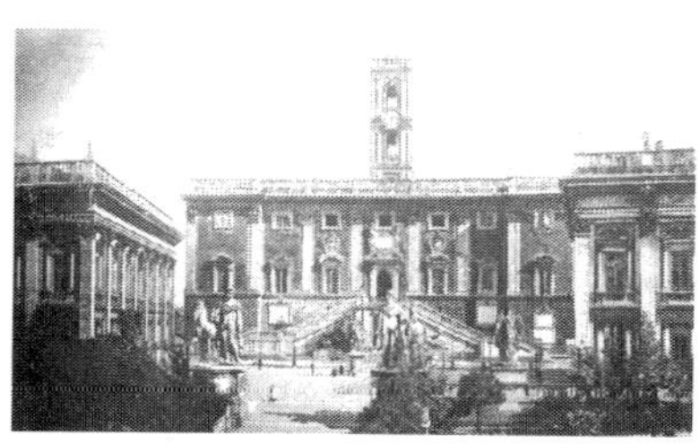

Figure 5. Photographic view of Campidoglio square. Palazzo Senatorio presents a single level, and the upper squared windows ('mezzanini') look on to Giulio Cesare Hall.

The gable roof with wooden pitched trusses was built between January 1576 and March 1578, as attested by the payment for the purchase of wooden beams and boards "to cover the roof of the great hall".[6] The sixteenth century closed with the completion of the façade towards the square in the forms we still admire today – due to Giacomo Della Porta and Girolamo Rainaldi. Later work inside the Senator's hall would be executed under Pope Paul V (1605-21) and restorations after the 1703 earthquake. After the unification of Italy, Palazzo Senatorio became the seat of the town hall of Rome and the main hall – adapted for city council meetings – was named the Giulio Cesare Hall.

The late XIX century work: the reasons

In June 1893 – after the fall of some portions of plaster from the vault of the Council hall – the chief engineer Moretti of the 3rd Division of the Technical Office of the Municipality of Rome (maintenance of buildings and museums owned by the city) carried out an inspection using a provisional scaffolding erected under the area concerned. He states in his report that:

> "the plaster is barely adherent to the vault and we had to remove it almost totally in the part of the vault that could be reached from the scaffolding. A similar condition can be evidently surveyed elsewhere and in some parts bulges are clearly visible".[7]

After removing the plaster significant cracks were detected on the masonry work of the vault and other cracks were also discovered in the vaulted surface still covered with plaster.

Based on the results of the inspection, Moretti suggested completely removing the plaster in order to assess the overall condition of the structure and, subsequently, working from the intrados, "restore the vault by repairing cracks with masonry infill" and "where necessary by inserting metal keys, hooks or needles or by applying special wire mesh".[8]

The work program was approved in July 1893 with the allocation of the amounts required to start the bidding. In mid-September, the contractor[9] had already completed the erection of the scaffolding and undertaken the removal of the plaster residues. Moretti wrote in a report dated September 22, 1893:

> "… after completely removing the plaster from the vault, significant faults were discovered ... and especially in the parts corresponding to the three windows that separate it from its springing. These three windows have flat arches and lintels that are completely crumbling and, consequently, the region of vault resting on them is faulty and broken. Therefore, it is essential, in my opinion, to reconstruct the three flat arches and (at least partially) the three rings of vault that rise from them. This consequently leads to the need for a falsework supporting the three rings of vault; and the cost of the intervention I am proposing will be significant". (Fig. 6)

Reading Moretti's report, it would appear reasonable to recognize the main cause of the surveyed distress in the thrust of the vault, insufficiently buttressed by the façade overlooking the square. The onset of a flexural mechanism in the vault, as a consequence of the unbalanced outward movement of the façade,[10] would have in fact determined significant intrados damage in the vault's haunch, in addition to the classical extrados crack opening, because of the presence (and geometry) of the lower pitch vaults corresponding to the three windows.

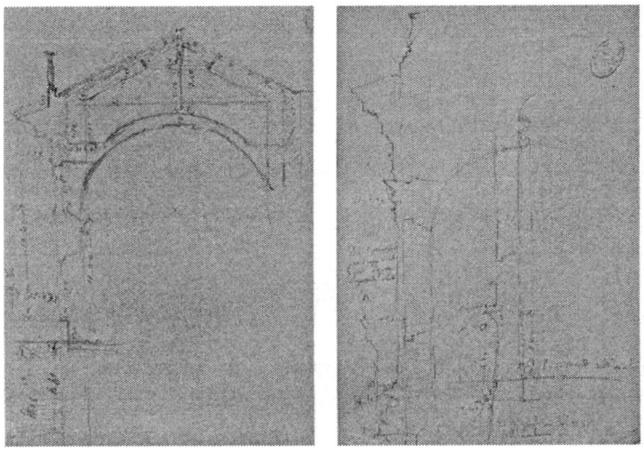

Figure 6. The late XVI century vault and wooden trusses before the substitution work. Archivio Storico Capitolino.

That would have justified the "faulty and broken" condition surveyed in this area of the vault. In any case, the suspension of work – in late September 1893 – started a long period of reflection for the definition of a new plan of interventions.

The definition of the intervention: arguments, variations and financial assessments.

The assessment of the vault damage was entrusted to a commission of experts [11] who, after an inspection carried out in early October 1893, expressed a rather concerned opinion:

> "... the conditions of the vault are such as to fill the technicians with serious apprehensions ... the technical difficulties for the restoration of the vault could be overcome, but regardless of the expense, as the restoration, or renovation, would certainly require, because of its difficulty, an expense not less than that required for the total renovation; moreover major restorations would be required for the façade wall".[12]

Based on these indications, the Municipal Technical Office drew different design proposals, to compare costs, from the restoration of the vault to its complete replacement.

As for the latter, five different solutions were identified in a few months: metal floor framing with wooden coffered intrados placed (1) below [13] or (2) above the level of the second order windows; (3) metal framing with finish brick floor and plane plastered intrados with painted decorations; (5) light vault supported by metal trusses; (6) masonry vault.

The solutions were submitted to the Building Commission, which, in April 7 1894, rejected both the restoration of the existing vault and its reconstruction in masonry work accepting, among the replacement proposals, the light vault with metal trusses and the flat floor with wooden coffered intrados above the second order of windows. The two solutions were also compared form the viewpoint of their cost: £120,000 the former, £57,000 the latter. Nevertheless, in May 1894, the decision was made to demolish the sixteenth century vault, with the support of the unanimous opinion of another expert committee which declared:

> "... the main cause of the serious cracks surveyed on the vault had to be found in its structure consisting of a mass of masonry concrete, 80 cm wide at the haunch and 60 cm wide at the crown, ... poorly constructed and badly springing ...". [14]

The aforementioned insufficient buttressing offered by the building's façade seems here indirectly confirmed by the statement that the vault is "badly springing"; while a further suggestion to explain the surveyed distress can be derived from the judgement according to which the vault is considered "poorly constructed". Both considerations are, moreover, closely related, since a masonry concrete vault, by virtue of its own compactness, would have certainly exerted a lesser thrust on its abutments. These findings leave no doubt about the reasons that led to the final design decision to replace the original masonry vault with a light vault supported by metal trusses. (Fig. 7)

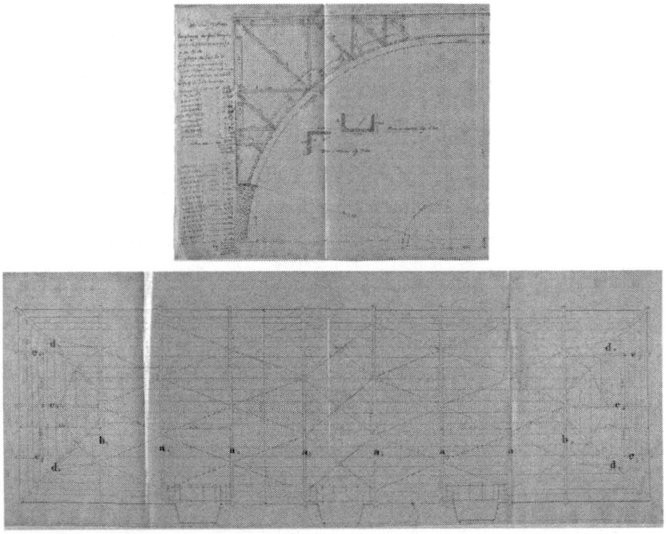

Figure 7. Design drawings for the substitution of the masonry vault: plan of the iron trusses (bottom) and detail of a diagonal truss (top). Archivio Storico Capitolino.

The approval of the project to replace the vault and ... the wooden roof

In October 16, 1894, Moretti transmitted the construction drawings and specifications for the reconstruction of the hall's vault. In the attached letter he explained that the increase in expense was due to the additional work foreseen for the wooden roof:

> "... the repeated investigations have revealed organic defects that could not be detected when all the attention converged on the vault and nothing seemed to be faulty on the roof. ... The repair of the roof is of such a nature that it cannot be executed without also reconstructing the vault and therefore it is necessary to decide that things are part of the same contract and provide for a spending difference of £14,000".[15]

The decision to dismantle the wooden trusses erected by Giacomo Della Porta in the late sixteenth century [16] was completely unexpected, since, in the preliminary studies, it had never been mentioned and the work to be executed on the roof was limited to localized improvements and strengthening of wooden elements and their supports.[17]

Instead, the final project lists the following major interventions:

> "1) building a complete falsework for the existing concrete vault to be demolished step by step; 2) restoring the perimeter walls above the vault impost and adding there new masonry; 3) dismantling and re-building the roof of the hall by re-using part of the old material for pitched trusses, purlins and rafters and adding new iron elements for trusses". (Fig. 8)

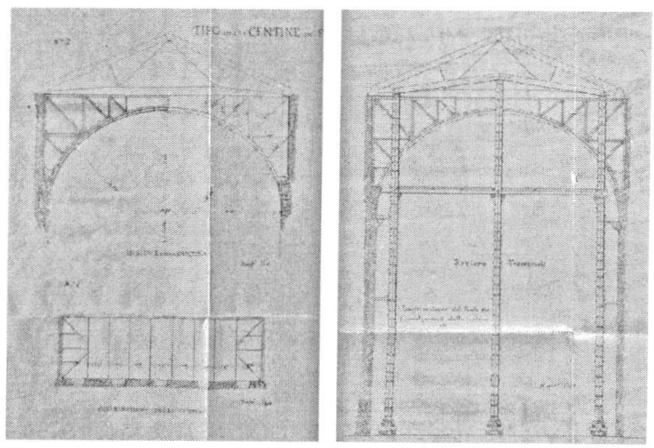

Figure 8. Design drawings: the new vault and the composite Polonceau trusses. Archivio Storico Capitolino.

The decision to dismantle the original roof does not seem to find, in the archival documents, reasons as compelling as those supposed for the reconstruction of the underlying vaulted structure. The impression we receive from reading the documents – rather generic about the real distress condition of the roof structures – is that of an intervention motivated more by a desire to simplify the execution of the work than by the actual need to fix a situation of unacceptable precariousness.

The execution of the project: construction contract and work-in-progress reports

The work began in January 1895. [18] Two scaffoldings were installed on the vault extrados and above the roof, this latter projecting over the way of the Arch of Septimius Severus, and a provisional shelter made of 'tarpaulins to cover the dismantled parts of the roof during the reconstruction' was set up before starting the removal of the tile roofing.

The problematic dismantling operation was carried out step by step, removing consecutively two bays at a time, putting up immediately the new pitched truss and the overlaying purlins and performing simultaneously the interventions on the perimeter walls (to improve quality and create the supports for both timber and metal trusses). The aim was to minimize execution time, so that bad weather conditions would not jeopardize the structures.

The great wooden elements of the sixteenth century pitched trusses were disassembled, selected and set aside to be reused as compression members of the new composite Polonceau trusses. In fact, the construction contract specified that:

> "... eleven timber struts will be obtained from the lower chords of the old pitched trusses, squaring their transverse sections off and planing them perfectly; the other eleven struts will be obtained from new chestnut beams".

The new Polonceau trusses were illustrated by detailed drawings mentioned in the design report. We have not found these drawings, but the description contained in the construction contract is accurate:[19] the new trusses would be made:

> "of two chestnut struts 6.80 m long, 25 cm thick and 20 cm wide, cast iron diagonal struts, iron ties with eye-shaped forged heads, threaded pins secured by nuts, molten iron boxes for the heels."

Purlins were partially made with reused materials too,[20] and "new chestnut beams 3.40 m long, 18 cm thick and 15 cm wide", joined to the Polonceau rafters by means of iron elements.

Finally, the completion of the roof involved the "nailing of rafters, layering of thin bricks, positioning the pan-and-roll tiling and rebuilding the chimney, gutters and two skylights ...".

Once the new roof was completed, the demolition of the vault was started, following the directions in the construction contract, i.e. "in small transverse sections, [from the crown of vault] up to the impost of the new metal trusses".

The supporting recesses of the metal trusses were then made ("recesses to cut in the perimeter walls in order to build in the new trusses") and the 'projecting pillars' supporting the dismantled sixteenth century trusses were demolished (Fig. 5a) ("the pillars that supported the lower chords of the old pitched trusses ... rested on the vault, were simply leaning against the walls and without any connection with these"). The interventions on the masonry walls of the Giulio Cesare Hall changed substantially the inner leaf of the façade above the impost of the big masonry vault. (Figs 9-10)

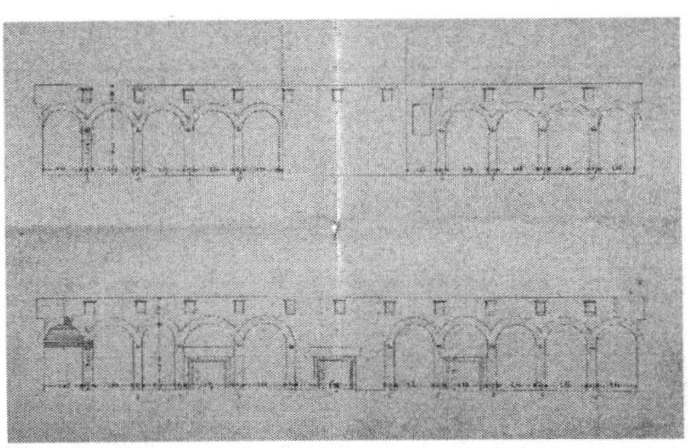

Figure 9. Design drawing: upper part of the longitudinal walls of the Giulio Cesare Hall with the recesses supporting the Polonceau trusses. Archivio Storico Capitolino.

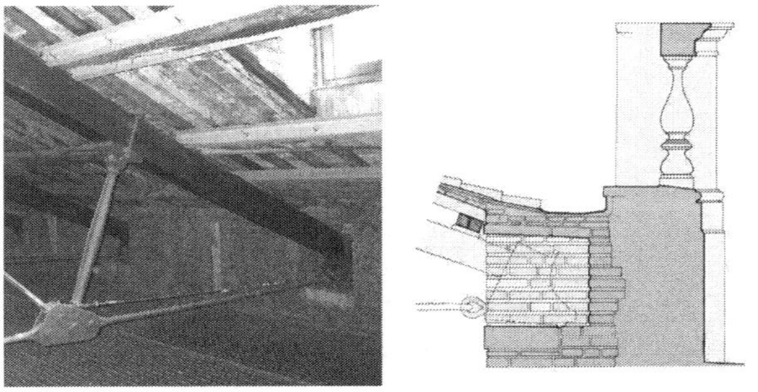

Figure 10. Details of the recesses supporting the Polonceau trusses.

These interventions were carried out both to provide proper support for the new structures (steel trusses of the new vault and Polonceau trusses of the roof) and to improve the masonry work quality.

The supports for the metal trusses of the vault were first carved out in the existing masonry and then completed with insertions of effectively bonded bricks.[21] At a higher level wider areas were made to receive the heads of the Polonceau trusses: the areas were defined by normal brickwork visible on both the wall facing and the inner surfaces of the rooms.[22]

The bases of both supporting areas were provided with "travertine slabs acting as cushions for the roof and vault trusses, their horizontal faces perfectly planed and bonded to masonry with a thick layer of mortar". (Fig. 10)

A document dated January 8, 1896 shows that the execution of the described work on walls had exceeded the costs foreseen in the project.[23]

To justify this increase in expenditure, the work director produced a detailed report describing the state of distress of the façade wall, thus explaining the greater amount of work carried out to improve the "poor quality of the perimeter walls and especially the one overlooking the square".

The weakness of the wall emerged during the execution of the new roof, when it was observed that:

> "the entire thickness of the upper part of the wall, above the vault, 1.30 m wide, was made of three different structures: the inner one with tufa stones in horizontal courses …; the intermediate one, with bricks and tile fragments, without any form of bonding with the former to the point that it still had large portions of the plaster and painting which decorated the inner face of the hall; the third and outer structure made of a coursed rubble with tufa and bricks …".

Because of this, an intervention was carried out for both longitudinal perimeter walls based on the introduction of travertine blocks (some 80 cm long) in order to bond the different masonry leaves.

The recent survey

Figure 11 shows the detailed survey of one of the nineteenth century Polonceau trusses drawn for the static restoration project, whose execution has been recently completed.

It is easy to recognize the general structural layout just outlined in the late nineteenth century drawings (Fig. 8), with the metal boxes connecting the main timber rafters and metal tie-rods, the joints between metal tie-rods and diagonal cast-iron struts, the raised lower chord of the truss. Moreover, we can recognize the details of the structural assembly about which archive documents give no information.

Some of these details deserve to be mentioned because they evidently violate the canons of the rule of art as they can be deduced form the nineteenth century treatises. And that seems to have played a decisive role in the development of the forms of distress that finally led to the collapse of one of the trusses.

First of all, the centroidal axes of the wooden struts and metal tie-rods do not converge in the heel and summit joints – contrary to a mandatory rule for trusses;[24] secondly, only the central member of the lower chord is equipped with a turnbuckle.

The misalignment of the axes produces secondary bending stresses in the joints (moreover amplified by long-term wood deformations) that can undermine – and, in fact, undermined in one of the trusses – the strut and tie connections. While the absence of turnbuckles makes it impossible to tighten the lateral tie-rods of the lower chord, causing further malfunctioning of the trusses. Naturally, the recent restoration project focused primarily on these constructional flaws.

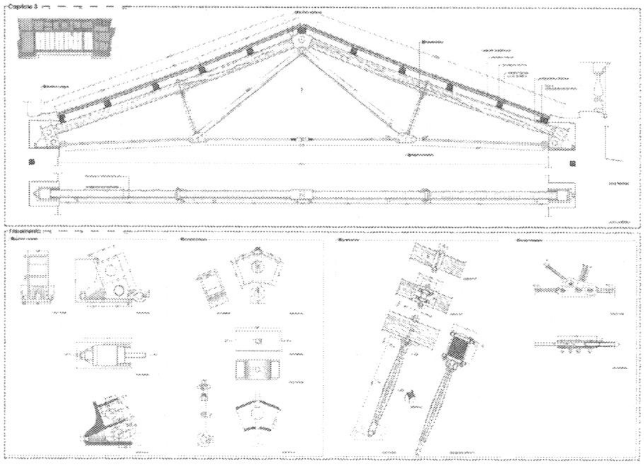

Figure 11. Detailed survey of the Polonceau trusses drawn for the 2009 project.

Conclusions

The historical reconstruction of the intervention carried out in the late nineteenth century on the vault of the Giulio Cesare Hall in Palazzo Senatorio is interesting for several reasons even beyond the importance of the building and site.

First, it should be noted that both the metal trusses supporting the vault and the composite Polonceau trusses of the roof are examples of a rather rare technology in late nineteenth century Roman construction.

Secondly, the story of Giulio Cesare Hall seems to reveal an approach towards the existing buildings which, at the end of the nineteenth century, was completely indifferent to the preservation of historic matter, unless it regarded the exterior surface of monuments, such as the wooden structure of a magnificent roof or the masonry work of a great vault.

Finally, a further question emerges that relates to the attitude of the designers with respect to the building that they were called to restore. Such a question is all the more significant since the work was carried out in a crucial period for the development of theories of restoration.[25]

The replacement of the vault of the Giulio Cesare Hall and the dismantling of the sixteenth century timber trusses demonstrate a twofold attitude: on the one hand, there seems to be an evident desire not to alter the exterior architectural aspect; on the other, we find great freedom from a merely technical-constructional point of view.

On the contrary, in the last restoration project, recently completed, the decision was made to maintain, as far as possible, the original structure – at this point the one of the nineteenth century – acting in accordance with the universally shared assumptions of minimum intervention and reversibility – at least as far as safety needs allow.

Notes and references

[1] The restoration project for the XIX century pitched trusses was drawn up by the Technical Office of the Municipality of Rome (Operational Unit for Monumental Buildings) with structural consultancy by C. Tocci and C. Carocci, C. Circo, D. Indelicato. The work, started in July 2015, was recently completed.

[2] Concerning the construction phases of the Palazzo Senatorio, see: C. Pietrangeli, Le prime fasi architettoniche del Palazzo Senatorio, Rome, 1959.

[3] Rests of the loggias were found during the late nineteenth century work and the more recent ones of the late 1950s. See: Tittoni M.E. (ed.), La facciata del Palazzo Senatorio in Campidoglio: Momenti di storia urbana, Pisa, 1994, pp. 44-47.

[4] Compare with the view of P. Isaacsz reproduced in B. Contardi, 'La storia della facciata tra Michelangelo e Della Porta', in Tittoni M.E. (ed.), La facciata del Palazzo Senatorio in Campidoglio: Momenti di un grande restauro a Roma, Pisa, 1995, p. 51. In this view, certainly post 1561 (year in which the equestrian statue of Marcus Aurelius was put in place) the façade of the Palazzo already had the monumental double stairway, the two levels of windows and the upper corridor.

[5] In 1573 payments are mentioned for "walls made in the Palazzo Senatorio … and partly the great vault above them and the cornice …, brick finish floor in the hall, insertion of three tie-rods, masonry work in the lower pitch vaults of the windows, … as to estimate and measure made and signed by Jacopo della Porta architect of the Roman people …". P. Pecchiai, Il Campidoglio nel Cinquecento sulla scorta dei documenti, Rome, 1950, p. 92.

[6] Ibid., pp. 93-94.

[7] Archivio Storico Capitolino, Ufficio V, Divisione III, n. catena 4; fasc. 1, sottofascicolo 1: corrispondenza, "SPQR, anno 1893-4, Amministrazione del Comune di Roma, Ufficio V, Divisione 3°, Palazzi e Musei, Oggetto: Palazzo Senatorio. Aula Massima Consiliare: Restauro della volta (relazione).

[8] Ibid., Moretti's report included the financial assessment for the repair and restoration of the intrados plaster which would be "thinner, ... could be built with a more cohesive mortar, and anchored with iron nails and somewhere with wire mesh ...".

[9] Company "Eugenio Mattia", contractor responsible for the "maintenance of municipal buildings in Rioni (districts) X and XII and the Teatro Argentina for the period 1893-95".

[10] It is worth noting that the chronicles of Palazzo Senatorio report an out-of-plumb for the façade wall overlooking the square and that repairs were necessary after the 1703 earthquake. See: Pietrangeli, *Palazzo Senatorio*, (Note 2) pp. 13-16.

[11] The commission was formed by the architects-engineers: Francesco Vespignani, Eurdeo Gui e Pio Piacentini.

[12] Commission report, November 19, 1893.

[13] This solution would have produced 18 new rooms for offices. The opinion of Moretti was different and he wrote: "building a floor at the level of the vault impost gives rise to a space that can be used between the floor itself and the roof, but it can change, and very disadvantageously, the proportions of the great Capitoline hall and deprive it of much light ...".

[14] Draft of the speech of the Mayor at the City Council meeting of May 18, 1894.

[15] The increase in spending in fact goes over the estimate by £ 75,000 to £ 89,000.

[16] The description of the trusses to be dismantled is contained in the contract specifications of the project: "... roof pitched trusses, each composed of tie-beam, rafters, cushion rafters, queen posts, straining beam, iron brackets, corbels, etc".

[17] The preliminary project provided for the "general arrangement of the roof after completing the work [for the reconstruction of the vault], with improvements and rehabilitation of scuppers, provision and arrangement of the galvanized iron sheets at the base of the new skylights", as well as the reinforcement of the truss heels with "iron beams and brackets" and of the rafters and cushion rafters using "iron brackets, 7 cm thick and 5 cm wide, and iron bars with diameter 3 cm and with the necessary threading, slots, nuts, wedges".

[18] In the construction contract the timeline for the work is implicitly indicated (Capitolato d'Appalto dei lavori murari per la ricostruzione della volta e dei lavori tutti occorrenti per la riforma del tetto dell'Aula Massima del Palazzo Senatorio al Campidoglio January 5, 1895). The construction site was prepared by using a part of the way of the Arch of Septimius Severus to store the "timber beams and assembly of the new trusses".

[19] Nevertheless, the survey carried out for the recent project made it possible to explain the details of the nineteenth century intervention and identify the elements described in the archive documents.

[20] The reuse of the existing purlins is confirmed by the direction: "reduction of old purlins ..." (Capitolato d'Appalto dei lavori murari ..., January 1895).

[21] Ibid., "masonry work for the improvement of recesses hollowed in the perimeter walls to receive the heads of the metal trusses of the vault, ...".

[22] Ibid, "brickwork for renewal of walls, vaults and flat arches to be executed with fine mortar of high quality ... including cutting the old wall, by chisel or where necessary pickaxes".

[23] Application for approval of exceeding work in the vault of the Giulio Cesare Hall, letter of the Chief Engineer of the Division II to the Director of Office V, January 8, 1896.

[24] And strictly observed in the drawings of composite iron-wood trusses shown in the late nineteenth century treatises (see, for example: C. Formenti, La pratica del fabbricare, 2nd ed., Milan: Hoepli, 1909, tav. L-LI).

[25] In 1883 the IV National Congress of Engineers and Architects was held in Rome, whose final vow, written by Camillo Boito, is considered the first Italian Restoration Charter.

The roof of the Gallery Vittorio Emanuele II in Milan: reconstructing the original building technology

Iva Stoyanova
Independent Researcher

Introduction

Gallery Vittorio Emanuele II (1865-77) in Milan is a milestone in the development of the European arcade. Glazed shopping arcades were complex social, economic, urban, and architectural phenomena and emerged in Paris following the French Revolution (1789–1799).[1] A typical shopping arcade was several things at once: retail space (a pedestrian street symmetrically lined with shops); a street (shortcut between two equally busy nodes in dense mediaeval urban fabric); a manifestation of an emerging middle-class (representative bourgeois venue); an architectural innovation (sky lit space).[2] Wrought iron and cast iron became two of the main materials used to build the roofs of shopping arcades in combination with glass plates.

The arcade evolved throughout the nineteenth century and reached its peak with the Milan example during the so-called Monumental Phase (1860-80).[3] The term 'Gallery' (capitalized) will be used in this paper to refer to the gallery 'Vittorio Emanuele II'. Unlike many other examples of nineteenth-century glazed arcades, which unfortunately were demolished during the twentieth century, the Gallery still exists. It consists of two streets, or passages, that cross perpendicularly with an octagonal space at their intersection. This cruciform plan is covered with four barrel vaults, while the central space is surmounted with a monumental dome and cupola. (Fig. 1)

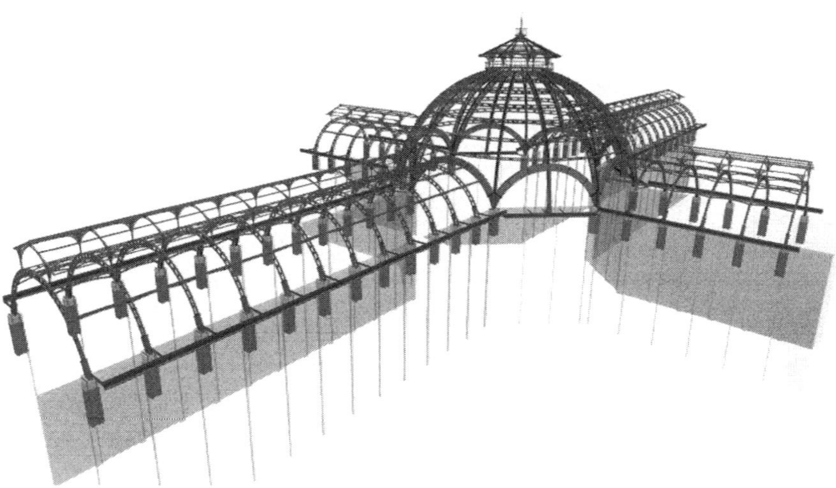

Figure 1. Three-dimensional model of the roof structure. (Image: Iva Stoyanova, Tihomir Stoyanov)

Yet the immaturity of the iron industry in post-liberation Italy made the construction of the roof a challenge; its builders required inputs from more developed countries.[4] The Gallery has been recognized as the successful result of international collaboration[5] thanks to the architect Giuseppe Mengoni (1829–77), who managed to bring together English financing with French engineering know-how and iron production.[6]

Compared with other arcades of the time, the Gallery's roof was unprecedented in its dimensions and form. It was especially celebrated when newly completed for the size and spatial effect of the central dome[7], and it has been recognized in twentieth-century literature as a significant achievement in nineteenth-century iron-and-glass architecture.[8]

Nevertheless, 20th-century writers have not elaborated on the construction and glazing technologies of the roof. Works written on the occasion of the hundred-year anniversary (1967) of the Gallery have referred to the roof as a characteristic part of the overall monumental effect. More recent academic research[9] treating the roof's construction technology has relied on the available archival documentation. The focus has been on the iron framework, which has been discussed in the general context of the construction technology of the Gallery. However, the glazing techniques originally used have remained unclear due to a lack of information in contemporary documentation. In addition, the complicated system of maintenance facilities in the roof has been insufficiently explored.

The main goal of this paper is to reconstruct the original building technology of the roof through a virtual model. This three-dimensional model puts together all the available technical data about the main roof components, technical solutions, and construction details. These data have been collected and analysed by the author in her doctoral dissertation. The research draws on original drawings and archival sources dealing with the technology of the Gallery's roof, as well as nineteenth-century technical texts and previous academic research. Gaps in this information were then filled with information obtained from five graphic plates – detailed drawings of the Milan iron roof – that were prepared for the World Exhibition of 1867 in Paris. They are reproduced as technical drawings in the appendix to this paper. These plates supply more precise information on the wrought-iron and cast-iron components of the roof, especially about the glazing bars, and on the various assemblies of the roof components. Based on these sources, the main characteristics of the roof's components and assemblies as originally built can be reconstructed, illustrated, and analysed.

The roof systems

The Gallery roof consisted of several interrelated systems: the main body or framework, the integrating system, the glazing system, and the maintenance system. The main body was composed of four barrel vaults covering the wings of the structure, which intersected in a central space that was crowned with a dome. A smaller half dome closed the end of the vault on one of the long wings, which also covered a diagonal entrance from 'Piazza della Scala' located to the north of the Gallery. The vaults were topped with linear lanterns, while a circular lantern or cupola projected from the centre of the monumental central dome. The dome cupola was often called a "cupolino" in architectural literature, and that is how it will be referred to in this paper.

All the parts of the main body were developed through a primary structure, which supported the glazing and the maintenance facilities. The integration of this complex iron-and-glass organism into the supporting masonry walls and the surrounding Gallery buildings was achieved through the integrating system.

Primary structure

The vaults

The four vaults had the same width, a 14.96 m span, but differed in length according to the wings they covered: the eastern and western wings were both 31.09 m long, the northern wing 71.12 m, and the southern wing 64.70 m.[10] The main iron components of the vaults were crosswise arches and lengthwise purlins. (Fig. 2)

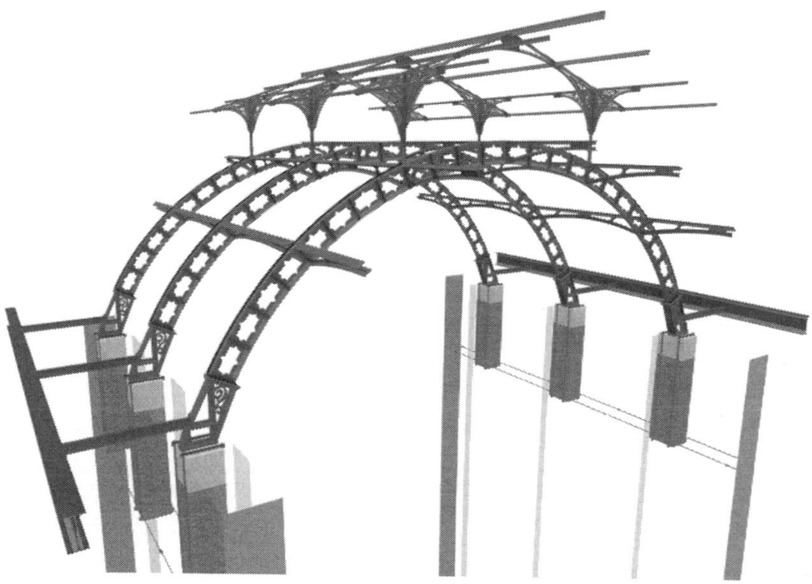

Figure 2. Three-dimensional model of the primary structure of the Gallery vault and lantern. (Image: Iva Stoyanova, Tihomir Stoyanov)

Each primary arch component was preassembled from six curved segments fabricated of T's and connecting plates, and had an I cross section and a perforated web. (Appendix, Plate 5, top image) The arches ending the vaults at the dome were doubled because they supported the dome structure.

The primary vault arches were braced lengthwise by five purlins per span, for a total of 190 purlins. Each purlin weighed 5 kg.[11] They were connected at their ends to the arches by means of wrought-iron brackets and 12 bolts, so that a structural node was created. (Appendix, Plate 5, bottom image)

Two main types of purlins can be seen in the technical documentation, differentiated according to their location at the summit or the sides of the vault. These two kinds differed in the connecting plates that held together the horizontal top and the curved bottom of the purlin. The summit purlins had fewer plates, or stiffening elements, because they supported less weight: the lantern ran above them, and there was no glazing on the arches under the lantern.

The primary arches of the vaults stepped onto the supporting walls by means of consoles made of cast-iron[12] in order to resist compression.[13] The console was partly visible and partly concealed: the visible part was decorated where it protruded from the façade while the rest was integrated into the masonry. The console transferred the lateral thrust of the vault arch to a peripheral system of wrought-iron beams. The bottom flange of each console was supplied with circular openings for four anchoring bolts, which secured a rigid attachment to a granite block topping the supporting masonry.

The vault lanterns

Lanterns ran the length of the vaults except at the ends where maintenance stairs were installed over the glass canopy. The lanterns comprised columns, a glazed pitched roof, and additional elements that stiffened the whole structure in space. (Fig. 2)

The original columns had an X-shaped cross section (100 mm x 100 mm), as found by an onsite investigation of the historic roof structures in the 1980s.[14] The lantern roof was developed through a primary structure of crosswise rafters (T-section 69 mm x 65 mm) and lengthwise purlins, which supported the glazing. (Appendix, Plate 5, central series of crosswise sections) Archival documentation and the 1980s investigation[15] reveal four different types of lantern purlins: a ridge purlin (I-section 160 mm x 48.5 mm), an intermediate purlin (I-section 102 mm x 42 mm), a purlin bracing the column tops (T-section 72 mm x 70 mm), and a purlin bracing the rafter tails (L-section 74 mm x 50 mm). In addition, the lantern was braced both crosswise and lengthwise at the juncture of the columns, and the rafters and purlins, by curved knees with T-profiles (69 mm x 65 mm).[16] The bolted decorative knee braces contributed significantly to stiffening the lanterns.[17]

The lantern columns were bolted to the vaults underneath at the points of intersection between a vault arch and purlins in order to obtain a spatial structural node. Thus, structural integration of the loadbearing members of the vault and of the lantern was achieved.

The dome

Previous research has discussed the Gallery dome in the context of the vast panorama of experiments in dome construction. Notable domes of the time include those of the Halle au Blé in Paris (1809), London Coal Exchange (1847), Exhibition buildings in New York (1853) and Dublin (1853), Leeds Corn Exchange (1860), and Exhibition building in London (1862).[18] Geist further suggested a parallel between the Gallery dome and that of Saint Peter's Cathedral in Rome, as the Gallery dome had very similar dimensions in plan.

Physically, the dome is a hemisphere with a circular base (39 m external diameter).[19] (Fig. 3) The structure is 30.15 m above the pavement , and its own height is 12.35 m (cupolino excluded).[20]

The primary framework of the dome consisted of 16 wrought-iron arches, which will be termed 'meridians' in this paper. (Appendix, Plate 1) Each of them was preassembled from six curved segments, which had a compound double I-profile (1000 mm x 300 mm).[21] All the segments were 3,057 m long except the ones at the very top, which were slightly shorter at 3,050 m.[22]

A16-point structural scheme with three types of technical solution was adopted for the support of these meridians. In addition, this scheme had to be coordinated at the two different levels where the meridians discharged loads: the octagon walls at 25.07 m[23] and the vault arches at 30.15 m, from the pavement.

The supports for the meridians can be divided into three main types (I, II, and III in this paper) according to their locations, as indicated in the original technical documentation.[24] The different technical solutions resulted from the superimposition of the circular base of the dome onto the octagonal room formed at the intersection of the Gallery wings. The meridians with supports of type I and II needed to be extended in order to reach the octagon where they discharged their loads.

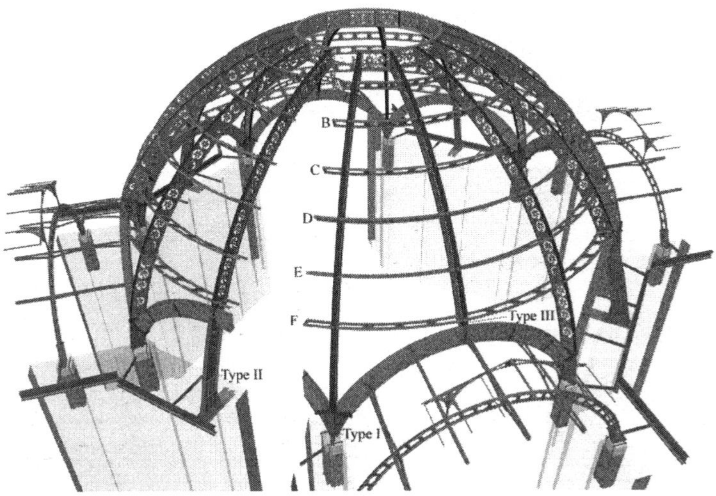

Figure 3. Three-dimensional model of the structure of the Gallery dome and its supports of type I, II, and III. (Image: Iva Stoyanova, Tihomir Stoyanov)

Supports of type I were used at the eight angles of the octagon, and they supported not only the feet of eight meridians but also the ends of the double vault arches spanning the wings, and the blind arches along the sides of the octagon. This complicated combination was resolved with a special shoe made of cast iron that was bolted to the masonry wall. It was composed of four pieces set at an angle of 135° degrees (the obtuse angle of the octagon) in order to provide the necessary support in the relevant elevation plane. The meridian extensions and the cast-iron shoes were hidden behind decorative eagle sculptures.

Supports of type II were located behind the four masonry walls that formed sides of the octagon. The meridians supported by type II required a complementary 6-meter extension. The arch foot was attached to a ribbed, cast-iron shoe, which was carried on a pair of transverse beams (I-profile 300 mm x 280 mm).[25] One end of these beams was anchored into the masonry wall. The other end was connected to a wrought-iron beam that was a member of the integrating system. Thus, any lateral thrust due to expansion or contraction of these meridians was transmitted to the surrounding buildings.

Supports of type III were used where the meridians stepped directly onto the double vault arches (1000 mm x 340 mm) by means of appropriately shaped cast-iron wedges. (Appendix, Plate 4, central right image)

The rest of the framework of the dome consisted of a central ring and successive rings of lateral braces. The upper ends of the meridians attached to a wrought-iron ring made of I-profile members (1325 mm x 200 mm)[26], which had a perforated web. The meridians were braced laterally with six levels with wrought-iron rings, which will be referred to as 'parallels' named A to F, with A being the uppermost one. (Appendix, Plate 3, bottom left images) The parallels were discontinuous because they were formed from separate segments, which were probably bolted in-situ between two consecutive meridians. The segments of the parallels had a cross section of a double-T profile[27] with a perforated web. Sources showing the original construction indicate that the parallel rings differed from one to another by 10 cm in section depth. Thus, each parallel could adequately respond to resistance requirements that decreased from the bottom to the top. The lowest ring, F, was the deepest (1000 mm x 300 mm) while the upper ring, A, reached half its depth (500 mm x 300 mm).

Decorative consoles were located in the connections between the meridians and the parallels. These varied in height in order to accommodate the difference resulting from the consistent depth of the meridians and the changing depth of the parallels. It can be assumed that these consoles played a significant role in the installation process. Once the meridians and the consoles were installed, the segments of a parallel were then positioned onto the consoles. Next, the parallels were appropriately adjusted so that they could be bolted in their precise location. In the long term, the consoles contributed to the spatial stiffening of the dome's primary structure.

The dome cupola or lantern (cupolino)

The cupolino structure has been described often in original technical documents due to its structural complexity and significance as the "crown" of the entire Gallery roof. It consisted of a cylindrical body (10.00 meters in diameter and 5.25 meters tall)[28] and a cone-like glazed roof. (Fig. 4) The cylindrical body was shaped from eight columns located at the eight meridians springing from the corners of the walls of the Gallery octagon. (Appendix, Plate 2, top image) The columns were fabricated from several simple profiles: a flat wrought-iron section (150 mm x 15 mm) and two wrought-iron T-profiles (128 mm x 65 mm). (Appendix, Plate 3, centre right image) Each column had a cast-iron shoe with a strap at its base that was bolted to the top dome ring.

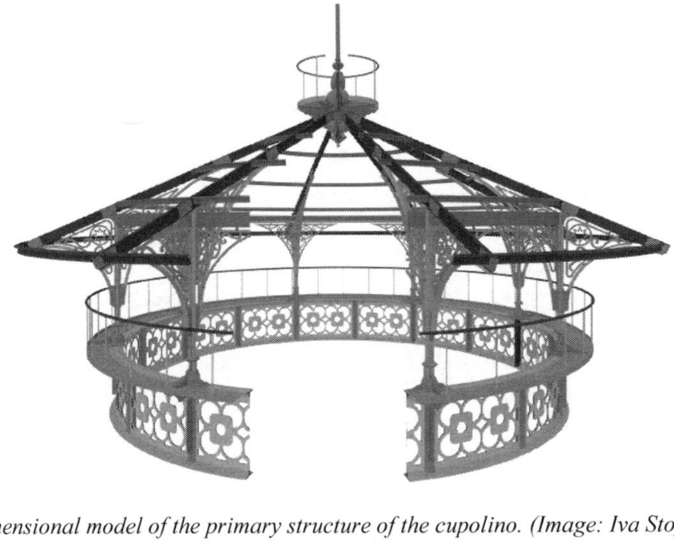

Figure 4. Three-dimensional model of the primary structure of the cupolino. (Image: Iva Stoyanova, Tihomir Stoyanov)

A ring (Π-section 250 mm x 55 mm) braced the column tops. Like the columns, it was composed of simple profiles: two L-sections (60 mm x 40 mm) and a flat bar (250 mm x 15 mm). (Appendix, Plate 3, top left image)

The cone-like glazed roof had a primary structure that supported the glazing. Eight roof rafters (I-section 200 mm x 110 mm) rested on the columns. In addition, the rafters were braced lengthwise by purlins on four levels. The purlins at the lowest level had the deepest section (150 mm x 45 mm) while the rest had identical I-profiles (100 mm x 45 mm).

According to the technical drawings, all the connections between the construction members of the cupolino were achieved through riveted wrought-iron braces. Bolts were used to connect the columns to the dome's upper ring and to the glazing bars. Therefore, it can be suggested that the primary structure of the cupolino could have been preassembled in advance. Unfortunately, no confirmation of this has been found in original documentation or previous research.

Integrating system

The integrating system was designed by engineer Gerolamo Chizzolini (1824-97) who was at that time the head of the Construction Works Department.[29] The aim of this system was to constrain lateral thrust caused by expansion or contraction of the primary roof arches supported by the masonry walls. The adoption of visible horizontal tie-rods was prohibited by the building contract. Thus, an integrating system was devised, made of wrought-iron beams and vertical ties that were distributed in accordance with the vault arches and the dome meridians with support from type I.[30] (Fig. 5) Horizontal ties connected the lower ends of the vertical ties. Granite blocks topped the masonry walls under each arch foot and contributed to distributing the load from the iron roof frames more uniformly to the supporting brick pilasters.[31] The rigid connection between the arch foot and the block was crucial for the successful functioning of the system.[32] In case of expansion or contraction the arch was constrained to move upwards by the rigid connection at its foot and 4-meter-long ties anchored in the supporting brick walls. Any lateral thrust left over was transferred to the surrounding buildings by means of crosswise (I-section 200 mm x 100 mm) and peripheral (I-section 600 mm x 300 mm)[33] wrought-iron beams.

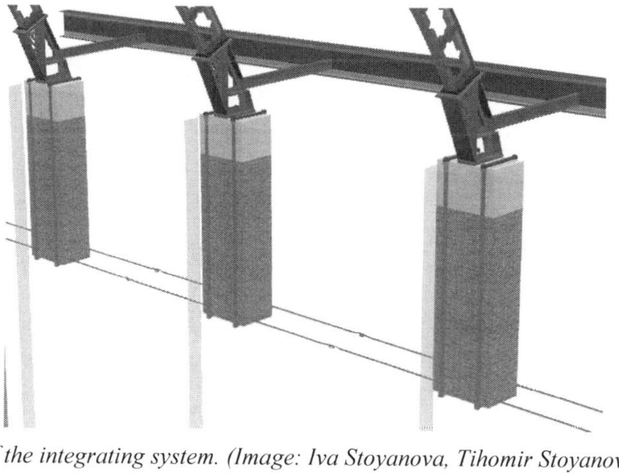

Figure 5. Components of the integrating system. (Image: Iva Stoyanova, Tihomir Stoyanov)

The integrating system was criticized in its time as an avoidable financial expense, especially in the case of the statically stable hemisphere of the dome.[34] The vertical ties were reproved because movement could damage the stucco ornaments of the internal facades.[35]

Chizzolini designed the integrating system using the same structural blend that was chosen to build the edifices encompassing the Gallery.[36] Wrought iron, cast iron, brick masonry, and granite blocks were combined in a joint system, which has been acknowledged in previous academic research[37] as a 'hybrid' between traditional Lombard building techniques and modern technologies. The integrating system contributed to the monumental spatial effect inside the Gallery by making possible the successful balance of the span of the vaults and the dome without visible tie-rods between the springings of the arches.[38]

Glazing system

Rolled wrought-iron glazing bars were adopted for the glazing. Different types of cross sections were employed according to their locations, and different technical solutions were required for their connections to the purlins.

Cross-shaped glazing bars with indentations in the rebates were used to glaze the vaults and all the lanterns.[39] (Appendix, Plate 2, centre left series of cross sections) They were semi-circular or curved for the vaults and linear for the lantern roofs. The cruciform sections were imbedded in the vault purlins (Appendix, Plate 5, bottom image) while in the cupolino they were suspended by means of additional planks or supported by L-profiles to which they were screwed. (Appendix, Plate 2, centre left series of cross sections)

In addition, T and L sections were employed in the lanterns along the primary arches. This is mentioned in the archival documentation made on the occasion of the first large-scale campaign to repaint the original ironwork (the interior surfaces) in 1907. T-profiles (35mm x 35 mm x 5mm) with indentations were claimed to have been employed for the integral glazing of the dome.[40] In addition, L-profiles (35mm x 35 mm x 5mm) were attached with set-screws to the meridians.[41] But the 1907 documentation referred to the dome glazing bars as cruciform in section, which raises doubts whether the T-profile was actually employed in the construction of the roof.

The original glass plates, supplied by Saint-Gobain, were made of flat ribbed glass.[42] The plates were consistent in their 6-mm thickness and 0.60-m width. Their lengths varied according to their locations, but two lengths were most prevalent: 0.88 m and 1.70 m.[43] The glass plates were equipped with a V-shaped bottom edge and were laid so that one overlapped the previous plate. Metal fixings secured the glass plates to the glazing bars.

The glass plates over the dome were additionally supported by lead wedges, which gave them the necessary inclination.[44] Although lead wedges were used for the entire glass cladding, as indicated in technical documentation, they probably fell out of use due to the negative effects of electrochemical action between lead and wrought iron in the presence of moisture.[45] Subsequent campaigns to maintain the glazing do not refer to the use of lead wedges.[46] The iron-and-glass connection was depicted as a zinc cap made of folded zinc sheets (0.80 m long) that overlapped 0.05 meters along the glass plates.[47] However, the adoption of such a protective cap has not been confirmed.

Maintenance system

The maintenance system provided access from the surrounding buildings to the roof. It included a service corridor on the top floors of the buildings surrounding the Gallery, a gutter at the base of the dome, and a system of boardwalks and stairs over the glazing. The largest part of the components of these maintenance facilities were produced from sheet iron and wrought-iron bars, in the case of some stairs.[48] (Fig. 6)

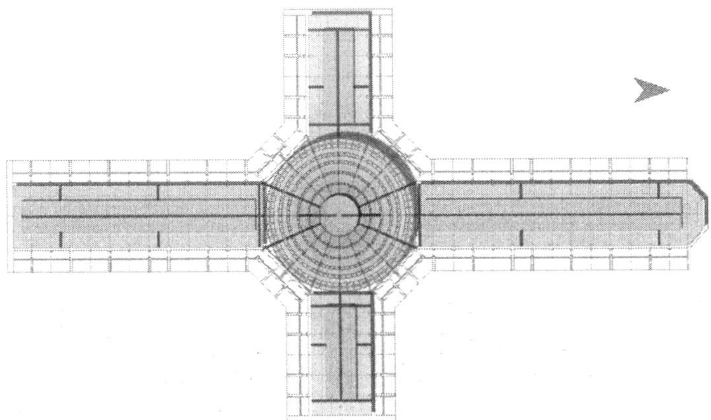

Figure 6. Plan of the Gallery roof showing also the location of main maintenance facilities. (Image: Iva Stoyanova, Tihomir Stoyanov)

The service corridor (2.15 m x 1.50 m)[49] ran along the periphery of the four wings and the octagon. This corridor served as the place for collecting snow thrown down from the roof by maintenance workers. The accumulated snow was then pushed through perpendicular branches of the corridors into the internal courts of the surrounding buildings. Furthermore, the service corridor provided access to the vaults. Each long vault was equipped with four sliding and two fixed stairs, while the short vaults had two sliding and four fixed stairs. Fixed, inclined stairs provided access to the boardwalks that ran along the lantern tops.[50]

The vault stairs gave access to the main gutter encircling the base of the dome. Dome boardwalks were developed at three levels: parallel D, parallel B, and the upmost ring at the base of the cupolino. The gutter and the boardwalks were connected vertically with 20 fixed stairs.[51] On top of the cupolino was developed a round platform, which was accessible from the highest boardwalk of the dome through two inclined stairs.

This elaborate system of maintenance facilities was reported in the original technical documentation to have been supported by the primary structure of the vaults and the dome. However, the glazing bars also contributed significantly to supporting the boardwalks and stairs.[52] In particular, the stairs sliding over the vaults were mounted on longitudinal rails that ran on three levels. Thus, the cross sections of the glazing bars had also to resist the live loads during sliding.

Conclusions

The Gallery roof combined primary, integrating, glazing, and maintenance systems into a coherent organism. At the base of this intricacy lay a few simple wrought-iron sections and sheets, which were employed in a diversity of composite profiles and technical solutions.

The primary system was characterized by structural nodes between the composite wrought-iron sections. The primary structure of the dome and its base, involving three types of supports, exemplified how the combination of different technical solutions could achieve the wide diameter of 39 m and support it on masonry walls at a significant height.

The integrating system was the invisible part of the Gallery roof, which penetrated the supporting brick walls and the surrounding buildings. It exemplified how the structural hybrid typical for the Gallery edifices was applied, in order to incorporate the made-in-Paris iron roof into local building traditions in Milan, where brick masonry was a dominant material. The employment of I-sections in the integrating system and the dome supports showed how the adoption of similar profiles ensured the interaction between the systems. The cruciform glazing bars were also significant members, which allowed a variety of technical solutions involving connections to other elements. They served as a supporting system for the maintenance stairs and boardwalks.

A large part of this complex roof structure still stands in place today and proves that the original building technology could endure for the long term. Despite its intricacy and the experimental character of such a large iron structure erected in a place with little experience in iron construction, the Gallery roof was a success. The iron-and-glass roof was appreciated for its aesthetics – its seemingly light and ephemeral qualities. It became a feature of the new type of national monumental architecture, as it was followed by the Naples gallery 'Umberto I' (1887-90).

Appendix

'Combles en fer du passage Victor-Emmanuel, à Milan, construits par H. Joret' kept at Musée des arts et métiers\Conservatoire national des arts et métiers, Photothèque: Inventory N° 13571.1837/1 – 5.

The original drawings were executed on vellum by Brzozowski on the occasion of the World Exhibition of 1867 in Paris. They also contain precise measurements in millimetres. The drawings were exposed in room 53 of the exhibition along with another project by Joret '13571-1813. Combles en fer du hangar de Grenelle, construits par M. Joret (1 pl.)'.

COMBLES EN FER

Pl. №1

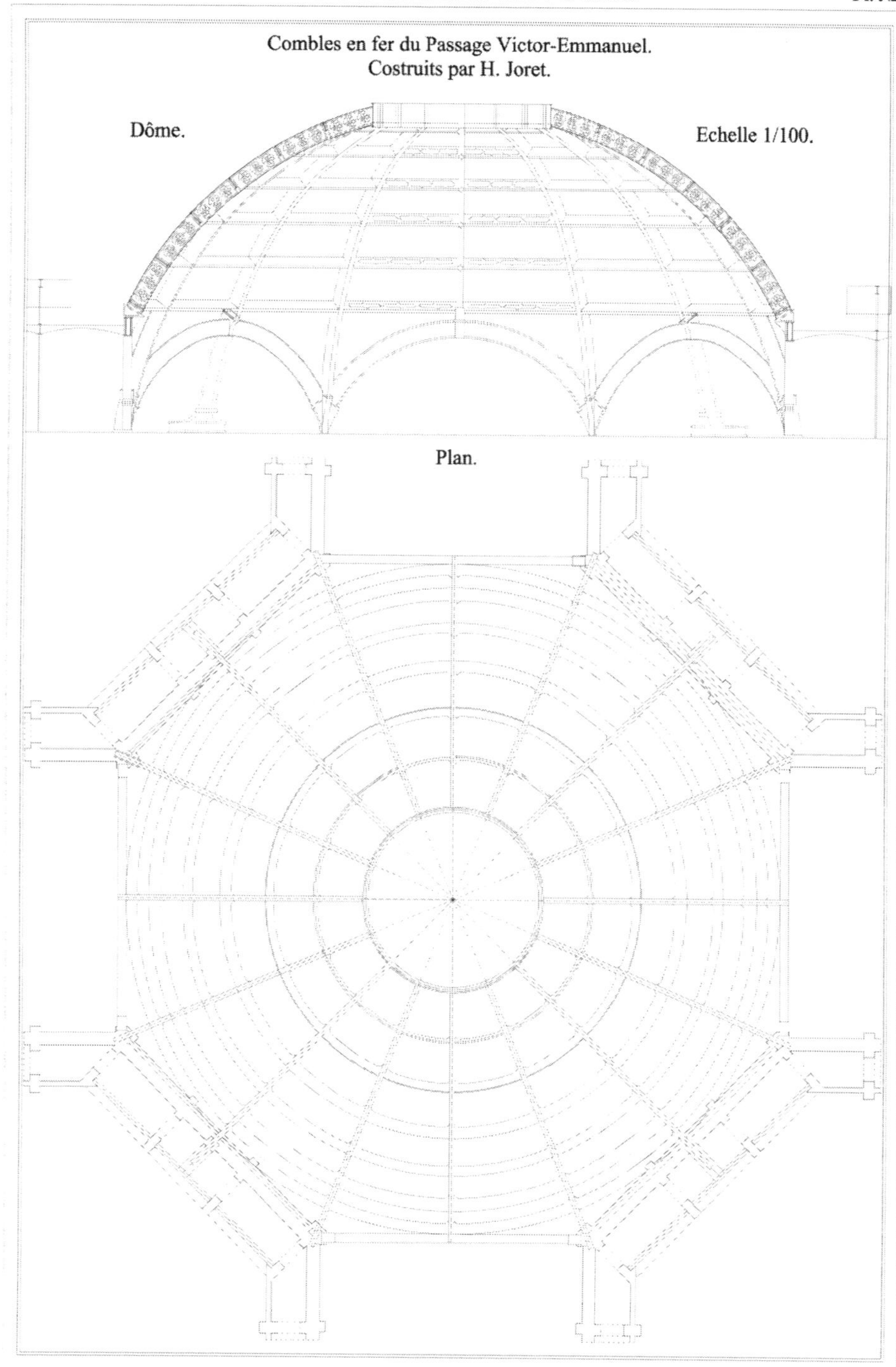

COMBLES EN FER

Pl. №2

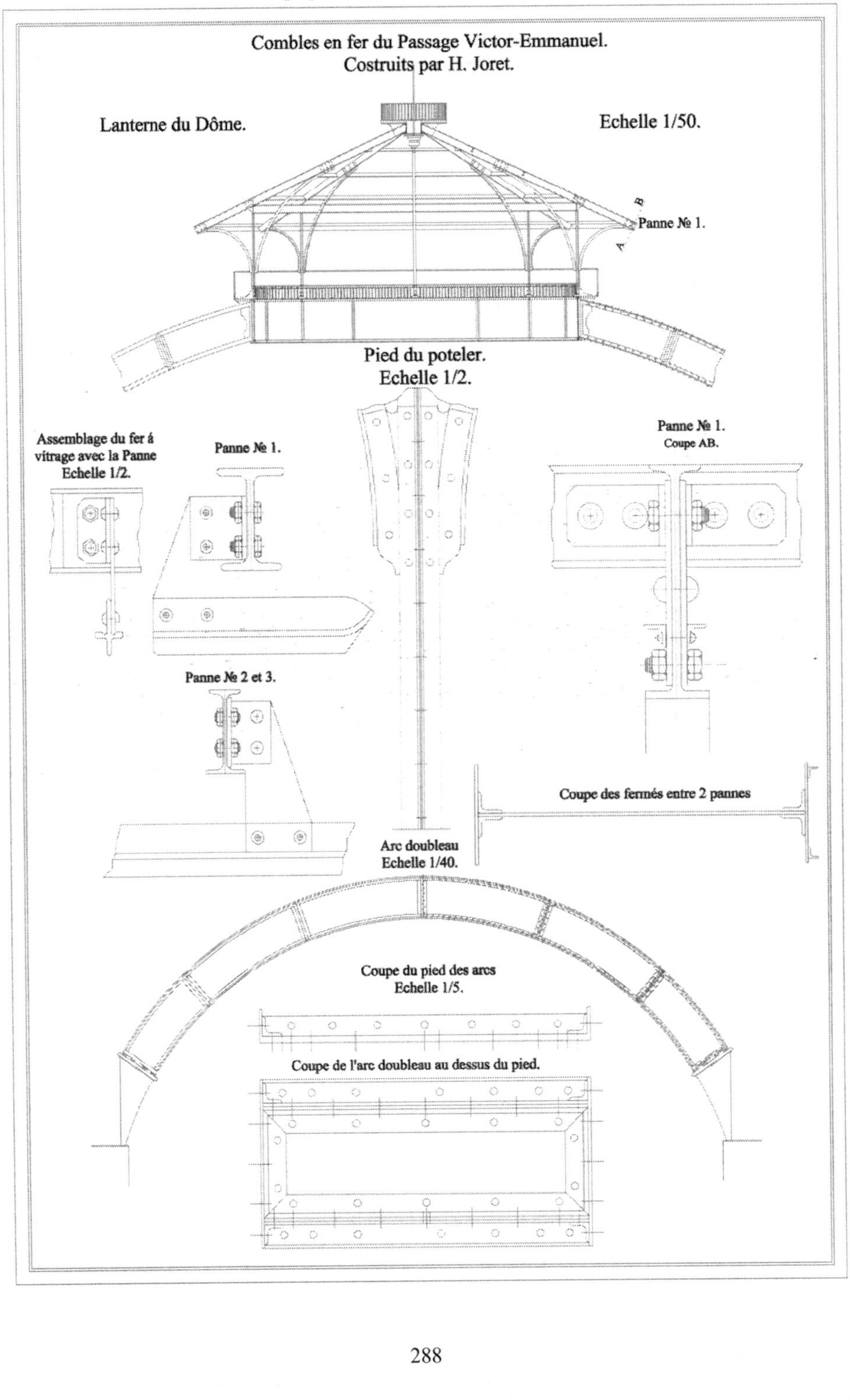

COMBLES EN FER

Pl. №3

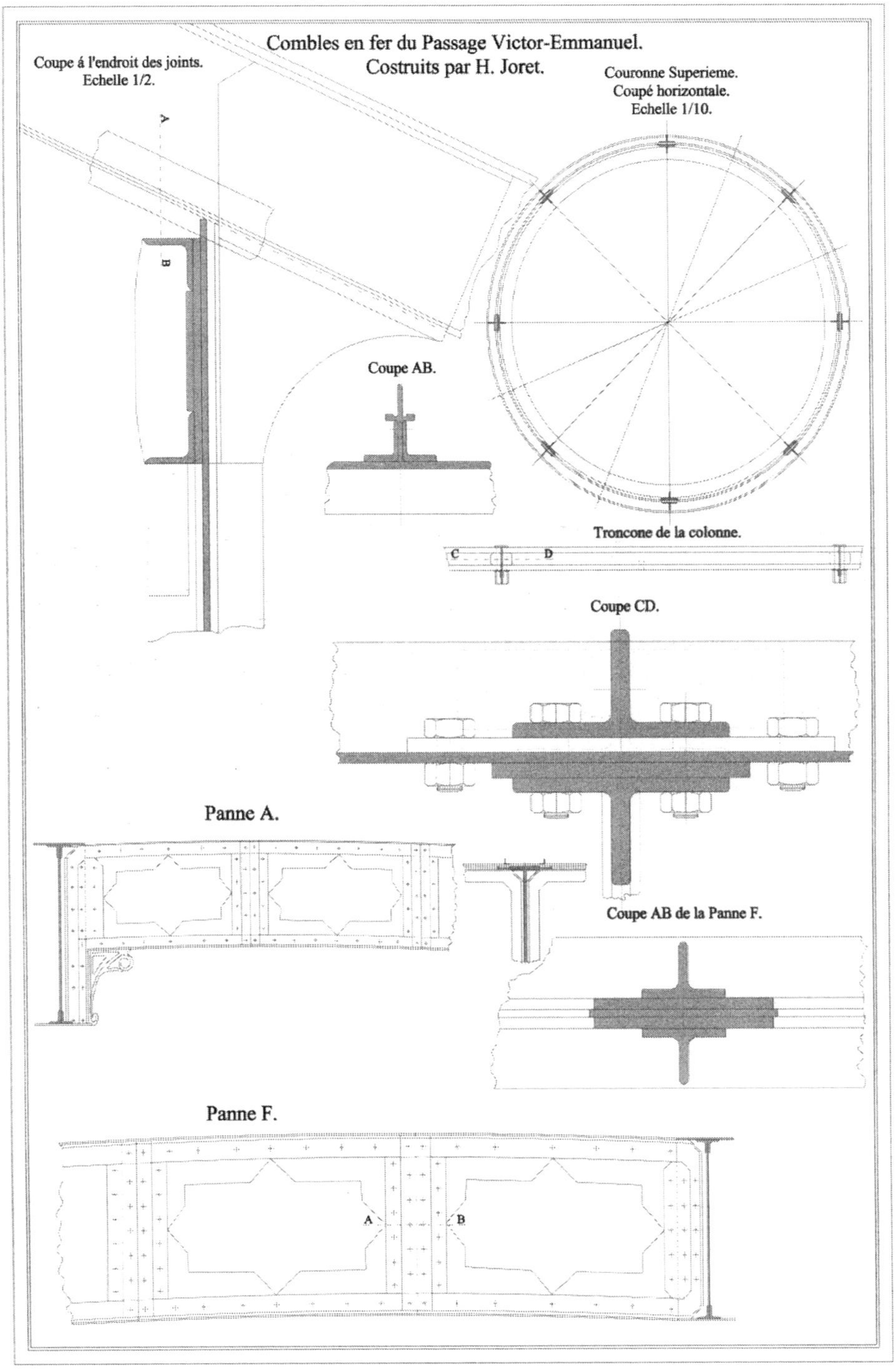

COMBLES EN FER

Pl. № 4

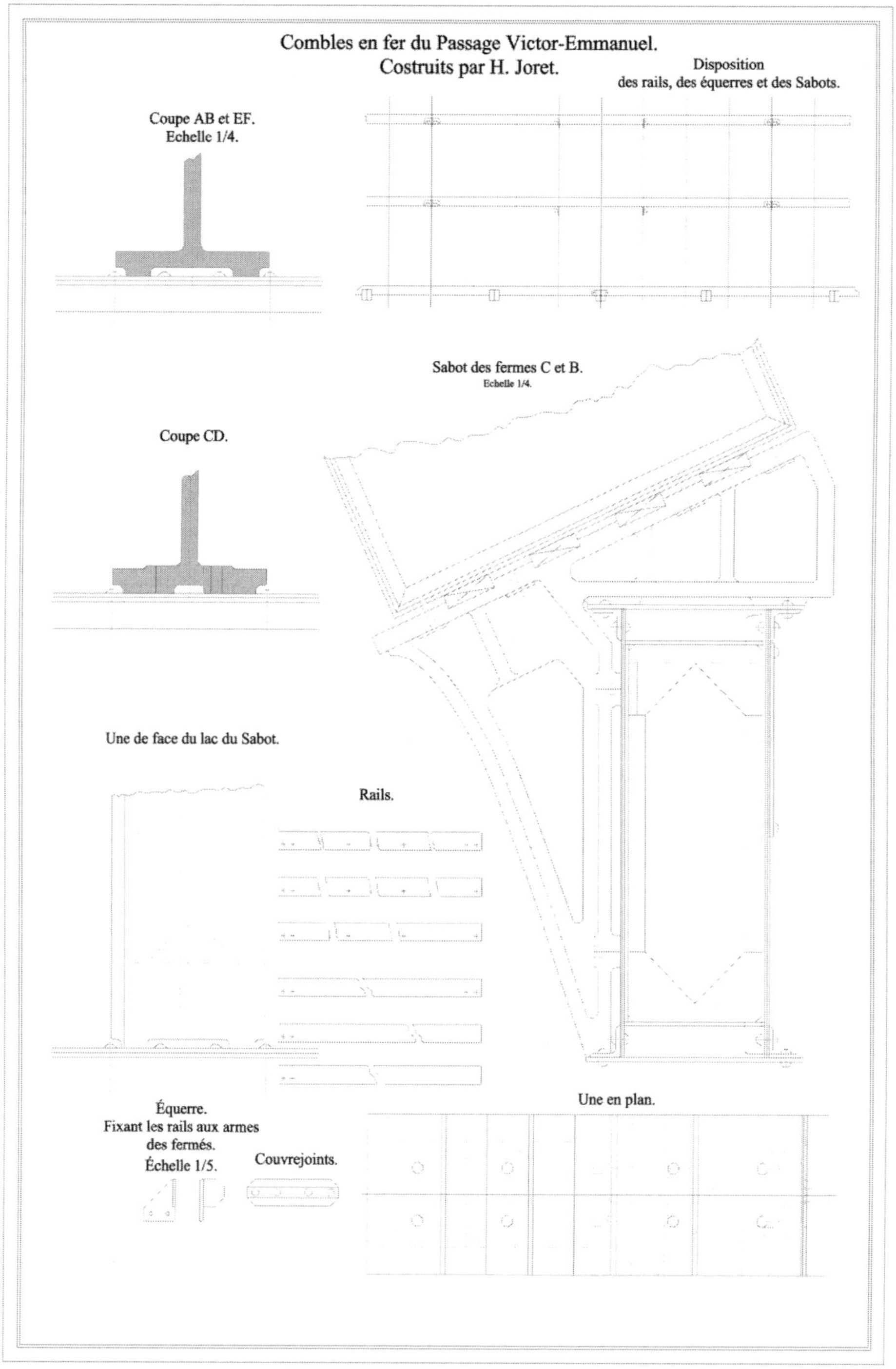

COMBLES EN FER

Pl. № 5

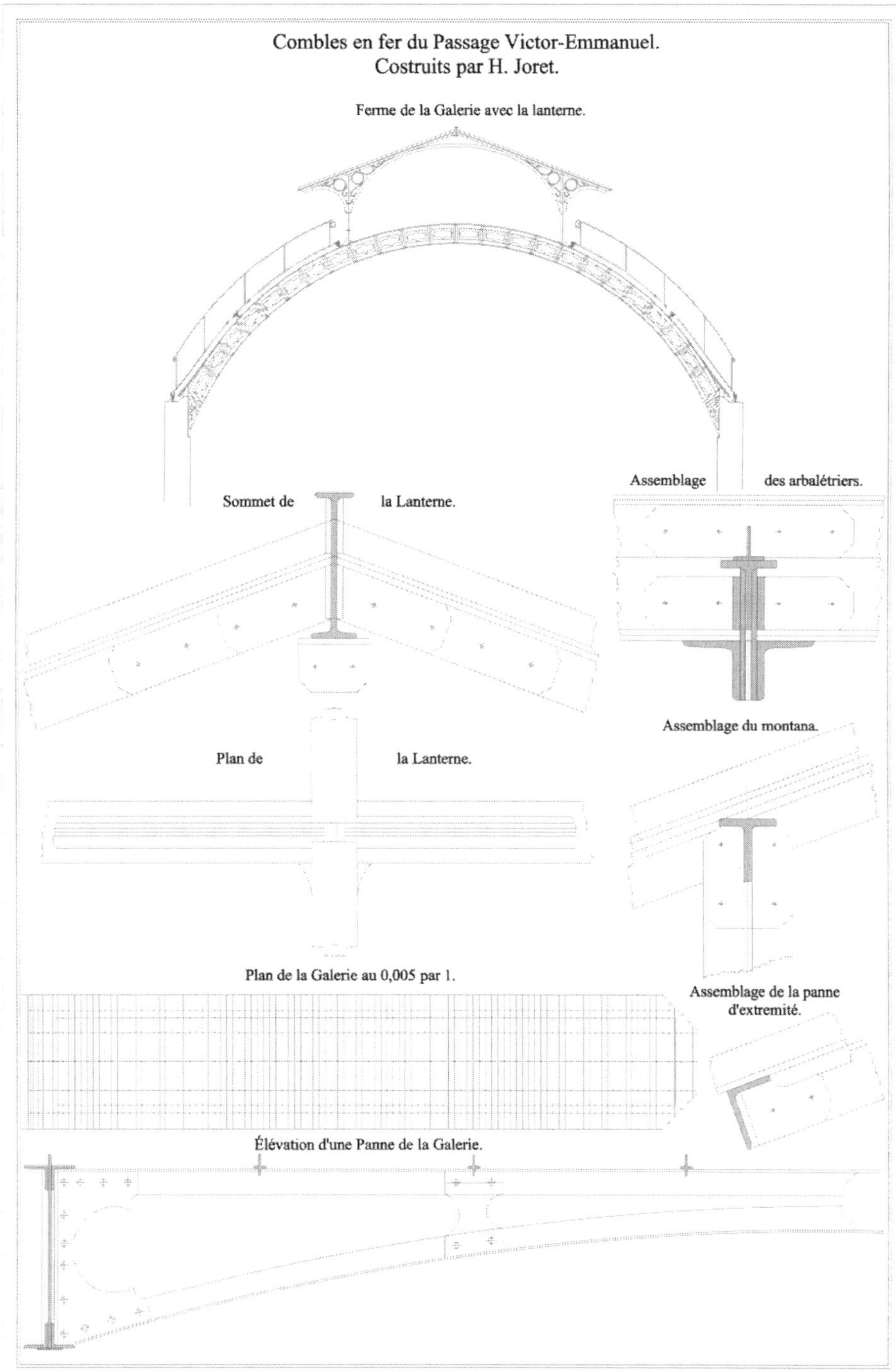

Acknowledgements

Very special thanks to Prof. Sara Wermiel for the thorough editing of the paper.

References

[1] J. F. Geist, *Arcades: The History of a Building Type*, Cambridge, Massachusetts: MIT Press, 1985. pp. 59-62.
[2] Geist, *Arcades*, (Note 1), p. 12; P. de Moncan, *Les passages couverts en Europe*, Paris: Les Editions du Mécène, 2003. p. 13; P. de Moncan, *Le passage couvert. Une trajectoire patrimoniale européenne,* Paris: Les Editions du Mécène, 2003. p. 21.
[3] Geist, *Arcades*, (Note 1) pp. 74-76.
[4] R. Jodice, *L'architettura del ferro. L'Italia, 1796-1914*, Roma: Bulzoni, 1985. p. 15
[5] Geist, *Arcades*, (Note 1) p. 74.
[6] O. Selvafolta, 'La Galleria Vittorio Emanuele' in A. Castellano, O. Selvafolta, (Eds) *Aspetti e problemi di storia edilizia*, Milan: Electa, 1983. p. 221.
[7] 'La copertura della Galleria di Vittorio Emanuele di Milano' in *L'architettura del ferro: raccolta di motivi per costruzioni civili, ferroviarie ed artistiche compilata col concorso dei migliori ingegneri, architetti e costruttori italiani*, Milan: Prem. Litog. e Tipog. degli ingegneri Milano, 1885; A. F. Jorini, 'La cupola di Vittorio Emanuele', *L'Edilizia moderna*, vol. 2, 1892. p. 6.
[8] N. Pevsner, *A History of Building Types,* Princeton, N.J.: Princeton University Press, 1976. p. 265; H.-R. Hitchcock, *Architecture: Nineteenth and Twentieth Centuries,* Harmondsworth: Penguin Books, 1985. pp. 75, 120, 146; M. Mackeit, *The History and Conservation of Shopping Arcades*, London, New York: Mansell, 1986. pp. 40-43.
[9] Selvafolta, 'La Galleria', (Note 6); L. Gioeni, *L'affaire Mengoni: la Piazza Duomo e la Galleria Vittorio Emanuele di Milano: i concorsi, la realizzazione, i restauri*, Milan: Guerini a Associati, 1995.
[10] G. Chizzolini & F. Poggi, 'Piazza del Duomo e Galleria Vittorio Emanuele' in AA. VV., *Milano tecnica dal 1859 al 1884*, 1885. pp. 211–212.
[11] 'Parte II^{da} che comprende i quattro bracci della Galleria. Lavori in ferro', N° 52, *Perizia della Copertura in ferri e vetri della Galleria Vittorio Emanuele* (kept at Archivio Storico Civico di Milano, Fondo Piano Regolatore, folder 1382, file 2).
[12] 'Ferri speciali di sicurezza', N° 72, *Perizia della Copertura*, (Note 11).
[13] 'Materiali impiegati', *Perizia della Copertura*, (Note 11).
[14] A. Vallatta, *Relazione sullo stato delle strutture in ferro della copertura della Galleria Vittorio Emanuele II*, Milan: Municipality of Milan, 1981. pp. 14-15.
[15] Ibid.;'Parte II^{da} che comprende i quattro bracci della Galleria. Lavori in ferro', N° 58, 57, *Perizia della Copertura*, (Note 11).
[16] 'Parte II^{da} che comprende i quattro bracci della Galleria. Lavori in ferro', N° 54-56, *Perizia della Copertura*, (Note 11).
[17] Vallatta, *Relazione*, (Note 14) p. 19.
[18] Jodice, *L'architettura*, (Note 4) p. 274.
[19] 'La copertura', (Note 7).
[20] Chizzolini & Poggi, 'Piazza del Duomo', (Note 10) p. 216.
[21] 'La copertura', (Note 7) Table VI.
[22] *Perizia della Copertura*, (Note 11) Table VIII.
[23] Chizzolini & Poggi, 'Piazza del Duomo', (Note 10) p. 212.

a copertura', (Note 7) Table V.
id.
a copertura', (Note 7) Table IV.
erizia della Copertura, (Note 11) Table XI.
Chizzolini & Poggi, 'Piazza del Duomo', (Note 10), Table XIV; 'La copertura', (Note 7) Table IV.
] I. Stoyanova, I. Wouters & I. Bertels, 'Glazed Wrought-Iron Arcades: Building Technologies and Spatial Effects', *Construction History*, Vol. 30, No. 2, 2015. pp. 45-65.
0] 'La copertura', (Note 7).
31] Stoyanova, Wouters & Bertels, 'Glazed', (Note 29) p. 56.
[32] I. Stoyanova, 'Gallery Vittorio Emanuele II in Milan: The Iron-Glass Cover: Innovation, Conservation, Continuity' (Ph.D. thesis, Polytechnic University of Milan, 2015), pp. 159-169.
[33] 'La copertura', (Note 7) Table I.
[34] 'Apprezzamento delle opere addizionali', *Perizia della Copertura*, (Note 11).
[35] 'Premessa', *Perizia della Copertura*, (Note 11).
[36] I. Stoyanova, 'Promoting a Nineteenth-century Italian Technology: the Crystal Skies of the Milanese Gallery Vittorio Emanuele II' in M. Boriani, L. Toniolo & G. Guidi, (Eds) *Built Heritage: Monitoring Conservation Management*, Milan: Springer, 2014. pp. 257-270.
[37] Selvafolta, *La Galleria*, (Note 6) p. 261.
[38] Stoyanova, Wouters & Bertels, 'Glazed', (Note 29) pp. 45-65.
[39] Ibid.; Stoyanova, 'Gallery', (Note 32) pp.130-136.
[40] 'La copertura', (Note 7); Jorini, 'La cupola', (Note 7) p. 6.
[41] 'Armatura dell'Ottagono', N° 13, *Perizia della Copertura,* (Note 11).
[42] Chizzolini & Poggi, 'Piazza del Duomo', (Note 10), p. 217.
[43] 'Nozioni sulla tettoia', *Perizia della Copertura*, (Note 11).
[44] 'Parte VII^{a}. Lavori in piombo', N° 181, *Perizia della Copertura*, (Note 11).
[45] R. McGrath & A. C. Frost, *Glass in Architecture and Decoration*, London: English Heritage, 1961. p. 572.
[46] Stoyanova, 'Gallery', (Note 32) p. 135.
[47] "Parte VI^{a}. Lavori in zinco", N° 173, *Perizia della Copertura*, (Note 11).
[48] "Parte III^{a}. Lavori d'aggiunte diverse in ferro specialmente annesse alla cupola dell'Ottagono" and "Parte III^{a}. Lavori d'aggiunte diverse in ferro specialmente annesse ai quattro bracci della Galleria", *Perizia della Copertura*, (Note 11).
[49] 'La copertura', (Note 7) Table I.
[50] Ibid.
[51] Ibid.
[52] Stoyanova, 'Gallery', (Note 32) p. 138.

Education for construction: engineering education in Trinity College Dublin in the 1840s

Ronald Cox and Dermot O'Dwyer
Department of Civil, Structural & Environmental Engineering, Trinity College Dublin

Introduction

The School of Engineering in Trinity College Dublin (TCD) is among the oldest in the English-speaking world [1]. Although this paper deals specifically with engineering education in TCD it can be taken to be representative of the moves across the UK in the middle of the nineteenth century to provide university courses in engineering. These developments were part of a general movement of the profession away from the master and apprentice system of tuition that had previously been the model in the UK, resulting in the gradual closing of the gap between the analytical treatment given to engineering in continental Europe and engineering practice in the UK [2].

Mathematics in Trinity College Dublin in the nineteenth century

Although TCD did not have a particularly strong reputation in the area of mathematics at the start of the nineteenth century, the situation was markedly different by the 1840s. This reform was begun by Bartholomew Lloyd following his appointment to the Erasmus Smith Chair of Mathematics in 1813. Bartholomew Lloyd broke from the fluxions tradition that had held back mathematics in the United Kingdom and introduced the analytical methods that had been developed on the continent. Dionysus Lardner, a TCD alumnus, described this sea change in the preface of his *Elements of the Theory of Central Forces*, published in 1820, as *"... the study of mathematics has leaped a chasm of 100 years"* [3].

John Brinkley, Professor of Astronomy, was also an able mathematician and these professors were followed closely in TCD by William Rowan Hamilton, Humphrey Lloyd and James McCullagh, mathematicians who worked in the areas of mechanics and optics [4]. Hamilton was famously appointed Professor of Astronomy in 1827 at the age of twenty-two, before he had graduated. Humphrey Lloyd, Bartholomew Lloyd's son, was appointed to the Erasmus Smith Chair of Natural and Experimental Philosophy in 1831 and James MacCullagh was appointed Professor of Mathematics in 1835. Mathematics in TCD was ahead of Cambridge at this time in part because the reformers were appointed to chairs relatively young [4].

Humphrey Lloyd instigated the establishment of the School of Engineering in TCD in 1841. His deep interest in engineering is clear from his *Praelection on the studies connected with the school of engineering* [5], delivered on the occasion of the opening of the School of Engineering in 1841. In his address he details the development of engineering science, primarily citing research carried out on the continent. He is also passionate about steam engines and their application. It seems clear that Bartholomew Lloyd, Humphrey's father and the then Provost of TCD, must have favoured the idea. Earlier in his career, in 1822, Bartholomew Lloyd had moved from the Erasmus Smith Chair of Mathematics to the Erasmus Smith Chair of Natural and Experimental Philosophy. Bartholomew Lloyd's text *An Elementary Treatise of Mechanical Philosophy* covers both the theory and the application of mechanics [6]. This treatise includes sections on the equilibrium of roofs, arches and domes, considers framed structures and includes the analysis of statically determinate trusses. The work also contains a section on the elastic curve, the term used to describe the deflection of a statically determinate beam. Lloyd's description of how a king-post truss functions is a model of clarity. His comment that the king-post truss form provides a means of spanning most spaces perhaps explains why the widespread application of static analysis to roof trusses did not develop until the construction of large-span railway passenger sheds provided the requirement.

The TCD School of Engineering

The original intention was to found a school for civil engineers and architects, but, like the then recently formed professional body, the Institution of Civil Engineers of Ireland (founded 1835), architecture was quickly dropped in order to pursue solely the requirements of the engineering profession.

The University Calendar for 1847 [8] stated that the School of Engineering (had been) established "*with a view to combining, as far as is practicable, the theoretical and practical instruction requisite for the Profession of Civil Engineering and of imparting to the Members of that profession the other advantages of academical education*".

The scientific basis of the course of education is highlighted by Humphrey Lloyd's comments on his research into the methods of teaching in the French *École Polytechnique* [1]:

> "...we shall, I believe spend part of the autumn in Paris. I mean to make myself up there in the French plan of instruction for Engineers, with a view to borrowing whatever will bear transportation...".

The course in civil engineering was initially of two years duration, being extended to three years in 1845. Entry to the engineering course was open to students who had completed the Junior Freshman (first year) Arts course in the university, which consisted of Mathematics, Mechanics, Latin and Greek.

At the beginning, the engineering course structure was as follows:

The first (or Junior) year consisted of Mathematics, taught by Thomas Luby, the Principles of Mechanics and Hydrostatics, taught by Andrew Searle Hart, and Chemistry & Geology, taught by James Apjohn. The Junior Year was designed to cover the basic principles with an orientation towards machines, materials, geology and mining.

Mathematics consisted mainly of geometry, plane and spherical trigonometry with practical applications, logarithms and the construction of tables. An effort was made to make the course practical by including formulae connected with machinery, instruments, surveying, etc. The principles of analytical geometry were included, as was the description of curves.

The Mechanics course was comprehensive for the time. It included the laws of motion, equilibrium of forces, moments, funicular polygon, centre of gravity, the catenary, construction of arches and domes, virtual velocities, Kepler's laws, moment of inertia, the pendulum, collision of bodies, laws of small oscillations and applications to machines in motion. There was also a section on hydrostatics and pneumatics.

The Chemistry course consisted of two main parts – general and applied chemistry. The latter was oriented towards what civil engineers needed to know and included topics such as water and its analysis, heat and combustion, distillation, quarrying and building materials and assaying and smelting of ores. The Geology section included topics under the heading of economic geology such as the relative value of different rocks as road materials, slates and fine clay bricks. Mineral veins and faults were also covered.

The second (or Senior) year consisted of Practical Mechanics, Heat & the Steam Engine, taught by Humphrey Lloyd, and Practical Engineering, taught by John Macneill, with assistance from Henry Laws Renny, who also taught Drawing and Surveying. [1]

A notebook [9], used by Thomas H Going, when a senior year student in 1848-49, has survived and indicates some of the topics covered by Professor Apjohn in his chemical laboratory course. These included studies of the properties of limestone, iron, lead, bituminous coal, and other minerals, such as quartz, zinc, manganese, and cobalt. The notebook also contains numerical examples, such as the method of finding the amount of super-elevation required on railway curves, the ratios of cohesive (tensile) to compressive force in wrought and cast iron. Ratios of widths of top and bottom flanges of girders, transverse strain, and the deflection of beams, cantilevered and simply supported, were covered, as were suspension bridges. The rules of perspective and the laying out of railway curves were also included.

Engineering Textbooks

A small specialist library was established for the use of students in the School of Engineering. This library was stocked partly by purchases, but also by the transfer of volumes from the Lending Collection of the university's main copyright library. Texts for students, written by members of staff, included Mathematics (Luby)[10], Mechanics (Hart)[11], and Hydrostatics (Hart)[12] and there were any number of texts available on the subjects of drawing, surveying and levelling.

In the Preface to Hart's *Elementary Treatise on Mechanics*, he explains that the application of mathematical analysis to the solution of mechanical problems was frequently beyond the reach of the student of the day, who is acquainted only with the elements of geometry. Hart goes on to say:

> "The difficulty of finding a treatise on Mechanics free from this inconvenience has long been felt in the University of Dublin, and had been brought more immediately under the notice of the Author by his connexion with the School of Engineering. In the hope of contributing to its removal, he has been induced to publish the following treatise, in which he has endeavoured, by means of simple geometrical constructions, to render the most important fundamental propositions easily understood by all classes of students".

In notes at the end of each chapter, Hart developed solutions using algebra and the calculus, and referred readers to Bartholomew Lloyd's more comprehensive text.

In the 1840s, the design, layout, construction, and operation of railways were rapidly becoming part of the engineering curriculum and the early students were fortunate to have access to the experience and wisdom of the School's first professor, Sir John Macneill (Fig. 1). Apart from George Semple's pioneering treatise on *Building in Water*, published in 1776 [13], there were few English language texts dealing with civil engineering, as distinct from military engineering.

With the increase in interest in railways, surveying texts began to include chapters on railway curves and earthworks and often claimed to be "*courses in civil engineering*", e.g. John Gregory's treatise of 1842-43, first published in Dublin [14]. On the title page of his treatise (Fig. 2), Gregory described himself as "*Resident Director of the College for Civil Engineering, Mining, and Agriculture in Ireland*".

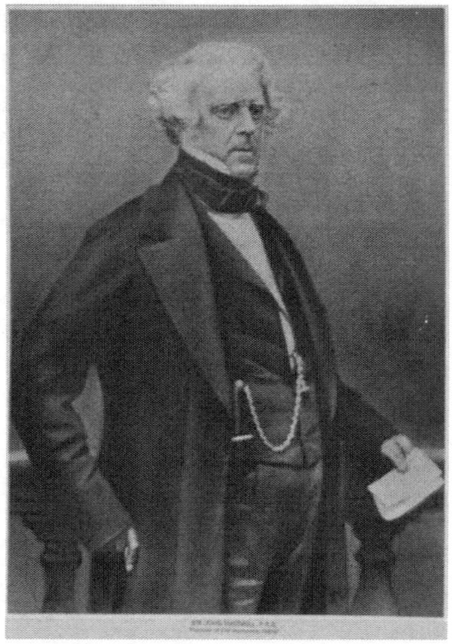

Figure 1. Sir John Macneill F.R.S., Professor of the Practice of Engineering 1842-52.

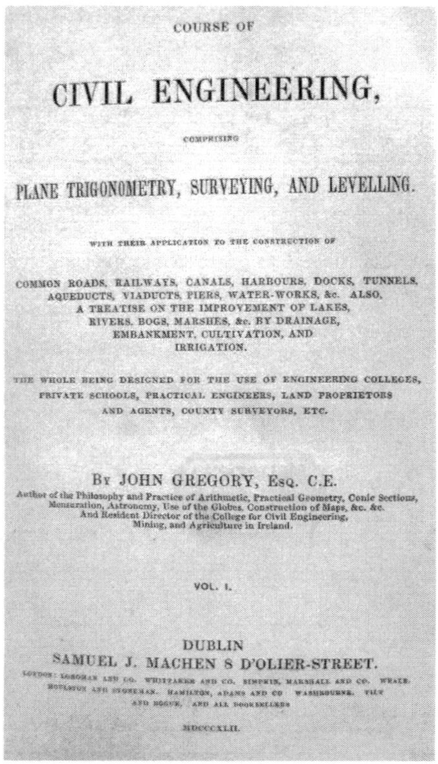

COURSE OF

CIVIL ENGINEERING,

COMPRISING

PLANE TRIGONOMETRY, SURVEYING, AND LEVELLING.

WITH THEIR APPLICATION TO THE CONSTRUCTION OF

COMMON ROADS, RAILWAYS, CANALS, HARBOURS, DOCKS, TUNNELS, AQUEDUCTS, VIADUCTS, PIERS, WATER-WORKS, &c. ALSO, A TREATISE ON THE IMPROVEMENT OF LAKES, RIVERS, BOGS, MARSHES, &c. BY DRAINAGE, EMBANKMENT, CULTIVATION, AND IRRIGATION.

THE WHOLE BEING DESIGNED FOR THE USE OF ENGINEERING COLLEGES, PRIVATE SCHOOLS, PRACTICAL ENGINEERS, LAND PROPRIETORS AND AGENTS, COUNTY SURVEYORS, ETC.

BY JOHN GREGORY, ESQ. C.E.

Author of the Philosophy and Practice of Arithmetic, Practical Geometry, Conic Sections, Mensuration, Astronomy, Use of the Globes, Construction of Maps, &c. &c. And Resident Director of the College for Civil Engineering, Mining, and Agriculture in Ireland.

VOL. I.

DUBLIN
SAMUEL J. MACHEN 8 D'OLIER-STREET.

LONDON: LONGMAN AND CO. WHITTAKER AND CO. SIMPKIN, MARSHALL AND CO. WEALE. HOULSTON AND STONEMAN. HAMILTON, ADAMS AND CO WASHBOURNE. TILT AND BOGUE. AND ALL BOOKSELLERS

MDCCCXLII.

Figure 2. Title page of John Gregory's Course of Civil Engineering.

This was at the time when the TCD School of Civil Engineering was being established. Gregory may have had some connection with TCD because in the Preface to his book he refers to "*our University extending the sphere of its usefulness by having recently established a professorship of Engineering...and a new College (sic) of Engineering...*" [14].

In dealing with survey topics, such as trigonometrical surveying, Gregory refers to the survey of Ireland, which was then being carried out under the direction of the military engineer, Colonel Colby. Railway surveying included descriptions of plans and sections and, in particular the determination of the elevation of the outer rail of a railway track curved in plan. This topic appears on the examination paper for 1843, the question using a 5ft railway gauge as the Irish gauge had yet to be standardised at 5 feet 3 inches [15]. Much space in Gregory's book was taken up with such topics as the drainage of bogs (an essential requirement for engineers working in Ireland), but there was nothing on structures or buildings. This seems strange to a modern engineer, given that Gregory was by profession a mathematician who might be expected to gain satisfaction from structural analysis. However, at the time building was regarded as the preserve of architects and builders, whereas Civil Engineering was generally seen to be concerned with infrastructure. Robert V. Dixon made this point on his retirement in 1854 in *Scientific Training for Practical Pursuits: A Farewell Address to the Students of the School of Engineering, Trinity College, Dublin* [16].

The many early nineteenth century books on surveying and levelling (plane and trigonometrical) naturally included descriptions of instruments and methods of surveying, the most used being the chain (for distance), the theodolite (for direction) and the level (for elevation). Practical surveying classes were always a feature of civil engineering courses.

Two other books with the title *A Course in Civil Engineering* that appeared around the time the School was established were made available to the early students. One of these was Mahan's *An Elementary Course of Civil Engineering*, which was published in Glasgow, and edited by Professor Barlow of the Royal Military Academy, Woolwich [17]. Dennis Hart Mahan was a Professor of Military and Civil Engineering in the U.S. Military Academy. He refers to the only other work (to his knowledge) being that of the French engineer, Joseph Matthieu Sganzin, the third edition of whose *Cours de Constructions* was translated into English and published by Hilliard Gray & Co. of Boston, Mass. in 1837 [18]. It treats of materials, roads, railroads, viaducts, bridges, canals, aqueducts, and marine works and is accompanied by a large atlas containing extensive illustrations of construction methods. A copy held by the university library, which is the 4th edition in French [19], would no doubt have provided a mine of information for the engineering students of the day (Fig. 3).

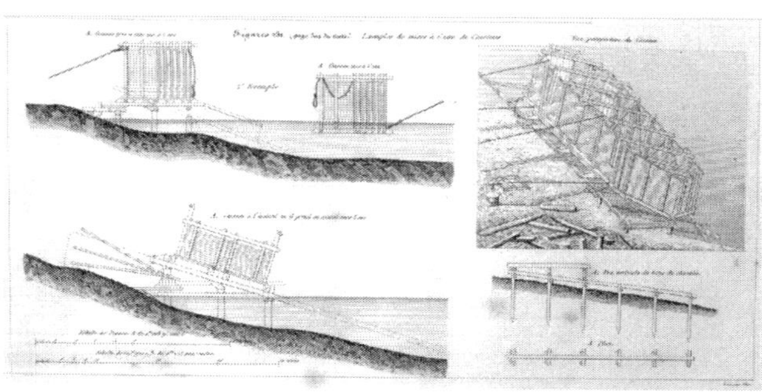

Figure 3. A detail from Cours de Constructions [19] showing the launch of a cassion.

John Millington (an English professor of civil engineering at William & Mary College in Virginia, USA) published in 1839 *Elements of Civil Engineering*, but again this contains no structural analysis, apart from the treatment of masonry arches and a reference to the use of iron links in suspension chains, such as used by Telford at Menai [20].

The computation and setting out of masonry arches, in particular the more complicated nature of skewed arches, was an important part of the curriculum and students were supported by such texts as George Watson Buck's *Oblique Bridges* [21], published in 1839. The School of Engineering archive contains a heavily used and annotated copy, which was obviously a recommended text for students (a second edition was published in 1857). Figure 4 illustrates the artistic standard achieved by one student for whom the subject of oblique bridges appears to have attracted his attention, albeit if only to record the lecturer in full flight, if not the spelling of the word oblique. On the reverse of one of the plates, a student wrote a stanza of a poem on "learning", which was signed HHN. On checking the alumni registers, it turns out that HHN received his diploma in 1855 and is recorded as Horatio Horace Nelson!

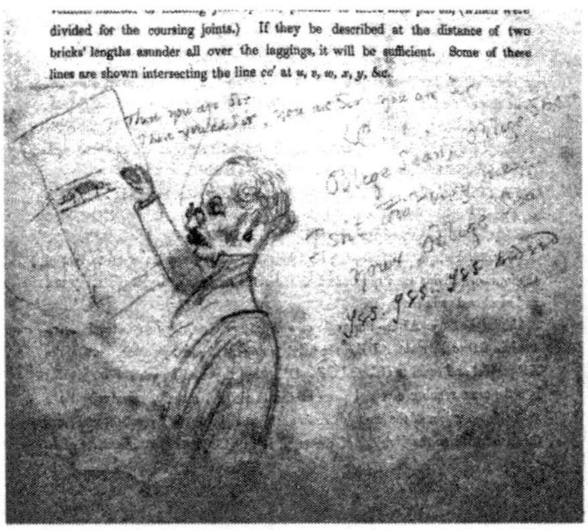

Figure 4. Artistic efforts of an early engineering student.

Henry Parnell's *A Treatise on Roads* [22], published in 1833, provided a comprehensive overview of their construction. Parnell, in an introductory chapter, quoted liberally from a contemporary French encyclopedia referring to the École des Ponts et Chaussées under Perronet as the main driving force in the development of road engineering. Parnell goes into considerable detail regarding the principles on which roads should be constructed, citing examples of plans and specifications used by Telford on the Holyhead Road, but also including a specification for "*forming a road over a peat bog in Ireland*". Macneill had worked for Telford and would have been very familiar with Parnell's book, including as it did an appendix describing Macneill's road indicator for ascertaining the power required to draw a carriage over a line of road, and for comparing the relative merits of different road surfaces. Telford, in one of his many reports to parliament [23] stated that "*I consider Mr Macneill's invention, for practical purposes on a large scale, one of the most valuable that has been lately given to the public*".

Parnell dealt with the formation of cuttings and embankments, but provided little, if any, guidance as to the numerical design of retaining walls and other structures. Again, he cited Macneill's tables for the calculation of the volumes of earthworks, such as cuttings and embankments [24]. Proper drainage was, of course, considered vital in road formations as was the foundation supporting the carriageway. However, the building of all but small masonry bridges was considered to be outside the scope of the treatise. There were useful sections on road materials, instruments, legislation, contracts, and maintenance.

Examinations

The engineering syllabuses, textbooks and student notes give much information on the topics covered by engineering students. The final primary evidence comprises the examination papers. Not all the engineering exam papers have survived but in addition to the papers sat by the engineers there are some mechanics papers from this time that indicate the standards achieved by students.

The 1840 Humphrey Lloyd Exam in mechanics survives and question seven from this paper gives an indication of the level of analysis expected of the students:

> "7. Deduce the differential equation of the curve, in which a body descending by the force of gravity presses equally against the curve in all points."

This question shows that the development and manipulation of differential equations was on the mechanics curriculum at the time the engineering school was founded.

Although this paper predates the foundation of the school it is clear that TCD, in common with other UK universities were already starting to address engineering education. In the case of TCD this is clear from Lloyd's 1826 treatise on mechanics. In a similar manner William Whewell's *The Mechanics of Engineering* [25], which was intended for instructing engineering students, was published before Cambridge, where Wheeler was a lecturer, had established an engineering school. The fact that TCD and other universities were effectively training future engineers before the establishment of formal schools is demonstrated by students like William Bindon Blood, who graduated from the University of Dublin in 1839, having studied Mathematics and Physics. Blood subsequently worked under I.K. Brunel before being appointed Professor of Civil Engineering in Queen's University Galway in 1850 [23]. Blood's paper to the ICE in 1851 shows a high level of analytical training [26].

The earliest TCD engineering examination papers that survive date from 1843, the year the first engineering students graduated. These papers include the *Physics* paper, the *Chemistry and Geology* paper and the *Practical Engineering* paper. These exams are notable for the applied nature of the questions and for the fact that they show evidence that the latest technical developments were being examined.

Physics paper

The 1843 Physics paper for the engineers was published in the University Calendar for 1844 [8]. The Calendar carried a note that the students were also examined in mathematics and in mechanics, both theoretical and practical. The questions asked on the general mechanics papers from this period are remarkably similar to the questions a current maths-physics student would be expected to solve. The physics paper was clearly designed for the engineering students. This can be deduced from the fact that a large proportion of the questions are of direct engineering relevance. For example, there are questions on the empirical formulae of Tredgold and Navier on steam, a question of the principal improvements to the steam engine introduced by Watt and a question on the method of transforming reciprocal motion into circular motion. The most interesting aspect of the paper is how up-to-date it was for the time. There was a question on the temperature compensating bars used in the ordnance survey and a particularly interesting question concerning railway gradients, namely:

> "21. What is the effect of the air's resistance, as affecting railway gradients?"

In 1838, when he detailed the factors that limited railway gradients, Peter Barlow senior, the professor of Mathematics in Woolwich, did not consider wind resistance as an important factor [27]. However, within a few years this accepted view had changed. In his seventh edition of *The steam engine explained ...etc.* , published in 1840, Dionysus Lardner commented that air resistance had begun to be considered only recently and he detailed a series of experiments he had performed to assess its effect. Lardner commented that this recent work had not been contained in earlier editions of his book [28].

Chemistry and Geology

The Chemistry and Geology examination was quite extensive, comprising a total of seventy-eight questions. Approximately a quarter of the questions are classic questions from the fields of chemistry or geology. The rest have a clear focus on engineering applications, thus there are a number of questions relating to hydraulic limes, a number of questions on the properties of iron and steel and other questions related to building materials and the improvement of soil. For example:

> "22. What is the cause of the setting of common, and of hydraulic mortar?"
>
> "52. What are the differences in chemical constitution of malleable iron, steel and pig iron?"
>
> "65. What qualities should be found in a good stone for metalling roads? and what rocks are found to possess these in the highest degree?"

Interestingly John Gregory's civil engineering text from the same period also includes a section on methods of improving soil.

Practical Engineering

The role of John Macneill must not be forgotten. Lloyd and the other lecturers were clearly very mathematically able, but they would not have had Macneill's practical experience [29].

The description *Practical Engineering* describes the content of this exam very accurately. If the paper, which is contained in an appendix, is read without any knowledge of the theoretical examinations in mathematics, mechanics, physics and chemistry that the students also sat one might underestimate the level of their analytical training, because the level of analytical difficulty in the practical engineering exam is moderate. Unfortunately, although copies of the general mechanics papers from this time survive, the papers taken by engineering students do not. The students studied mechanics texts written by their lecturers and, as mentioned previously, these give a good overview of the material they studied. However, the practical engineering exam shows the level of practical technical competence that engineering students were expected to have achieved. This exam is where Macneill's influence on the course of study can clearly be seen.

The examination paper comprised two sections. The first set of 71 questions formed the basis of a *viva voce* and the second set comprised 11 "*Questions for Calculation...*". The first 21 questions in the *viva voce* section and the first four questions requiring calculation where concerned with survey work. The remaining questions relate to construction and examine the students' knowledge of engineering practice, construction materials and structural design. The fact that some questions relating to arches and retaining walls are in the *viva voce* section indicates that engineering students were expected to be familiar with "rules of thumb". Thus questions 32, 33 and 54 from the *viva voce* section required students to give suitable dimensions for arches and a retaining wall without calculation while questions 5 and 6 from the calculation section, which also treat arches and retaining walls, clearly required solutions based on an analysis of the mechanics of each problem.

On the particular question of structural analysis, it is clear that students were expected to be able to calculate the safe load for beams in bending and to calculate the deflection of a cantilever. Question 41 from the *viva voce* section and question 8 from the calculation section relate to cast iron and its use in structures. These questions are of particular interest when one realises that they predate the collapse of Robert Stephenson's cast-iron railway bridge over the river Dee and the subsequent inquiry into the use of iron in railway structures [30].

Structural Analysis in 1840s

The 1843 practical examination demonstrates that students were expected to be able to analyse the bending of statically determinate beams. Student notebooks from the same period confirm this. However, the question of whether these early engineering students had any exposure to the analysis of statically indeterminate structures is worth considering. There are three reasons for exploring the question despite the lack of any reference to indeterminate beams in the surviving examination papers. Firstly, in 1836 John Macneill had published an English translation of Navier's book on Railways [31], thus it is highly likely that he would have been familiar with Navier's *Leçons* [32]. Particularly, as Macneill's experimental work on the resistance of barges [33] and his introduction of wrought-iron lattice railway girders [34] show he was interested in the theoretical aspects of engineering. Navier's text contains the earliest analysis of statically indeterminate trusses and of continuous beams. Moseley produced the first English presentation of Navier's methods in 1843 [35] but at this time there is clear evidence that engineering practice was running in parallel with or in advance of published theoretical work. This is perhaps best illustrated by the fact that the next significant work on continuous beams was contained in Clark's account of construction of the Britannia Bridge, published in 1850 [36, 37].

In 1846, at about the same time as the construction of the Britannia Bridge, Macneill first presented a scheme for a three-span continuous lattice girder to span the river Boyne at Drogheda (Fig. 5) [38].

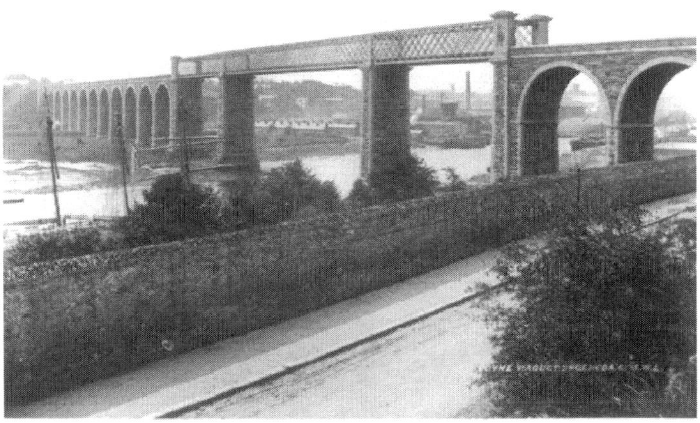

Figure 5. The original Boyne Viaduct [Courtesy of the National Library of Ireland].

This viaduct was on a very large scale: the two side spans were of 141 feet (43 m) and the central span was of 267 feet (81.4 m). Macneill had first applied the lattice girder form in the construction of wrought-iron railway bridges in the 1840s.

Two other notable TCD engineering alumni were connected with the design and execution of the Boyne viaduct, James Barton and Bindon Blood Stoney. Barton was a member of the first class to graduate from the School of Engineering in 1843 and he later presented a detailed paper on the calculation of the forces in the diagonal members of lattice girders to the Institution of Civil Engineers in London in 1855 [39]. Bindon Blood Stoney, who would later write "*The Theory of Strains in Girders and Similar Structures...*" [40], and which would become the standard reference on girder design, was an engineering alumnus from TCD in 1850. Stoney, employed as Resident Engineer for the Boyne Viaduct under Barton, carried out experimental tests on lattice girders [41] and undertook many of the detailed calculations. Barton's paper to the ICE concentrated primarily on the fact that the bridge had been designed such that the sizes of the members had been selected in proportion with the loads they carried. The paper describes testing during construction where the true positions of the points of inflection of the three-span continuous girders were compared against the calculated positions. Barton suggests in the paper that such calculations were well understood.

Unfortunately James Barton and Sir John Macneill fell out publically over where the credit for the design of the bridge should rest [38]. One result of this dispute was the publication of much of the correspondence between Macneill and Barton. This correspondence makes it clear that A.S. Hart, who lectured mechanics to the engineering students, had been involved in checking the calculations for the Boyne Viaduct.

Conclusion

In his 1854 farewell address to the students of the School of Engineering, Trinity College Dublin, Rev. Robert V. Dixon extolled the benefits to an engineer of a university education at some length. However, buried deep in his address is the following pragmatic appraisal:

> "... Of two engineers, one who comprehends the equilibrium of structures, and the action of material forces, must be a more able designer than one who merely works by empirical rules."

Dixon was reflecting on the fact that engineering was in transition. Many practicing engineers had learned their profession by working under the tutelage of established engineers; however, the benefits of a formal education were becoming clear. Sources concerning the engineering syllabus, textbooks, student note books and engineering examinations in TCD in the 1840s give a good indication of the material that students studied, and of the emphasis on ensuring that the material could be put to practical use. The examination papers indicate clear parallels between early engineering practice and current practice.

The level of mechanics taught in TCD in the 1840s, when taken in conjunction with the application of mechanics to real-world problems, and the evidence that the first professor and the first graduate were designing and constructing continuous statically indeterminate girders, provides additional insight into the early analysis of statically indeterminate structures.

The material presented all relates to engineering in TCD. However, Ireland at the time was part of the UK and Irish and English engineers worked in both countries and were members of the same professional organisations. Therefore the practice in TCD was probably mirrored by the early engineering schools, such as those being established in London, Glasgow and Durham.

Appendix

Practical Engineering
Professor Macneill and Mr. Renny.

1. How would you proceed to lay down a plan from a survey made by the chain alone? and how from a survey made by the chain and theodolite?
2. What scale do you consider the best for laying down a plan of an estate, a parish, a townland, a road, a railway, or a canal?
3. In a section of a turnpike road, what scales would you employ for the longitudinal distances and vertical heights? and what scales for a railway or canal?
4. How would you represent elevations of mountains, hills &c., on a plan?
5. How would you proceed to make a chart on Mercator's projection? and what is the use of this projection?
6. How would you proceed to survey a road actually constructed?
7. How would you proceed to survey a town?
8. How would you proceed to survey an estate or parish?
9. How would you calculate the superficial contents of such a survey, viz. of an estate or parish?
10. How do you determine the true meridian, so as to ascertain the magnetic variation?
11. How would you proceed to survey a bay or harbour?
12. What precautions would you take to ascertain the state of the tides at the moment of taking the soundings?
13. How do you adjust the Y level, Troughton's level, and Gravatts' level?
14. Where is it necessary to make allowance for the curvature of the earth–and what is the amount of such allowance?
15. How do you adjust the theodolite?
16. How do you take a section with the theodolite?
17. How do you take a section by the barometer?
18. How would you make a survey for a new line of road?
19. How would you make a survey for a railway?
20. What particular circumstances ought to be noticed, in making a survey for a canal?
21. How would you lay out a turnpike road, preparatory to commencing the work?
22. What dimensions would you allow for the carriage-way, the foot-path, side drains, and fences?
23. How would you form the roadway, before the materials were put on it?
24. What description of materials would you prefer for a turnpike road?
25. How would you distribute the materials, and what thickness of earth would you put on?
26. What precautions would you take to secure a good drainage?
27. What curve would you give to the surface of the carriage way?
28. How would you proceed to form a road through a bog?
29. What declivity would you consider desirable for a turn-pike road?
30. How would you determine the proper size of the culverts and bridges on a line of road?
31. What dimensions would you consider necessary for the cross-drains in a wet soil?
32. If you had to build a culvert of six feet span, having abutments five feet high, what rise would you give the arch? What thickness would you give the abutments and the arch, if the material to be employed were brick? And what would be the cost, if the bricks were 20s. per thousand, lime 1s. per barrel of thirty gallons, sand 2s. per cubic yard, bricklayers' wages 16s. per week, and labourers' 9s.?
33. If you had to build a bridge of rubble masonry of thirty feet span, the abutments of which are to be eight feet high, what thickness would you give to the abutments and to the arch, supposing it to be a circular segment rising one-third of the span?
34. If an embankment should be required on a line of road, what width would you give it at top, and what slopes according as the soil happened to be clay, loam, or sand? How would you fence it, and what precautions would you take in forming the embankment?
35. What slopes would you consider necessary in a clay cutting, and what in a bog?
36. How would you found a bridge or culvert in a bog?
37. What price, per cubic yard, should be allowed for cutting a road through lime-stone rock, and through green stone?
38. What precautions would you take to keep a road in repair, for a year after it was formed?
39. If a plan of an arch, with its piers and abutments, were given, how would you proceed to determine if it were in equilibrium or not?
40. How would you calculate the lateral thrust against the abutments?
41. What form of section do you consider best for a cast-iron girder of a bridge?
42. At what distance would you place cast-iron girders of a bridge from each other; and how would you fill the space between the girders?
43. How would you secure the cast-iron girders to the abutment?
44. If you had to construct a timber platform or road-way, meeting on stone piers, the space being thirty feet, what dimensions would you consider necessary for the main-beams, and how near to each other would you place them, the greatest weight to cross over the bridge being supposed to be ten tons? How thick would you make the sheeting?
45. What proportion of sand would you put to lime for rubble-work, in the abutments and piers of bridges, and what for the arch and inside work?
46. In what parts of the bridge would you introduce cement, and in what proportions would you mix sand with cement?
47. In making use of sand-stone and free-stone, what precautions would you take?
48. What are the different descriptions of brick in use in this country?
49. What bond would you employ in bridge-work, and in a retaining wall?
50. In what situations are timber bridges preferable to those of stone?
51. If you wished to put sheets under a beam of a bridge of fifty feet span, what length would you give to the sheets? at what angle from the face of the abutment would you place them? and how would you secure them to the abutments?
52. What description of timber would you prefer for a bridge, and what for piles and platforms?
53. In what situations are suspension bridges preferable to cast-iron bridges and stone bridges?
54. If you had to build a retaining wall of brick, twenty feet high, to support a bank of sand, how thick would you make

it at the bottom and at the top, and what form would you give to it? If the wall were to be of rubble-masonry, what dimensions would you give it? and if you introduced counter-ports, what dimensions would you give them?
55. What form do you consider best for a tunnel through clay soil?
56. What thickness would you give to the side walls and arch of a brick-tunnel in clay, the width being thirty feet?
57. How would you proceed to lay out a line of railway, preparatory to commencing the work?
58. How would you lay down the curves on the ground?
59. How would you lay out the lines of the top of the slopes in cuttings, and the bottoms of the slopes in embankments?
60. What thickness of ballasting would you consider necessary?
61. How would you determine the velocity of a river – the inclination of the surface and form of the channel being given?
62. How would you calculate the time of filling a lock from the upper level?
63. What angle do you consider the best for lock-gates?
64. How would you calculate the pressure against a lock-gate?
65. What slope would you give to the embankment of a dam or reservoir?
66. How would you guard against the water of the basin overflowing the banks?
67. How would you protect the slopes of a reservoir?
68. What form of wall would you adopt for a sea-wall?
69. What form of wall would you adopt for a dock-wall?
70. What thickness would you give to a dock-wall thirty feet high, built in a soft clay or mud?
71. How would you secure a dock-wall, if built on a sandy foundation?

Questions for Calculation in Practical Engineering.

1. Given the angle taken by a sextant, in a boat at sea, between two points on shore, slightly elevated, $= 60^\circ 40'$, also the angles of depression of the boat taken by theodolites from the points on shore $\begin{cases} 1^\circ 10' \\ 0^\circ 50' \end{cases}$, required, the horizontal angle at the boat between the two points.
2. Having, by means of a theodolite, observed, on the 7th October, 1843, at 9 hours A. M., in latitude and longitude nearly of Dublin College Observatory, the elevation of the Sun's centre to be $20^\circ 7'$, the magnetic bearing of Sun's centre $159^\circ 24'$, also the magnetic bearing of a distant steeple $45^\circ 6'$. Required the bearings with true meridian of the Sun's centre, and of the distant steeple? also the variation of the compass?
3. Given AC 30 miles, $\angle A$ $60^\circ 4' 10''$, $\angle B$ $49^\circ 46' 17''$, $\angle C$ $70^\circ 9' 42''$; required the error of observation of angles, if any? Required also the length of sides AB and BC, calculated on geodetic principles?
4. Having observed with barometer,

Height of mercury, top of hill, $= 28.924$ inches $\begin{cases} \text{Attached thermometer, } 60^\circ. \\ \text{Detached thermometer, } 54^\circ. \end{cases}$

Height of mercury, top of hill, $= 30.630$ inches $\begin{cases} \text{Attached thermometer, } 68^\circ. \\ \text{Detached thermometer, } 60^\circ. \end{cases}$

Required the height of the hill?
5. A segmental arch of 135°, having a span of 40 feet, thickness of masonry above the key stone 5 feet, depth of voussoirs 2 feet, the extrados a horizontal line, and height of abutments, 30 feet; required the thickness of abutment?
6. An embankment of earth of 24 feet height, having a natural slope of 45°, is to be supported by a retaining wall of masonry, having an inner batter of two feet: the specific gravity of masonry being to that of earth as 4:3, required the thickness of the wall?
7. The dimensions of a cutting are, base, 30 feet; slopes of sides, 2; base to 1, perpendicular; height of cutting at one end, 50 feet, at the other end 10 feet; the length of cutting 500 feet; required, the cubic yards of cutting, and verify the calculation by Mac Neil's table?
8. A case iron beam, resting on two props 20 feet distant, has to sustain 15 tons without injury to its elasticity, the breadth of the beam is to be one-fourth of the depth; required the depth of the beam?
9. A beam of Riga fir 6 inches deep by 4 inches broad, projects 10 feet from a wall, and supports a weight at its extremity; required the greatest weight it can bear without breaking? also the ultimate angle of deflection?
10. The radius of curvature of the curved part of a rail-road being 5000 feet, the velocity of carriages being 30 miles per hour, and distance between rails being 5 feet; required the height of outer rail to obviate centrifugal force?
11. Having to lay down points for a curved portion of a rail-road, the radius of curvature being 6000 feet, and chord of curved part being 1200; required the ordinates for chords, subtending at the centre of the circle, angles of 2° and 4°? Also, in employing Mr. Bourne's method, required the distance between the extremity of a chord 100 feet long, and the extremity of the adjacent chord produced to a distance of 100 feet?

References / Bibliography

[1] R.C. Cox, *Engineering at Trinity*, Dublin: School of Engineering, Trinity College Dublin, 1993.
[2] S. B. Hamilton, 'The French Civil Engineers of the Eighteenth Century.' *Transactions of the Newcomen Society*, 1941; 22(1), pp. 149-159.

[3] T.D. Spearman, 'Humphrey Lloyd 1800-1881', *Hermathena*, 130, 1981, pp. 37-52.

[4] R. Flood, 'Taking Root: Mathematics in Victorian Ireland', *Mathematics in Victorian Britian*, R. Flood, A. Rice and R. Wilson (Eds), Oxford: Oxford University Press, 2011.

[5] H. Lloyd, *Praelection on the studies connected with the School of Engineering delivered on the occasion of the opening of the School, the 15 November, 1841*, Dublin: Milliken, 1841.

[6] B. Lloyd, *An elementary treatise of mechanical philosophy: Written for the use of the under-graduate students of the University of Dublin*, Dublin: Richard Milliken, 1826.

[7] R. Cox (Ed.), *Engineering Ireland*, Cork, Collins Press, 2006.

[8] University of Dublin Calendars (1840-1853), Dublin: Milliken and Son, 1840-53.

[9] T.H. Going, Student notebook, Held in the School of Engineering Archive, Trinity College Dublin, 1849.

[10] J. Luby, *The Elements of Geometry in General terms ...etc.*, Dublin: J. J. Ekens, 1833.

[11] A. S. Hart, *An elementary treatise on mechanics*, Dublin: William Curry, Jun., and Company, 1844.

[12] A. S. Hart, *An elementary treatise on hydrostatics and hydrodynamics*, Dublin: William Curry, Jun., and Company, 1846.

[13] G. Semple, *A Treatise On Building in Water.: In Two Parts. Part I. Particularly Relative to the Repair and Re-building of Essex-Bridge, Dublin, ... Principally Addressed and Peculiarly Adapted to Young and Unexperienced Readers.* Dublin: printed for the author, by J. A. Husband, 1776.

[14] J. Gregory, *Course of civil engineering, comprising plane trigonometry, surveying and levelling*, London: Samuel J. Machen, 1846.

[15] B. Share, 'Railway Gauges', *Encyclopedia of Ireland*, Brian Lalor (Ed.), Gill & McMillan, Dublin, 2003, p. 912.

[16] R. V. Dixon, *Scientific Training for Practical Pursuits: A Farewell Address to the Students of the School of Engineering, Trinity College, Dublin*, Dublin: Hodges and Smith, 1854.

[17] D. H. Mahan, *An Elementary Course in Civil Engineering, edited by Professor Barlow*, Glasgow: Archibald Fullarton & Co., 1838.

[18] J.M. Sganzin, *An Elementary Course in Civil Engineering*, Boston: Hiliard, Gray and Company, 1837.

[19] J.M. Sganzin & M. Reibell, *Programme ou Résumé des Leçons Cours de Construction avec des applications tirées spécialement de l'art de l'ingénieur des Ponts et Chaussées*, Paris: Carilian – Goeury et Vor Dalmont, éditeurs, Library des Corps Royaux des Ponts et Chaussées et des Mines, 1839-1841.

[20] J. Millington, *Elements of Civil Engineering.* J.Dobson, Philadelphia: J. Dobson, 1839.

[21] G. W. Buck, *A practical and theoretical essay on oblique bridges*, London: John Weale, 1839.

[22] H. Parnell, *A treatise on roads: Wherein the principles on which roads should be made are explained and illustrated, by the plans, specifications, and contracts made use of by Thomas Telford, Esq. on the Holyhead Road*, London: Longman, Rees, Orme, Brown, Green & Longman, 1833.

[23] P. Cross-Rudkin and M. Chrimes (Eds), *Biographical Dictionary of Civil Engineers in Great Britain and Ireland, Vol 2: 1830-1890*, London: Thomas Telford Publishing, 2008.

[24] J. Macneill, *Tables for Calculating the Cubic Quantity of Earth Work in the Cuttings and Embankments of Canals, Railways, and Turnpike Roads*, London: Roake and Varty, 1833.

[25] W. Whewell, *The Mechanics of Engineering, Intended for use in Universities, and in Colleges of Engineering*, Cambridge: J. & J. Deighton, 1841.

[26] W. T. Doyne & W. B. Blood, 'An investigation of the strains upon the diagonals of lattice beams, with resulting formulae. (Including Appendix)', *Minutes of the Proceedings of the Institution of Civil Engineers*, 1852 11:1852, pp. 1-10.

[27] Irish Railway Commission. *First & Second Reports of the Commissioners Appointed to Inquire Into the Manner in Which Railway Communications Can Be Most Advantageously Promoted in Ireland ...*, London, Dublin: H.M.S.O., 1837-1838.

[28] D. Lardner, *The steam engine explained and illustrated with an account of its invention and progressive improvement, and its application to navigation and railways etc.* 7th Ed., London: Taylor and Walton, 1840.

[29] P.J. Geraghty, 'Sir John Macneill (1793–1880): King of the Irish Railways', *Transactions of the Newcomen Society*, 2008, 78:2, 207-234

[30] D. Yeomans, *How Structures Work, Design and Behaviour from Bridges to Buildings, 2nd Ed.*, Chichester: Wiley Blackwell, 2016.

[31] C. H. Navier, *On The Means Of Comparing The Respective Advantages Of Different Lines Of Railway; and on the use of locomotive engines, translated from the French by John MacNeill*, London: Roake & Varty, 1836.

[32] C. Navier, *Résumé des Leçons Données sur L'Application de la mécanique a L'establissement des constructions et des machines*, 2nd Ed., Paris: Chez Carilian-Goeury, 1833.

[33] J. B. Macneill, *Canal navigation.: On the resistance of water to the passage of boats upon canals, and other bodies of water, being the results of experiments*, London: Roake and Varty, 1833.

[34] G. W. Hemans, 'Lattice bridge over the Royal Canal Dublin and Drogheda Railway', *Transactions of the Institution of Civil Engineers of Ireland*, vol. 2, 1848, pp. 98-104.

[35] H. Moseley, *The mechanical principles of engineering and architecture*, London: Longman, Brown, Green & Longmans, 1843.

[36] T.M. Charlton, *A history of the theory of structures in the nineteenth century*. Cambridge: Cambridge U.P., 1982.

[37] E. Clark & R. Stephenson, *The Britannia and Conway tubular bridges: With general inquiries on beams and on the properties of materials used in construction*, London: Day and Son and John Weale, 1850.

[38]R. Cox, 'Bridging the gap: the Boyne Viaduct 1855 – conception, design and construction', *Ríocht na Midhe: Records of the Meath Archeological and Historical Society*, Vol. XVII, 2006, pp. 223-253.

[39] J. Barton, 'On the economic distribution of material in the sides or vertical portion, of wrought-iron beams. (Including Plate)', *Minutes of the Proceedings of the Institution of Civil Engineers*, 1855 14:1855, pp. 443-458.

[40] B. B. Stoney, *The Theory of Strains in Girders and Similar Structures: With Observations On the Application of Theory to Practice and Tables of the Strength and Other Properties of Materials. 2nd ed.*, London: Longmans, Green, and Co., 1869.

[41] B. B. Stoney, 'Description of some experiments made at the Boyne Viaduct in 1854', *Transactions of the Institution of Civil Engineers of Ireland*, vol. 5, 1860, pp. 135-143.

The professionalization of Belgian general contractors (1877-1914): an analysis of the construction journal *La Chronique des Travaux Publics, du Commerce et de l'Industrie*

Jelena Dobbels, Inge Bertels, and Ine Wouters
Department of Architectural Engineering, Vrije Universiteit Brussel (VUB), Belgium

Introduction

In Belgium, nineteenth-century industrialization caused - together with Belgian independence and the associated public building projects - a booming Belgian construction industry with ever larger architectural and infrastructure projects. Henceforth, there was a growing need to standardize the process of work organization, meaning more projects were put out to tender. In this context 'general contractors' emerged who gradually took on complete construction projects and became increasingly responsible for the work organization and execution. This caused a redrawing of working relations on site, with an increasing polarisation between clients and designers on the one hand and executors on the other.[1] This nineteenth-century construction industry has been studied mainly through the eyes of 'traditional' building actors, such as architects and engineers, with a focus on their position and professionalization[2], leaving the (hi)story of general contractors largely untouched, undeservedly because they played a pivotal role in the evolving construction industry. Indeed, they had to devise technical solutions to realize the architects' and engineers' designs, assemble and manage large bodies of men, plan and organize the work, usually in tight commercial competition with rivals.[3] (Fig.1) Only recently have these contractors received proper research attention by looking at the overall picture of the contractors[4] and by focussing on their intellectual and cultural profile,[5] drawing up biographies of major contractors[6] and discussing definitional aspects of 'the contractor'[7]. Research on Belgian contractors focused especially on their emergence in the nineteenth century[8] and on their involvement in the introduction of new construction materials and techniques,[9] leaving their professional development from the 1870s onwards underexposed.

Initial research has shown that general contractors should have experienced a professionalization process similar to that of architects and engineers.[10] The research discipline 'sociology of professions' offers a general method to study this professionalization.[11] Traditionally, knowledge and expertise are seen as important conditions for professionalization. Recent research also puts forward other aspects, such as legal regulation and the improvement of position in wider society.[12] In addition, the professionalization studies of architects and engineers offer interesting frameworks. The selection of the following key issues seems relevant to map the professionalizing trajectory of the Belgian general contractors: organisation and association, institutional and legal aspects, and relations with other building actors. These aspects are not only used nowadays in research on professionalization processes, but were also defined as important issues by the contractors' associations themselves. Until now the first aspect, the professional organisation, has been mainly highlighted in tribute publications on the initiative of the professional associations[13], or in research that focused on one particular association.[14] These publications allow us to contextualise the emergence of contractors' associations. Contractors were traditionally united in guilds and trade associations, but the French *Le Chapelier* Law (1791), extended to Belgium in 1795, prohibited these artisan organizations. From 1830 onwards, they became legal again, with the exception of trade unions, which remained prohibited until 1866. From then on, different local contractors' organizations were established: the Antwerp *Cercle des Entrepreneurs de Travaux Publiques* (1874), the Brussels *Chambre syndicale des entrepreneurs de travaux publics* (1879) and the *Cercle des Entrepreneurs de Travaux Publics et Civils du Pays de Liège* (1880). Currently, an in-depth view of the cooperation between and development of these organizations is still missing, as well as an overall picture of the contractors' legal context and their relation with other construction actors.

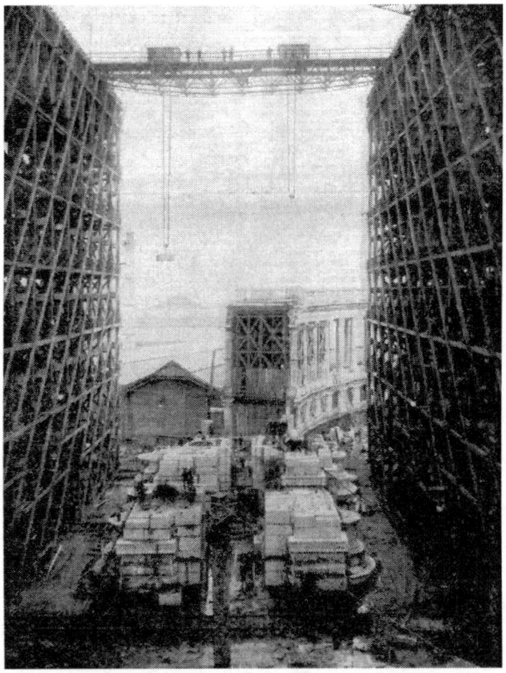

Figure 1: Contractors at the construction side of the triumphal arch in the Brussels' Cinquantenaire. 'L'arcade du cinquantenaire', La Chronique des Travaux Publics', 30 April 1905.

This paper therefore examines the three afore-mentioned key aspects, based on a discourse analysis of the journal *La Chronique des Travaux Publics, du Commerce et de l'Industrie* for the period 1877-1914. Previously, this journal has only been studied sporadically.[15] However, its continuous publication until 1971 offers longitudinal research opportunities on the evolution of topics covered. On the international level, the long-term analysis of professional journals - more specifically architectural journals - has proven to be a very suitable method to map professionalization processes of architects.[16] This paper uses this line of research in order to outline the professionalization trajectory of Belgian general contractors.

La Chronique des Travaux Publics, 'le journal spécial des entrepreneurs'

The weekly journal *La Chronique des Travaux Publics, du Commerce et de l'Industrie* was first published in 1877 by the Brussels-based *Imprimerie des Travaux Publics*. In the early years, the journal included articles on political and financial aspects, international exhibitions and also on activities of different professional associations. This large number of topics covered is reflected in the changing title: *Travaux Publics, Commerce et Industrie* (1877), *Travaux Publics, Finance, Commerce et Industrie* (1881) and *Travaux Publics et Finance* (1890). Because of the government's announcement in 1883 that it would no longer publish the bulletin of public tenders, the journal decided to include an overview of these tenders and their allocation from then on.[17] The publishing house received the lists of public tenders from the different government departments and completed this with private tenders, in order to offer their readers a comprehensive overview. In 1881 the contractors first described the journal as *le journal spécial des entrepreneurs*.[18]

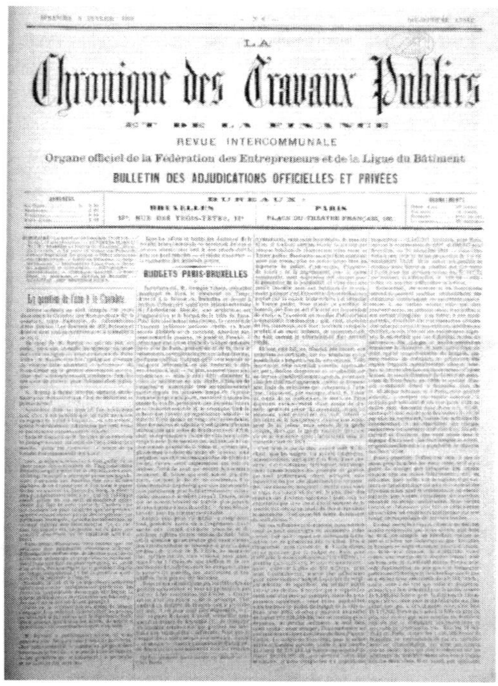
LA
Chronique des Travaux Publics
ET DE LA FINANCE
REVUE INTERCOMMUNALE
Organe officiel de la Fédération des Entrepreneurs et de la Ligue du Bâtiment
BULLETIN DES ADJUDICATIONS OFFICIELLES ET PRIVEES
BUREAUX
BRUXELLES
PARIS
BUDGETS PARIS-BRUXELLES

Figure 2. Front page of the journal La Chronique des Travaux Publics, *3 February 1893.*

This link with the contractors was formalized in 1892, as the journal became the official organ of the nationally-orientated contractors' associations *Fédération des Entrepreneurs* (°1880) and the *Ligue de l'Industrie du Bâtiment* (°1884) (Fig. 1). *La Chronique des Travaux Publics* narrowed its focus to the construction industry, with extensive coverage of important construction projects, the publication and analysis of building specifications, reports of activities of the contractors' associations, etc. Although the journal was the official organ of the contractors, it remained published by the independent *Imprimerie des Travaux Publics* and also contained reports of meetings and conferences of the architects' associations, and to a lesser extent of the engineers' associations. The journal can thus best be described as a broad construction journal, rather than a contractor's journal. This shifted focus coincided with an increasing number of advertisements and ever-growing lists of tenders, which resulted in the publication of these tenders in an additional volume from 1892 onwards. The success of the journal is reflected in the growing number of pages per journal issue: from four pages in the 1870s up to 64 pages in the 1910s. (Fig. 2) The journal title no longer included a link with the contractors' associations from 1907 onwards. However, a content analysis has shown that *La Chronique des Travaux Publics* remained the mouthpiece of these associations.

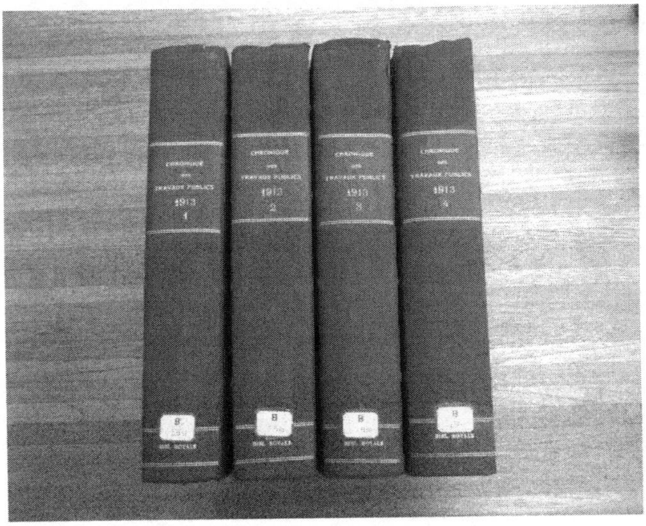

Figure 3: Four volumes of La Chronique des Travaux Publics for the year 1993. Royal Library.

« *L'Union fait la force* »: professional organisation and association

An analysis of the wide variety of articles about the contractors' associations - correspondence, meetings and conference reports, etc. - published in the journal allows the completion, adjustment and nuancing of previous research findings on the contractors' professionalization. For instance, the Brussels contractor's association was first a part of the trade union. Indeed, an article in *La Chronique des Travaux Publics* (1878) calls on the Brussels contractors to organize themselves into a *Chambre syndicale* within the trade union.[19] But the contractors resigned from this trade union in 1880 because the focus was too much on the industry and the specific interests of the contractors were inadequately defended. The journal analysis brought out that this was a pivotal moment in the contractors' organisation: the Antwerp, Brussels and Liège association then decided to create their own national federation.[20] The journal analysis places the establishment of this national association in 1880, a year earlier than was generally assumed, and indicates that the idea of a national umbrella organisation was already discussed earlier that year, at the Brussels association and during the preparatory meetings for the creation of the Liège association. In 1880 a provisional board was appointed, the bylaws and goals were discussed and a year later the official board was voted. The Brussels *Chambre Syndicale* merged with this national federation at its emergence in 1880. The idea behind this federation was to have strong local organisations that united in a strong national organisation, because "*l'union fait la force*". Therefore, a new Brussels-based organisation was highly needed: the *Ligue de l'industrie du bâtiment* was founded in 1884.[21] The national federation was furthermore extended with other local divisions, for instance in Ghent (1881), and became more representative of the Belgian contractors. They outlined the need for their professional association themselves by highlighting the different interests of the construction actors. On the one hand, there were the government architects and engineers who drafted the building specifications, using their experience with previous construction projects to add clauses to protect the government's interests. But on the other hand there were the individual contractors, always rivals, who often did not have archives or sufficient knowledge of precedents, and had to make an offer in a very short time period. The construction industry therefor craved, more than any other sector, the creation of an organisation that would represent their common interests towards the public authorities.[22]

The general contractors thus united to safeguard their position in the construction sector. In order to do so, they focussed on important aspects, such as the system of calls for tender and general building specifications. The contractors' associations pled for the system of public tenders and protested against restricted tenders - where only a limited number of contractors was invited to bid - and projects that were 'given' to a particular contractor without any tender procedure.[23] They also asked for an appropriate amount of time between the announcement and the date of tender, to allow the contractors sufficient time to make a decent offer, and for sufficient project information, detailed plans, a building estimation, etc. The contractors advocated that these tender documents should always be printed, and not hand-drawn, to ensure they could be easily read and analysed. In addition, they asked that these documents could be consulted in an appropriate room with enough space and long opening hours, to allow as many contractors as possible to study them.[24] Furthermore, the contractors asked for a correct application of the successive general building specifications (1863, 1881 and 1891) since not all government departments followed these completely. The 1881 building specifications, for instance, prohibited the specification of the brand name of a product or of its place of origin. However, in 1885 the Liège contractors' association protested that the Department of Railways had prescribed specific asphalt from Val-de-Travers and they requested that any asphalt could be used, as long as it had an equivalent quality.[25] Furthermore, the contractors found that the general building specifications gave the contracting government too much power, since they could easily refuse the contractor with the lowest offer if they felt that insufficient guarantees were put forward. The contractors' associations therefore argued very intensively for the review of these building specifications, which was only realized in 1891, but allowed the contracting government still to deviate from the normal course of business.[26]

The contractors' associations undertook action on these issues, for instance through extensive communication. Local associations reported local issues to the national federation, which contacted the responsible government officials. Secondly, in order to form a well-founded opinion, certain issues were discussed at the meetings of the contractors' organisations. They tried to enable as many contractors as possible to attend these meetings. For this reason, the Liège association changed its meetings from Monday to Sunday. In the beginning, the national federation met every two months, at the offices of each member association in turn, while the extraordinary meetings took place in Brussels. From 1896 on they met more regularly and always in Brussels, in the office of the *Ligue de l'Industrie du Bâtiment* that was situated near the Brussels town hall (Fig. 3).[27] The general assembly was organised in December and alternately took place in the offices of the five associations that were first part of the Federation (Antwerp, Brussels, Liège, Ghent and Verviers). Thirdly, recurring and persistent issues were covered at the (inter)national conferences. The Liège association took the lead in the organisation of the first conference in 1881, where among others the building specifications were studied. The large numbers attending this conference reflected the international resonance of these matters. There were foreign contractors present as well as representatives of foreign contractors' associations (like the *Chambre syndicale des Entrepreneurs de Versailles*) and journalists of professional journals, such as *Revue d'architecture, The Architect, The Contract Journal*. This resulted in the creation of a permanent organisation committee and the organisation of succeeding (inter)national conferences in Liège (1905), Paris (1907), Brussels (1909, 1910), Charleroi (1911), Ghent (1913) and Ostend (1914).[28] (Fig.4) Finally, the associations used various publications to inform contractors and other construction actors of their key points and on the actions taken. Their mouthpiece, *La Chronique des Travaux Publics*, offered an overview of their communication, meetings and conferences. This ties in with other construction journals, mentioned above, that were used in the contractors' professionalization process. In addition other publications, such as conference proceedings (Fig. 5) and yearbooks were distributed.[29]

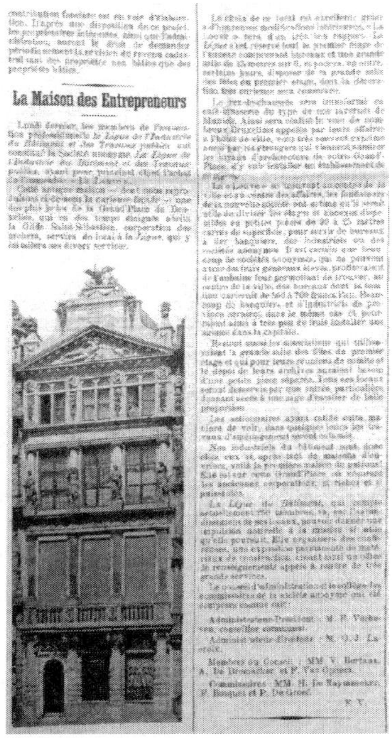

La Maison des Entrepreneurs

Figure 4: Article on the offices of the Ligue. 'Maison des Entrepreneurs', La Chronique des Travaux Publics, 16 December 1900.

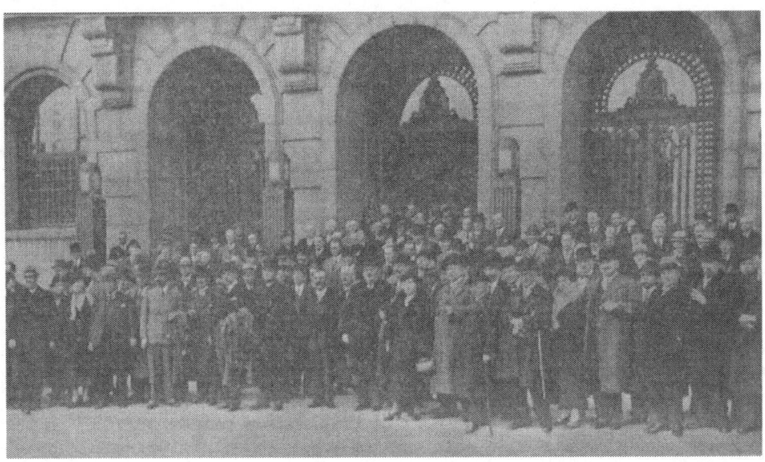

Figure 5: Contractors at the conference in Charleroi. Archives of the Federatie van Algemene Bouwaannemers (Federation of General Building Contractors).

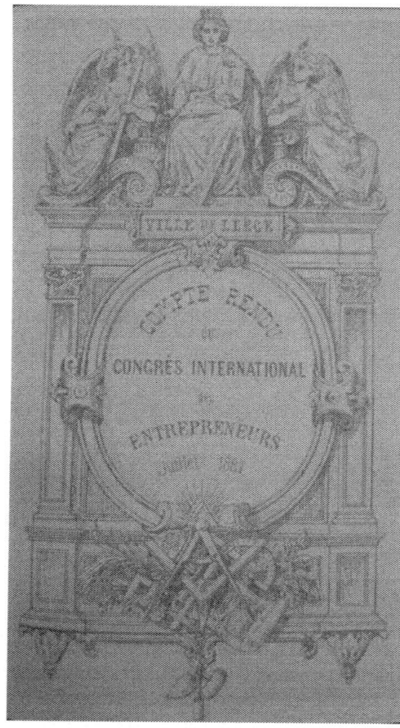

Figure 6. Front page of the proceedings of the first conference in 1881 in Liège. Archives of the Federatie van Algemene Bouwaannemers (Federation of General Building Contractors).

Over the years, the national federation grew steadily, resulting in a larger number of affiliated local organisations, but also in the creation of an additional organisational level in some areas. For example, in 1908 the *Fédération provinciale des Entrepreneurs du Hainaut* was created with the contractors associations *du Borinage, du Centre, du Tournais et du Pays de Charleroi* and in 1912 the coastal association and the contractors from Bruges and Roulers created the *Fédération provincial de Flandre Occidentale.*[30] This was in line with the Belgian bottom-up approach where local contractors could take the initiative to create local associations that afterwards could become part of the national federation. This was not the case in Switzerland, for instance, where the national *Société Suisse des Entrepreneurs* worked top-down and set out the rules for the creation of local associations.[31] The Belgian federation studied the organisation of other national contractors' federations (in Switzerland, the Netherlands, etc.) to ameliorate their own professional organisation. Because the growth of the Belgian federation - from three founding associations in 1880 up to 24 member associations with more than 3000 members in 1914 - asked for organisational adjustments as modifications of the bylaws in 1896 and 1905.[32]In the 1910s, a growing need for standardisation resulted in the formalisation of a number of rules on the possible exclusion of contractors, on an equal number of representatives of Flemish and Walloon associations in the national board, an increase of the annual contribution to allow the organisation of a national documentation centre, the adjustment of the voting procedure at national conferences, etc.[33] After outlining the general professional development, the next paragraph will discuss the legal context of the contractors and their relationship with other construction actors.

Institutional and legal context

While at the beginning of the nineteenth century architects regulated the design, building control, and execution of the work, the nineteenth-century industrialization led to a redrawing of working relations. From then on, architects focused more on the design aspect and on the oversight of executed projects, while general contractors were responsible for the organization and execution of work on site.[34] However, the legal framework then in force was still the *Code Civil* (1804) and the contractors mentioned that the relevant articles 1787-1799 "*règlent un peu trop vaguement les responsabilités en matière de travaux et établissent une sorte de solidarité entre l'architecte et l'entrepreneur*".[35] Therefore, from the end of the nineteenth century onwards, contractors tried to adapt the legal framework to this modified working context. For instance, at the Liège conference in 1905 they discussed the responsibility of the contractor and that it should be limited to hidden construction defects and mistakes in violation of the building specifications, while the architect and/or engineer would be liable for deliberately misleading plans or alignment problems.[36] These modified working relations would only become legally consolidated in the 1930s, when successively the degree (1936) and the title and profession of architect (1939) were protected.[37] This prohibited the combination of design and construction in one person/office. A decade later, in 1947, a law on the official recognition of general contractors was enacted, which focused on social and financial aspects. It was followed in 1958 by the law on business licenses (*Vestigingswet*), introducing a qualitative distinction between general contractors, based on educational training degrees, practical experience, and business liability.[38] However, the seeds for these architects' and contractors' laws were already planted in the 1880s.

In 1885 the *Société Centrale d'Architecture de Belgique*, the architects' association, published a passionate plea in *La Chronique*, in which they stressed the importance of a compulsory diploma to ensure that architects had sufficient artistic and scientific knowledge. This was studied more in-depth during the following years, for instance at their conference in 1897[39] and the architects' association petitioned in parliament for the establishment of the compulsory diploma in 1908.[40] At the same time, they asked the contractors to no longer draw plans themselves and to leave the design aspect of construction projects to architects.[41] This was discussed at the contractors' conference of 1910, where the contractors outlined they would keep on drawing plans themselves until a legal limitation of the profession of architect prohibited them from doing so. These discussions on a diploma for architects gave rise to the idea of a legal framework for contractors. They knew this would take a while, but they acknowledged the importance and relevance of this legal context and they were sure that, over time, legislation and training for all construction trades would be established.[42]

Relation with other construction actors

The legal demarcation, or lack thereof, seriously affected the relationships between contractors and other construction actors. Although outsiders often saw architects and general contractors as one group, there were a lot of differences and disputes about the responsibilities of the contractor and the architect, which sometimes led to lawsuits.[43] However, both contractors and architects, and to a lesser extent engineers, acknowledged the necessity for cooperation and sent for instance representatives of their professional associations to conferences and meetings, organized by the other professions.[44] They also cooperated on the topic of experts who were called in to judge in lawsuits. In construction-related lawsuits, often the same experts - who were almost exclusively architects or surveyors - were selected. This intertwines with foreign examples, such as the eighteenth-century Parisian expert corps that was dominated by surveyors as well. These experts did not limit themselves to technical questions but also judged building designs and town-planning projects.[45] The Belgian contractors opposed this from 1884 onwards because the experts could not have all sufficiently encompassing knowledge and they proposed to use different experts for each specialisation.[46] Furthermore, they stated that architects and surveyors had knowledge of the general construction industry, but possessed little expertise of aspects such as the value of materials or labour costs, aspects that were seen as essential parts of the job responsibilities of general contractors.[47] Therefore, they also wanted contractors to be able to act as experts and they drew up a list of possible experts, while using a number of requirements, such as integrity, independence and competence, but also the ability to write a clear report.[48] Although initially the conflicting interests of contractors and architects predominated, they made a joint initiative to improve this situation. In 1910 different contractors' and architects' associations founded an arbitration tribunal in Brussels, which was evaluated as a successful initiative to resolve disputes between building professionals, because it included representatives of all building professions.[49]

Conclusion

An in-depth analysis of the Belgian journal *La Chronique des Travaux Publics* offers more insight into the professional organisation of general contractors, and allows a first analysis of the other key issues (their changing legal context and the relationship with other construction actors), which was missing previously. The professional associations clearly functioned bottom-up, with a strong local drive that led to the creation of a national umbrella organisation. Over the years, the growing number of members led to the need for formalization, both of their organisation and their legal context. The emergence of general contractors altered the working relations in the nineteenth-century construction sector. Although this was only contextualised legally from the 1930s onwards, the journal analysis proves this was already a 'hot topic' in 1880. Architects took the lead with their plea for a compulsory diploma, which prompted the contractors to think about the protection of their own profession. This inter-professional interaction also proved important outside the legal context. Although there were tensions and conflicts, contractors and architects worked together in many areas. If the cooperation between contractors and engineers was expected to be similar, the journal analysis proved otherwise. A supplementary analysis of research on Belgian engineers could possibly provide more information on this topic.[50] The contractors' professionalization trajectory seems influenced by both internal motivations - the level of professional organisation - and by external motivations, following the architects' initiatives on legal stipulations.

The journal still offers additional research opportunities, such as the long-term evolution of the studied key issues (1870-1970), a more quantitative approach (via analysis of the number of members), a biographical approach (profile analysis of the succeeding chairmen), an iconographical analysis (of the published pictures and drawings) or a wider network analysis, which focuses not only on the relationship with architects, but also on the interaction with other actors such as the government, subcontractors and customers. Furthermore, the professionalization process can be compared internationally, to gain more insight in the similarities and differences with other contractors' organisations.

Acknowledgements

This research is funded by the Strategic Research Program on Construction History of the Vrije Universiteit Brussel. (http://www.vub.ac.be/ARCH/ae-lab/projects/groeier).

Notes and references

[1] I. Bertels, 'Building the city. Antwerp 1819-1880' (Ph.D. thesis, KULeuven, 2008), p. 203.

[2] L. Verpoest, 'Architectuuronderwijs in België, 1830-1890. Aspecten van de institutionele geschiedenis' (Ph.D. thesis, KULeuven, 1984).; D. Van de Vijver, 'Ingenieurs en architecten op de drempel van een nieuwe tijd (1750- 1830)' (Ph.D. thesis, KULeuven, 2003).; A. Saint, 'Architect and engineer: a study in construction history', *Construction History*, vol. 21, 2005, pp. 21-30.; P. Raeymaeckers, 'Makers van een nieuwe wereld. De socioprofessionele geschiedenis van ingenieurs in België 1850-1914' (Ph.D. thesis, KULeuven, 2013).; W. Linssen, 'Engineers in Belgium 1830-1865. Archaeology of a Profession' (Ph.D. thesis, KULeuven, 2013).

[3] H. Ferguson and M. Chrimes, *The contractors,* London: ICE Publishing, 2013, p. 4.

[4] Ferguson and Chrimes, *The contractors*, (Note 3).

[5] I. Bertels, 'The contractors' intellectual profile: knowledge and training of nineteenth-century public works' contractors in Antwerp, Belgium' pp. 379-91 in M. Dunkeld et al (Eds), Proceedings of the 2nd International Congress on Construction History, Cambridge 2006, Cambridge: Construction History Society, 2006.; V. Nègre, 'Les figures de l'entrepreneur. Inventer et représenter la technique au tournant des XVIIIe et XIXe siècles', Lecture at the Seminar *Entreprendre dans le bâtiment aux époques médiévale et moderne Oser, risquer, gérer,* organized by Le Laboratoire de médiévistique occidentale de Paris, Le Centre de théorie et analyse du droit and Le Laboratoire Géométrie-Structure-Architecture, Paris, 2nd of June 2014.; I. Bertels and J. Dobbels, 'Cataloging contractors know-how. An analysis of late nineteenth- and early twentieth-century library catalogues of Belgian Industrial schools' pp. 211-218 in B. Bowen, D. Friedman, T. Leslie and J. Ochsendorf (Eds), Proceedings of the Fifth International Congress on Construction History, Chicago 2015, Chicago: Construction History Society of America, 2015.

[6] S. Wermiel, 'The Rise of the General Contractor in 19th Century America', *FMI Quarterly,* 3, 2008, pp. 116-129.

[7] H. Vérin, *Entrepreneurs, entreprise. Histoire d'une idée*, Paris: Classiques Garnier, 1882.

[8] Bertels, 'Building the city', (Note 1).

[9] R. Devos, 'Modern at Expo 58. Discussions on post-war architectural representation' (Ph.D. thesis, UGent, 2008).; S. Van de Voorde, 'Bouwen in beton in België. Samenspel van kennis, innovatie en experiment' (Ph.D. thesis, UGent, 2011).; S. Van de Voorde, I. Bertels and I. Wouters, *Post-war building materials in housing in Brussels 1945-1975*, Brussels: Vrije Universiteit Brussel, 2015.

[10] A. Van der Woud, 'Professionalisering en integratie' pp.165-174 in H.W. Lintsen (Ed.) *Geschiedenis van de techniek in Nederland: de wording van een moderne samenleving 1800-1890*, Zutphen: Walburg Pers, 1992.

[11] A. Abbott, *The system of professions. An essay on the division of expert labour*, Chicago-London: The University of Chicago Press, 1988.; M. Burrage and R. Torstendahl (Eds), *Professions in theory and history: rethinking the study of the professions*, London: Sage, 1990.

[12] M. Saks, 'Defining a Profession: The Role of Knowledge and Expertise', *Professions & Professionalism*, vol. 2, no.1, 2012, pp.1-10.

[13] P. Lombaerde and M. Dussene (Eds), *Bouwen is leven, leven is bouwen: jubileumboek uitgegeven ter gelegenheid van de 50ste verjaardag van de Nationale Confederatie van het Bouwbedrijf*, Brussel: Nationale Confederatie van het Bouwbedrijf, 1996.; Nationale Confederatie Bouw (Ed.), *De bouwnijverheid, Studies uitgegeven ter gelegenheid van de 20ste verjaardag*, Brussel: Nationale Confederatie van het Bouwbedrijf, 1966.

[14] I. Bertels, 'Building Contractors in late-Nineteenth-century Belgium: from Craftsmen to Contractors', *Construction History*, vol. 26, 2011, pp. 1-18.; J. Venstermans, 'De aannemer en zijn beroepsorganisatie' pp.27-86 in Nationale Confederatie Bouw (Ed.), *De bouwnijverheid,* (Note 13).

[15] Bertels, 'Building the city', (Note 1) p. 199.; Venstermans, 'De aannemer', (Note 14) p. 40.; J. Cornilly,

'Architect/Ambtenaar. De betekenis van het ambt van provinciaal architect voor de 19e-eeuwse architectuur in West-Vlaanderen' (Ph.D. thesis, KULeuven, 2013).

[16] J.-M. Leniaud and B. Bouvier (Eds), *Les périodiques d'architecture, XVIIIe-XXe siècle; Recherche d'une méthode critique d'analyse*, Paris, Ecole des chartes, Etudes et rencontres de l'Ecole des Chartes, series, 2001.; M. Woods, 'The "American Architect and building News" 1876-1907' (Ph.D. thesis, Columbia University, 1983).

[17] , 'Avis', La Chronique des Travaux Publics, 7 January 1883.

[18] 'Rapport annuel présenté à la Chambre', La Chronique des Travaux Publics, 13 February 1881.

[19] 'Aux entrepreneurs de travaux publics', La Chronique des Travaux Publics, 27 January 1878.

[20] 'Chambre des Entrepreneurs de Travaux Publics de Belgique', La Chronique des Travaux Publics, 6 March 1881.

[21] Over the years, this Brussels-based *Ligue de L'industrie du Bâtiment* became nationally orientated.

[22] 'Rapport de la Fédération des entrepreneurs de travaux publics de Belgique. Année 1880-1881', La Chronique des Travaux Publics, 22 January 1882.

[23] 'Ligue du Bâtiment', La Chronique des Travaux Publics, 1 February 1891.; 'Les adjudications restreintes', La Chronique des Travaux Publics, 16 June 1895.

[24] 'Chambre des Entrepreneurs', La Chronique des Travaux Publics, 7 February 1885.

[25] 'Chambre syndicale des Entrepreneurs de Liège', La Chronique des Travaux Publics, 27 September 1885.

[26] 'Ligue de l'industrie, du bâtiment et des travaux publics', La Chronique des Travaux Publics, 20 January 1889.; 'Commentaire du Cahier des Charges Type', La Chronique des Travaux Publics, 5 April 1891.; 'Ligue de l'industrie du bâtiment et des travaux publics', La Chronique des Travaux Publics, 24 January 1892.

[27] 'Fédération des entrepreneurs', La Chronique des Travaux Publics, 3 May 1896. 'La Maison des entrepreneurs', La Chronique des Travaux Publics, 16 December 1900.

[28] 'Le banquet de la fédération', La Chronique des Travaux Publics, 25 February 1906.; 'Fédération nationale du bâtiment et des travaux publics', La Chronique des Travaux Publics, 10 August 1913.

[29] 'Annuaire belge des bâtiments des travaux publics, et des industries qui s'y rattachent', La Chronique des Travaux Publics, 17 September 1899.; 'A nos lecteurs', La Chronique des Travaux Publics, 17 May 1894.

[30] 'Fédération nationale du bâtiment et des travaux publics', La Chronique des Travaux Publics, 8 December 1912.; I. Bertels, 'De uitvoerders op het terrein. Een braakliggend onderzoeksdomein' pp. 177-191 in J. Cornilly, S. De Caigny and D. Dendooven (Eds), *Bouwen aan wederopbouw 1914/2050. Architectuur in de Westhoek*, Ieper: Erfgoedcel CO7, 2009.

[31] 'L'organisation des entrepreneurs suisses', La Chronique des Travaux Publics, 14 April 1912.

[32] 'Ligue du bâtiment', La Chronique des Travaux Publics, 1 March 1914.

[33] 'Fédération nationale belge du bâtiment et des travaux publics', La Chronique des Travaux Publics, 25 January 1914, 'Le comité fédéral', La Chronique des Travaux Publics, 24 November 1912.

[34] I. Bertels and J. Dobbels 'VBA 1936-2016. Van vereniging voor burgerlijke bouwkunde tot vertegenwoordiger van grote bouwbedrijven/ADEB 1936-2016. Quand une association du génie civil devient la représentante des grandes entreprises de construction' pp. 10-33 in AAM (Eds), *1936-2016. België Bouwt/ La Belgique construit*, Brussels: Archives d'Architecture Moderne, 2015.

[35] 'Nos architectes', La Chronique des Travaux Publics, 27 December 1885.

[36] 'Premier congrès internationale de l'industrie du bâtiment et des travaux publics', La Chronique des Travaux Publics, 24 September 1905.

[37] Verpoest, 'Architectuuronderwijs in België', (Note 2).

[38] Bertels, 'Building the city', (Note 1), p. 175.

[39] 'Nos architectes', La Chronique des Travaux Publics, 27 December 1885.; 'L'esthétique des villes', La Chronique des Travaux Publics, 8 August 1897.

[40] 'Le congrès nationale des architectes', La Chronique des Travaux Publics, 20 September 1908.

[41] 'A la Chambre syndicale des entrepreneurs et fournisseurs de travaux publics et civils', La Chronique des Travaux Publics, 12 December 1909.

[42] 'Nos architectes', La Chronique des Travaux Publics, 27 December 1885; 'Nos architectes', La Chronique des Travaux Publics, 17 December 1911.

[43] 'A bon entendeur', La Chronique des Travaux Publics, 3 June 1894.; 'Commentaire du nouveau cahier des charges-type', La Chronique des Travaux Publics, 14 June 1891.

[44] 'Congrès des Entrepreneurs (25-26 juillet 1881)', La Chronique des Travaux Publics, 6 March 1881.; 'Chez les architectes', La Chronique des Travaux Publics, 13 December 1914.

[45] R. Carvais and V. Nègre, 'Parisian Surveyors (1690-1792): founding an expert corps' pp. 383-394 in Bowen, Friedman, Leslie and Ochsendorf, Proceedings (Note 5).

[46] 'Congrès national des Travaux publics', La Chronique des Travaux Publics, 2 May 1909.

[47] M. Woods, *From Craft to Profession: The Practice of Architecture in Nineteenth-Century America* (Berkeley: University of California Press, 1999).

[48] 'Les expertises', La Chronique des Travaux Publics, 4 October 1885.; 'Ve Congrès national des Bâtiment et des Travaux Publics', La Chronique des Travaux Publics, 24 August 1913.

[49] 'IIIe congrès nationale du bâtiment et des travaux publics', La Chronique des Travaux Publics, 6 August 1911.

[50] Linssen, 'Engineers in Belgium 1830-1865', (Note 2).

An English company's role in the 19th century water supply to Cartagena

---

F. J. Pérez de la Cruz[1], J. García León[1], C. Díaz García[1], and A. Trapote Jaume[2]

1. Technical University of Cartagena, Spain; 2. Technical University of Alicante, Spain

Introduction

Throughout its history, the city of Cartagena has had to face many problems related to regional water shortages and ensuring sufficient water to meet the needs of the local population. This is a situation that dates back from the time of the first settlers and has continued to the present. This has led to a number of different measures being taken in order to alleviate this problem and seek available water resources. The absence of permanent water resources and the poor quality and shortage of the water drawn from the subsoil have frequently marred the development of the city and presented a challenge which was not overcome until the middle of the 20th century when water was brought from the river Taibilla.

Weather and existing resources

The coast of Cartagena is located in the south-east of the Iberian Peninsula and is characterized by its semi-arid climate, with little rain (rarely more than 300 millimetres per year) and a lot of sunshine (between 2,500 and 3,000 hours per year), which makes it "the driest region of Spain and one of the driest in Europe"[1].

In 1929, José Mediavilla, Deputy Mayor of the city, said:

> "water is simply a product from heaven, and when it lands at the depths or on the earth's surface, the earth is a mere temporary container for this liquid element. If water has to come from heaven, and in Cartagena this does not happen, then it is normal that there are not many permanent springs with abundant flow, neither in Cartagena nor in the surrounding areas"[2].

Moreover, the composition of the lands makes the existent springs both limited in number and poor in quality.

Precedents to the 19th century

The city of Cartagena was founded as *Qart Hadasht* by the Phoenicians in the year 227 B.C. who maximised the city's position as a natural port and as a main base of operations for Carthage in Iberia, as well as a source of silver for the maintenance of the army in the Second Punic[3]. These first settlers fulfilled their water requirements via the excavation and construction of wells and tanks within the city, where they collected the rainwater.

By the middle of the 1st century B.C. the city was under Roman rule and as a consequence of the ensuing demographic growth, the demand for water increased. In order to solve this problem, an aqueduct was built which carried water from the *caput aquae* located in the town of Fuente Cubas (Fig. 1); a spring located two kilometres to the north of the city, to the *castellum aquae* which is thought to have been located in the hill of El Molinete[4]. The existence of this water infrastructure is evident due to the following: testimonies discovered both during restoration works of the Roman theatre's museum and from the ruins found in the aforementioned hill; the aligned appearance of what was believed to be the foundations during the excavation of a car park in Alameda de San Antón.

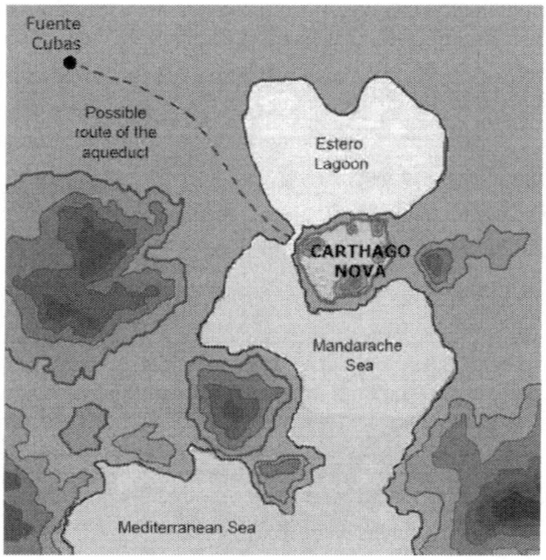

Figure 1. Location of Fuente Cubas and the aqueduct in the Roman city of Carthago Nova. Design: Javier Pérez de la Cruz

Despite obtaining water from Fuente Cubas, the Romans continued building water tanks in the main city. These were made with *opus caementium* and waterproofed with *opus signinum*. The fact these tanks were built was probably motivated by the limited water supply, or by the high salinity of the available water, which meant that it was not suitable for human consumption, despite being usable for other needs.

When the population declined during the Middle Ages, the water supply was further reduced to being solely obtainable from wells and reservoirs for rainwater.

It was not until the middle of the 16th century that the population was, once again, faced with a shortage of water. This became a worrying issue for the authorities who needed to find solutions, not only in supplying water to the population, but also to irrigate the land and supply the port. This was reflected in a document written by King Philip II to the City Council in 1564, which explained that, due to the shortage of water galleys, they decided not to spend the winter at this port[5].

Numerous reports or briefs were written between the 16th and 18th centuries which referred to various projects and attempts to supply water to the southeast of Murcia (Lorca and Cartagena) from the Castril and Guardal rivers, located north of Granada[6]. Unfortunately, all these attempts failed, including one which was supported by King Philip V in 1742. Nevertheless, the population continued to grow due, in part, to the construction of the

Military Arsenal. Thus, the problem of water shortages worsened because, as the population grew, the water levels decreased.

In the middle of the 18th century, some works took place in order to build public fountains and improve the existing ones, therefore trying to make the most of the minimal water flow emanating from the nearby springs. This was not the solution for the problem of supply, however, since the water obtained had a high saline content and, therefore, wells and reservoirs still represented critical elements for the population's supplies.

Water companies in the 19th century

Due to the incompetence of the public administrations who were unable to solve the problem, a private initiative tried to benefit from the situation. This led to the emergence of private companies during the last quarter of the 19th century who, attracted by the economic growth of the area due to the mining industry, offered definitive solutions to the city's water issues. However, these companies confirmed how pointless these attempts would be, due to the high costs and limited benefit[7].

The main source of available information regarding these companies was the "Report related to the drinkable water supply in the city of Cartagena", written by Luis Mariano Vidal and Lucas Mallada in 1914[8]. The following table displays the main characteristics of these companies:

Table 1. Data regarding the main companies that supplied water to the city of Cartagena at the end of the 19th century. Source: Vidal and Mallada, 1914

Company	Date	Intake area
Aguas de Santa Bárbara	1887 - 1945	Los Puertos
Aguas de los Cartageneros	1883 - 1890	Galifa
Aguas de la Suerte	1880 - 1889	Los Patojos
Agua Inglesa	1886 - 1945	Perín

Of all these companies, we will mainly focus on two: Aguas de los Cartageneros (Los Cartageneros Waters) and La Compañía Inglesa (The English Company).

Los Cartageneros Waters

In 1883, water-pumping works began in Galifa; a district located six kilometres from Cartagena. These were established due to the existence of some small springs, such as the ones of La Muela, Los Higueros or Pozo de la Torre, in the nearby western slopes of the La Muela and Morteral mountains. Approximately 300 cubic metres were obtained daily and scoring works were performed from a waste water pipe located in the Munguía cliff where the inputs were brought to a tank located in the hill of Odón, just 1 kilometre to the west of Canteras.

In 1890, this company was taken over by the English company that worked in Perín, their infrastructure was an important part of the new company, especially the intakes from Fuente Vieja. Its water quality was considerably worse than the rest, to the extent that some pathogenic microorganisms were discovered.

An English company's role in the 19th century water supply to Cartagena

La Compañía Inglesa (The Carthagena Water Co. Ltd.)

Founded in 1889, "The Carthagena Water Works" was a company based in Manchester, subsequently named "The Carthagena Mining and Water Co. Ltd.", which supplied the city from the locality of Perín, 15 kilometres to the west of the city.

The amount of water supplied by the company reached, on average, 1,000 cubic metres daily, which was not enough to supply the population. Furthermore, the quality of the drinking water was deteriorating over the years.

This company was the most important and active one at the beginning of the 20th century and maintained its functions until the middle of the century, when the water of the Taibilla solved the water problems of Cartagena. Its closure took place in 1955.

Infrastructure of the The Carthagena Water Co. Ltd.

In order to supply water to the population, this company collected water, not only from the surface area, but also from underground. Later, it transported the water (through galleries or flow free channels and pressure pipes) to a group of tanks where it was kept until subsequent distribution. Filters were used throughout the whole system in order to improve the quality of the water.

This system was appreciated for such significant elements, as the water tanks built in the village of Canteras (5 kilometres from Cartagena) and the final distribution tank of Monte Sacro, within the urban area of Cartagena. However there were serious drawbacks overall regarding both the design as well as functioning capabilities. This happened due to the fact that, as mentioned previously, it was constructed by a private company. Therefore, there is no record of the project in the city files.

The fieldwork performed here has enabled us to totally recreate the system. This work has been complemented by the discovery of various original plans belonging to local individuals. It is thanks to them that the original toponymy of many elements has been recovered and suggested hypotheses have been verified, together with unknown aspects that otherwise would not have been discovered.

In order to present a clear description of the system, we will distinguish between the areas where the catchment was performed and those where the storage took place, plus the subsequent water transportation.

Intake system of Fuente Vieja

The place known as Fuente Vieja is located 10 kilometres to the west of Cartagena, and was the main intake source for the Los Cartageneros company, by maximising the surface water which occasionally ran through the ravines of Giménez and Cabezo Negro, as well as of its underground water which supplied (and continues to supply) the water source after which the location is named. The water, which came from various sources, converged in a small tank (popularly known as the filter house of Fuente Vieja), where a first decantation took place in order to begin its course towards Cartagena through an underground gallery.

The main intake was from the Cabezo Negro ravine, where a dam is settled over 1,000 metres up-river from the filter house. (Fig. 2). On the right bank of the aforementioned dam there is a side point through which the water was brought to the so-called Giménez tank, through a 350 metre long rectangular-shaped channel which lies in parallel to the ravine.

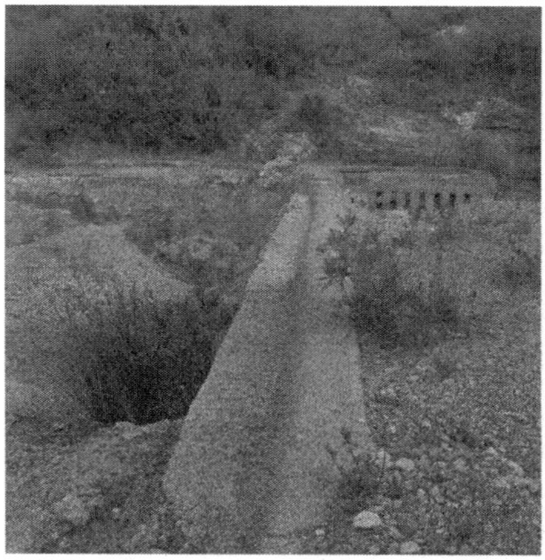

Figure 2. Dam in the ravine of Cabezo Negro. Photo: Javier Pérez de la Cruz, 2015

The Giménez tank (Fig. 3) had a trapezoidal cross-section, with a capacity of 1,100 cubic metres and is the first central collection point of the system. It had a roof although, nowadays, most of this closing structure has been lost. From this tank, through an iron pipe measuring 0.15 metres in diameter, the water was transported to the filter house. This way, its contribution could be regulated through the corresponding valves located at the exit point of the tank.

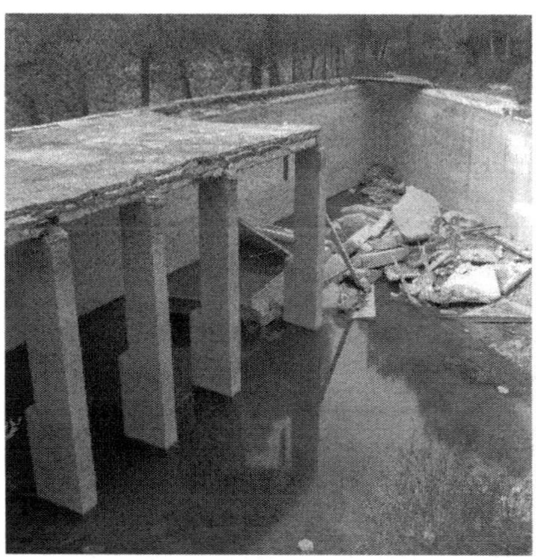

Figure 3. View of the Giménez tank. Photo: Javier Pérez de la Cruz, 2015

Downstream from the initial dam, and over the Cabezo Negro ravine, three more dams were built. The first was located close to the tank of Giménez, while the others were built upstream from the filter house. The function of the two first dams was to attenuate the erosive effect of the water in the ravine by laminating as much as possible, the floods and by retaining the extracted sediment (which was, subsequently, removed by opening the floodgates located in the body of the dam). The second one was also used as a collection point, enabling water transportation to the filter house through an iron pipe measuring 0.15 metres in diameter.

The intake in the Giménez ravine was performed through a dam that, nowadays, is completely covered. It collected all the contributions from the ravine, together with the run-off from the right bank of the ravine, which was guided to that point via a small 40 centimetre wall. These led to the ravine just a few metres upstream from the dam. On the left bank of the dam, water abstraction was performed for the streams, which needed to be moved from this ravine to the Cabezo Negro ravine.

In order to create the diversion, the Los Cartageneros company arranged a system of wells which, via a simple system of communicating channels, enabled water transportation from one catchment area to another. The initial well, located 5 metres from the dam of the Giménez ravine, linked with the second one through a gallery measuring 110 metres. A channel started from the wellhead of the second well, which flows into the Giménez tank. This enabled a connection between the two intake areas to those ravines in a common collecting point.

Finally, for the collection and use of the Fuente Vieja underground water, a gallery was created which was perpendicular to the design of the ravine of Cabezo Negro. This gallery flows into the filter house and is still working today. The inspections performed in this area have identified five wells that belong to the underground building. These elements allow us to follow the trace of the gallery on the surface.

In the 1920s, some changes of the system were made by the English company in order to increase the water collection capacity, and this resulted in a greater guarantee of the service to the population. Thus, a project was designed and built consisting of a tank in the vicinity of the Giménez tank, known as tank of La Manda. (Fig. 4). This tank had a rectangular cross-section and a capacity of 8,000 cubic metres.

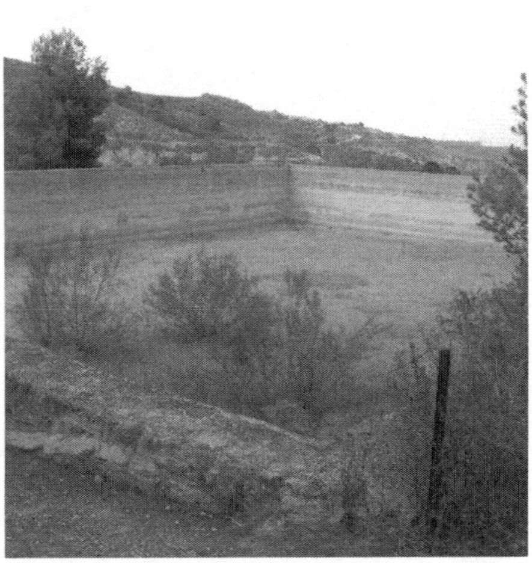

Figure 4. La Manda tank. Photo: Javier Pérez de la Cruz, 2015

According to the initial plans, the tank was supposed to have a roof, however, this closure was never performed. This tank was supplied by derived flows of the Giménez tank, which was considerably smaller and noticeably increased the regulation capacity of the Fuente Vieja system. It also increased the collection capacity due to its ceramic pipe, which led from the head dam to the filter house. The aforementioned pipe, which went through the banks of the ravines, has suffered considerable damage due to successive floods, although some remnants of the design remain.

Once all the water was collected in the filter house, it continued its way through an underground gallery, which led to a tank located in the area of Galifa, known as El Bancal Blanco (it has a trapezoidal cross-section and a capacity of 5,000 cubic metres from which it continued its way to Canteras). This pipe which started from the tank was withdrawn and a new one was built, based on a small middle tank (measuring no more than 600 cubic metres) in the area of Loma Asomada, which transferred the catchment water flows to the tanks in Canteras.

Intake system of Arjona

The town of Arjona is located in the district of La Torre de Nicolás Pérez, 11 kilometres to the west of Cartagena. This water abstraction system gathered water in different ways: via a spring, with the exploitation of the run-off thanks to the use of small walls and through an intake point located in the La Torre ravine.

The first intake point is in a spring settled on the left bank of the La Torre ravine. Starting from this point, the English company built an underground gallery which, starting from the spring, was used to transport the water which was obtained from deep under the ground. Only 200 metres away from the first well, a dam was built in the ravine with the aim of adding to the gallery the catchment flows from the ravine.

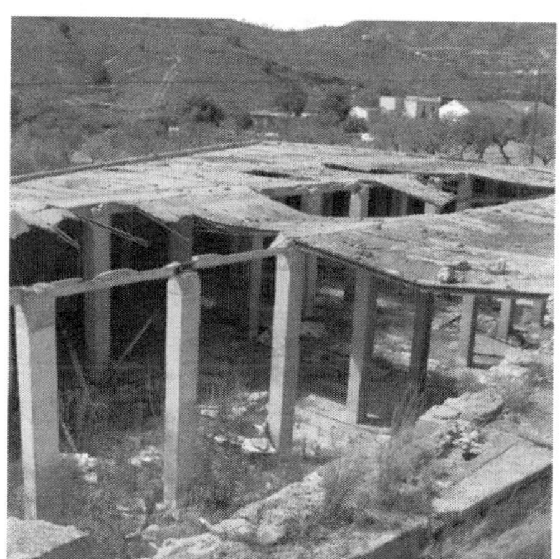

Figure 5. Arjona tank. Photo: Javier Pérez de la Cruz, 2015

Another important element of the Arjona's system is the tank of the same name (Fig. 5), located downstream from the intake point of the ravine. It has a trapezoidal cross-section and a capacity of 5,000 cubic metres, towards which water could be diverted from the intake point of the ravine through some pipes in the tunnel, which began at the dam. The run-off flows, collected via a series of small walls arranged in the slope of the hill of La Cárcel, were also collected culminating in a pool located over the tank. Thus, this tank constitutes the main water-collecting element of this system.

It is important to highlight that the water collected in the Arjona pool could be sent to the tank or to the estate where the company had its headquarters. This took place via a channel, which ended at one of the two collection tanks, which the estate used for water consumption for the workers, as well as for the pipe factory located in the same place.

The underground gallery from where the system starts, continues downstream from the ravine essentially following its trace. The tank can add to the water flow of the gallery, regulating the same through specifically made valves. The circulating water that flows through the gallery can follow two paths: either following a continuous path to the town of Canteras or be diverted via a filter to, subsequently, be incorporated into the Perín system.

Perín intake system

The Perín system, located in a district located 12 kilometres west of Cartagena, was entirely built by the Cartagena Water Co. Ltd. This system, the most complex of the three, could collect both the surface water, which circulated through the local ravines, as well as underground water, through a series of wells and galleries.

The collection of surface water was established at four different points, which covered the entire basins of the area and reflected the highest exploitation of the resource. From these surface points, we can highlight the one settled on the Sagena cliff. The aforementioned dam, as well as the ones described in the system of Fuente Vieja, shows a tailgate in order to clean the retained sediments. Currently, it is in a tumbledown state, presumably caused by the effect of local flooding. The collected water was carried through a channel to a pool; the first point of collection.

The collection of underground water took place in three areas; the ravines of Los Jarales, Los Barbastres and a gallery in the village of Perín. This water was carried through galleries measuring about 6 kilometres and which can still be traced via the 32 existing wells.

The water collected from deep underground was treated by two filters placed at the end of the galleries. From these filters there was the possibility of sending the water directly to the city of Cartagena. However, most of the water which went through the filters led to an estate located 5 kilometres from the village of Perín known as "Casa de las Aguas" ("House of Water"). Here, the main tank was located as part of the system and was where the company could collect the water. This enabled them to regulate its consumption according to demand through a series of existing sluices and a flowmeter. Furthermore, the company had a decantation tank of substantial capacity where any surface water collected could be treated if it was substandard for consumption. (Fig. 6).

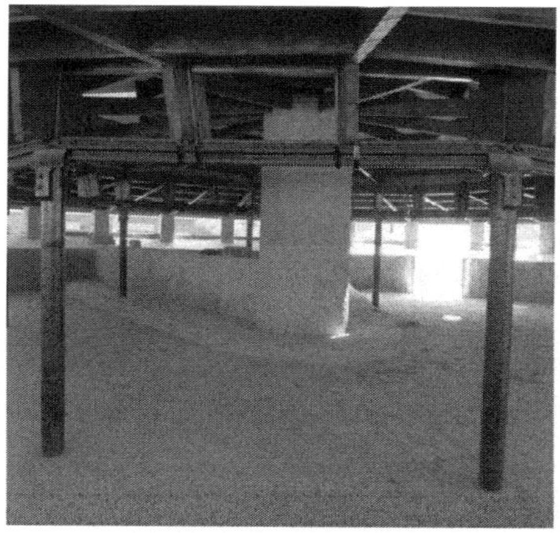

Figure 6. Decanter in Casa de las Aguas. Photo: Javier Pérez de la Cruz, 2014

Water was sent from this tank to the tanks the company had in the neighbouring town of Molinos Marfagones.

Points of collection and transportation to Cartagena

The final collection in the city of Cartagena took place in a tank located on top of Monte Sacro (Fig. 7) from where it was transported to subscribers through lead pipes. In order to build this tank, the company needed the permission of the Real Orden (Royal Order) of 10th of June 1896, since the tank was built inside the defence area of the city, in front of the number one bastion of the wall of Charles III.

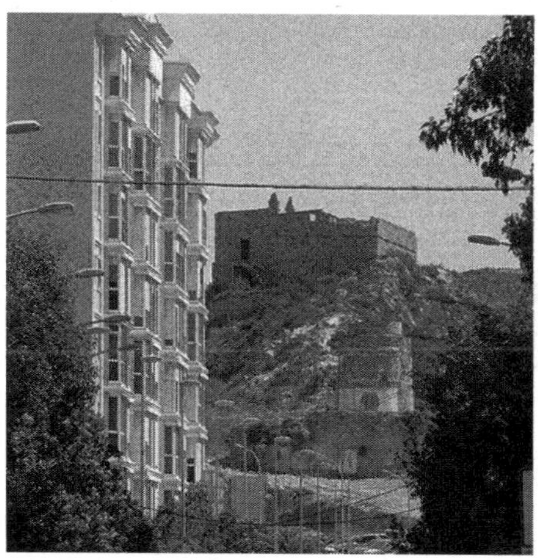

Figure 7. Tank of Monte Sacro. Photo: Javier Pérez de la Cruz, 2015

Water was transported to this tank via two specific ways: one coming from the tanks built by the society of Los Cartageneros in Canteras or, two, via those built by the English company close to Molinos Marfagones.

In Canteras there are two tanks and a filter that received the water from the Fuente Vieja system and the one derived from the system of Arjona. The first one, the tank of Odón (Fig. 8), can be found in the place known as Casas de Belmonte, barely 1 kilometres from the town of Canteras. This tank has a capacity of 10,300 cubic metres representing the largest tank within the entire infrastructure of the company. It displayed an arched roof made of reinforced concrete, which, at present, is almost destroyed.

The second tank was called Serna (Fig. 9), found at the highest part of the locality of Canteras, close to the sandstone quarry. It had a roof, a rectangular cross-section and was glass-closed by semi-cylindrical surfaces with a capacity of 3,300 cubic metres. The water could be led to one or another well independently, making the exploitation of the system easier.

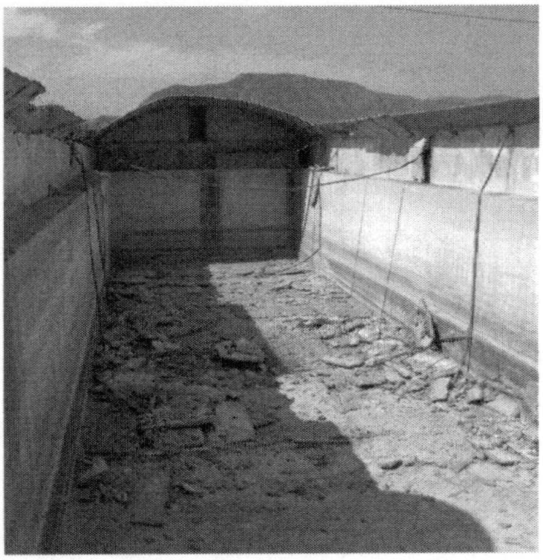

Figure 8. Odón Tank. Photo: Javier Pérez de la Cruz, 2015

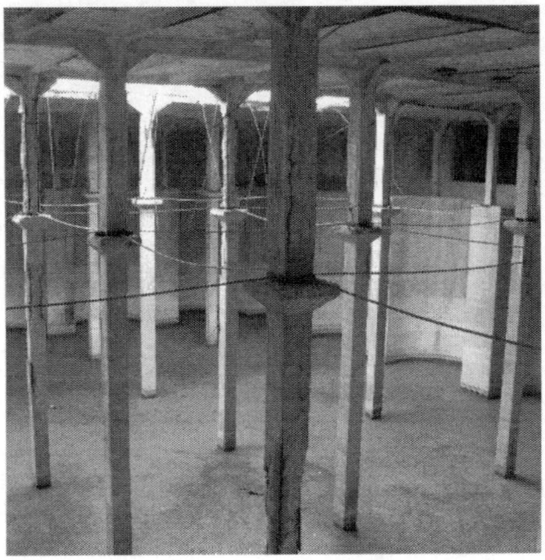

Figure 9. The inside of the Serna tank. Photo: Javier Pérez de la Cruz, 2014

Finally, the water collected in both tanks passed through the filter placed in front of the church of Canteras (Fig. 10). It has two rectangular cross-section chambers with a total capacity of 280 cubic metres. These chambers were filled with sand and gravel in order to filter the water that ran through iron pipes until reaching the final tank of Monte Sacro, and after going through a metering house, which was destroyed at the end of the 20th century.

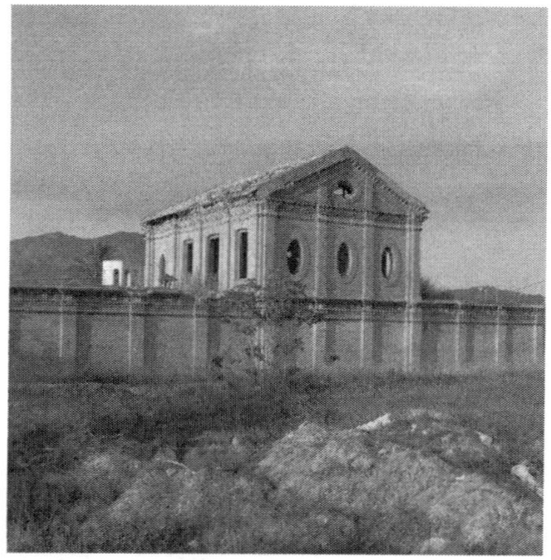

Figure 10. Canteras Filter. Photo: Javier Pérez de la Cruz, 2014

The second way the water reached the final tank was from the tanks of the English company in Molinos Marfagones. There, the water arrived through the Perín system while the flows derived from the Arjona system. Nowadays, we do not have any kind of data regarding these tanks, except for the ones noted by Vidal and Mallada (1914), which show their existence and location in the aforementioned locality.

Conclusions

The aim of this work has been to identify the infrastructure of the Carthagena Water Co. Ltd., initially based on the limited data available in documents, as well as via extensive fieldwork, which had its drawbacks. Once the general functioning of the system has been established, the subsequent aims are to provide a thorough characterization of the system via the elaboration of a water model that allows us to know the amount of water that the company had and its distribution over time. Finally, this enables us to make a mathematical model which allows us to reproduce the entire system in order to fully comprehend the total functioning of such an interesting infrastructure as the Carthagena Water Co. Ltd.

Notes and references

[1] G. Arnaud, 'La région la plus sèche d'Espagne', Annales de Géographie, no. 34, 1925

[2] J. Mediavilla, Cartagena y las aguas de la región murciana. Murcia: Consejería de Política Territorial y Obras Públicas, 1989.

[3] J. M. Blázquez, 'Explotaciones mineras en Hispania durante la República y el Alto Imperio Romano',

Anuario de Historia Económica y Social en España. Madrid: Facultad de Filosofía y Letras de la Universidad Complutense de Madrid, 1969

[4] A. Egea, 'Características principales del sistema de captación, abastecimiento, distribución y evacuación del agua de Carthago Nova', *Empuries*, no. 53, 2002

[5] A. de la Piñera, 'Breve historia del abastecimiento de las aguas de Cartagena', Cuadernos del Estero, no. 4, 1990.

[6] C. Tornel, A. Grandal y Á. Rivas, Textos para la Historia de Cartagena (ss. XVI - XVII). Granada: Ayuntamiento de Granada, 1985.

[7] M. C. Berrocal y A. Egea, 'El abastecimiento de agua de Cartagena en el siglo XIX y comienzos del XX. La época de las compañías de aguas', Revista Murciana de Antropología, no. 14, 2007

[8] L. M. Vidal y L. Mallada, Memoria sobre la traída de aguas potables a Cartagena y su puerto. Cartagena: Ayuntamiento de Cartagena, 1914

References

G. Arnaud, 'La région la plus sèche d'Espagne', *Annales de Géographie,* no. 34, 1925.

M. C. Berrocal y A. Egea, 'El abastecimiento de agua de Cartagena en el siglo XIX y comienzos del XX. La época de las compañías de aguas', *Revista Murciana de Antropología,* no. 14, 2007.

J. M. Blázquez, 'Explotaciones mineras en Hispania durante la República y el Alto Imperio Romano', Anuario de Historia Económica y Social en España. Madrid: Facultad de Filosofía y Letras de la Universidad Complutense de Madrid, 1969.

A. de la Piñera, 'Breve historia del abastecimiento de las aguas de Cartagena', *Cuadernos del Estero*, no. 4, 1990.

A. Egea, 'Características principales del sistema de captación, abastecimiento, distribución y evacuación del agua de Carthago Nova', *Empuries*, no. 53, 2002.

J. Mediavilla, Cartagena y las aguas de la región murciana. Murcia: Consejería de Política Territorial y Obras Públicas, 1989.

C. Tornel, A. Grandal y Á. Rivas, Textos para la Historia de Cartagena (ss. XVI - XVII). Granada: Ayuntamiento de Granada, 1985.

L. M. Vidal y L. Mallada, Memoria sobre la traída de aguas potables a Cartagena y su puerto. Cartagena: Ayuntamiento de Cartagena, 1914.

Timbers, palm boards and construction materials of eighteenth and nineteenth century architecture in the Dominican Republic

Virginia Flores-Sasso
Pontificia Universidad Católica Madre y Maestra, Dominican Republic

Introduction

The great forest treasure which as well as the great variety of palms and trees that exists in the Caribbean Islands was used for medicinal purposes, to build their homes, vessels, buildings, fuel for boilers of the sugar mills and other industrial dedications. The wood became an important commodity of the economy of the European colonies in the Caribbean.

By the early decades of the sixteenth century, uncontrolled extraction of wood caused scarcity on various occasions, resulting in the prohibition of tree-felling without the permission of the Spanish crown.

In the late sixteenth century and early seventeenth century, the Spanish colonies in the Caribbean fell into decadence, leading to a significant population exodus, leaving the island with few inhabitants. This encouraged other European kingdoms to take over some Caribbean islands, leading to economic and social change.

After the Spaniards, the first to arrive to the Caribbean were the British, occupying Bermuda (1612), San Cristobal (1623), Barbados (1625), Nevis, Antigua, Montserrat, Anguilla, Tortola, Providence (1633) and Jamaica (1655). The French occupied San Cristobal (1625), an island shared with the British for many years, and later Tortuga (1629), Guadalupe (1635) and Martinique (1635).

The Dutch also arrive to the Caribbean and occupied Saba, St. Maarten, St. Eustatius, Curacao, Bonaire, Aruba, Tobago, St. Croix, Tortola, Anegada, Virgin Gorda, Anguilla and for a short period Puerto Rico. In 1672 they created the Dutch West India Company headquartered in Saint Thomas. In 1697, Spaniards formally ceded to France a third part of Hispaniola islands, divided into two colonies with two different languages and cultures. The western part called Saint Domingue (now Haiti) and eastern called Santo Domingo (now Dominican Republic).

The eighteenth and nineteenth centuries were very difficult times for the Spanish colony of Santo Domingo, characterized by a great austerity, conflicts, pirate's attacks, loss of most of the territory, illicit trade, abandonment and finally the struggle for independence. Despite these events, the population of the colony always tried to maintain a social and economic level inside the colony.

However, the presence of these empires generated a strong trade between the Caribbean islands. According to customs documents in the eighteenth century, 70% of the vessels that touched port on Hispaniola came from an insular or continental Caribbean port. During these times the merchandise trading was diverse, but one of most commonly traded products was the Caribbean timber that became an important part of the economy in those centuries. Amongst them were *lignum vitae*, mahogany, logwood and oak.

In the eighteenth and nineteenth centuries, mahogany logging was an extractive industry that largely relied on two main modes of production: clear cutting and selective cutting. Clear cutting is the procedure in which all the trees across a wide area are felled Selective cutting is a more selective method in which a distinctive species of tree is selected and only those in particular are removed.[1] The arrival of the Industrial Revolution, with new machines that streamlined and changed the way of building as well as increasing trade between islands and the European powers, transformed the landscape and the way of life

The timber during the eighteenth century

The early eighteenth century was a time of great tension and hostility in the Caribbean as a result of the previous century, characterized by a general crisis of hunger, diseases, wars and political conflicts among the European powers and other countries. Spain lost its leading role in the region in one of the most complicated moment of its history, during the "War of Succession" (1700-1713), which resulted in the establishment of the new Bourbon dynasty headed by Felipe V of Bourbon.

At the beginning of the eighteenth century Caribbean wood began to be very popular, especially mahogany which was highly esteemed for building, carpentry, joinery, cabinetmakers and manufacture vessels. The timber trade was intensified. In 1702, an advertisement in *The London Gazette*, announced: *"On Wednesday.., will be... exposed to Publick Sale.., the Cargo of the Galeon called the Tauro.., consisting of... Cocoa, Brazelletto, Mohogony"*.[2] There were many other advertisements announcing for sale by auction Caribbean timber, in particular Hispaniola mahogany, such as that in Bonner and Middleton's *Bristol Journal*. (Fig.1)

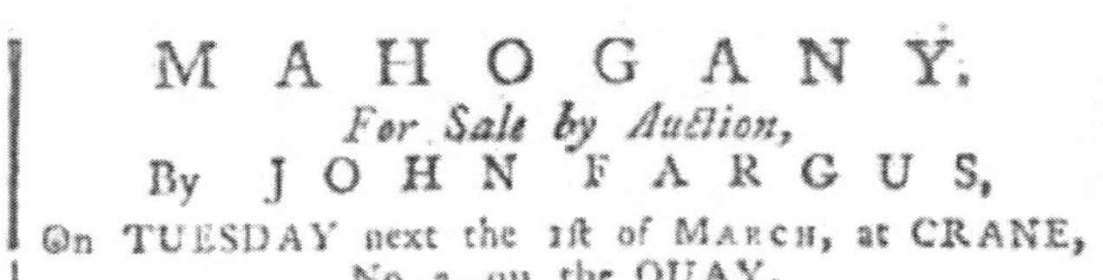

MAHOGANY.

For Sale by Auction,

By JOHN FARGUS,

On TUESDAY next the 1ſt of MARCH, at CRANE, No. 3, on the QUAY,

ABOUT 14,000 Feet of very fine *Hiſpaniola* MAHOGANY, in 11 Lots, from 10 to 12 Hundred Feet in a Lot. This Parcel of Mahogany is nearly as fine as any imported into Briſtol theſe ſeven Years, a great Part of it appearing fit for Veneers, and will be ſold without Reſerve.

The Sale to begin exactly at Half paſt Twelve o'Clock, and continue till ſold.

Removed for the Conveniency of SALE,

And to be Sold by Auction,

Fig.1. Advertisement in Bonner and Middleton's Bristol Journal of 1785 for the auction of mahogany from Hispaniola (Dominican Republic).. Photo: BCC Library Service

The British politician and Chancellor of the Exchequer, Robert Harley in 1711 formed a private commercial organization, The South Sea Company, that was granted the exclusive rights of trade with South America, Central America and Caribbean, through the monopoly of "Asiento" - a thirty-year trade agreement with Spain which permitted British merchants to trade up to 500 tons of goods per year, tax free, which could be sold in the Spanish colonies of Veracruz, Cartagena or Portobelo; together with an unlimited number of slaves. Soon the merchants increased that to 650 tons.[3]

In exchange for these concessions, the British promised not build stone structures in their American territories. This demanded the use of timber in the colonies and the establishment of timber traders and carpenters.[4] The development of trade was so important that the company needed to establish three operational centres in America: Jamaica, its favourable location that had connections with most of Spanish Colonies; Barbados, connecting to Caracas and its hinterland; and Buenos Aires, covering Chile and Peru.[5]

Taking advantage of the "Asiento", the Spanish settlers of Hispaniola prefered to trade with the British and sell the timber or exchange it for slaves. There are documents that prove how common it was for Spaniards to trade slaves for wood with French and British merchants. As a consequence, smuggling and piracy increased and affected the relationship between Britain and Spain resulting in the war of 1727-1729, after which Britain granted Spain the right to stop British ships to ensure that the terms of the agreement were being respected.

In 1733, Sir Robert Walpole, the first Prime Minister of Great Britain, ordered the abolition of taxation on imported goods, including those from the Caribbean, increasing the timber trade from the Caribbean to Europe. In October 1739, Walpole declared war on Spain, called The War of Jenkins' Ear. Demand for Caribbean wood (especially mahogany) amongst the European and settler's aristocracy and the nouveau riche, continued to grow. However, in 1742 after The War of Jenkins' Ear, supplies Jamaican mahogany were nearly exhausted and colonial mahogany supplies decreased rapidly, and what was left of it had outrageous prices.[6]

Nonetheless, the Caribbean timber trade remained important to the European powers. For example, that of the United Kingdom, grew 700% in ten years. Five hundred and twenty five tonnes of wood that were imported in 1740, had grown to 3,688 tons by 1750[7]. This growth affected Caribbean producers, including the Spanish colony of Santo Domingo.

The English historian Jennifer Anderson has said that in the 1760's mahogany began to be imported from the Caribbean region and has documented the proliferation of geographical monikers as a consequence of two types of Mahogany that grows in West Indies: *Swietenia Mahagoni and Swietenia Macrophylla.* The first one is known as Hispaniola, Spanish Mahogany, San Domingo, Santo Dominga, Cuban, Jamaican or True Mahogany. The other species was known as Honduran Mahogany or Mosquito wood.[8]

From 1760, the Industrial Revolution, with its inventions, economic growth and new capitalist models, among other things also stimulated population increase and the growth of cities in Europe. This coincided with the growth of the America independence movement and the increase of north American demand for Caribbean timber.

Increased trade activity and movement between the Caribbean colonies, together with the establishment of free ports in several Caribbean colonies, stimulated an exchange of knowledge and materials in the construction industry. . The free ports in Caribbean colonies were: Curaçao (1675), Saint Thomas, Saint John, Martinique,

Guadeloupe (1763), Saint Lucia and Saint-Domingue (1767). That time was characterized by excessive timber cutting and an intensive timber trade.[9] As a onsequence of Britain's desire for free trade laws, four free ports of Jamaica were declared at Kingston, Lucea, Montego Bay, and Savanna-la-Mar. Also, Barbados was used as a refreshment station for the South Sea Company.[10] All those actions increased timber trade in the Caribbean.

Shipping logs record that sailing vessels left from ports in Saint-Domingue to Kingston with provisions including timber and prisoners, presumably captives from the Seven Years' War (1756-63) and an illegal trade in molasses and rum developed between Saint-Domingue and Jamaica. Before the passing of the Free Port Act in 1766, all tropical goods had to be shipped to and redirected through Britain to non-British colonies or territories.[11]

Hispaniola's Wood architecture of the eighteenth century

During most of the eighteenth century, Hispaniola's architecture was timber, except in Santo Domingo and some other place where settlers determined they should achieve a certain architecture dignity as befitted the seat of government for which they used stone, brick or rammed earth to construct some of the houses, religious, public and government buildings.

According to reports, the typical timber houses had wood boards or mud walls and were thatched with palm leaf cover, palm leaves and wood shingle called *tejamanil*. Usually, the walls were sided with palm board and the roof was of shingle made from one of the resistant Caribbean hardwoods, like mahogany (*Swietenia mahagoni*), oak (*Catalpa longissima*), caya yellow (*Sideroxylon foetidissimum*), baitoa (*Phyllostylon rhamnoides*) and lignum vitae (Guaiacum officinale) among others.

This type of architectur was very common and was fundamental to most of the domestic architecture in the island. It remained for hundreds of years as a model for rural and urban housing and is known as *bohío*, the indigenous name adopted by the Spanish. (Fig.2)

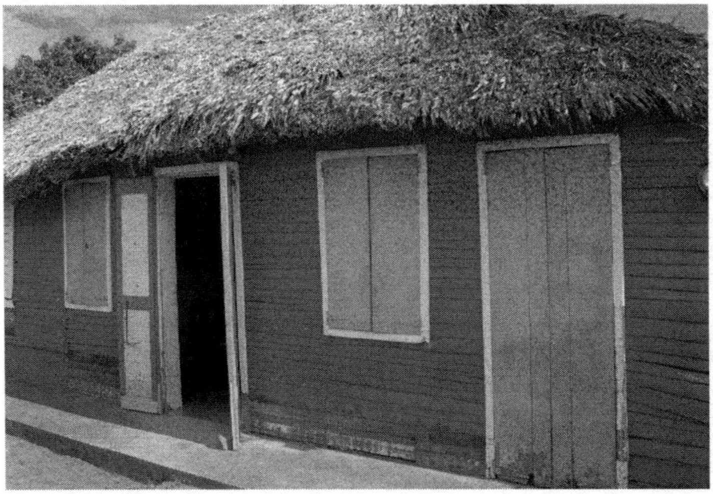

Fig.2. A typical bohio made with palm board and cover with cana (palm leaf) Photo: Virginia Flores, 2013

The *Bohio* of palm board was thus the results of combining indigenous and Spanish traditions with special social and climatic conditions. It has a rectangular plan with a simple practical structure formed of load-bearing wooden walls composed of vertical and horizontal posts.

The vertical posts are called *horcón* and the horizontal elements or sills are called *solera* and placed a doorway's height. All the post carry the loads[12]. In the four corners of the structure there are wooden posts wider than others. Those corner posts are the principals and usually they were made with hatchets from of logs of hard wood like mahogany, cedar or oak among others. In addition to corner posts, intermediate post of the same or smaller scantling might have been placed at intervals. The wall's structure was covered by wooden board or palm board with handmade nails made from wrought iron. The length of the corner posts determined the height of the building from ground to upper sill.

The two types of roofs commonly used were the gable roof with double slopes or the hip roof with four slopes. (Fig.3) This structure was formed by a ridge board or *cumbrera*, hip rafters *limatesa* and common rafters *chorros*, joist *llave*, collar bean and king post *pie de amigo*, all made with wooden post. Over these structures, as alternative for roof they tied the palm leaves that could be *cana*, *guano*, *yarey* or *yagu*a or in some houses they used a wooden shingle call *tejamani* nailed to random-width boards or to shingle laths.[13]

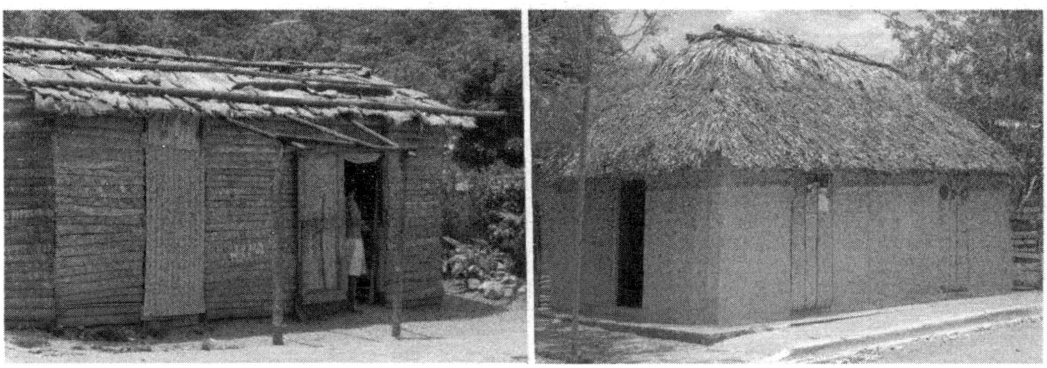

Fig.3. Two types of bohio's roofs: with double slopes or the hip roof with four slopes and the wall with palm board and the other with post and mud. Photo: Virginia Flores, 2013

No two houses have the same dimensions, maybe because they cut the timber as desired, but some old *bohios* that are still in existence measure between 4.60m by 8.30m and 5.7m by 7.60m. The small size of the houses is due to their use almost exclusively as bedrooms, a product of the lifestyle of those that live in tropical regions such as the Caribbean islands of Hispaniola. In addition, the stability against the forces of nature such as earthquakes or hurricanes loads of this simple construction system is extraordinary.

Despite the excellent timbers available in Hispaniola, most settlers preferred to trade them and keep their houses simple with palm board walls and *cana*, *yagua* or wooden shingle roof. The cause was the intensive timber trade that emerged since the eighteenth century with Britain and her colonies, principally with the Thirteen Colonies where timber was the main building material in most of the British colonies.[14]

Timbers, palm boards and construction materials of eighteenth and nineteenth century architecture in the Dominican Republic

In 1730 a French Jesuit priest, Pierre Francois Xavier de Charlevoix, described the Cibao region and said: "..*the houses made of interlaced branches of trees, roofed with palm leaves and a church made of similar material*".[15] In 1764, another French traveller, Daniel L'Escalier, described several villages of the Hispaniola and said that there was little population and housing "..*all made of wood*".[16] According to an inventory of 1766, the church of the newly founded settled of San Joaquin de Dajabón, was "..*24 yards long and eight feet wide*" (8.10m by 2.40m) *roofed with mahogany's shingles*..."[17]

In 1770, as part of the foundation of the town of San Miguel de la Atalaya, newly founded in 1768, the Royal Audience of Santo Domingo, at the request of the prosecutor Vicente Herrera, made an offer to all residents to build "..*a house of bahareque with shingle roof, with a living room and two rooms*"[18]. These houses were built and served as models for the rest of the houses that were built in the region during those years.

The timber trade in Hispaniola did not stop at any time during the eighteenth century. In the customs records there are a lot of papers related to timber sales (board, post and rafter). In 1774 Santiago Cavani, a French doctor living in San Rafael exported 1,598 feet (487 metres) of wooden boards. In 1781 Antonio Linares leads 27,000 feet and the Spanish sergeant Manuel de Castro, 4,000 feet of mahogany timber and 1,000 feet of *amacey* (*Tetragastris balsamifera*) timber. Juan Martinez sold 2,500 shingle, Santiago Cavan 12,000 shingle and Mr. La Pier 385 feet of plank[19].

In 1776, the French lawyer Médéric Louis Elie Moreau de Saint Mery describes housing in Hispaniola as "..*simple huts made with single wooden, surrounded by boards and post, all covered with palm leaves*..." and lit up "...*with slivers of pine, with torches and pieces of cuaba*". Its furnishings are simple and made "..*with native woods usually mahogany and other hardwoods*"[20].

The sale of wooden board and shingles increased. The commodity was sold through the French ports of Saint Domingue to Jamaica and France. Spanish settlers sold their goods through the border. In 1777, several settlers acquired orders to extract timber for building houses. Santiago Saldaña sold 3,000 shingles; Cavani 15,0000 shingles and 200 boards; Gabriel Mendoza 30,0000 shingles; Santiago Familias 11,500 shingles, 200 stakes and 100 posts; Madame Porlier 8,000 mahogany shingles; Antonio Linares y Mr. Sulier 80 posts each of "yaya" (*Oxandra lanceolata*). Also Santiago Camacho extracted 216 boards, 22 stakes and nine ridge posts; Francisco Reinoso 300 palm boards for covering; Mr. Jaime Paler 8,000 shingles and others 7,000 roof shingles from Barón de la Atalaya's forest.[21] In 1778 Luis Peres Guerra extracted 15,750 shingles, 10 stakes, 21 poles and 770 boards. In the same year, Perez Guerra acquired three black slaves in exchange for wood. In 1779 the logging continued in similar proportions. In 1790 Francisco Verde transported 12,500 shingles and 4,000 boards; Javier León 8,000 shingles and others Spaniards sold small amounts of wooden boards and shingles.[22] Unfortunately, none these timber buildings are standing: there are only the records and descriptions of travellers, traders, businessmen and authorities from the island.

The progress of the nineteenth century

The coming and going of passengers and traders kept the Spanish colony of Santo Domingo informed about new scientific and industrial advances, including the architectural stylistic trends of the moment. The development of the modern technology and machinery allowed the standardization of products and processes in construction. Even though the machines designed in the 1800's ran with water power, those provide elements that can be exploited to improve processes, maximize the raw materials utility, reduce time, cost and recycling of the waste.

Over the years a few rudimentary tools were introduced to help streamline and improve efficiency of production. But, at the beginning, most of the new machines required human or animal labour to operate. However, around 1827, Great Britain began manufacturing and exporting the first portable wooden houses to the United States and the first steam engines were installed for cutting boards and wood turning. The Caribbean markets began to attract new siding styles like tongue and groove, lapboard, clapboard and board and batten; as well wooden decorative items, metal roofing, nails, industrial paints and others materials used for construction purposes that were not available in the local market. Also, there were many different choices of materials for manufactured these coatings such as pine, oak, mahogany, palm tree and others.

Since the early eighteenth century timber had also been exported from the United States to Hispaniola. In 1818 a brig, that travelled from New York to Puerto Plata, was wrecked and lost all the timber cargo.[23] Even during the Haitian Occupation (1821-44), logging continued at Hispaniola betweens 1825-37, with an average of 2.5 million feet of mahogany exported and in the last Haitian period between 1838 and 1842, this amounted to 5 million feet of mahogany exported.[24]

From 1830 emerged in the United States a new building system for wooden buildings called "Balloon Frame", which was warmly welcomed by the population and builders. That became popular and quickly spread throughout the country and in regions where they had commercial relations, such as the Caribbean. For example, during 1833, 150 houses were erected in Chicago in one spring and summer alone. This occurred so rapidly that Chicago was almost entirely balloon framed before the fire of 1871. The balloon frame became infamous, following the building of the entire west of the city, mostly in light timber.[25] This construction system lasted for over 100 years because it had the ability to adapt to the different styles that were emerging, adapting to urban and rural housing and provided flexibility to add or combine decorative elements with a lot of freedom. But the best of that system was that it could be accommodated to the diverse styles that emerged in north America during the Victorian period (1837-1901) like: Gothic Revival (1840), Gingerbread (1860), Folk Victorian (1870), Shingle Style (1874), Queen Anne (1880), Craftsmen (1880-1905) and Georgian Revival (1895).

This new architecture became fashionable among the rich and the new middle class that was emerging, was very manageable, easy to transport and assemble and even sold by catalogue. This architecture's revolution changed the landscape of cities, towns and even the countryside. You could order and buy all types of buildings: homes, schools, churches, stables and barns among others.

The new architectural model had the advantage of being adaptable to different climatic conditions and did not require an expert builder to do it, which stimulated its rapid acceptance especially in people living faraway from big cities or in places outside the United States territory. This gave the opportunity to have a new building in anywhere it was wanted. (Fig.4)

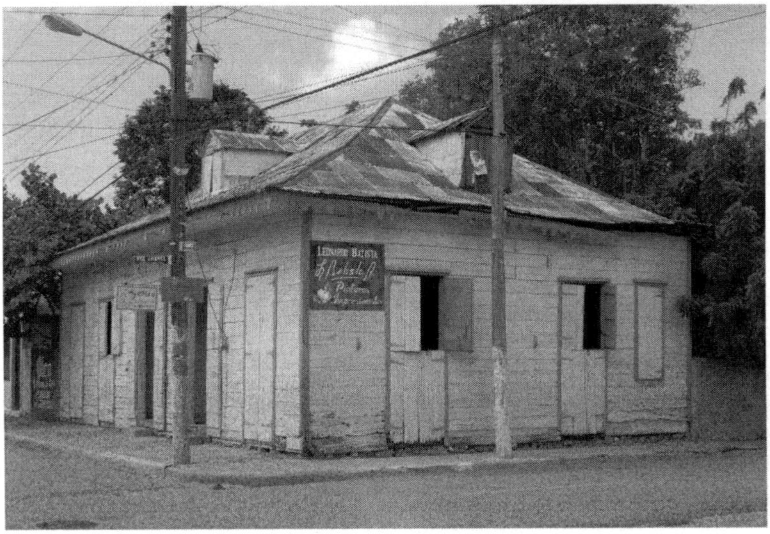

Fig.4. Timber house building with pine board in 1860, Montecristy, Dominican Republic. Photo: Virginia Flores, 2011

In the Caribbean, agents for the many brands, emphasized the rewards that these kinds of buildings offered, successfully conquering the unfamiliarity of most of the inhabitants and consequently this timber architecture became a symbol of modernity and progress. Some replaced the *bohio* with a "Balloon frame" timber house decorated with artistic grilles, brackets and others ornaments. Some people ordered and bought the plans, the whole house or just the catalogue as reference. Everything was sent by sea and was assembled in the country.

Since 1864, books and guides had been published about building wooden houses, such as that of George E, Woodward, who published several editions of "*Practical Construction of dwelling houses for the Country, Suburb and village with full and complete sets of specifications and an estimate of the cost of each design*".[26] In 1878 A.J. Bicknell & Co, published "*Specimen Book of One Hundred Architectural Designs*" showing plans, elevations and views of buildings. The price of the book and catalogue was one dollar. The catalogue contained drawings, floor plans, elevations, specifications, cost estimates, interior perspectives, doors, windows, shutters, hinges, handles, sanitary wares, selling and all suppliers. On buying the buildings, they were sent the instructions, patterns and diagrams sufficiently clear and explicit so anyone could make their house without being an expert.

Economic stability and increased trade relations with European countries favoured the establishment and representation of many foreign firms and trading houses in Dominican Republic. Most of them were American, probably because of geographical proximity. Trading houses were installed in Montecristi, Puerto Plata, Samaná, Sánchez, San Pedro de Macorís, Santo Domingo, Azua, Barahona, Santiago, La Vega, San Juan de la Maguana and El Seibo. Thus, the new architecture reached the entire population, urban and rural.

At that moment, the most important traders were: Rotschild, Coen & Co., J.B. Bouví, Ginebra Hnos., J.B. Cambiaso, Pellerano y Maggiolo, Jules Grandgerard, T.S. Heneken and Nicolás Durocher[27]. Importers established in the northern region were: C.J. Neuman & Co., C.S. Passailaique, W.O.Bartlett, Lithgow Brothers and Arzeno & Co.[28]

Over the time and the acquisition of knowledge by the Creole carpenters, the population began to imitate the imported model and build their own homes using some prefabricated elements and other, locally made for lower costs using native woods or combined with imported timber, always maintaining the proportions and style. (Fig.5)

In Hispaniola everyone wanted to have a timber house with decorative details built by a Creole carpenter. A record of 1864 said "*..three particular timber houses arrived*" from the United States to Santo Domingo. Those portables houses were sold by catalogue and "*sent by mail*". It is still not known how many arrived in the country.

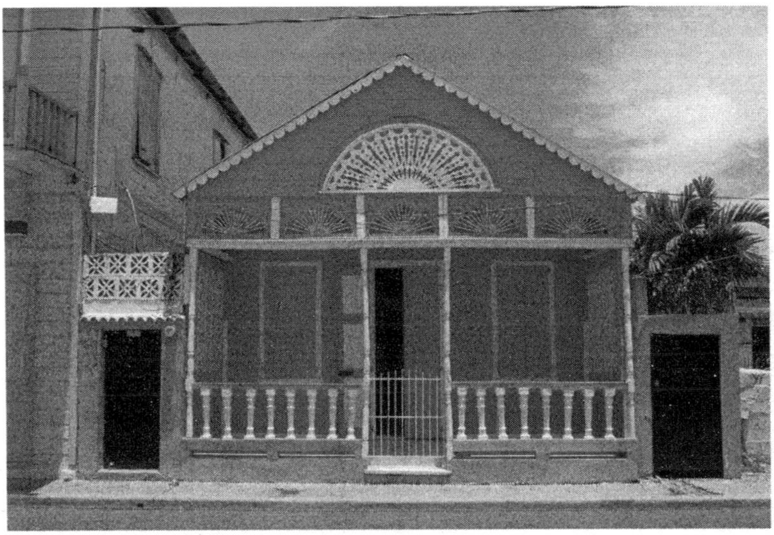

Fig.5. Timber house built in 1885 by Creole carpenter with artistic grilles, balusters and brackets, Puerto Plata, Dominican Republic. Photo: Virginia Flores, 2014

Most of the goods that arrived came from the ports of Pennsylvania, Massachusetts, New York, Maine, South Carolina, London, Liverpool, Glasgow and Bristol and from other European ports in Belgium, France and Germany. Towards the Caribbean, 61.5 per cent of exports come from New York, 14.3 per cent from New Orleans, 9.9 per cent from Baltimore; 9.35 per cent from Boston and Maine and 4.94 per cent from Philadelphia.[29] Between's 1891-92 the United States posted the biggest profit in history for foreign trade and most of that trade were buildings, including their "*Houses by Mail*".

Local and imported timber was processed in modern sawmills. The first established was at La Vega, with others later in Santiago by 1889. These were steam-powered and used their own sawdust as fuel. Also established were brush machines, clapboard machines, moulding machines, among others. Another product used was palm board which was cut and prepared with more rudimentary tools. Most urban and rural houses put on the front façade, sawn timber and on the sides and the rear façade, palm board, thus reducing the building cost but maintaining the appearance of wealth. (Fig.6)

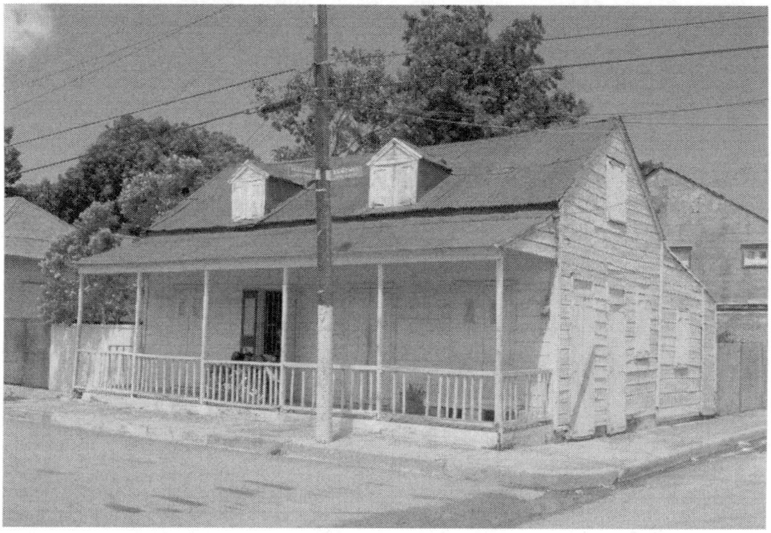

Fig.6. Timber house building in 1890, Montecristy, Dominican Republic. Photo: Virginia Flores, 2011

In the late nineteenth century the "novelty"siding board for use on the facades became very popular in North American and West Indies, arriving in Hispaniola around 1890. The board had the top rounded with a "scallop" and the shiplap edge created a shadow on the wall surface. In the warehouses could be found diverse type of board, such as : brushed tongue and groove, 6, 9, 10 and 12 inches wide by 1 inch thick; un-brushed, 6 inches wide; brushed on both sides without tongue and groove to make frames; board with drawstring at the centre and on both sides; floor boards, 4 and 4½ inches wide. Also available were mouldings, artistic grilles, balusters, brackets and different type of ornaments, most of these made with Creole wooden. (Fig.7)

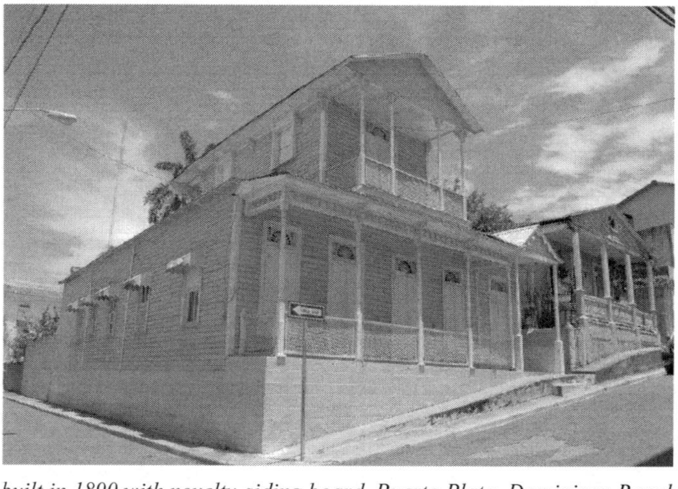

Fig.7. Timber house built in 1890 with novelty-siding board, Puerto Plata, Dominican Republic. Photo: Virginia Flores, 2014

Over time the balloon frame was replaced by the platform frame, the fundamental difference of which was construction floor by floor, so that the fabric of the walls prevents or disrupts the continuity of the pillars between the first and the second level, generating individually visible levels.

Conclusions

Certainly prefabrication and industrialized materials was an important contribution to the development of the Caribbean islands. The new architectural model changed the landscape and the appearance of Caribbean cities, becoming part of the identity of the region.

The bulk of the architecture was created by non-professionals but included good Creole carpenters, craftsmanship and cabinetmakers. They made buildings with beautifully decorated details and stylistic features such as decorative elements above doors, windows, balconies. The fashion and novelty of foreign products maintained the import of large quantities of goods like pine wood, boards, decorative pieces, joints, and other wooden products. This material often arrived in a raw state and was converted by local sawyers at point of use.

In 1844, the Spanish colony of Santo Domingo achieved independence and the new republic sought a new identity through architecture, building in line with the modern times and other islands and the regions of the Caribbean in an endeavor to show the new trends, trying to forget the colonial times and the 22 years of Haitian Occupation.

Notes and references

[1] Jennifer L. Anderson, Mahogany. *The costs of luxury in Early America.* London: First Harvard University, 2015.

[2] Newspaper Archives (1665 - 1913), *London Gazzette*, February 22-25, 1702, No. 3891/3.

[3] Margarita Rodríguez García, *Compañías privilegias del comercio con América y cambio político (1706-1765).* Estudios de Historia Económica, N°46. Madrid: Banco de España, 2005.

[4] Geoffrey J. Walker, *Política española y comercio colonial, 1700-1789.* Barcelona: Ariel, 1979.

[5] Georges H Nelson. *'Contraband Trade under the Asiento. 1730-1739'*, London, The American Historical Review, Oxford University Press, Vol. 51, No. 1, Oct., 1945, pp. 55-67

[6] George Newton Lamb, *The Mahogany Book.* Chicago, Illinois: Published Mahogany Association, Inc. 1947.

[7] Adam Bowett. "*'The 1721 Naval Stores Act and the Commercial Introduction of Mahogany, Furniture History, XXX* ". National Archives, United Kingdom, 1994, pp. 42-56

[8] Anderson, (Note 1), p.35

[9] Nadine Hunt. 'Contraband, free ports, and British merchants in the Caribbean world. 1739-1772', in *Diacronie Studi di Storia Contemporanea.* N°13, 1. Contrabbandieri, pirati e frontiere: per una storia delle pratiche informali nell'America Centrale (XVII-XXI secolo), Italy: 2013.p.7

[10] Nadine Hunt. 'Expanding the frontiers of western Jamaica through minor Atlantic ports in the eighteenth century', in *Canadian Journal of History*, No.45, March 2010, pp.485-501.

[11] Hunt. (Note 10) p.4

[12] Esteban Prieto Vicioso. 'El bohío como expresión de la arquitectura vernácula dominicana en la Región Sur'. (Ph.D. thesis, Universidad Michoacana de San Nicolás de Hidalgo, Morelia, México, 2008), pp.

[13] The traditional way to made de wooden shingle was to rive (hand split) them from straight grained, knot free,

sections of logs pre-cut to the desired length known as bolts. The wood species varied according to available local woods, but only the more durable heartwood, or inner section, of the log was usually used.

[14] Marcus Whiffen. "The Eighteenth-Century Houses of Williamsburg. A study of Architecture and Building in the Colonial Capital of Virginia". Charlottesville, Virginia: The Colonial Williamsburg Foundation, University Press of Virginia.1990.

[15] Pierre Francois Xavier Charlevoix. "Historia de la Isla Española o de Santo Domingo. Escrita particularmente sobre las memorias manuscritas del Padre Jean Bautista Le Pers, jesuita, misionero en Santo Domingo y sobre los documentos originales que se conserven en el depósito de la Marina". Sociedad Dominicana de Bibliófilos, Inc., Santo Domingo, R. D.: Editora de Santo Domingo, 1977.

[16] Manuel V. Hernández González. "La colonización de la frontera dominicana 1680-1795". Archivo General de la Nación Vol.XXV, Academia Dominicana de la Historia Vol. LXXI, Colección Investigaciones 5, Santo Domingo: Editora Búho, 2006.

[17] Ibíd., p.138

[18] Ibíd., p.204

[19] Ibíd., pp.181-182

[20] M. L. Moreau de Saint-Mery. "Descripción Topográfica y Política de la Parte española de la Isla de Santo Domingo, traducido en 1944". Sociedad Dominicana de Bibliófilos, Inc. Santo Domingo, R. D.: Editora de Santo Domingo, 1976.

[21] Archivo Histórico Nacional (A.H.N.) Ultramar. Libro 769. Libro de la administración de San Rafael de la Angostura desde 1774 a 1786. España.

[22] A.H.N. Ultramar. Libro 769. Libro de la administración de San Rafael de la Angostura desde 1774 a 1786. España.

[23] Archivo General de la Nación. Expediente relativo a varias ventas y pérdida de maderas. Marzo a diciembre 1818, No. 10, Depósito especial, DO AGN JPI.1.6.A159-2 Santo Domingo, R. D.

[24] Roberto Cassá."Historia social y económica de la República Dominicana", Tomo I. Santo Domingo, R. D.: Editora Alfa & Omega, 2003

[25] Colin Davies. *The Prefabricated Home*. London: Reaktion Books, 2005. pp.44-47

[26] George E. Woodward, Edward G. Thompson. A V. "A Victorian housebuilder's guide : "Woodward's national architect" of 1869 / George E. Woodward / Edward G. Thompson". New York: Dover Publications.1988

[27] Cassá (Note 26) p.16

[28] Ibíd. Pp.34-38

[29] Port through which commodity were departures to West Indies (1853-90): **New York** (3): Port Jefferson, New York, Staten Island. **Pennsylvania** (1): Philadelphia. **Massachusetts** (9): Boston, New Bedford, Salem, Bass River, Danversport, Provincetown, Harwich, Fall River, Nantucket. **Delaware** (1): Wilmington. **South Carolina** (1): Charleston. **North Carolina** (1): New Bern. **Rhode Island** (1): Newport, Providence. **Maine** (26): Bucksport, Searsport, Columbia Falls, Thomaston, Belfast, Bangor, Portland, Calais, Damariscotta, Camden, Rockland, Ellsworth, Yarmouth, Castine, Machias, Wiscasset, Bath, Georgetown, Boothbay, Milbridge, Gloucester, Rockport, Bookhaven, Bucksport, Waldoboro, Richmond. **Ohio** (1): Cleveland. **Maryland** (1): Baltimore. **Virginia** (1): Accumack. "National Archives and Records Administration (NARA)", United States and "Immigrant Ships Transcribers Guild LLC. 1850-90

From de l'Orme's to Hetzer's arch roofs: engineering the elegance

Louis Vandenabeele, Inge Bertels, and Ine Wouters
Department of Architectural Engineering, Vrije Universiteit Brussel (VUB), Belgium

Introduction

It is hard to imagine what current timber construction would look like without glued laminated timber (glulam). Timber arches spanning more than 150 metres or ten-storey buildings are some of the recent examples which would not have been possible without glued laminated products. With today's revival of timber as a structural material, this technology, which allows us to go beyond the restraints of solid timber with regard to its natural growing dimensions and properties, still has a promising future.

The invention of modern glulam can be attributed to Otto Hetzer, a German master carpenter and sawmill owner who patented several casein-glued elements in the 1900s. Hetzer's pioneer work has been documented in several studies, among others by Hengeveld (1979), Meschke (1989), Rug (1996, 2006) and Müller (1998). [1] The paternity of Hetzer's invention is usually credited to the French Colonel Emy's laminated arches, first built in 1825 in France, which were themselves inspired by Philibert de l'Orme's system (1561). These early nineteenth-century developments of de l'Orme's and Emy's arches, as well as their historical structural understanding, have been investigated by Booth (1971), Quagliarini (2003), Campa (2006), Hahmann (2006) and Mongelli (2006). [2] More recently, the nineteenth-century applications of de l'Orme's system in Bavaria – whose last built example dates from 1875 – have been traced back by Säbel (2012).[3] In England, Bell (2015) discovered surviving examples of Emy-type arches, which were erected between 1840 and 1864.[4]

As can be seen, most research on the origin of glulam focusses on the renowned trinity of de l'Orme, Emy and Hetzer.[5] Nevertheless, the study of nineteenth- and early twentieth-century technical literature on timber construction reveals that many other timber arch roofs were developed before Hetzer's invention, as improvements or alternatives to de l'Orme's and Emy's systems, especially after the criticisms levelled by Captain Ardant against laminated arches in 1840.[6]

Therefore, this paper sheds light on these less known yet remarkable timber arches designed between 1840 and 1910, based on their representation in the historical technical literature. By positioning these arch roofs in their chronological and technological frameworks, the present research aims at nuancing, detailing and broadening the historical background preceding the glulam invention by Otto Hetzer.

The precursor works of de l'Orme and Emy

Before discussing the developments which followed the inventions of de l'Orme and Emy, it is worth briefly reviewing the main characteristics and applications of these two precursor arch roof systems.

In 1561, Philibert de l'Orme, architect of King Henri II, published a treatise in which he presented a new laminated arch roof system.[7] He composed his arches from two staggered vertical layers of short boards (about 1.3 metres). These arches were positioned very close to each other (about 0.6 metre) and connected with horizontal *liernes*, which also ensured the bond between each layer of boards using wooden pegs. (Fig 1.a) Applied to a few castles in the 1540-50s, the invention of de l'Orme fell into disuse during the two following centuries, until 1783, when the architects Legrand and Molinos excelled in applying the system to the cupola of the *Halle au blé* in Paris, with a span of 40 metres.[8] Praised for its aesthetics, de l'Orme's system was transposed in the following decades to numerous arch roofs in France.[9] In Germany, the architect David Gilly popularized the technique with his 1797 treatise. He also modified de l'Orme's system by joining two or three layers of boards with iron nails and by increasing the spacing between the arches up to 3 to 4 metres, thereby creating what is more in the way of a purlin roof.[10] (Fig. 1.b)

In 1819, Colonel Amand Rose Emy was commissioned to design a roof with a span of 21 metres for a military horse riding hall in Libourne, according to the system of de l'Orme. On this occasion, Emy noticed that the cutting of curved boards generated a lot of material waste, and it required an important recourse to skilled craftsmanship.[11] Consequently, he developed his own roof system which consisted in assembling long flexible boards (about 10 metres) in horizontal layers (between five and eight), which were retained in that position using iron bolts.[12] In 1825, he had the opportunity to first apply his innovative method to a riding hall in Marac (Fig. 1.c), followed the next year by Libourne (Fig. 1.d). Besides de l'Orme's legacy, Emy also credited his invention to the previous work of Carl Friedrich von Wiebeking in the 1800s.[13] Indeed, during the construction of the Altenmarkt Bridge (Austria) in 1809, Wiebeking employed thin boards of timber which he glued together in order to obtain long continuous arches.[14] Although Emy admired the lamination principle, he did not believe that the glue was an efficient solution regarding the arch's durability.[15]

In the first decades of the nineteenth century, the systems of de l'Orme and Emy gained a European fame thanks to their unrivalled elegance. However, diverging views started to call into question their structural behaviour in the early 1840s. One of the main contributor to these criticisms was Captain Paul-Joseph Ardant, who published his *Études théoriques et expérimentales sur l'établissement des charpentes à grande portée* in 1840.[16]

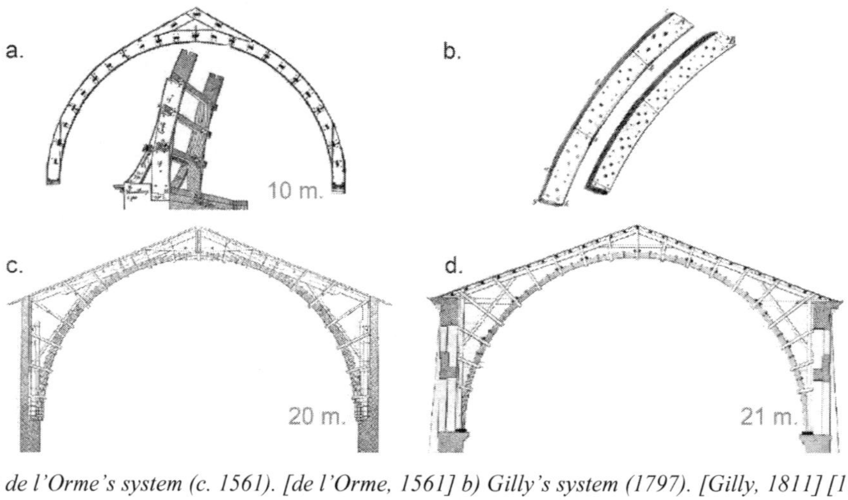

Figure 1. a) de l'Orme's system (c. 1561). [de l'Orme, 1561] b) Gilly's system (1797). [Gilly, 1811] [17]c) Emy's roof in Marac (1825). [Emy, 1841] d) Emy's roof in Libourne (1826). [Emy, 1841].

Arches from straight elements

Although Emy was convinced – through his own experiments – that his laminated arches were sufficiently rigid to avoid any horizontal force on their supports, this statement was discredited by the theoretical and experimental investigations of Ardant. Financed by the French Ministry of War, Ardant's work demonstrated that the arches of Emy, but also those of de l'Orme, were much more flexible than widely believed at the time: not only were laminated arched easily subject to local bucking, they also always exerted horizontal forces at their feet. Ardant mentioned:

> "It seems that if curved arch roofs keep some advantage over roofs composed of straight elements, it is only for having a more graceful shape, and that on the important aspect of solidity and economy, the first ones are very inferior to the latter".[18]

Because Ardant also claimed that curved arch roofs were much more expensive than roofs composed of straight members, he developed several alternatives which attempted to preserve the elegance of the timber arch while improving its cost and structural efficiency. (Figs 2.a & 2.b) Ardant's conclusions were immediately adopted by the Ministry of War and his frames became very popular from the 1840s onwards, as shown by their omnipresence in the technical literature until the turn of the twentieth century. Nevertheless, the lateral stability of Ardant's roofs was inadequate due to their poor triangulation, which still left room for improvement.[19] Attempts to solve this problem consisted, for example, in increasing the number of tangential members (Fig. 2.c) or in combining Ardant's frame with a semi-circular arch (Fig. 2.d).

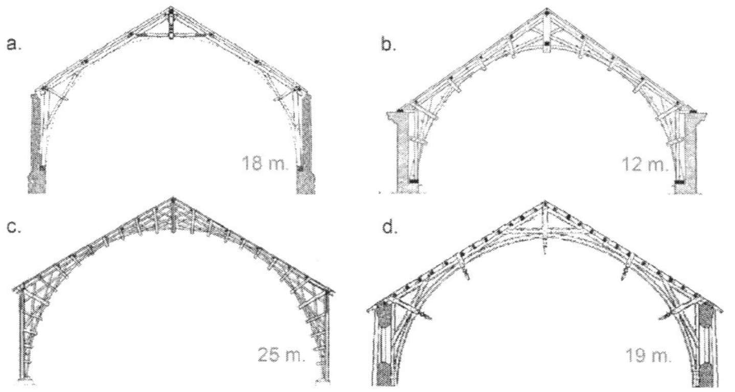

Figure 2. a) & b) Ardant's systems (c.1840). [Böhm, 1911] c) Modification of Ardant's system (undated). [Oslet, 1890][20] d) Modification of Ardant's system (undated). [Böhm, 1911]

In 1846, the imperfections of Ardant's system were addressed by Captain Victor Hippolyte Fabré who was responsible for building a new military horse riding hall in Castres using Ardant's typology. Fabré proposed an alternative system, an inverted funicular arch, which was not approved for the construction. Nevertheless, the *Comité des fortifications* asked him to test the invention, which he did in 1849. His successful results were then communicated to contemporary engineers through his 1851 treatise.[21]

Fabré's principal idea consisted in matching the shape of the timber arch with the funicular polygon corresponding to the system of forces applied on the roof. (Figs 3.a & 3.b) By doing so, large bending moments were avoided in the arch, leading to important savings in material; for identical spans, his system required about 60% less timber than the Ardant's frame, while still offering an increased resistance.[22] Because the shape of the graphically-determined funicular polygon varied in response to asymmetrical loadings (snow, wind and workers), he made sure that the funicular could in any case be drawn between the upper rafters and the lower arch, in such a way that the forces could always be redistributed on the internal elements if necessary. Hence, these diagonal bracing struts ensured the lateral stability of the whole.

In his treatise, Fabré repeatedly referred to suspension bridges with iron chains which were in widespread use at the time. He compared his roof system to an inverted bridge where the iron chain would be the timber arch and the iron ties the vertical timber struts.[23] He even dedicated a small chapter of his book on the application of his theory to iron bridges, which is noteworthy. Indeed, Fabré advised suspending two iron chains in a vertical plane, and placing between these chains several vertical cast iron elements, in the same spirit as his timber struts positioned between the arch and the rafters. The shape of the chains would thus not vary in response to the asymmetrical loads, thereby limiting oscillations and the risk of damage to the deck. According to Fabré, the chains could even be replaced by several iron frames. An application of this brilliant idea can still be observed on the outer spans of the London Tower Bridge built between 1886 and 1894.

Although the paternity of funicular timber roofs might certainly be credited to Fabré,[24] another French captain, Pierre-Félix Michon, described in a comparable way a very similar roof structure as early as 1848, (Figs 3.c & 3.d) a year before Fabré's experiments. This type of roof was thus quite popular and discussed within the French military engineers' circles in the 1840-50s. Michon also put forward the great resistance and economic use of material resulting from this new roof system compared to Emy's system. However, he thought that semi-circular arches remained more graceful than funicular ones,[25] which might explain why such arches did not make a breakthrough in the construction field during the years that followed their invention.

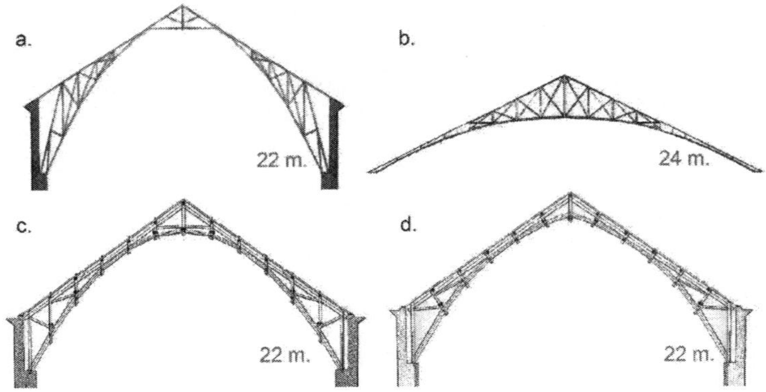

Figure 3. a) & b) Fabré's funicular arches (c.1846). [Fabré, 1851] c) & d) Michon's funicular arches (c.1848). [Michon, 1848]

Upgrading de l'Orme's and Emy's arches

Semi-circular and funicular arches composed of straight elements were a way to cope with Ardant's criticisms. Another interesting approach consisted in upgrading the existing systems of de l'Orme and Emy – somehow considered to be more pleasant to the eye – whilst taking into account their then-known weaknesses.

In order to increase the stiffness of Emy's arch, a first solution was to construct an additional arch inside the usual system which was left unchanged. (Fig. 4.a) The internal arch was built from the assembly of five layers of boards, while the thickness of the external arch varied from nine layers at the foot to seven at the top. Eventually, these two semi-circular arches were connected using a braced network of timber members, as seen in Fabré's funicular system. The resulting roof had an internal span of about 24 metres which is somewhat larger than the traditional arch roofs of Emy.

One of the main criticisms against the Emy's arches was related to the lateral forces at their feet, which could overturn the supporting walls. For example, this defect was taken into account in the design of the Saint-Germain station (Paris Region) which was erected around 1845 by the French architect Alfred Armand.[26] (Fig. 4.b) Indeed, an iron tie allowed the taking up of thrust forces, ensuring the stability of the construction. Not surprisingly, this rational solution was also applied to de l'Orme's system. In Germany there was a renaissance of this system in the second half of the nineteenth century thanks to Gilly's improvements, an example being the 1869 gymnasium built in Karlsruhe by the architect Heinrich Lang.[27] (Fig. 4.c) Just as for Saint-Germain station's roof, the thrust forces were borne by a tie.

Unlike Michon, the Spanish architect Antoni Gaudí admired the architectural qualities of funicular arches. Around 1883, he was commissioned to design his first medium-sized building: a bleaching factory for the *Cooperativa Obrera Mataronense*, which required a span of 12 metres.[28] Gaudí, who was acquainted with the treatise of Emy, opted for de l'Orme's system of vertical boards and applied the latter to a funicular shape. (Fig. 4.d) Instead of using nails in Gilly's way, Gaudí joined three layers of boards with iron bolts, the lengths of these boards varying in function of the arch's curvature. From a structural perspective, the arch followed the shape of a parabola, that is to say the funicular polygon corresponding to a distributed vertical load. Yet, as noticed by Brullet Tenas (2006) who renovated the structure, the load in this case was concentrated close to the top of the arch.[29] The parabolic form, which is thus not the optimal shape here, was clearly chosen for its elegance. The premises of Gaudí's architectural quest are perceptible through this early work, where the timber funicular arch regained its nobility.

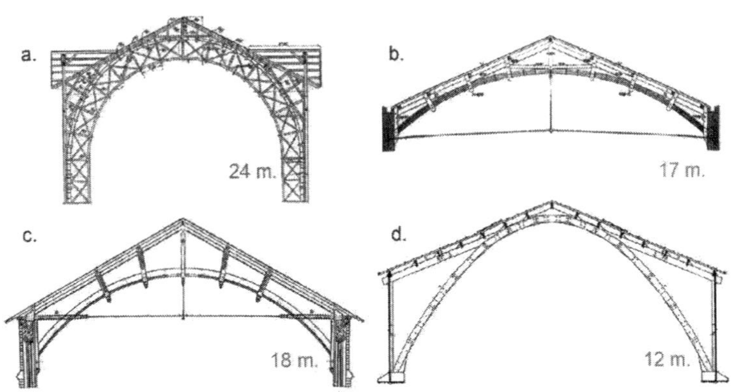

Figure 4. a) Upgrade of Emy's arch (undated). [Oslet, 1890] b) Upgrade of Emy's arch by Armand (c. 1845). [Böhm, 1911] c) Upgrade of de l'Orme's arch by Lang (1869). [Böhm, 1911] d) Upgrade of de l'Orme's arch by Gaudí (c.1883). [Pane, 1964][30]

Towards efficient timber cross-sections

The laminated systems developed by de l'Orme and Emy had drastically improved the formability of timber. Nevertheless, the above-mentioned laminated arches were all built from the stacking of boards in one given direction, forming a square-profile. As a next step, a very significant innovation may be traced back to the construction of the French pavilion during the International Exposition held in Vienna in 1873. The construction can be attributed to Philippe Bosc whose *Modèle de charpente pour espace carré, voûté, à grande portée* had been selected in order to represent French progresses in architecture and civil engineering.[31] His ingenious elliptical arch combined the system of de l'Orme with that of Emy, shaping an efficient bolted I-section. (Fig. 5.a) Certainly for the first time, the I-profile – which was already in use in iron construction since the mid-1830s[32] – was applied to a timber arch. The resulting gain of strength and the saving of material were immediately acknowledged in the 1874 edition of the *Zeitschrift des österreichischen Ingenieur- und Architekten-Vereins* (Journal of the Austrian Engineers and Architects Association).[33] The success of Bosc's system in the Germanic world is also shown by its implementation in the hall of the *Sängerfest*, built in Vienna in 1890, which had an incredible span of 56 metres.[34] (Fig. 5.b)

Bosc's system opened the way towards a more rational use of timber thanks to an efficient arrangement of the boards. Indeed, in the same year, the German architect and *Hofzimmermeister* (master carpenter) Philipp Stephan developed a new roof system with the idea of improving the stiffness of the arch by increasing the moment of inertia of its cross-section, in order words, by enlarging the distance between the flanges.[35] These flanges were composed of nailed boards – measuring between 6 and 8 metres – which were bent in the vertical plane. The flanges were then connected by a network of diagonal members forming a lattice truss. (Fig. 5.c) With a span of about 20 metres, the first versions of this system were stabilized by a timber tie-beam, which was replaced by iron in later versions, such as the one built in 1907 for the *Sängerbundesfesthalle* of Wrocław (span of 33 metres).[36]

Around 1893, the German *Hofzimmermeister* Ernst Noack built a somewhat similar system in order to shelter a temporary working area which had to be used during the construction of the *Carolabrücke* in Dresden. (Fig. 5.d) The flanges were made of horizontal and vertical layers of boards forming two U-profiles, one of which was horizontal. With its diagonals, the resulting structure can be regarded as a Warren truss with a span of 20 metres. This arrangement also facilitated the sizing of the structure, thanks to the available graphical calculation methods which had initially been developed for iron structures.

Another remarkable structure built by Noack was realized for the Third German Arts and Crafts Exhibition held in Dresden in 1906. (Fig. 6.a) Just as Fabré and Gaudí before him, Noack opted for the efficient inverted funicular shape in order to span 18 metres. The arch's section was made of two U-profiles, each consisting of bolted vertical boards – similarly to Gaudí's arch – whose lengths depended on the curvature, and of horizontal boards bolted in Bosc's fashion. The two U-profiles were maintained at close distance by a sort of internal timber truss. Finally, the arch's thrust force was taken up by a moment-resisting frame which had been anchored to the ground.

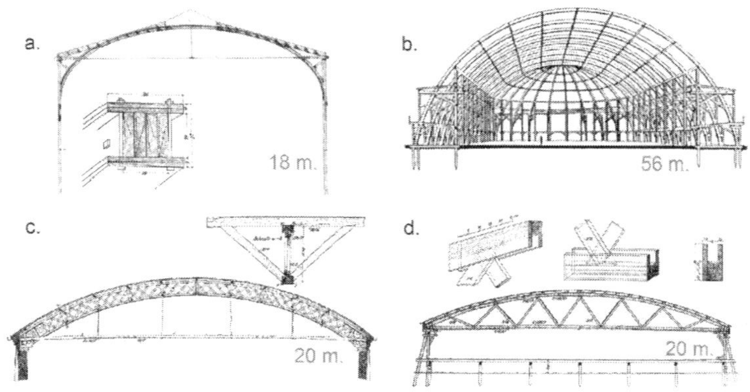

Figure 5. a) Bosc's arch (1873). [Rada, 1874] b) Sängerfest Hall of Vienna (1890). [Meschke, 1989] c) Stephan's arch (c.1890). [Böhm, 1911] d) Noack's truss (c.1893). [Böhm, 1911]

Recontextualizing Hetzer's invention

Karl Friedrich Otto Hetzer, a German *Hofzimmermeister* and sawmill owner, is known as the inventor of modern glulam. He launched his firm in 1872 and – due to his very good knowledge of the properties, processing and applications of timber – filed five patents between 1892 and 1907.[37] He created optimized elements by carefully selecting and combining different types of wood. Because he was not satisfied with the rigidity achieved with bolts or nails when connecting timber boards, he decided to use a casein glue prepared by himself.[38] This glue, as many other animal adhesives, was already known since the second half of the eighteenth century.[39] In the nineteenth century, it is reported that the above-mentioned Altenmarkt Bridge (1809) and several English roofs were assembled thanks to such adhesives.[40]

Using casein glue, Hetzer patented in 1906 a glued laminated arch composed of horizontally arranged boards. From 1907, thanks to efficient advertising, many companies bought the licence and started to erect roof frames according to this system in Germany, Switzerland, Scandinavia and the Netherlands.[41] The cross-sections of these first structures were always laminated I-profiles, which had already been patented by Hetzer in 1900. This I-profile was strongly similar to that of Bosc (1873), apart from the fact that Hetzer had replaced the bolts by glue.

Another key point was the shape of these structures, whose cross-section's depth followed the bending moment diagram in order to save material. In the same spirit of efficiency, several of these early glulam arches were designed according to a funicular shape, an idea which has already been related to the works of Fabré (1851), Gaudí (1883) and Noack (1906). (Fig. 6.b & 6.c) Moreover, many of these glulam structures were built as three-hinged arches, which are statically-determinate systems and therefore easy to size with precision. This typology had been realized for the first time – as a full iron truss – by the German engineer Johann Wilhelm Schwedler in 1865.

Finally, one year before Hetzer's death, a milestone in the development of his arch roof occurred during the Brussels International Exposition of 1910, announcing the worldwide success of glulam. His system was applied to the German Railway hall which had a considerable span of 43 metres. (Fig. 6.d) At the time, the poor corrosion resistance of iron led to its replacement by timber in railway buildings, chemical industries, salt depots, etc.[42]

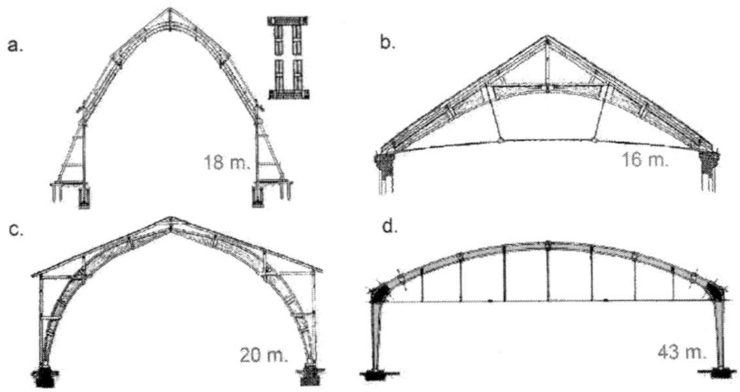

Figure 6. a) Noack's funicular arch (1906). [Böhm, 1911] b) & c) Hetzer's glulam arches (c. 1908). [Böhm, 1911] d) Hetzer's Railway Hall (1910). [Müller, 1998]

Conclusions

From de l'Orme to Hetzer, we have traced back the numerous developments of the ingenious idea which consists in assembling small timber pieces in order to produce great arches.

Starting from the structural criticisms addressed in the 1840s against de systems of de l'Orme and Emy, we have identified two main structural and formal responses. A first radical choice was to create arches from the assembly of straight elements; while a second group of builders adopted a more respectful approach by trying to preserve the elegance of de l'Orme's and Emy's arches. In the 1870s, a major step was achieved with the design of very efficient cross-sections through the combination of de l'Orme's and Emy's systems. From then onwards, most innovations occurred in the Germanic world, a transition which is perfectly illustrated by the construction of the French pavilion of the Vienna International Exposition in 1873.

The analysis of the construction principles and architectural aspects of Hetzer's glulam arches resurrects the majority of these previous developments, as described in the last section of this article. Moreover, the influence of iron engineering has been pointed out several times: as a source of inspiration for the structural behaviour (suspension bridges, Warren trusses, three-hinged arches), as well as for the construction details (I-profiles) of timber arches.

Although the aesthetic aspect was never far from the discussion, it is thanks to the improvement of their structural efficiency that the elegance of timber arches could be preserved until the invention of modern glulam at the turn of the twentieth century. Consequently, as highly engineered structures, glulam arches remain today one of the most graceful, economical and sustainable ways of spanning large distances.

Acknowledgments

The authors wish to thank Stefan M. Holzer for his valuable remarks. The present research could be realized thanks to the funding of the Agency for Innovation by Science and Technology (IWT).

References

[1] D.J. Hengeveld and H. van Putten, Het gelamineerde hout in Nederland, Delft: Delftse Universitaire Pers, 1979.
H.-J. Meschke, 'Baukunst und -technik der hölzernen Wölbkonstruktionen : Vom Bogentragwerk zum Stabnetzwerk' (Ph.D. thesis, Rheinisch-Westfälischen Technischen Hochschule Aachen, 1989).
W. Rug and F. Rug, 'Innovation in Timber Engineering: The Hetzer Method', Vol.4, pp. 435–42 in V.K.A. Gopu, (Ed.), *Proceedings of the International Wood Engineering Conference*, New Orleans 1996, New Orleans: Louisiana State University, 1996.
W. Rug, '100 Jahre Hetzer-Patent', Bautechnik, Vol.8, no.83, 2006, pp. 533–40.
C. Müller, 'Entwicklung des Holzleimbaues unter besonderer Berücksichtigung der Erfindungen von Otto Hetzer - ein Beitrag zur Geschichte der Bautechnik' (PhD thesis, Bauhaus-Universität Weimar, 1998).
[2] L.G. Booth, 'The Development of Laminated Timber Arch Structures in Bavaria, France and England in the early nineteenth century', *Journal of the Institute of Wood Science*, Vol.5, 1971, pp. 3-16.
E. Quagliarini, A. Stazi, and M. D'Orazio, 'Evolution of the analysis criteria for wooden arch structures between the 16th and the 19th century', pp. 1657–68 in S. Huerta (Ed.), *Proceedings of the First International Congress on Construction History*, Madrid 2003, Madrid: Instituto Juan Ferrera, 2003.
M.R. Campa, '"Le Nouvelles Inventions pour Bien Bastir et a Petits Fraiz" by Philibert de l'Orme: a New Way to Conceive Wood Roof Covering', pp. 525–42 in J. Campbell (Ed.), *Proceedings of the Second International Congress on Construction History*, Cambridge 2006, Cambridge: University Press.
L. Hahmann, 'How stiff is a curved timber plank? Historical discussions about curved-plank structures', pp. 1501-16 in J. Campbell (Ed.), *Proceedings of the Second International Congress on Construction History*, Cambridge 2006, Cambridge: University Press.
A. Mongelli, 'A new wood roofing system: Marac's barracks and Colonel Armand Rose Emy's innovative system', pp. 2241–60 in J. Campbell (Ed.), *Proceedings of the Second International Congress on Construction History*, Cambridge 2006, Cambridge: University Press.
[3] A. Säbel and S. Holzer, '19th century curved board roofs in Bavaria', *Journal of Heritage Conservation*, No. 32, 2012, pp. 115–21.
[4] P.W.R. Bell, '19th century laminated timber roofs in England', pp. 171-9 in B. Bowen, D. Friedman, T. Leslie and J. Ochsendorf (Eds), Proceedings of the 5th International Congress on Construction History, Chicago 2015, Chicago: The Construction History Society of America .
[5] Hengeveld (1979) and Meschke (1989) included a description of the arches of Philipp Stephan, which are discussed in the fifth part of this paper (Towards efficient timber cross-sections). Meschke also mentioned the French pavilion of the 1873 International Exposition in Vienna.
[6] P. Ardant, *Etudes théoriques et expérimentales sur l'établissement des charpentes à grande portée*. Metz: S. Lamort, 1840.
[7] P. de l'Orme, *Nouvelles inventions pour bien bastir et à petits fraiz*, Paris : Federic Morel, 1561.
[8] M.K. Deming, *La Halle au blé de Paris*, Brussels: Archives d'Architecture Moderne, 2014. pp. 177-9.
[9] ibid., p. 184.
[10] Hengeveld, Hout, (Note 1) p. 13.
[11] A.R. Emy, *Traité de l'art de la charpenterie*, Paris: Carilian-Goeury & Anselin, 1841. pp. 194-5.

[12] Before Emy's arch roofs, several timber arch bridges had already been built. However, their curvature was not obtained from the bending of thin boards, but from the assembly of curved cut or naturally bent timber. See for example Navier's description of the Choisy Bridge (1810) in C.L.M.H. Navier, *Projet pour l'établissement d'une gare à Choisy*. Paris: Firmin Didot, 1811. p. 62.

[13] ibid., p. 424.

[14] C. F. Wiebeking, *Traité contenant une partie essentielle de la science de construire les ponts*, Munich, 1810. p. 98

[15] Emy, Charpenterie, (Note 11) pp. 425-6.

[16] Ardant, Etudes, (Note 6).

[17] D. Gilly, *Anweisung zur landwirthschaftlichen Baukunst*, Halle: Renger, 1811.

[18] Ardant, Etudes, (Note 6) p. 75.

[19] T. Böhm, *Handbuch der Holzkonstruktionen*, Berlin: Springer, 1911. pp 380-1.

[20] G. Oslet, *Traité de charpente en bois*, Paris: Chairgrasse Fils, 1890.

[21] V.H. Fabré, *Théorie des charpentes*, Paris: E. Thunot, 1851

[22] ibid., p. VI.

[23] ibid., pp. 26,57.

[24] H. Résal, *Traité de mécanique générale*, Vol. 5, Paris: Gauthier-Villars, 1880. p. 267.

[25] P.-F. Michon, *Cours de construction. Stabilité des constructions. Instruction sur la résistance des matériaux*, Metz: École d'Application de l'Artillerie et du Génie, 1848. p. 265-6.

[26]P. Smith, 'Les chemins de fer atmosphériques: Deuxième partie', *In Situ*, No. 10, 2009. p. 12.

[27] Säbel, Bavaria, (Note 3).

[28] M. Brunel Tenas, 'Remodelació i restauració de la nau de blanqueig de la Cooperativa Obrera Mataronense projectada per Antoni Gaudí', *Quaderns d'arquitectura i urbanisme*, No. 250, 2006. p. 106.

[29] ibid., pp. 106-7.

[30] R. Pane, *Antoni Gaudí*, Milan: Comunità Editions, 1964.

[31] *Exposition universelle de Vienne, 1873: France, produits industriels*, Paris: Commissariat général, 1873. p. 464.

[32] B. Addis, 'The iron revolution: How iron replaced traditional structural materials between 1170 and 1870' in M. Rinke and J. Schwartz (Eds), *Before steel*, Zürich: Niggli, 2010. p. 42.

[33] E. Radda, 'Ueberdeckung der Hofräume der französischen Abtheilung des Industriepalastes bei der Weltausstellung 1873 in Wien', *Zeitschrift des österreichischen Ingenieur- und Architekten-Vereins*, 1874. pp. 93-4.

[34] Meschke, thesis, (Note 1) p. 113.

[35] Böhm, Holzkonstruktionen, (Note 18) pp. 391-2.

[36] ibid., pp. 392-3.

[37] W. Rug, '100 Jahre Hetzer-Patent', *Bautechnik*, Vol. 8, No. 83, 2006. p. 534.

[38] Casein is the main protein constituent of milk.

Hengeveld, Hout, (Note 1) p. 23.

[39] S. Ebnesajjad, *Handbook of Adhesives and Surface Preparation: technology, applications and manufacturing*, Amsterdam: Elsevier, 2011. p. 137.

[40] L.G. Booth, 'Henry Fuller's Glued Laminated Timber Roof for Rusholme Road Congregational Sunday School and other early Timber Roofs', *Construction History*, Vol. 10, 1994. pp. 29–45.

[41] M. Seraphin, 'On the origin of modern timber engineering', pp. 1845–54. in S. Huerta (Ed.), *Proceedings of the First International Congress on Construction History*, Madrid 2003, Madrid: Instituto Juan Ferrera, 2003. p. 1847-48.

[42] ibid., p. 1848.

The Twentieth Century

The exception, not the norm: pre-1940 concrete-framed commercial offices in England

Jonathan Clarke
Department of Art History, University of Cambridge, UK

Introduction

At the start of the 20th century British architects and engineers had at their disposal skeleton frame construction in either steel or reinforced concrete. Both techniques offered comparable advantages including strength, stability, spatial openness and non-combustibility, yet such were the economies of reinforced concrete (which typically required only a third of the amount of steel that a steel frame required), and its unrivalled suitability for forming other parts of buildings - floors, foundations and basement retaining walls - that even before 1914 some foresaw it replacing the more familiar steel frame. This proved otherwise, for steel-skeleton construction triumphed as the standard means of erecting multi-storey buildings between the wars, with concrete frames used only to a limited extent, mostly in factories, warehouses and other industrial buildings. Bowley [1], Yeomans [2] and others have offered explanations for this state of affairs, including the steel-mindedness of engineers habituated in the more established technique, a lack of promotion on the part of the cement industry (for whom framed structures were a small part of their market), and the relative complexity of reinforced concrete, in both the processes of design and construction.

The intention of this paper is to document the employment of concrete-framing in commercial offices in England up to 1940, a building type that early on realised the advantages of iron and steel-framing [3]. Beginning with the early pioneers in London and other cities, this paper looks at how and why concrete was selectively used in commercial office buildings, at the effect of building regulations and codes, and at why concrete framing increased markedly in the late 1930s, prefiguring post-war developments.

1903-1913: Unregulated experimentation and promulgation

If cost-saving was the overriding factor in the adoption of reinforced concrete for warehouses, mills and other multi-storey industrial buildings in the years before the First World War [4]' then for offices in the same period it seems to have been technical interest on the part of the architect or patron, or the material's expediency in specific circumstances. Architects proceeded cautiously at first, incorporating reinforced concrete floors and other elements within brick loadbearing walls, as with Dunn and Watson's extension to the premises of the Clerical, Medical and General Life Assurance Society, St James's Square, London (1903-4; architects) [5] and Sir Edwin Lutyens's offices for *Country Life* magazine, Tavistock Street, London (1904) [6]. Both used Hennebique concrete, concealed behind more architecturally palatable Portland stone – a disguise shared by virtually all English offices built in the subsequent three decades, whether in stone (natural or 'cast'), brick or faience. Britain's first commercial office block to be wholly framed in concrete was probably Lion Chambers, Glasgow (1904-07; Salmon and Son and Gillespie, in collaboration with the engineer Louis Gustave Mouchel) [7], but

London, in spite of its more restrictive building regulations, was not far behind. Richard Norman Shaw, an architect well versed in steelwork, wanted to try his hand with the newer material, declaring in a letter to Lethaby that 'Reinforced concrete ought to do a lot for us... do you say to have a turn on those lines?'. He got his 'turn' with Portland House, the headquarters of the Associated Portland Cement Manufacturers (1908; internally rebuilt), which was built on a Kahn-system frame by one of its British licensees, DG Somerville and Co. working under the general contractor Holland and Hannen [8]. It closely followed Friars House, New Broad Street (1907-8; internally rebuilt), an eight-storey speculative office block erected by the same specialist concrete firm and general contractors, but in that case it was the building owners - also Holland and Hannen - and not the architect, Arthur Blomfield junior, who chose concrete rather than steel framing, and for pragmatic reasons, not novelty (Figure 1). These were stated as rapidity of erection, non-combustibility and the replacement of the usual heavy and expensive "Scotchman" crane with a small electric hoist, there being no heavy members to lift [9]. As one of the growing array of contractors that were 'prepared to tender on Reinforced Concrete Work in the Kahn System', [10] it was in Holland & Hannen's interest to broadcast the advantages of the Kahn system in a prominent commercial building. Another, subtler, stated advantage of using a concrete frame was structural continuity between the beams, columns and slabs, enabling slabs with a maximum thickness of 7in. and floors of up 17ft width to be spanned without beams. Such continuity was inherent in the monolithic nature of the material, and was fully exploited in the disposition of the distinctive 'Kahn Trussed Bar' reinforcing, with 'continuity bars inverted over beams giv[ing] continuous beam action, their shear members reaching downward onto the slab on either side'[11].

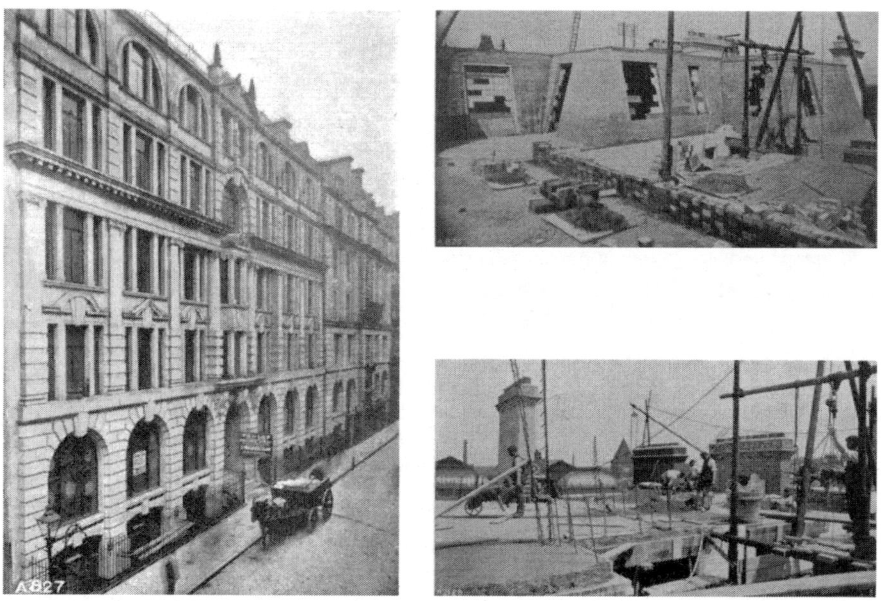

Fig. 1. Friars House, New Broad Street, London (1907-8)

Reinforced concrete construction was particularly suited to the employment of wall beams, where entire walls - interior or exterior - were designed to act as beams. They enabled open spaces on lower floors to be spanned without the usual heavy beams projecting deeply from the ceilings. This facility does not however seem to have been recognised or exploited before *c*1909, mainly in industrial and institutional buildings such as and the Manchester YMCA building (1907-11; Woodhouse, Corbett & Dean, architects; Kahn system) [12]; Clay's Printing works, Southwark (1909-10; G.F. Collinson, architect; Kahn system) [13], and Peek, Frean & Co's biscuit factory extension, Bermondsey (1911-12; architect/engineer H. M. De Colleville of W. Moss & Sons; Moss system) [14]. A seemingly rare instance of its use in office building was a seven-storey building in central Birmingham on the corner of New Street and Temple Street (1912-1; Nicol and Nicol, architects; Wells system) [15] (Figure. 2). Yeomans suggests that architects were seemingly unaware of the potential for this kind of structure, possibly stemming from a tendency to plan in terms of frames [16]. This must have been true for the most part, but as far as speculative offices were concerned, multiple open floors interrupted principally by columns rather than solid, immovable walls were preferred, enabling the flexible configuring of non-structural partitions to suit individual clients' needs. In the Birmingham office, the architects maintained some degree of interior flexibility by setting the wall beams over one another such that the removal of any one would not affect the integrity of those above.

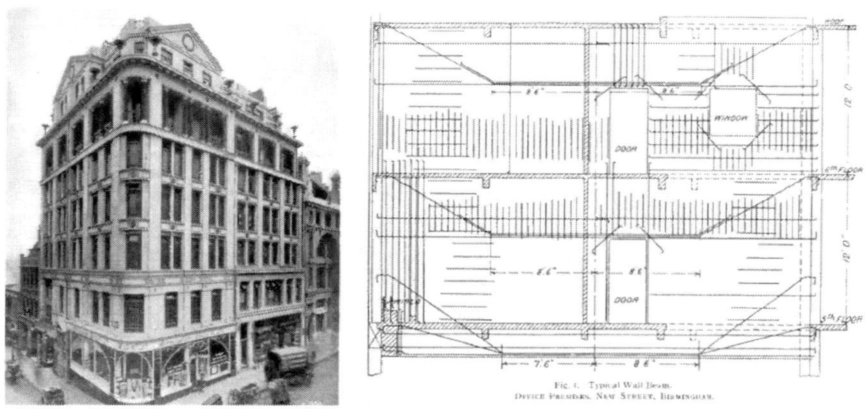

Fig. 2. Speculative office in Birmingham built on the Wells system and which (unusually) employed wall beams

Reduction of exterior wall thickness to make a difficult site financially viable was the principal reason that 'Cross House', Newcastle-upon-Tyne (1911-12) was framed in concrete. The walls of this wedge-plan building, including its Portland stone cladding, were 'only 12in. thick over all', suggesting that the architects, Cackett and Burns Dick, won a waiver from the building authority [17]. This however was considerably thicker than the 4-inch-thick exterior, non-load-bearing panel-walls used in Lion Chambers, Glasgow, which enabled some 88 per cent of that building's cramped (33 x 46ft) footprint to be extracted as lettable floor space[18].

Concrete's monolithic strength and solidity saw its use in one specialised form of office building perhaps begin to approach that of structural steel. Part industrial, part commercial, newspaper offices almost always required thick raft foundations, substantial retaining walls and deep pits and piers that supported the heavy printing presses. Reinforced concrete lent itself to these structures, and it made sense to use this for the frame and walls also, rather than employ steelwork contractors in addition to concrete specialists. Offices, or extensions to existing premises, for the *Dundee Courier*, Dundee (1905-7; Niven & Wigglesworth, architects; Wells system) [19]; the *Northern Echo*, Darlington (1908-09; W.H. Brown, architect; Hennebique system) [20]; the *Liverpool Daily Post* (1912-13; Aubrey Thomas, architect; Hennebique system; *dem.*) [21], were all framed in concrete, with the material's inherent fire-resistance an additional reason for its selection in the Liverpool building.

These, then, were some of the specific reasons for the choice of reinforced concrete over steel for framing offices in the Edwardian period. Mostly however, where concrete frames can be identified, the motive cannot.

Generalised patterns of development relating to firms, architects, regulations and architectural expression are nevertheless discernible. The most prominent firms/systems were Mouchel-Hennbique, Kahn, Considère and Coignet, with Kahn the most popular. Whilst the dominance of Kahn is explainable in terms of the dual operational strategy of the Trussed Concrete Steel Company (marketing and licensing the Kahn system to suitable contractors as well as using it themselves), perhaps equally important was the firm's concern with getting its product into street architecture as well as industrial and engineering structures. That the second edition of its general catalogue, published in 1913 (a year before the launch of the bi-monthly *Kahncrete Engineering*) comprised two sections, one architectural, the other engineering, is symptomatic of this desire to promulgate on multiple fronts. In this sense, it was adopting Mouchel's earlier strategy of reaching out to architects: Cussack noted how 'Mouchel and his assistant T. J. Guentte both attached importance to the architectural use of reinforced concrete and no doubt welcomed the employment of architects to give their material an *artistic advantage*' [emphasis added] [22]. Through architect-licensed contractor associations, direct marketing, or other means, the Kahn system was used to frame other (mostly insurance) offices besides those already mentioned, including the Scottish Union and National Insurance Company's offices, Leeds (1909; Perkin and Bulmer, architects) [23]; Aldine House, Buckingham Street, London (1909-11; E Keynes Purchase, architect) [24]' Atlas House, Leeds (1910; Perkin & Bulmer, architects) [25]' the International Buildings and Kingsway Hall, Kingsway, London (1910-11, Gordon and Gunton, architects) [26]; and the Cunard Building, Liverpool (1912-16; Willink & Thicknesse, architects) [27]' The Considère and Coignet systems did not enjoy anything like the same success in terms of office buildings, and documented instances of their employment are hard to find. A triangular block of insurance and speculative offices in Infirmary Street, Leeds was framed with Coignet concrete (1910, *dem.*; GD Martin & Sidney D Kitson, architects) [28], but the only large-scale use of Considère concrete was seemingly for the Royal Insurance Company's offices in Lombard Street - a steel framed building with concrete foundations, a two-storey basement, strong room, floors and dome (1910-11; Gordon & Gunter, architects) [29]. The Hennebique system seems to have achieved better market penetration than these newer, rival French systems, framing (besides those already mentioned) two offices in Edinburgh (*c*1906), and others in Lambeth (*c*1910), Manchester (*c*1911) and Liverpool (1908-11) [30]. This last named, the Royal Liver Building, Pierhead, Liverpool (W. Aubrey Thomas, architect), was Britain's tallest, biggest and most prestigious office building, and not only a resplendent advertisement for the Hennebique system, but also a towering feat of rapid construction that rivalled that of steel-frame construction (Figure 3). The first seven floors of this 17-storey 'skyscraper' were constructed in an average time of 19 working days per (5000 sq. yd) floor, and it was only the exceptionally heavy, complicated work required for the support of the two towers that prevented such rapidity from being maintained throughout [31].

As with early steel-frame construction, the main provision within metropolitan and provincial building regulations inhibiting concrete framing was that relating to wall thickness, which effectively barred thin, low-cost, panel walls. Some municipal authorities were more lenient, either in their published minima or willingness to waive them, and in that sense London was less hospitable than most (although Mouchel's declaration that it was 'the only town in the civilised world where ferro-concrete constructions are actually prohibited' [32] was clearly overstatement). However, until the passing of the Steel Frame Act of 1909, which sanctioned thin-walled steel-skeleton construction, concrete frames were no more repressed by building regulations than were steel frames. Even after that (at least until 1915 when the LCC finally published equivalent regulations governing reinforced concrete; see below) there was regulatory parity, Cussack noting 'from about 1908 more local authorities, including the LCC, began to permit reinforced-concrete framed buildings with reduced wall thicknesses ...' [33].

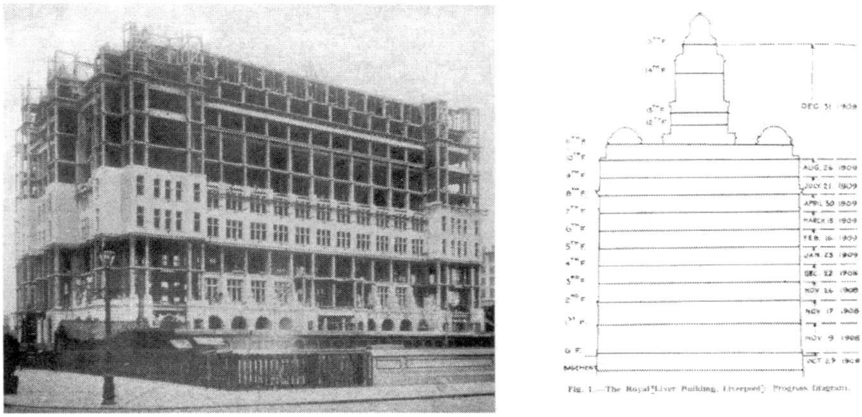

Fig. 3. Construction of the Royal Liver Building, Pierhead, Liverpool (1908-11)

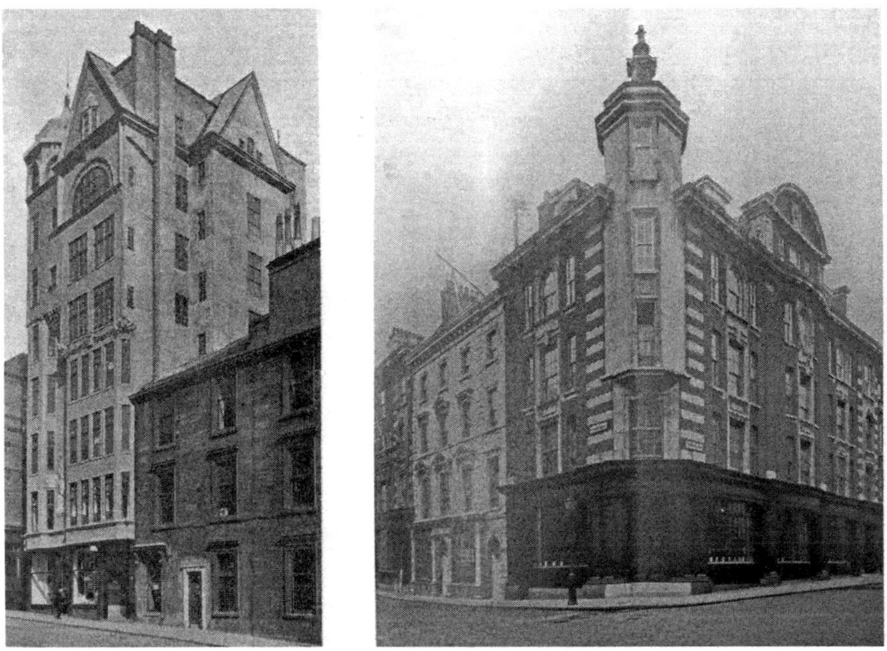

Fig. 4. Lion Chambers, Glasgow (1904-07) (left), and Aldine House, London (1909-11) (right)

Thus the building regulations do not really factor into the disproportionately fewer concrete-framed, compared to steel-framed, offices in the decade before the First World War, a disparity epitomized by the ratio of steel-framed to concrete-framed offices on Kingsway by1915, which was at least 10 to 1 [34]. But, in those instances where they permitted reduced wall thicknesses, they did give some architects greater license to express the architectural character of the material: Lion Chambers, the mansard storey of Friars House, and the corner turret of Aldine House (Figure 4) all made play of the material's planar, faceted character when suitably shuttered. Most architects however preferred to conceal the material behind thick veneers of stone, brick or terracotta to give it style and decorum; a columnist for *Kahncrete Engineering* referred to this as 'masked treatment', acknowledging that it was equally applicable - and hence indistinguishable - to a steel-framed building [35]. Certainly no pre-1914 offices of the 'unmasked' character of the former Clays Printing Works in Paris Garden, Southwark appears to have been built - a mildly expressionistic building that Saint identifies as 'unmistakably a concrete building, with the bluntness and weight that is one characteristic of the material' [36].

1914-18: Wartime stimulus and official regulations

The period 1914-18 saw an imposed curb on steel construction that briefly favoured concrete as a construction material. Two London west end offices document this 'artificial' fillip. One was a speculative office/shop building at No. 299 Oxford Street by Delissa Joseph. Designed originally with a steel frame, the Ministry of Munitions demanded that it be redesigned with a concrete frame in 1916 when construction started. Delayed further by the Ministry's general building embargo, it was eventually completed in 1920, with Summerville, Ltd and G. Munday & Sons jointly responsible for the concrete construction [37]. The other was the Commercial Bank Building, an 11-storey, 130ft-tall block of mostly speculative offices on Gracehcurch Street by F.R. Gould Wills (Figure 5). The foundations were prepared in 1914, but it was not until 1918-20 that the concrete superstructure was built, designed according to the London County Council's (hereafter, LCC) regulations governing reinforced concrete construction. Published in 1915 and effective the year after, this was the first codified British design and construction guidance, based largely on the Second Report of the Joint Committee on Reinforced Concrete (1911) [38]. The Commercial Bank Building was the first building to be designed according to its provisions. Because of the general embargo on unregulated private building in 1916-18, it was not until after the war that the 1915 regulations were used.

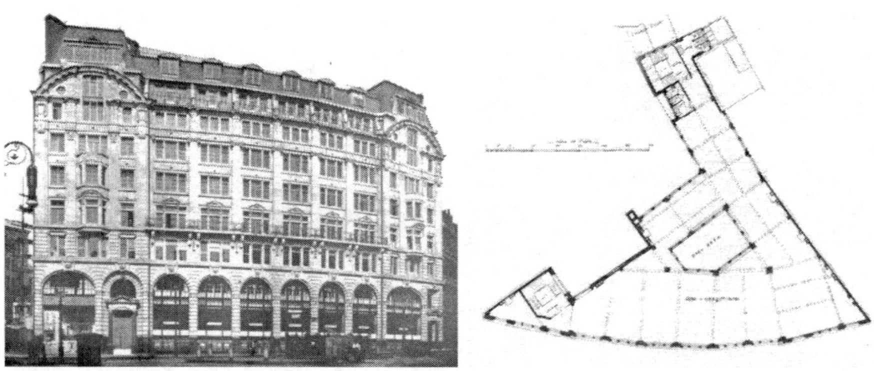

Fig. 5. The Commercial Bank Building, Gracehcurch Street, London: the first building to be designed according to the LCC's 1915 regulations

1919-33: Regulated, repressed but resourceful employment

Outside London there were no regulations governing reinforced concrete construction, and for most of the inter-war period local authorities, 'and practically all writers and lecturers on reinforced concrete '[39]adopted the LCC's 1915 regulations. According to one structural engineer they 'influenced the whole of English reinforced concrete design and practice' [40]. Unfortunately this had the unintended effect of making concrete frames more costly for many types of buildings, since the regulations were unduly conservative in terms of specified superimposed loads and working stresses. Engineers and reinforced concrete contractors bemoaned its restrictions, particularly as regards column thicknesses (one noting they demanded 'a larger section of column than any other set of Regulations on the Continent or in America') [41], and many called for immediate amendment [42]. Revision did not come for another 15 years, in which period an increasingly polarised debate on the relative merits of steel and concrete raged, with Oscar Faber defending the former from Owen Williams's criticisms [43], and which saw the formation of the Reinforced Concrete Association (est.1932) in response to The British Steelwork Association (est. 1929) [44]. What is clear is that steel-skeleton construction triumphed as the standard means of building commercial offices in the interwar period to the virtual exclusion of concrete. Those rare instances of the use of concrete frames show that designers were often concerned with making the most effective, economising use of the material, or with exploiting those structural possibilities or building forms to which it was better suited than steel.

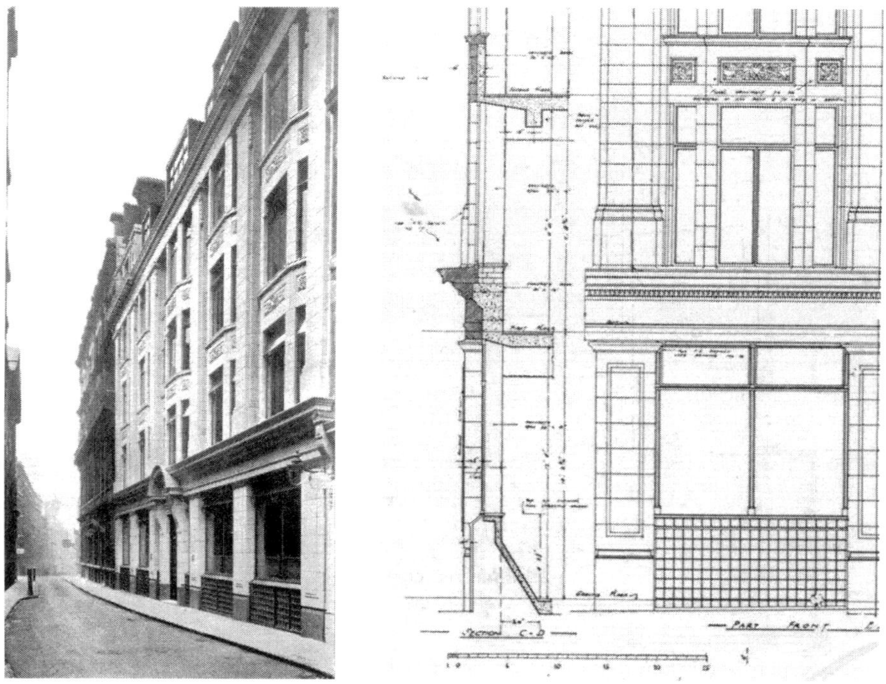

Fig. 6. No. 13 Rood Lane, a speculative office built c1929 for Rood Lane Properties to designs by Gordon & Gordon

For the Liverpool & London & Globe Insurance Co.'s offices in Charing Cross (*c*1922-5), the architects Gordon & Gordon in concert with the Considère Construction Co. employed two-way reinforced floors 'so as to avoid projecting beams in the ceilings below' [45]. These were 8-in-thick and spanned between a rear party wall and curved beams that ran between the front perimeter columns. *The Architects' Journal* remarked that forming these curved members 'in concrete was a comparatively easy matter, but it would have been extremely difficult in any other form of construction' [46]. The same architects employed 7in-thick floors, reinforced both ways, at No. 13 Rood Lane (*c*1929) - a rare instance of a concrete-framed speculative office, built for Rood Lane Properties, Ltd (Figure 6). On the upper floors only two detached reinforced concrete columns were required, the remainder forming part of the walls. The detached columns were spirally reinforced to make them as slender as possible, suggesting that the Coignet system was used. Because of the narrowness of the street, obtaining the maximum amount of light was vital and this was achieved by using canted window bays and by inverting the floor beams over the window heads so that they were carried above the ceilings [47].

In the singularly gifted hands of Owen Williams, concrete was able to show mastery over steel. For the extension to the Daily Express building in Fleet Street (1929-31; consulting architects H.O. Ellis & Clarke), Williams both supported and extended the existing steel-framed offices using advanced techniques of concrete framing. The existing steel building at the back of the site was carried on a basement-level portal frame resembling a giant table, with eight pyramidal legs and a deep slab top [48]. Wider and longer than the building it supported, this powerful structure could accommodate the runs of new press machines, which according to Serge Chermayeff was 'one of the deciding factors for the adoption of concrete construction in preference to steel' [49]. For the better known and publicised extension to this building, Williams employed a series of stacked long-spanning cantilevered concrete portal frames to maximise floor space, create a dramatic overhanging loading bay and permit near-continuous curtain wall glazing. Williams's design, with its optimised, concrete-specific forms, was both structurally and aesthetically superior to the steel-framed design originally proposed by Ellis & Clarke, and, wrapped as it was in curvilinear, clear and black vitrolite glass, was 'widely acclaimed as a revolutionary piece of British architecture' [50].

As with the pre-1914 generation of concrete offices, the precise reasons as to why the material was used are often unclear. For example, a small, four-storey office and shop for Twining Brothers in George Street, Oxford was built on a concrete frame (*c*1924; Gilbert T. Gardner, architect) [51]. Possibly the architect or client had some association with (or was enticed by the marketing of) the specialist contractor, the Birmingham Concrete Steel Company. For the construction of two additional upper storeys to one of the Prudential Assurance Company's Holborn Bars buildings, the choice of concrete seems especially puzzling given the earlier and extensive use of structural steel by the architect, Paul Waterhouse, and his father, Alfred [52]. Possibly it was because of the on-site adaptability of concrete to unexpected design changes compared to steel, which had to be cut and fabricated off-site in advance: the contemporary description noted 'In many cases it was not possible to obtain exact dimensions and important particulars until the existing work was removed, but to avoid holding up the work provision was made for a certain amount of adjustment upon the spot, taking up irregularities here or there by means of additional laps between the bars and by other little "tricks of the trade". [53]

In spite of the interest in the surface treatment of concrete through colour and texture in the 1920s, as far as office buildings were concerned, the 'masked' handling of the pre-1914 continued. However, recognition of the plastic richness of concrete saw it used for architectural elements in otherwise steel-framed elements. Examples include the jutting Egyptianizing cornice of Britannia House, Shaftsbury Avenue (1929; Hobden and Porri, architects) and the fire escape staircase to the internal courtyard of Melbourne House, Kingsway (1929-30; Trehearne & Norman, architects), described as a 'graceful and unique concrete structure ... not a mere excrescence in cast iron of standard sections'. [54]

1934-39 Revitalized use

Following mounting agitation for a revision of the outdated, unduly stringent and inelastic 1915 regulations, 1934 saw the publication of the first British code of practice (as opposed to regulations) for reinforced concrete design. The LCC which had instigated the research behind it did not publish its new regulations until 1938, although in the intervening period it exercised its powers of waiver, accepting designs that followed the new code. Other local authorities probably did likewise. [55] The effect on concrete frame buildings was dramatic, one (albeit biased) publication remarking in 1938 on the 'great increase in the proportion of buildings erected, or in course of erection, with reinforced concrete frames'. [56] This increase in popularity was particularly marked with flats, hotels and hospitals, but concrete-framed office blocks saw a definite upsurge in the late 1930s as designers capitalised on their freedom to design more optimised, cost-effective structures.

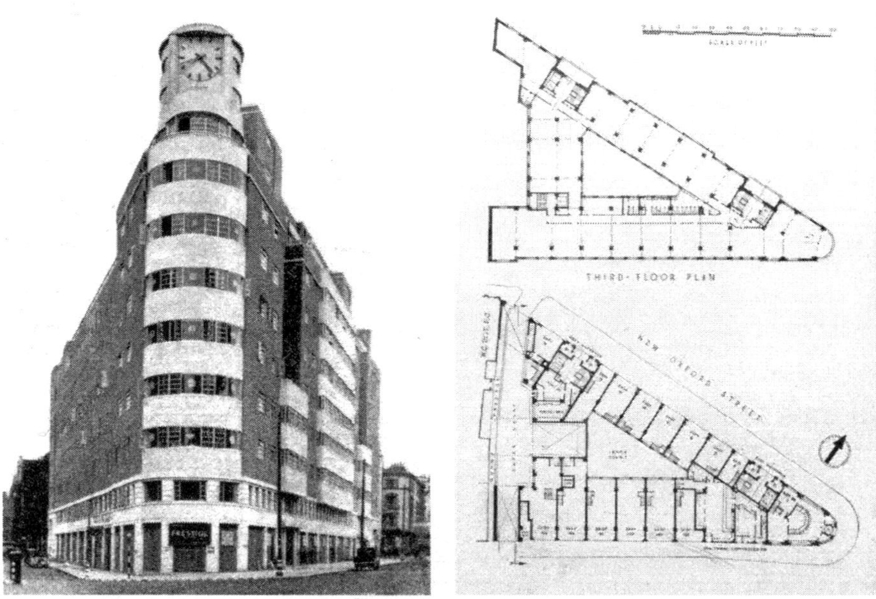

Fig. 7. Commonwealth House, New Oxford Street (1938-9; H.P. Cart de Lafontaine, architect)

The 1934 code, and 1938 regulations, made exploitation of the space and material-saving advantages of continuous beams more compelling, since they provided simple formulae for calculating the bending moments. Hitherto, the difficulty of calculating such indeterminate structures had been a 'long-standing objection to taking continuity into account in designing frames'. [57] Commonwealth House, New Oxford Street (1938-9; H.P. Cart de Lafontaine, architect) used columns set-back a few feet from the perimeter 'in order to reduce the depth of the main beams and increase headroom' (Figure 7). [58] Great Westminster House, an enormous, 250,000 sq ft stand-alone speculative office block in Horseferry Road (1936-7; T.P. Bennett & Son, architects) also used set-back columns, albeit just 4½ inches inside the external wall, but it seems this was more for architectural and services-planning reasons (enabling horizontal strip windows and space for heating pipes) than structural efficiency and economy. Also by T.P. Bennett & Son, Cleland House, Page Street, Westminster (1938-9) capitalised on the less conservative widths to be assumed for the flanges of T or L-beams, employing 4 ft 6in-high concrete wall-beams in the exterior to carry the windows and brick facing (Figure 8). The reinforced flanges of these 'apron beams', forming the window heads and cills, provided the lateral stiffness, allowing the webs to be just 5 in thick. Their projecting heads carried a 4½ in.-thick brick facing which was necessary to comply with the regulation for a panel wall of 9 in. minimum thickness. [59]

7" wall.

1934 new code, lower requirements.
" revitalised use of concrete
readymix saved space
electric vibrator -> faster bldg
Bulley Sq - less than 1y
One of largest concrete bldg in Europe

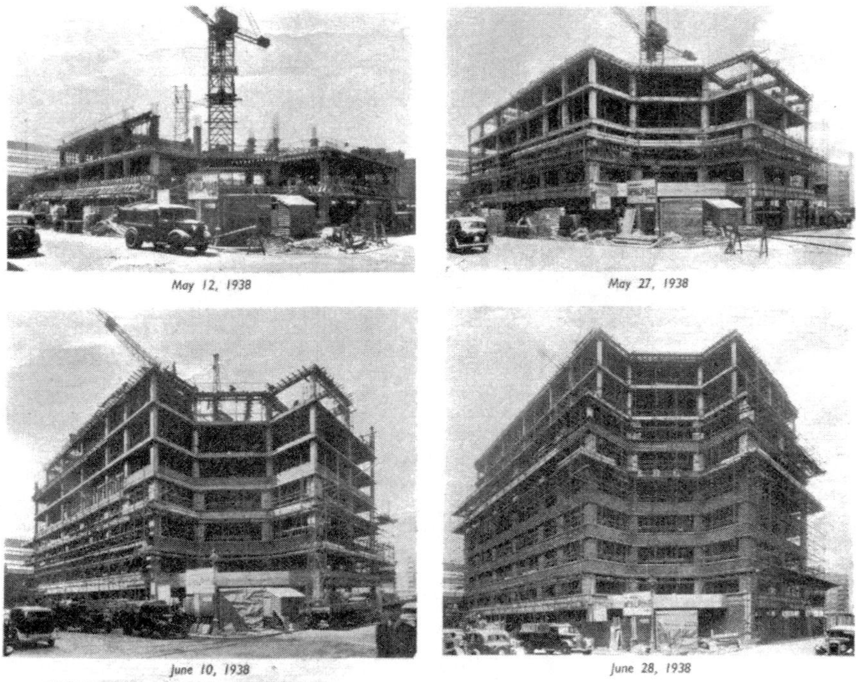

Fig. 8. Rapid construction at Cleland House, Page Street, Westminster (1938-9; T.P. Bennett & Son, architects)

The new code and regulations also allowed increased permissible stresses for different concrete mixes and for the steel reinforcement, which ecomised on materials. For the ten-storey Provincial Newspaper Offices in Salisbury Square, London (1935-37; *dem.*) architect-engineer Owen Williams employed box-wall construction since the footprint measured just 30ft by 35ft. The walls and floor slabs were just 7in.-thick, formed from concrete with a direct compressive strength of 1,150 lbs. per sq. in. (almost double that permitted by the 1915 regulations) and reinforced with steel designed with a tensile strength of 18,000 lb. per. sq. in. LCC waivers, ahead of the 1938 regulations, permitted these working stresses. [60] No columns were used, the floor slabs being designed to span across the external side walls and an interior wall that separated the office from the service functions. This enabled the front and rear elevations to be extensively glazed. [61] Sven Bylander - a structural engineer who generally preferred to work in steel - employed the higher strength, 'Quality A' concrete as defined by the new regulations in his skeleton for Egton House, Langham Street (*c*1938, dem.). This took account of workmanship as well as mix proportions, and according to Bylander the result was 'cheapness and small scantlings'. [62]

Other factors, in addition to more permissive and economical design guidance and regulations, encouraged the use of concrete frames in the late 1930s. The introduction of ready-mixed concrete, delivered by drum truck mixers to the job as required, reduced the congestion in tight, urban sites since the need to store mounds of aggregate and cement was dispensed with. Similarly, the supply of reinforcement, bent already to the necessary shape, freed up space that would otherwise had been required for stacking and bending bars. [63] One of the first British offices to make use of the former was the ten-storeyed Waterloo Bridge House, Southwark (1937-38; Howard and Souster, architects) (Figure 9). The concrete was delivered by the Express Supply Concrete, Ltd, and was pumped to delivery position using plant supplied by the Concrete Pump Co. Ltd. Electric vibrators - another recent innovation - were used to compact the concrete. [64] By this date rapid-hardening Portland cement was coming into ordinary use, which advantaged concrete frames *vis-à-vis* speed of construction. Berkeley Square House in Berkeley Square, London, was one of the largest office buildings in Europe when completed, and also a ringing endorsement of the advantages of concrete-frame construction (Figure 10). Providing 280,000 sq feet of naturally-lit office space, this prestigious speculative block was completed in less than a year, a feat indubitably facilitated by the employment of rapid-hardening Portland cement concrete. However, it was also made possible by meticulous planning and particularly close collaboration between the architects (Gordon Jeeves), mechanical engineers (J. Stinton Jones and Partners) and consulting engineer (William Leslie Scott) so that all special openings, holes and recesses required for mechanical services were provided in the various members at the time of construction. [65]

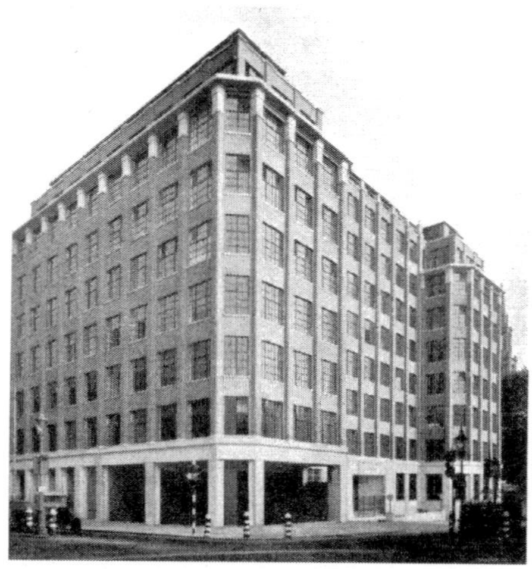

Fig. 9. Waterloo Bridge House, Southwark (1937-38; Howard and Souster, architects)

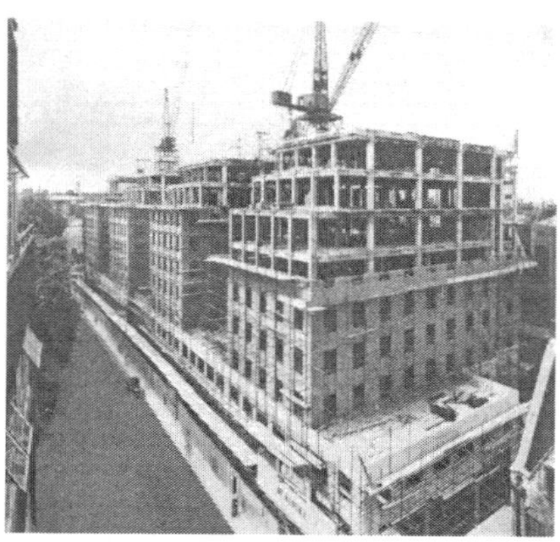

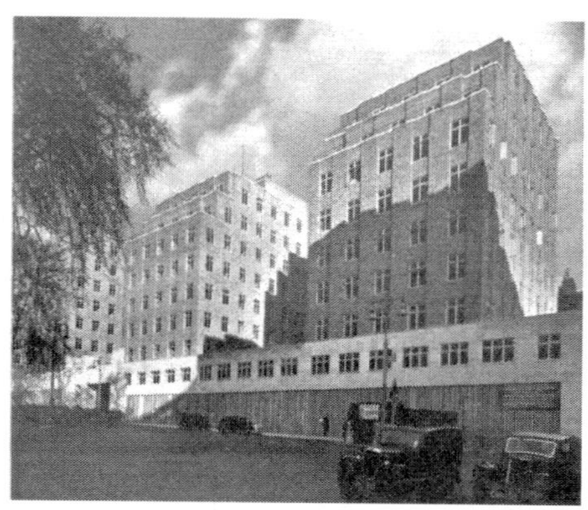

Fig. 10. Berkeley Square House, Berkeley Square, London (Gordon Jeeves, architect)

Conclusions

The increasing use of reinforced concrete frames in office building during the later thirties was a trend that continued after the war, albeit gradually. Even in 1956 Professor A.L.L. Baker could observe that 'In the heart of

London and most of our big cities at the present time tall steel frames are rising', whereas 'Most other countries have abandoned the use of structural steel in favour of reinforced concrete for building frames up to 25 storeys in height for economic reasons'. [66] Nevertheless, this was possibly an overstatement, since most of the buildings cited in a report on office buildings erected in London in 1945-60 were concrete-framed. [67] The main innovation in concrete in that period, devised by the engineer Felix Samuely in collaboration with Grenfell Baines, was the use of external pre-cast concrete load-bearing frames, which saved on plywood shuttering and steel, both of which were in short supply. [68]

The reasons for the unpopularity of the concrete frame across most building types for most of the interwar period are many and complex, and have been explored elsewhere. That other countries in Europe, as well as America, reaped the economic advantages and exploited the greater flexibility in design offered by the material suggested, to one observer in the 1920s 'a national and deep-rooted conservatism ... [amounting] ... almost to prejudice'. [69] Reinforced concrete, as Yeomans points out, entailed a more complex design process, and demanded more supervision in construction. Steel was simpler, and to a generation of builders, engineers and architects trained in or familiar with steelwork, it made sense to continue with what they knew, even in the face of strong countervailing opinion and practice. That 'steel-minded' conservatism began breaking down in the 1930s thanks partly to a new generation of architects and engineers, many associated with the Modern movement. Most were drawn to designing residential flats, but hospitals, town halls, shops, garages and industrial buildings

all saw new or renewed interest. [70] As far as commercial offices were concerned, the decisive change was the adoption of reinforced concrete by a new generation of big property developers and their preferred architects, such as Associated London Properties and T.P. Bennett & Son. With the financial means to build on the largest of scales, often involving specialist engineers such William Leslie Scott, this tipped the balance in favour of concrete, setting the mould for the post-war period.

Acknowledgements

I should like to thank David Yeomans and Kathryn Morrison for reading and commenting on an earlier draft of this paper.

References

[1] M. Bowley, *The British Building Industry: Four Studies in Response and Resistance to Change*. Cambridge: Cambridge University Press, 1966, pp. 39-67.

[2] D. Yeomans, *Construction Since 1900: Materials*. London: Batsford, 1997, pp. 112-14; 124-26.

[3] See J. Clarke, *Early Structural Steel in London Buildings*, Swindon: English Heritage, 2014 pp. 191-237

[4] A. Saint, 'Some thoughts about the architectural use of concrete', *AA files* no. 21, 1991 Spring, p.6.

[5] See P, Cusack, 'Reinforced Concrete in Britain: 1897-1908' (unpublished PhD thesis, University of Edinburgh, 1981), p. 370.

[6] Cusack, *ibid*, p. 518.

[7] 'A Reinforced Concrete Office Building', *The Builders' Journal and Architectural Engineer* (*BJ&AE*) (Concrete and Steel Supplement), 30 January 1907, p. 12. Maximisation of interior space through the use of thin panel walls seems to have been the lead motive for the use of concrete.

[8] A. Saint, *Richard Norman Shaw* (2nd ed.) Yale University Press, 2010, p. 417.

[9] 'A Reinforced Concrete Office Building in London', *Concrete & Constructional Engineering* (C&CE) v (1908), pp. 113-116.
[10] For a list of contractors using the Kahn system, see *Kahncrete Engineering* v1 (May 1914), p. 24.
[11] 'A Reinforced Concrete Office Building ...' (Note 9).
[12] A. Lakeman, 'The YMCA building', *C&CE* v6 (1911), pp. 368-77.
[13] *C&CE* v7 (1912), pp. 325-332.
[14] Albert Lakeman 'Messrs. Peek, Frean & Co.'s Factory Extension', *C&CE* v7 (1912), pp. 875-83.
[15] 'Office Premises, New Street, Birmingham', *C&CE* v8 (1913), pp. 525-29.
[16] Yeomans, *Construction* (note 2), p. 114.
[17] '"Cross House,", Newcastle-upon-Tyne', *The Building News*, 26 September 1913, p. 437
[18] 'The area of the site is 1,578 sq. ft., and after deducting the space occupied by the outer walls, lobbies, stairs and lift, the lettable area of the 9 floors of shops and offices was 11,070 sq. ft'. 'A Reinforced Concrete Office Building', *The Builders' Journal and Architectural Engineer* (*BJ&AE*) (Concrete and Steel Supplement), 30 January 1907, p. 12
[19] 'A Reinforced Concrete Newspaper Office', *BJ&AE*, 23 May 1906, pp. 7-11.
[20] L.G. Mouchel & Partners Ltd., *Mouchel-Hennebique Ferro-Concrete: List of Works Executed in the UK 1897-1919* (n.d. c.1920), p. 21.
[21] 'New Offices for the "Liverpool Daily Post", *C&CE* v8 (1913), pp. 363-4.
[22] See P. Cusack, 'Architects and the Reinforced Concrete Specialist in Britain 1905-08', *Architectural History* Vol. 29 (1986), p. 185.
[23]'The Utility of Reinforced Concrete', *Architects' Journal*, 26 January 1921, p.100.
[24] '"Aldine House,", Bedford Street, W.C.', *The Builder*, 20 August 1915, p. 141; 'Aldine House, Bedford Street, W.C.', *Kahncrete Engineering*, March 1918, pp. 34-38.
[25] *Kahncrete Engineering,* July 1914, p.34.
[26] 'The Buildings of Kingsway', *The Architectural Review* v38 (1915), p.132.
[27] 'The Cunard Building, Liverpool', *Kahncrete Engineering* (May 1917), pp. 68-69; W.E. Willink, 'The Cunard Building, Liverpool', *Kahncrete Engineering* (Sept. - Oct. 1921), pp. 76-79.
[28] 'Reinforced Concrete and Terra-Cotta Office Building', *The Builder*, 27 August 1910, pp. 243-44; 'Offices and Business Premises, Infirmary Street, Leeds', *The Building News*, 28 October 1910, p. 617.
[29] 'Reinforced Concrete at the Royal Insurance Building', *C&CE* v6 (1911), pp. 811-820.
[30] Mouchel & Partners, List of Works, note 20.
[31] 'Reinforced Concrete in Building Construction. III. – Rapid Building', *The Builder*, 22 January 1926, pp. 157-58.
[32] L. G. Mouchel, 'Monolithic Constructions in Hennebique's Ferro-Concrete', Jnl R.I.B.A. v12 (1904), p. 50, as quoted in P. Cusack, 'Agents of Change: Hennebique, Mouchel and ferro-concrete in Britain, 1987-1908', *Construction History*, Vol. 3 (1987), p. 66.
[33] *ibid*, p. 67.
[34] see 'Kingsway', *The Architectural Review* (note 26), p. 131.
[35] 'The Architectural Treatment of Reinforced Concrete', *Kahncrete Engineering*, July 1914, pp. 33-35.
[36] Saint, 'architectural concrete' (note 3), p. 10.
[37] 'No. 299, Oxford Street, W', *The Builder*, 2 January 1920, p. 30.
[38] See M. Bussell, 'The development of reinforced concrete design and guidance' in J. Sutherland, D. Humm and M. Chrimes, (Eds), *Historic concrete: background to appraisal. London*: Thomas Telford, 2001, pp. 84-5; Yeomans, *Construction* (note 2), p.104.
[39] W.E.J. Budgen 'The Concrete Code', *The Architects' Journal*, 1 February 1934, p. 179.

[40] *ibid.*

[41] 'Reinforced Concrete', *The Architects' Journal*, 24 January 1923, p. 200.

[42] *ibid.*

[43] Oscar Faber 'The Portent of Concrete: An Answer to Sir Owen Williams', *The Architects' Journal*, 20 January 1932, p. 121.

[44] Advertisement in *Kahncrete Engineering*, August-September 1932, p. 48.

[45] 'A New Building at Charing Cross', *The Architects' Journal*, 18 February 1925, p. 293

[46] *ibid.*

[47] 'Office Building in the City', *The Architects' Journal*, 25 December 1929, p. 984.

[48] For a detailed account of how this was achieved, with construction photographs, see D. Yeomans and Cottam, D, *The Engineer's contribution to contemporary architecture: Owen Williams*. London: Thomas Telford, 200, pp. 68-70.

[49] As quoted in Yeomans and Cottam, *Williams* (note 48), p. 68.

[50] D. Cottam, *Sir Owen Williams: 1890-1969*. London: Architectural Association, 1986, p. 68.

[51] 'New Premises, George-Street, Oxford', *The Builder*, 26 September 1924, p. 480.

[52] See Clarke, *Steel*, note 3, pp.153-57.

[53] 'Adding a Storey to the Prudential Building', *The Architects' Journal*, 10 November 1920, pp. 527-28.

[54] 'Kingsway Architecture: Melbourne House', *The Architects' Journal*, 29 January 1930, p. 199.

[55] See Yeomans, *Construction* (note 2), pp.118-19.

[56] 'Reinforced Concrete Frame Buildings: Rapid Development in Recent Years', C&CE v33 (1938) (supplement), p. 1.

[57] *ibid.*

[58] 'Commonwealth House, New Oxford Street, W.C.1', *The Architect & Building News*, 16 February 1940, p. 183.

[59] Morris L Winslade, 'Cleland House, Westminster. The Growth of a Building II. - Structure and Finishings'. *The Architect & Building News*, 21 April 1939, pp. 68-71.

[60] 'An Office Building in Central London', C&CE, January 1938, p. 39.

[61] 'A Model in Minimum Planning. No. 2 Salisbury Square, E.C.4.', *The Architect & Building News*, 2 July 1937, pp. 22-24; Cottam, *Williams* (note 48), p.167.

[62] S. Bylander 'The Design and Construction of Modern Buildings', *The Structural Engineer*, March 1939, p. 177.

[63] 'Reinforced Concrete Frame Buildings' (note 56), p. 2.

[64] '"Waterloo Bridge House," Waterloo Road, S.E.', *The Builder*, 14 January 1938, pp. 111-12.

[65] '"Berkeley Square House," Berkeley Square, W', *The Builder*, 2 December 1938, pp. 1068-72, 1081-82.

[66] As quoted in Bowley, *British* (note 1), p. 40.

[67] Robert Thorne, 'Post-war Listing: Informative Report on Office Buildings in London 1945-60' (unpublished typescript for English Heritage dated October 1987), p. 4.

[68] For this information I am grateful to David Yeomans who notes that the technique was first employed by Samuely and Baines at the Thomas Linacre School, Wigan (1952).

[69] 'Colour and Concrete', *Architects' Journal*, 23 May 1923, p.

[70] see 'Reinforced Concrete Frame Buildings' (note 56), pp. 1-34. For structural innovations in flat construction, see Ove Arup, 'Planning in Reinforced Concrete. Part 1', *Architectural Design & Construction* v5 (1934-5), pp. 297-307.

Fine-tuning and demolition: the first acoustics laboratory at Britain's Building Research Station

Fiona Smyth
Harvard University, Dept. of the History of Science & Trinity College Dublin, School of Engineering

Introduction

The first government laboratory in Britain specifically dedicated to building science research in acoustics was at the Building Research Station (BRS). The laboratory, which operated from 1923 until 1925, was the site of significant research in materials testing. However, despite its significance for twentieth-century building science and construction, neither the location nor the physical construction of the laboratory have been addressed in the published literature. The details of the building and its site have become somewhat occluded over time.

The majority of BRS laboratories, prior to 1926, were located in reconditioned army huts housed on a plot of land in East Acton. They were leased from what was then known as the Acton Urban District Council (UDC). Extant BRS land files (1920-1927)[1] contain no specific reference to the lease of a supplementary site during this time, and in later years it seems to have been assumed that the acoustics laboratory was amongst the central cluster at East Acton. However, separately archived documents which include unpublished letters, memoranda and an acoustics research report (marked "confidential" at the time of its issue in 1925) clearly demonstrate that the acoustics laboratory was not located on the main BRS campus at Acton. It was a satellite laboratory housed in a disused munitions factory in Harlesden, and it had to be very particularly reconditioned for experimental work in acoustics.

This paper draws on recent archive work to present details of that forgotten laboratory. It discusses the necessity of locating the acoustics lab offsite, the modification of the factory building for use as an acoustics laboratory, and the inherent impact of both site and structure to the evolving building science research in acoustics.

The Forgotten Laboratory

The BRS was one of six government-funded Research Stations established in the interwar years by the Department of Scientific and Industrial Research (DSIR) in Britain.[2] The primary catalyst for its foundation was the housing crisis, which had been recognised for some decades, and had rapidly worsened in the aftermath of World War I. The BRS began operating under the remit of the Building Research Board (BRB) in mid-1921 with the brief of '... serv[ing] as a central laboratory at which the essential scientific work could be conducted on a broad basis.'[3] As a Research Station, the BRS was to focus specifically on matters associated with the construction industry. It was founded to function independently of the National Physical Laboratory (NPL) which had been established in 1900, however there was an inevitable degree of overlap in the research agendas of both institutions. This was particularly the case in the arena of architectural acoustics, and in the early decades of formalised research, a spirit of manifest collaboration was fostered between the two.

The site of the earliest such collaborations was the first BRS acoustics laboratory.

Sources and Documentation

The first specific details of an acoustics laboratory to be contained in an official BRB publication are to be seen in the Board's report for the period ended 31st December 1926.[4] By this stage, the BRS had proved its worth in terms of scientific and industrial research, and had become a firmly established entity. After five years of operation from temporary premises in East Acton, the Station had moved to a permanent site at Garston near Watford, taking up residence there in April 1926.

The frontispiece of the 1926 report shows a site plan of the new BRS premises which was located on a large country estate, some 17 miles from central London. In the main, the laboratories were organised in collective blocks (A-D). The acoustics laboratory, a small, stand-alone construction, sits slightly south of the main buildings. The building depicted was the first *purpose*-designed laboratory for architectural acoustics at the BRS, but it was not the first laboratory to have been utilised by the Station in that capacity. Acoustics research had first been instigated at the BRS in 1923, with a laboratory coming into operation in the summer of that year.[5]

The 1926 report, which summarises the first five years of research at the BRS, contains a précis of the acoustic work undertaken between 1923 and 1925 but makes little mention of the laboratory building itself, or of the manner in which it had been conditioned to facilitate work in architectural acoustics. The report does indicate that the acoustic research had been undertaken at an undefined location in Park Royal (Harlesden) in a facility which then became suddenly unavailable in 1925.[6] This is the first hint in a publication that the acoustics laboratory was a satellite of the central Station facilities at East Acton. No information about the location or construction of an acoustics laboratory is contained in the BRS land files for that period.[7] Likewise, the extant land files contain no specific reference to the lease of a supplementary site for acoustics during this time. For some reason, despite its fundamental role in twentieth-century building science, the acoustics laboratory at Park Royal seems to have slipped through the cracks.

Intriguingly, the most comprehensive details of the laboratory are contained in a short report, circulated as a confidential internal document in 1925,[8] and contained in one of the BRS separate project files.[9] It summarises acoustic research which was undertaken on behalf of the Government of India for a legislative chamber designed for the new Imperial capital at Delhi. The research utilised a reductive method for materials assessment which had been formulated by the physicist Wallace Clement Sabine in Harvard at the turn of the century.[10] In the BRS implementation of this, the building itself provided the baseline for assessment. The absorptive quality of materials was established relative to the percentage reduction of reverberation in the laboratory.

In recognition of the relevance of physical context to that research, the report pays due regard to the site of the experimental work, and includes a set of plans and sections as well as photographs of the laboratory. This internal document is the most complete source of information on the laboratory and on the research processes instigated therein. The document remained internal and confidential until the BRS files from that era were released under public record in the 1970s. (Fig.1)

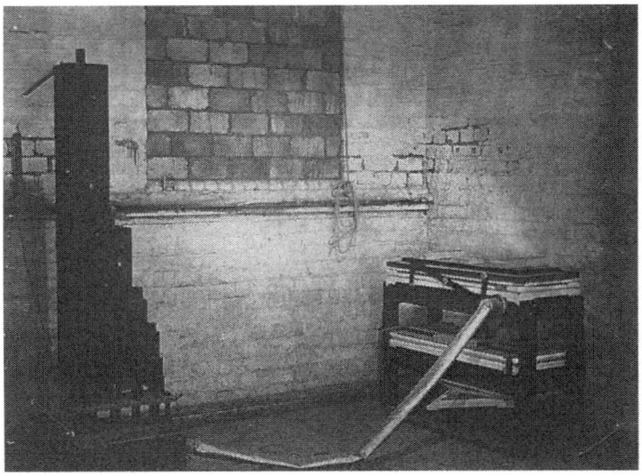

Fig. 1 - Interior of Acoustics Laboratory, courtesy of National Archives.

Numerical quantification of the reverberant condition of the laboratory does not occur anywhere in this report. However this data does appear in a study on contemporary methods of calibration which was published by the NPL in 1926.[11] The BRS laboratory was one of two case studies which formed the basis of the NPL evaluation. Reverberation time data for the laboratory are given across the frequency range from 64 Hz to 2000 Hz. The existence of this study is mentioned in a short exchange of correspondence between the BRS and NPL,[12] and the laboratory is identifiable in the study from its volume, and the description of its surface materials.

In addition to these reports, further unpublished government papers and the personal and professional letters of those involved in research at the laboratory (both the architects and scientists who implemented the research as well as those who commissioned it) are of value in contributing a rounded picture of the context of the work and of its significance in establishing a more extensive acoustics research agenda at the BRS.

With respect to the building which had been re-conditioned to facilitate the laboratory, construction progress schedules for the munitions factories are held in the Ministry of Munitions files at the British National Archives in Kew.[13] The methods and nature of the construction of munitions factories were addressed in a relatively circuitous fashion in contemporaneous publications. For the most part, the factories had been constructed at great speed under classified conditions. Given the sensitive nature of the work undertaken in the factories, their construction received little exposure in architectural or engineering periodicals until after the war. Even then, coverage was sparse and the factories were not identified by name or location. Although not overtly referenced, Park Royal is identifiable by its substantial acreage (1,200 acres) from amongst the immediate post-war discussion of factory construction.[14]

Though solid in construction, the very specificity of the munitions factory buildings made them transient in nature. Determined by the authorities to have limited suitability for re-purposing, the majority were destroyed in the years following the war, and the land on which they had been sited was sold.[15] The munitions factory at Park Royal was replaced with industrial buildings in the 1930s leaving no physical trace of the laboratory on the site and no hint of its role at the instigation of acoustics research at the BRS.

The Instigation of Acoustic Research

"Fundamental Research" versus "Special Difficulties"

As the BRS had been established in large measure to expedite and economise the construction of new housing, acoustics was initially seen as somewhat peripheral to its foundational remit. Whilst the Director of Building Research, H.O. Weller, was keen to bring acoustics on board from the outset,[16] the Advisory Council of the DSIR did not see it as a priority, considering it to be neither pressing nor immediately relevant to the housing industry. No accommodation was made in the planned layout at East Acton for its pursuance.

Although as yet undefined in scope, the potential of building science was well-recognised. Accordingly, the structure of the BRS accommodated two research streams: "General Research" and "Intelligence and Special investigations". The former division followed an agreed research agenda of issues deemed pressing or "fundamental". The latter division made provision for pursuit of external commissions beyond that established research agenda. In contrast to the "fundamental science" of general research, these were denoted "special difficulties".[17] Acoustics was one such "special difficulty" which came on board initially as an external commission. The research was required for a high-profile project and was instigated on behalf of the Government of India.

The Delhi Commission

Curvilinear in plan, with a large dome that reached a height of 57 feet (17.4 metres) at its crown, the initial design of the new legislative chamber planned for Delhi promised to be acoustically complex.[18] Its architect, Sir Herbert Baker, engaged an acoustic consultant, Hope Bagenal, to ensure that the chamber would function as intended and that speech would be intelligible within. Bagenal determined to reduce the height of the dome and to treat it with acoustic materials so that it would function as an absorber of sound rather than a reflector. He worked on the chamber initially using ray-tracing techniques and estimates of the acoustic performance of various materials. In the absence of British data, these estimates were based on American data and trade literature. However, it quickly became apparent that data more specific to the intended construction would be required to maximise the chances of success for the new Legislative Chamber.

Prior to 1923, the bulk of research on the acoustic performance of construction materials had been undertaken in the US. The available data was not fully apposite either to the materials and practices of the British construction industry or the Delhi climate. Likewise, the majority of commercial sound-absorbing materials had been developed and manufactured in the US. When, in January 1923, it appeared that supply of acoustic materials from America might be interrupted subsequent to a conflict with the manufacturers, Baker contacted H.O. Weller, director of research at the BRS to discuss potential experimental work in acoustic materials.[19]

Having been anxious to incorporate acoustics on the BRS agenda for some time, Weller was pleased to acquiesce, and fund the research to some extent from the BRS budget. However he was conscious of the Advisory Council's opinion on acoustics and its lack of fit with what was termed "fundamental research". He insisted that the commission come as a formal request from the Government of India to the DSIR with a small token fee in order to "regularise" the work.[20]

The token fee of £200 requested of the Government of India was to cover expenses only, and everything was to be implemented on a tight budget. Weller determined the research to be a sufficiently valuable opportunity for the Station to garner expertise in a new branch of building science and thus no fees were levied for the research hours.[21] He began assembling a team of experts immediately, including Hope Bagenal, the acoustic consultant who had called for the data in the first instance, and Major Tucker of the Signals Establishment at Woolwich.[22] They were soon joined by P.W. Barnett and W.H. Glanville of the BRS and the physicists Sir William Bragg, G.A. Sutherland, and G.W. Kaye became involved shortly thereafter.

From the perspective of Sir Herbert Baker, the architect who had instigated the research commission, the arrangement was ideal. The Chief Engineer at Delhi shared the view of the DSIR Advisory Council as to the peripheral significance of acoustics and was reluctant to mortgage any great financial outlay on the commission of scientific research in a relatively unestablished field. However the new Legislative Chamber was a high-profile project and clarity of speech within the completed chamber would be integral to its success. The token expenditure requested by the BRS for research and development on something so essential could not be faulted. Furthermore, the commissioned research meant that materials and experimental work would be advanced in England where the developments and data could potentially be re-used in further construction projects. The Royal Institute of British Architects (RIBA) leant their support to the endeavour, keen to have a body of data that would be specific to national construction practices. The commission was approved. Acoustic research was to go ahead.

The next issue was to locate a suitable premises for a laboratory.

From Old Oak Common Lane to Acton Lane

The BRS campus at East Acton was at Long Drive on Old Oak Common Lane.[23] It had been inherited from a research division within the Ministry of Health, and leased on a temporary basis from Acton UDC.[24] Licensure for research facilities on the site was subject to bye-law complications, and had to be renewed annually. Constrained by the temporary nature of the tenure and an exceptionally tight budget, Weller had procured a number of army huts to serve as the first BRS laboratories and installed them at Acton. Secured on a 9 x 9 inch concrete curb foundation, these were of timber-frame clad in rebated weatherboarding. The roofs were corrugated asbestos sheeting.[25] The only concrete construction on site was a small unit which housed the lavatories.[26] Although less than ideal, and described as "pretty poor" for "an imperial undertaking",[27] the insubstantial nature of the temporary accommodation was adequate for most types of experimental work on the BRS agenda. In its first two years of operation as a Research Station, a valuable corpus of work emerged despite minimal resources.[28] However, there were two prerequisites to acoustic research facilities distinct from the other building science laboratories.

A primary requirement was that external noise be excluded from work in acoustics so as not to skew the measurements. A much more substantial construction than the wooden army huts was required to provide adequate sound insulation. Secondly, as the work was based on measuring and tempering the acoustic context of the laboratory, the laboratory itself had to be excessively reverberant: much more so than was feasible with the scale and material of the huts. The work on sound-absorption and materials assessment could not be completed in the facilities available at Acton. It was hoped initially to undertake the research at the Signals Experimental Establishment in Woolwich,[29] but when these plans fell through, attention moved towards locating an appropriate BRS premises.

No. 3 Filling Factory

Pragmatism, especially the urgency of the time constraints, dictated the identification and choice of premises. Like its sister laboratories at Acton, the building that was to serve as the acoustics laboratory was the product of war-time surplus. In the absence of suitable accommodation at East Acton, the Disposals and Liquidations Commission were consulted. Temporary access to part of a disused munitions factory about three miles away in Harlesden was secured and the laboratory was established there. The heavy construction with its booming, resonant interior was eminently more suited to purpose than the laboratory accommodation at East Acton. From a promising base-line, the premises was reconditioned into a reverberant chamber appropriate for subtractive assessment. The building, which had been in operation as part of a munitions factory for almost three years, was to function as an acoustics laboratory for a little under two.

The postal address, discerned from the correspondence with the manufacturers who provided material samples for analysis, was No. 3 Filling Factory, Acton Lane, Park Royal.[30]

Fine-tuning: "As bad as acoustically possible"

The stand-alone unit leased to the BRS for acoustics work was part of a larger factory complex. The site was also relatively isolated from urban noise as a prerequisite of its designation as a munitions factory had been distance from populated areas.

Those parts of the factory designed for handling High Explosive (HE) material were of heavy-weight construction with externally revetted walls. The exception to this was the roofing. In general, roofing over these areas was as lightweight as possible in order to minimise the impact of accidental explosions. To avoid sparking from the HE components of ammunition, internal surfaces within the Filling Factory were relatively smooth, but were insufficiently reflective to create a reverberant chamber of required specification. Floors were of asphalt, formulated to a particular gritless composition, likewise to minimise HE ignition.[31]

The BRS set to work in Harlesden, tempering the interior of the laboratory within the munitions factory to make it "acoustically as bad as possible."[32] Once experimental work began, the intent was to measure the relative improvement with the introduction of each different sample of construction material.

The nine windows of the factory building were bricked in, flush with the walls. The new brickwork remained unpainted. Projecting elements, including the coved skirting of the factory walls, were removed to leave planes that were as flat as possible. A new resonant ceiling was installed and finished in "Sirapite", an exceptionally hard, rapid-set patent plaster formulated with fully-hydrated gypsum. [33] The surface, once dry, was worked to a smooth, highly-polished finish to maximise its reflective qualities. A replacement floor was of cement render, polished until "words spoken by one occupant were almost unintelligible to another standing at the opposite end of the room."[34] Any enamelled-cloth lining left over from the munitions work was removed and the brick walls were left unplastered. Data for the acoustic characteristics of brick was later to form a fundamental component of the experimental work on wall materials.

The dimensions of the laboratory were 44 feet 1 inch (13.4 metres) in length, 16 feet 1 inch (4.9) in width and 13 feet 7 inches (4.14) in height. It had a total volume of 9,622 cubic feet (272.47 cubic metres). When the reconditioning had been completed, it was calibrated using organ pipes and the human ear to gauge the reverberance of the chamber.

With a laboratory fully set up, the BRS were now in a position to assess and rank construction materials in terms of acoustic absorption. Materials for assessment were purchased where necessary, otherwise samples were borrowed or acquired from the manufacturers in exchange for a promised return of acoustic data.

Materials were assessed in 100 square foot (9.3 square metre) samples with the exception of carpets. 100 square foot (9.3 square metre) equivalency for these was calculated from the larger sample sizes provided by manufacturers.

Test signals were generated using an electric organ manufactured by Norman and Beard. A pedal-inflated compensating bellows was used for air supply. Tests were implemented at octave intervals encompassing the range from C1 to C7 (64 - 4096 Hz). A morse writer borrowed from the Central Telegraph Office was used as part of a circuit, linked to a pendulum and tapping key to graphically record reverberation, synchronised with the cessation of the organ note. The organ was located centrally along one of the short walls.[35]

Within the laboratory, seven points of maximum intensity were identified by ear relative to the test signal "at which the notes sounded loudest." These were marked on the floor as receiver positions. Two observers – described as "sets of ears" - assessed each material from these locations. 20-30 observations were made for each material at each octave. Measurements were spread over a number of days to avoid ear fatigue.

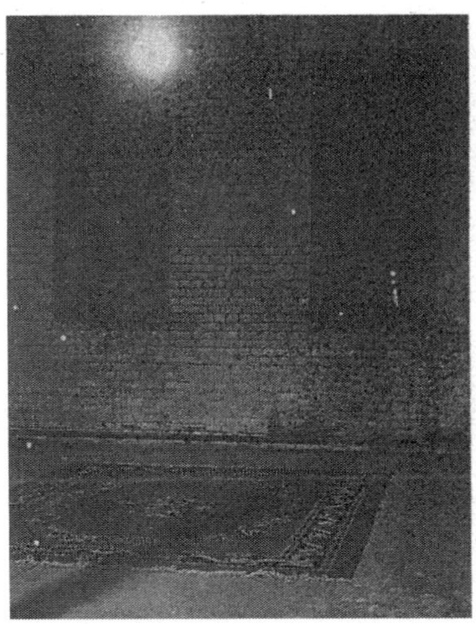

Fig. 2 Carpet under assessment in the Laboratory (Courtesy of National Archives)

After the first tentative experiments - based on values for US materials derived from trade literature and personal contacts in America - a system was established. The materials specific to the laboratory construction were central to this system. Not only were construction materials analysed in terms of percentage reduction of the reverberance in the laboratory environment, but values specific to the floor and wall materials of the laboratory provided the constants in determining the results. Sound-absorption values for brick and cement render (depending on whether wall or floor materials were under assessment) were slotted into a mathematical formula as additive constants to obtain relative values for sound-absorption in the construction materials under analysis. (Fig.2)

As the experiments for the Government of India drew to the close, the NPL began to use the laboratory to experiment with sound intensity and signal propagation. Use of an electro-magnetic loudspeaker as a sound source for reverberance work was trialled in the laboratory. The baseline data for the room were re-calibrated as a result, and the construction materials data revised accordingly. The published report on this NPL experiment seems to be the only source which provides numerical data for the acoustic specification of the laboratory. At mid-frequencies (500 Hz), the reverberation time (Rt) of the laboratory was found to be 2.5 seconds.[36]

Demolition

The physical construction of the laboratory was appropriate to acoustics research, infinitely more so than would have been possible in the buildings at East Acton. However the external conditions and the terms of the lease were less appropriate. The Park Royal site had been earmarked for industrial development and the laboratory lease was subject to sudden termination as site clearing and development progressed.

Within six months of commencing the acoustic tests, the destruction of buildings surrounding the Park Royal laboratory had begun. The depth and solidity of the factory walls was no match for the noise generated by adjacent demolition. Objective testing became increasingly difficult as external noise interrupted the measurements and corrupted the data.

For each incidence of external noise infiltration, testing had to be ceased, and the whole time-consuming process of repeated observations re-instigated at a quieter juncture. Initially, a lookout was stationed outside the laboratory to give warning of any impending demolition noise, but in the end the destruction of the surrounding factory buildings was too all-pervasive for research to continue. The building which housed the laboratory was itself on the list for demolition and it was destroyed in 1925. By this stage, the BRS had been consolidated and was to move to permanent premises, at Garston in Hertfordshire. From the experimental work and body of data generated in the first laboratory, acoustics had proven its worth as "fundamental research" in the eyes of the Advisory Council. In the months before the laboratory ceased operation, a joint BRS-NPL acoustics committee was formally established, and an agenda was set for further building science research in acoustics to extend the work which had begun at Park Royal. The legacy of the Park Royal Chamber was further reflected in the design and construction of a new acoustics laboratory - the one depicted in the 1926 Report - at the recently-acquired BRS premises in Garston.

Conclusion

The chamber at Park Royal operated as an acoustics laboratory from 1923 to 1925. Within that short time-frame, equipped only with skeleton staff and a minimal budget, laboratory work undertaken here had provided not just the foundation for subsequent experimental work in architectural acoustics, but had produced pioneering research with far-reaching applications. From this forgotten laboratory, there emerged the first set of sound-absorption data specific to the British construction industry and developments in the formulation of proprietary plasters for sound absorption, building on recent US advances in the same field.

Although of great significance to the development of acoustics within both the BRS, and the NPL, the Park Royal test chamber, has, in many ways become a forgotten laboratory. Perhaps the nature of the building in which it was housed as well as the timing and manner of its acquisition contributed to this, or perhaps the neglect was accidental. Regardless of the reason, by the time the laboratory ceased operation in 1925, acoustic research at the BRS was no longer limited to what was termed "special investigations". It had been officially recognised as an essential component of the housing agenda and featured proudly as one of only three BRS Standing Committees:[37] It was the *only* branch of environmental science that was so represented.

Acknowledgements

The author gratefully acknowledges the support of grants from the Royal Irish Academy, the British Society for the History of Science and a Marie Sklodowska-Curie Fellowship which made this, and related work, possible. She also wishes to express her thanks to the Modern Sciences Working Group and colleagues at Harvard for their support and advice, and to staff at the Loeb Architectural Library, The RIBA Archives and the National Archives at Kew.

Notes and References

[1] National Archives, DSIR 4/62 (1920-1927) 'Acton Experimental Station: Lease of land and erection of Station'

[2] The other Research Stations were concerned with chemicals, food, forest products, roads and water pollution. For an overview, see chapter two of N.J. Vig, *Science and Technology in British Politics*, Oxford: Pergamon Press, 1968.

[3] Department of Scientific and Industrial Research, Report of the Building Research Board for the Period Ended 31st December, 1926. London: HMSO, 1927, p. 2.

[4] DSIR, Report of BRB for 1926 (Note 3).

[5] Archives of the Royal Institute of British Architects (Victoria & Albert Museum), BaH/61/1 Sir Herbert Baker Archive, letter of H.O. Weller to H. Baker, 22 June 1923.

[6] DSIR, Report of BRB for 1926 (Note 3) p. 5. and p.82.

[7] NA, DSIR 4/62 (1920-1927) 'Acton Experimental Station: Lease of land and erection of Station'(Note 1).

[8] P.W. Barnett & W.H. Glanville, (May 1925) Report on Acoustic Experiments Carried out for the Government of India. DSIR. Confidential Report No. 250, May 1925 in National Archives DSIR 4/139 'Sound absorption tests on building materials carried out by Building Research Board at request of Government of India' (Sept. 1923 Sept - Oct. 1926).

[9] National Archives DSIR 4/139 'Sound absorption tests on building materials carried out by Building Research Board at request of Government of India' (Sept. 1923 - Oct. 1926).

[10] W.C. Sabine, *Collected Papers on Acoustics,* Cambridge Massachusetts & London: Harvard University Press & Oxford University Press, 1922.

[11] A.H. Davis, & N. Fleming, 'The Loudspeaker as a Source of Sound for Reverberation Work' in *London, Edinburgh and Dublin Philosophical Magazine*, vol. 2, no. 7, 1926, pp. 51-61.

[12] NA DSIR 4/139 'Sound absorption tests on building materials carried out by Building Research Board at request of Government of India' (Note 9).

[13] See National Archives MUN 4 'Ministry of Munitions'.

[14] F. Baines,'War Factories and Sheds: Their Construction and Adaptation to Future Needs' in *Journal of the Royal Institute of British Architects,* vol. 26, no. 10, 1919 pp. 230-40 & vol. 26, no. 11, 1919, pp. 249- 59.

[15] A notable exception to this is the Filling Factory at Rotherwas in Herefordshire which was retained and reused in World War II. Archaeological traces of certain of the factories, notably that at Banbury, can still be observed. See C. Appleby, W. Cocroft, & J. Schofield, *The Home Front in Britain 1914-18,* York: Council for British Archaeology, 2015.

[16] Noted in a memorandum of 1921. See F.M. Lee, (1971) *Science and Building: A History of the Building Research Station*, London HMSO, 1971, p. 67.

[17] DSIR, Report of BRB for 1926 (Note 3).

[18] The height was subsequently reduced by 11'. See H. Bagenal 'The acoustics of the new legislative chamber at Delhi' in *Architect & Building News*, vol. 121,1929, p. 851-853. See also reports by Hope Bagenal contained in the Baker Archive at the RIBA.

[19] Archives of the Royal Institute of British Architects (Victoria & Albert Museum), BaH/61/1 Sir Herbert Baker Archive, letter of H. Baker to H. Keeling, 25 Jan. 1923.

[20] Archives of the Royal Institute of British Architects (Victoria & Albert Museum), BaH/61/1 Sir Herbert Baker Archive, letter of H.O. Weller to H. Baker, 25 Jan. 1923.

[21] NA DSIR 4/139 'Sound absorption tests on building materials carried out by Building Research Board at request of Government of India' (Note 9) See DSIR Advisory Council: Confidential Memorandum on Sound Absorption Tests of Building Materials Carried out by the BRB at the Request of the Govt of India., 9 April 1924.

[22] Archives of the Royal Institute of British Architects (Victoria & Albert Museum), BaH/61/1 Sir Herbert Baker Archive, letter of H.O. Weller to H. Baker, 8 Feb. 1923.

[23] NA DSIR 4/62 'Acton Experimental Station: Lease of land and erection of Station' (Note 1). See Site Plan.

[24] NA DSIR 4/62 'Acton Experimental Station: Lease of land and erection of Station' (Note 1) Letter of J. Carmichael to G.W. Humphries, 29 Mar. 1921.

[25] NA DSIR 4/62 'Acton Experimental Station: Lease of land and erection of Station' (Note 1) See 'Brief Specification RE: Huts for proposed Building Research Experimental Station'

[26] NA DSIR 4/62 'Acton Experimental Station: Lease of land and erection of Station' (Note 1) See Block D in 'Building Research Board Proposed Experimental Station Sketch Plans'. Corresponding Specification in 'Brief Specification RE: Huts for proposed Building Research Experimental Station' (Note 25).

[27] Comment by R.H.H. Stanger, Vice -president of the Institution of Structural Engineers in R. Stradling, 'Building Research: Paper read before the Institution of Structural Engineers" in *The Structural Engineer*, 1927, pp. 137-45. (p. 143).

[28] For an overview of progress and publications see DSIR, Report of BRB for 1926 (Note 3)

[29] See DSIR, Report of BRB for 1926 (Note 3) & RIBA letter of Weller to Baker , 8 Feb. 1923, (Note 22).

[30] NA DSIR 4/139 'Sound absorption tests on building materials carried out by Building Research Board at request of Government of India' (Note 9), letter of P.W. Barnett to R.A. Stoffert, 3 Nov. 1923.

[31] Baines, 'War Factories ' (Note 14).

[32] Barnett & Glanville, 'Report on Acoustic Experiments' (Note 8) p. 1

[33] Further detail on Sirapite is contained in G.A.T. Middleton, *Building Materials, Their Nature, Properties and Manufacture: A Text-Book for Students and Others.* 1905, Reprint. London: Forgotten Books, 2013. pp. 143-4.

[34] Barnett & Glanville, 'Report on Acoustic Experiments' (Note 8) p. 1

[35] Barnett & Glanville, 'Report on Acoustic Experiments' (Note 8).

[36] 'Davis & Fleming, 'The Loudspeaker as a Source of Sound' (Note 11).

[37] The other two were the Chemical and Weathering Committee and the Structures Committee.

Why did modern post-tensioned floors flourish in the US and not in Europe – a matter of tradition?

Marc Sanabra-Loewe
UPC – Barcelona Tech

Introduction

Unlike in Europe, prestressed concrete with post-tensioned reinforcement came to be a standard technique in building construction in the US. Kenneth Bondy has been the only one who has made a significant contribution to clarify why this occurred, by writing about his insights on the origins of post-tensioned floors in the United States. His vision is completed here with new data and put into context. Moreover, the American and European situations are compared in an attempt to explain why things developed so differently on each side of the Atlantic.

What does 'technology tradition' mean in this study?

The construction industry tends to be one of the least flexible, and the market for structure and construction is one of the more resistant areas to technological change. Among the reasons for that are: the risk involved in the construction of structures, the high cost of buildings, and the fact that the prescriber (architect, engineer) uses a very different logic to make decisions from that used by other involved agents, such as the contractor, the developer or the final user.

We normally use the term 'tradition' to mean a custom kept for generations. Its origins are rarely known or questioned, but it is kept regardless. In this work, the word 'technology tradition', or simply 'tradition', means a technology that at a certain moment achieved a strong position[1] in one market segment and was able to keep it for a time, remaining almost unquestioned during that period. The features of such a 'tradition' are described next, but are not scientifically proven. The concept must be understood as a conjecture, which may show its validity only by its utility to explain the lack of flexibility of the market of structural systems in the construction industry.

The strong position of a 'technology tradition' typically originates when a strong technological shift occurs, which is when the new technology appears under the shape of several equivalent variant technologies. Each variant will fight the others to obtain a segment of the market, which is being shaken up and offers important positioning opportunities. In the struggle, each of the variants may or may not succeed in gaining a part of the total market.

As described by Trout, the *order* in which each of the variants appears in a certain market and the initial expansion speed are the most critical factors determining the size of the market for each variant. The first variant will have the largest effect: the first will hit the strongest. The more time the second takes to appear, the more difficulty it will have gaining market share. However, as there are only slight objective differences between competitors, factors other than initial speed may have an influence on the final market segmentation. These may include: the support of skilled pioneering engineers and/or determined capital investors; good advertising (which is not easy in this industry); and the ability to survive the initial struggle long enough for the technology to become a real 'tradition'.

After a time, say one or two decades, the market segmentation has been set and it remains almost constant. Once this state is achieved, it is reinforced by several factors, including: advertising, industry associations, scientific or technical publications, and academia which altogether establish links between a technology and its applications. This state or tradition will remain until a new technology arrives that will again disrupt the market.

Notice that because the order of appearance is very important, the idea of a technological tradition is tightly linked to the history of a particular local market. Thus, the validity of the idea would explain why some variants of a technology are well rooted in certain geographies but not in others.

The four main variants of prestressed concrete

Prestressing is simply the introduction of loads to a structure to improve its performance. In the case of concrete structures, using steel as the prestressing agent is the cheapest method, as steel is already needed in any concrete structural element.

There are two main variants of the use of steel to prestress concrete:

[1] *Prestressed concrete with pretensioned steel*: Concrete is poured on top of steel wires kept under strong tension. Once the concrete has hardened, the tension of the steel is released so that prestress force is transferred to the concrete.

This technique is typically used for precast components produced in precasting plants

[2] *Prestressed concrete with post-tensioned steel*: Concrete is poured to form a structural element. After concrete hardening, the steel strands are put into tension[2] and anchored at the ends of the concrete element to transfer the prestress force to the concrete element.

This second variant is often referred to as 'post-tensioned'.

As the prestressing force acts upon hardened concrete, the force may also have the function of holding together several elements cast separately. Therefore, post-tensioning can be divided into three main variant techniques:

[2a] Post-tensioned on a single cast-in-situ concrete element

[2b] Post-tensioned on elements precast away from the job

[2c] Post-tensioned on elements precast at the job

To what extent variants are equivalent

From the point of view of structural efficiency, there are reasons why post-tensioned structures are far more efficient than prestressed precast elements, and much more efficient than reinforced concrete structures. However, each square foot of post-tensioned floor is currently more expensive than either of the other two technologies. This makes it *prima facie* not evident to see which of the technologies to use. That is why we may say that those are, to a certain extent, equivalent technologies.

Other factors influence the structural floor choice, such as the depth of the floor, the weight of the floor, the speed of construction, the span between bearings, etc. That is why, depending on the relative importance of the involved factors within each market, one technology or another may be more prevalent in a particular market. The primacy of one factor over another may very well be influenced by the same factors that shape a technology tradition.

Origins of modern prestressed concrete use in France

It has been argued that the advent of modern prestressed concrete is closely related to the ability to predict the loss of prestress force,[3] which is complex because it results from many interacting factors.

The most difficult part of this breakthrough effort was achieved by the French civil engineer Eugène Freyssinet through a series of studies performed from 1907 to 1929.[4] In 1928, he applied for his patent for prestressed concrete with prestressed steel **[variant 1]**, and in 1939 for his patent for prestressed concrete with post-tensioned steel **[variant 2]**.

Soon after his patents were filed and during the rest of his career, Freyssinet successfully used three of the four variants described above **[1, 2a, 2b]** and went to considerable effort to disseminate the knowledge and broaden the usage of his methods.

How modern prestressed concrete arrived the US

Freyssinet's inventions greatly disrupted the structure-construction situation in both Europe and in the US, even though on the American continent Freyssinet was a virtual unknown. His inventions took root in the US after the end of World War II thanks to the influence of the Belgian Gustav Magnel. He designed and built the Walnut Bridge in Philadelphia in 1948-49, which left a fabulous footprint in the mind of American engineers.[5][6] It must be highlighted that with this bridge, Magnel was the first to put into practice the fourth of the main prestressed concrete techniques mentioned above: post-tensioned segments precast at the job **[2c]**. It typically consists of precasting large elements lying on the ground and then lifting them into their final position.

How did post-tensioned floors flourish in the US: Bondy's testimony and its context

Unlike in Europe, in the US prestressed concrete with post-tensioned reinforcement became a standard technique in building construction. How this occurred has been outlined by Kenneth Bondy, who was a direct witness to this technical evolution.[7][8]

Why did modern post-tensioned floors flourish in the US and not in Europe – a matter of tradition?

Below is a chronology of the main events he described, each preceded by (-). To ease contextualization, several facts have been added, each preceded by (+).

(+) 1929-30: The French H. Sauvage patents that can be considered the antecedent of modern lift-slab.[9] All concrete floor slabs of a building are poured at the ground floor, piled in a stack, and then moved to their definitive level using telescopic columns.

(+) 1944: The Frenchman B. Laffaille patents a new lift-slab system in France.[10] This is where slabs are elevated using a "lifting apparatus" which has a sort of rack with a backstop mechanism.[11] In the US, Laffaille patented only the "lifting apparatus".

(+) 1948: The two first modern US lift-slab patents, almost simultaneously, were licensed to a group of companies owned by the Texan tycoon Thomas B. Slick. One of the patents, developed by P. N. Youtz,[12] (Fig. 1), was clearly influenced by Laffaille's patent. The other patented technique, developed by Slick,[13] was less evidently also influenced by the French.

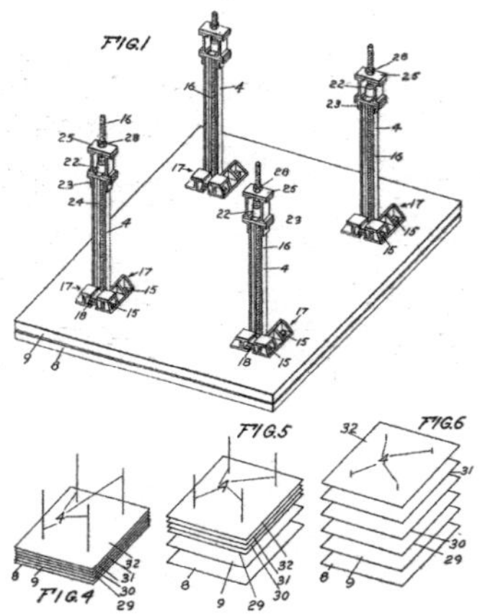

Figure 1. Drawings of patent for lift-slab system applied for by Youtz in 1948. US 700346, US Patent Office

(-) Mid 1950s: According to Bondy, the lift-slab method was used for the first time in the US. Concrete slabs were typically solid and very shallow, with only mild steel reinforcement (no prestressing). The slenderness of slabs, necessary to reduce their weight, led to excessive deflection. Moreover, slabs tended to stick to each other during the lifting process.[14]

(-) Mid to late 1950s: Modern post-tensioning was used for the first time in building construction in lift-slab buildings. This allowed the use of shallow slabs while avoiding both excessive deflection and the problem of stuck slabs. These post-tensioned slabs typically used a Swiss anchorage system developed by BBRV, which was called the "button-headed tendon".

Because lift-slab companies obtained good results controlling deflection in slender slabs, other companies, not affiliated to the lift-slab method, decided to purchase licenses to install BBRV anchorages. Lift-slab companies then used defensive tactics to prevent tendon-installing companies (called 'post-tensioning companies' by Bondy) to enter bids for jobs where lift-slab was used.[15]

(-) 1962: Edward K. Rice[16] established the company Atlas Prestressing and applied for the first patent for a post-tensioning anchorage for an unbonded monostrand tendon, which included conic wedges to anchor the strand (Fig. 2). This sort of anchorage enabled an easier and faster installation of tendons, which soon made BBRV anchorage totally obsolete. Nonetheless, lift-slab companies stayed defensive and never abandoned the "button-headed tendon".

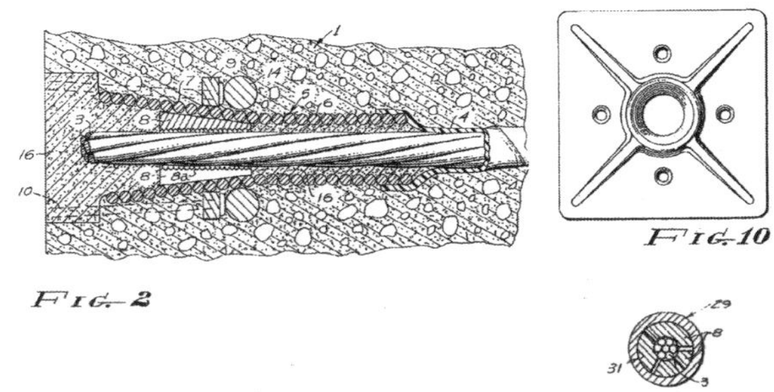

Figure 2. Drawings of the patent for the monostrand anchorage system applied for by Rice in 1962. US 3293811, US Patent Office

(-) 1963: T. Y. Lin published the "load balancing method", which made it much easier to design post-tensioned slabs.[17]

(-)1960s: Atlas Prestressing forged alliances to outcompete the lift-slab companies in erection speed. The key alliance was made with companies using flying forms, a sort of form that was very fast to put in place and to remove.

(-) Late 1960s: Post-tensioning companies wiped lift-slab companies out of the market, thanks to the alliance of cast in place post-tensioning and flying forms, and to the fact that lift-slab companies never adopted Rice's new anchorage. According to Bondy, this last factor was the fatal mistake that killed lift-slab.[18]

As a result, post-tensioned floors were no longer made out of precast elements precast on the job **[2c]**. Post-tensioning was then exclusively performed upon slabs cast in place **[2a]**.

Additions to Bondy's insight

Bondy's first-person testimony is hardly questionable. However, now that some decades have passed, a more general perspective may possibly help identify some things that were difficult to see at the time. That is why this work humbly attempts to suggest some additions to his insights. This is done by describing three factors that may have had an influence on the birth of modern American post-tensioned floors:

(a) The first American post-tensioning 'tradition' in building construction

Why did modern post-tensioned floors flourish in the US and not in Europe – a matter of tradition?

(b) The similarity between the Walnut Bridge and lift-slab construction logic

(c) Possible British roots of American modern post-tensioned floors

First American tradition (a)

- *1872-1888:* Peter H. Jackson developed several patents for post-tensioned floors[19]'[20]'[21] made of stone, brick or concrete, mainly for building construction. Jackson thought his invention was particularly interesting because of its fireproof properties, as he stated in his first patent on the matter in 1872. This reasoning was not too original, as fireproofing was one of the main advantages attributed to reinforced concrete structures versus steel or timber structures. Jackson designed by intuition, as he had no formal engineering education, so his post-tensioning designs were not able to control losses, as he could not even have suspected the complexity of that phenomenon. As a result, his designs must be considered rather rudimentary when compared with modern post-tensioning. This led him to abandon his defence of post-tensioned concrete floors against solutions made of reinforced concrete,[22] which were very well backed by highly qualified engineers, such as Ransome and his colleagues at the Technical Society of the Pacific Coast.[23] However, Jackson's rudimentary post-tensioned floors had a certain importance at the time, as they were present for decades in a very widespread construction manual written by Frank E. Kidder. While reinforced concrete ended up being an almost all-purpose structural material, Kidder still credited Jackson's post-tensioned systems as particularly suitable for fireproof structures.[24]'[25]

- *1890-1894:* Thomas A. Lee followed in the footsteps of Jackson, and obtained his own patent for 'fire-proof' post-tensioned floors.[26] As in Jackson's 1872 patent, Lee mentions that blocks may be made of natural stone, artificial stone or brick. However, his drawings clearly show that Lee mainly thought of hollow ceramic bricks (Fig. 3). To exploit his inventions, he soon founded the Lee Fire Proof Construction Co., which specialized in post-tensioned floors made of blocks held together by prestress force **[2b]**. Lee's systems were soon included in Kidder's book.

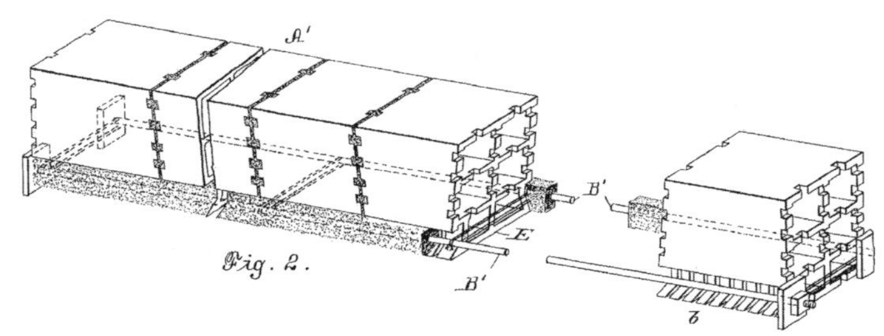

Figure 3. Drawings of the patent for a post-tensioned fire-proof floor, applied for by Lee in 1962. US 461028, US Patent Office

- *1940s to 1960s:* Jackson's and Lee's rudimentary post-tensioned floors, along with several similar Scandinavian inventions of the first decades of the twentieth century, were the basis of an entire industry, known as Dox Plank (Fig. 4), which was flourishing across the US in the 1940s and 1950s. In the 1950s there were 25 production plants in 15 States. There was an industrial association, the Dox Plank Manufacturers Association, and their design was regulated by the ACI code. This phenomenon has been well described by Dolhon.[27] Most of the systems included in the association shared the basic features found in Jackson's 1872 original patent: a) very primitive prestress techniques and materials; and b) precast concrete or tile blocks held together by the prestress force. During the 1960s most of this industry was replaced by modern prestressed concrete technology imported from Europe.

Most Dox Plank plants were in the west and mid-west of the US, but there was also one plant in Pharr, Texas, the state where the modern post-tensioned technique was used for the first time in building construction. In all, it is not unreasonable to assume that the footprint of a 90 year "tradition" of fireproof post-tensioned floors influenced American engineers in the 1950s and 1960s to use modern post-tensioned floors.

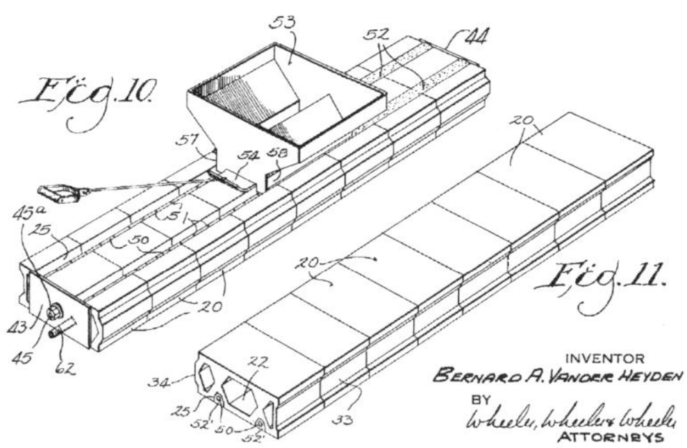

Figure 4. Drawings of a patent for post-tensioned floor made of lightweight concrete blocks applied for by B. A. -Doc- Vander Hayden in 1944. This system, known as Doc's Planks or Dox Plank, became the basis of an entire industry. US 2696729, US Patent Office

The Walnut Bridge and lift-slab buildings (b)

In the 1950s, Dox Plank was reaching the peak of its usage, while the lift-slab industry was just starting. At the same time, the modern prestressed technique had just arrived in the US with the Walnut Bridge built in 1948-49 and it was about to completely transform the industry. The erecting logic of this bridge was very similar to that of lift-slab: large elements precast on the job and then lifted and placed into their final position. The only difference was that the Walnut Bridge included post-tensioning **[2c]**.

For the lift-slab industry, where problems with deflection were a main concern, post-tensioning in slabs to improve their performance could have been an attempt to address such problems. This approach may have been inspired by the example of the famous bridge, known to any well-informed engineer at the time, if we think that both bridge and building construction methods were not too separate.

Possible British roots for the second American tradition (c)

When reviewing British patents of the 1940s and 1950s on post-tensioning, it has been found that they were quite early and original compared with the American equivalents, to the point that an influence of the former on the latter cannot be totally dismissed.

The following chronology includes some outstanding examples:

Why did modern post-tensioned floors flourish in the US and not in Europe – a matter of tradition?

- *1942:* P. W. Abeles and K. W. Mautner, both exiled from German-speaking countries during World War II, patented each one of the UK systems to erect modern post-tensioned floors for building construction by joining together precast concrete elements **[2b]**. Abeles' proposals were quite abstract and general,[28] but Mautner's were much more specific.[29] This makes the latter more realistic, which could be a reason to credit Mautner with being the first to design a modern post-tensioned floor. This patent proposed the use of very thin tendons with very small anchorages. It all it looks very similar to use of monostrands and anchorages patented by Rice in the US 20 years later.

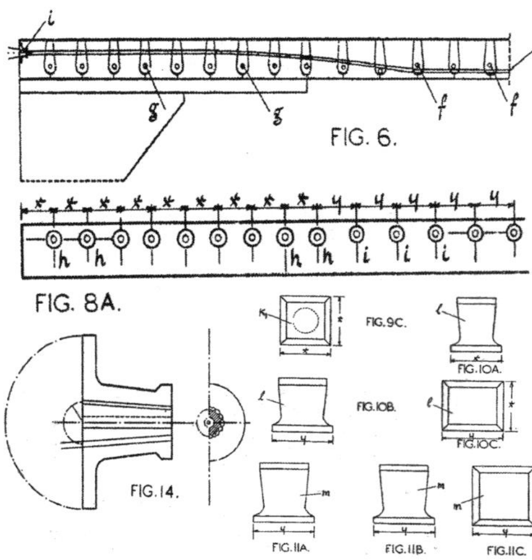

Figure 5. Drawings of the patent for the first modern post-tensioned floor system applied for by Mautner in 1942. GB 556570, UK Intellectual Property Office

- *1952:* American Curzon Dobell, working for the contractor erecting the Walnut Bridge, the Preload Company of NY, applied for a patent for post-tensioned precast floors,[30] citing Mautner's patent as a reference. Two years before that, in the ACI journal, he had published a paper establishing the most important patents and references for prestressed concrete.[31] His being involved in the Walnut Bridge construction and his paper in the ACI would make him a quite influential person in this industry at the time. This could possibly mean that American industry may not have been opposed to Mautner's idea to post-tension structural floors.

- *1953:* British Udalls Prestressed Concrete Ltd. applied for the patent for an anchorage system for post-tensioning known as the Gifford-Udall anchorage,[32] which would be one of the most used in the US in the following decades. This anchorage was well known among the most skilled American engineers of the period, probably including some who worked for lift-slab companies.

- *1954:* Udalls Prestressed applied for the patent for a system of post-tensioned slab-on-the-ground. The slab was lifted from the ground with jacks, just after post-tensioning, to avoid problems associated with soil-slab friction (Fig. 6).[33] This technique was extremely similar to that used in lift-slab buildings and could have been an inspiration for American lift-slab engineers to solve their problem of slabs sticking together during the lifting operation. Notice that Bondy wrote that the lift-slab industry started to post-tension slabs by the end of the 1950s. By that time American lift-slab engineers who knew of Gifford-Udall anchorages might have also heard about other Udall prestressed products, such as post-tensioned slabs-on-the-ground.

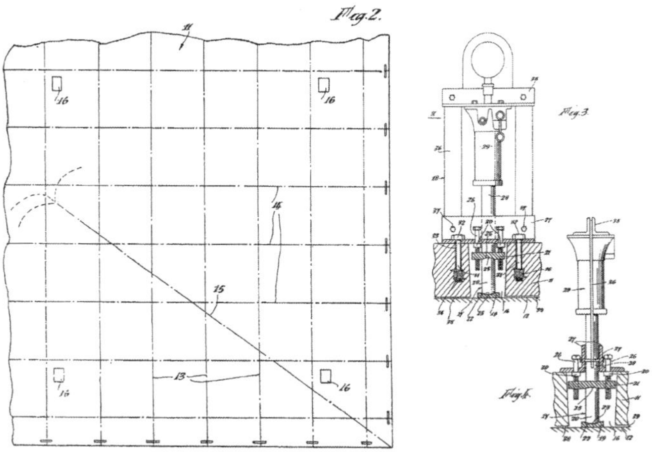

Figure 6. Drawings of patent for post-tensioned slab-on-ground applied by Udalls Prestressed Concrete Ltd. in 1954. GB 773890, UK Intellectual Property Office

- *1958:* Karl H. Middendorf, working for the Texan Prescon Corporation, applied for a patent for the construction of waffle post-tensioned floors, good both for slabs cast in place and for slabs used in the lift-slab method.[34] Patents similar to this one were used by lift-slab companies to protect their technology. Two features of this patent are particularly interesting. On the one hand, the anchorage system used is that of the Swiss of BBRV –which coincides with Bondy's depiction of the state of the art at the time. [35] On the other hand, the patent cites as a reference Mautner's patent of 1942. Therefore, lift-slab companies already knew about their British predecessor.

The second American tradition of post-tensioned floors

Viewing all the above topics under the perspective of the idea of 'technology tradition', we may summarize the whole using the following approach.

The four variants of modern prestressed concrete arrived the US at the same time, and each had to fight the others to gain a place in the market. While all four variants found application in civil engineering, in building construction they did not have quite the same fortune. Prestressed concrete with prestressed steel **[1]** soon became very popular, as in Europe, because it was cheap, fast and easy-to-use. Via lift-slab, post-tensioned concrete also entered the building construction industry under the variant **[2c]** and soon after post-tensioned cast in situ slabs were also used **[2a]**. So, less than 15 years after the Walnut Bridge, modern prestressed concrete was already used in building construction under three of its four main variants. However, due to the lift-slab companies' lack of strategic vision, they failed to predict the importance of the new generation of anchorages, and finally succumbed, reducing the living variants to two **[1 and 2a]**.

Thus the foundations of the second tradition of post-tensioned floors for building construction in the US were built, which lasts to this day.

Why did modern post-tensioned floors flourish in the US and not in Europe – a matter of tradition?

What happened in Europe?

A number of reasons can be found to explain why post-tensioned floors did not take root in Europe after World War II, but the most critical factor was how the war determined the way Freyssinet's inventions spread across the continent. The patents of his two main inventions **[1, 2]** were granted 17 years apart from each other, which is a long time in terms of 'technology tradition'. However, the most influential factor was the war that occurred during the time between these two patent publications. His first invention, modern prestressed precast **[1]** appeared in 1930, in the inter-war period,[36] and expanded very fast. It was probably considered war technology and was pushed to massive production levels by the Germans and the British.[37] During the war, the patents of the German E. Hoyer -to a considerable extent copied from Freyssinet[38] - virtually invaded Europe in parallel with German expansion.[39]'[40]

Freyssinet had filed his post-tensioning patent **[2]** in 1939, but this technology only made it to the market in large scale after the war, and only in the field of civil engineering.[41] By the time this occurred, precast concrete (prestressed or not) had already taken a very strong position in the market as a cheap and easy-to-use technique that was able to solve most of the massive and urgent needs of building construction. At that time, the expertise in prestressed concrete design was almost exclusively in the hands of civil engineers devoted to infrastructure and of industrial engineers devoted to precasting production. Those experts were busy reconstructing the continent, and had little time and incentive to innovate. Technologies proven effective during the war were simply used over and over. Civil Engineering was the exception, as Freyssinet pushed hard his whole life for his ideas to succeed. He used post-tensioning in audacious bridges and other important infrastructure, and he soon succeeded in demonstrating that his proposals made sense and were cost efficient.[42]

Another very important factor, which prevented post-tensioning from entering the European building construction market, was the lack of capital devoted to research as there was a lack of funds following the war. This is evident when we see that European and American inventors in the 1940s and 1950s had a similar number of productive patents related to post-tensioned floors, but in Europe they were not able to raise capital to invest in their ideas. The same could be said of lift-slab technology. Modern lift-slab was invented in France and was soon applied to post-tensioning in the UK, but none of these inventions were properly backed by venture capital. This lack of investment and engineering endeavour finally led to a situation where Europeans could not take advantage of key American inventions related to post-tensioned floors for buildings, such as monostrand tendons and anchorages or the balanced load design method.

Indeed, it can be said that, as a whole, World War II determined the technology tradition of prestressed concrete in Europe.

Conclusion

The order of events, i.e. the history of the technology, might have had a very strong role in determining why post-tensioned floors flourished in US in the 1950s and are still commonly used today, and why this technique has never had similar strength in European building construction. If we look at the history of prestressed concrete as a 'technology tradition' as described above, two answers are found. On the one hand, the spread of the two main variations of modern prestressed concrete in Europe was interrupted by the war, while just after the war all variations of prestressed concrete appeared in the US. On the other hand, the stagnation present in post-war Europe made it difficult to innovate, while innovation was very much a part of the dynamic U.S. economy. The market distribution resulting from these first critical decades of modern prestressing concrete created a solid basis for a 'technology tradition' that was very different on each side of the Atlantic and which will be very hard to alter unless a new technology is able to disrupt the status quo.

Notes and references

[1] J. Trout, 'Positioning is a Game People Play in Today's me-too Market Place', *Industrial Marketing*, vol.54, no.6, June 1969, pp.51-55

[2] A proper arrangement of the reinforcement must allow its free tensioning without leading to tensions onto surrounding concrete due to reinforcement-concrete bonding. A number of solutions exist to enable this.

[3] M. Sanabra-Loewe & J. Capellà-Llobera, 'The Four Ages of Early Prestressed Concrete Structures', PCI Journal, vol.59, no.4, Fall 2014, pp.93-121

[4] J. A. Fernández Ordóñez, *Eugène Freyssinet*, Barcelona: Xarait, 1978

[5] G. D. Nasser, 'The Legacy of the Walnut Lane Memorial Bridge', *Structure Magazine*, October 2008, pp.27-31

[6] D. P. Billington, 'Historical Perspective on Prestressed Concrete', *PCI Journal*, vol.49, no.1, January-February 2004, pp.14-30

[7] S.C. McCraven, 'Post-Tensioned Concrete: Five Decades of American Building Construction, An interview with Kenneth B. Bondy', *Concrete Construction*, December 2001, pp.1-6

[8] K. Bondy, 'Post-Tensioned Concrete Buildings. Past and Future. An Insider's View', *PTI Journal*, December 2006, pp.91-100

[9] H. Sauvage, 'Ossature pour bâtiments et édifices de toute nature et système d'érection de ces bâtiments', French Patent 684089, filed 2 February, 1929, and issued 20 June, 1930

[10] B. Laffaille, 'Procédé perfectionné de mise en œuvre des matériaux de construction', French Patent 909771, filed 24 October, 1944, and issued 17 May, 1946

[11] B. Laffaille, 'Appareil de levage', French Patent 912526, filed 24 October, 1944, and issued 12 August, 1946

[12] P. N. Youtz, 'Slab lifting apparatus', US Patent 2686420, filed 30 November, 1948, and issued 17 August, 1954

[13] T. B. Slick, 'Apparatus for erecting a building', US Patent 2715013, filed 26 July, 1948, and issued 9 August, 1955

[14] Bondy, Post-Tensioned (Note 8)

[15] McCraven, Post-Tensioned (Note 7)

[16] E. K. Rice, 'Anchorage for concrete stressing tendons', US Patent 3293811, filed 1 June, 1965, and issued 27 December, 1966

[17] T. Y. Lin, 'Load Balancing Method for Design and Analysis of Prestressed Concrete Structures', *Journal of the American Concrete Institute*, vol.60, num.6, June 1963, pp.719-742

[18] McCraven, Post-Tensioned (Note 7)

[19] P. H. Jackson, 'Improvement in girders', US Patent 126396, issued 7 May, 1872

[20] P. H. Jackson, 'Building or bridge construction', US Patent 366839, filed 7 January, 1886, and issued 19 July, 1887

[21] P. H. Jackson, 'Construction of artificial-stone or concrete pavements', US Patent 375999, filed 27 October, 1886, and issued 3 January, 1888

[22] Sanabra-Loewe & Capellà-Llovera, Four Ages (Note 3)

[23] S. E. Wermiel, 'California Concrete, 1876-1906: Jackson, Percy, and the Beginnings of Reinforced Concrete Construction in the United States' in Proceedings of the Third International Congress on Construction History, Cottbus, 2009, Cottbus: Brandenburg University of Technology, 2009

[24] ibid.

[25] F. E. Kidder, *The Architect's and Builder's Pocket-book (12th edition)*, New York: John Wiley & Sons, 1895

[26] T. A. Lee, 'Artificial fire-proof joist for floors or roofs', US Patent 461028, filed 20 December, 1890, and issued 13 October, 1891

[27] A. M. Dolhon, 'Performance Evaluation of Dox Plank', in M. Ettorney, (Ed.), AEI 2008: Building Integration Solutions, Denver 2008, Denver: ASCE Publications, 2008

[28] P. W. Abeles, 'An Improved Manufacture of Structures from Reinforced Materials', UK Patent 556572, filed 3 March, 1942, and issued 11 October, 1943

[29] The Pre-Stressed Concrete Company Ltd. & K. Mautner, 'Improvements in and relating to Flat Slabs or Slabs Spanning in Two Directions with Precast Elements in Pre-stressed Concrete', UK Patent 556570, filed 28 August, 1942, and issued 11 October, 1943

[30] C. Dobell, 'Method of erecting prestressed floor sections', US Patent 2776471, filed 9 January 1952, and issued 8 January 1957

[31] C. Dobell, 'Patents and Codes Relating to Prestressed Concrete', Journal of the American Concrete Institute, vol.46, num.5, May 1950, pp.713-722

[32] Udalls Prestressed Concrete Ltd., 'Improvements in or relating to Means for Tensioning Rods and the like', UK Patent 746033, filed 24 February, 1954, and issued 7 March, 1956

[33] Udalls Prestressed Concrete Ltd., 'An Improved Method of Pre-Stressing Reinforced Concrete of Large Area, and Apparatus for Carrying Out Said Method', UK Patent 773890, filed 17 August, 1955, and issued 1 May, 1957

[34] K. H. Middendorf, 'Concrete building construction', US Patent 3152421, filed 17 November, 1958, and issued, 13 October, 1964

[35] McCraven, Post-Tensioned (Note 7)

[36] E. Freyssinet & J. Seailles, 'Procédé de fabrication de pièces en béton armé', French Patent 680547, filed 2 October, 1928, and issued 1 May, 1930

[37] J. Grote & B. Marrey, *Freyssinet, la précontrainte et l'Europe. Der spannbeton und Europa. Prestressing and Europe. 1930-1945*, Paris : Éditions du Linteau, 2000

[38] Fernández Ordóñez, Freyssinet (Note 4)

[39] E. Hoyer, 'Procédé pour faire du béton armé', French Patent 837141, filed 26 April, 1938, issued 2 February, 1939

[40] E. Hoyer, 'Einrichtung zur gleichzeitigen Herstellung einer gröβeren Zahl langer Betonkörper mit vorgespannter Bewehrung', German Patent 711506, filed 24 May, 1938, and issued 2 October, 1941

[41] E. Freyssinet, 'Système d'ancrage de câbles sous tension destines à la réalisation de constructions en béton précontraint', French Patent 926505, filed 26 August, 1939, and issued 3 October, 1947

[42] Fernández Ordóñez, Freyssinet (Note 4)

Home delivery. English temporary prefabricated housing in Bilbao: the testing of a new construction system in 1947.

Francisco Javier Muñoz Fernández
University of the Basque Country

I.

After the Spanish Civil War, during the 1940s, housing shortage was one of the most important problems of the industrial metropolitan area of Bilbao and other urban sites.[1] It was a period of deep economic crisis, in which the few construction works carried out were delayed or paralyzed due to a lack of financial support, energy, transportation, skilled labour and, especially, construction materials, whose prices were constantly rising. Housing policies, mainly fostering private initiatives with public resources, were also managed by different public institutions with no coordination, when not in direct conflict with one another.

As a result, the housing problem was not resolved, and became worse in the following years with the intense growth of Bilbao and its metropolitan area; so much so that living in crowded slums or in shacks became more common than in previous years. In the context of a harsh dictatorship, this situation motivated an increasing, but silent, social unrest, and debate on the housing shortage became more active and dynamic than in years before. Some architects, entrepreneurs, religious organizations, local institutions and newspapers asked for direct and higher aid for housing, proposed alternative and smaller sized houses, as well as the use of new construction systems, such as the prefabricated houses used in the USA and the UK.

A local entrepreneur Antonio Menchaca de la Bodega, who wanted to provide affordable housing to the workers of his factories, asked the architect Eugenio de Aguinaga for new and quick solutions. In 1947 the architect decided to try the Uni-Seco prefabricated housing system which, together with other proposals, was being used to mitigate the housing shortage after the Second War World in the UK. Prefabricated housing was also a profitable business with high public investment that Aguinaga thought might be possible in Spain.

II.

The housing shortage during and after the Second War World, prompted the UK and the USA to pay special attention to prefabricated construction, which was also of interest to other countries.[2] The USA was a pioneer in prefabrication that served as a model to the UK but even Spanish professional magazines, and local newspapers in Bilbao, published articles on the North American experiences from 1942 onwards.[3] (See Figure 1.)

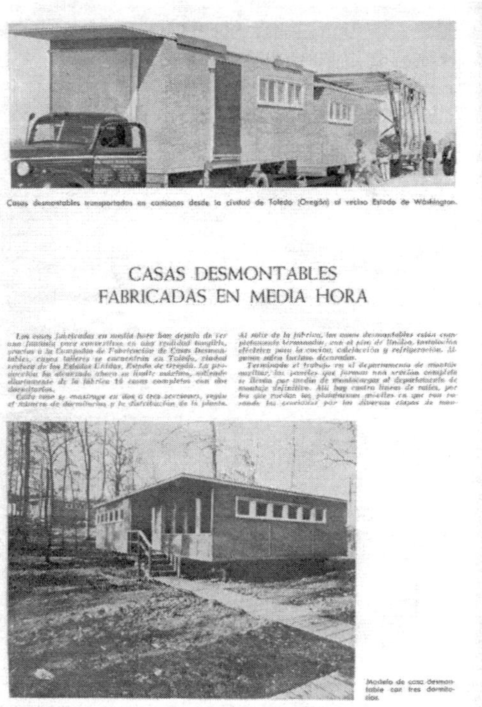

Figure 1. 'Demountable houses manufactured in half an hour'. Prefabricated houses manufactured in Toledo (Oregon) and transported to the nearby state of Washington. Revista Nacional de Arquitectura, No.42, June 1945.

Prefabrication had been used earlier in the UK and had been tested in military camps and temporary accommodation during the war. In fact, the war set the agenda for reconstruction, and a massive reconstruction programme of peacetime rebuilding and housing policy lay ahead. By the end of 1942 a variety of initiatives by central and local governments had been set up to look at different aspects of housing. The most important was the Burt Committee, an interdepartmental committee on house construction formed in February 1942 under the chairmanship of George Burt. The Committee was briefed to investigate a range of different systems suitable for alternative, and non-traditional, methods of house construction including prefabrication. In February 1944, the Ministry of Works, who had contributed to the work of the Burt Committee,, announced the design of a new temporary dwelling known as the Portal Bungalow, named after the then Minster of Works, Lord Wyndham Portal. The Ministry also encouraged three manufacturers: ARCON, Tarran Industries and Uni-Seco Structures to supply bungalows based upon a single-storey prototype with modern planning and design. They were finished and exhibited at the Tate Gallery in London in May 1944, and set the standard by which all subsequent prefabs were designed.[4]

Soon afterwards, in October 1944, still during the war, the Housing Temporary Accommodation Act was passed, earmarking £150 million for an emergency Temporary Housing Programme (THP), which planned to build 300,000 prefab houses over the next four years. As a result, during the coalition government headed by Winston Churchill, prefabricated homes, a new type of state-subsidized houses, were adopted as a temporary answer to the housing shortage during the war and, principally, the years immediately after it. In fact the THP was implemented, together with other housing policies, by the Labour Party which, in July 1945, fought and won the election with a promise of five million new homes.

The UK government knew that it would take considerable work to persuade the British public that the prefabs, houses with an estimated ten-fifteen years life and intended for rent, were suitable accommodation. It was for this reason that the construction program was developed with a favourable propaganda campaign. The BBC broadcast programmes analyzing the virtues of prefabrication for answering the housing crisis; and prefabrication was also promoted in a flurry of publications aimed at architects and the general public. The prefab debate was carried out through high-brow architectural debates down to cartoons in newspapers and magazines, and the majority of architects in the UK were keen to accept the challenge, though some members of the profession had reservations because they considered prefabs a waste of time, labour and material resources.

From 1944 to 1949, under the THP, some 156,623 prefabricated houses were produced by different companies which contributed to the war industry. Apart from the Portal Bungalow, the first prefabricated design that was never produced due to its high cost, eleven different types of houses were manufactured: the Aluminium Bungalow (also called the B2 or the AIROH manufactured in aluminium), the American (imported from the USA and also called the USA), the Arcon Mark I to V, the Isle of Lewis type [What was this?: a type of prefab, only 50 were manufactured and all of them were built in the Isle of Lewis], the Miller, the Orlit, the Phoenix, the Spooner, the Tarran, the Uni-Seco and the Universal.

Of the various types of bungalows produced under the programme, four were made in quantity: the Tarran (19,014), the Uni-Seco (28,999), the Arcon (38,849) and the Aluminium (54,500). Only the Aluminium was wholly prefabricated, and most were versions of steel or timber frames with asbestos or concrete cladding. The prefabs were made of different pieces manufactured in various factories, which were quick and easy to assemble by unskilled labour in the desired location.

The Ministry of Works established a standard prefab type with a minimum floor size of 59 square metres in a single-storey and a maximum of 2.3 metres wide to allow transportation by road. The layout of the house had a standard two-bedroom format, a living room and a "service unit": a prefabricated kitchen that backed onto a full bathroom. The houses were completed with a plot of land and a shed, a cottage on its own plot with a futuristic design. The prefabs also offered hot water, central heating and a refrigerator, which together with an indoor bathroom and living in a single-storey with a plot of land were a luxury at the time.

Thousands of quirky bungalows sprouted in the suburbs of the largest towns in the UK, mainly in the ones that had suffered the most during the war. The layout of big settlements tended to be more elaborate with roads, footpath access and alleys. Local authorities, the owners of the land on which the prefabs were erected, decided on their location depending on the land available and their future use, and also decided who should live in them and set their rent. Priority was given to people with children or special medical requirements, but most residents had no money and/or had been made homeless because of the war. They were generally people from a working-class background, some of them ex-servicemen.

Spanish architectural magazines and the local newspapers from Bilbao published different prefabs experiences from the UK. In this way the initiatives developed in Cheltenham, Birmingham and other cities were known[5], together with some permanent prefabricated housing projects.[6] (Fig. 2)

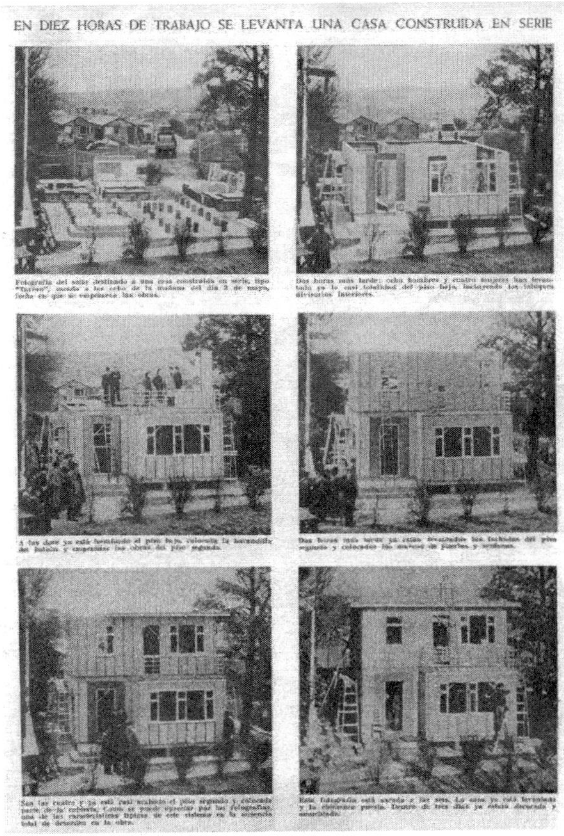

Figure 2. 'Ten working hours to assemble a house manufactured in series'. Tarran prefabricated houses in England. Revista Nacional de Arquitectura, No.31, July 1944.

In 1946 the British Council invited the Spanish General Director of Architecture, Pedro Muguruza, to visit prefabricated houses in Bath, Birmingham, Bradford, Liverpool, Manchester, Oxford and Stratford. Muguruza described his travel in a book with references and pictures of the AIROH, the Uni-Seco and the Universal prefab types[7]. Aguinaga also had notice of the prefabricated houses used in the UK and other countries thanks to the architectural magazines he received in his domicile: *Architectural Review* from England, *Architectural Record* and *Architectural Forum* from the USA and *Baumeister* from Germany.[8]

III.

The entrepreneur Antonio Menchaca de la Bodega asked Eugenio de Aguinaga, who had carried out various projects for him since 1940, to design new houses for the workers of his factories. Menchaca wanted to build cheap houses with affordable rent not just for some of his employees but for all of them. Aguinaga understood that prefabricated housing could be a possible answer. Initially he tried timber houses, and in 1946 he wrote to two architects established in Madrid, Luis García Palencia and Luis Moya, because he was interested in their proposals for prefabricated housing in timber. On 17 May Aguinaga ordered a prefabricated house with a layout designed by him, of which he wanted to manufacture between 80 or 100 houses, but which were never produced.[9]

Later, in May 1947, Aguinaga opted for the Uni-Seco prefabricated houses. The London-based company, founded in 1940, was achieving great success[10], and was considering the manufacturing of their prefabs under licence in Madrid and in Casablanca, adapting the design to local needs and features[11]. The Spanish builder Agromán was interested in building prefabs for his workers in the hydroelectric projects he was developing across the country; and Uni-Seco was also in contact with Ramón Quijano de la Colina, a manufacturer of high tension wires and concrete beams, with a view to manufacture prefabricated homes in a number of Spanish cities.[12]

Aguinaga got in touch with the General Director of Uni-Seco, Bernard Brunton, expressing his interest in using their prefabs, as well as in the possibility of setting up a new business with them in Bilbao. Around June 1947, Brunton sent the architect a film about the Seco building system which Aguinaga showed to a small number of colleagues[13]. Even though the architect pointed out the high cost of the materials needed, it did not discourage him from trying a housing system and a business "very convenient under the current circumstances in Spain"[14]. If the project went ahead, the architect intended to build a factory based on the Uni-Seco prefab licence to manufacture 60 houses per week.[15]

On 12 June 1947 Aguinaga sent Brunton the layout of two "ultra-small and ultra-economic" houses that could be modified if needed "but always within the minimum dimensions" established[16], as a construction proposal. The London based factory realised this in a semi-detached house signed by the Uni-Seco architect, R. G. Booth, and Eugenio de Aguinaga. (Fig. 3)

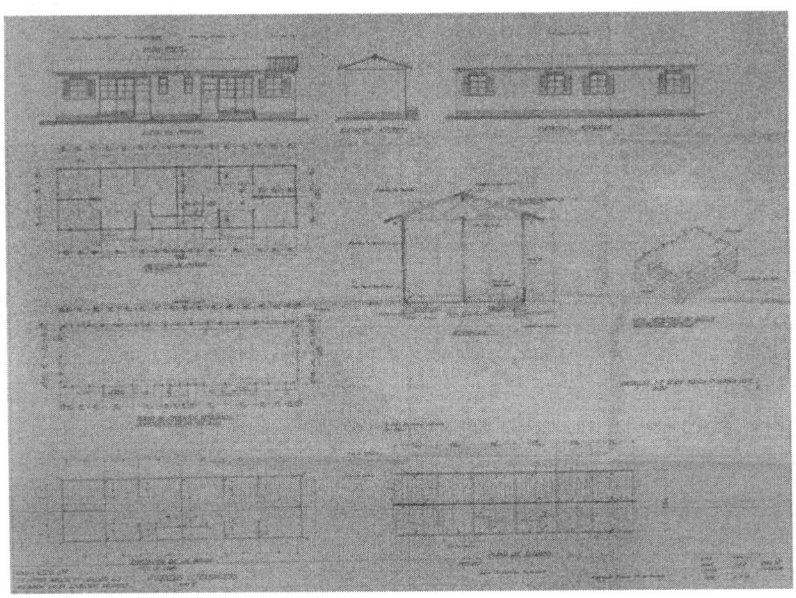

Figure 3. Plan of the Uni-Seco semi-detached house signed by R. G. Booth and Eugenio de Aguinaga. Archivo General de la Universidad de Navarra (AGUN)/ Eugenio de Aguinaga.

Some months later, on 21 October 1947, Aguinaga and the entrepreneur Pedro Ybarra y Mac-Mahon obtained the authorization of the Firestone Hispania factory in Basauri, close to Bilbao, to build the "prefabricated minimum house"[17]. Aguinaga's uncle, Restituto de Azqueta, was the Managing Director of the American-Spanish company and had, since that September, started building on the Firestone Estate.[18] In fact, the architect chose this location because the company could be a potential customer for the prefabs and, at the same time, it could be a great opportunity to compare both a traditional and a prefabricated construction system.

By the end of October there was the possibility of importing the semi-detached house from London to Bilbao. But the customs tax of 100,000 pesetas, four times the price paid for the house, made the project unviable.[19] Aguinaga asked for and obtained a tax reduction from Francisco Prieto Moreno, the new General Director of Architecture[20]. Soon afterwards, at the beginning of December, Brunton announced his intention to go to Madrid and later to Bilbao to oversee the assembly of the house. [21]

In December, the Uni-Seco bungalows made of a timber and concrete frame, steel reinforcement, and tiles and with Uralita cover for a pitched roof, which was not used in the UK, were assembled after 182 working hours. (Figs 4-7)

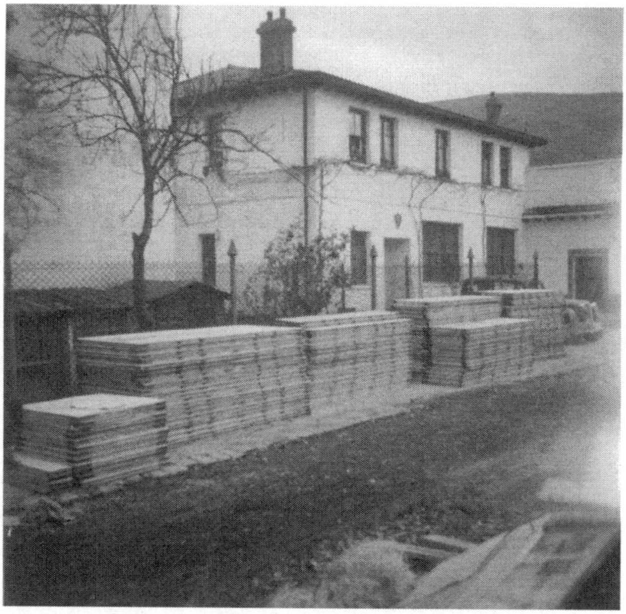

Figure 4. Uni-Seco semi-detached house before being assembled in December 1947. Photo: unknown author. AGUN/ Eugenio de Aguinaga.

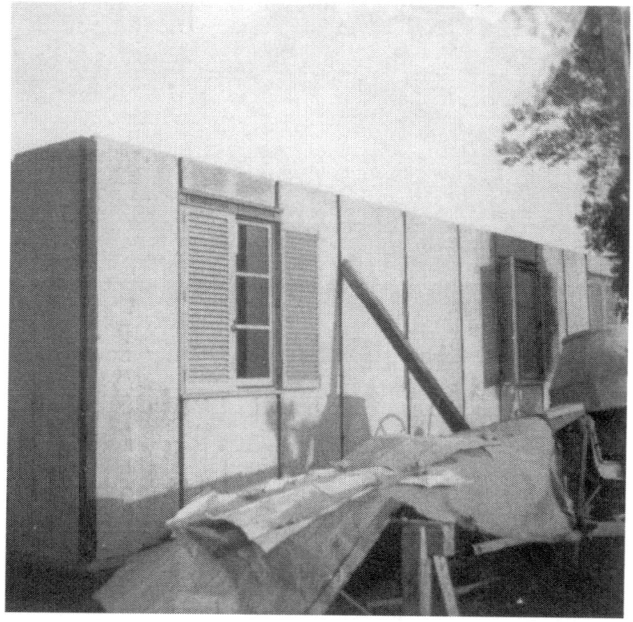

Figure 5. Uni-Seco house being assembled in December 1947. Photo: unknown author. AGUN/ Eugenio de Aguinaga.

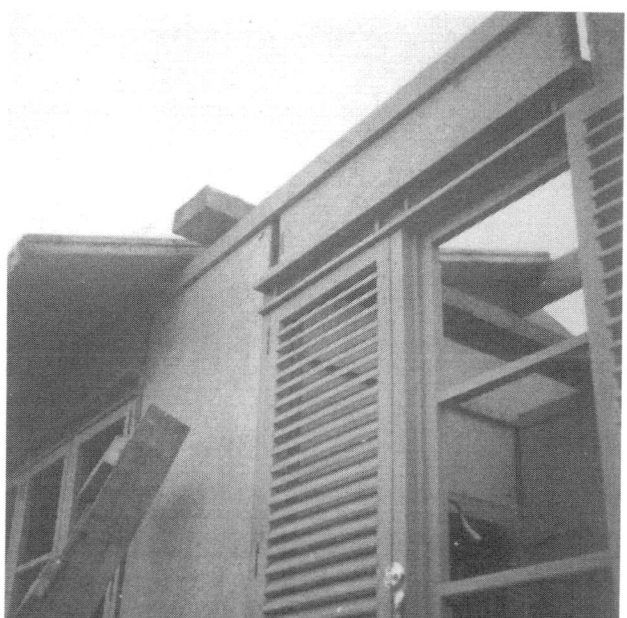

Figure 6. Uni-Seco house being assembled in December 1947. Photo: unknown author. AGUN/ Eugenio de Aguinaga.

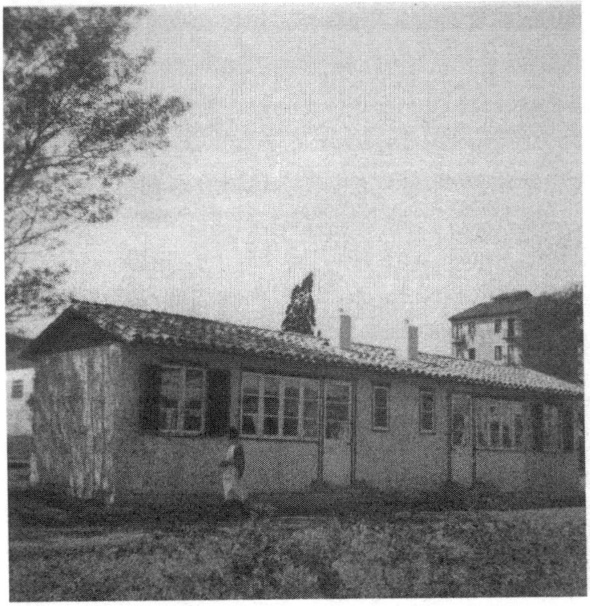

Figure 7. Uni-Seco house, picture taken April-May 1948. Photo: unknown author. AGUN/ Eugenio de Aguinaga.

The result was two houses of rectangular dimensions (14.22 x 3.55 metres; 50.48 m^2) and 2.44 metres high. The layout was composed of a central area used as a kitchen and dining-room from which there was access to two bedrooms and to a very small W.C.. Months later Pedro Ybarra furnished the houses,[22] which did not have the "service unit" found in those manufactured in the UK.

The total cost of the prefab was 45,505.72 pesetas, without the customs taxes. Of this, 20,331.17 pesetas were for the prefabrication in London (18,591.17 for materials and 1,740 for the workforce), and the remaining 25,174.55 pesetas were for the assembly (11,680.55 for materials, 5,020 for the workforce and 8,474 for facilities, painting, glass and transportation)[23]. The assembly was carried out by the local company Macazaga Constructions, owned by Esteban Macazaga, who regularly collaborated with Aguinaga.[24]

By the end of January 1948, before the Firestone Estate was completed, Menchaca, Ybarra, Macazaga and Aguinaga met with the intention of offering Firestone Hispania a project to manufacture the prefabricated houses needed by the company using the Uni-Seco licence. They concluded that they would need the machinery to manufacture the prefab and the technical support of a technician from the London based factory, to deal with problems related to the manufacture and the assembly. They would also have to address the lack of some construction materials.

The local entrepreneurs and Aguinaga opted for the prefabricated houses because the constant steady increase in construction prices, apparently, made the quick prefabricated system cheaper[25]. However, their initiative did not prosper, possibly because the materials needed, especially Uralita, and the final cost of the houses were too expensive. In addition, Spain did not have a modern construction industry, and, unlike traditional housing, prefabs did not have any institutional support and were unknown to professionals and commissioners usually resistant to innovation, whereas a traditional house was cheaper and permanent, as Aguinaga could verify with the Firestone Estate that he was building at the same time.

The Firestone Estate was a 5,000 m^2 and 3 km long urban development located on a hillside, close to the American-Spanish factory. The buildings, following the wishes of the commissioners, were inspired by vernacular architecture. The estate was composed of 60 semi-detached houses and a square with a church, a school, shops and houses for three teachers and a priest. (Fig. 8.)

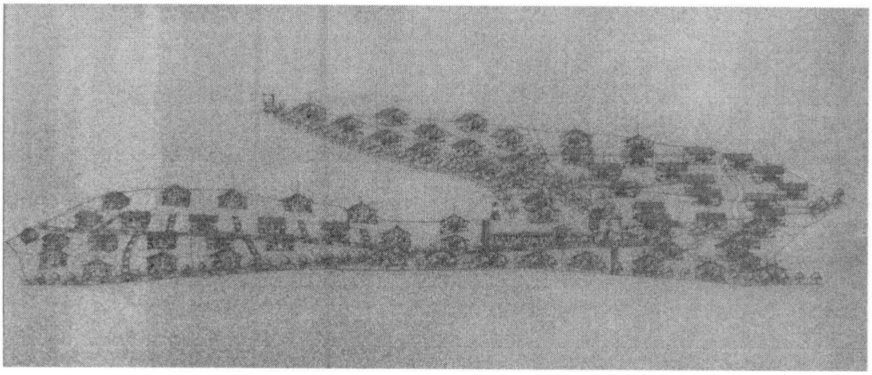

Figure 8. General perspective of the Firestone Hispania Estate designed by Eugenio de Aguinaga in May 1951. AGUN/ Eugenio de Aguinaga.

Aguinaga was commissioned by Firestone-Hispania to build the project at the beginning of June 1944.[26] The first design was completed by 17 August 1945 and its construction was delayed until 27 September 1947, twenty days after it was officially approved by the Spanish Government to receive financial and construction materials support. In two years' time, by 9 November 1949, two houses were completely finished and furnished ready to be exhibited.[27] The rest of the houses were gradually completed until 1 December 1954.

The houses' foundations were made of mass concrete, while reinforced concrete was used in the structure, including poles and beams and the pitched roof which was covered with tiles. Facades and internal partition walls were made of brick, and the exterior had rough plaster walls with plinths of natural stone. Wood was used in carpentry and for floors except in the kitchen, dining-room and bathroom where cement tiles were used.

In order to prevent monotony Aguinaga designed eight types of semi-detached houses with differences in the roofs and the colours of the walls (brown, green and red). Each of the 120 houses had a plot of land and on average was 103 m^2, a dimension the architect considered excessive for this kind of house, but was demanded by the company[28]. The houses were distributed on two or three floors, with a hall, a dining-room, a kitchen and a pantry on the ground floor; and a bathroom and three bedrooms or more on the upper floors. (Figs 9-10).

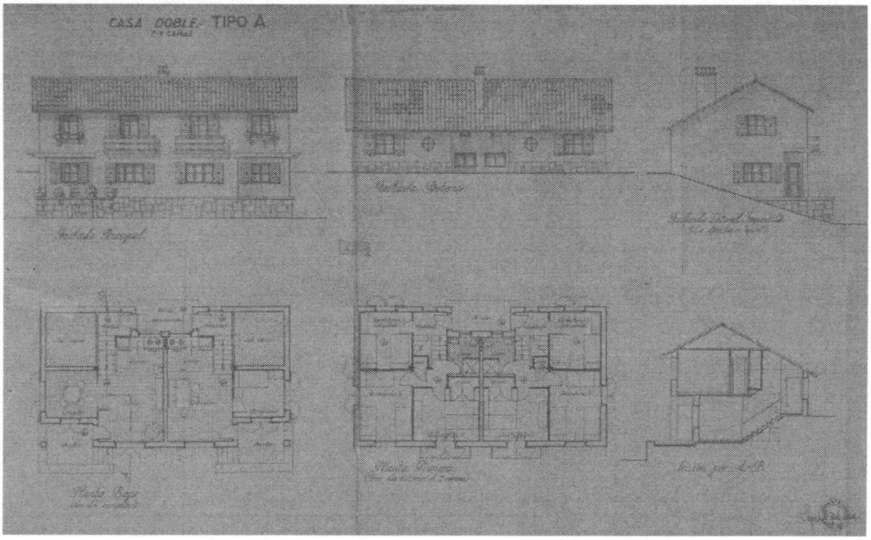

Figure 9. Firestone Hispania Estate, type A semi-detached house, designed by Eugenio de Aguinaga in March 1949. AGUN/ Eugenio de Aguinaga.

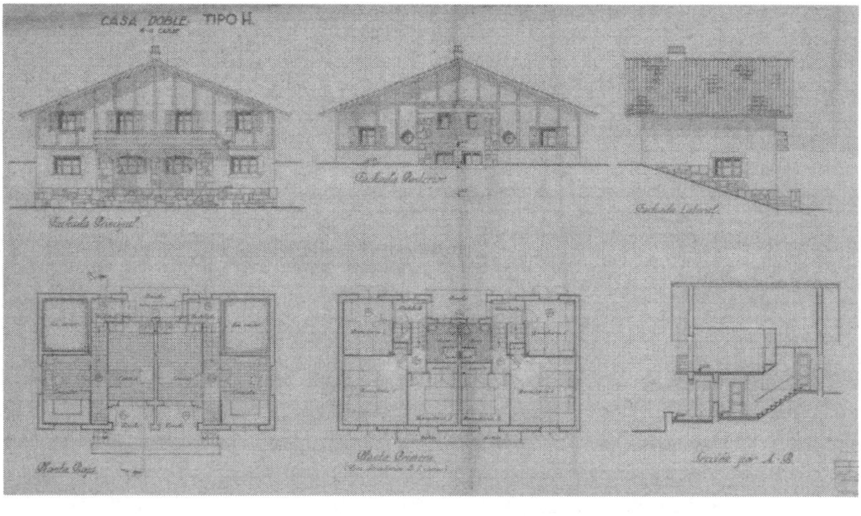

Figure 10. Firestone Hispania Estate, type H semi-detached house, designed by Eugenio de Aguinaga in March 1949. AGUN/ Eugenio de Aguinaga.

The total cost of the village was 17,367,098.22 pesetas[29], almost double the estimate of October 1946 which was 9,667,196.07 pesetas.[30] Each semi-detached house cost 75,188.29 pesetas[31], far from the 47,340.37 pesetas estimated in 1946[32], but in any case less than a prefab.[33]

IV.

In 1952, Aguinaga assessed the two Uni-Seco prefabricated houses that were never occupied. He confirmed the good resistance and the good condition of the structure and carpentry; they had even weathered recent storms which had caused serious damage to other buildings. Inside there was some humidity,possibly because they had not been ventilated as they were not inhabited. This humidity caused the electricity cables and the metallic parts of the doors to rust.[34]

Aguinaga had predicted that prefabs would have a lot of difficulties due to the materials required. It is also significant that Aguinaga asked Brunton to bring to Bilbao the book *Flats. Modern developments in apartment house construction* by Hippolyte Kamenka[35], indicating that the architect was more interested in high dwellings which were more economic and more typical of his architecture, than either the Uni-Seco proposal he was testing or the Firestone Estate he was building to the instructions of his commissioners.

Aguinaga was attracted by the prefabs built in the UK because they were quick and easy to assemble and to produce, they did not require skilled labour[36], and had the economic support of the government. However, he ignored the finding that prefabs did not provide instant homes at the low prices originally promised.[37] Even the 1944 government reports pointed out that traditional housing would provide the vast majority of the accommodation needed because its construction was cheaper than aluminium, the material used by the vast majority of prefabs.[38] Government support for prefabricated houses was a measure to redeploy, so as to avoid collapse, of war industry factories, specialized in steel engineering, and which employed a great number of workers.[39] At the same time prefabs, fitted with a range of luxuries for the time, appeared in a period in which housing and the whole development of the mechanism of the welfare state was to emerge. Prefabricated dwellings were promoted during the war as the herald of the changes that were to come in peacetime.[40] Therefore, in an era of reconstruction and hope in the post-war period, prefabs, thanks to their media profile, became objects typifying new opportunities, and offering a new way of life and comfort as well as the idea of a reward to a society who had fought and suffered during the war. [41]

Consequently, British prefabs were developed in a particular context, which was not present in Bilbao, where technical and financial resources were very different, there was no opportunity for business, and where traditional housing was still cheaper and permanent. Despite this, Aguinaga wanted to try new construction techniques and to adapt the prefabs to a country where building construction experienced constant delays and rising prices, and he saw tprefabrication as a possible alternative and a business opportunity.[42]

Even though the Uni-Seco system trialled was not successful, Aguinaga predicted that prefabrication would become the future of construction because it could be cheaper and could provide accommodation to the large numbers of people living in deplorable conditions. In fact, when the economic situation of the country and the construction industry faced new building challenges, from 1960 on, new permanent prefabricated housing proposals were developed in Bilbao and in Spain, which coincided with the promotion by public authorities of prefabrication as a real possibility to deal with the serious housing shortage: but this is already part of another history.[43]

Acknowledgements

I would like to express my gratitude to the people working at the General Archive of the University of Navarre (Archivo General de la Universidad de Navarra) for their kindness and generosity.

Note and References

[1] A. Santas Torres, *Urbanismo y vivienda en Bilbao. Veinte años de posguerra,* Bilbao: COAVN, 2007. F.J. Muñoz Fernández, *Arquitectura racionalista en Bilbao (1927-1950). Tradición y modernidad en la época de la máquina,* Bilbao: Universidad del País Vasco, 2011.

[2] Many countries, among them the English-speaking countries, had a long tradition in the construction of demountable houses. After the First War World the prefabricated housing industry became more specialized in the USA, the UK and other European countries but, apart from some exceptions, it did not have any impact in Spain. For the few cases developed in Bilbao consult: Muñoz Fernández, Arquitectura (Note 1) pp.404-5 and 343-6.

[3] 'Casas de papel', La Gaceta del Norte (23 April 1942), p.3. 'Casas para la defensa nacional en los Estados Unidos', Revista Nacional de Arquitectura, No.14, (Feb.), 1943, pp.77-88. 'Noticiario. Las nuevas casas transportables', Revista Nacional de Arquitectura, No.25, (Jan.), 1944, pp.29-30. 'Casas desmontables para obreros, en Norteamérica', Obras, No.54, (Apr.), 1944, pp.113-7. 'Casas desmontables fabricadas en media hora', Revista Nacional de Arquitectura, No.42, (Jun.), 1945, pp.240-1. 'Sistemas de fabricación en los Estados Unidos', Revista Nacional de Arquitectura, No.42, (Jun.), 1945, pp.242-4. 'Sección extranjera. La arquitectura moderna en los EE.UU. Un grupo de casas baratas', Revista Nacional de Arquitectura, No.43, (Jul.), 1945, pp.273-5. 'Casas prefabricadas de acero en los Estados Unidos', Reconstrucción, No.84, (Jun.-Jul.), 1948, pp.231-6.

[4] E. Blanchet, *Prefabs Homes*, Oxford: Shire Publications, 2014, N. Bullock, *Builidng the Post-War World. Modern Architecture and Reconstruction in Britain*, London. New York: Routledge, 2002, C. Davies, *The Prefabricated Home*, London: Reaktion Books, 2006, B. Finnimore, *Houses from the Factory. System Building and the Welfare State, 1942-74*, London: Rivers Oram Press, 1989, G. Stevenson, *Palaces for People. Prefabs in Post-War Britain*, London: Batsford, 2003, T. Smith, *Prefab Homes for Heros*, (Essay, London Architectural Association, 1974), B. Vale, *Prefabs. A History of the UK Temporary Housing Programme*, London: E & FN Spon, 1995.

[5] 'Construcción de casas', La Gaceta del Norte (25 May 1944) p.1. 'Casa de aluminio', La Gaceta del Norte (31 March 1945), p.4. 'Casas experimentales de acero en Inglaterra', Revista Nacional de Arquitectura, No.42, (Jun.), 1945, pp.236-40. 'El método Mulberry aplicado a la construcción', La Gaceta del Norte (23 February 1946), p.10. 'Viviendas para construcción urgente', La Gaceta del Norte (7 April 1946), p.10. 'Casas para los campesinos ingleses', La Gaceta del Norte (27 May 1946), p.3. 'Un nuevo pueblo, de aluminio', La Gaceta del Norte (23 October 1946), p.3. '16.000 casas de aluminio en Inglaterra. Una vivienda cuesta 1.365 libras y se monta en 45 minutos', *Obras*, No.64, (Jul.-Sep.), 1947, pp.95-100.

[6] 'En diez horas de trabajo se levanta una casa construida en serie', Revista Nacional de Arquitectura, No.31, (Jul.), 1944, pp.267-8. 'La casa Wates. Solución de vivienda barata industrializada', Cortijos y Rascacielos, No.54, 1949, pp.30-2.

[7] P. Muguruza, *Notas de un viaje por Inglaterra*, Madrid: EPESA, 1946.

[8] E. Aguinaga Churruca, 'Recuerdos entre bastidores' in: *Aguinaga. Obras. Lanak*, Bilbao: COAVN. Bizkaia, 1992, p.14. For Aguinaga see also: A. Fernández Per, (Ed.), *Eugenio Aguinaga*, Vitoria-Gasteiz: Gobierno Vasco, 2000.

[9] Letter of Eugenio de Aguinaga to Luis García Palencia dated 17 May 1946. Archivo General de la Universidad de Navarra (AGUN)/ Eugenio de Aguinaga. For Moya see: A. Capitel and J. García- Gutiérrez Mosteiro, *Luis Moya Blanco. Arquitecto 1904-1990*, Madrid: Electa. Ministerio de Fomento, 2000, J.M. Otxotorena, (Ed.), *Luis Moya Blanco 1904-1990,* Pamplona: t6, 2009. About different prefabrication experiences after the Spanish Civil War consult: P. Cassinello, (Ed.), *Eduardo Torroja 1949. Strategy to Industrialise Housing in Post-World War II*, Madrid: Fundación Eduardo Torroja. Fundación Juanelo Turriano, 2013.

[10] By 1950 Uni-Seco structures had appeared on over six hundred sites, and nearly 200 firms had engaged in the work of erection different types of buildings. Uni-Seco Structures Ltd., *'Seco' Unit System. General Information and data Sheets*, London: Hunt, Bernard and Co., 1950?, p.A2.

[11] Letter from Aguinaga to Brunton dated 11 November 1947 and letter from Brunton to Aguinaga dated 24 November 19947. AGUN/ Eugenio de Aguinaga.

[12] Letter from Brunton to Aguinaga dated 28 May 1947. AGUN/ Eugenio de Aginaga.

[13] It might have been the film 'Homes While You Wait' made by British Pathé in October 1945.

[14] Letter from Aguinaga to Brunton dated 12 June 1947. AGUN/ Eugenio de Aguinaga.

[15] Letter from Aguinaga to Prieto dated 28 November 1947. AGUN/ Eugenio de Aguinaga.

[16] Letter from Aguinaga to Brunton dated 12 June 1947. AGUN/ Eugenio de Aguinaga.

[17] Letter from Aguinaga to Brunton dated 21 October 1947. AGUN/ Eugenio de Aguinaga.

[18] Firestone Hispania SA. Grupo de 124 viviendas en Urbi. 1945-1959. AGUN/ Eugenio de Aguinaga. 'Inauguración del poblado Firestone-Hispania en Basauri (27 de septiembre)', Boletín Oficial de la Diócesis de Vitoria, No.10, (Oct.), 1947, pp.604-5. E. Aguinaga, 'Poblado Firestone Hispania, Bilbao', Revista Nacional de Arquitectura, no.153, October 1954, pp.5-10. Fernández Per, Aguinaga (Note 8) pp.89-93, Santas Torres, Urbanismo (Note 1) pp.291-6. For Firestone see: J.M. González García, 'Los orígenes de la industria del caucho en el País Vasco (1923-1950)', Vasconia, no.25, 1998, pp.187-93.

[19] Earlier,, at the end of August 1947, Aguinaga wrote to Prieto Moreno to obtain the approval of the Ministry of Industry and Commerce. Letters from Aguinaga to Prieto Moreno dated 28 August 1947 and 28 October 1947. AGUN/ Eugenio de Aguinaga.

[20] Between 8,000 and 10,000 pesetas. Letter from Aguinaga to Brunton dated 11 November 1947. AGUN/ Eugenio de Aguinaga.

[21] Letter from Brunton to Aguinaga dated 2 December 1947. AGUN/ Eugenio de Aguinaga.

[22] Letter from Ybarra to Aguinaga dated 28 November 1949, with the invoice for the furniture dated 30 November 1948. AGUN/ Eugenio de Aguinaga.

[23] Uni-Seco Limited. Time taken for erection of prototype of small houses, Bilbao. December 1947. Letter from Aguinaga to Brunton dated 23 November 1948. AGUN/ Eugenio de Aguinaga.

[24] Letter from Macazaga to Aguinaga with the invoice for the furniture dated 5 April 1948. AGUN/ Eugenio de Aguinaga.

[25] Letter from Aguinaga to Brunton dated 23 January 1948. AGUN/ Eugenio de Aguinaga.

[26] Initially the architect Anastasio de Telleria also collaborated with the project, but he was not involved in it by the time the construction began.

[27] Letter from Aguinaga to Firestone Hispania dated 29 November 1949. AGUN/ Eugenio de Aguinaga.

[28] Aguinaga, Poblado (Note 18) p.7.

[29] Poblado Firestone. 13 February 1959. AGUN/ Eugenio de Aguinaga.

[30] Firestone Hispania S.A. Grupo de 124 viviendas protegidas en Urbi. Memoria descriptiva y ordenanzas. AGUN/ Eugenio de Aguinaga.

[31] Poblado Firestone. 13 February 1959. AGUN/ Eugenio de Aguinaga.

[32] Firestone Hispania S.A. Grupo de 124 viviendas protegidas en Urbi. Memoria descriptiva y ordenanzas. AGUN/ Eugenio de Aguinaga.

[33] The cost of each square metre was: 229.80 pesetas in 1946, 364.99 in 1954 (from estimations made in 1959), and 372.36 in 1947 for the prefabs.

[34] By this date Uni-Seco wrote a letter to Aguinaga asking for information about the erected houses. Letter from Brunton to Aguinaga dated 17 November 1952, and another one dated 9 April 1952 in which Brunton thanks Aguinaga for the information provided. AGUN/ Eugenio de Aguinaga.

[35] H. Kamenka, *Flats. Modern Development in Apartment House Construction*, London: Grosby Lockwood & Son, 1947. Letter from Aguinaga to Brunton dated 27 November 1947. AGUN/ Eugenio de Aguinaga.

[36] Some prefabs were built by German and Italian prisoners of war. In 1946, over 400,000 German prisoners were still in British camps, and were used as forced labour in construction and in agriculture. J. Grindrod, *Concretopia. A Journey Around the Rebuilding of Postwar Britain*, London: Old Street Publishing, 2014, p.31.

[37] The houses produced under the aegis of the 1944 THP, represented over six per cent of the new permanent temporary houses and flats built in the UK until 1949. Vale, Prefabs (Note 4) p.170.

[38] Smith, Prefab (Note 4) unp.

[39] Finnimore, Houses (Note 4), p.36.

[40] Ibid., p.26. Vale, Prefabs (Note 4) p.167.

[41] Blanchet, Prefabs (Note 4) p.44.

[42] In 1954 Aguinaga designed for Menchaca a timber prefabricated house in La Reineta, in La Arboleda, a mining municipality in the metropolitan area of Bilbao. AGUN/ Eugenio de Aguinaga.

[43] The housing developer and technician from Bilbao José Luis Calvo Casas went to France to find out about the prefabrication techniques used there. Afterwards, in 1960, he founded the company Previcasa (Prefabricados de Vizcaya S.A.) and he started using prefabricated houses in Bilbao, Biscay and other Spanish provinces. In the following years some other companies dedicated to prefabricated houses or prefabricated construction elements were created: Precosa and Prefabricados Ygla S.A. in 1963, and Poly-Plac Iberia and Preycon in 1964. At the same time, the Instituto Técnico de la Construcción (Construction Technical Institute) located in Madrid sent technicians to different countries to study the construction techniques used. It gave detailed information about them in its journals and publications and even trialled them. L. Bilbao, 'Algunas consideraciones sobre la historia de la industrialización de la construcción de viviendas durante el Desarrollismo (1960-1975): la aportación bilbaína al debate de la industrialización de la vivienda', Madrid, *Informes de la Construcción*, vol.58, no.502, 2006, pp.49-62.

Motel: building techniques and architectural features of the Italian repertoire (1954-1969)

Laura Greco

Department of Civil Engineering, University of Calabria, Rende, Italy

Introduction

The motel is an architectural form that originated in the United States of America during the years between the two world wars. The word motel, derived from the contraction of motorist hostel or motor hotel, was coined by the US architect Arthur Heineman to indicate tourist accommodation reserved for motorists. The use of this form in the USA is generally demonstrated by the presence of numerous cottages arranged around open courtyard layouts, which became known as motel courts in the period 1920s-1930s. The war created a crisis in tourism and for this type of accommodation, then the more isolated buildings were abandoned.

After the war, the recovery of the automobile industry, the development of tourism and the localization of manufacturing activities in the semirural areas of the country favoured conditions for the evolution of the phenomenon towards the modern motel operated by large national chains.

As a consequence of these social and economic transformations the architectural form evolved into a form without the motel court. The location of motels was carefully studied, taking into account car flows, but overall the amount of long-distance traffic directly related to the market of motels. The chosen site was located in some cases along highways, and in others near tourist routes characterized by natural attractions (beaches, sights, parks), or along routes affected by manufacturing activities.[1] The economic sector related to motels attracted investments from the major hotel chains, such as Sheraton, National Auto Haven and Holiday Inn, whose presence affected the design and construction process of the buildings. The picturesque style of motel court disappeared. Modern buildings were basic constructions that delegated the strength of the commercial message to the impressiveness of billboards and neon. The policy of a low cost strategy was applied to the buildings, while more investments were planned for interior design in order to ensure higher comfort conditions than motel courts had typically offered.

In the early 1950s the presence of major clients encouraged further changes in the design and construction process of this architectural form. A recurring layout considered for multi-storey buildings arranged facing rows of rooms served by a peripheral corridor and toilets grouped in the corner of the plan. At the end of the 1950s, hotel companies again used multi-storey plans but with a central corridor and elevator. In the same period, the increasing number of motels and the need to ensure low cost services favoured the use of industrialized building systems, as in the Holiday Inn policy. In this case, Kemmons Wilson, founder of the hotel chain concluded an agreement with Wallace Johnson, manufacturer of prefabricated building systems.

The late 1950s coincided with a new stage in the architectural type evolution. In those years highway motels arose that were distinguished for their greater attention to architectural character, approaching the style of urban hotels, so much so that the difference between hotel and motel became less evident.[2]

The development of the motel in Italy. State of the art and new analysis opportunities

Motels in Italy were part of the motorway architecture developed as consequence of the construction of the national motorway system. Autogrills, bars and motels became the icons of the modernization process which affected the country in the 1950s. Studies of the architectural and construction characteristics of motels in Italy highlighted the evolutionary outlines of the phenomenon, the main promoters and the building techniques used.

In particular, the study published by the author of this paper in 2010,[3] analyzed the Italian repertoire with reference to the work developed by the Azienda Generale Petroli Italiana (Italian General Petroleum Company) which became known as Agip. The company was established in 1923 and in 1953 joined the Ente Nazionale Idrocarburi (National Hydrocarbons Agency) which became known as Eni.

In the research presented in 2010, the author examined unpublished documents of the Archivio Storico Eni (Eni Historical Archive) from which a preliminary analysis was formulated. The results highlighted similarities with the American contemporary experience and peculiarities of the Italian repertoire, to which the author in this paper refers.

The motel form became widespread in Italy in the 1950s. The phenomenon came from the development of the national road system and the subsequent increase of tourism through the country. The motel was established as economy accommodation, strictly connected to suburban car flows. The major promoter was Agip, already known as a leader in the distribution and retail of fuel in the country.

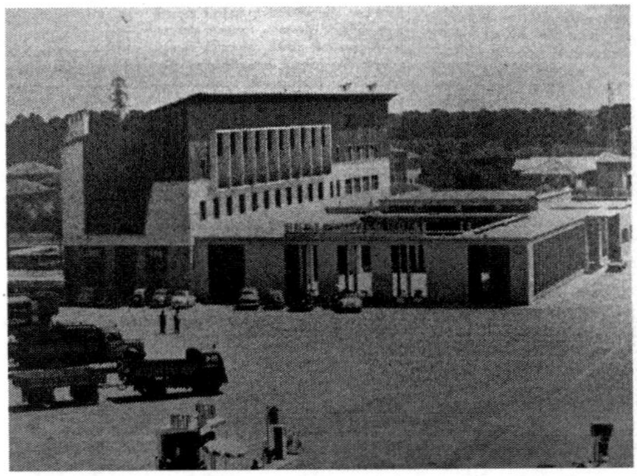

Figure 1. Motel for truck drivers, San Donato Milanese. Architect, Mario Bacciocchi. 1954. Photo: Eni Historical Archive, Rome (ASE).

As mentioned, in 1953 Agip became part of Eni and launched a program for the upgrading of its motorway assistance system, starting with their service stations. In 1954 Agip expanded its activity to the motel sector, and constructed its first building. It was a motel for truck drivers, designed by the Milanese architect Mario Bacciocchi (1902-74) in San Donato Milanese near Milan (Fig. 1). The building was expanded two years later by the Milanese architects Ugo Ratti (1922_94) and Marco Bacigalupo (1922-80). The site plan was arranged around a courtyard enclosed by a colonnade and a low block. The motel was in the background, located in a two-storey building with a pitched roof.

The program for the Agip motels prefigured a network of hotels located along highways. At the end of 1962 the Agip group included thirty motels.[4]

The other Italian motorway restaurant chains, such as Pavesi and Motta, were not interested in these facilities, except for some projects by Pavesi where the autogrill included the motel.[5]

The influence of the American experience in the Italian context, and in particular in the Agip program, was emphasized by the oil company, whose policy used the US image to present and display these type of facilities in the national arena.[6]

However, the Italian case was independent from the phenomenon of the temporary housing style that characterized the American context. The design process was conducted by the technical offices of Agip and of Società Nazionale Metanodotti (Snam), another Eni company. In some cases, projects were developed, as mentioned, by architects such as Mario Bacciocchi, Ugo Ratti and Marco Bacigalupo who worked in collaboration with the design departments of the Italian petrol company. In these cases, Agip coordinated the designs defining the general technical requirements. A substantial part of the repertoire, however, was linked to the design activities of the internal technical departments.

In the period of more important development of the motel repertoire (1954-69), Agip's strategy was based on the research of standardization of spaces and construction techniques which progressively guided the designs of this Italian company. This, on one hand ensured the identification and consistency of services through the country, and on the other hand, this approach was conditioned by the Italian cultural and construction context, whose technological delay in the building industry led to choices of materials and building techniques that were not coherent with the objectives of standardization established by Agip in its general program. In other cases, the models developed were inappropriate to the need for flexibility that usually affected this type of building, as the layout and technology adopted were inflexible. In the mid-1960s, the search for industrial construction technologies and the adoption of prefabricated components became part of the Agip program.

The study of the Italian motel repertoire can now benefit from the use of new documentary sources. In 2015, the author of this paper analyzed some unpublished documents of the Historical Archive of Eni that highlight original aspects of the Italian experience, concerning the development of the motel type between 1956 and 1961. These are drawings regarding the project of a motel with an adjacent service station (1956) and the preliminary studies of the motel type named 1961. The results of the analysis are presented in this paper.

Architectural and construction standardization. The Agip case: Motels 1959, 1961, 1968

Previous architectural and construction research on the motel type suggested that this form first appeared in Italy in 1959.[7] Instead, from recently acquired evidence, it is possible to demonstrate the presence of previous projects. In fact, a drawing of 1956, discovered in 2015 due to the cataloguing of a new part of the Eni Historical Archive heritage, illustrates the project of a restaurant-motel to be built with an adjacent service station. The project, developed by Mario Bacciocchi, was never realized, but it represented an important premise for subsequent solutions. The multi-storey building had a rectangular plan.[8] The typical floor included 15 rooms with a central distribution corridor. The project provided for a reinforced concrete structure cast on site and external and internal walls constructed from hollow blocks. The geometrical scheme of the framed reinforced concrete structure was not modular. The longitudinal bays were, in fact, different due to the dimension of twin rooms separated by a service-supporting wall for walk-in closets. In another case the distance between bays was conditioned by the dimensions of the master bedroom, or determined by the dimensions of the staircase. In the transverse direction the layout included two side spans (4.40 meters) and one central larger span (5.10 meters) that incorporated the corridor and the bathrooms. A cantilevered portion, reserved to balconies, concluded the scheme (Fig. 2).

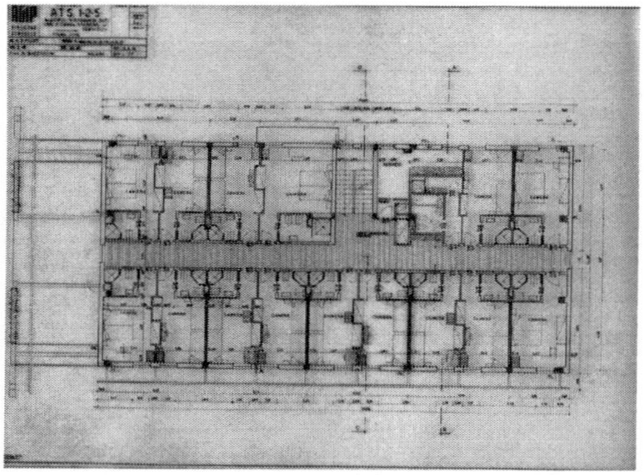

Figure 2. Project of an Agip restaurant-motel. Architect, Mario Bacciocchi. Plan. The proposal was never realized. 1956. Source: ASE.

In the project of a motel type known as 'motel 1959' some traces of the study developed by Bacciocchi in 1956 were present. In fact, the multi-storey building (3-4-5 levels) had a rectangular plan (Fig. 3). The ground floor was destined for common services. However, 'motel 1959' was distinguished due to the attempt to standardize construction elements. The framed reinforced concrete structure cast on site was organized on a geometric module in the longitudinal direction (3.30 meters). This motel design was distributed along the Italian motorway system, representing the project connoting the image of Agip in this sector of motorway service assistance.

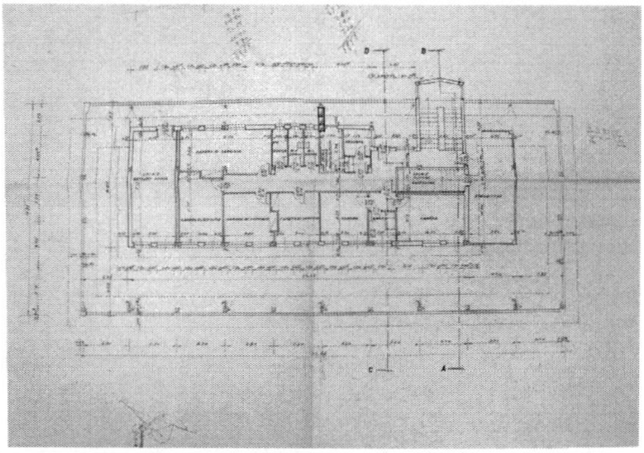

Figure 3. Project of the motel type 1959. Plan. The project realized along the national motorway system. 1960. Source: ASE.

In some cases, such as the Motel in Gela (Sicily), the building was completed by a shop block arranged on one level. Also in this part of the construction, the reinforced concrete structure was cast on site and organized in the longitudinal direction on a geometric module (3.30 meters).

In 1960, Agip considered the project of a removable prefabricated motel with a steel structure, but it was never built. The proposal included a rectangular plan articulated into a basement for systems, a ground floor for common facilities and the first floor destined for rooms. The construction choices were inspired by industrialization criteria. The design covered a metal structure composed of HE profiles for pillars and beams combined with steel sheet floor slabs and self-supporting panels. The panels used the US patent Steelox and were produced in Italy by Armco-Finsider. The modular system was chosen to guarantee rapid assembly, disassembly and re-use of the structure. The scheme showed an almost industrial aesthetic experience, which was very different in construction terms from the traditional style of the 'motel 1959', so that this prefabricated solution was not used in the subsequent Agip motel program.

The discovery in the Historical Archive Eni of some drawings concerning the preliminary project of 'Motel 1961' allowed for an improvement of knowledge on this phase of the standardization strategy conducted within the Eni program. These three drawings showed some site plans and preliminary studies of the typical room for the motel.[9]

The plans are of interest because they suggest a new point of affinity between the Italian repertoire and the US case. The site plans had layouts very similar to American motel courts. In fact, they covered open courtyard plans, prepared for rectangular areas of different dimensions (Fig. 4). In general, three preliminary projects were based on the presence of a service core, arranged near the entrance and adjacent to the road. Facilities included a service station, bar, reception, restaurant and kitchen. The rooms were in the inner part of the area, arranged in two-storey buildings, in one case rotated by 60°. In all solutions, rooms on the ground floor were provided with a garden and private parking, while those upstairs were completed by a balcony. All the plans adopted an almost square module (6.00x5.50 meters). Two solutions planned expansions of the motel in one direction (longitudinal or transversal), taking into account the original site plan. These proposals were never realized in Italy. A further variant was developed a year later.

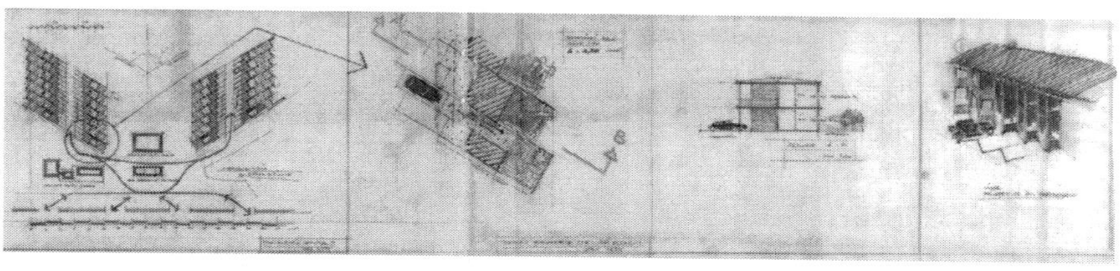

Figure 4. Preliminary studies Motel 1961. Site plans. 1960. Source: ASE.

In a drawing of 1961, recently discovered in the Eni archives, showed standard windows and doors of the 'Motel 1961/b' type. The drawing showed the façade onto the garden for a one-storey building. The façade was finished with colored plaster and prefabricated panels combined with an external layer of thermal insulation and a white aluminum sheet (Fig. 5). This coating was anchored to the façade through a metallic substructure fixed to reinforced concrete pillars and slabs. The windows of this motel type utilized a natural anodized aluminum frame. This project was developed by Agip's technicians in partnership with the architects Ratti and Bacigalupo who in the same year designed a motel in Pisticci, whose construction was completed in 1964. The building in Pisticci was an application, albeit modified, of 'motel type 1961/b'. In this case, the building was organized in two levels, but the façade to the back was resolved with a solution similar to that described in the drawing of 1961.

In any case, 'motel type 1961' was not so widely used as the 'motel 1959' type. Recently acquired documentation suggests that its use would determine a more articulated development of the Italian repertoire, improving affinity with the American case due to the use of extensive layouts. Probably the relationship established in Italy between the motorway system and motels suggested a preference for multi-storey buildings (4-5 levels), in this case more affordable than one-storey buildings.

However, preliminary studies of 1960-61 highlighted some issues of Agip's strategy recurring in the subsequent years. The architectural and construction research was oriented towards the study of adaptable layouts, the definition of designs inspired by standardization of spaces and construction elements and the use of industrialized building techniques.

These themes were developed in the late 1960s. In 1968, Agip launched a competition for a new motel type.[10] The archival documents allow us to see the essential aspects. The call for the motel type required a building suitable for different areas, with a capacity of two hundred beds, increasing up to three hundred and reducible to one hundred, in addition to common facilities.

In reference to the evolution study being developed in this paper, it is useful to consider the solution proposed by the group led by the Italian architect Costantino Dardi (1936-91) from the projects presented to the competition. The project focused its program on the interaction of two aesthetic, construction and structural systems: the reinforced concrete modular private space of the typical room and the public spaces of the motel identified by the metallic grid structure (Fig. 6). The reinforced concrete system combined industrialized precast elements and parts cast on site. The basic element was formed by a rectangular slab of the same dimension of the typical room. The slab had bidirectional wire-mesh reinforcement, stiffened by ribs. Each room was formed by assembling four slabs. The overlap of adjacent modules formed a box-shaped system whose cavities were used to arrange the additional reinforcement and cast the concrete for the connection of precast elements.

In a motel proposed for Mestre, near Venice, designed by Dardi between 1969 and 1970 but never built, there were some traces of the project of the competition of 1968. It is an urban motel with public facilities. The plan of the complex was developed from a large basement on which the prism (33 meter side) of the motel was placed. In the basement storage rooms for plants and staff were arranged. This part was completed by a system of open spaces and a swimming pool with related services. The ground level accommodated the common facilities. The nine floors of the motel were served by a gallery distribution walkway overlooking a central atrium (Fig. 7). The reinforced concrete structure of the motel was combined with the metallic roof of the common facilities. The layout of the framed reinforced concrete structure was organized on the module of the typical room (3x6 meters). Pillars supported the metallic grid structure of the roof. Beam and block floors (thickness 18 centimeters) completed the structure of the motel. As mentioned, the floor of common areas and the roof of the winter garden located in the central atrium used a metallic grid structure formed by a pyramidal module with square plan (120 centimeters side).

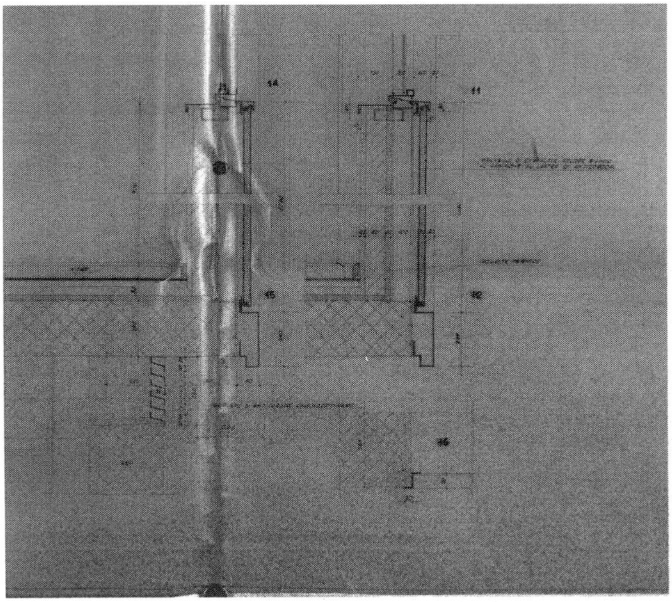

Figure 5. Project of the motel type 1961/b developed by Agip. Detail of the façade finished with prefabricated panels. 1960. Source: ASE.

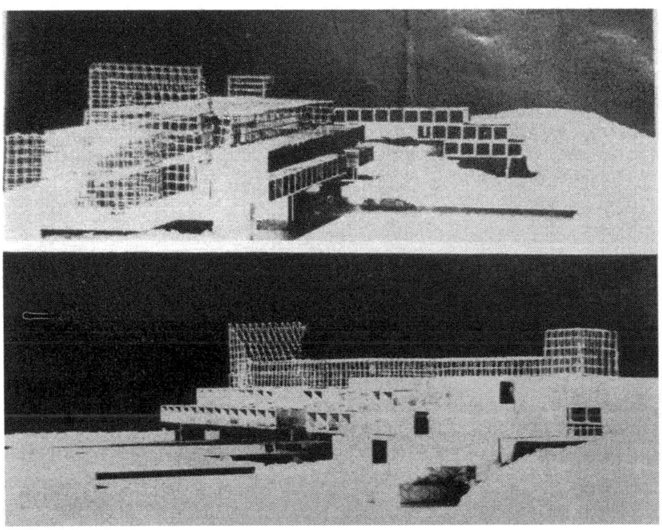

Figure 6. Design Competition for a new Agip motel type. Architect, Costantino Dardi. 1969. Source: Casabella, no. 338, 1969.

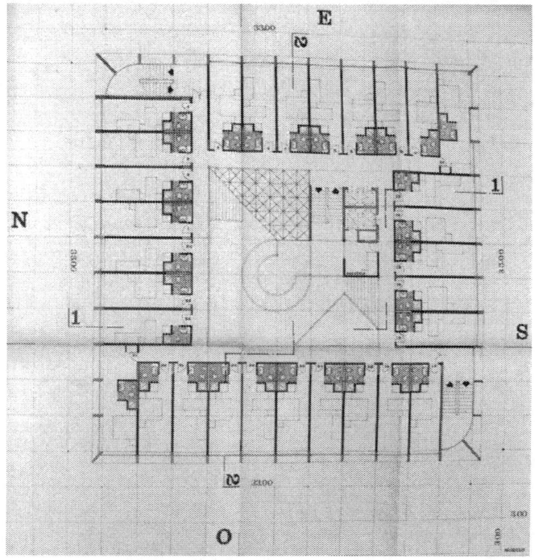

Figure 7. Project for the motel Agip in Mestre. Plan. Architect, Costantino Dardi. 1969-70. Source: ASE.

An example of building industrialization: the motorway motels

The development of Italian motorways, the construction of which culminated with the realization of the Autostrada del Sole (1956-64), favoured the spread of motorway motels. This phenomenon affected the Agip repertoire. As mentioned before, these types of building originated in the USA where their architecture proved very similar to urban hotels. In Italy, at the beginning of 1960s, an evolution of the motels occurred towards an architectural style with an urban character similar to that developed in the USA in the 1950s. This happened because of the proximity of the motels to office urban districts or urban areas in general. The location of the motels became the symbolic modern-day gate to the city.

These projects and realizations were distinguished by the dimensions or peculiarity of the architectural features of buildings. Belonging this group of edifices were the motel in San Donato Milanese, near Milan, and the motel in the motorway service area of Florence, both built between 1961 and 1963 along the Autostrada del Sole in association with the major service areas. In the first case, the value of the area was determined by the presence of the headquarters of Eni (offices and laboratories) in San Donato Milanese; in the second case, the motel of Florence was located in association with one of the more important traffic junctions of the Autostrada del Sole (Fig. 8). In addition to traditional facilities, a motel, a bank, a restaurant, offices, a mechanical workshop, and the Church of San Giovanni Battista designed by the Italian architect Giovanni Michelucci (1891_1991), articulated the layout of the service area in Florence, giving it a functional, architectural and cultural quality unusual for the Italian experience at that time.

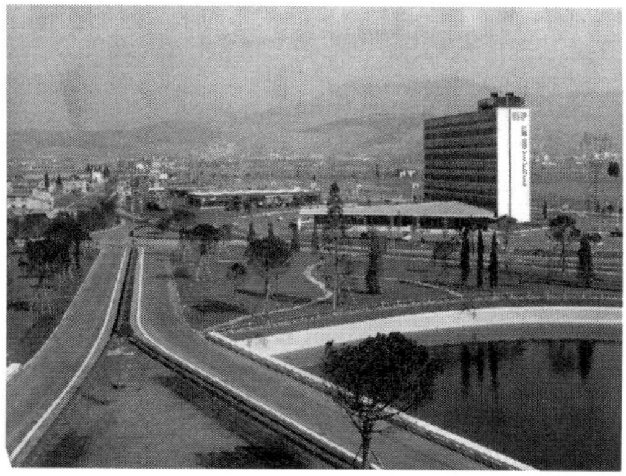

Figure 8. Motel Agip in motorway service area of Florence. Architects, Ugo Ratti and Marco Bacigalupo, 1963. Source: ASE.

In both cases the project was developed by the Milanese architects Ugo Ratti and Marco Bacigalupo. The designers aimed to define the motel as the pivot of the service area layout, using an international architectural style.

Ratti and Bacigalupo developed the project for the motel in Florence in collaboration with Snam technicians and simultaneously to that in San Donato Milanese.[11]

The complex in Florence was completed in 1963. The motel, with rectangular plan (8.45x54.75 meters) and 29.25 meters high, provided a functional layout articulated in a basement and a ground floor for common services and eight levels for rooms (fifteen on each floor).

The motel was connected to the restaurant by a reinforced concrete canopy. The restaurant, with a triangular plan and the base arranged parallel to the long side of the motel had a basement and a ground level, while the shops consisted of a one-storey building organized in a Y scheme. All edifices had reinforced concrete structures cast on site.

The curtain wall was the construction element characterizing the motel, giving an aesthetic experience similar to that of urban business districts. The façade of the motel emerged in the motorway landscape as a modular surface, punctuated by the texture of the metal uprights and by the regular composition of windows, spandrel panels and metal sheet string courses. The curtain wall was organized on the geometric module of 1.75 m. The documentation of the project available today concerns different phases of elaboration of the adopted solution.[12] The design of the façade was developed in collaboration between Snam Progetti and Alsco Malugani, a leader in the field of curtain walls in Italy. Unlike that observed in the motel in Pisticci, where Ratti and Bacigalupo directly defined the detail of the construction, in this case the definition of the façade system seems to have been developed by Snam. Available details concern construction and assembly aspects of windows and panels. The system used a substructure of iron uprights to connect opaque and transparent panels of the façade. The spandrel component was externally insulated and completed by a precast concrete panel 1 meter high and 3 centimeters thick. The concrete panel was supported at the extrados of the reinforced concrete slab and held from two other points at the top, where it was connected through metal brackets to the iron uprights of the substructure. String courses consisted of a metal sheet that closed the cavity formed at the intrados of the slab for the passage of air conditioning system ducts.

The facade of the motel in San Donato Milanese, realized by Alsco Malugani, was characterized by a similar general composition. The geometric module of 1.75 meters was organized into three parts using precast concrete spandrel panels, enamelled sheets for windows and string courses (Fig. 9).

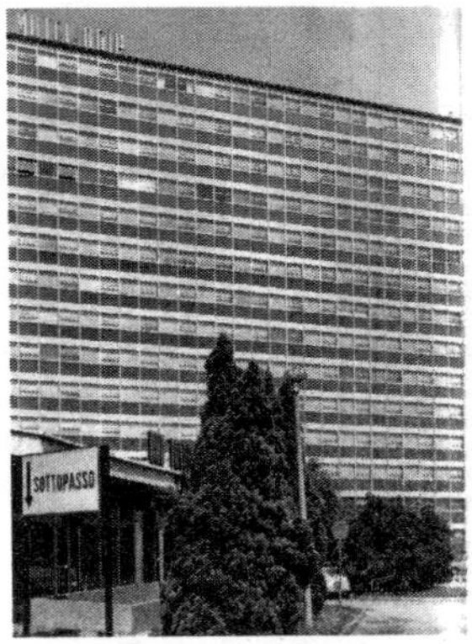

Figure 9. Motel Agip in San Donato Milanese. Architects, Ratti and Bacigalupo, 1963. Source: ASE.

Among the motorway motels, the proposed design of the motel Agip in Settebagni (1968-69), near Rome, developed by the Italian architect Mario Ridolfi (1904-84) stood out. The project, another one which was never built, was for a tower over 40 meters high. It was an unusual interpretation of the motorway architectural theme, whose figurative power and originality of construction solution were affected by the cultural background of the architect. Ridolfi did not adopt current industrialized systems. The reinforced concrete cast on site structure was completed by the hollow block external walls and *ad hoc* designed prefabricated panels (Fig. 10). The geometry of plan and volume, the articulation of floors and the originality of construction solutions defined the uniqueness of the Settebagni proposal. Ridolfi worked for Agip a few years but did not join the commercial and construction program of the company.[13] He preserved his cultural and technological independence. His experience is comparable to that of Pier Luigi Nervi (1891-1979) who worked for Motta, an Italian leading company in the motorway restaurants sector, developing some studies and an autogrill in Limena near Padua. [14] Nervi, like Ridolfi, did not yield to the established program of the company, but transferred his experience, his iconographic and technological references to the design of the autogrills. For this reason the motel in Settebagni does not represent a typical step in the cultural and commercial program of Agip. However, its construction would have been an unprecedented developmental trajectory for motel design in Italy. In any case, it contributed to prove, beyond the commercial policies of petroleum and restaurant companies, the relationship between the 1950s and 1960s Italian architectural culture and the motorway architecture (service stations, motels, autogrills) due to the work of architects and engineers as Ridolfi, Bega, Dardi and Nervi, protagonists of the general cultural debate that developed in Rome and Milan in particular.

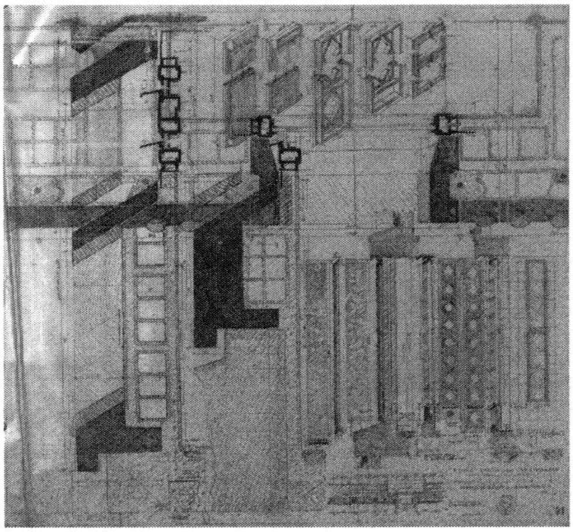

Figure 10. Project of motel Agip in Settebagni. Studies of prefabricated panels. Architect, Mario Ridolfi, 1969. Source: ASE.

Conclusion

The analysis of new documents concerning Italian motels conducted in this paper in continuity with the studies published by the author in 2010 allows the addition of further elements to the knowledge of the evolutionary process of this architectural style in Italy during the 1950s-1960s, with particular reference to the role played in Italian research by designs that were never realized.

The scheme developed by Bacciocchi in 1956 suggests considering the motel type 1959 designed by Agip in the light of the Milanese architect's contribution, by linking and comparing two proposals. The plan of 1956 strongly influenced the solution of 1959. The studies of 1960 and 1961 on one and two-storey motels arranged in open courts document the architectural research carried out in Italy on extensive layouts similar to cottages designed in the USA during the decades between the two world wars. Research on modular design and the extensibility of buildings testify as to the interest in 1960-61 for flexible and adaptable construction, providing a reference for the subsequent experimentation of 1968.

Motels in San Donato Milanese and Florence designed by Ratti and Bacigalupo confirm the Italian contribution to research on the urban motel type, whose architectural style finds correspondence in the American 1950s repertoire. The dimension and the peculiarity of the context reinforce the singular character of two motels, turning them away from the trajectory of the standardized motel.

The evolution presented in this paper shows that motels represent a style sector in which the complex spread of industrialized building systems in Italy is confirmed. Particular reference is made to the 'motel 1959' type that was born to represent a standardized building but was realized with traditional handcrafted techniques. This question was determined by the conditions of the Italian technological and cultural context in which these buildings were developed. The coexistence of desire for standardized solutions and the use of traditional or proto-industrialized techniques joined, in fact, this style to the general condition of the Italian construction context during the 1950s-1960s.

Notes and References

[1] See G. Baker, B. Funaro, *Motels*, New York: Reinhold Publishing Corporation, 1955, pp. 1-14.

[2] See H. C. Liebs, *Main street to Miracle mile. American roadside architecture*, Boston: Little Brown, 1985, pp. 188-189.

[3] The study is L. Greco, *Architetture autostradali in Italia. Progetto e costruzione negli edifici per l'assistenza ai viaggiatori*, Rome: Gangemi, 2010.

[4] See D. Deschermeier, *Impero Eni. L'architettura aziendale e l'urbanistica di Enrico Mattei,* Bologna: Damiani, 2008, p. 168.

[5] See L. Greco, (note 3), p. 182.

[6] The American motels were illustrated on the magazine of Agip "Gatto Selvatico". A series of articles published between 1959 and 1962 outlining the evolutionary characters of the new typology.

[7] See L. Greco, (note3).

[8] See Drawing no. 25427 "Albergo Ristorante con e senza stazione di servizio", 26 Aug. 1956 (Eni Historical Archive, from now on ASE).

[9] See Drawings no. 101/1, 101/2, 101/3, "Progetto di massima motel 1961", 15 Nov. 1960 (ASE).

[10] The commission closed the evaluation process on 12 Feb. 1969. See Casabella, no. 338, 1969.

[11] Preliminary studies on motel also concerned the project of a motorway bridge-building restaurant related to the motel. The hypothesis was abandoned.

[12] See Drawing "Motel Agip Firenze – Corpo Albergo. Particolari pannelli e serramenti", no. 4062/173, 2 Aug. 1960 (ASE). A subsequent series of drawings was developed by Alsco Malugani. See Drawing Alsco Malugani, "Motel Agip Firenze - Serramenti tipo C", no. 2112/46, 8 May 1961 (ASE).

[13] Ridolfi developed in 1968 another project for a Motel in Belgrado.

[14] See L. Greco, 'Building techniques and architectural quality of motorway restaurants in Italy. The case of Mottagrill by Pier Luigi Nervi and Melchiorre Bega', pp. 745-751 in E. Kurrer at al (Eds.), Proceedings of the Third International Congress on Construction Historey, Berlin: Neunplus 1, 2009.

Building Technology and Corporate Image: a case study of ENI, a leading Italian company

Stefania Mornati

Department of Civil Engineering and Computer Science Engineering – "Tor Vergata" University of Rome

Introduction

During the period of Enrico Mattei's presidency of the *Ente Nazionale Idrocarburi* (ENI),[1] Italy's National Hydrocarbons Authority, the entrepreneurial activities of this State-run company focused on a major expansion and its building activities took a radical turn. Over the course of Mattei's nine years at the head of the company, from 1953 until his untimely death in 1962, "SNAM Progetti" – ENI's construction division – was responsible for the majority of the company's constructions across Italy. Alongside a massive promotional campaign, Mattei intended to tell the outside world about the innovation and technological modernisation of the company he managed, through the projects it built. Regardless of ideological entanglements or theoretical references, this vast building programme – comprised of an extensive network of natural gas pipelines, industrial sites, residential developments, sports facilities, office complexes, service facilities for employees and their families, hotels, motorway service and refuelling stations – pursued a pragmatic value focused on functionality, rapid construction and a decidedly modern image: achievable only through an agile organisational structure, recourse to prefabrication and the use of innovative construction techniques. These objectives occupied an anything but secondary role in establishing ENI's new corporate image, in the full awareness that this increased visibility would only benefit the company. This programme included the construction of three office buildings between 1956 and 1961, two in San Donato Milanese (near Milan) and one in Rome, and a sports centre in San Donato Milanese (1955-56). In the Italian architectural panorama they represent interesting examples of applied research in building construction and were among the strongest demonstrations of Mattei's sensitivity toward the modernisation of building techniques in Italy. While the ENI building laboratory was not immune to the general tendency of Italian construction sites in using established traditional building techniques, nevertheless it demonstrated an organisational structure, technical expertise and programming skills that, for most of Italy, were looked upon as revolutionary.

Though much has been written about ENI, very little has been said about the building techniques and construction practices adopted in the realisation of its architectural and industrial legacy. The investigation of these aspects is intended as a contribution to the understanding of Italian post-war construction and as a tool useful in the preparation of possible restoration programmes.

The Italian Context

From the end of the 1940s and throughout the following decade, at an international level the construction industry was swept up in an experimental impulse driven by the urgent need for reconstruction. Of course the issue of housing polarised debates between specialists, with the consequent emergence of a demand to increase productivity, to build a great deal, soundly and in a short time. This led to studies focused on improving building techniques and the organisation of construction sites. Italy, characterised by small enterprises and a slowness in modernising construction methods and operating practices, answered the call more by discussing these issues in conferences and specialised publications than in introducing any actual changes on site. A shortage of trained labourers represented one of the primary limits to real change in an industry that should have been evolving toward large-scale prefabrication, industrialisation and a more rational organisation of the phases of work. Northern Italy, the more industrially developed part of the country, responded with more interest and vivacity to the demands for change. In particular, the city of Milan became the centre of this process with the establishment in 1946 of the *Centro Industriale Lombardo di Coordinamento per l'Edilizia* (Lombardy Industrial Centre for Building Coordination). Albeit briefly, the Centre published the magazine *Cantieri* (Construction Sites), which served to promote and disseminate the most advanced Italian and foreign experiences. The greater part of Italian companies only timidly welcomed these constructive impulses toward innovation, preferring instead to continue with tried and tested practices more suitable to a largely unskilled and numerically abundant workforce.

There was, however, a small group of enlightened clients who, conversely, considered architectural research and innovation in building techniques useful tools for conveying the image of a modern company: among them was ENI under the direction of Enrico Mattei, the brilliant entrepreneur who, in addition to revolutionising company policy and its internal organisation, also encouraged technical and scientific research among its various subsidiaries, drawing inspiration from the most advanced models being applied in the United States. Based on these models, at the end of the 1950s SNAM *Progetti* developed a set of guidelines, formulated from experiences primarily in the sector of mechanical manufacturing. In addition to defining the organisational structure of the office, it also spelled out the essential criteria to be followed in the design and construction of building works.[2] A mention of this document serves to introduce a theme that is inextricably intertwined with the experimental atmosphere that reigned over projects from this period and the autonomy afforded to external professionals invited to collaborate with the company; however, in general, this highly useful tool served to support the efforts at coordination required by the rationalisation of operational and technical procedures.

Functionality, speed of construction, quality and economy were the keywords governing the laying of gas pipelines as much as the construction of the company's most representative buildings. As mentioned, the ideas for controlling different aspects of the design and construction phases came from organisational models employed overseas, where the techniques of work planning, industrialisation, the use of serial building components and constant cost-control were widely credited with optimising production processes in all industrial sectors. This reorganisation directly involved the functional organisation of ENI's design office. It was employed to identify tasks, responsibilities and review and checking procedures based on a clear framework that assigned each parameter with a specific value. The theme of industrialisation thus acquired an important role, defined in relation to the specific characteristics of what was to be built, sacrificing the spectacular by adopting the criteria governing the activities of the SNAM Progetti division. Unlike the rest of Italy, in the world of ENI the industrialisation of the construction sector was considered a means for improving the quality of buildings and each important occasion to build something represented a chance to establish a record in Italy (the use of a steel structure, the expanse of a glass façade, innovative plant systems) and to quickly better it.

The Architecture of ENI

In the early 1950s ENI purchased a large plot of land in the municipality of San Donato Milanese, adjoining the territory of Milan. It was initially intended as the site of a large centre for pipeline maintenance and a compressed natural gas station serving transport vehicles. With the expansion of ENI's business, this initial programme was soon expanded to include a motel, housing, a shopping centre, laboratories, office buildings, a church and other services for employees, taking on the characteristics of a true urban centre named *Metanopoli*, 'Methane City'.

During this decade ENI built two office buildings in Metanopoli, identified by the ordinal numbers "first" and "second", and its new main headquarters in Rome's EUR neighbourhood. Together with the goal of unifying the offices of its various business groups, these buildings, all strikingly modern, also represented the company to the outside world. Mattei himself directly commissioned the design of the "first" building in 1955 by Marcello Nizzoli (1887-1969), a well-known architect and former designer of typewriters for the Olivetti group, who in turn brought on the architect Mario Oliveri (1921-2007). The building was completed in 1957. The projects for the headquarters in Rome and the "second" building near Milan were assigned to Marco Bacigalupo (1922-94) and Ugo Ratti (1922-80) in 1959. The building in Rome was completed in 1961, followed by the inauguration of the offices in Metanopoli in 1963. Bacigalupo and Ratti, unlike Nizzoli, were two young and little-known Milanese architects, introduced to the world of ENI by the engineer Sante Tibaldi, their classmate at the Politecnico di Milano and employee of the group since 1950.[3]

Though different from one another, the three buildings acted as a common laboratory for technological experimentation that extended from structure to envelope, and from finishes to mechanical and electrical engineering, placing ENI at the forefront of companies contributing to the modernisation of building technologies.

In fact, the use of steel structures and curtain wall systems were evident indicators of new technological horizons. In Italy, traditionally more favourable toward the use of concrete, steel structures were still rare, though the curtain wall was gradually gaining ground.

The three buildings in Metanopoli and Rome all adopted site-welded steel structures and curtain wall envelopes. The first responded to the company's objectives of optimising production: rapid erection, simplified installation of mechanical equipment and the most advanced technological services, reduced foundation costs with respect to a concrete structure and increased useable volume thanks to the smaller dimensions of columns and minor depths of floor slabs. This approach required that conventional processes be reduced to a minimum, in favour of finishing elements suitable to the elastic behaviour of a steel structure and the greater precision offered by industrialised production. For Italy, the curtain wall was emblematic of a new aesthetic frontier and a modern way of conceiving the external wall; together with the famous six-legged dog [the ENI logo – TN] and the myriad of petrol stations distributed across the country, the serial repetition of glazing panels, defined in accordance with more or less international models, proved to be the most effective tool for propagating the corporate image ENI wished to present.

For the "first" office building, Nizzoli and Oliveri developed a complex comprised of two buildings, inaugurating a pattern that would be repeated in the other two designs: a low, rather ordinary block for general services attached to a taller landmark volume. (Fig. 1) The originality of this architectural *parti*, unprecedented in Italy, at the time just approaching the construction of office skyscrapers, coupled with the particular figurative qualities of the envelope, interpreted Enrico Mattei's desire for "something ... modern and extraordinary, a building no one [had] ever made".[4] This approach immediately placed the building among the most representative late-1950s examples of experimental types, of which the office building proved to be one of the most interesting fields.

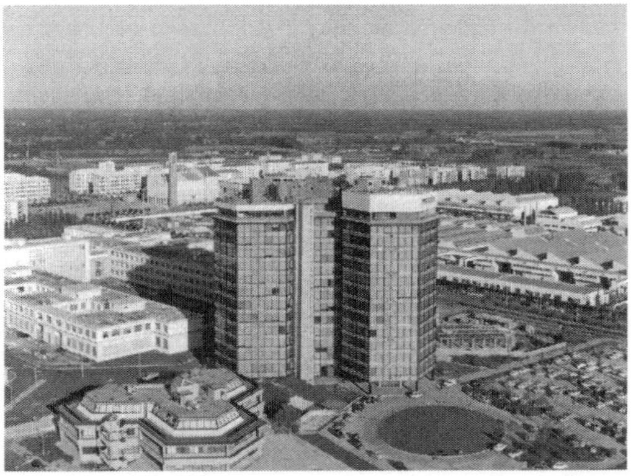

Figure 1. The "first" ENI building in Metanopoli: general view (ENI Historical Archive)

The design of the building's steel structure, among the first in Italy for a skyscraper, was driven by the need to accommodate the unusual configuration in plan generated by the joining of 4 hexagonal volumes with 12.50 m long sides meeting at an angle of 120°, creating no less than 17 façades. (Fig. 2) Soaring fifteen stories above the ground, the tower established a landmark in the vast expanse of the Po Valley. Architectural critics at the time immediately grasped the reference to typical tower constructions of Lombardy, as well as to the new icons of the methane industry whose most readily-identifiable iconic element was the gas holder.[5] Designed by the engineers L. Finzi and G. Magenta, the structural system employs a frame with rigid connections and primary spans of 12.50 m. Unifying the connections at different floors are a series of composite 'I' profiles made from welded plates for struts and main beams, and 'IPN' profiles for the secondary beams. The multi-directional framing of the beams defined an extensive space frame that proved particularly efficient in resisting horizontal forces. This made it possible to hang the reinforced concrete stair cores from the steel structure, eliminating their function as bracing elements. The complex connections between frames resulting from the hexagonal configuration of 120° angles required some 11,000 meters of welds.

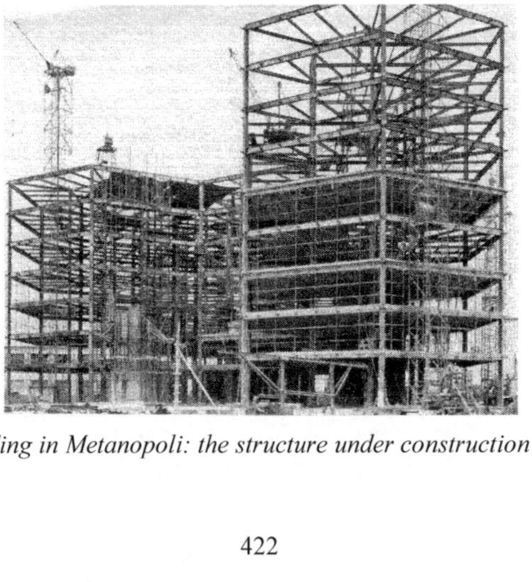

Figure 2. The "first" ENI building in Metanopoli: the structure under construction (ASE)

The obligation to respect the reduced tolerances typical of steel fabrication was further accentuated in this case by the highly original plan, which required special attention and a further refinement of the techniques employed by the Pessina company, responsible for setting out the foundations and completing the traditional building works. Engaged in particularly advanced topographical activities, the contractor encountered no shortage of difficulties in guaranteeing the precision of the foundation geometries. A further novelty was the use of special formwork suspended from the secondary beams and used to cast the composite masonry and concrete floor slabs.

With the exception of the foundations and floor slabs, all ordinary building works were replaced here by building components compatible with the elastic properties of steel: false ceilings, lighting fixtures, cabinetry and modular partition walls were all designed in response to the main structure and employing a repertoire of the era's most modern technical solutions.

Construction began in October 1956 and was completed in February 1957.[6]

The other two buildings, designed by Bacigalupo and Ratti, were much less emphatic and therefore able to adopt a more regular structural system.

The twenty-one storey office building in Rome, situated at the eastern end of the artificial lake in the EUR, is a rectangular block measuring 87 x 16 meters, with a total height of 73 m. (Fig. 3) The long elevations are completely glazed, while the narrow ends are clad in slabs of travertine.

The structure, again the work of L. Finzi, assisted here by E. Nova, consists of a series of steel frames with rigid connections, set at intervals of 7.20 m and spanning the entire width of the plan without intermediate supports. (Fig. 4)

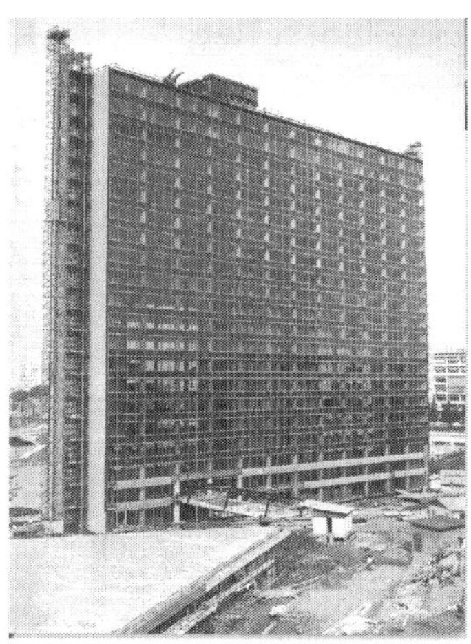

Figure 3. ENI Headquarters in Rome: general view (ASE)

The presence of reinforced concrete bracing cores is evidence of a more common practice in Italy, where the absence of a specific building regulation suggested maintaining a rigid frame portal structure even in the presence of reinforced concrete cores. The secondary beams, spanning 2.40 m and running parallel to the main façades, support 10 cm thick reinforced solid concrete slabs, all with the same dimensions and the same reinforcing.[7] The synchronisation of building works was carefully planned to meet the construction timetable. For the casting of the floor slabs, ENI technicians designed special, recoverable and self-supporting steel formwork, braced once again by a steel structure, as in the "first" building. This permitted the construction of a full slab every 7 days, during which time it was possible to complete an entire floor, including mechanical and electrical systems, with the exception of the façade.[8] Two hoists for lifting concrete and other materials were accommodated in specially designed scaffolding that, contrary to typical practices, was raised as the structure grew in height. Similar organisational methods were also applied to the installation of the façades: as the steel structure neared the uppermost level, the curtain wall had already been applied to the first four storeys, working from the interior and eliminating the need for traditional platforms. Additionally, an innovative system was adopted for the fire protection of the structure, at the time generally entrusted to asbestos coatings; in Rome this hazardous material was replaced by gypsum panels. As their behaviour had not yet been verified by the Fire Department, full scale samples had to be tested to validate their actual resistance in the event of a fire. The excellent results of these tests would see this solution adopted in other projects.

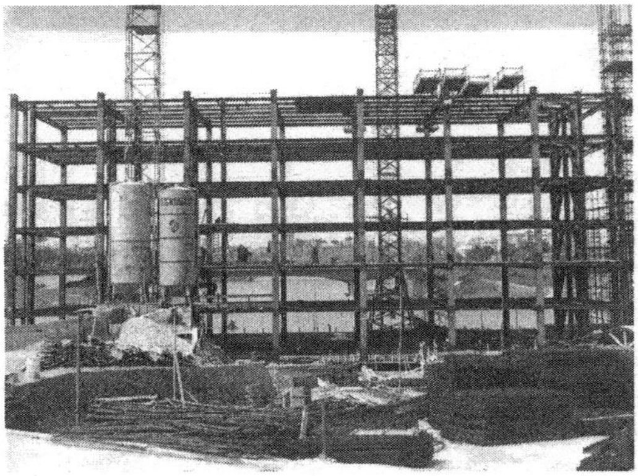

Figure 4. ENI Headquarters in Rome: the structure under construction in April 1961 (ASE)

For the second building in Metanopoli, Bacigalupo and Ratti chose a 'Y' shape, whose arms spread apart by 120°. Each arm measured 14.9 x 36 meters and was completely glazed. (Fig. 5)

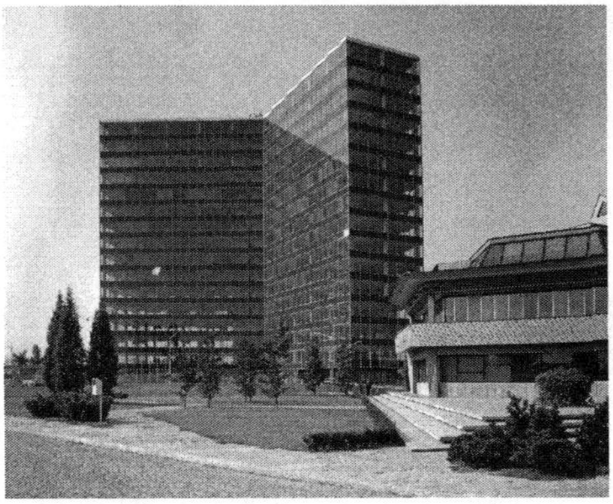

Figure 5. The "second" ENI building in Metanopoli: general view (ASE)

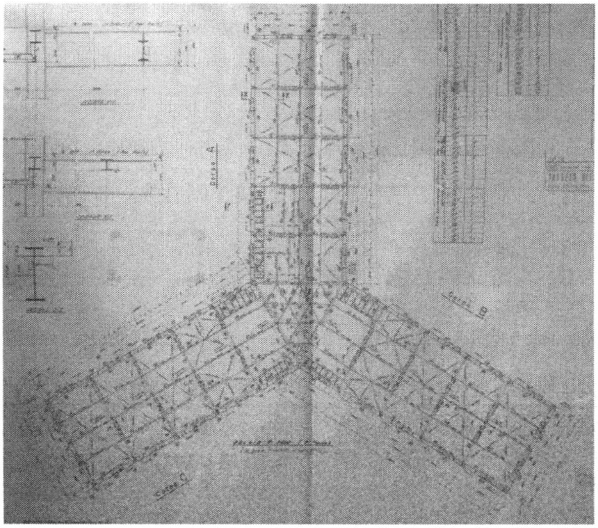

Figure 6. The "second" ENI building in Metanopoli: structural carpentry of the typical floor plate (ASE)

"This expression of uncompromised modernism"[9] rose seventeen storeys above the ground. The Officine Bossi, responsible for the structural design, construction and erection of the building[10] responded to the architectural constraints with a succession of two-bay steel frames. The structural *parti* was based on the maximum standardisation of building components and allowed for two different schemes: the intermediate frames had poor transversal stiffness, while those at the extremities featured rigid connections between beams and columns that replaced the stiffening elements, given the absence of reinforced concrete perimeter walls to hold the bracing trestles. The frames, consisting of two 6.80 meter wide bays placed every 7.20 m, converge toward a central section in the form of an equilateral triangle, whose sides measure 13.60 meters. This structural element increased the rigidity of the structure thanks to the use of additional horizontal framing based on a double order of similar equilateral triangles. (Fig. 6) The floor slabs were realised in prefabricated reinforced masonry sections.

As in the other cases, the need for rapid construction was detailed in a rigorous erection programme, closely coordinated with the supply of materials to the site.

The fully glazed façades of each of the three buildings, all realised by the Fratelli Greppi Company of Milan, were based on the most modern criteria. While façades made from lightweight opaque or transparent glass panels were gradually being adopted in Italy in 1950s, this technology was still in an experimental phase. Their advancement was made possible by the collaborative efforts of the industrial sector, architects and engineers, all searching for the most appropriate technical and architectural solutions. The many problems entailed by the use of a curtain wall system, for example issues of thermal insulation or the necessary tolerances during assembly and the life of a building, were the subject of constant study and continuous checks on site, with the growing number of examples regularly proposing new metal profiles. In this field as in others, as a client, ENI was an exemplar of technological advancement and the modernisation of the image of architecture. Moreover, the race for supremacy in this sector found its most emblematic representations precisely in ENI's buildings, with the scale of each façade setting a new record in Italy.

The façades of the building designed by Nizzoli and Oliveri were composed of a framework of anodised black aluminium alloy profiles and fixed glass panels. Ventilation was assured by an air conditioning system that also regulated the varying degrees of solar heat gain on each of the seventeen façades. The mullions, in both square and 'Y' sections (the latter also functioning as guides for the window cleaning platforms) were anchored to the structure by means of galvanised steel brackets welded to the structural steel beams. They were interrupted every 3.40 m and connected to one another by a vertical slip joint which allowed for the deformations of each single element and those of the slab. Two cross members were installed at each joint, one fixed to the upper rail and the other to the lower rail. The ends of the two cross members featured a comb-like shape that allowed for relative movements. The glazing panels, insulated where they span the floor slabs and serve as parapets, declared the architects' independence from the most common models of the International Style. The unusual treatment of the panels, softened by the use of coloured geometric decorations, served as a counterpoint to the rigid Cartesian matrix of the envelope and stood out as a unique case among the many buildings from this period.

The façades of the other two buildings are very different and more openly inspired by examples found overseas. The common authorship of the designs led to the replication – unique to the development of the curtain wall – not only of the layout of the elevations, with vertical aluminium mullions at 1.80 m on centre and horizontal mullions at 1.15 and 2.25 meters, but also of the sections of the profiles themselves. At the same time, the adoption of different systems for anchoring the mullions to the building structure highlighted the typical problems of the curtain wall and the fact that it was the object of continuous experimentation.

The building in Rome, the first to be completed, utilised 'Bauer steel', already employed overseas and introduced in Italy precisely by Greppi for the façades of the Pirelli skyscraper in Milan (1956-61). This steel, which was to have guaranteed the necessary elasticity of the connections to the building structure, was positioned in the floor slab formwork and thus incorporated within the cast in-situ structure; a bracket fixed to the steel provided for the connection to the vertical mullions, while oval fixing slots containing the connectors ensured the correct tolerances between the various components of the joint. However, the use of the Bauer steel elements immediately proved to be a complicated affair, due to the difficulties in inserting these elements in the formwork and the need to respect reduced tolerances (less than 10 mm) during the site casting of the floor slabs. Naturally, these difficulties had repercussions on site during successive phases of assembly, giving rise to a series of disputes that lengthened construction times and increased costs.[11]

Based on events in Rome, for the subsequent construction in Metanopoli the anchoring structure for the 14,000 square meter curtain wall was fixed to the columns, with an interposed horizontal steel bar at each storey, supported by 56 cm long projecting steel brackets. This system eliminated any interference with the casting of the floor slabs.

The sports centre in Metanopoli

The construction of the sports centre in Metanopoli was another component of the corporate strategy that characterised the years of ENI under Enrico Mattei, focused on the opportunity to provide health and social service facilities to the employees and families of the holding he presided over. The sports complex, at the time the largest in Italy,[12] was immediately appreciated for its architectural quality and state-of-the-art equipment. It was once again Mattei who requested a very modern building, complete with football pitches, a swimming pool and indoor and outdoor tennis courts. Other than confirming an understanding of the needs of its employees, this approach would also heighten the company's visibility. Among the various constructions, the indoor tennis court structure stands out for its thin shell vault, measuring 45 meters in width and 63.15 in length and spanning the entire playing surface. The architectural design, developed in 1954-55, was entrusted to the architect M. Baiocchi (1902-74), a member of the group responsible for the urban planning of Metanopoli and other projects in the city. An expert in his field, he was accustomed to working with Mattei, to whom he was also linked by a bond of friendship. The design consisted essentially of a large vaulted roof whose spring points were modelled on the exterior to form two long cantilevers. (Fig. 7) The end walls were fully glazed with "*ferrofinestra*" (steel frame) windows with horizontally-pivoting opaque glass fins, operated by a lever from below. The walls and underside of the vault were clad with a special acoustic insulating material to avoid the reverberations typical of indoor sports facilities.

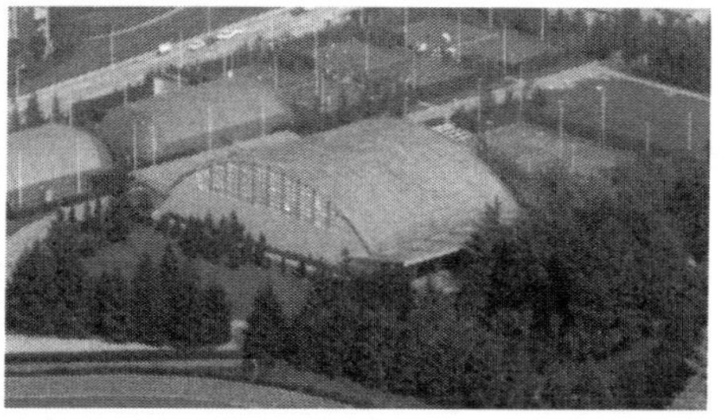

Figure 7. The indoor tennis courts in Metanopoli: general view (from Il Laterizio. Bollettino Tecnico RDB, 1956)

The vault structure was designed by the engineer C. Fermi and consisted of a series of elementary arches sealed with cement mortar, realised using prefabricated beams denominated 'SAP20',[13] all with the same curvature. (Fig. 8) The directrix assumed the form of a low arch, an arrangement that most closely reflected the loading curve. A series of 6.50 meter long curved beams formed the large segments of the arches, in turn connected by longitudinal reinforced concrete ribs. A 4 cm thick concrete topping slab brought the total thickness of the vault to 24 cm. This dimension was increased at the spring points. The arches were tied to a trapezoidal section edge beam supported by triangular frames set every 5.23 meters. To contain the thrust of the vault, steel chains were inserted in correspondence with the support points. The chains were run in passageways beneath the floor and placed in tension 40 days after completion of the concrete casting.[14]

The realisation of a vault with such a long span with respect to its height was a novelty for the Piacenza-based contractor RDB, responsible for the curved beams; as late as 1958, the data sheets published in the company's technical periodicals continued to prescribe the use of SAP20 beams for spans up to a maximum of 40 m. In 1956 the vault over the indoor tennis courts in Metanopoli had the honour of being published on the cover of issue n. 37 of the RDB Technical Bulletin, accompanied by an article.

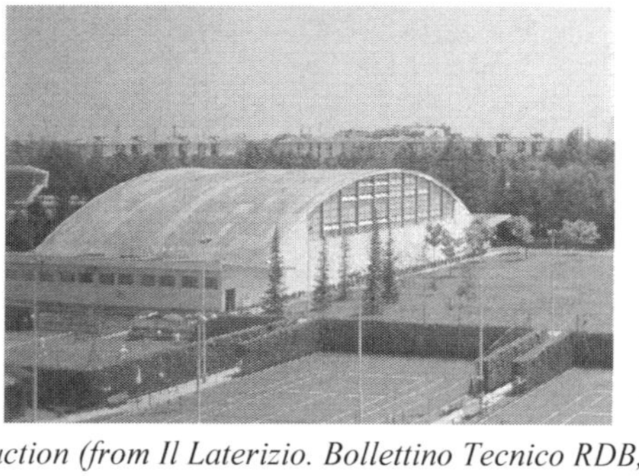

Figure 8. The vault under construction (from Il Laterizio. Bollettino Tecnico RDB, 1956)

Conclusions

When the buildings presented here were designed and built, Italy demonstrated an evident contrast between the drive toward technological innovation and a tendency to conform to methods and techniques more familiar to Italian labour. Compared to this more conservative convention, the buildings realised by ENI stood out in sharp contrast. They highlighted the importance of technological development, both in the form of technical improvements and the streamlining of organisational procedures, to the construction of an architectural image that would serve as a showcase of corporate identity. In addition, these case studies exemplify the driving role of experimentation in the building sector, promoted by enlightened clients in many subsequent projects developed in Italy.

Notes and References

[1] The *Ente Nazionale Idrocarburi* was instituted under Italian law n. 136 on 10 February 1953 to unite and coordinate the State's petroleum companies AGIP Mineraria, AGIP, SNAM and ANIC.

[2] SNAM-Progetti (Ed.), 'Organizzazione delle attività di un servizio di costruzioni edilizie', *Edilizia Popolare*, vol.33, 1960, pp.42-47.

[3] V. Gandolfi, 'Intervista con l'ingegnere Sante Tibaldi', 17-18 May 1990, ENI Historical Archive (ASE), Fund Interviews, vol.29, 21.

[4] Ibid., p. 30.

[5] M. Oliveri, 'La nostra storia', in B. Gravagnuolo, (Ed.) *Gli studi Nizzoli. Architettura e design 1948-1983*, Milan: Electa, 1983, p.40.

[6] L. Finzi, G. Magenta, 'Il palazzo uffici E.N.I. a san Donato Milanese', *Acciaio*, vols. 7-8, 1961, pp.411-47; L. Greco, 'The first Eni-Snam headquarters in San Donato Milanese: some features of industrialisation in construction techniques applied to office buildings in the Post Second World War period in Italy', in R. Carvais et al., (Eds.) *Nuts and bolts of construction history. Culture, technology and society*, vol.3, Paris: Picard, 2012, pp.439-47.

[7] Construction of the facility was entrusted to the Milanese firm Bossi; the concrete work to Genghini of Rome; S. Mornati, 'La facciata leggera del complesso direzionale ENI a Roma tra produzione industriale e tecnica artigianale', G. Mochi, (Ed.) Proceedings of the International Seminar *Teoria e pratica del costruire: saperi, strumenti, modelli*, vol.2, Oct. 2005, pp.819-38.

[8] L. Finzi, E. Nova, 'Il centro Direzionale E.N.I. all'E.U.R. di Roma', *Acciaio*, No. 2, 1962, pp.5-12.

[9] G. Zucconi, 'La vicenda architettonica e urbanistica', in *Metanopoli: Attualità di un'idea*, Milan: SNAM, 1995, p.34.

[10] F. Goeta, 'Le strutture del secondo Palazzo Uffici della 'S.N.A.M.' a S. Donato Milanese', *Acciaio*, vol.12, Dec. 1964, pp.623-27.

[11] Mornati (Note 7).

[12] G. Buffa, 'Per gli sportivi di Metanopoli attrezzature moderne', *Il Gatto Selvatico*, vol.2, Feb. 1963, pp.7-11.

[13] This code refers to the 20 cm thick masonry beams produced by RDB of Piacenza.

[14] Work supervision was entrusted to the engineer S. Tibaldi; construction was entrusted to *Costruzioni Edili Affini* (C.E.A.) of Milan; C. Fermi, 'Copertura a volta SAP su luce di 45 M.', *Il Laterizio. Bollettino Tecnico RDB*, vol.37, Apr. 1956, pp.202-04.

Glass and glazing in post-war Belgium (1945-70). The rise of double glazing.

Stephanie Van de Voorde
Department of Architectural Engineering, Vrije Universiteit Brussel (VUB), Belgium

Introduction

Although the history of glass dates back several centuries,[1] thanks to continuous technological progress, it is one of those materials –together with for example steel and concrete- that have caused a revolution in modern architecture. Advances in glass technology have been decisive for the development of several building types and construction techniques, from stained and coloured glass in church buildings and *Art Nouveau* buildings, over the Crystal Palace, the *Glashaus Pavillon*, and several other *Palais* and *Maisons de verre*, to endless glass curtain walls in the skyscrapers of the International Style. Glass holds an important position in the history of architecture and construction as the *matériau de lumière*: "L'évolution de la civilisation, si l'on y songe, résulte pour une très large part de l'amélioration de la fabrication du verre".[2] This quote by the architectural journalist Pierre-Louis Flouquet was published in a themed issue of the Belgian architectural journal *La Maison* on glass in 1959. Also in a 1959 themed issue of another Belgian journal, *Architecture*, glass was praised: "Le verre ne constitue plus, comme par le passé, un simple moyen d'obturation laissant à la pierre la faveur de créer un style".[3] And Le Corbusier stated that "Le Verre [est le] matériau fondamental de l'architecture moderne".[4]

Despite being recognized as one of the fundamental materials of modern architecture, and the remarkable and diverse development of new types of glass and glazing in the twentieth century and the post-World War II period in particular, glass has received relatively little attention in architectural and construction history research. Notable and interesting exceptions are the publications edited by Franz Graf and Francesca Albani,[5] English Heritage,[6] and the Getty Conservation Institute.[7] Focusing on Belgium, the history of glass production has been synthesized in *Le verre en Belgique, des origines à nos jours* in 1989.[8] More recently Leen Lauriks[9] and Liesbeth Dekeyser[10] published on particular aspects of nineteenth- and twentieth-century glass technology in Belgium. In addition, a large number of publications has been written on stained glass and leaded glass windows, in Belgium[11] and abroad.[12] Despite these laudable efforts, many gaps in our knowledge of the production and the use of twentieth-century window glass still need to be filled. While the preservation, conservation and restoration of glass in particular case studies has been relatively well covered, generic yet detailed overviews on glass production techniques, different types of glass products, the practical application and relation to other building materials are far less numerous. This paper will shed light on the development and application of innovative types of glass and glazing used in 1945-70 in Belgium. Key aspects such as advances in production techniques, popular glass products, the structure of the glass industry, and the introduction of new types of glass and glazing in post-war architecture, in particular double glazing, will be discussed. The research is based on archival research (in particular company catalogues and technical documentation from important glass manufacturers[13]), literature study (focusing on contemporary architectural and technical journals), on site research (visits to post-war houses in Brussels in which the original glass was preserved) and interviews with glaziers who were active in the post-war period.

Glass production in post-war Belgium

After a few difficult years immediately following WWII, the glass manufacturing industry in Belgium experienced a very dynamic and productive period from the middle of the 1950s onwards. By the end of the 1950s, production levels of window glass had again reached the record level of the end of the 1920s, with a combined annual output of 280,000 tonnes. The production continued to increase, to 642,000 tonnes in 1963 and even 930,000 tonnes of flat glass in 1973. The increase is ascribed to, among other things, the trend towards ever larger (and therefore thicker) glazed surfaces and the success of double glazing.[14] The most striking feature of the glass industry in the post-war period, however, was not quantity but its versatility: new production techniques and treatments were developed or improved, resulting in an increasing range of products in 1945-70, from regular window glass, mirror glass and float glass, to decorative cast glass, safety glass, coloured glass, insulating glass, solar glass, etc.[15] (Figs 1-2) The architectural possibilities were seemingly endless, while the list of extra functions that glass could fulfil became longer and longer, for instance blocking UV and/or infrared radiation, providing thermal and acoustic insulation, and greater resistance to breaking.

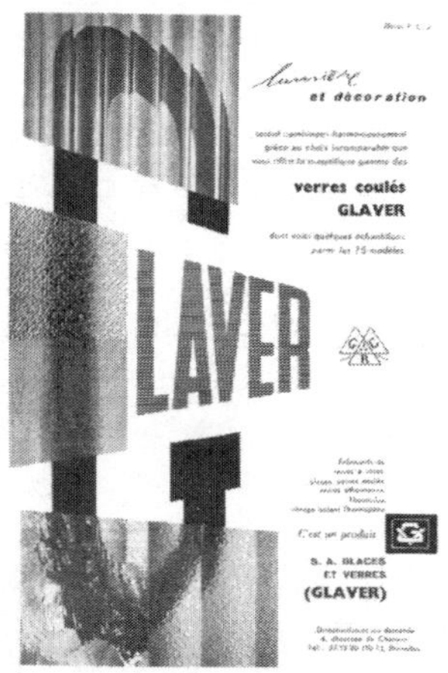

Figure 1. Cast glass by Glaver. La Maison, vol.13, no.6, 1957.

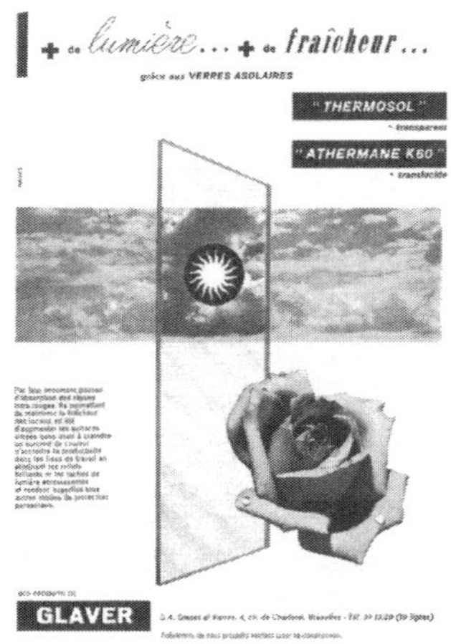

Figure 2. Solar glass by Glaver. La Maison, vol.15, no.7, 1959.

Production techniques

The production of glass, traditionally made out of silica and chemical compounds, is a labour and energy intensive process. This process can be manipulated in various ways to create different types of glass, e.g. by shaping the glass in different ways, by adding specific ingredients to the mixture or by means of mechanical treatment.[16] In the twentieth century, the historical production techniques of blowing and casting glass evolved and were supplemented by new production techniques for drawn glass and float glass. Drawn glass was invented by the Belgian engineer Émile Fourcault in the early twentieth century: he had proposed drawing a melted glass mixture through a slot or *débiteuse* and pulling it upwards between rollers to create a long, vertical ribbon of glass that was cut into pieces after cooling.[17] During the 1950s, another method to produce glass was developed by the British glass manufacturer Sir Alastair Pilkington.[18] In the Pilkington process, or float glass process, melted glass was poured onto a bath of melted metal, usually tin, creating a sheet with a uniform thickness, perfectly smooth on both sides. At the end of the bath the glass sheet was lifted onto rollers and cut into pieces. Float glass was introduced in Belgium during the 1960s: it caused the almost complete disappearance of polished cast mirror glass, yet drawn window glass was still used on a large scale, despite its lower quality, often showing imperfections or a striped surface.[19] Today approximately 90 per cent of the flat glass used throughout the world is float glass.[20]

Also the treatment of glass underwent some important changes over the years. While glass used to be ground and polished manually, during the twentieth century the transition was made to mechanical treatment and just before WWII machines were developed to polish both sides of glass panes at once.[21]

Types of glass and glazing

Many types of glass and glazing have been developed, based on particular production techniques, compositions, treatments, or combinations. In order to categorize the different types, the Belgian Building Research Institute drafted a 'Terminology of the main glass products used in the building industry' in 1962, defining eight categories: mirror glass, window glass, cast glass, blown glass, glass blocks, special types of sheet glass, processed glass, and glass treatments.[22] Each category included a number of sub-categories. For example, coloured glass and athermic glass were special types of sheet glass; safety glass, double glazing and insulating glass were examples of processed glass. Not every type of glass was commonly used in post-war architecture, e.g. cast glass and blown glass.

Flat, transparent sheets of polished cast mirror glass (*glace coulée et polie*) and drawn window glass (*verre à vitre étiré*) were the most common types of glass used in house building, until the rise of float glass. While window glass was polished by fire, mirror glass was polished mechanically. Mirror glass existed in thicknesses between 2 and 40 mm (commonly between 3.5 and 8 mm), while window glass varied between 0.6 and 20 mm. The maximum size was related to the thickness and transportation possibilities. Theoretically, lengths up to 5 m for window glass and 6 m for mirror glass or more were possible in the 1960s, yet difficult to achieve in practice.[23] Both the Pittsburgh and the Libbey-Owens technique were commonly used in post-war Belgium for drawn window glass.[24] The Pittsburgh vertical draw technique, which can be considered as an improved version of Fourcault's technique, was used by the Belgian company Univerbel, In the Libbey-Owens technique, used by Glaver, the glass was drawn upwards but then bent over 90 degrees before proceeding horizontally through the annealing oven, in which the glass was polished by fire.

Another popular product in the post-war period was double glazing: this consisted of two glass panes with a layer of dehydrated air between them, hermetically sealed around the edges to avoid condensation on the inside of the unit. The glass panes were usually between 3 and 10 mm thick, while the layer of air could be almost 20 mm. In Belgium, double glazing was produced from 1947-48 onwards; during the 1950s it became commonly available.[25] (Fig. 3) The theoretically largest size for double glazing in the 1960s was 6 m by 3 m. Double glazing became very popular because of its insulation capacities: it reduced heat loss by 50 per cent over single glazing, and retained 40 decibels compared to 20 decibels for single glazing.[26] Instead of just two glass panes, it was also possible to use three, or even four or five, panes of glass to create triple, quadruple and quintuple glazing – these were advertised in Belgium already in the 1950s.[27]

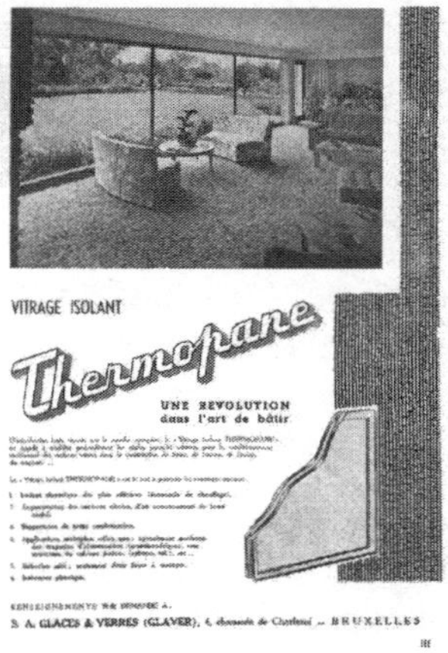

Figure 3. Early advertisement in La Maison for Thermopane by Glaver. La Maison, vol.4, no.12, 1949.

The Belgian Building Research Institute's list of main types of glass products also included various ways to treat glass, either industrially or artisanally. For instance, by applying a very thin coat of metal to one side of the glass infrared rays were reflected. Another example is enamelled glass, a specific type of opaque glass: a layer of coloured enamel was applied to the glass and thermally treated to assure a complete vitrification. Enamelled glass needed little maintenance and resisted mechanical and thermal shocks and atmospheric agents very well. For these reasons, it was ideal for sandwich panels in curtain walls or parapets. And as it enabled lively colour schemes, enamelled glass fitted perfectly with the optimistic, modernistic architectural style of the 1950s.[28]

Glass manufacturers in Belgium

Throughout history, Belgium has been an important manufacturer of glass. During the nineteenth century, the glass companies grew in number and also became larger, more professional, and better equipped. Belgium became one of the most important producers and exporters of window glass worldwide, in direct competition with the American glass industry.[29] Even at the end of the 1920s and during the 1930s, when the glass industry relapsed due to the economic crisis and the emergence of industrial production techniques in other countries, Belgium was still one of the most important exporters of window glass with 50 per cent of the market worldwide.[30] Belgium had been able to maintain this position, thanks to a reorganisation of the sector, responding to the need for a mechanized and rationalized industry that was felt since the early twentieth century. The rationalisation led to important mergers in the early 1930s, creating three main companies, which were still leading companies in the 1950s, namely Univerbel, Glaver, and Glaceries de la Sambre.

Univerbel was created in 1930 out of the union of 14 small glass factories in Belgium – hence the full name 'Union des verreries mécaniques belges'- and became the largest glass manufacturer in Belgium. The annual production of Univerbel in the 1930s amounted to 60,000,000 m^2 glass.[31] One of the most important types of glass produced by Univerbel was drawn glass: after switching from the Fourcault technique to the Pittsburgh technique, they further improved this and promoted it as the Univerbel technique. (Fig. 4) Other hit products produced by Univerbel in the post-war period were enamelled glass Colorbel and double glazing Polyverbel.

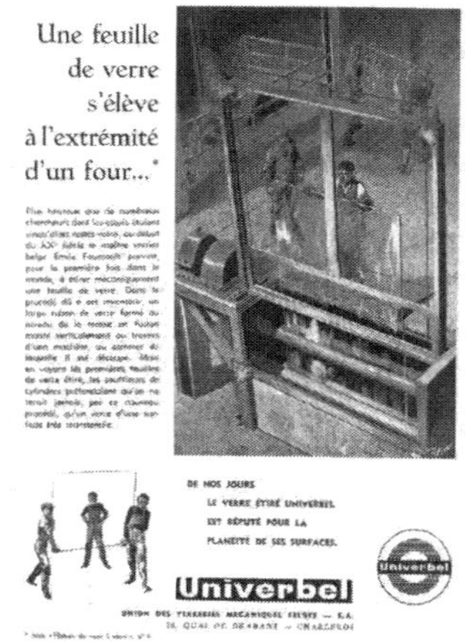

Figure 4. Drawn glass by Univerbel. La Maison, vol.11, no.12, 1955.

One of Univerbel's direct competitors was Glaver, the 'Société anonyme nouvelle Glaces et Verres'. Glaver was created in 1931, also by merging several companies. One of those companies was the 'Compagnie Internationale pour la fabrication mécanique du verre Libbey-Owens-Mécaniver' or Mécaniver, founded in 1921 and holding the exclusive rights to produce Libbey-Owens drawn glass in Europe.[32] Glaver took over Mécanivers's rights to produce drawn glass L.O.B., or 'Libbey-Owens-Belgium'. Glaver became one of the major glass manufacturers in the world, producing almost every type of glass in the post-war period, including window glass L.O.B., double glazing Thermopane, insulating glass Thermolux (translucent glazing with a thin layer of glass fibres between two panes of glass), cast glass G.C.R., and opaque coloured glass Marmorite.

The third important company was Glaceries de la Sambre, created in 1932 also out of a merger of several companies, producing mainly cast mirror glass. In the post-war period the company was mainly known for its production of double glazing Polyglass, solar glass Filtrasol, two-sided polished glass Duplex, and tempered, enamelled glass Panoroc.

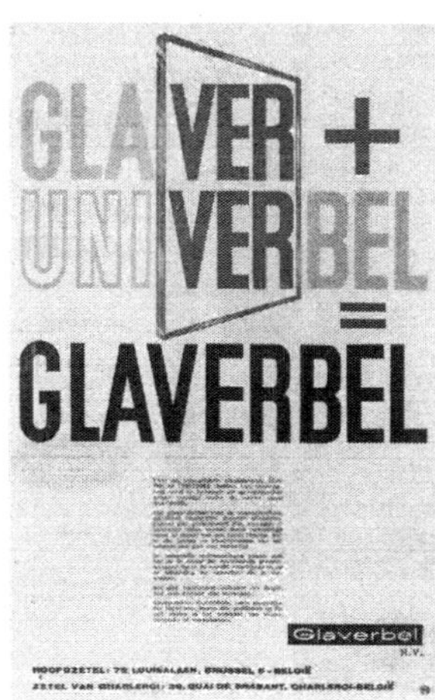

Figure 5. Merger of Glaver and Univerbel. Bouwen en Wonen, vol.9, no.8-9, 1961.

The interwar period and the early post-war period was marked by the transition to an almost complete mechanized industry: production was centralized and the equipment was perfected, enabling Belgium to maintain its dominant market position.[33] Even if it took some time for the glass companies to adjust, the efficiency level significantly increased: between the early 1930s and the early 1960s, the monthly output of Univerbel rose from 400,000 m^2 to 1,000,000 m^2.[34] Yet still, in the 1960s, a second important rationalisation operation became inevitable, responding to international competition and the new scale of the post-war industry and economy. Glaver and Univerbel, which had an annual production output of 28,800,000 m^2 and 43,200,000 m^2 respectively in 1960,[35] merged into Glaverbel in 1961. (Fig. 5) In 1966, Glaceries de la Sambre became Glaceries de Saint-Roch, without changing much in the product range. The size of the new Glaverbel company again raised the market position of Belgian flat glass sheets. At the end of the 1960s, Glaverbel employed over 10,000 people and produced 80,000,000 m^2 of glass each year, of which 75 per cent was exported.[36] Before the merger, both Glaver and Univerbel produced most types of glass, so choices had to be made in the reorganisation. The new Glaverbel range consisted of, among other things, drawn glass (produced by both the Pittsburgh/Univerbel technique and the Libbey-Owens-Belgium technique), double glazing Thermopane (the production of Univerbel's Polyverbel on the other hand was cancelled), insulating glass Thermolux, enamelled glass Colorbel, solar glass Stopray, cast glass, etc. While new production lines were started, for float glass for instance, the old, familiar products like Thermopane were further improved.

Double glazing

One of the most important developments in the post-war glass industry is the emergence of double glazing. Still a somewhat expensive feature in the early post-war period, double glazing gradually became a standard, established building material. Double glazing, marketed under the brand name Thermopane, was invented in the 1930s in the USA.[37] Thermopane became a generic term for double glazing worldwide. After Glaver had successfully introduced Thermopane (Fig. 6) on the Belgian market in 1947/1948, Univerbel and Glaceries de la Sambre also started to produce double glazing in the 1950s, under the brand names Polyverbel and Polyglass.[38] For each of the manufacturers, double glazing was a top seller in its product range. All three highlighted more or less the same advantages: reducing heat losses, lowering heating costs, increased window sizes, avoiding condensation, higher comfort levels because sharp temperature falls near the windows were avoided and better acoustic insulation. The thermal performance of the various brands of double glazing was similar: the thermal transmittance or U-value varied between 3.0 and 3.5 W/m^2K, compared to 5.8 to 6.4 W/m^2K for single L.O.B. glass panes.[39] A third layer of glass decreased the thermal transmittance to approximately 2.3 or 2.1 W/m^2K.[40] On the other hand, the connection and the composition of the glass panes differed in the three brands.

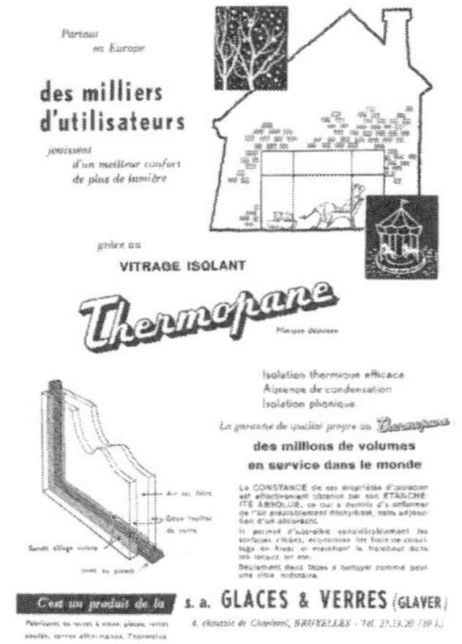

Figure 6. Thermopane by Glaver. La Maison, vol.12, no.9, 1956.

Thermopane

In October 1934, Charles D. Haven applied for a patent for a 'Multi-Ply Glass Sheet Glazing Unit', which he called Thermopane. Haven specified that "Preferably, the separators [between the two glass panes] are made from sheets of a laminated rubber compound covered on both sides with a suitable fabric".[41] Yet it seems that the rubber compound did not perform as hoped for, as in 1937 Haven applied for a new patent in which "glass sheets are first provided with fused metallic coatings to which the metal spacer strips are then soldered, whereby an effective and durable seal is provided".[42] This description matches to the double glazing units Thermopane with a Bondermetic seal that were marketed by the Libbey-Owens-Ford Glass Cy.[43] A 1946 brochure showed over a dozen houses, schools, factories, etc. that were equipped with Thermopane windows. It also listed four important advantages of Thermopane over single glazing: better insulation, perfect seal, clearer vision and only two surfaces to clean."[44]

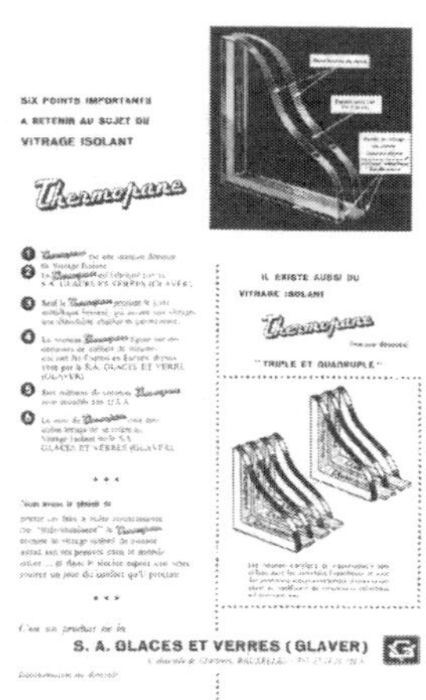

Figure 7. Triple and quadruple glazing Thermopane by Glaver. La Maison, vol.13, no.10, 1957.

In Belgium, Thermopane window units were produced by Glaver.[45] The metal-to-glass joint applied by Glaver consisted of lead and copper: a copper strip was attached to the perimeter of each glass pane, after which a lead strip was welded between them – from the 1970s onwards, glued aluminium strips were used to maintain the space between the two panes. A typical thickness for Thermopane units was 14 mm, including two panes of glass of 3 mm each. The internal layer of filtered, dehydrated air was between 6 and 12 mm thick. When installing Thermopane in window frames, with putty and possibly glazing beads, contact between the glass and the frame needed to be avoided. Thermopane units up to 6 m^2 were possible with regular window glass, while Thermopane units with polished mirror glass were made in sizes up to 18 m^2. Thermopane could in fact be produced with almost any kind of glass, including cast glass, mirror glass, athermic glass, sandblasted glass, and tempered glass, and not just two but also three, four or five panes of glass. (Fig. 7)

To convince the building industry of the benefits of Thermopane windows, Glaver conducted an extensive propaganda campaign, mainly emphasizing reduced heat transfer. The promotion campaign seems to have succeeded: approximately 100,000 Thermopane windows were put in place throughout Europe in 1955 and in 1960 Glaver celebrated the installation of the one millionth square meter of Thermopane. During the 1960s, the technology of Thermopane had improved to a point that Glaverbel raised the period of warranty against diminished visibility, condensation, and dust on the inside from five to ten years. In 1968 'Thermopane pret à placer' was put on the market, in 47 standard dimensions, ready to be delivered on site within two weeks. In the same year, Glaverbel also started to promote Thermopane for renovations, without having to change the existing window frames.

Polyverbel

Polyverbel was Univerbel's brand of double glazing: two (or more) panes of drawn window glass Univerbel were enclosed in a rigid frame of stainless steel with a layer of dehydrated air between them, sealed by a wear-proof, hydrophobic, plastic joint – without specifying the composition thereof however.[46] For double glazed Polyverbel window units, panes of 3 to 7 mm could be used. With 6 to 13 mm of air between, the total thickness was between 14 and 27 mm. For triple glazing, the individual glass panes were 4 or 6 mm thick, with 6 mm of air in between, giving 27 or 34 mm in total. To enjoy the five year warranty, Polyverbel had to be correctly placed, i.e. on supporting lead or neoprene blocks and with lateral distance pieces, to avoid direct contact with the window frame, while a plastic putty created a waterproof connection around the edges. Thanks to the reduced heat losses, the extra cost of double glazing Polyverbel was said to be recovered in six to seven years.

Polyglass

Glaceries de la Sambre's double glazing unit Polyglass was made with two-sided polished mirror glass, perfectly flat and clear, without distortions or stripes.[47] The flexible joint between the two panes was made with a silicone gel and steel holders. The whole was enclosed within a U-shaped profile in polyethylene and a robust, stainless steel frame. The maximum dimensions of the panes were 3 m by 5 m. In 1961, the range of Polyglass consisted of 13 types of double glazing, four types of triple glazing, one type of quadruple glazing, and even one type with five panes of glass. The thinnest type of double Polyglass was 'D143': the 'D' stood for double glazing, '14' for the total thickness, and '3' for the thickness of the two glass panes. This type of Polyglass weighed 16 kg/m^2. The heaviest type with two glass panes was D4012, which weighed 61 kg/m^2. Polyglass came in several varieties, with different types of glass (Fig. 8), for instance combining regular mirror glass pane with blueish mirror glass that absorbed infrared rays, or with a grey, polished solar glass Filtragrey – in the latter case the unit was called Polygrey. Another possibility was to use two panes of window glass instead of polished mirror glass – this was called Polyver.

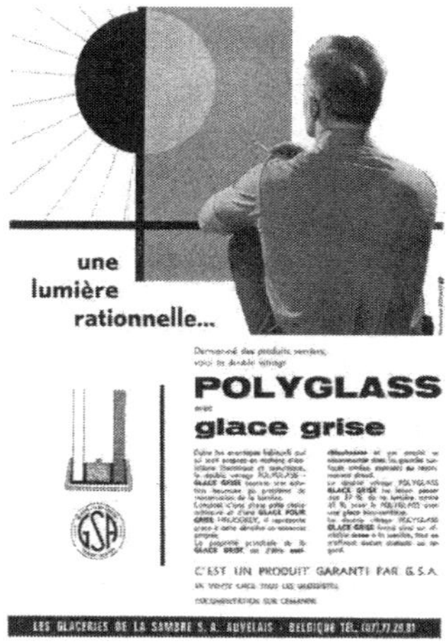

Figure 8. Double glazing Polyglass with translucent grey glass. La Maison, vol.17., no.8, 1961.

Early applications of double glazing

An analysis of the contemporary architectural journals shows that double glazing was used from the 1950s onwards: focusing on the descriptions of newly built houses in the Brussels Capital Region, published in the architectural journals *La Maison* and *Architecture* between 1945 and 1970, 43 articles give details about the type of glass that was used; 20 of those mentioned double glazing, sometimes even saying which brand was used.[48] Thermopane was the most popular (or most mentioned) brand: it was used at least six times, compared to four applications of Polyverbel and one reference to Polyglass. The first reference to double glazing was published in 1952, concerning an apartment building designed by Josse Franssen in 1950.[49] Although the article literally says 'double vitrage', this was a very particular kind of double glazing: the space between the two glass panes was several centimetres wide, and sliding shutters were fitted within this space. A few years later, Franssen applied 'genuine' double glazing Thermopane: in a 1952 apartment building in Ukkel (Fig. 9), he had advised the individual owners to use Thermopane, after which the majority of them followed his advice.[50] In addition to this sample of case studies, field research has yielded some other early, surviving examples of double glazing, for instance the house Durieu by architect Jacques Dupuis in Sint-Jans-Molenbeek (1954) and the private house of architect Georges Volckrick in Watermaal-Bosvoorde (1958) – the inscription of the brand name in the metal-to-glass joint makes it easy to identify them..[51]

Double glazing was used in every type of construction, from traditional masonry, over concrete skeletons, to timber frame constructions. Although Willy Van Der Meeren applied Thermopane in the social high-rise apartment building 'Ieder Zijn Huis' (Fig. 10), double glazing nevertheless was still a rather exclusive or luxury article initially. In a number of cases, for instance the aforementioned house Durieu by Dupuis or a private house in Sint-Pieters-Woluwe by architect Homez,[52] double glazing was only used in the living areas or rooms with an unfavourable orientation.

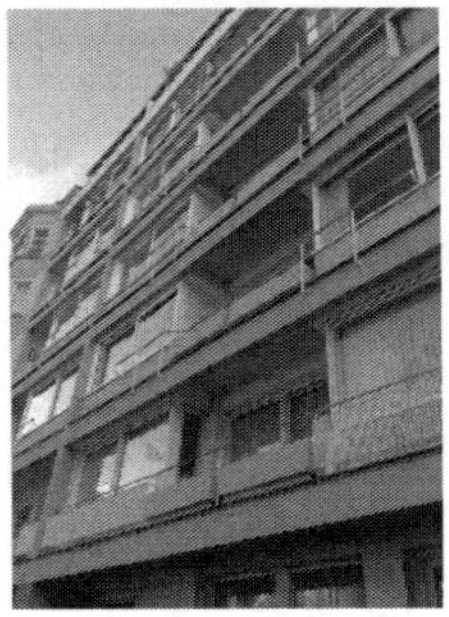

Figure 9. Apartment building, Ukkel. Architect, Josse Franssen. 1952. Early application of Thermopane double glazing. Photo: Stephanie Van de Voorde, 2015.

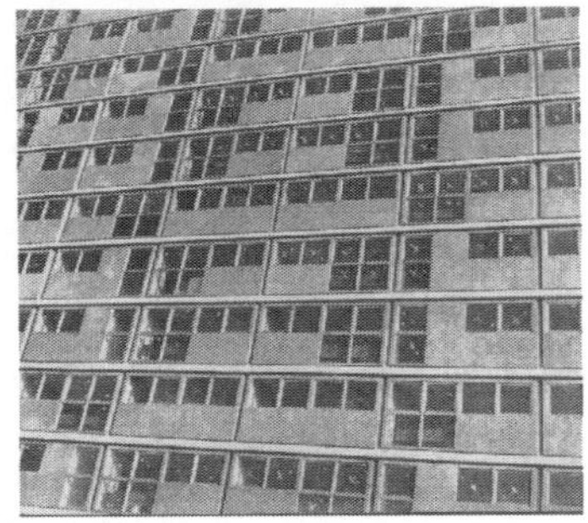

Figure 10. Apartment building 'Ieder Zijn Huis', Evere. Architect, Willy Van Der Meeren. 1954-1960. Use of double glazing in social housing. Architecture, vol.38, 1962, p.693.

Since double glazing was thicker than single glazing, not every type of window frame could hold a double glazing unit. An important manufacturer of metal window frames in Belgium, Chamebel, adapted its production range accordingly: in approximately 1960 two series of aluminium window frames were available, of which one was specifically designed for double glazing.[53] Yet the question remains: to what extent were these window frames for double glazing used? Likewise, the catalogues of the glass manufacturers and the architectural journals show that double glazing was commercially available from the 1950s onwards, but these are not necessarily representative in common building practice.

Conclusion

Glass technology has experienced a remarkable development in the twentieth century. The production of glass was 'big business', especially in Belgium, with numerous new and improved production techniques, brands and products. Double glazing is one of those new glass products, used from the 1950s onwards in housing and gradually gaining foothold, to become used almost exclusively. Yet research into other post-war building types, like office buildings for instance, might show completely different evolutions, accents or popular products. To gain insight into the history of architecture and construction in Belgium, it is necessary to map such developments and applications. This also applies to other building materials that were invented or innovative in the post-war period: knowledge of technical detailing, production techniques, implementation in the building practice and relation to other building materials is often still lacking, despite the increase in research dealing with post-war architecture and construction. More specific information is needed to fully understand the material nature of our post-war heritage and the importance of certain materials, techniques and applications, especially because so many novel materials and innovative construction techniques were used during *les trentes glorieuses*. Documenting and analysing these innovations, therefore, are essential for the assessment of post-war architecture and construction.

Acknowledgments

This paper fits within the framework of a research project funded by the Brussels Capital Region through the "Innoviris Strategic Platform Environment 2012" (www.brusselsretrofitxl.be). The research resulted in a trilingual book and website on *Post-war building materials in housing in Brussels 1945-1975*.[54]

References

[1] D. Kula & E. Ternaux (Eds), *Materiology*, Amsterdam: Frame, p.54

[2] P.-L. Flouquet, 'Le verre, matériau de lumière', *La Maison*, vol.15, no.7, 1959, pp.200-202.

[3] P. Gillard, Éditorial, *Architecture*, vol.30-31, 1959, pp.314-315.

[4] Le Corbusier, 'Le Verre, matériau fondamental de l'architecture moderne', *Tchéco-Verre*, vol.2, no.1-4, 1935 (http://west86th.bgc.bard.edu/translated-text/glass-modern-architecture.html# Consulted on Jan. 15 2016).

[5] F. Graf & F. Albani (Eds), *Glass in the 20th Century Architecture: Preservation and Restoration*. Mendrisio: Mendrisio Academy Press, 2011.

[6] R. Pender et al., *Glass and glazing. English heritage. Practical building conservation*, Farnham: Ashgate, 2011.

[7] T. Jester et al., *Twentieth-Century Building Materials: History and Conservation*, Los Angeles: Getty Conservation Institute, 2014.

[8] L. Engen (Ed.), *Le verre en Belgique, des origines à nos jours*, Antwerp: Mercatorfonds, 1989.

[9] L. Lauriks, 'Contribution of the glass cladding to the overall structural behaviour of 19th century iron and glass roofs' (PhD thesis, Vrije Universiteit Brussel, 2012); L. Lauriks, 'Technical improvements in 19th-century Belgian window glass production', in H. Thienpont (Ed.), *Proceedings of SPIE*, Bellingham: SPIE, vol.8422, 2012.

[10] L. Dekeyser et al. 'Marbrite Fauquez opalescent and mass coloured glass', pp.1106-1113 in J. Jasienko (Ed.), *Proceedings of the International Conference on Structural Analyses of Historical Constructions*, Wroclaw: DWE, vol.2, 2012.

[11] See for instance the work by Yvette Vanden Bemden, Aletta Rambaut and Zsuzsanna Böröcz.

[12] See for instance M. Archer, *An introduction to English Stained Glass*, London: HMSO, 1985; V. David & M. Hérold (Eds), *Vitrail: Ve-XXIe siècle*, Paris: Ed. du Patrimoine, 2014; H. Janse (Ed.), Restauratievademecum, Zeist: RVMZ/'s-Gravenhage: Staatsuitgeverij, 1985-98.

[13] The documentation on building materials –mainly company catalogues- is rarely dated. The catalogues, consulted at the Archives d'Architecture Moderne (AAM) in Brussels, are not inventoried.

[14] Engen, *Verre*, (Note 8) p.345, 348.

[15] Catalogues of glass manufacturers, kept at the AAM, Brussels.

[16] Pender, *Glass*, (Note 6) p.3-30.

[17] E. Fourcault, *Apparatus for the Manufacture of Glass Sheets or Plates*, United States Patent Office, n° 901,800, Oct. 20 1908 (filed April 5 1904); E. Fourcault, *Method of and Apparatus for Drawing Continuous Sheets of Glass*, United States Patent Office, n° 941,866, Nov. 30 1909 (filed May 15 1905).

[18] L. Pilkington, *Manufacture of Flat Glass*, United States Patent Office, n° 2,911,759, Nov. 10 1959 (filed Dec. 6 1954).

[19] Engen, *Verre*, (Note 8) p.347.

[20] M. Patterson, *Structural glass facades and enclosures*, Hoboken: Wiley, 2011, p.24.

[21] P. Bot, *Vademecum: historische bouwmaterialen, installaties en infrastructuur*, Alphen aan de Maas: Veerhuis, 2009, p.463.

[22] *Terminologie van de voornaamste in het Bouwbedrijf verwerkte glasproducten. Technische Voorlichtingsnota*

nr. 25, Brussels: WTCB, 1962.

[23] Ibid.

[24] Based on the analysis of documentation on building materials kept at the AAM, Brussels.

[25] 'Les Vitrages Isolants', La Maison, vol.15, no.7, 1959, pp.227-228; company catalogue of Glaver, kept at the AAM, Brussels.

[26] Catalogues of Glaver and Univerbel, kept at the AAM, Brussels.

[27] Catalogues of Glaver and Glaceries de la Sambre, kept at the AAM, Brussels; Advertisements appeared in *La Maison* in Oct. 1952, Oct. 1957.

[28] *Terminologie* (Note 21).

[29] Engen, *Verre*, (Note 8) p.218.

[30] Ibid., p. 208.

[31] Ibid., p.207.

[32] Ibid., p.206.

[33] A. Norrenberg, Aperçu historique, *Architecture*, vol.30-31, 1959, p.316.

[34] Engen, *Verre*, (Note 8) p.345.

[35] Ibid., p. 345.

[36] Catalogues of Glaverbel, kept at the AAM, Brussels.

[37] C. Haven, *Multi-Ply Glass Sheet Glazing Unit*, United States Patent Office, n° 2,030,869, Feb. 18 1936 (filed Oct. 12 1934).

[38] The first advertisements for Polyverbel and Polyglass appeared in *La Maison* in 1955 and 1956 respectively.

[39] Catalogues of Glaver, Univerbel and Glaverbel, kept at the AAM, Brussels.

[40] Catalogue of Glaceries de Saint-Roch, kept at the AAM, Brussels.

[41] Haven, *Multi-Ply*, (Note 37).

[42] C. Haven, *Multiple Glass Sheet Glazing Unit and Method of Making the Same*, United States Patent Office, n° 2,234,680, Mar. 18 1941 (filed July 14 1937).

[43] Thermopane and Bondermetic Seal were registered as trademarks in 1941 and 1948. https://trademarks.justia.com/ (Consulted on Jan. 15 2016).

[44] *Thermopane*, Libbey-Owens-Ford Glass Company, 1946 (brochure).

[45] The following paragraphs are primarily based on catalogues by Glaver and Glaverbel, Univerbel, Glaceries de la Sambre and Glaceries de Saint-Roch, kept at the AAM, Brussels, and advertisements in *La Maison* and *Bouwen en Wonen*, published in 1950-70.

[46] Ibid.

[47] Ibid.

[48] The articles can be downloaded at the website http://postwarbuildingmaterials.be.

[49] J. Franssen, 'Immeuble d'appartements', *Architecture*, vol.5, 1952, pp.144-146.

[50] J. Franssen, 'Immeuble à appartements', *La Maison*, vol.12, no.9, 1956, pp.259-260.

[51] On-site visits in 2014-15, interviews with current owners Pascale Durieu and Marie-Elisabeth Volckrick in 2014-15.

[52] R. Homez, 'Habitation à Woluwé-St-Pierre', *La Maison*, vol.16, no.3, 1960, pp.69-70.

[53] Catalogue of Chamebel, kept at the AAM, Brussels. The catalogue is not dated, but it shows pictures of buildings of the 1950s.

[54] S. Van de Voorde, I. Bertels, I. Wouters, *Post-war building materials in housing in Brussels 1945-1975*, Brussels: VUB, 2015; http://postwarbuildingmaterials.be.

Building with air: the pneumatically powered construction systems of Dante Bini

Will McLean
Faculty of Architecture and the Built Environment, University of Westminster

Introduction

In July 1964, Italian Architect Dante Bini (1932–) successfully constructed (in three hours) a 12 metre diameter, 6 metre high hemispherical reinforced concrete shell structure (Fig. 1) on the outskirts of Bologna. Bini had tested (for the first time) his unique system of inflated fabric formwork to lift and shape the concrete. Bini had been inspired by the concrete shell structures of Pier Luigi Nervi (1891-1979), but was simultaneously frustrated by the expense, time and material wastage associated with the timber formwork necessary to construct such forms. By using a low-pressure inflatable membrane (which Bini entitled pneumoform) to both lift and form the concrete, Bini managed to entirely obviate the need for timber formwork. The 1964 prototype subsequently became the *Binishell*, a patented technology licensed across the world to construct housing, sports facilities and industrial buildings such as agricultural stores.

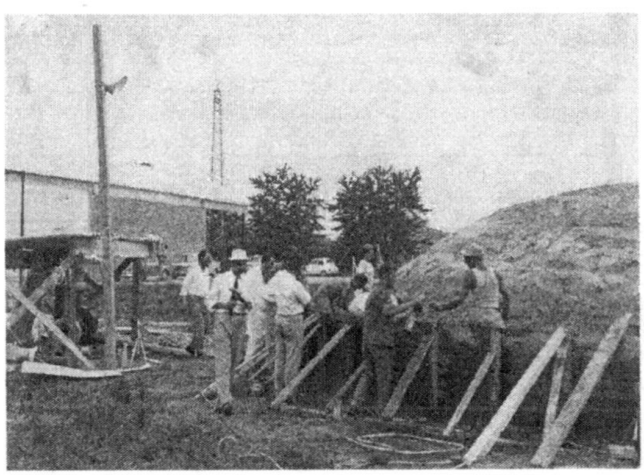

Figure 1. Crespellano, Italy. Architect, Dante Bini. The first Binishell under construction, 1964. Private archives of Dante Bini.

The paper will explore the development of the *Binishell* construction process as well as the subsequent family of pneumatic construction systems developed by Bini including the *Binix*, *Binistar* and *Minishell* systems. I will also examine the relative industrial success of these systems and the perceived difficulty in the commercial acceptance of such novel technological inventions and innovations. The paper has been written using primary sources including site visits, interviews and conversations with Dante Bini, and original documents including previously unpublished photographs, and commercial ephemera such as brochures.

The origination of the Binishell

Dante Bini recounts a story of playing a game of tennis in an air-supported fabric dome in January 1963 in Bologna. Having finished their game, Bini and his tennis partner were unable to leave the dome because during play almost half a metre of snow had fallen, temporarily blocking the entrance. What struck Bini was the heavy mass of snow that was being supported by the dome. “I did a quick calculation of the approximate weight of the snow amassed on the surface of the structure which, inflated at low pressure, was supported by just a few hundredths of an atmosphere – in technical terms, only 3.45 kPa (0.5 psi) literally supporting tons of weight!”[1] Only a year and a half later Bini was able to realise his first version of what became known as the Binishell. Through a series of iterations between 1964–68, Bini utilised an inflated pattern-cut membrane to lift and form concrete shell structures, which was common to all of the prototypes and early commissions. The developments and innovations through the iterative construction process explored differing cross-sectional geometries, alternative fabric types, and perhaps most importantly, alternative methods of steel reinforcement and of resisting the pressure during the lifting process.

The steel reinforcement for Bini’s first dome was a series of circular concentric steel rods connected with steel chains (Fig. 2) and the concrete was kept in position with specially cut sections of galvanized chain link fence attached to the steel rods when the dome was fully inflated the bi-directional transverse chains would eventually resist the air-pressure from inside the fabric dome. Bini tested this system ‘dry’ without concrete to make sure of a smooth transition from flat to dome shape before the first lift. For the first dome, concrete was poured at ground level with a variable thickness from the edge to the centre. After the air pressure had successfully lifted the dome using only a single fan, the texture of the concrete was cracked and crumbly and was re-compacted and smoothed by hand, using trowels. Bini himself admits that the original development of his construction process was empirical and with each prototype adjustments and innovations were made.

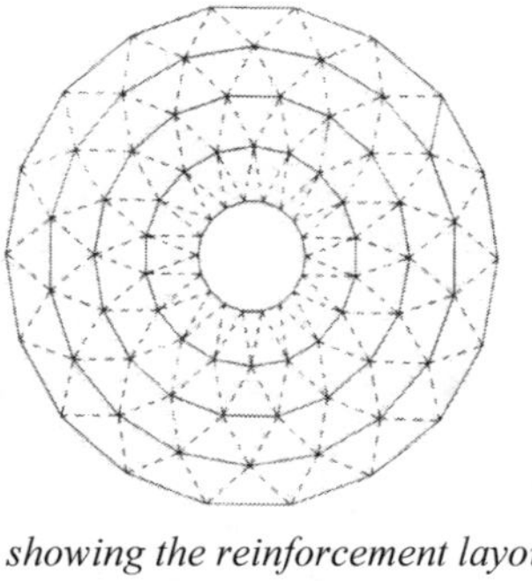

Figure 2. Architect, Dante Bini. Drawing showing the reinforcement layout of the Crespellano Binishell with the concentric circles indicating steel rods and the dotted radial elements are steel chains, 1964. Private archives of Dante Bini.

One of the major problems Bini experienced was the controlling of the concrete lifting process. For a 30 metre diameter dome of over 700 square metres, the pneumatic formwork has to lift approximately 200 tonnes of wet concrete using a fan-generated pressure of approximately 5 kPa. Photographs taken during the lifting of Bini’s first 30 metre diameter dome at Castelfranco Emilia, illustrate how the unconstrained concrete bubbled and swayed during the inflation process (Fig. 3). The first 30 metre dome (Fig. 4) was successful and still stands today, but Bini knew that he needed to successfully industrialize or systematize his unique construction process for it to become a marketable product. Through another leap of imagination Bini had the idea to use a network of steel springs stretched flat across the circular base at tangents to the perimeter (Fig. 5). These springs would contain steel reinforcement rods inside, fixed at the perimeter and overlapping at the centre. The springs would serve four purposes: Firstly to control the lifting of the concrete with their opposing force, secondly to house the reinforcement bars, thirdly to prevent the concrete slumping to the edges, and finally to introduce a degree of post-tension into the concrete once set. Another issue that Bini had encountered was the crumbling of the concrete during the lifting process and the need to re-consolidate. Bini had initially used local craftsmen to hand trowel the exterior, which was effective, but not systematic and labour intensive. The use of a second, external membrane was subsequently introduced, which as well creating a uniform outer skin finish, allowed a concrete vibrating machine to be run across the surface, post inflation. The mobile vibrating trolleys, which Bini also developed were hung from a central spigot at the pole of the dome and towed around the surface to reconsolidate the concrete around the steel springs and reinforcement rods.

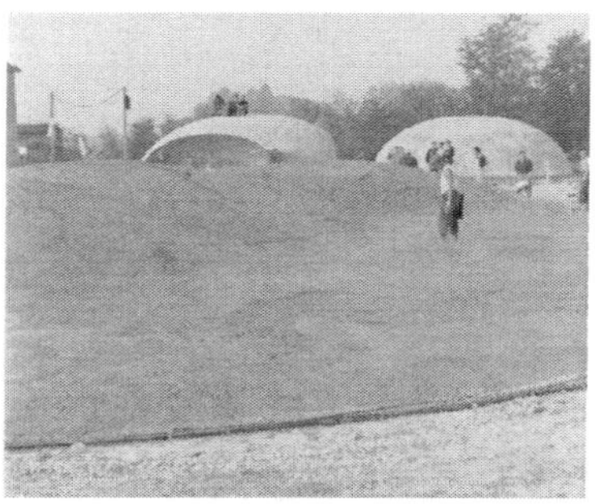

Figure 3. Castelfranco Emilia, Italy. Architect, Dante Bini. The first 30 metre diameter Binishell during inflation, 1967. Private archives of Dante Bini.

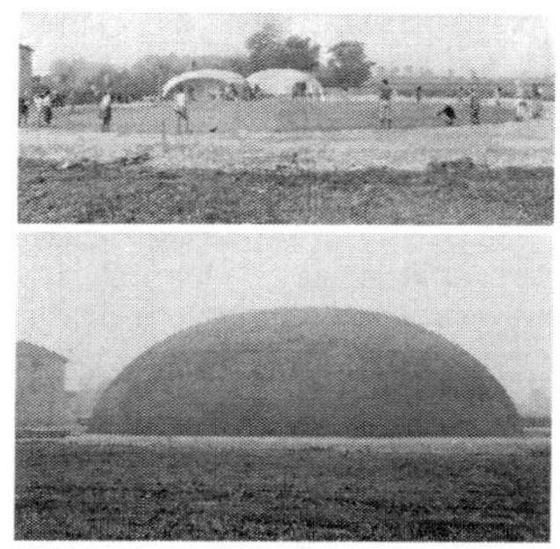

Figure 4. Castelfranco Emilia, Italy. Architect, Dante Bini. The first 30 metre diameter Binishell before and after construction, 1967. Private archives of Dante Bini.

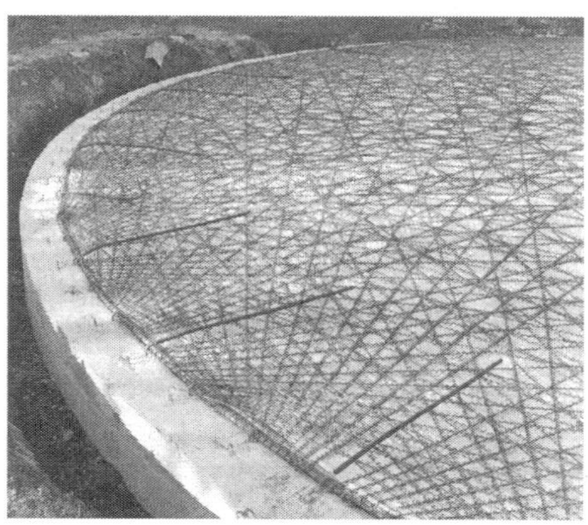

Figure 5. New South Wales, Australia. Architect, Dante Bini. Detail of spring network (with internal steel reinforcement bars), 1973. Photo: Max Dupain. Private archives of Dante Bini.

The engineering of the Binishell

> "Look, today I saw an amazing thing! If you were an engineer you would never have conceived of such nonsense"[2]

Mario Salvadori

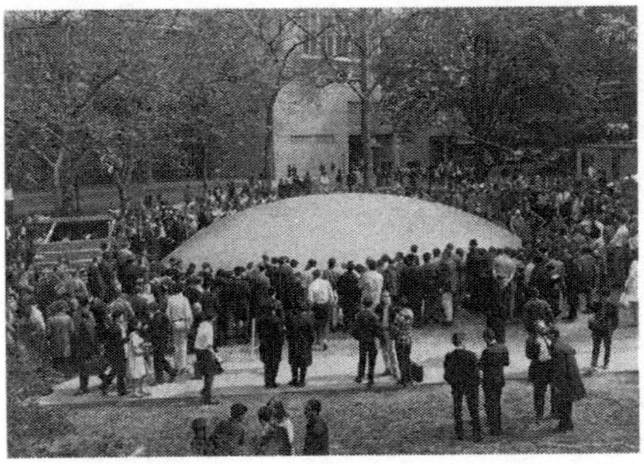

Figure 6. New York City. Architect, Dante Bini. Demonstration construction of a 15 metre diameter Binishell at Columbia University at the invitation of Mario Salvadori, 1967. Private archives of Dante Bini.

In 1966, the structural engineer Mario Salvadori and professor of Civil Engineering and Architecture at Columbia University, New York corresponded with with Dante Bini. Salvadori had read an article about Bini's first dome and invited him to New York to explain his process. Salvadori had himself; working with architect Elliot Noyes constructed a number of thin-shelled concrete buildings in 1954 using inflatable formwork. The process that Noyes and Salvadori used was based on an inflated formwork system devised by Wallace Neff[3] in 1942. The Neff system differed insomuch as it employed an inflated static form, on which reinforcement is placed and then sprayed with concrete (Gunite). Salvadori's invitation was as much of a challenge to Bini whose process sounded unbelievable to him. After their initial meeting, Salvadori was invited to Italy to witness the construction of a Binishell with his own eyes. The demonstration was successful and Salvadori invited Bini to create a demonstration Binishell on the campus of Columbia in New York City, which was successfully realised in May 1967 (Fig. 6).

The New York demonstration was widely publicised including an appearance on the front page of the New York Times, which helped to globally promote the work of Dante Bini and the Binishell Company. The meeting with Mario Salvadori had been a challenge to Bini, requiring him to reverse engineer his empirically developed structures and to provide proof of their engineered strength and characteristics. Following testing at the Institute of Construction, Turin Polytechnic under the supervision of Guido Oberti, Bini published a paper entitled 'A New Pneumatic Technique for the Construction of Thin Shells' as a part of the Proceedings of the 1st International Colloquium on Pneumatic Structures in May 1967.[4] Simultaneously Mario Salvadori published 'Technical Problems in the Design and Construction of Thin Shells'[5] where he highlights the advantages of the Binishells system over the Neff system, which obviates the need for costly scaffolding required for spraying the concrete and replaces the more expensive Gunite with a lightweight concrete. Salvadori also details methods of dome analysis and design explaining that a better understanding of the structural properties and behaviour of such structures was critical to their wider adoption within the construction industry.

The experimental testing ground of the 'Mushroom Field'

In 2013, I accompanied Dante Bini to the site in Castelfranco Emilia, which had been nicknamed the 'Mushroom Field' by local farmers and visiting engineer Mario Salvadori. This former agricultural yard near Modena, surrounded by vineyards had been the test site for Bini during the inception and subsequent developments of his pneumatically lifted and formed thin shell reinforced concrete shells. Whilst the site has long since been abandoned, many of the original structural experiments still stand. Formerly used as industrial stores and even temporary housing, each structure tells a different story in relation to its geometry, casting process, reinforcement method, and material make-up. As a testing ground and showroom of his inventiveness, the *Mushroom Field* allowed Bini to experiment with different concrete mixes, plasticisers, retarders, aggregates and reinforcing systems all at 1:1.

There was also a good deal of experimentation with the form of the shells themselves. For example, one elegant (and site-specific) configuration offers a prototype dwelling for Liberia, where a tangential slice of the dome is removed, rotated (180 degrees in plan) and then reconnected to form a concave and self-shading entrance (Fig. 7). Another of the surviving 7 metre diameter domes is an insulated shell, where lightweight woodwool slabs are incorporated as a part of a permanent formwork. Whilst the woodwool slab has mostly rotted away, this idea of casting-in lightweight formers was to be repeated in one of Bini's later construction systems.

In a search of Bini's personal archive, I could find only one documented example of a scale model (a pressurised elastic membrane at 1:10 scale), which was used to refine the cross-sectional profile of the Binishell. In the mid- to late-1960s, Bini was clearly able to marshal all the local craft skill required for the construction of these thin-shell reinforced concrete domes at a variety of different dimensions, but all at full scale. The site at Castelfranco Emilia afforded a unique workshop environment or test bed for the development of Dante Bini's ideas in way that parallel's the work of Pier Luigi Nervi and his invention and construction of the Ferro cement Pavilion at Magliana in Rome, 1945.[6]

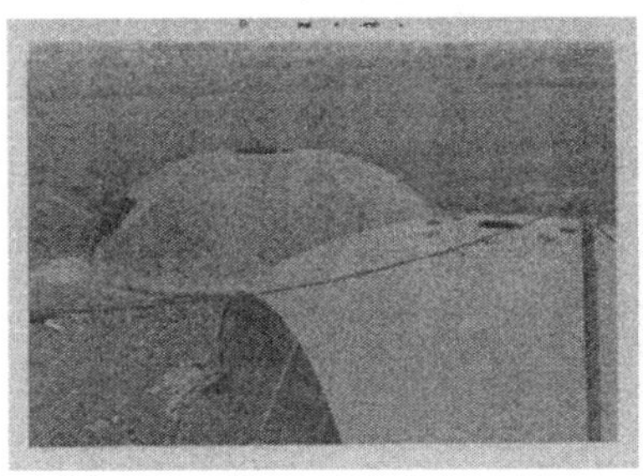

Figure 7. Castelfranco Emilia, Italy. Architect, Dante Bini. Early Binishells at the 'Mushroom Field' showing (foreground) a housing prototype developed for Liberia, 1966.

The Refining of the Binishell

> "It is not just the physics that have to work in the successful launch of new construction technologies, it is also other, external factors ... the metaphysics."
>
> Dan Ptacek[1][7]

In one of his most successful projects, Dante Bini was employed by the Department of Education in New South Wales (NSW), Australia, to deliver over 20 educational buildings under a very tight schedule and budget. Bini was contacted in 1971 and visited by a delegation from Australia who visited a number of Binishell structures across Italy including sports arenas and swimming pools. The tight timescale of the Australian projects was perfectly suited to the Bini methodology, and the result was an exemplary project, matching programmatic need to technological fix and spatial flexibility (circular, clear span, etc.). Given the imperative of construction speed and cost (allied to political promises), Bini, now well-rehearsed with his unique technology of pneumatic formwork, standardised the diameters of the domes to 18 metre and 36 metre and successfully delivered the projects (in a variety of cosmetically different versions) on time and on budget. In order to facilitate the project, Bini clearly set out the Binishell construction process in a set of instructional documents that included diagrams of key details and was subsequently published[8]. The construction of the Ashbury Public School administration building an 18 metre diameter dome new Sydney, NSW, was recorded by the renowned Australian photographer Max Dupain and provides one of the most complete documents of the construction of a Binishell (Fig. 8). Following the completion of the NSW schools projects, the Concrete Institute of Australia and the NSW Public Works Department hosted a Bini-Shells Seminar[9]. In a ten-page publication to accompany the event, diagrams, photographs and technical drawings illustrate the construction process, and finished buildings. The document includes drawings of two of Bini's key innovations, which enabled their construction; the mobile concrete vibration cart for concrete consolidation and the footing (or edge beam) detail[10]. (Fig. 9) This detail incorporates an ingenious 'figure of eight' profiled, pneumatic edge tubing. This tube is used during the pouring of the edge beam to produce a groove in the concrete foundation near the surface. The tube is latterly re-inflated in order to pneumatically anchor the pneumoform ground membrane during the lifting of the dome.

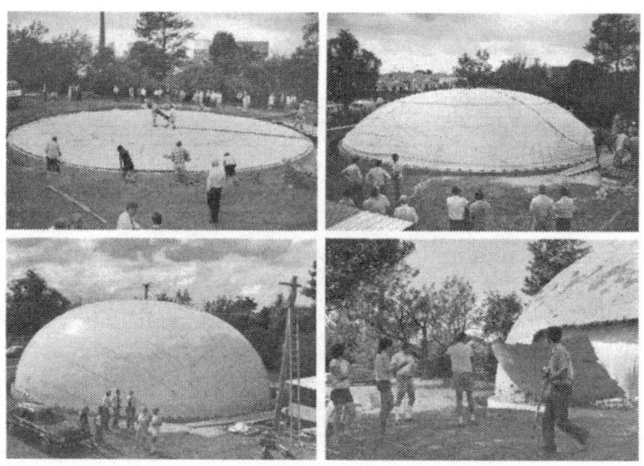

Figure 8. New South Wales, Australia. Architect, Dante Bini. Construction of Ashbury Public School administration building, 1973. Photographs: Max Dupain. Private archives of Dante Bini.

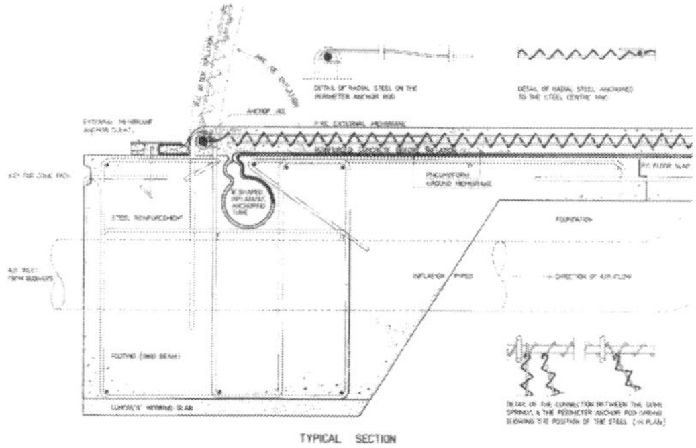

Figure 9. Architect, Dante Bini. Detail drawing of edge beam footing showing inflatable anchoring tube for pneumoform, 1974. Private archives of Dante Bini.

Whilst Bini had previously licensed his patented technology (with mixed results), it is arguable that his presence on the ground as the designer/contractor was a large contributory factor in the success of the NSW projects. The Binishell system is a patented technology and as such the construction methodology is clearly expressed and its products eminently repeatable, but it is perhaps Bini's role as 'craft contractor' in the manner of his great inspiration Pier Luigi Nervi, which might be seen to be most successful. The Binishell technology was licensed in the UK at the same time as Parashell and was used to create what was thought to be the only extant example of a Binishell in the UK, Michael Godwin's (Godwin & Cowper) 'Edinburgh Dome'[11], built in Malvern in 1977. Following a visit to Italy in 1974 to view a number of Binishell projects, Michael Godwin used Bini's system to create a 36 metre diameter school sports hall for Malvern Girls College, which was officially opened on May 4th 1978 by Prince Philip, the Duke of Edinburgh. The entire dome is raised on a series of eight concrete pilotis to provide natural light reflected from the surrounding pool. So in this case the dome forms a 'lid' atop large columns with the elevated ring-beam holding the dome in place. In May 2009 the 'Edinburgh Dome' was given a Grade II listing in recognition of its rare (and seemingly unique in the UK) construction method and quality of architectural execution. I have recently discovered that there is in fact another Parashell dome still in existence at Mildenhall in Suffolk and I am currently in contact with the original job architect Simon Conolly to ascertain more details of its construction.

In a conference paper from 1993[12], Bini reported that between 1970 and 1990 over 1,600 Binishells were successfully constructed across 23 countries, three of which subsequently suffered failures[13] and were demolished or rebuilt.

The Proliferation of Bini Systems

During his time in Australia, Bini also developed and prototyped a number of other structural systems. The Minishell system can be viewed as a development of the original Binishell patent and is designed to produce small, 8 metre x 8 metre low-cost, square or octagonal-based, monolithic, reinforced concrete shell structures, provided with openings at the corners which result from the construction process. Bini had observed the difficulties (especially with the large 36 metre diameter domes) of maneuvering, positioning, anchoring and folding of the inflatable membrane. The largest membranes (for a 36 metre diameter Binishell) had a surface area of 1000 square metres and could weigh over 1500 kg. The 8 metre x 8 metre Minishell system was designed to use less than 5 cubic metres of concrete and could be formed (excluding site preparation and foundation) in only 30 minutes. Interestingly, the protruding upturned edges formed around the openings during inflation help to create a raised 'lip' around the edge of the openings, which acts to stiffen the arch formed openings. Several tourist villages in both Australia and Italy were built using this system including Cairns in Queensland, Australia, of which Bini designed and oversaw construction of and was completed in 1980.

Another system prototyped in Australia although not further developed, was Binix (Fig. 10). Binix was not a shell structure, but a ribbed (or lattice) dome structure, which employed a system of prefabricated lightweight polystyrene 'void-formers' laid flat in a diagrid across a membrane. A grid of steel reinforcement was then laid in the channels between the chamfered polystyrene forms, which were then filled with concrete. The membrane was then inflated to lift the reinforced concrete lattice dome, which, when the formers were removed was more redolent of a geodesic frame. Bini notes, that "The only problem experienced during the construction of the prototype was the difficulty in re-compacting and vibrating concrete inside the raised form network."[14] Bini claimed that the Binix patented method of construction could produce hexagonal-based monolithic reinforced concrete framed dome structures with spans of up to 100 metres[15]. Bini also adds that the Binix system "...had even greater potential than the Binishell itself, because in addition to its aesthetic appeal, it would provide the necessary thickness of steel cover for reinforced concrete required by building codes across the world."[16]

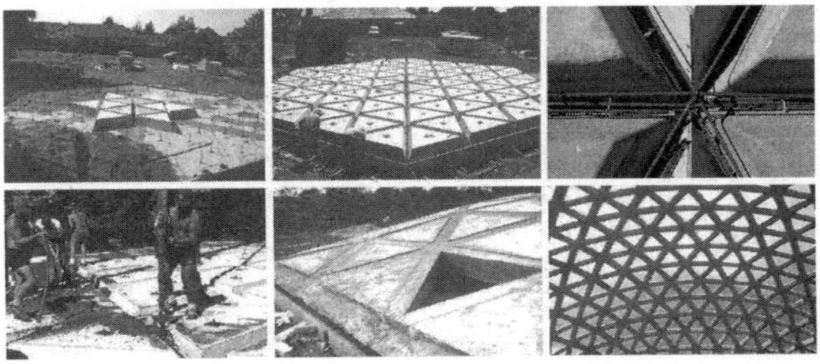

Figure 10. New South Wales, Australia. Architect, Dante Bini. Sequence showing the only built prototype of the Binix system, 1976. Private archives of Dante Bini.

By the 1980s, Bini was starting to explore fabric-covered space-frames, and in a successful collaboration with the Gruppo Dioguardi construction company he realised a number of these structures, notably for FIFA's Italia 90 World Cup. This new construction system was called Binistar (Fig. 11) and it employed an air-filled membrane to lift the structure, which was a space-frame composed of extendable strut members that would lock together when the fabric was fully inflated. The PVC membrane used for the structural erection process was then left in place as the building skin. This process of 'building with air' (which became the English title of his memoir of his life in architecture and construction) became the main focus of his subsequent research projects.

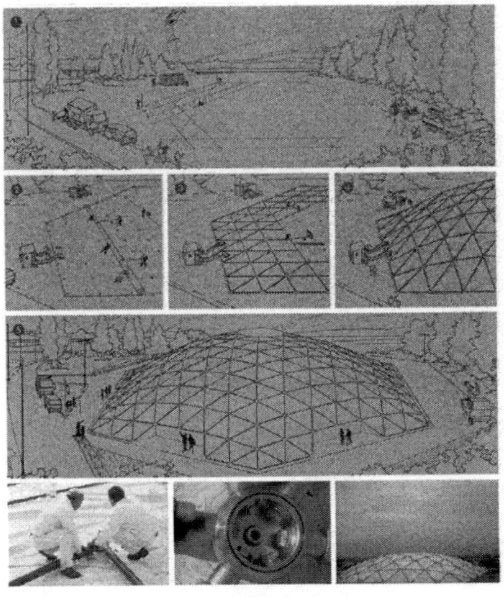

Figure 11. Architect, Dante Bini. Assembly sequence of the Binistar system, with photographs of system assembly and fabric connections to external frame, 1982. Private archives of Dante Bini.

Through his built work and contributions to conferences and congresses, Bini was increasingly invited to act as a specialist construction consultant. One such invitation took him to Japan to work with the Shimuzu Corporation.

Amongst the many highly speculative projects Bini worked on with Shimuzu was his contribution to TRY 2004, a prototypical megastructure designed for one million inhabitants at Tokyo Bay. The proposed structure was a pyramidal tower of 2004 metres high and one of the most difficult technical challenges was how to build such a structure, which Bini answered with giant pneumoform spherical forms that would use compressed air to assemble the giant modules. At a more modest scale was the Air Lift-Up System[17] (or ALU) (Fig. 12) where Bini in collaboration with Shimuzu developed an idea for a multi-storey construction system that used air (in both positive and negative pressure) to push up and pull up concrete slabs (cast in situ) around a series of columns.

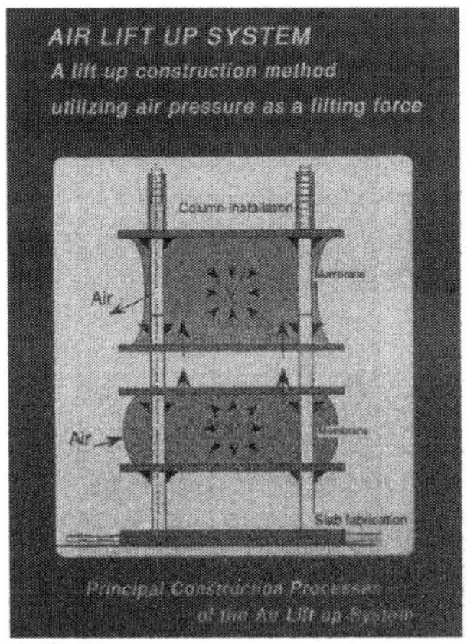

Figure 12. Architect, Dante Bini. Air Lift-Up System developed with Shimuzu, 1982. Private archives of Dante Bini.

Conclusion

The work of architect Dante Bini and in particular his Binishell system for lightweight 'domed' concrete shells developed in the early 1960s was technologically inventive, but remained largely a niche construction product looking for a client. It was arguably the exposure of Bini's ideas following his demonstration Binishell at Columbia University, New York that both legitimised this new technology and launched Bini's career. Throughout that career as variously an architect, inventor and builder Dante Bini has utilised the inexpensive, safe and ubiquitous material of air as a motive force and forming medium. Common to almost all his projects the use of differential air pressure as a means to lift and form heavy materials like concrete embodies an approach, which is both influenced by the great concrete craftsman architect and engineer Pier Luigi Nervi and simultaneously the "doing more with less" philosophy of Richard Buckminster Fuller.

The unique test bed of the 'Mushroom Field' at Castelfranco Emilia afforded Bini a series of demonstrable building systems and products, which although experimental, did not simply remain ideas on the drawing board. His empirical testing of both the properties and qualities of the new Binishell forms at the start of 1960's can find a parallel in the sheet metal experiments of French architect Jean Prouvé. Prouvé's work was also an exercise in material exploration and with the seminal work at his Maxéville factory he was both the designer and fabricator of architectural artefacts from furniture to prefabricated buildings. There are other parallels with Prouvé to whom the construction process of any given project was an integral part of the design. Bini was, and continues to be fascinated by what he calls Construction Automation and sees one of his key jobs as a systems designer to make the system easily (or more easily) buildable. With renewed interest in Fabric Formwork of which we can include

Bini as a pioneer, a wider evaluation of his work and perhaps more specifically his working method is long overdue.

Notes and References

[1] D. Bini, *Building with Air*, London: Bibliotheque McLean, 2014. p.28.

[2] ibid., p.59.

[3] M. G. Salvadori, 'Technical Problems in the Design and Construction of Thin Shells', Paul Weidlinger Consulting Engineers, May 1967. p.3.

[4] D. Bini, 'A Pneumatic Technique for the Construction of Thin Shells' pp.52–55 in D. Feder (Ed.), International Association for Shell Structures (IASS), Proceedings from the 1st IASS International Colloquium on Pneumatic Structures. Stuttgart, May 11th – 12th 1967, Stuttgart: IASS, 1967.

[5] M. G. Salvadori, 'Technical Problems in the Design and Construction of Thin Shells', Paul Weidlinger Consulting Engineers, May 1967. p.3.

[6] T. Lori, *Pier Luigi Nervi*, Milan: Motta Architettura, 2009. p.25.

[7] D. Ptacek, (2013). *The Adjacent Possible*. London: University of Westminster. Available from https://youtu.be/XOIYSR2tsVI (Consulted on 01/12/15).

[8] D. Bini, 'Concrete Domes', *NSW Builder: Official Journal of the Master Builders' Association of New South Wales*, vol.3, no.7, 1974, pp.326–334.

[9] D. Bini, 'Binishell Seminar conducted by The Concrete Institute of Australia and NSW Public Works Department', *Constructional Review*, May 1976.

[10] Ibid., p.6.

[11] M. Godwin, 'Malvern sports centre – an architect's adventure story', *Concrete*, Vol.12, no.4, April 1978, pp.20–25.

[12] D. Bini, 'Automation in construction of shells, space, multi-storey, super high-rise and extra-terrestrial structures' pp.1526–1536 in G.A.R. Parke, C.M. Howard, (Eds), Fourth International Conference for Spatial Structures, Space Structure Research Center, Space Structures 4, Vol. 2, University of Guildford 1993, London: Thomas Telford, 1993.

[13] D. Bini, 'The causes of the collapse of the Pittwater Binishell', *Engineers Australia*, no. 63, 3rd May 1991, pp. 5–8.

[14] D. Bini, 'Automation in construction of shells, space, multi-storey, super high-rise and extra-terrestrial structures' p.1528 in G.A.R. Parke, C.M. Howard, (Eds), Fourth International Conference for Spatial Structures, Space Structure Research Center, Space Structures 4, Vol. 2, University of Guildford 1993, London: Thomas Telford, 1993.

[15] ibid., p. 1528

[16] D. Bini, *Building with Air*, London: Bibliotheque McLean, 2014. p.102.

[17] H. Nakazawa, S. Matsumoto, H. Takada, D. Bini, 'Air-Lift-Up Construction System', Construction Beyond 2000 – Future of Construction – Construction of the future: First International Symposium of CIB Working Commission W82: Construction Beyond 2000, Futures (sic) Studies of Construction. June, 1992 Espoo, Finland.

Better than Bucky: 'domes' for sports halls

David Yeomans

Independent scholar, UK

Introduction

Buckminster Fuller's advocacy of domes as an ideal form of construction hardly had much practical effect. It was supposed to be economical but, although his ideas had some influence on students in the 1960s, they were hardly taken up by the building industry at large. Although it was hardly 'architecture' there might have been more occasions in which it could have been used as a cheap form of enclosure. Perhaps one of the difficulties was that Fuller did not explore variations on the form that might have made it a more practical proposition for a variety of situations; a circular dome has only limited applications. However a firm of architects in Ipswich took up the idea and, in collaboration with Felix Samuely and Partners, developed it through a sufficient number of projects to show how it could be used effectively. The architects eventually produced a spiral bound book that has been deposited in the RIBA library and which gives full details of their buildings.[1] The majority of these still survive and this is reappraisal of their development following a visit to the survivors in April 2011.

The architects

During the school building programme that followed WWII several novel forms of construction were tried either to cope with the scarcity of materials or looking for economies of scale through the development of building systems, and this seems to have led to a general pioneering mood among architects. A small number of basic structural ideas were taken up by individual architects, a good example being the hyperbolic parabaloid roof that was used for a number of school halls. One of the firms that used this on occasions was the Ipswich firm of Johns, Slater and Haward who also built schools using a pyramid roof form of their own devising. However, they also became interested in Buckminster Fuller's ideas about geodesic domes.

In 1963 they built a small experimental dome just 6.4m diameter using the icosadodecahedron geometry proposed by Fuller. This used 2inch (50mm) square section timbers, which were extended by having flat metal plates attached to the ends. The plates overlapped within the joint so that they could simply be bolted together. This was just an idea that the firm was interested in exploring but it was from this that the idea came to use the technique for sports halls of various kinds. By the mid 70s they had built several sports halls of varying shapes and sizes.

There are three trails to follow here: the development of the geometry used for these buildings, the development of the method of connecting the components and the development of the structural analysis. The first is the most significant because they quickly moved from Buckminster Fuller's geometry to a much simpler one that provided greater flexibility. Within Felix Samuely and Partners, it was Frank Newby who was involved with these buildings. The size, geometry, dates of building and methods of connection are summarized in a table produced by Newby who took a particular interest in these jobs probably because of an interest in Fuller's ideas (Fig. 1). [2]

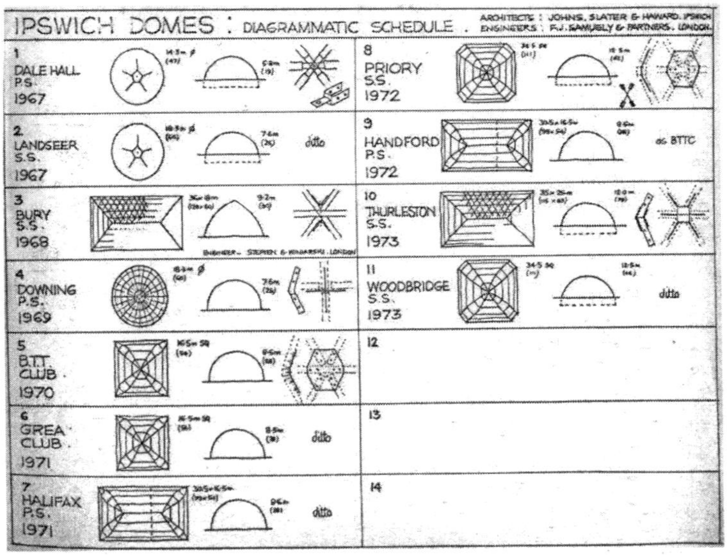

Figure 1 Chart of the various structures drawn by Frank Newby.

Icosadodecahedra

Two domes were built using icosadodecahedra, advocated by Fuller, a small one for a primary school, which still survives, and a larger one for a secondary school, which has been demolished along with the school itself. The two domes for Dale Hall Primary School and Landseer Secondary School were essentially the experimental structure writ large. The small sports hall for Dale Hall School was the first practical demonstration of the approach as a method of construction (Fig. 2).

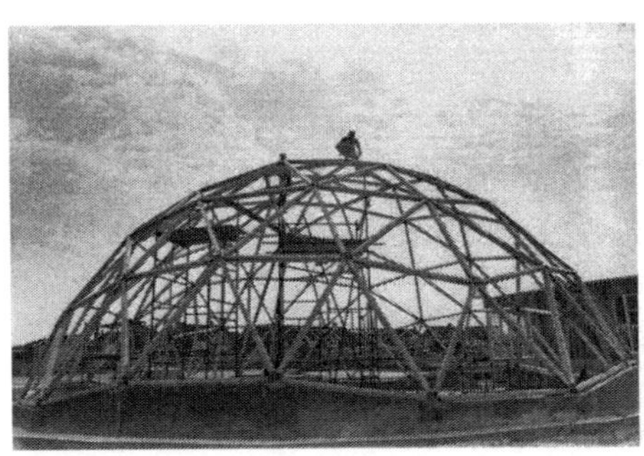

Figure 2 Dale Hall dome under construction.

Apart from the geometry, the basis of these designs was to use simple timber sections and metal fasteners, as used in the experimental structure. That would make the structures economical and simple to make. Only a small enclosure was needed at Dale Hall, a mere 47ft 6ins (14.5m) diameter and, because there was no overriding functional requirements on the plan, the overall size was decided by determining the most efficient use of 8ft x 4ft plywood sheets that were to be used for roofing. The structure was of 4" (100mm) square timber sections to which the 9mm ply was nailed, except for the top ring where a thicker ply was used just below the rooflight.[3] Apart from those timbers defining the geometry there were additional timber noggins to help support the plywood.

Members were joined with rather simple connectors, a yoke fastened to the timbers with two bolts and welded to a plate with just a single bolt through the overlapping plates (Fig 3). Because of the geometry "the shape built itself as if by magic" with erection carried out from scaffold towers.[4] As the dome was then given a fibreboard lining the connections cannot now be seen.

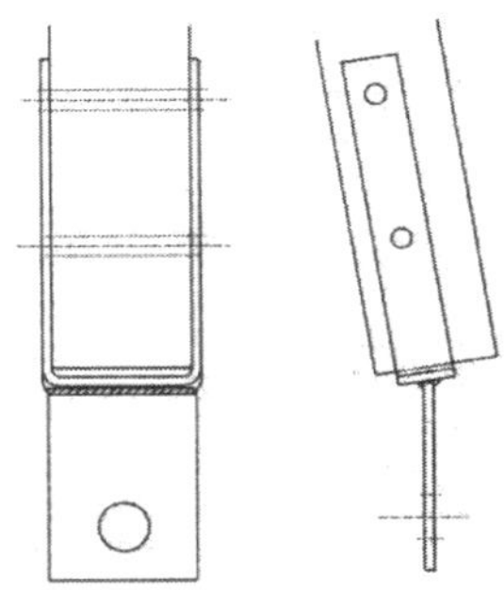

Figure 3 Basic connector used for Dale Hall and Landseer School domes made from 6mm steel plate.

Dale Hall School immediately demonstrated the limitations of the Fuller approach. A hemispherical dome may be fine in theory but for practical purposes something less that a hemisphere is wanted. The upper part of the volume is hardly very useful and simply increases the surface area and the volume that has to be heated. A more functional shape uses something a little less than a hemisphere. Unfortunately the bottom of a dome cannot be a level circle so that the base upon which it is to be fastened must rise and fall to accommodate the geometry of the structure above (as seen in Figure 2), a clear problem for construction.

In the larger Landseer School dome built in the same year the base to which the timber structure was attached was cast level and steel make-up pieces were used to connect to the higher nodes to it. This dome was 60ft (18m.) diameter also had a central roof light and the size was determined by the need to accommodate a badminton court. The ply sheathing was cut from 10ft x 4ft sheets and the frame members changed to 4ins. x 3ins. (100 x 75mm). Both domes were covered with 'Evode' bituminous roofing felt with a silvered finish and that became the standard for all the structures they built.

Bury School

In 1968 the architects designed a large rectangular structure for Silver Jubilee School, Bury St Edmunds (now called King Edward VI School) using a singly curved form, a vaulted structure with 'hipped' ends (Fig 4). The plan shape was determined by the need to accommodate a tennis court and that precluded the use of a dome. Construction was quite different from the other sports halls that they built but should be considered in the light of the later rectangular structures. Z.S. Makowski reviewed this structure acknowledging Stepien and Winiaski as the structural engineers, and commented on the quality of the building and the cheapness of the architect's buildings generally.[5] It's not clear why different engineers were used for this project but it was probably because they were engaged for other buildings on the site.

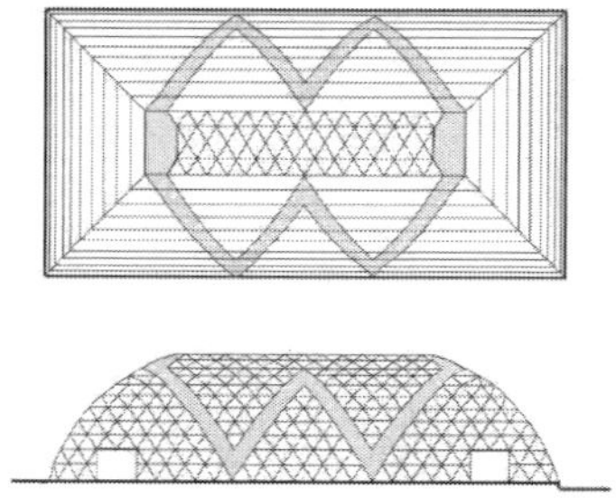

Figure 4 Plan and elevation of the Bury St Edmunds School. The W shaped area indicates plywood wind bracing.

The geometry chosen was a triangular layout of timbers, which were butted against each other as shown in Figure 5. In some ways this was a curious decision. One might have assumed that they could have used a lamella form as this had been used for similar sized structures in America, the details for which had been published in a standard American text on timber design.[6] A lamella offers the advantage that jointing is relatively simple and the continuity of members across the joints must increase the overall stiffness of the structure. Makowski points out that until the advent of computer analysis the vaults and domes used by the Ipswich architects would have been analysed assuming pin-jointed connectors.

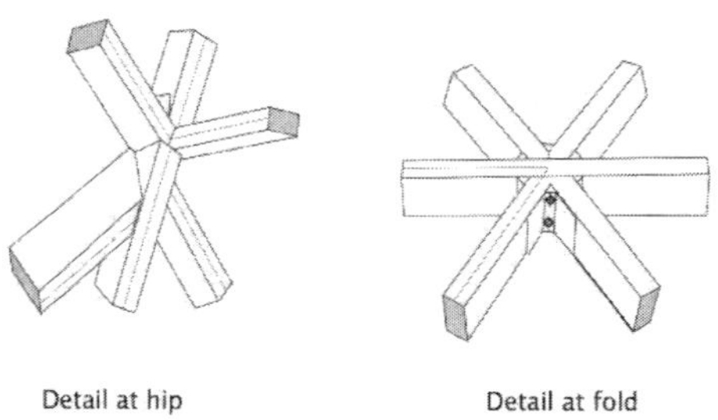

Figure 5 Connections between members of the Bury St Edmunds structure.

At Bury St. Edmunds with the timbers butting together at the joints, the ends of members had to be accurately cut and the associated costs made this a comparatively expensive structure. What seems to have been taken from this experience however was the adoption of a triangular geometry for the surfaces of subsequent buildings. Although some of the later structures had already been built by the time he was writing, what Makowski did not say was that the Bury St Edmunds building was rather more expensive than all the others, neither did he point out that Newby was the engineer for other buildings by these architects in spite of naming them.[7]

A radial dome

An experiment in building a dome of radial members did not prove a great success. This was a relatively small dome still surviving (although only just) at Downing Primary School at the time of my visit. The idea of radial members was that the dome would have a level base and structural action would be simple. In the event it proved difficult to erect and there were also functional difficulties. It was lined with battens, which proved to be a mistake because there were no clear straight lines within the space. As a result badminton players had nothing in their peripheral vision to give them direction when they were looking up at the shuttlecock. It has also proved difficult to gain access to the central rooflight to clean off the dirt that has built up on it and, as it began to leak, there was no easy access to affect repairs. Of all the surviving structures this one is in the worst condition and one has the impression that it has not proved a particular asset to the school in recent years.

Square 'domes'

Some small square domes followed and their geometry set the pattern for all those that followed. They adopted a rationalization of the triangular geometry used at the Bury St Edmunds school. Using triangular panels on four sides curved to give a semicircular cross section left four areas at the corners to be filled with 'gussets' (Fig. 6). This had the merit that most of the members and connectors were exactly the same with the only variation contained within the gussets and their connections with the triangular panels. The majority of the connectors were simple 'flat' plates bolted through the timbers (Fig. 7). Connectors on the hips, which required thicker timbers, were folded and let into the thickness of the timber.

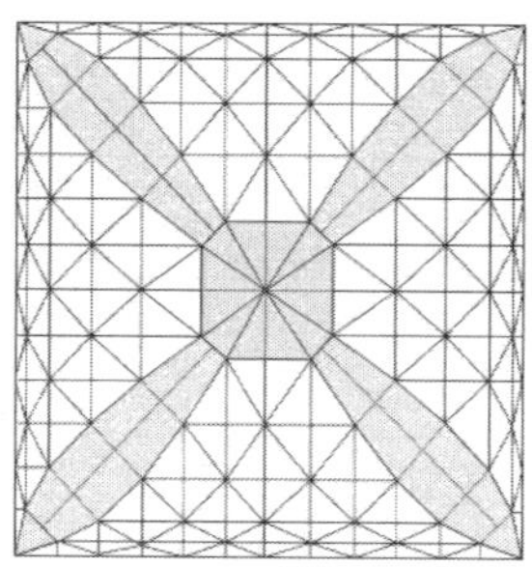

Figure 6 Plan of the framing for the Britannia Table Tennis Club building.

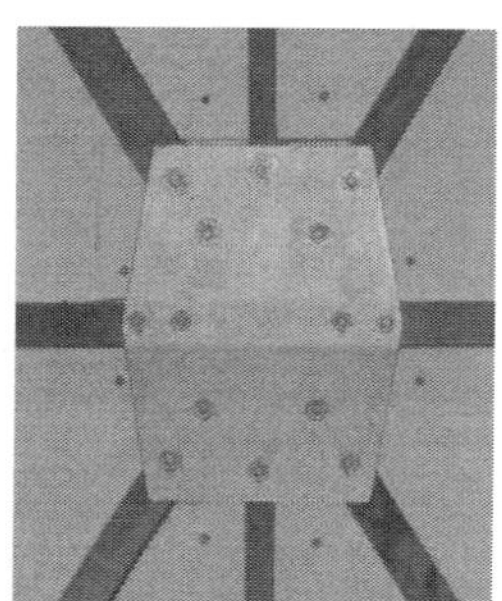

Figure 7 Flat plate connector as used in the Britannia club building and the Halifax and Handforth schools.

Three such domes were built: the first for the Britannia Table Tennis Club in Ipswich, which still survives, and two similar sized domes for Guardian Royal Exchange Athletics Club, one at Ipswich and the other at Lytham St Annes. These later two have been demolished as a result of redevelopment of their sites. The table tennis club, like all later domes, has the walls lined out internally at the base using plywood with the structure exposed above. The sports club buildings for the insurance company housed badminton courts and those buildings incorporated windows near the floor. There are no windows in the table tennis club.

Wind loading on these domes proved problematic and a complication was that a pair of timbers was added at the corners to provide hold down forces against the uplift generated by the wind. Calculations were initially by hand but when the structure was built for the Guardian Royal Exchange Athletics Club, these additional corner members were omitted following a computer analysis of the structure (see below).

Halifax and Handforth Primary Schools

The next stage of development was the design of two rectangular structures. The first came about because of a change in the client's brief. The original plan at Halifax Primary School was to have a circular domed sports hall of 60ft diameter. However, there were delays in funding so that the project was put on hold. When it was later revived it was decided to adopt the form that had been used for the Britannia Table Tennis Cub. Then there was a last minute additional requirement for a swimming pool and it was thought possible to build a rectangular structure to cover both sports and swimming areas with a dividing wall between them. This involved complete redesign of the structure with the internal dividing wall made loadbearing.

These structures were being built at a time when computer based analysis of structures was just becoming a practical design tool and it was for Halifax Primary School that computer analysis was now adopted. The effect of moving from hand calculations to computer analysis was that the designers no longer needed to make the simplifications that had been necessary for the former to be manageable. Although calculations could now be more precise, we must presume that with the same simple connector plates the assumption was still that the structure would be pin-jointed. However, the noticeable effect was a reduction in the hold-down forces needed at the corners that had been predicted by the hand calculations. It would have been possible to omit these additional corner members incorporated into the early square domes. However, by the time the analysis had been completed for Halifax School the rather well-organized contractor had already planned out his ordering and erection, which included these additional corner members, and so they were left in. They were however omitted from the very similar structure at Handforth Primary School.

The additional feature of both these buildings, compared with the badminton club buildings, is the inclusion of small windows near the base and of roof lights at the top. The result is a pleasant, well-lit interior (Fig. 8).

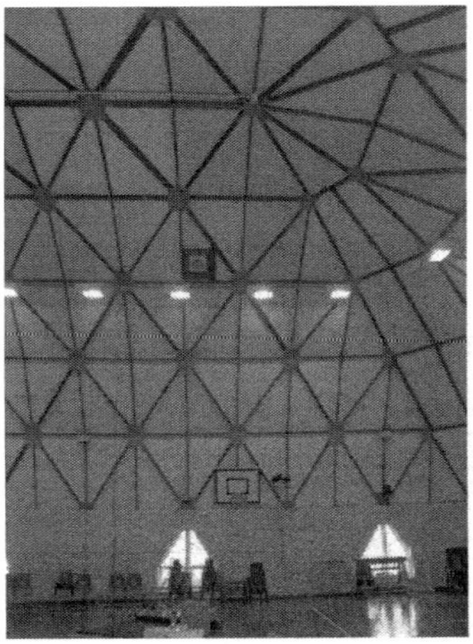

Figure 8 Interior of Handforth School sports hall.

The large structures

The final phases of design development involved the building of very large sports halls, initially a large 'square'. The triangular geometry was clearly a sound arrangement and was now expanded for much larger sports halls. Increasing the span of the square from the 54ft (16.5m) span of the table tennis club to the 34m span sports halls. The first to be built was for Priory Heath Secondary School (Fig 9), with a similar structure later provided for Woodbridge School, a private school outside Ipswich. Retaining the same geometry with a semicircular cross section would have resulted in an excessively high space. However, by simply leaving out two rows of triangles from the base the height of these was reduced to 12.5 m. Of course, the plan was no longer square but a square with the corners cut off and with the gusset between the curved triangles coming down onto the clipped corner, clearly seen in Figure 9.[8]

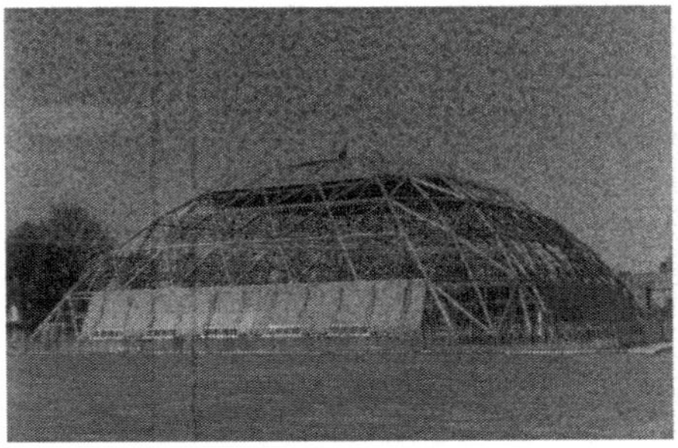

Figure 9 Priory Heath dome under construction. Felix Samuely and Partners archive.

Naturally, with the increased size, forces were increased and the connection design was modified. Slots were cut in the now larger, 150 x 150mm timbers into which the plates were let. Unfortunately these connectors proved to be inadequate because large deflections were observed following some strong winds. A more sophisticated computer analysis showed that the bolt-hole tolerances allowed some movement of the connector bolts within the timbers and remedial work was necessary to stiffen the structure at the connections. To do this additional steel connectors were screwed to the face of the timbers at each joint. In Figure 10 it is possible to see an original connector plate and the additional connector that was added. The additional members comprise 'intersecting' plates to carry some bending moments over the joint and welded to long plates screwed to the structural timbers of the vault. This is clearly a retrofit because the new connectors are attached over the internal plywood boarding at the base.

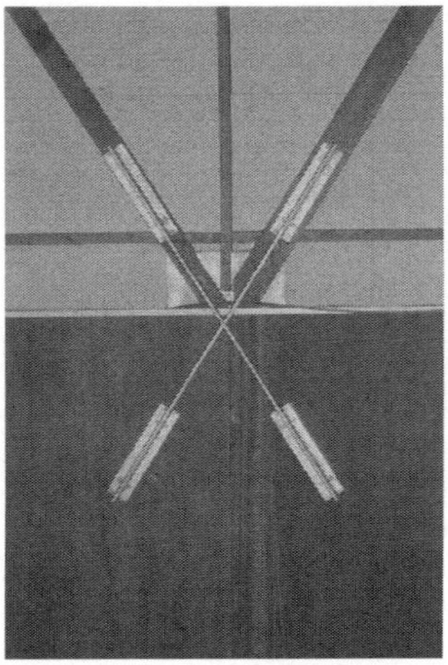

Figure 10 Interior of Priory Heath dome showing retrofitted connector. The original flat plate connector can be seen underneath.

A modified connector detail was then used for the rectangular structure built for Thurleston School, which was much the same height, and for a very similar 'dome' at Woodbridge School. For these two a new connector design was adopted, again with the steel of the connector let into slots cut into the timbers. However, the steel was now perpendicular to the surface of the structures, enabling a more satisfactory bolting pattern, and with additional plates at the junction welded over them, top and bottom (Fig. 11).

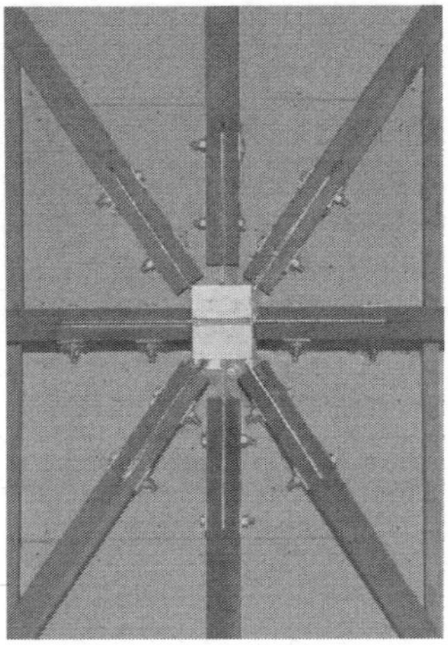

Figure 11 Jointing arrangement used at Thurston and Woodbridge Schools.

The rectangular building for Thurleston School (Fig. 12) is wider than that built at Bury St Edmunds its form determined from a cost analysis after an increase in timber prices. Changing rooms of traditional construction were incorporated into the building, 'inserted' into one side of the timber structure. This can be seen to the right in the photograph, which is of the hipped end of the building. Note also the ventilators built into the surface. As the changing rooms are partly within the envelope of the shell structure the roof of this block that is within the hall is used as a viewing gallery.

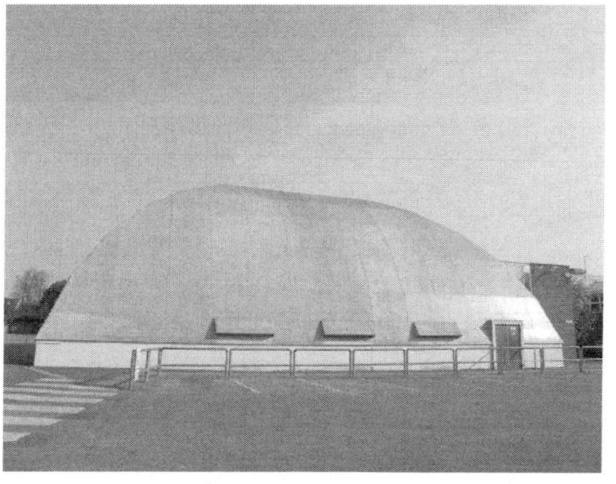

Figure 12 Thurleston sports hall viewed from the end. The changing rooms can be seen to the right.

Assessment

One could hardly regard any of these as elegant buildings. Externally the rectangular buildings are rather overpowering in contrast to the more human scale of the school buildings they stand next to, especially for the smaller primary schools. The generally silver grey finish of the 'Evode' roofing felt is not particularly attractive in such necessarily large areas. However, internally those at the Halifax and Handford schools are rather pleasant, largely as a result of the rooflights and the windows close to the floor. It seems rather a pity that some form of natural lighting was not provided for the much larger sports halls. Nevertheless the manager at Woodford School expressed satisfaction with his building. They fall into the category of 'a good job and cheap' and that these structures have lasted for half a century, mostly with minimal maintenance, is a testament to the basic soundness of the design that was developed.

The simple combination of timber members, plywood sheathing and steel connectors has proved structurally sound and, once the triangular geometry was adopted, capable of being adapted to much larger structures than the small squares that it was first used for and to rectangular as well as square buildings. As Makowski pointed out, the analysis of structures of this kind improved with the development of computer analysis. Nevertheless, the early hand calculation methods resulted in a robust design. Thus, that even when joints were found to be inadequate in the large structure at Priory School, the problem could be remedied with a simple retrofit and an improved joint design easily substituted for the two subsequent structures.

The detailing round doors, windows and ventilation openings has for the most part given few weathering problems and simple maintenance of the covering has been all that has been generally required. If there are any major complaints about the performance of these buildings it is because of the difficulty of adapting the spaces to uses other than the sports for which they were designed. They are poorly insulated and, while that is something that could be remedied by retrofitting insulation, their height makes them difficult to heat. This has proven to be problem when the buildings are used for holding examinations. The method of heating is by high-level, fan-assisted heaters and the fans are very noisy – not so much a problem for sports but clearly a problem for those grappling with examination papers.

In spite of these disadvantages the method of construction produced a form that was relatively simple to build and certainly simple to maintain. The survival of those not demolished because they were no longer wanted on the site is a testament to the latter.

One might well assume that this building type would be attractive to commercial clients, so it seems curious that, like Buckminster Fuller's domes, this simple and more adaptable structural form was not more widely used. Presumably that is because of the process of procurement. The professionals involved, the architects and the engineers, were consultants whose job it was to solve other people's problems. The local authority wanted cheap sports halls for its schools and their consultants provided that. The sports clubs that needed small buildings were local and would easily have become aware of the idea. Similarly the private school would have easily known about the large hall at Priory Secondary School. The architects and engineers were not entrepreneurs and apparently not interested in selling the idea as a commercial enterprise. Had it been taken up by a commercial company it might well have been more widely used for workshops, warehouses or farm buildings. The shape is unusual but the result is hardly less elegant than precast concrete portal frames that were widely marketed for such commercial purpose.

Notes and References

[1] *Timber Domes Developed in the Ipswich Area Since 1963*, Ipswich: Johns, Slater & Haward, 1975.

[2] Newby had become the senior partner of the firm following the death of Felix Samuely in 1959. He had met Fuller when the latter visited England and while in London had also visited the site of the Snowdon Aviary at London Zoo – a 'tensegrity' structure.

[3] There is a difference here between the written description and the drawings. The former says 15mm while the drawings show only 12mm ply.

[4] Op. cit. note 1, p. 20.

[5] Makowski, Z.S. "History of Development of Various Types of Braced Barrel Vaults and Review of Recent Achievements All over the World." In *Analysis, Design and Construction of Braced Barrel Vaults*. London: Taylor and Francis, 1985.

[6] Timber Engineering Company. *Timber Design and Construction Handbook*. New York: F.W. Dodge Corporation, 1956. Chapter 6.

[7] Possibly because Makowski had been in dispute with Frank Newby over the authorship of the stressed skin roof for the London UIA conference building in 1961.

[8] At the time of my visit Priory Heath School had become a technical college and the plan was to move it to a new site. Thus the sports hall will probably be demolished.

Architect-entrepreneurs in post-independence Pune (India)

Sarah Melsens, Priyanka Mangaonkar-Vaiude, and Yashoda Joshi
Department of Architectural Engineering, Vrije Universiteit Brussel (VUB), Belgium; Department of Architecture, BRICK school of Architecture, Pune, India

Introduction

At the time of Independence in 1947, India counted 200 to 300 qualified architects[1] and about 5000 degree-level engineers and thousands of technically trained construction assistants[2]. These British-trained professionals carried forward the western building practice, which by then had largely replaced traditional native construction practice.

The disproportionate number of architects to engineers reflects the educational and work opportunities for Indians under colonial rule. Major nation-wide infrastructure works had required technical skills and natives were trained as early as the 1840s at various institutes for working as overseers, clerks of work, and technical and executing assistants. These institutes rapidly evolved into engineering schools offering licentiate courses in civil engineering. There existed 36 such schools at the time of Independence[3]. In comparison, the first and only diploma course of architecture in India was started in 1913, merely four decades before Independence, in the economically flourishing city of Bombay. As opposed to the Indian engineers who mostly worked with the government - either as employee or as government contractor - Indian architects usually catered to the wealthy native business clientele emerging in the cities in the 1930s. In general, these native architects had a well-to-do and cultured background.

While historic construction practice in India has gained increasing scholarly attention recently,[4] less is known about its further development and spreading beyond the major colonial cities after India's independence in 1947. This paper forms part of a larger research project that aims to fill this lacuna by analysing Pune's post-independence building culture. The choice for Pune, a second tier city in which few architects were based pre-independence, is hence a conscious one in the attempt to gain knowledge on the production of everyday buildings.

Building involves a collaborate effort of patrons, designers, contractors and suppliers. Based on interviews with senior practitioners we have listed the noteworthy Indian actors in these categories practicing in Pune between 1947 and 1982[5]. This paper focuses on the role of architects in particular. From the group of 36 architects, the (family members of the) most senior architects were approached. In this manner we narrowed down on three practices that were willing to collaborate and could provide study material for this paper: U.M Apte, V.V. Badawe and Architects United (a partnership between V.V. Ghotge and A.B. Sharma).

This study is built on data of the period 1947-1982, collected from interviews with the architects themselves or their relatives (who took over the business) and on office archives. The archives contain hand drawings, communication in the form of letters and notes, library books and photographs. The first part of this paper analyses the academic and practical training of these architects, the type of projects the firms were working on and the procedures and organisation of design and construction. The second part discusses the defining characteristics of the buildings of the era, in terms of style and construction techniques. As such, this study will shed light on how, in a post-colonial situation, western models of construction practice were translated into the Indian context.

Establishing a new profession: the path of tree architectural practices

After independence, the newly founded socialist government became the main patron for building activity. An estimated 20 to 40 per cent of the architects were employed at the government's Public Works Department (P.W.D.) or public sector undertakings[6]. Earlier research shows that independent architects found the average quality of architecture produced by architects at these government departments inferior. Secondly, private architects criticised engineer-contractors, surveyors and *mistris* (skilled craftsmen) offering design-and-build services, which they proclaimed hampered the recognition of their profession[7]. An analysis of Pune Municipal Corporation's list of 'licensed surveyors' from the year 1952-53 confirms this[8]. Only designers with a municipal surveyor's license were authorized to submit building permit applications. Out of 83 licensed surveyors included in the list only five were holder of a graduate degree in architecture while the majority had a Bachelor degree in Engineering. One of the three Pune-based architects mentioned in this list, U.M. Apte (1913-1977), is studied in this paper.

The father of architect U.M. Apte was an avid photographer and painter who worked as a drafting assistant in colonial service and had successfully passed an exam in 'Elementary Architecture' conducted at the Sir Jamsetjee Jeejebhoy School of Art (J.J. School of Art) in Mumbai in 1899. His son, U.M. Apte, graduated in 1939 as an architect from the same J.J. School of Art, where by then architectural education had developed into a full time government recognised and RIBA accredited diploma course[9]. He was a student of the British architect Claude Batley, a principal of the renowned firm Gregson Batley & King who practiced in Bombay and India-wide at that time. After his graduation U.M. Apte responded to a newspaper advertisement of a job offer at the office of architect Anderson in Lahore. He was offered the post and moved there together with his classmate from the J.J. School of Arts Anand, who hailed from Lahore. While working full-time at the office of Anderson for about eight years, he and Anand founded the practice Anand & Apte in Lahore. Through the connections of Anand they obtained important commissions like the design and construction of Lahore's prime movie theatres 'Rattan' and 'Odeon'. (Fig.1) After India's Independence in 1947 and the subsequent partition that led to the creation of India and Pakistan, both architects were forced to move back to India where their collaboration ended. On advice from his father U.M. Apte set up practice in Pune the same year and remained active there till the end of his career in 1974. U.M. Apte has designed a variety of projects from 'bungalows' (free-standing family-owned houses) to temples, industrial buildings, office buildings and hospitals. He became particularly famous for his specialization in the design of educational institutes, which proliferated in Pune.

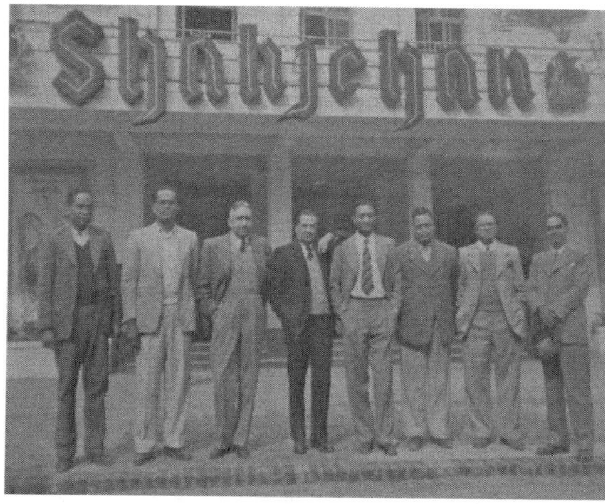

Fig. 1: U.M Apte (second from left) in front of Rattan Theatre, 1940s, Lahore. Photo: unknown. Private archives of Kiran Apte.

The founders of the two other practices studied, architect V.V. Badawe and Architects United, gradated more than two decades later and belong to Pune's second-generation of architects. Architect V. V. Badawe was born in Pune in 1936 and has no family background in design or construction. He joined the Sir J.J. College of Architecture in 1953, the year after which the architecture department had separated from the Sir J.J. School of Art. There, he obtained his degree in Architecture in 1958. At that time the first generation of Indian (but British-trained) architects was teaching at the J.J School of Art. Mumbai architect G.B. Mhatre - one of the pioneers to re-interpret the International Style in an Indian context[10] - was his design professor. V.V. Badawe subsequently worked part time shifts with several Indian architects and engineers in Mumbai in order to save money to pursue a post-graduate course in London. Together with two other Indians, he studied Tropical Architecture at the AA School of Architecture in 1959-1960 under Otto Koenigsberger and Jane Drew. After briefly working with architect Michael Lyesle & Associates in London, he was employed for a year at the architecture studio of Mogens Black-Petersen in Copenhagen. He returned to India in 1962. For a few months he worked in the office of architect B.V. Doshi in Ahmadabad, then he decided to start his own practice in Pune in 1963. The portfolio of architect V.V. Badawe includes a range of residential, industrial, commercial and cultural projects amongst which several movie theatres. His most famous buildings in Pune city are the public auditorium '*Tilak Smarak Mandir*' (Fig.4) and the '*Lokmangal*' building (headquarter for the Bank of Maharashtra, 1977-78).

Architect V.V. Ghotge (1939-2003) and architect A.B. Sharma (1939-2004), partners of the firm Architects United, graduated together from the Sir J.J. School of Architecture in 1959 (Fig.2). US-trained architect Charles Correa (1930-2015) had been one of their design teachers in Mumbai. Both partners worked for one year with Santh-Gothing-Dongre, a first generation architectural practice where many Pune based architecture graduates have gained initial job experience. In 1961 they founded Architects United and started their career with the design of bungalows. At the end of the 1960s the first commissions for apartment-schemes and a private hospital assignment gave a boost to the practice. The 1960s-1980s portfolio consists of residential, industrial and commercial projects.

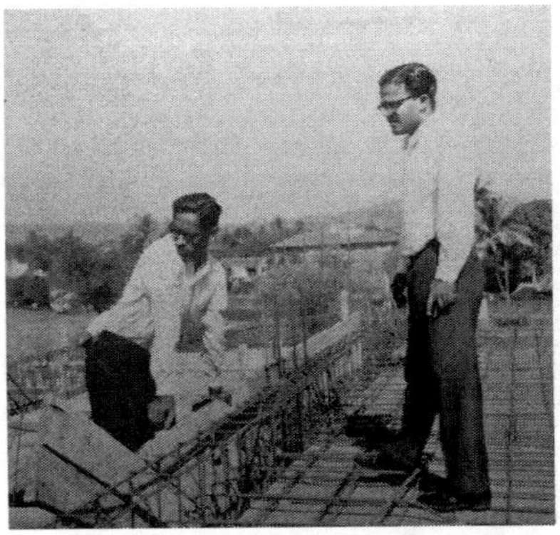

Fig. 2: A.B. Sharma (left) and V.V. Ghotge (right) on one of their construction sites, [place, year unknown], Photo: unknown. Office archives of Architects United.

In the period 1947-1982, the majority of these architects' clientele consisted of the urban elite of businessmen and white-collar workers. None of the studied architects pursued the design of public projects and the rare projects undertaken for government bodies were obtained through personal invitation rather than on a competitive basis. The public projects were generally found to be more time-consuming and complex because of mandatory procedures and funding issues[11].

Professional practice and circulation of knowledge in the architect's office

It is noteworthy that although the number and size of projects undertaken by architect U.M. Apte left a significant mark on the city, the firm mostly remained a one man's practice which only sporadically relied on one or two drafting assistants. Apte's maternal uncle, R.W. Nene, was an engineer and the structural consultant for most of his projects. General contractors were appointed on a cost competitive basis both for public and private clients and the firm did not have contractors they repetitively worked with.

Interviews and the correspondence in the archives of Architects United show that construction practice and the responsibilities of various building professionals until the 1980s largely followed the western modes of production first introduced by the British. The architect would head and gather a construction team. He would be in charge of supplying drawings and specifications for tendering and supervise the work on site, in a few cases assisted by an independent clerk of works who would be paid by the client to supervise the construction site. In private practice the architect used to coordinate the entire process as opposed to usual practice at in-house government departments, where architects were often subordinate to engineers who were responsible for site supervision, specifications and cost management[12].

At Architects United's studio the first architect employees were hired at the end of the 1960s when larger projects were commissioned. Until then, both partners even did the structural design of smaller projects themselves. From the mid 1970s to the '80s the firm counted approximately ten architects and additional administrative staff. From that time they often collaborated with structural engineers Kanetkar-Kulkarni. As opposed to common Indian construction practice today, the making of bills of quantities, construction work planning, acoustic and services design and sanctioning were the architects' tasks. Professional interior designers were not common and some drawings of interior design and made to measure furniture in the archives of V.V. Badawe testify that for bespoke public projects (banks, movie theatres) architects designed the interiors as well. The house that U.M. Apte designed for contractor B.G. Shirke (Fig.3) also features intricately designed internal doors and staircases as well as fixed furniture designed by the architect.

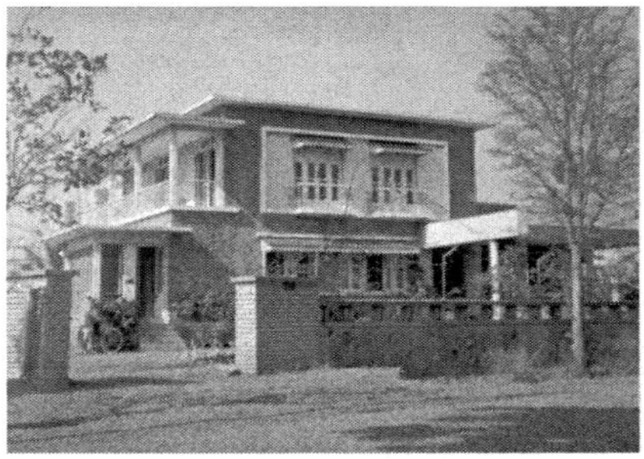

Fig. 3: Shirke house, Pune. Architect, U.M. Apte. Year: 1957. Photo: Unknown. Personal archives of Kiran Apte.

All studied architects combined professional practice with teaching at Pune's '*Abhinav Kala Vidyalaya*', the first college to start a full-time diploma course in architecture in 1954. While U.M. Apte started teaching after years of practical experience, Badawe, Sharma and Ghotge taught since the very beginning of their careers. From approximately 1963 to 1968, Architects United additionally ran an independent 'Institute of Architecture' at which they conducted evening courses that prepared students for the exam of Bachelor in Architecture at Sir J.J. College of Architecture. In total an estimated 80 to 90 students have followed these classes[13].

V.V. Badawe and Architects United distinguished themselves from U.M. Apte in the organisation of their office work. The second-generation architects numbered their projects consistently. Both offices also made intricate scale models (Fig.4), whereas there is no indication of scale models having been made in U.M. Apte's practice. In addition, V.V. Badawe and Architects United possessed in-house reference libraries of professional books, which were numbered and classified. In Badawe's library the approximate 1000 books are numbered chronologically by date of procurement. In Architects United's library books are classified based on content categories. The library of Architects United was used by students at their Institute of Architecture and hence also served their teaching endeavours. At the time of this study the Architects United library was not entirely accessible.

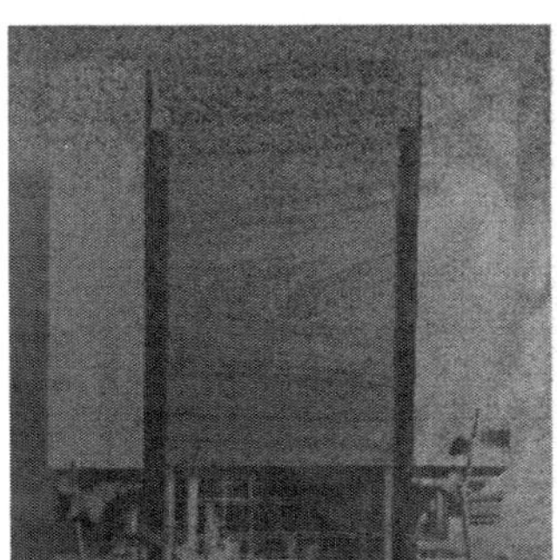

Fig. 4: Scale model of Tilak Smarak Mandir, Pune, Year: Unknown, Photo: Unknown. Office archives of V.V. Badawe.

A detailed analysis of the office library of V.V. Badawe sheds light on the origin and content of the 349 books that were acquired before 1982. The topics of almost half of the books are design related. This category encompasses – in descending order of representation - architectural, interior, structural, urban and landscape design. About 26 per cent of the books concern professional practice, laws and regulations. Books on construction, containing text and/or construction details make out 13 per cent of the collection. The remaining books, gathered under the miscellaneous category include – in descending order of representation- books on art, drawing and model making skills, travel books and philosophy books. Almost equal shares of all books have been published in India and England (ca. 30 per cent each), whereas 19 per cent was published in the U.S.A. and the remaining 16 per cent in continental Europe and Japan. The figure below shows within each content category the proportionate shares of the countries of origin of the books. (Fig.5) The large majority of books on construction were published in England and the 20 per cent of books published in India are mostly colonial P.W.D. handbooks written by British engineers, or derivates thereof. The legacy of British colonial engineers hence proves influential until the 1980s. Indian books are poorly represented in the design category, in which more than 80 per cent of the books are published in the west (Europe and the U.S.A). As will be discussed later, western sources of inspiration reflect in the designs of the architects. Out of Indian design books only nine books relate to architectural design, six to structural design, one to urban design and one to landscape design. On the other hand, books published in India make out the majority (74 per cent) of books on professional practice, laws and regulation.

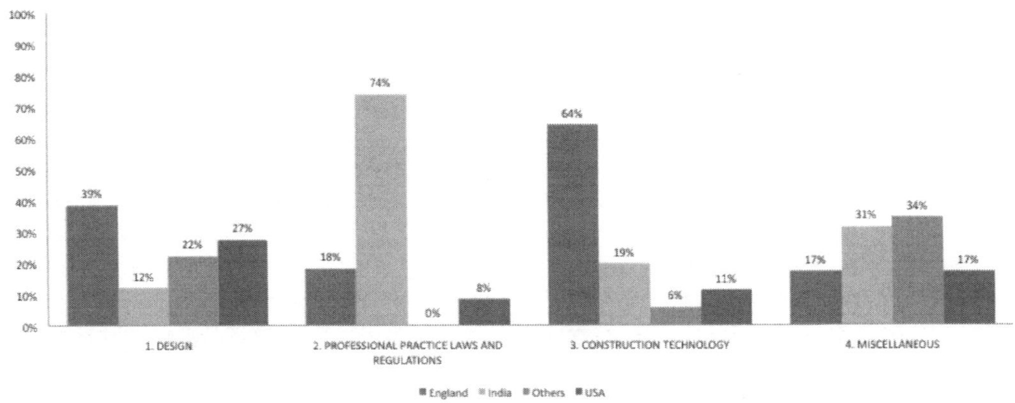

Fig. 5: Proportional provenance of the books in V.V. Badawe's office libarary per content category. Produced by authors.

Iconic books by western architects who practiced in India after independence -such as Le Corbusier's *Modulor* (1948) and *Modulor 2* (1955) and *Tropical Architecture* by Maxwell Fry and Jane Drew- were found at the library, along with 10 books on Danish design and architecture. These reflect V.V. Badawe's continued affinity with the places where he studied and worked. The libraries did not contain journals but U.M. Apte and Architects United where familiar with the American magazines: *Progressive Architecture* (U.M.Apte, Architects United), *American Architecture* (U.M.Apte) and *Architectural Record* (Architects United)[14]. At the time, two noteworthy Indian architectural design magazines existed, *Design* and *MARG*[15]. These magazines did not have a large readers public however, and only V.V. Badawe remembers *MARG* from his student time in Mumbai.

The above indicates that the education, methods of practice and knowledge sources on which Pune's architects relied after independence were substantially western-based. Yet, the architects practiced in an Indian context. How did this translate in the buildings they designed?

Regional and modern design influences

U.M. Apte's early work indicates experimentation with styles. His versatile application of ornamental Art Deco, Indian revivalist and modernist facades in the same time period and for diverse functional programs is striking. The Western India House, built for an insurance company, and his design for a biscuits factory derive their Art Deco character from similar elements: staggering facade planes, an accentuation of the entrance and coloured plaster bands with smaller windows (Fig.6).

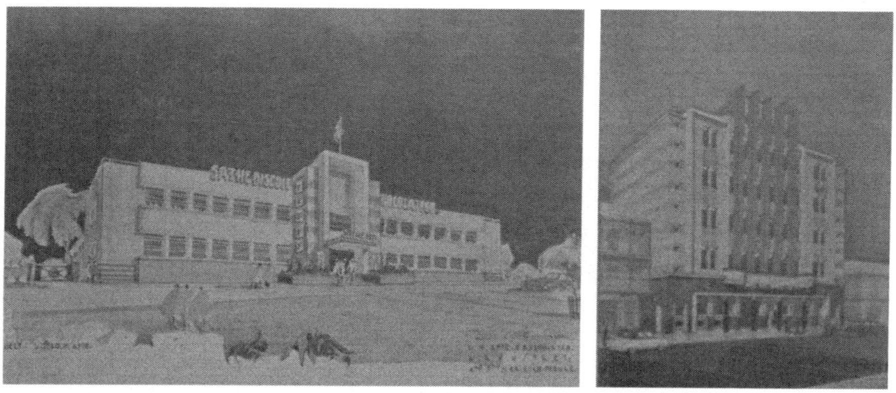

Fig. 6: Sathe Biscuits Factory, Yerawada, 1949 (left). Western India Building, Pune, 1953 (right). Rendered perspective drawings. Architect, U.M. Apte. Private Archives of Kiran Apte.

His Bank of Maharashtra building (Fig.7) however shows an eclectic blend of Art Deco and traditional Indian elements not unlike Ballardie, Thompson and Mattews' famous design of Akshvani bhavan (All India Radio building) in Calcutta (1957-58).

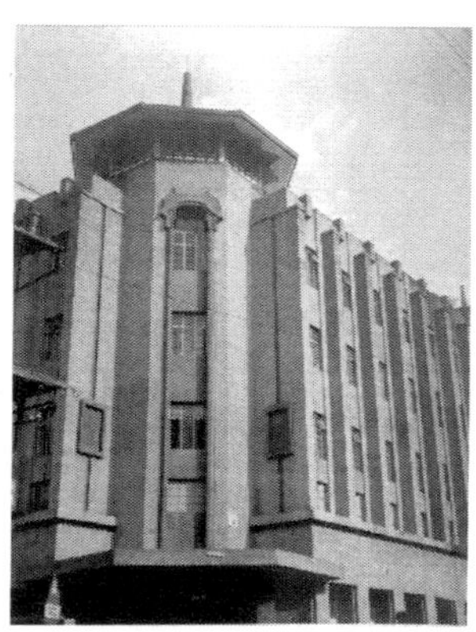

Fig. 7: Bank of Maharashtra building, Pune. Architect, U.M. Apte. Front facade, 1956. Photo: unknown. Private archives of Kiran Apte.

Contrastingly, Lahore's *Rattan* Theatre and Pune's *Ayurved Mahavidyalaya Bhavan* (Fig.8) are designed in a stripped-down modernist style. Only the sunshades add dynamics to their pragmatic and no-nonsense uniformly plastered facades. This adaptation of international modernism met climatic conditions and more restricted building budgets.

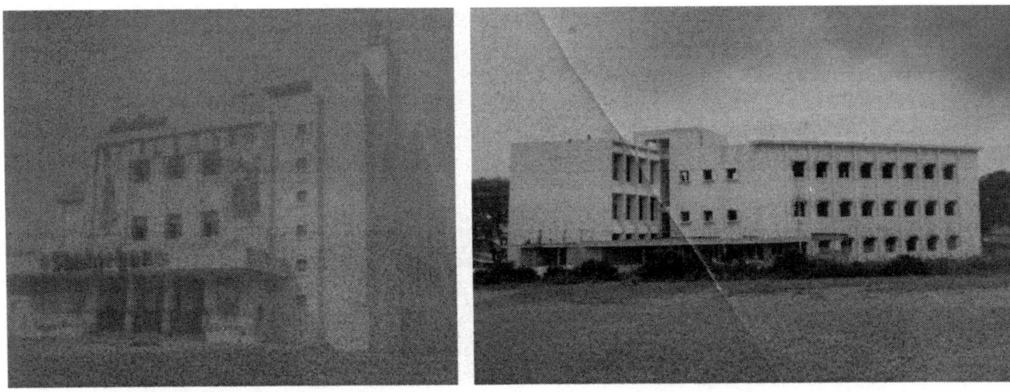

Fig. 8: Top: Rattan Theatre, Lahore, 1940s. Architects, Anand & Apte. Bottom: Ayurved Mahavidyalaya Bhavan, Pune, late 1950s. Architect, U.M. Apte. Photos: Unknown. Private Archives of Kiran Apte.

V.V. Badawe and Architects United's work can largely be seen as a continuation of this 'utilitarian modernist'[16] style, characterised by flat roofs, plainly plastered facades and concrete strips or screens to shade windows (*chajjas*). In Architect United's more elaborate versions of this design language, perforated concrete screen walls (*jaalis*) for ventilation and cantilevering canopies and various decorative plaster finishes render sculptural and unique qualities to each building (Fig.9).

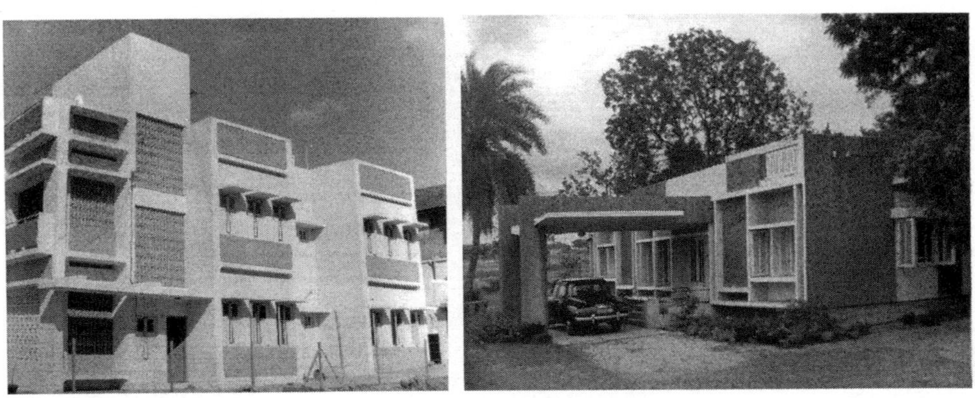

Fig. 9: Left: Bungalow for Dr.R.S.Rao, Pune, 1964. Right: Bungalow for Kalyani cloth merchants, Pune, 1965. Architects United. Office Archives of Architects United.

Some works of V.V. Badawe have a Brutalist flair. His *Tilak Smarak* building (Fig.4), Agashe house (Fig.10) and *Lokmangal* building were some of the first buildings with exposed concrete in Pune. This supports Scriver's assertion that the Brutalist aesthetic resurfaced during the 1960s in India, in particular because the second generation of Indian architects returned home from work and study experience in Europe[17].

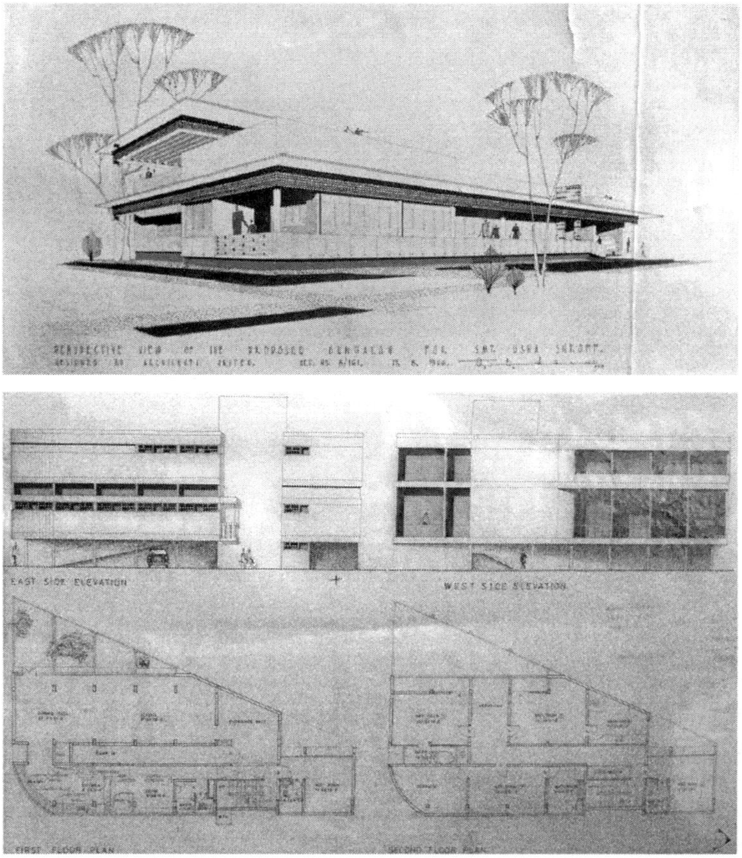

Fig. 10: Top: perspective view of Shroff Bungalow, Pune, Architects United, 1966. Office archives of Architects United. Bottom: Drawings for Agashe House, Pune. V.V. Badawe, 1964. Office archives of V.V. Badawe.

The external appearance of Badawe's Agashe house, with its *pilotis*, sun breakers and access ramp carries the signature style of Le Corbusier's India projects, yet the internal space built-up accommodates the Indian household. It provides for a *Puja* corner for religious worship, and has both a westernised kitchen (with raised counter) and an Indian kitchen with *mori* (wet area for washing and bathing) and gas stove at floor level.

In their Shroff bungalow, Architects United used Frank Lloyd Wright's Prairie style (Fig.10) to carve out shaded verandas, which are similar to the places where traditionally the head of the Indian family would receive guests.

Hence, in residential design of the 1960s and 1970s, the designs were more characteristic of foreign influence in their facades than in the interiors. A functional space layout based on the local climate and Indian social customs prevailed. A staggered plan helped to improve cross-ventilation. The kitchen was usually separated from the dining space and often located at the back of the house. It often had a separate access for household personnel, which lead to an outdoor washing area. Other characteristic features are a lavatory basin in the entry hall or near the dining area for the washing of hands. Several houses by Architects United and V.V. Badawe were designed for joint families: parents and sons with their respective families traditionally share a house. This was accommodated in the designs by providing separate attached bathrooms to each bedroom or dividing the house in different quarters with their own kitchen and gathering spaces.

Prevalent building tectonics

While architectural aesthetics evolved rapidly between 1947-1982, developments in construction technology and tectonic detailing occurred at a slower pace.

In U.M. Apte's buildings stonework was common. Natural stone-faced brick walls make up the facade of his Bank of Maharashtra (Fig.7) and Shirke house (Fig.3). The entrances of plastered Art-Deco buildings like the Western India House are clad in polished natural stone. Stonemasons were not readily available in Pune and had to be sourced from outside[18]. In projects of the 1960s and '70s by V.V. Badawe and United Architects entire facades in stone masonry were less common. Stone was used more often for accentuating a single exterior wall. In the projects by Architects United the combined use of different types of decorative plasters and finishes such as 'stonecrete' was popular.

Roof terraces of the early projects were sealed with a mosaic floor made up of broken pieces of household porcelain and later tiles (*china mosaic)*. Its glazing reduced surface porosity and reflected the heat. Since the 1960s cement screeds with waterproofing admixtures and without mosaic were more commonly used.

The Shirke house by U.M. Apte is the only of all studied projects that had a structural system made up of load bearing masonry walls. Multi-storey buildings in the 1950s, and even single and two-storey houses in the '60s and '70s were designed as 'concrete frame -masonry infill' structures with floor slabs in reinforced concrete. Since the 1920s and especially after independence in 1947, concrete became an economically viable construction material because the Indian cement industry had picked up production and because labour working under the guidance of site engineers, was more abundantly available in cities than craftsmen.

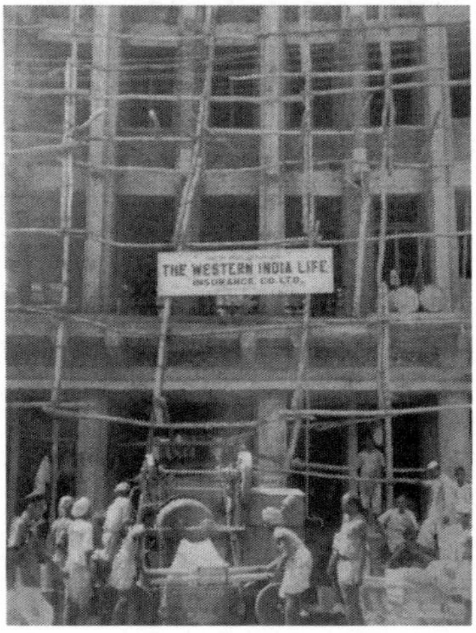

Fig. 11: Western India Life Insurance building, Pune. Architect, U.M. Apte. Building under construction, 1952. Photo: Unknown. Private archives of Kiran Apte.

Until today labour intensive cast in-situ concrete remains a considerably cheaper option than prefabricated structural elements in concrete or steel.

Conclusions

The education, methods of practice and knowledge sources on which U.M.Apte, V.V, Badawe and Architects United relied after independence were substantially western-based. This was valid for the first-generation architects, who practiced since the 1940s, and the second-generation architects, who started practice in the 1960s. The first-generation architects studied and worked under British architects present in India before Independence. The second generation architects -Badawe, Sharma and Ghotge- studied after 1947 yet their education was still foreign influenced since teachers were foreign-trained or they pursued post-graduation degrees abroad. A study of the books acquired by V.V. Badawe between 1947 and 1982 sheds light on the architectural knowledge circulation of the time. Eighty per cent of the design books in V.V. Badawe's library are published in Europe or the U.S. The majority of books on construction are published in England. Only in the category of books on professional practice, laws and regulations do India-published books form the majority.

The upkeep of a classified office library and codification of their design projects suggests that the practice of the second-generation architects was more organised than that of the first generation. U.M. Apte possessed no personal library and his professional knowledge was presumably more based on his practical experience in Lahore and family network (his father was an architectural assistant and his uncle an engineer).

The Anglo-Indian educational, training and knowledge background of these offices is most easily discerned in the stylistic characteristics of the buildings they designed and particularly in their facades. Inner spatial layouts were generally less susceptible to influence of foreign trends than the facades, and would consider climatic and Indian user patterns. U.M. Apte's projects of the 1950s show more diversity in terms of style, material use and structural systems than the projects by the second-generation architects. In the 1960s a typically Indian design language emerged, a utilitarian modernism adapted to climatic needs.

In the decades after independence architects mostly catered to elite clients. Parallel models of building practice -in which engineers or *mistris* where in charge of the design and production of buildings- deserve further investigation.

Acknowledgments

The authors express their gratitude to V.V Badawe, Kiran Apte, Prakash Apte, Deven Ghotge, Uma Ghotge and Ajay Shirke for their time and for disclosing their archives.

References

[1] J. Lang, M. Desai, M. Desai, *Architecture and independence: The search for identity-India 1880 to 1980*. New Delhi: Oxford University Press, 1997. 190.

M. Chatterjee, 'The evolution of contemporary Indian Architecture' in [no editor], Architecture in India, Paris: Electa Moniteur, 1985. pp.124-127.

[2] *Pursuit and promotion of science: The Indian Experience.* New Delhi: Indian National Science Academy, 2001.

[3] *Report of the university education commission (december 1948-august 1949) Volume I* (report 1962). New Delhi: Ministry of Education and Culture, Government of India. 1963.

[4] P. Chopra, *A Joint enterprise: Indian elites and the making of British Bombay*, Minneapolis: University of Minnesota Press, 2011.
P. Scriver, A. Srivastava *India: Modern architectures in history,* London: Reaktion books, 2015.
Lang, Architecture and independence, (Note 1)

[5] V.V. Badawe, G. Doshi, P. Deshmukh, U.Ghotge, D.Ghotge, H.M. Kadam, Peshwe, Pundalik, V. Sardesai, interviewed by authors, 2015.

[6] C. Deshpande, 'Employed architects' woes' *Journal of the Indian Institute of Architects*, Vol. 38, no.4-5-6, 1972, pp. 9-10.
R.M. Valavalkar, 'Problems faced by the self-employed and employed architects' *Journal of the Indian Institute of Architects*, Vol. 49, no.1, 1984, pp. 9-10.

[7] S. Melsens, I. Bertels, 'Shaping India's cities: The changing role of stakeholders in construction since Indepenence (1947)' pp. 575-581 in B. Bowen, D. Friedman, T. Leslie, J. Ochsendorf (Eds), Proceedings of the Fifth International Congress on Construction History, Volume 2, Chicago 2015.

[8] 'List of licensed surveyors' Pune Municipal gazette, Vol. 3, No. 21, (August), 1952, pp. 13-16.

[9] J.B. Fernandes, 1967. "Brief history of the I.I.A." *Journal of the Indian Institute of Architects*, Golden Jubilee number.

[10] Scriver, India, (Note 4) p. 113.

[11] Deven Ghotge, son of V.V. Ghotge, interviewed by Sarah Melsens, 2015.
V.V. Badawe, interviewed by Sarah Melsens, 2015.

[12] Melsens, Shaping India's cities, (Note 6).

[13] Deven Ghotge, interview, (Note 10).

[14] Kiran Apte, son of U.M.Apte, interviewed by Sarah Melsens and Priyanka Mangaonkar-Vaiude,2015.
Deven Ghotge, interview, (Note 10).

[15] Scriver, India, (Note 4), p. 219.

[16] Lang, Architecture and independence, (Note 1), p. 278.

[17] Scriver, India, (Note 4), p. 226.

[18]Ajay Shirke, son of B.G. Shirke, interviewed by Sarah Melsens and Priyanka Mangaonkar-Vaiude, 2015.

St Pancras Vict. construction ~~[illegible]~~ photo
George G. Scott

See also old goods room at Leeds GI
Gothic style train shed.
~~Several Gothic~~
Several styles pressure – Fruh, etc.
Robert Thorne

Scaffolding is v. clever
May have had a RIBA lecture about it

Simon Bradley 2 x books

Italy
PhD lists being collected

Bill Addis

Italy SIXXI [illegible]
history ERC grant

Executive
IABSE Swiss
construction history Bridge Engineers
older organisation

Italy 2016 UK [illegible] group mtg
Cambridge

– heritage mtg

Eng. History & Heritage J.
– Engin – existing structures
run by Inst of Civil Engineers
Also web based resource
here for eng. in conservation
– links
+ Addis – 3000 y of bldg – book
+ wiki – Constr. History

RCAHMS @
IHA downloads + Sheridan

~~[illegible]~~ photography docs

Warwick course
save as searchable pdf – photos of [illegible]!

Bertels

Very exp Firm

Hussey plates – NT history

photos, notes re other chamber ~1750
or sketches

Advertising contracts

French CHS – online text book.
Nantes 2017

online (for members) new journal 2017 ~~2~~ 2/year
multilingual peer review.

content online

portugal/spain Active. oporto congress
Int^n congress in S. America

Germany – new society
new chair of construction history

Belgium – post 2014

"Assoc" Francophone
D'histoire de la construction"

Brussels research centre for cons. history
4 orgs, Vrije VUB, Unilore.

Stefan Holzer.
workshops eg timber trade marks & nails
Construction Histories Brussels

ICCH 2018 9–13 July Brussels Eur cong

Westminster

find USV actual site?

church archaeol site

Tom Peters